Research Methods for
Arts and Event Management

Research Methods for Arts and Event Management

A. J. Veal and Christine Burton

PEARSON

Harlow, England • London • New York • Boston • San Francisco • Toronto • Sydney
Auckland • Singapore • Hong Kong • Tokyo • Seoul • Taipei • New Delhi
Cape Town • São Paulo • Mexico City • Madrid • Amsterdam • Munich • Paris • Milan

PEARSON EDUCATION LIMITED
Edinburgh Gate
Harlow CM20 2JE
United Kingdom
Tel: +44 (0)1279 623623
Web: www.pearson.com/uk

First published 2014 (print and electronic)

© Pearson Education Limited 2014 (print and electronic)

ISBN: 978–0–273–72082–9 (print)
      978–0–273–72086–7 (PDF)
      978–0–273–78113–4 (eText)

British Library Cataloguing-in-Publication Data
A catalogue record for the print edition is available from the British Library

Library of Congress Cataloging-in-Publication Data
Veal, Anthony James.
  Research methods for arts and event management / A.J. Veal, Christine Burton.
    pages cm
  ISBN 978-0-273-72082-9
1. Special events–Research. 2. Special events–Management. 3. Special
events–Planning. 4. Arts–Management. 5. Arts–Research. I. Title.
  GT3405.V43 2014
  394.2–dc23
                    2014017941

10 9 8 7 6 5 4 3 2 1
18 17 16 15 14

[Insert any freelance text designer, illustrator or cartoonist credits as required]
[Insert name of freelance cover designer as required]
[Insert any credit line from back cover of book]

Print edition typeset in 9.5/12.5 pt Charter ITC Std by 71]
Print edition printed and bound by Ashford Colour Press, Gosport

NOTE THAT ANY PAGE CROSS-REFERENCES REFER TO THE PRINT EDITION

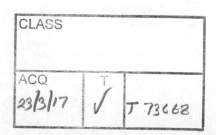

Contents

List of figures   xi

List of tables   xvii

List of Case Studies   xviii

Guided Tour   xix

Preface   xxi

Acknowledgements   xxii

Part 1 Introduction

1 Introduction to research: what, why and who?   3

Introduction   3

What is research?   5

Why study research?   8

Who does research?   14

Who pays?   17

Research outputs   18

Terminology   22

Summary   23

Test questions   23

Exercises   24

Resources   24

References   25

2 Approaches to research in the arts and events   29

Introduction   29

Disciplinary traditions   30

Approaches, dimensions, issues, terminology   31

Summary   46

Test questions   46

Exercises   46

Resources   47

References   48

3 Starting out: research plans and proposals   51

Introduction   51

Planning a research project   51

The research process in the real world   74

Research proposals   79

Summary		82
Test questions		83
Exercises		83
Resources		83
References		85

4 Research ethics 88

Introduction		88
Institutional oversight of research ethics		90
Ethics in the research process		91
Ethical issues in research		92
Access to research information		103
Summary		104
Test questions		104
Exercises		105
Resources		105
References		106

5 The range of research methods 108

Introduction		108
The major research methods		108
Subsidiary/cross-cutting techniques		115
Multiple methods		127
Policy/management-related research-based techniques		129
Choosing methods		129
Summary		132
Test questions		133
Exercises		134
Resources		134
References		137

6 Reviewing the literature 143

Introduction		143
The value of bibliographies		144
Searching: sources of information		145
Obtaining copies of material		148
Compiling and maintaining a bibliography		149
Reviewing the literature		149
Referencing the literature		154
Referencing and referencing systems		156
Referencing issues		160
Summary		161
Test questions		161
Exercises		161
Resources		162
References		163

Part 2 Data collection

7 Secondary data sources and measurement   167

Introduction	167
Measurement in the arts and events sectors	168
Introduction to secondary data sources	178
Administrative/management data	179
National cultural/events participation surveys	180
Economic/industry data	186
The population census	188
Documentary sources	190
Opportunism	190
Summary	191
Test questions	191
Exercises	191
Resources	191
References	194

8 Observation   198

Introduction	198
Types and possibilities	199
Main elements of observational research	205
Use of technology	209
Just looking	211
Case studies	212
Summary	213
Test questions	213
Exercises	213
Resources	214
References	215

9 Qualitative methods: introduction and data collection   217

Introduction	217
The nature of qualitative methods	218
Merits, functions, limitations	218
The qualitative research process	220
The range of qualitative methods – introduction	221
In-depth interviews	222
Focus groups	226
Participant observation	227
Analysing texts	228
Biographical research	229
Ethnography	230
Validity and reliability, trustworthiness	230

Early qualitative research   231

Summary   232
Test questions   233
Exercises   233
Resources   233
References   234

10 Questionnaire surveys: typology, design and coding   237

Introduction   237
Definitions and terminology   238
Roles   238
Merits   239
Limitations   240
Types of questionnaire survey   243
The household questionnaire survey   243
The street survey   245
The telephone survey   246
The mail survey   248
E-surveys   252
Visitor/user/on-site/surveys   254
Captive group surveys   257
Questionnaire design   258
Coding   278
Validity of questionnaire-based data   282
Conducting questionnaire surveys   284

Summary   287
Test questions   287
Exercises   288
Resources   288
References   289

11 Experimental research   292

Introduction   292
Principles of experimental research   293
Validity   294
Quasi-experimental designs   295
Experimental methods in arts/event research   297

Summary   305
Test questions   306
Exercises   306
Resources   306
References   307

12 The case study method   309

Introduction   309
Definitions   310
Validity and reliability   311

Merits of the case study approach   313
Design and conduct of case studies   313
Analysis   315
Case studies in practice   316

Summary   320
Test questions   320
Exercises   320
Resources   321
References   321

13 Sampling: quantitative and qualitative   324

Introduction   324
The idea of sampling   324
Samples and populations   325
Representativeness   325
Sample size   330
Weighting   336
Sampling for qualitative research   337

Summary   338
Test questions   339
Exercises   339
Resources   339
References   339
Appendix 13.1   341

Part 3 Data analysis

14 Analysing secondary data   345

Introduction   345

Summary   355
Exercises   356
Resources   356
References   356

15 Analysing qualitative data   358

Introduction   358
Data storage and confidentiality   359
Case study example   360
Manual methods of analysis   362
Qualitative analysis using computer software – introduction   366
NVivo   367

Summary   377
Test questions   377
Exercises   377

Resources   378
References   378

16 Analysing quantitative data   380

Introduction   380
Survey data analysis and types of research   381
Spreadsheet analysis   383
IBM SPSS Statistics Software (SPSS)   386
Preparation   387
SPSS procedures   395
The analysis process   410

Summary   410
Test questions   410
Exercises   411
Resources   411
References   412
Appendix 16.1   413

17 Statistical analysis   417

Introduction   417
The statistics approach   418
Statistical tests   423
In conclusion   451

Summary   451
Test questions/Exercises   452
Resources   452
References   453
Appendix 17.1   455
Appendix 17.2   459

Part 4 Communicating results

18 Research reports and presentations   463

Introduction   463
Written research reports   463
Other media   477

Summary   479
A final comment   479
Test questions/Exercises   479
Resources   479
References   480

Index   481

List of figures

1.1   Arts and events   5
1.2   Types of research   6
1.3   Why study research?   9
1.4   Examples of policies, plans and management activity   10
1.5   The rational–comprehensive planning/management process   11
1.6   Example of planning/management tasks and associated research   12
1.7   Research in the stages of exhibition development   13
1.8   Who does research?   14
1.9   Managers/policy makers and research topics   16
1.10 Who pays?   17
1.11 Research report formats   18
2.1   Disciplines and examples of research questions   31
2.2   Terminology: approaches/dimensions/issues   32
2.3   Circular model of the research process   40
3.1   Elements of the research process   52
3.2   Examples of research topics from different sources   53
3.3   Reasons for re-visiting theories/propositions/observations from the literature   54
3.4   Purposes of research   57
3.5   Roles of the literature in research   59
3.6   Development of a conceptual framework   62
3.7   Exploration of relationships between concepts – example   62
3.8   Concept map example   63
3.9   Examples of concepts – definition and operationalisation   64
3.10 Conceptual framework as quantifiable model   65
3.11 Conceptual framework: market research study   66
3.12 Conceptual framework: customer service quality study   66
3.13 Research question vs hypothesis format   67
3.14 Information needs for the market research study   69
3.15 Research strategy components   69
3.16 Example research budget   71
3.17 Research programme: diagrammatic representation   72
3.18 Research project timetable   72
3.19 The research process in the real world   74

3.20	Facility use study: conceptual framework	76
3.21	Facility use study: concepts, definitions and operationalisation	77
3.22	Facility use study: research questions	77
3.23	Facility use study: information needs and likely sources	78
3.24	Facility use study: research strategy	78
3.25	Research proposal checklist: self-generated research	80
3.26	Research proposal checklist: responsive research	82
4.1	Ethics in the research process	92
4.2	Free choice 'grey' areas	94
4.3	Information for research participants: checklist	97
4.4	Example of a consent form	97
4.5	Ethics guidelines for anonymous questionnaire-based surveys	98
4.6	Personally identifiable data	101
5.1	The range of major research methods	110
5.2	Qualitative data-collection methods	113
5.3	Types of questionnaire-based survey	114
5.4	Subsidiary, cross-cutting and multiple techniques/methods	116
5.5	Action research process	117
5.6	A simple network	123
5.7	Examples of psychographic/lifestyle categories	125
5.8	Repertory grid: example	126
5.9	Scales for arts/events-related topics	127
5.10	Triangulation	129
5.11	Policy/management-related research approaches/techniques	130
5.12	Considerations in selecting a research method	130
6.1	The roles of the literature in research	144
6.2	Sources of information	145
6.3	Types of literature review	150
6.4	Questions to ask when reviewing the literature	151
6.5	Making sense of the literature	153
6.6	Standard/generic reference formats	154
6.7	Examples of reference formats	155
6.8	Reference systems: features, advantages, disadvantages	159
7.1	Typology of individual cultural engagement	169
7.2	Measures/indicators of engagement in cultural activities/events	170
7.3	Local/non-local participants in culture/events	172
7.4	Counting heads in arts/events settings: sources and methods	173
7.5	Models of national statistics gathering/dissemination arrangements	174
7.6	Culture cycle	174
7.7	Framework for cultural statistics domains	175

7.8	Populating a cultural map	177
7.9	Advantages and disadvantages of using secondary data	179
7.10	Types of secondary data	179
7.11	Management data	180
7.12	National cultural participation surveys: composite international publications	181
7.13	National cultural participation survey details	182
7.14	Participation rates in arts/events by reference period, persons aged 16+ England, 2003	184
7.15	Household expenditure: cultural items	187
7.16	Examples of non-financial measures of output/supply	188
7.17	Census data: geographical levels of availability	189
7.18	Census data available	189
7.19	Documentary sources	190
8.1	Types of observational research	199
8.2	Situations for observational research	200
8.3	Visitor movement patterns in a museum	202
8.4	Steps in an observation project	205
8.5	Counts of site use	207
8.6	Mapping of observed data: outdoor event	208
8.7	Observation recording sheet: counts	209
8.8	Observational technology	209
9.1	Sequential and recursive approaches to research	220
9.2	Qualitative methods: summary	221
9.3	Questions, responses and interview types	222
9.4	Example of a checklist for in-depth interviewing	224
9.5	Interviewing interventions – Whyte (1982)	225
10.1	The use of questionnaire surveys compared with other methods: examples	240
10.2	Interviewer-completion compared with respondent-completion	242
10.3	Types of questionnaire survey: characteristics	243
10.4	Factors affecting mail survey response	249
10.5	Mail survey follow-ups	250
10.6	Mail survey response pattern	251
10.7	Types of e-survey	253
10.8	Questionnaire design process	259
10.9	Question wording: examples of good and bad practice	263
10.10	Open-ended vs pre-coded questions: example	263
10.11	Example of range of replies resulting from an open-ended question	264
10.12	Range of information in arts/events questionnaires	266
10.13	Economic status, occupational and socio-economic groupings	269
10.14	Household type and visitor group type	271

10.15 Life-cycle stages 272
10.16 Housing information 273
10.17 Opinion or attitude question formats 274
10.18 Filtering: examples 277
10.19 Coding open-ended questions: example 279
10.20 Completed questionnaire 280
10.21 Data from 15 questionnaires 281
10.22 Questionnaire surveys: threats to validity 282
10.23 Fieldwork planning tasks 284
10.24 Pilot survey purposes 286
11.1 Classic experimental design 294
11.2 Threats to validity of experiments 295
11.3 Quasi-experimental research designs 296
11.4 Types and contexts of experiments in arts/events research 297
11.5 Experimental model of policy projects 298
11.6 Experimenting with mail survey incentives 301
11.7 Cultural events: attributes, values and preferences 303
11.8 Example of museum choice scenario 304
12.1 The case study method: demographic and geographic levels 311
12.2 Case study research: theory and policy 312
12.3 Trends in theatre attendance, Australian adults 15+,1991–2010 316
12.4 Theatre attendance by income, Australia, 2010 317
12.5 Role variance of arts leaders: Renstchler (conceptual framework) 319
13.1 Normal curve and confidence intervals 332
13.2 Selected qualitative sampling methods 338
14.1 Summary of secondary data analysis case studies and data types 345
14.2 Relationship between income inequality and cultural participation, Europe, 2007 347
14.3 Estimating likely demand for a leisure facility 349
14.4 Catchment/market area 351
14.5 Studies of cultural consumption/taste and social status 352
14.6 The long tail 353
14.7 Symphony orchestra finances 355
15.1 Circular model of the research process in qualitative and quantitative contexts 359
15.2 Outline conceptual framework for a study of activity choice 360
15.3 Interview transcript extracts 362
15.4 Developed conceptual framework for qualitative study of activity choice 363
15.5 'Crosstabulation' of qualitative data 365
15.6 NVivo procedures covered 367
15.7 Create NVivo project procedure 368
15.8 Classification of nodes – procedure 369

15.9	Cases and attributes – procedure	369
15.10	Importing documents – procedure	370
15.11	Linking documents and cases – procedure	371
15.12	Setting up a coding system – procedure	371
15.13	Modelling – procedure	372
15.14	Coding text – procedure	373
15.15	Activity Choice project summary	375
15.16	Queries – procedure	375
15.17	Matrix coding query – procedure	376
16.1	Research types and analytical procedures	381
16.2	Questionnaire survey data: spreadsheet analysis	384
16.3	Questionnaire survey data: spreadsheet analysis steps	385
16.4	Survey analysis – overview	387
16.5	Variable names, labels and values	389
16.6	Starting an SPSS session	392
16.7	Blank Variable View and Data View windows	393
16.8	Variable View window with variable names and labels	394
16.9	Data View window with data from questionnaires/cases	394
16.10	Procedure starting an SPSS analysis session	395
16.11	Descriptives procedure and output	395
16.12	Frequencies for one variable: procedure and output	397
16.13	Multiple response procedures and output	398
16.14	Recode procedures and output	400
16.15	Means procedures and output	402
16.16	Campus Entertainment Survey 2012: statistical summary	403
16.17	Crosstabs procedures and output	405
16.18	Data types and graphics	407
16.19	Graphics procedures and output	407
17.1	Drawing repeated samples and the normal distribution	420
17.2	Dependent and independent variables	423
17.3	Types of data and types of statistical test	423
17.4	Alternative expressions of hypotheses	424
17.5	Chi-square test – procedures	425
17.6	Distribution of chi-square assuming null hypothesis is true	426
17.7	Presentation of chi-square test results	427
17.8	Chi-square and t distributions	428
17.9	Comparing means: t-test: paired samples – procedures	430
17.10	Comparing means: t-test: independent samples – procedures	431
17.11	Comparing a range of means – procedures	432
17.12	Comparing means and variance procedures	433

17.13	One-way analysis of variance – procedures	434
17.14	A table of means – procedures	435
17.15	Factorial analysis of variance – procedures	436
17.16	Relationships between variables	437
17.17	Correlation procedures	439
17.18	Correlation matrix – procedures	440
17.19	Regression line	441
17.20	Regression analysis – procedures	442
17.21	Regression line: curve fit – procedure	443
17.22	Regression: curve fit, non-linear – procedures	444
17.23	Multiple regression – procedures	446
17.24	Structural equation modelling	446
17.25	Binary and scale variable graphic	447
17.26	Simple manual factor analysis	448
17.27	Plots of 'clusters'	449
17.28	Dendrogram	450
17.29	Multiple correspondence analysis: from Pierre Bourdieu's diagram of the spaces of social position and lifestyle	450
18.1	Types of research report	464
18.2	Report style and components	466
18.3	Example report list of contents	467
18.4	Main body of report: technical aspects	468
18.5	Dot point list example	469
18.6	Table and commentaries	471
18.7	Conventional academic article structure	473
18.8	Report as narrative – structure	475

List of tables

7.1   Time use, Britain and Australia*   186

7.2   Cultural industry sectors and revenue, employment and exports (UK, 2001)   188

13.1   Confidence intervals related to sample size   332

13.2   Necessary sample sizes to achieve given confidence intervals   333

13.3   Confidence intervals applied to visit numbers   335

13.4   Sample size and population size: small populations   336

13.5   Interview/usage data from a site/visitor survey   337

13.6   Weighting   337

14.1   Income inequality and cultural participation, Europe, 2007   346

14.2   Cinema attendance by age   350

14.3   Study town and national age structure compared   350

14.4   Estimating demand for cinema attendance   350

List of Case Studies

2.1	Cinema attendance vs museum attendance – inductive and deductive approaches	41
3.1	Facility use: research design process	75
4.1	Examples of ethical issues in arts and events research	89
8.1	Movement patterns in a museum	202
8.2	Children's behaviour	212
8.3	Observation studies of museum visitor behaviour	212
9.1	Early qualitative research: *English Life and Leisure*	231
10.1	Example questionnaires	260
11.1	Exhibit layout and labels	300
11.2	Experimenting with research methods	301
11.3	Discrete choice experiments: examples	303
12.1	Activity profile: theatre attendance in Australia	316
12.2	Managing opera houses	317
12.3	The production and consumption of music	318
12.4	The entrepreneurial arts leader	318
12.5	How a museum dies	319
14.1	The *Spirit Level* and cultural participation	346
14.2	Estimating likely demand for a cultural facility	348
14.3	Facility catchment area	351
14.4	International study of cultural omnivorousness	352
14.5	Big data	353
14.6	The perilous life of symphony orchestras	354
15.1	Activity choice qualitative study	360

Guided Tour

Each **part opener** summarises the main themes of each chapter and how they relate to other parts within the book.

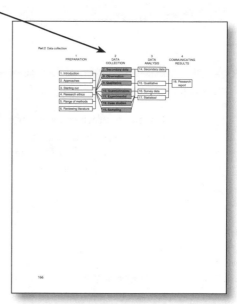

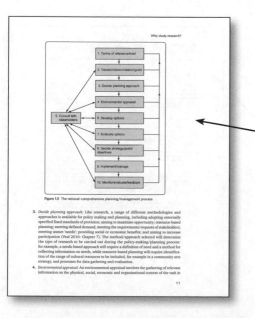

Figures and tables illustrate key points, concepts and processes visually to reinforce your learning.

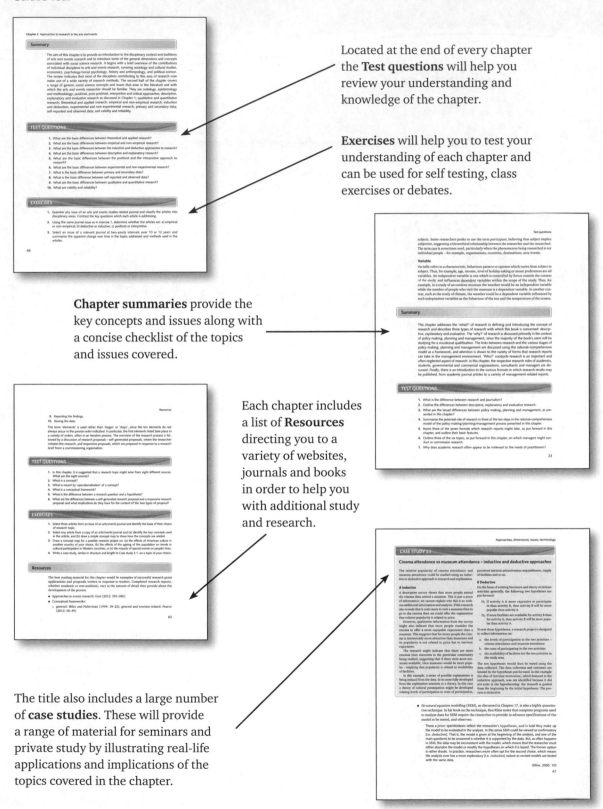

Located at the end of every chapter the **Test questions** will help you review your understanding and knowledge of the chapter.

Exercises will help you to test your understanding of each chapter and can be used for self testing, class exercises or debates.

Chapter summaries provide the key concepts and issues along with a concise checklist of the topics and issues covered.

Each chapter includes a list of **Resources** directing you to a variety of websites, journals and books in order to help you with additional study and research.

The title also includes a large number of **case studies**. These will provide a range of material for seminars and private study by illustrating real-life applications and implications of the topics covered in the chapter.

Preface

The aim of this book is to introduce research methods to students, policymakers and managers in the arts, cultural and events management sector, both as a skill required by students planning a professional career and as initial preparation for those embarking on research degrees. We seek to provide a 'how to do it' text and also to offer an understanding of how research findings are generated in order to assist students and practising managers to become knowledgeable consumers of the research of others.

Three software packages are used to demonstrate quantitative and qualitative data analysis (Excel, SPSS and NVivo). The particular packages selected did not arise as the result of a 'consumer test' of available packages, but are simply the packages with which we are familiar and which have been available to the students in the universities where we have taught. We can vouch for the usefulness of the packages demonstrated but are not in a position to compare the packages used with others available.

Regarding presentational style, we have sought, in the interests of readability, to reduce the amount of overt referencing in the body of the text, with references to literature offering examples of the use of various methods and techniques being provided in case studies or in the Resources sections at the end of each chapter. All URLs were checked in February 2014.

The book is modelled on an existing text, *Research Methods for Leisure and Tourism: A Practical Guide* (Veal, 2011), and a companion volume devoted to sport (Veal and Darcy, 2014). The three texts follow the same chapter structure, with much generic material in common, but with sector-specific demonstration data-sets and exercises. An advantage of this is that in those institutions where arts/events studies students are taught together with leisure, sports and tourism studies students, the specialist students can use their own subject-specific version of the text with relevant examples and source material.

Readers may wish to consult the online material available at www.pearsoned.co.uk/veal, which includes:

- copies of all figures, tables and some dot-point lists in PowerPoint files;
- copies of statistical and qualitative data-sets used in the book;
- Lecturer's guide;
- *errata* – which will be corrected in reprints following discovery.

A. J. Veal
Christine Burton
Sydney, November 2013

References

Veal, A. J. (2011) *Research Methods for Leisure and Tourism: A Practical Guide*, Fourth Edition. Harlow: Financial Times Prentice Hall.

Veal, A. J. and Darcy, S. (2014) *Research Methods for Sport Studies and Sport Management: A Practical Guide*. London: Routledge.

Acknowledgements

We are grateful to the following for permission to reproduce copyright material:

Figures

Figures 1.2, 1.3, 1.5, 1.8–1.11, 2.2, 2.3, 3.1–3.15, 3.17–3.19, 3.25, 3.26, 4.1, 4.3–4.6, 5.1–5.8, 5.10, 5.12, 6.1–6.3, 6.5, 6.6, 6.8, 7.4, 7.9–7.11, 7.15, 7.18–7.20, 8.1, 8.2, 8.4, 8.5, 9.1–9.5, 10.1–10.10, 10.12–10.24, 11.1–11.3, 11.5, 12.1, 12.2, 13.1, 13.2, 15.1, 15.5, 15.10, 15.15, 15.16, 16.1–16.4, 16.6, 16.11–16.19, 17.1–17.23, 17.27, 17.28, 18.1–18.5, 18.7 and 18.8 from or adapted from *Research Methods for Leisure and Tourism*, 4th ed., Pearson Education (Veal, A.J. 2011) Copyright © Pearson Education Limited 2006, 2011; Figures 7.6 and 7.7 adapted from *2009 UNESCO Framework for Cultural Statistics*, UNESCO Institute for Statistics (UIS) (2009) Figures 1 and 2, http://www.uis.unesco.org/datacentre; Figure 7.8 adapted from Cultural mapping and sustainable communities: planning for the arts revisited, *Cultural Trends*, Vol. 17 (2), pp. 65–96 (Evans, G. and Foord, J. 2008), p. 80, Figure 2, reprinted by permission of the publisher, Taylor & Francis Ltd., http://www.tandf.co.uk/journals, and the author; Figure 8.3 adapted from *The Ulysses Factor: Evaluating Visitors in Tourist Settings*, New York: Springer-Verlag (Pearce, P.L. 1988) pp. 100–101, Figures 5.2, 5.3, © Springer-Verlag New York Inc. 1988, with kind permission of Springer Science + Business Media; Figure 10.11 from *Port Hacking Visitor Use Study*, Centre for Leisure and Tourism Studies, University of Technology, Sydney (Robertson, R. W., and Veal, A. J. 1987); Figure 11.8 adapted from Retaining the visitor, enhancing the experience: identifying attributes of choice in repeat museum visitation, *International Journal of Nonprofit and Voluntary Sector Marketing*, Vol. 14 (1), pp. 21–34 (Burton, C., Louviere, J. and Young, L. 2009), Copyright © 2008 John Wiley & Sons Ltd.; Figure 12.5 from *The Entrepreneurial Arts Leader: Cultural Policy, Change and Reinvention*, Brisbane: University of Queensland Press (Rentschler, R. 2002) p. 59; Figure 14.7 adapted from *The Perilous Life of Symphony Orchestras: Artistic Triumphs and Economic Challenges*, New Haven, CN: Yale University Press (Flanagan, R.J. 2012) Figure 2.2, Copyright © 2012 by Robert J. Flanagan; Figures 15.7, 15.9, 15.12–15.16 NVivo software screenshots from QSR International Pty Ltd., reproduced with kind permission from QSR International; Figures 16.7, 16.8 and 16.9 IBM SPSS Statistics software screenshots reprinted courtesy of International Business Machines Corporation, © International Business Machines Corporation. SPSS Inc. was acquired by IBM in October 2009. IBM, the IBM logo, ibm.com, and SPSS are trademarks or registered trademarks of International Business Machines Corporation, registered in many jurisdictions worldwide. Other product and service names might be trademarks of IBM or other companies. A current list of IBM trademarks is available on the Web at "IBM Copyright and trademark information" at www.ibm.com/legal/copytrade.shtml.

Tables

Tables 6.4, 13.1, 13.2, 13.4, 13.5 and 13.6 from *Research Methods for Leisure and Tourism*, 4th ed., Pearson Education (Veal, A.J. 2011), Copyright © Pearson Education Limited 2006, 2011.

Text

Case Studies 2.1, 3.1, 8.1, 9.1, 10.1, 11.3, 14.2, 14.3 and 15.1, from or adapted from *Research Methods for Leisure and Tourism*, 4th ed., Pearson Education (Veal, A.J. 2011), Copyright © Pearson Education Limited 2006, 2011; Appendices 16.1, 17.1 and 17.2 from or adapted from *Research Methods for Leisure and Tourism*, 4th ed., Pearson Education (Veal, A.J. 2011), Copyright © Pearson Education Limited 2006, 2011.

In some instances we have been unable to trace the owners of copyright material, and we would appreciate any information that would enable us to do so.

PART 1

Introduction

This part of the book contains six chapters:

- Chapter 1, 'Introduction to research: what, why and who?', and Chapter 2, 'Approaches to research in the arts and events', set the context for research generally and for the background to research in the field of arts/events.

- Chapter 3, 'Starting out: research plans and proposals', considers the all-important process of designing a research project and provides a framework for the various components of research discussed in the rest of the book.

- Chapter 4, 'Research ethics', introduces the topic of the ethical conduct of research, which relates to moral as well as legal and administrative issues.

- Chapter 5, 'The range of research methods', provides an overview of the range of social science research methods and techniques used in arts and events contexts, which is discussed in more detail in the rest of the book.

- Chapter 6, 'Reviewing the literature', discusses the fundamental task of examining published and unpublished research relevant to the project in hand.

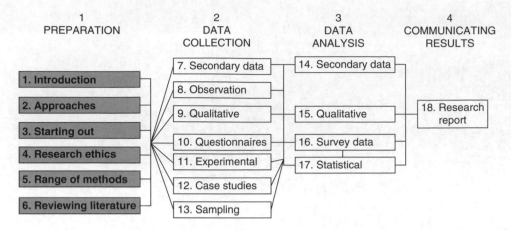

1 PREPARATION	2 DATA COLLECTION	3 DATA ANALYSIS	4 COMMUNICATING RESULTS

1. Introduction
2. Approaches
3. Starting out
4. Research ethics
5. Range of methods
6. Reviewing literature

7. Secondary data
8. Observation
9. Qualitative
10. Questionnaires
11. Experimental
12. Case studies
13. Sampling

14. Secondary data
15. Qualitative
16. Survey data
17. Statistical

18. Research report

Chapter 1

Introduction to research: what, why and who?

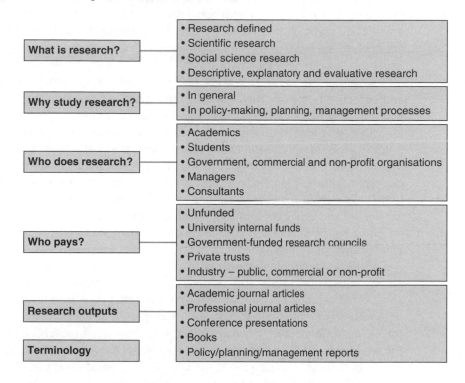

What is research?	• Research defined • Scientific research • Social science research • Descriptive, explanatory and evaluative research
Why study research?	• In general • In policy-making, planning, management processes
Who does research?	• Academics • Students • Government, commercial and non-profit organisations • Managers • Consultants
Who pays?	• Unfunded • University internal funds • Government-funded research councils • Private trusts • Industry – public, commercial or non-profit
Research outputs	• Academic journal articles • Professional journal articles • Conference presentations • Books
Terminology	• Policy/planning/management reports

Introduction

Information, knowledge and understanding concerning the natural, social and economic environment have become the very basis of cultural and material development in contemporary societies and economies. Recent controversies over the research basis of the global climate change predictions offer a dramatic demonstration of this. An understanding of how information and knowledge are generated and utilised and an ability to conduct or commission research relevant to the requirements of an organisation can therefore be seen as key skills for managers in any industry sector and a key component of the education of the modern professional. Research is not just a set of disembodied skills, however; it exists and is practised in a variety of cultural, social, political and economic contexts. The purpose of this book is to provide an introduction to the world of social research in the context of the arts and events, as an industry sector, a public policy concern and a field of academic inquiry and reflection. The aim is to provide a practical guide to the conduct of research and an appreciation of the role of research in the policy-making, planning and management processes of the arts/events sector and to foster a critical understanding of existing theoretical and applied research.

The focus of the book is the arts and events. While research methodology can be seen as universal, various fields of research – including the arts, but less so events studies, which is a relatively new field – have developed their own methodological emphases and bodies of experience. In some fields of research scientific laboratory experiments are the norm, while in others social surveys are more common. While most of the principles of research are universal, a specialised text such as this reflects the traditions and practices in its field of focus and draws attention to examples of relevant applications of methods and the particular problems and issues that arise in such applications.

The field of the arts and events is a large one, encompassing a wide range of individual and collective human activity. The arts can be defined as creative activities and products which convey beauty and/or insight into the human condition. The arts can be viewed as an activity engaged in by individuals and groups, but also as a service industry involving public-sector, non-profit and commercial organisations and facilities as diverse as a one-person pottery studio and major arts theatre complex and its resident companies. There is clear conceptual and material overlap with other domains such as entertainment and culture, both 'high' culture and popular culture. Of these, entertainment makes no claim to conveying beauty and/or insight into the human condition, although it may often do that, and it encompasses phenomena which are clearly not part of the arts, such as sport spectating, game shows and gambling.

Culture is a more complex term, with at least two meanings. The first meaning is virtually synonymous with 'the arts'. The second is equivalent to 'way of life'. But 'popular culture' is very close in meaning to entertainment. The emerging field of *events studies* is not concerned only with arts events but also with events in many other sectors, notably in sport, where the Olympic Games and the soccer World Cup are among the largest peacetime events in the world, while national, regional and local events are significant dimensions of culture in its broadest sense. Also covered in the book is the phenomenon of *cultural tourism*, which covers active involvement in the arts – as in a painting holiday – and passive involvement, such as travelling to attend a major show or visit historic cultural attractions. *Heritage* – in the form of valued historic and natural sites and as museum management – also falls within the purview of the arts and can be sites for events and cultural tourism. Similarly, craft and design are specific arts activities associated with museums or are displayed in specific design centres, often combining commercial opportunities for the maker but open to the public in the traditional way that museums operate.

In this book, the term 'cultural' is often used to encompass the arts, popular culture and leisure-based events, as in, for example, 'cultural participation' or 'cultural industries', and this can, of course, include events. See Figure 1.1.

Most of the book is concerned with *how* to do research, so the aim of this opening chapter is to introduce the 'what, why and who' of research. What is research? Why study research? Who does research?

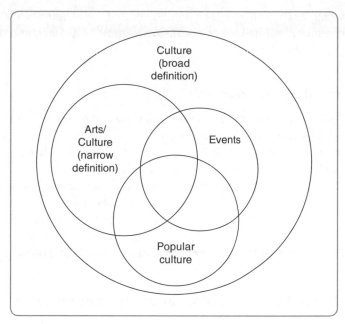

Figure 1.1 Arts and events

Research defined

What is research? Sociologist Norbert Elias defined research in terms of its aims, as follows:

> The aim, as far as I can see, is the same in all sciences. Put simply and cursorily, the aim is to make known something previously unknown to human beings. It is to advance human knowledge, to make it more certain or better fitting … The aim is … discovery.

Elias (1986: 20)

Discovery – making known something previously unknown – could cover a number of activities, for instance the work of journalists or detectives. Elias, however, also indicates that research is a tool of 'science' and that its purpose is to 'advance human knowledge' – features which distinguish research from other investigatory activities.

Scientific research

Scientific research is conducted within the rules and conventions of science. This means that it is based on logic and reason and the systematic examination of evidence. Ideally, within the scientific model, it should be possible for research to be *replicated* by the same or different researchers and for similar conclusions to emerge (although this is not always possible or practicable). It should also contribute to a cumulative body of knowledge about a field or topic. This model of scientific research applies most aptly in the physical or natural sciences, such as physics or chemistry, and in the biological sciences. In the area of *social science*, which deals with people as individuals and social beings with relationships to groups and communities, the pure scientific model must be adapted and modified, and in some cases largely abandoned.

Social science research

Social science research is carried out using the methods and traditions of social science. Social science differs from the physical or natural sciences in that it deals with *people* and their social behaviour, and people are less predictable than non-human phenomena. People can be aware of the research being conducted about them and are not therefore purely passive subjects; they can react to the results of research and change their behaviour accordingly. While the fundamental behaviour patterns of non-human phenomena are relatively constant and universal, people in different parts of the world and at different times behave differently. The social world is constantly changing, so it is rarely possible to produce exact replications of research at different times or in different places and obtain similar results.

Descriptive, explanatory and evaluative research

Elias's term *discovery* can be seen as, first, the process of finding out – at its simplest, therefore, research might just *describe* what exists. But to 'advance human knowledge, to make it more certain or better fitting', requires more than just the accumulation of information, or facts. The aim is also to provide *explanation* – to explain why things are as they are, and how they might be. In this book, we are also concerned with a third function of research, namely *evaluating* – that is, judging the degree of success or value of policies or programmes. Three types of research can be identified corresponding to these three functions, as shown in Figure 1.2. In some cases particular research projects concentrate on only one of these, but often two or more of the approaches are included in the same research project.

1 Descriptive research

Descriptive research is very common in the arts/events area, for three reasons: the relative newness of the field, the changing nature of the phenomena being studied, and the frequent separation between research and policy/management action.

Since arts/events is a relatively new field of study there is a need to map the territory. Much of the research therefore seeks to discover, describe or map patterns of behaviour in areas or activities which have not previously been studied in the field or for which information needs to be updated on a regular basis. It might therefore be described as *descriptive*. In some texts this form of research is termed *exploratory*. But because the other categories of research, including explanatory and evaluative, can also at times be exploratory, the term descriptive is used here.

1 Descriptive research	Finding out, describing what is
2 Explanatory research	Explaining how or why things are as they are (and using this to predict)
3 Evaluative research	Evaluation of policies and programmes

Figure 1.2 Types of research

One of the reasons why descriptive research is required is that the field of arts/events is constantly changing over time, for example:

● the popularity of different art forms or events changes;
● the cultural preferences of different social groups (for example, young people or women) change;
● new arts forms or events are introduced, such as the advent of hip-hop or 'installation' art;
● new technologies are introduced, for example, online live streaming of arts performances or the advent of 3D media;
● new/additional facilities are provided in local communities;
● new policy initiatives are taken, for example in marketing or in training of artists.

A great deal of research effort in the field is therefore devoted to tracking – or monitoring – changing patterns of behaviour. Hence the importance in the arts of *secondary data* sources, that is data collected by other organisations, such as government statistical agencies, as discussed in Chapter 7. A complete understanding and explanation of these changing patterns would be ideal, so that the future could be predicted, but this is only partially possible, so providers of cultural services must be aware of changing social and market conditions whether or not they can be fully explained or understood; they are therefore reliant on a flow of descriptive research to provide up-to-date information.

Descriptive research projects are often undertaken because that is what is commissioned. For example, a company may commission a *market profile* study or a local council may commission a *cultural needs* study from a research team – but the actual use of the results of the research, in marketing or planning, may be a separate exercise with which the research team is not involved: the research team may simply be required to produce a descriptive study.

2 Explanatory research

Explanatory research moves beyond description to seek to explain the patterns and trends observed. For example, explanations might be required for:

● the falling popularity of a particular art form;
● community opposition to the hosting of a major sporting event;
● the fact that some social groups have particularly low levels of participation in the arts.

Such questions raise the thorny issue of *causality*, where the aim is to be able to say, for example, that there has been an increase in A *because of* a corresponding fall in B. It is one thing to discover that A has increased while B has decreased, but to establish that the rise in A has been *caused* by the fall in B is often a much more demanding task. To establish causality, or the likelihood of causality, requires the researcher to be rigorous in the collection, analysis and interpretation of data. It also generally requires some sort of theoretical framework to relate the phenomenon under study to wider social, economic and political processes. The issue of causality and the role of theory in research are discussed further in later chapters.

Once causes are at least partially understood, the knowledge can be used to *predict*. This is clear enough in the physical sciences: we know that heat causes metal to expand (explanation) – therefore we know that if we apply a certain amount of heat to a bar of metal it will expand by a certain amount (prediction). In the biological and medical sciences this process is also followed, but with less precision: it can be predicted that if a certain treatment is given to patients with a certain disease then it is likely that a certain proportion will be cured. In the social sciences this approach is also used, but with even less precision. For example, economists have found that demand for goods and services, including cultural goods and services, responds to price levels: if the price of a product or service is reduced then sales will generally increase. But this does not always happen because there are so many other factors involved, such as variation in quality and the success of brand marketing. Human beings make their own decisions and are far less predictable than non-human phenomena. Nevertheless, prediction is a feature of some policy-related arts/events research.

3 Evaluative research

Evaluative research arises from the need to make judgements on the success or effectiveness of policies or programmes – for example, whether a particular cultural facility or programme is meeting required performance standards or whether a particular promotion campaign has been cost effective. In the private sector the levels of sales and profit are the main criteria used for such evaluations, although additional ratios may also be used. In the public and non-profit sectors, where facilities, services or events are not usually intended to make a cash profit, assessing community benefits requires research to assemble data as elementary as levels of use or attendance. Evaluative research is highly developed in some areas of public policy, for example education, but is less well developed in practice in the field of the arts, although it is subject to considerable debate, given that, because of the creative nature of arts practice, some forms of evaluation are seen as intrusive and are resisted.

The use of terms such as *evidence-based policy* and *performance indicators* heralds the advent of *managerialism* in the cultural sector, a process that is not without its critics. Schuster (1997: 254), for example, speaks of 'antipathy, if not outright opposition, to the use of performance indicators in the arts and culture', while Madden (2005: 217) notes that statistics are 'sometimes vilified in the arts'. A medical practitioner, discussing the proposition that the use of the arts in clinical settings should be evaluated, argues that such ideas are 'utterly absurd – an abuse not only of the arts culture but also of the science culture' (Baum, 2001: 306). In evaluation of arts projects, Matarasso (2003: 338) rejects 'uncritical scientism' in favour of 'an approach informed by practice', asserting that there are 'many ways of understanding the world and many legitimate forms of knowledge', a proposition explored further by Hemingway and Parr (2000). The public-sector part of the industry is, however, faced with the challenge of competing for funds with other parts of government in an era when governments are increasingly expecting expenditure to be evaluated in a formal manner (Hamilton *et al.*, 2003; HM Treasury, 2003). In event management, the idea of evaluation, and the formal measurement and research that go with it, has been a widely accepted part of the process of professionalisation of the field (see Allen *et al.*, 2000).

Why study research?

In general

Research and research methods might be studied for a variety of reasons, as summarised in Figure 1.3.

---

1. To understand research reports, etc.
2. To conduct academic research projects.
3. As a management tool in:
   - policy making
   - planning
   - management (individual/team/organisation)
   - evaluation.

Figure 1.3 Why study research?

- First, it is useful to be able to *understand* and *evaluate* research reports and articles encountered in an academic, professional or managerial context. It is advantageous to understand the basis and limitations of such reports and articles.

- Second, many readers of this book may engage in research in an academic environment, where research is conducted for its own sake, in the interests of the pursuit of knowledge – for example for a thesis.

- Third, most readers will find themselves conducting or commissioning research for professional reasons, as managers or consultants. It is therefore particularly appropriate to consider the role of research in the policy-making, planning and management process.

Of course, for many readers of this book, the immediate challenge is to complete a research-related project as part of an undergraduate or postgraduate programme of study. This book should, of course, assist in this task, but the task is a means to an end, not an end in itself. Research projects conducted as part of a curriculum are seen as a learning process to equip the student as a professional consumer, practitioner and/or commissioner of research in professional life.

Research in policy-making, planning and management processes

All organisations, including those in the cultural industries, engage in policy-making, planning and managing processes to achieve their goals. A variety of terms is used in this area and the meanings of terms varies according to the context and user. In this book:

- *policies* are considered to be the statements of principles, intentions and commitments of an organisation;

- *plans* are detailed strategies, typically set out in a document, designed to implement policies in particular ways over a specified period of time;

- *management* is seen as the process of implementing policies and plans.

Although planning is usually associated in the public mind with national, regional and local government bodies, it is also an activity undertaken by the private sector. Organisations such as developers of cinema complexes or event promoters are all involved in planning, but their planning activities are less public than those of government bodies. Private organisations are usually concerned only with their own activities, but government bodies often have a wider responsibility to provide a planning framework for the activities of many public- and private-sector organisations. Examples of policies, plans and management activity in cultural contexts are given in Figure 1.4.

Level	National Arts Council	Museum	Arts festival
Policy	Produce performing arts policy	Maximise visitation by all age groups	Decide overall purpose and emphasis of festival, e.g. international cinema
Plan	Publish five-year grant-aid strategy	Two-year plan to increase visits by older people by 50%	Prepare strategy plan for themes for next three years
Management	Distribute and monitor outcomes of grants	Implement morning guided tour/ lunch programme for seniors	Book films, etc. and venues, produce programme and implement year 1 marketing/sales programme

Figure 1.4 Examples of policies, plans and management activity

Both policies and plans can vary enormously in detail, complexity and formality. Here the process is considered only briefly in order to examine the part played by research. Of the many models of policy-making, planning and management processes that exist, the *rational–comprehensive* model, a version of which is depicted in Figure 1.5, is the most traditional, 'ideal' model. It is beyond the scope of this book to discuss the many alternative models that seek to more accurately reflect real-world decision making, but guidance to further reading on this issue is given in the Resources section at the end of the chapter. Suffice it to say here that these alternatives are often 'cut-down' versions of the rational–comprehensive model, emphasising some aspects of this model and de-emphasising, or omitting, others. Thus some reflect the view that it is virtually impossible to be completely *comprehensive* in assessing alternative policies; some reflect the fact that political interests often intervene before 'rational' or 'objective' decisions can be made; while others elevate community/stakeholder consultation to a central rather than a supportive role. In nearly all cases the models are put forward as an *alternative* to the rational–comprehensive model, so the latter, even if rejected, remains the universal reference point.

In most of these models a research role remains – sometimes curtailed and sometimes enhanced. It is rare that all of the steps shown in Figure 1.5 are followed through in the real world. And it is also rare for research to inform the process in all the ways discussed below. The steps depicted provide an agenda for discussing the many roles of research in policy-making, planning and management processes. An example of how the process might unfold in arts/events contexts is given in Figure 1.6.

1. *Terms of reference/brief*: The 'terms of reference' or 'brief' for a particular planning or management task sets out the scope and purpose of the exercise. Research can be involved right at the beginning of this process, in assisting in establishing the terms of reference. For example, existing research on levels of arts/events participation in a community may result in a government policy initiative to do something about it.

2. *Set values/mission/goals*: Statements of the missions or goals of the organisation may already be in place if the task in hand is a relatively minor one, but if it is a major undertaking, such as the development of a strategic plan for the whole organisation, then the development of statements of mission and goals may be involved. It is very much a task for the decision-making body of an organisation (such as the board, committee or council) to determine its mission and/or goals; research may be directly involved when there is consultation with large numbers of stakeholders, as discussed under step 4.

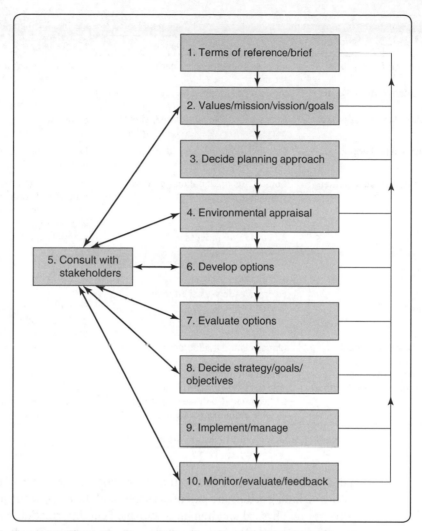

Figure 1.5 The rational–comprehensive planning/management process

3. *Decide planning approach:* Like research, a range of different methodologies and approaches is available for policy making and planning, including adopting externally specified fixed standards of provision; aiming to maximise opportunity; resource-based planning; meeting defined demand; meeting the requirements/requests of stakeholders; meeting unmet 'needs'; providing social or economic benefits; and aiming to increase participation (Veal 2010: Chapter 7). The method/approach selected will determine the type of research to be carried out during the policy-making/planning process: for example, a needs-based approach will require a definition of need and a method for collecting information on needs, while resource-based planning will require identification of the range of cultural resources to be included, for example in a community arts strategy, and processes for data gathering and evaluation.

4. *Environmental appraisal:* An environmental appraisal involves the gathering of relevant information on the physical, social, economic and organisational context of the task in

Steps in the planning/management process (see Figure 1.4)	Young people and the arts in a local community	
	Policy/planning/management	Associated research
1 Terms of reference/brief	Increase young people's participation in the arts	Existing research indicates 40% participation rate
2 Set values/mission/goals	Increase participation level to 60% over five years	–
3 Decide planning approach	Needs-based, demand-based, etc.: for discussion, see Veal (2010: Chapter 7)	As below
4 Environmental appraisal	Consider existing supply–demand	Existing programmes and infrastructure fully used
5 Consult with stakeholders	Consult arts organisations, schools, young people	Survey indicates support among all groups and confirms feasibility
6 Develop options	1. Publicity campaign 2. Free vouchers 3. Build more facilities 4. Promote events 5. Provide support to arts organisations /schools 6. Train leaders/teachers/directors	Review of experience of each option in other regions, based on published accounts and a survey
7 Evaluate options	Evaluate options 1–5	Each option costed; on basis of survey evidence, estimate made of cost effectiveness of each option
8 Decide strategy/goals/ objectives	Options 3 and 4 adopted	Options 3 and 4 recommended
9 Implement/manage	Implement options 3 and 4	–
10 Monitor/evaluate/feedback	Assess success in terms of increased participation. Continue programme: increase resources for training volunteers	Survey indicates participation increase to 45% after one year, but shortage of coaches/leaders

Figure 1.6 Example of planning/management tasks and associated research

hand. Information may relate to the organisation's internal workings or to the outside world, including actual and potential clients, and the activities of governments and competitors and physical and human resources. Such information may be readily to hand and may just need collation, or it may require extensive research (see cultural mapping, Chapter 7).

5. *Consult with stakeholders:* Consultation with stakeholders is considered vital by most organisations and, indeed, is a statutory requirement in many forms of public-sector planning. Stakeholders can include employees, clients, professional artists/performers, visitors, members of the general public, members of boards and councils, and neighbouring or complementary organisations. Research can be a significant feature of such consultation, especially when large numbers of individuals or organisations are involved.

6. *Develop options:* In order to develop a plan or strategy, consideration must be given to what policy options are available to pursue the goals of the organisation, their feasibility, their likely contribution to the achievement of the goals and the best way to implement them. Research can be involved in the process of *identifying* alternative policy or planning options, for example by providing data on the extent of problems or on stakeholder preferences.

7. *Evaluate options:* Deciding on a strategy involves selecting a course or courses of action from among all the possible options identified. This choice process may involve a

complex procedure requiring research to *evaluate* the alternatives. Typical formal evaluation techniques include cost–benefit analysis, economic impact analysis and environmental and social impact analysis, and the use of the *importance–performance* technique or *conjoint analysis* (see Resources section).

8. *Decide strategy/goals/objectives:* Evaluation processes rarely produce a single best solution or course of action. Thus, for example, option A may be cheaper than option B, but option B produces better outcomes. Final decisions on which strategy to pursue must be taken by the governing body of the organisation – the board, committee or council – based on political and/or personal values. A strategy should involve clear statements of what the strategy is intended to achieve (goals), with measurable outcomes and timelines (objectives).

9. *Implement/manage:* Implementing a plan or strategy is the field of *management*. Research can be involved in day-to-day management, for example in investigating improved ways of deploying resources, and in providing continuous feedback on the management process, for example in the form of audience surveys. However, the line between such research and the monitoring and evaluation process is difficult to draw.

10. *Monitor/evaluate/feedback:* Monitoring progress and evaluating the implementation of strategies is clearly a process with which research is likely to be involved. The process comes full circle with the feedback step. The data from the monitoring and evaluation step can be fed back into the planning or management cycle and can lead to a revision of any or all of the decisions previously made. The monitoring and evaluation process may report complete success, it may suggest minor changes to some of the details of the policies and plans adopted, or it could result in a fundamental re-think, going 'back to the drawing board'.

The above discussion is based on a generic model, Figure 1.5, which might apply to any policy-making, planning or management environment. Screven (1990) discusses the role of evaluative research in the context of a five-stage model of the development of an exhibition. This is summarised in Figure 1.7. The stages involve a mix of observation, interviews, experimentation, so the model relates to Chapters 8 (observation), 9 and 10 (qualitative and quantitative interview-based research) and 11 (experimental research).

Stage of development	Type of research	Methods
1 Planning	Front-end evaluation	Interviews, questionnaire-based surveys, focus groups with current and potential visitors regarding the concept/theme
2 Design	Formative evaluation	In relation to subjects viewing mock-ups of exhibits: interviews ('cued testing') and/or observation ('non-cued testing')
3 Construction/installation	–	–
4 Occupancy	Summative evaluation	Observation/tracking of visitors and/or visitor surveys
5 Remedial	Remedial evaluation	Responding to (negative) findings from summative evaluation, making changes to exhibits/layout, etc. over time – further observation and interviewing

Figure 1.7 Research in the stages of exhibition development

Who does research?

This book is mainly concerned with how to conduct research, but it also aims to provide an understanding of the research process which will help the reader to become a knowledgeable, critical consumer of the research carried out by others. In reading reports of research, it is useful to bear in mind why the research has been done and to a large extent this is influenced by who did the research and who paid for it to be done. Who does research is important because it affects the nature of the research conducted and hence has a large impact on what constitutes the *body of knowledge* which students must absorb and which managers draw on.

Research is undertaken by a wide variety of individuals and institutions, as listed in Figure 1.8. The respective roles of these research actors are discussed in turn below.

Academics

Academics are members of the paid academic staff of academic institutions, including professors, lecturers, tutors and research staff – in North American parlance: *the faculty*. In most academic institutions professors and lecturers are expected, as part of their contract of employment, to engage in both research and teaching. Typically a quarter or third of an academic's time might be devoted to research and writing. Promotion and job security depend partly (some would say mainly) on the achievement of a satisfactory track record in published research. Publication can be in various forms, as discussed under 'Research outputs' below.

Some research arises from academic interest and some arises from immediate problems being faced by cultural organisations. Much published academic research tends to be governed by the concerns of the various theoretical disciplines, such as sociology, economics or psychology, which may or may not coincide with the day-to-day concerns of the cultural industries. In fact, part of the role of the academic researcher is to 'stand apart' from the rest of the world and provide disinterested analysis, which may be critical and may not be seen as particularly supportive by those working in the industry. However, what may be seen by some as overly critical and unhelpful, or just plain irrelevant, may be seen by others as insightful and constructive.

Group	Motivation/purpose
Academics	Part of the job description. Knowledge for its own sake and/or to engage with industry/profession and/or benefit society.
Students	Coursework students: projects as learning medium and/or part of professional training. Research students: adding to knowledge and training/qualification for a research/academic career.
Government, commercial and non-profit organisations	Research to inform policy, monitor performance and aid in decision making. Relevant to the idea of 'evidence-based policy'.
Managers	Research to inform policy, monitor performance and aid in decision making.
Consultants	Research under contract to government, commercial and non-profit organisations.
Cultural observatories	Nationally based organisations which have a 'watching brief' to collate and disseminate cultural research, and may be funded from government, industry and/or non-profit sources.

Figure 1.8 Who does research?

Applied disciplines such as the fields of cultural planning, urban planning, business management, marketing or financial management focus specifically on aspects of the policy, planning and management process. While academic research in these areas can also be critical rather than immediately instrumental, it is more likely to be driven by the sorts of issues that concern the industry. However, this can also give rise to tensions among academics who wish to become involved with the cultural policy-making and planning process via research, while maintaining an independent/critical stance – as discussed, for example, by Scullion and Garcia (2005). Generally, academics become involved in funded research of a practically orientated nature when their own interests coincide with those of the agency concerned. For instance, an academic may be interested in ways of measuring what motivates people to engage or not engage in certain cultural activities and this could coincide with a cultural organisation's need for research to assist in developing a marketing strategy. Academics who specialise in applied areas are very often in a better position to attract funding from industry sources.

Students

PhD and Masters degree students are major contributors to research. Theses (or dissertations to use the term more common in North America) produced in recent years are mostly available in digital form and university libraries generally subscribe to various thesis databases (see Chapter 6).

In the science area research students often work as part of a team, under the direction of a supervisor who may determine what topics will be researched by individual students within a particular research programme. In the social sciences this approach is less common, with students having a wider scope in their selection of research topics.

PhD theses are the most significant form of student research, but research done by Masters degree and graduate diploma students and even undergraduates in the form of projects and honours theses can be a useful contribution to knowledge. The arts and events sector is not generally well endowed with research funds, so even, for example, a small survey conducted by a group of undergraduates on a particular cultural activity in a particular locality, or a thorough review of an area of literature, may be of considerable use or interest to others.

Government, commercial and non-profit organisations

Government, commercial and non-profit organisations conduct or commission research to inform policy, monitor performance or aid in decision making. A term coined to describe this relationship between policy and research is *evidence-based policy* (Pawson, 2006). Some large organisations have their own in-house research organisations – for example, at government level, the Office of National Statistics in the UK and the Australian Bureau of Statistics in Australia. Commercial organisations in the sector tend to rely on consultants for their social, economic and market research, although entertainment equipment manufacturers may conduct their own scientific research for product development.

Research reports from these organisations can be important sources of knowledge, especially of a more practically orientated nature. For example, in nearly every developed country some government agency takes responsibility for conducting nation-wide surveys of cultural participation rates (Cushman *et al.*, 2005; Schuster, 2002), as discussed in Chapter 7. This is descriptive research which few other organisations would have the resources or incentive to undertake.

- Current customers/members
- Market/community research: potential customers/community
- Environmental appraisal/cultural mapping
- Organisational performance
  - Sales
  - Efficiency
  - Staff performance/motivation
- Competitors
- Products/services
  - Existing
  - New

Figure 1.9 Managers/policy makers and research topics

Managers/policy makers

Professionals in the cultural/events sector who recognise the full extent of the management, policy-making and planning process see research as very much part of their responsibilities. Managers may find themselves carrying out research on a range of types of topic, as indicated in Figure 1.9. Since most of the readers of this book will be actual or trainee managers, this is an important point to recognise.

Successful management depends on good information. Much information – for example ticket sales or membership details – is available to the manager as a matter of routine and does not require research. However, the creative utilisation of such data – for example to establish market trends or seasonal patterns – may amount to research. Other types of information can be obtained only by means of specific research projects. In some areas of arts and event management even the most basic information must be obtained by research. For example, while managers of theatres routinely receive information on audience numbers from ticket sales, this is not the case for the manager of a museum with no entrance fee, a festival with multiple free open-air events, or broadcasters. To gain information on the number of users of this type of facility, event or service it is necessary to conduct a specific data-gathering exercise. Such data gathering may not be very sophisticated and some would say that it does not qualify as research, being just part of the management information system, but in the sense that it involves finding out, sometimes explaining, and the deployment of specific techniques and skills, it qualifies as research for the purposes of this book.

Most managers need to carry out – or commission – research if they want information on their audiences or customers, for example where they come from (the 'catchment area' of the facility or event) or their socio-economic characteristics. Research is also a way of finding out about customers' evaluations of the facility or service. It might be argued that managers do not themselves need research skills since they can always commission consultants to carry out research for them. However, managers will be better able to commission effective research and evaluate the results if they are familiar with the research process themselves. It is also the case that few managers in the arts/events sector work in an ideal world where funds exist to commission all the research they would like; often the only way they can get research done is to do it using their own and other available 'in-house' skills and time. Larger organisations have marketing, market research, or research and evaluation departments or units which employ specialist researchers who conduct, oversee or commission the sorts of research discussed in this book.

Consultants

Consultants offer their research and advisory services to government and commercial and non-profit organisations. Some consultancy organisations are large, multi-national companies involved in accountancy, management and project development consultancy generally, and which often establish specialised units covering the leisure/events/tourism sectors. Examples are PricewaterhouseCoopers and Ernst & Young. But there are also many much smaller, specialised organisations in the consultancy field. Some academics operate consultancy companies as a 'sideline', either because of academic interest in a particular area or to supplement incomes, or both. Self-employed consultancy activity is common among practitioners who have taken early retirement from employment in the culture industry.

Cultural observatories

Cultural observatories are nationally based organisations with a 'watching brief' to identify, collate and disseminate cultural research. Often a particular function is collation of statistical information. They are a relatively new phenomenon and a number have been established in the last decade or so, notably in Europe. They may be funded by government/research organisations, by non-profit trusts or by a combination of these sources together with consultancy work. Examples are listed in the Resources section.

Who pays?

Most research requires financial support to cover the costs of paying full-time or part-time research assistants, to pay for research student scholarships, to pay interviewers or a market research firm to conduct interviews, or to cover travel costs or the costs of equipment. Research is funded from a variety of sources, as indicated in Figure 1.10.

- *Unfunded*: Some research conducted by academics requires little or no specific financial resources over and above the academic's basic salary – for example, theoretical work and the many studies using students as subjects.
- *University internal funds*: Universities tend to use their own funds to support research which is initiated by academic staff and where the main motive is the 'advancement of knowledge'. Most universities and colleges have research funds for which members of their staff, and sometimes students, can apply.
- *Government-funded research councils*: Governments typically establish organisations to fund scientific research – for example, the UK Economic and Social Research Council or the Australian Research Council and the National Health and Medical Research Council. These or similar bodies often also provide scholarships for research students.

- Unfunded
- University internal funds
- Government-funded research councils
- Private trusts
- Industry – public, commercial or non-profit

Figure 1.10 Who pays?

17

- *Private trusts*: Many private trusts or foundations also fund research – for example, the Ford Foundation and the Leverhulme Trust. Trusts have generally been endowed with investment funds by a wealthy individual or from a public appeal.

- *Industry*: Funds may come from the world of practice – for instance from a government department or agency, a commercial company or a non-profit organisation such as a performing arts company run by a trust. In this case the research will tend to be more practically orientated. Government agencies and commercial and non-profit organisations fund research to solve particular problems or to inform them about particular issues relevant to their interests. Because of the scale of their available resources, governments in particular can have a significant effect on the patterns of research and data collection if they become interested in issues such as 'evidence-based policy' and 'accountability', as discussed by Selwood (2002).

Research outputs

Research outputs can be presented in a variety of forms and contexts. Some of these are listed in Figure 1.11 and discussed briefly below. The formats are not all mutually exclusive: a number of them may arise in various aspects in a single research project.

Academic journal articles

Publication of research in academic journals is considered to be the most prestigious form in academic terms because of the element of *refereeing* or *peer review*. Articles submitted to such journals are assessed (refereed) on an anonymous basis by two or three experts in the field, as well as the editors. Editorial activity is overseen by a board of experts in the field, whose names are listed in the journal. Arts and events research is published in specialist journals and a number in journals in cognate areas, such as leisure and tourism studies, and in mainstream disciplinary journals, such as in sociology, economics, marketing and psychology. Marketing discipline journals also cover audience research, including understanding

- Academic journal articles
- Professional journal articles
- Conference presentations/papers
- Books
- Policy/planning/management reports
  - Position statements/cultural maps
  - Market profiles
  - Market research
  - Market segmentation/lifestyle/psychographic studies
  - Feasibility studies
  - Cultural needs studies
  - Cultural tourism strategies/marketing plans
  - Forecasting studies
  - Impact studies
  - Industry/sector studies

Figure 1.11 Research report formats

the visitor experience in the areas of arts, heritage and events. Some of the main refereed journals in the arts and events areas are:

- Arts/culture

  Arts and Health
  Asia-Pacific Journal of Arts and Cultural Management
  Creative Industries Journal
  Cultural Trends
  Culture, Theory and Critique
  Curator Journal
  International Journal of Arts Management
  International Journal of Cultural Policy
  International Journal of Heritage Studies
  Journal of Arts Management, Law and Society
  Journal of Cultural Economics
  Journal for Cultural Research
  Journal of Cultural Management and Policy
  Journal of Museum Education
  Media International Australia (incorporating *Culture and Policy*)
  Museum Management and Curatorship
  Museums and Social Issues
  Popular Music and Society
  Poetics

- Visitor Studies

  Event Management (previously *Festival Management and Event Tourism*)
  International Journal of Event and Festival Management
  International Journal of Event Management Research
  Journal of Convention and Event Tourism
  Olympika (Olympic Games)

- Tourism studies journals containing significant events-related research

  Annals of Tourism Research
  Tourism Management

Academic research and publication is, to a large extent, a 'closed system'. Academics are the editors of the refereed journals and serve on their editorial advisory boards and referee panels. They determine what research is acceptable for publication. Practitioners therefore very often find published academic research irrelevant to their needs – this is hardly surprising since much of it is not designed for the practitioner but for the academic world. Students training to become professional practitioners in the arts/events area should not be surprised to come across scholarly writing that is not suitable for direct practical application to policy, planning and management. This does not mean that it is irrelevant, but simply that it does not necessarily focus explicitly on immediate practical problems.

Professional journal articles

Journals published by professional bodies for their members rarely publish original research, but may publish summaries of research of immediate relevance to practitioners.

Conference presentations/papers

Some academic conferences publish the papers presented in a hard-copy or online set of *proceedings*. In some cases such papers have been peer reviewed and have a similar status to academic journals, but this is rare in the arts/events field. Typically, research presented at conferences will also be published in journals or book form.

Books

Academic books can be divided into textbooks, like this one, and monographs, which may present the results of a single empirical research project or research programme, may be largely theoretical or may be a mixture of the two. Textbooks are not expected to present original research but may provide summaries and guides to research. Edited books with chapters contributed by a number of authors may be closer to the textbook model, or, if they contain original research, may be closer to the monograph model.

Policy/planning/management reports

Research conducted by commercial bodies is usually confidential but that conducted by government agencies is generally available to the public, increasingly via the internet. Such reports can invariably be found on the websites of national agencies, such as arts/events councils or tourism commissions and government departments, and local councils. Some of these documents are published, particularly when public agencies are involved, when they are typically made available on agency websites, often with invitations for public comment. In some cases, such as position statements and forecasting studies, they are inputs into later documents, such as strategic plans. Some may also appear, in summary form, in academic publications, in articles and as case studies in textbooks. Examples of published reports are listed in the Resources section. As indicated in Figure 1.11, such reports can take a variety of forms.

Position statements/cultural maps

Position statements, more recently referred to as cultural maps in the arts sector, are similar to the environmental appraisals discussed above in relation to the rational–comprehensive planning model. They are compilations of factual information on the current situation with regard to a topic or issue of concern, and are designed to assist decision makers to become knowledgeable about the topic or issue and to take stock of such matters as current policies, provision levels and demand. For example, if a local authority wishes to develop new policies for the arts in its area, a position statement might be prepared listing the existing public and non-profit arts organisations in the area and their memberships and programmes, the commercial arts-related facilities, their ownership, size and quality and usage, and patterns of cultural participation among the resident population.

Market profiles

Market profiles are similar to position statements but relate specifically to current and potential consumers and suppliers of a product or service. If an organisation wishes to start a project in a particular market it will usually require a profile of that market sector. How big is it, in terms of sales? What are its growth prospects? Who are the customers and what are their socio-demographic characteristics? What sub sectors does it have? How profitable is it?

Who are the current suppliers? Such a profile will usually require considerable research and can be seen as one element in the broader activity of market research.

Market research

Market research is a more encompassing activity than a market profile. Research on the actual or potential market for a product or service can take place in advance of a service being established but also as part of the on-going monitoring of the performance of an operation. Market research seeks to establish the scale and nature of the current market – the number of people who use or are likely to use the product or service, their expenditure and their characteristics – and actual and potential customer requirements, attitudes and motivations.

Market segmentation/lifestyle/psychographic studies

Traditionally, market researchers attempted to classify consumers into sub-markets or *segments* on the basis of their product preferences, including arts/events activities, and their socio-demographic characteristics such as age, gender, occupation and income. Later they sought to classify people using not only these background social and economic characteristics but also data on their attitudes, values and behaviour. Such lifestyle segments may be developed as part of any survey-based research project, but there are also commercially developed systems which survey companies may apply to a range of market research projects. Examples are discussed in Chapter 5.

Feasibility studies

Feasibility studies investigate not only current consumer characteristics and demands, as in a market profile, but also future demand and such aspects as the financial viability and environmental impact of a proposed development or investment projects. The decision whether or not to build a new arts/events facility or launch a new tourism product is usually based on such a feasibility study.

Cultural needs studies

Cultural needs studies, sometimes conducted as a part of a leisure needs study or cultural mapping exercise, are a common type of research in local planning, covering the arts, entertainment and events. These are comprehensive studies, usually carried out for local councils but sometimes for a consortium of arts organisations, examining levels of provision and use of facilities and services, levels of participation in cultural activities, and views and aspirations of the population concerning their own preferences and desired provision. In some cases a needs study also includes a cultural 'plan', which makes recommendations on future provision; in other cases the plan is in a separate document.

Cultural tourism strategies/marketing plans

Cultural tourism strategies/marketing plans may be separate exercises or a part of a general tourism strategy. Rather than referring to the *needs* of the local population, cultural tourism strategies or marketing plans refer to the cultural tourism *demands* of non-local populations to be accommodated in a destination area. Such studies usually consider the existing and potential attractions of an area and the capacity of the area to meet the demands of a projected number of tourists, in terms of accommodation, transport and existing and acceptable levels of environmental impacts.

Forecasting studies

Forecasting studies form a key input to many plans. They might provide, for example, projections of demand for a particular group of cultural activities/events over a specified period, such as ten years. Forecasting is intrinsically research-based and can involve predicting the likely effects of future population growth and change, changing tastes, changing levels of income or developments in technology.

Impact studies

Large built developments typically require an environmental impact to be undertaken as part of the process of gaining approval from planning agencies, covering matters such as noise, traffic generation and impacts on wildlife and cultural heritage. A common occurrence in the case of major events, particularly cultural events, is the conduct of an economic impact study to demonstrate that the costs incurred by the hosting of an event will be, or have been, offset by benefits, such as the generation of income and jobs and other types of legacy. Impact studies in the arts have increasingly covered economic and social impacts. The measurement of economic and social impact has been debatable and new ways of understanding the phenomena of impact have developed over the past decade (Centre for Economics and Business Research, 2013; Peterson, 2005; Reeves, 2002).

Industry/sector studies

Like many industries the arts have been subject to policy and structural changes in the past decade, while events have been subject to rapid change simply as a result of rapid growth. Policy changes in how the arts are funded have meant that the arts need to justify performance in relation to key measurements demanded by funders. For example, in Australia the Nugent Report (1999), which scoped and segmented the major performing arts companies, recommended continual funding based on artistic vibrancy among other indicators. Artistic vibrancy, itself a nebulous term, spawned other research to look at original compositions, audience acceptance of new work and the impact on the company in programming new work (Bailey and Du Preez, 2010). Similarly, digital technology has spawned a number of small to medium enterprises and microenterprises in the creative industries which are often suppliers to commercial or other non-profit cultural entities. Research has been undertaken to look at the skills deficit (particularly in relation to business acumen) in these companies with a view to ensuring their sustainability (Centre for International Economics, 2009). Sometimes such industry-wide studies are referred to as 'mapping' exercises, as discussed in Chapters 5 and 7.

Terminology

Like any field of study and practice, research methods has its own distinct terminology, some of which is familiar to the wider community and some of which is not. Most terms and expressions will be introduced and defined in the appropriate chapters which follow, but some are common to the whole research process and some key ones are described here.

Subject

Subject is used to refer to people providing information or being studied in a research project. For example, if a social survey involves interviews with a sample of 200 people, it involves 200 *subjects*. Some researchers prefer to use the term *participant*, believing that subject implies subjective, suggesting a hierarchical relationship between the researcher and the researched. The term *case* is sometimes used, particularly when the phenomenon being researched is not individual people – for example, organisations, countries, destinations, arts/events.

Variable

Variable refers to a characteristic, behaviour pattern or opinion which varies from subject to subject. Thus, for example, age, income, level of holiday-taking or music preferences are all variables. An *independent* variable is one which is controlled by forces outside the context of the study, and influences *dependent* variables within the scope of the study. Thus, for example, in a study of an outdoor museum the weather would be an independent variable while the number of people who visit the museum is a dependent variable. In another context, such as the study of climate, the weather could be a dependent variable influenced by such independent variables as the behaviour of the sun and the temperature of the oceans.

Summary

This chapter addresses the 'what?' of research in defining and introducing the concept of research and describes three types of research with which this book is concerned: *descriptive*, *explanatory* and *evaluative*. The 'why?' of research is discussed primarily in the context of policy making, planning and management, since the majority of the book's users will be studying for a vocational qualification. The links between research and the various stages of policy making, planning and management are discussed using the rational–comprehensive model as a framework, and attention is drawn to the variety of forms that research reports can take in the management environment. 'Who?' conducts research is an important and often neglected aspect of research: in this chapter, the respective research roles of academics, students, governmental and commercial organisations, consultants and managers are discussed. Finally, there is an introduction to the various formats in which research results may be published, from academic journal articles to a variety of management-related reports.

TEST QUESTIONS

1. What is the difference between research and journalism?
2. Outline the differences between descriptive, explanatory and evaluative research.
3. What are the broad differences between policy making, planning and management, as presented in this chapter?
4. Summarise the potential role of research in three of the ten steps in the rational–comprehensive model of the policy-making/planning/management process presented in this chapter.
5. Name three of the seven formats which research reports might take, as put forward in this chapter, and outline their basic features.
6. Outline three of the six topics, as put forward in this chapter, on which managers might conduct or commission research.
7. Why does academic research often appear to be irrelevant to the needs of practitioners?

EXERCISES

1. Choose a cultural organisation with which you are familiar and outline ways in which it might use research to pursue its objectives.

2. Choose an art/cultural institution and investigate the extent of its research activity. What proportion of its budget does it devote to research? What research has it carried out? How are the results of the research used, by the organisation or others?

3. Take an edition of a journal in the culture/events sector, such as one of those listed on page 19, and ascertain, for each article: why the research was conducted; how it was funded; and who or what organisations are likely to benefit from the research and how.

4. Repeat exercise 3 but using an edition of a journal outside the cultural field, for example a sociology journal or a physics journal.

5. Using the same journal edition as in exercise 3, examine each article and determine whether the research is descriptive, explanatory or evaluative.

Resources

Websites

National arts funding/promotion bodies typically sponsor and publish research and details are available on their websites. Major English-speaking examples are:

- Arts Council England: www.artscouncil.org.uk/what-we-do/research-and-data
- Australia Council: www.australiacouncil.gov.au/research
- Canada Council for the Arts: www.canadacouncil.ca/publications_e
- Cultural observatories: see IFACCA website below.
- Council of Europe: www.culturalpolicies.net/web/index.php
- National Endowment for the Arts (USA): arts.gov

International Federation of Arts Councils and Culture Agencies (IFACCA): www.ifacca.org Cultural observatories: for a listing, with websites, see: www.ifacca.org/links/cultural-observatories/

Publications

- Arts/arts management research: Perez-Cabanero and Cuadrado-Garcia (2011).
- Cultural mapping: see Chapters 5 and 7, Resources sections.
- Cultural strategies: Grogan and Mercer (1995).
- Cultural policy research: Bennett (2004), Schuster (2002).
- Cultural observatories: see Schuster (2002: 29–35) and IFACCA website above.
- Cultural tourism strategies/marketing plans – general: Evans and Foord (2008).
- Disciplines:
  o arts management: Chong (2009), Evrard and Colbert (2000), Ewebo and Sirayi (2009)
  o event studies: Getz (2002, 2012a: 5–7, 71–186, 2012b)

- Evaluative research:
  - general: Mertens (2009), Pollard (1987), Shadish *et al.* (1991)
  - arts: Radbourne *et al.* (2010)
  - arts festivals: Williams and Bowdin (2007)
  - leisure services: Veal (2010: Chapters 12, 13)
  - museums: Kelly (2004)
- Evidence-based policy: Eisner (1998), Nutley *et al.* (2007), Pawson (2006), Solesbury (2002).
- Exploratory research: Stebbins (1997).
- Feasibility studies: Docstoc (nd), Megadox.com (nd), Silberberg (1999).
- Forecasting – general: Veal (1987, 2010: Chapter 11).
- Government and research funding: Selwood (2002).
- Importance-performance technique – general: Martilla and James (1977); arts venues: Williams (1998).
- Impact studies – general: Reeves (2002), Peterson (2005),
- Industry/sector studies – examples:
  - arts/culture – cross-national: Gordon and Beilby-Orrin (2007); in UK economy: Centre for Economics and Business Research (2013)
  - arts festivals, UK: British Arts Festivals Association (2008)
  - cinema in Australia: Given and Goggin (2013)
  - creative industries, UK: Centre for International Economics (2009)
  - music, UK: National Music Council (2002)
  - national performing arts organisations, Australia: Nugent (1999)
- Managerialism/forms of knowledge: Hemingway and Parr (2000), Matarasso (2003).
- Market research – segmentation/lifestyle/psychographic studies:
  - general: Chisnall (1991), Veal (1993), Wells (1974)
  - museums: Dawson and Jensen (2011), Falk (2009)
  - arts participation: Australia Council (2010: 13)
- Models of planning and policy making Falk (2009) introductory discussions: Parsons (1995: 248ff), Veal (2010: Chapters 7–8).
- Practice-related research in the arts: Biggs and Karlsson (2010), Kershaw and Nicholson (2011), Smith and Dean (2009).
- Research in the exhibition planning process: Screven (1990).
- Researchers and arts organisations: Heidelberg (2010), Scullion and Garcia (2005).
- Segmentation/psychographics/lifestyle: see Market research.
- Terminology: Getz (2008, 2012a: 359–366).

References

Allen, J., Harris, R., Jago, L. K., and Veal, A. J. (Eds) (2000) *Events Beyond 2000: Setting the Agenda, Proceedings of a Conference on Event Evaluation, Research and Education, Sydney, July 2000*. Sydney: Australian Centre for Event Management, University of Technology, Sydney.

Australia Council (2010) *More than Bums on Seats: Australian Participation in the Arts*. Sydney: Australia Council, available at: www.australiacouncil.gov.au

Bailey, J. and Du Preez, K. (2010) *Artistic Reflection Kit: A Guide to Assist Arts Organisations to Reflect on Artistic Vibrancy and Measure their Artistic Achievements.* Sydney: Australia Council.

Baum, M. (2001) Evidence-based art? *Journal of the Royal Society of Medicine*, 94(3), 306–307.

Bennett, O. (2004) The torn halves of cultural policy research. *International Journal of Cultural Policy*, 10(2), 237–248.

Biggs, M. and Karlsson, H. (eds) (2010) *The Routledge Companion to Research in the Arts.* London: Routledge.

British Arts Festivals Association (2008) *Festivals Mean Business 3: A Survey of Arts Festivals in the UK.* London: BAFA.

Centre for Economics and Business Research (2013) *The Contribution of the Arts and Culture to the National Economy.* London: Arts Council England, available at: www.artscouncil.org.uk/media/uploads/pdf/CEBR_economic_report_web_version_0513.pdf

Centre for International Economics (2009) *Creative Industries Economic Analysis, Final Report.* Canberra: Centre for International Economics.

Chisnall, P. M. (1991) Market segmentation analysis. *The Essence of Marketing Research.* New York: Prentice-Hall, Chapter 6, pp. 76–91.

Chong, D. (2009) *Arts Management, Second Edition.* London: Routledge.

Cushman, G., Veal, A. J. and Zuzanek, J. (eds) (2005) *Free Time and Leisure Participation: International Perspectives.* Wallingford: CABI Publishing.

Dawson, E. and Jensen, E. (2011) Towards a contextual turn in visitor studies: evaluating visitor segmentation and identity-related motivations. *Visitor Studies*, 14(2), 127–140.

Docstoc (nd) *Feasibility Study Template.* Santa Monica, CA: Docstoc, available at www.docstoc.com

Eisner, E. W. (1998) Does experience in the arts boost academic achievement? *Art Education*, 51(1), 7–15.

Elias, N. (1986) Introduction. In N. Elias and E. Dunning, *Quest for Excitement: Sport and Leisure in the Civilizing Process.* Oxford: Basil Blackwell, pp. 19–62.

Evans, G. and Foord, J. (2008) Cultural mapping and sustainable communities: planning for the arts revisited. *Cultural Trends*, 17(2), 65–96.

Evrard, Y. and Colbert, F. (2000) Arts management: a new discipline entering the millennium? *International Journal of Arts Management*, 2(2), 4–13.

Ewebo, P. and Sirayi, M. (2009) The concept of arts/cultural management: a critical reflection. *Journal of Arts Management, Law and Society*, 38(4), 281–295.

Falk, J. (2009) *Identity and the Museum Experience.* Walnut Creek, CA: Left Coast Press.

Getz, D. (2002) Event studies and event management: on becoming an academic discipline. *Journal of Hospitality and Tourism Management*, 9(1), 12–23.

Getz, D. (2008) Event tourism: definition, evolution and research. *Tourism Management*, 29(3), 403–428.

Getz, D. (2012a) *Event Studies: Theory, Research and Policy for Planned Events*, Second Edition. London: Routledge.

Getz, D. (2012b) Event studies: discourses and future directions. *Event Management*, 16(2), 171–181.

Given, J. and Goggin, G. (2013) *Cinema in Australia: an Industry Profile.* Sydney: Australia Council.

Gordon, J. C. and Beilby-Orrin, H. (2007) *National Accounts and Financial Statistics: International Measurement of the Economic and Social Importance of Culture.* Paris: Statistics Directorate, Organisation for Economic Co-operation and Development (OECD).

Grogan, D. and Mercer, C. (1995) *The Cultural Planning Handbook: An Essential Australian Guide.* St Leonards, NSW: Allen and Unwin.

Hamilton, C., Hinks, S. and Petticrew, M. (2003) Arts for health: still searching for the Holy Grail. *Journal of Epidemiology and Community Health*, 57(6), 401–402.

Heidelberg, B. M. (2010) The need for arts researchers in arts organisations. *Journal of Arts Management, Law and Society*, 40(3), 235–237.

Hemingway, J. L. and Parr, M. G. W. (2000) Leisure research and leisure practice: three perspectives on constructing the research–practice relation. *Leisure Sciences*, 22(2), 139–162.

HM Treasury (2003) *The Green Book: Appraisal and Evaluation in Central Government*. London: The Stationery Office.

Kelly, L. (2004) Evaluation, research and communities of practice: program evaluation in museums. *Archival Science*, 4(1–2), 45–69.

Kershaw, B. and Nicholson, H. (eds) (2011) *Research Methods in Theatre and Performance*. Edinburgh: Edinburgh University Press.

Madden, C. (2005) Indicators for arts and cultural policy: a global perspective. *Cultural Trends*, 14(3), 217–247.

Martilla, J. A. and James, J. C. (1977) Importance–performance analysis. *Journal of Marketing*, 41(1), 77–79.

Matarasso, F. (2003) Smoke and mirrors: a response to Paola Merli's 'Evaluating the social impact of participation in arts activities'. *International Journal of Cultural Policy*, 9(3), 337–346.

Megadox.com (nd) *Feasibility Study for Cultural Arts Center (model document)*. Santa Monica, CA: Docstoc, available at: www.docstoc.com

Mertens, D. M. (2009) *Transformative Research and Evaluation*. New York: Guilford Press.

National Music Council (2002) *Counting the Notes: The Economic Contribution of the UK Music Business*. London: NMC, available at: www.nationalmusiccouncil.org.uk

Nugent, H. (1999) *Securing the Future: Major Performing Arts Inquiry Final Report*. Canberra: Department of Communication, Information Technology and the Arts.

Nutley, S. M., Walter, I. and Davies, H. T. O. (2007) *Using Research: How Research Can Inform Public Services*. Bristol: Policy Press.

Parsons, W. (1995) *Public Policy*. Cheltenham: Edward Elgar.

Pawson, R. (2006) *Evidence-based Policy: A Realist Perspective*. London: Sage.

Perez-Cabanero, C. and Cuadrado-Garcia, M. (2011) Evolution of arts and cultural management research over the first ten AIMC conferences (1991–2009). *International Journal of Arts Management*, 13(3), 56–68.

Peterson, R. A. (2005) Problems in comparative research: the example of omnivorousness. *Poetics*, 33(3), 257–282.

Pollard, W. E. (1987) Decision making and the use of evaluation research. *American Behavioral Scientist*, 30(6), 661–676.

Radbourne, J., Glow, H. and Johanson, K. (2010) Measuring the intrinsic benefits of arts attendance. *Cultural Trends*, 19(4), 307–324.

Reeves, M. (2002) *Measuring the Economic and Social Impact of the Arts: A Review*. London: Arts Council England.

Schuster, J. M. (1997) The performance of performance indicators in the arts. *Nonprofit Management and Leadership*, 7(3), 253–269.

Schuster, J. M. (2002) *Informing Cultural Policy: The Research and Information Infrastructure*. New Brunswick, NJ: Center for Urban Policy Research, Rutgers, State University of New Jersey.

Screven, C. G. (1990) Uses of evaluation before, during and after exhibit design. *ILVS Review*, 1(2), 36–66.

Scullion, A. and Garcia, B. (2005) What is cultural policy research? *International Journal of Cultural Policy*, 11(2), 113–126.

Selwood, S. (2002) The politics of data collection: gathering, analysing and using data about the subsidised cultural sector in England. *Cultural Trends*, 12(47), 13–73.

Shadish, W. R. Jr., Cook, T. D. and Leviton, L. C. (1991) *Foundations of Program Evaluation: Theories of Practice*. Newbury Park, CA: Sage.

Silberberg, T. (1999) The importance of market and financial feasibility studies. In G. D. Lord and B. Lord (eds), *The Manual of Museum Planning*. London: The Stationery Office, pp. 85–105.

Smith, H. and Dean, R. T. (eds) (2009) *Practice-led Research, Research-led Practice in the Creative Arts.* Edinburgh: Edinburgh University Press.

Solesbury, W. (2002) The ascendancy of evidence. *Planning Theory and Practice*, 3(1), 90–96.

Stebbins, R. A. (1997) Exploratory research as an antidote to theoretical stagnation in leisure studies. *Society and Leisure*, 20(2), 421–434.

Veal, A. J. (1987) The leisure forecasting tradition. *Leisure and the Future.* London: Allen and Unwin, Chapter 7, pp. 125–156.

Veal, A. J. (1993) The concept of lifestyle: a review. *Leisure Studies*, 12(4), 233–352.

Veal, A. J. (2010) *Leisure, Sport and Tourism: Politics, Policy and Planning.* Wallingford: CABI Publishing.

Wells, W. D. (ed.) (1974) *Life Style and Psychographics*. Chicago, IL: American Marketing Association.

Williams, C. (1998) Is the SERVQUAL model an appropriate management tool for measuring service delivery quality in the UK leisure industry? *Managing Leisure*, 3(2), 98–110.

Williams, M. and Bowdin, G. A. J. (2007) Festival evaluation: an exploration of seven UK arts festivals. *Managing Leisure*, 12(2–3), 187–203.

Chapter 2

Approaches to research in the arts and events

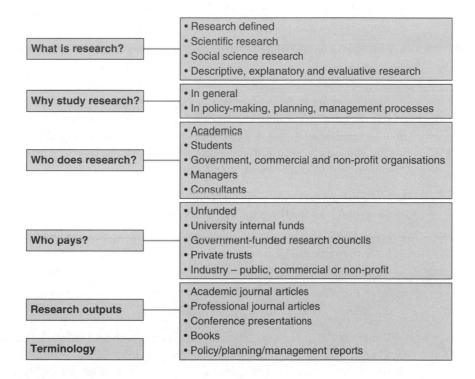

What is research?	• Research defined • Scientific research • Social science research • Descriptive, explanatory and evaluative research
Why study research?	• In general • In policy-making, planning, management processes
Who does research?	• Academics • Students • Government, commercial and non-profit organisations • Managers • Consultants
Who pays?	• Unfunded • University internal funds • Government-funded research councils • Private trusts • Industry – public, commercial or non-profit
Research outputs	• Academic journal articles • Professional journal articles • Conference presentations • Books
Terminology	• Policy/planning/management reports

Introduction

The aim of this chapter is to introduce a range of disciplines and paradigms within which arts and events research is typically conducted. The chapter examines:

- *disciplinary traditions:* reviews of a number of academic disciplines and their approaches to the arts and events research, including sociology, economics, geography, psychology, social psychology, history and philosophy;

- *terminology – approaches, dimensions, issues:* examination of a number of mainly dichotomous concepts which characterise research approaches and methods.

Disciplinary traditions

The bulk of published arts and events research has arisen not from the demands of the cultural and events industries but from the interests of academics who typically owe allegiance to a particular disciplinary field of study. Here we examine, very briefly, the contributions by academic disciplines that have been particularly significant in the field, namely:

- sociology and cultural studies
- economics
- geography/environmental studies
- psychology/social psychology
- history and anthropology
- political science.

Disciplines are characterised by the particular aspect or dimension of the universe with which they are concerned, the theories which they develop for explanation and the distinctive techniques they use for conducting research. An area as diverse as arts and events studies can hardly be considered a discipline, but can be seen as a multi-disciplinary, cross-disciplinary or inter-disciplinary *field of study*.

- *Multi-disciplinary* means that research from a number of disciplines is used – for example, the economics and the sociology of the arts.

- *Cross-disciplinary* means that issues, theories, concepts and methods which are common to more than one discipline are involved in a particular perspective or theory – for example, the cross-disciplinary dimensions discussed later in this chapter.

- *Inter-disciplinary* refers to sub-fields of research which do not fit neatly into any particular discipline – for example, time–budget research.

When reading in the area of the arts and events it should be noted that not all commentators keep the wide mix of disciplines consistently in mind. For example, when making comments on 'arts and events studies' they may in fact be discussing only 'the *sociology* of the arts and events'.

The relationships between arts and events research and the six disciplines are summarised in Figure 2.1, which presents examples of descriptive, explanatory and evaluative research topics/questions addressed by each discipline in relation to the arts and events.

A number of recognised areas of academic expertise are inter-disciplinary or multi-disciplinary in nature and sometimes claim disciplinary nature, for example management, planning, education, cultural studies. Typically, however, they draw on research methods and theory from the more established disciplines. These 'applied disciplines' or fields of study are discussed briefly below under 'Theoretical and applied research'.

Descriptive	Explanatory	Evaluative
Sociology		
● What proportion of the population and of various socio-economic groups participate in specific arts and events activities?	● Why do middle-class, highly educated people make greater than average use of the arts and events facilities/programmes?	● How successful was the hosting of an international arts event in increasing employment and incomes?
Geography/environment		
● What is the spatial area from which most users of a particular arts facility travel?	● What is the relative importance of distance and travel time in affecting use of a particular arts facility?	● How effective is the local council in meeting the cultural demands of all neighbourhoods in its area?
Economics		
● What is the size of the cultural /creative industry sector in a city?	● What is the relationship between level of income and expenditure on the arts and events?	● What are the costs and benefits of hosting the Olympic Games?
Psychology/social psychology		
● What satisfaction do people obtain from engaging in cultural events?	● To what extent is Maslow's hierarchy of needs theory relevant to the arts and events?	● How effective has a marketing policy been in boosting participation in cultural events among young people?
History/anthropology		
● How has the role of the arts and national celebratory events in shaping national identity changed over the last 25 years?	● What has caused the growth in the arts and events attendances over the last 25 years?	● Over the last 25 years have governments helped or hindered the development of the arts?
Political/policy science		
● What are the arts and major events policies of the main political parties?	● How is power exercised in the arts and events contexts?	● How effective have joint public–private partnerships been in arts and events development?

Figure 2.1 Disciplines and examples of research questions

Approaches, dimensions, issues, terminology

A number of approaches, dimensions, issues and associated terminology recur in the research literature and discourses on research, and at least a basic understanding of them is necessary if the literature and the discourses are to be understood. A number are listed in Figure 2.2. Those terms that arise in pairs, X and Y, are often presented in the literature as X *versus* Y. But X and Y are not always opposed to one another, they are often complementary, so here the form X *and* Y is used. It is not possible to analyse in detail all the terms and concepts in this introductory chapter, especially given that definitions vary in the literature. The coverage is quite extensive and can be viewed as a reference source for future consultation. Additional sources are provided in the Resources section of the chapter.

Ontology, epistemology, methodology

Ontology, epistemology and methodology are frequently encountered in discussions of research approaches, particularly in sociology.

Pairs/groups of terms	Brief definition	Associated terms
Ontology	Way of looking at the world.	Paradigm, philosophy
Epistemology	Relationship between the researcher and the subject of research.	
Methodology	Ways of designing research, particularly the gathering and analysing of information/data.	Technique
Positivist	Hypotheses are tested using objectively collected factual data. If supported, this produces scientific laws.	Scientific method, logical empiricist, functionalist, objectivist
Post-positivist	Hypotheses found to be consistent with the data deemed to be 'not falsified', establishing *probable* theories or laws.	
Interpretive	People provide their own accounts or explanation of situation/behaviour.	Phenomenology, phenomen-ography, symbolic inter-action, inter-subjectivity, ethnography, subjectivist, relativism
Critical	Research influenced by beliefs/values critical of the status quo in society.	Standpoint, transformative, emancipatory
Constructivist	People construct their own views of reality and the researcher seeks to discover this.	Social constructivism
Pragmatist	Located somewhere between positivist and interpretive /relativist position; often policy/management-focused.	Mixed methods, bricolage, eclecticism
Participatory	Researcher and subjects jointly influence the pattern of research.	Action research (see Chapter 5)
Research/practice	Research informs arts practice and arts practice informs research.	
Descriptive	Seeks to describe what is.	Exploratory
Explanatory	Seeks to explain relationships between phenomena.	Predictive
Evaluative	Seeks to test policy/management outcomes against benchmarks.	
Qualitative	Research in which words (and possibly images, sounds) are the medium.	
Quantitative	Research in which numbers are the main medium.	
Theoretical	Research which results in general propositions about how things/ organisations/people behave.	Pure research
Applied	Use of research to address particular practical, policy /management issues.	Evidence-based
Experimental	Research where the researcher seeks to control all variables.	Controlled experiment
Naturalistic	Research where subjects are researched in their 'natural' environment where the researcher's control is minimal.	Real life context
Reflexive	The process of examining the relationship between the researcher and the subject of the research.	Intersubjective
Empirical	Research involving data – quantitative or qualitative or both.	
Non-empirical	Research involving only theory and the literature.	Theoretical
Inductive	Hypotheses/explanations/theory are generated from examination of the data.	Exploratory
Deductive	Data collected to test a priori hypotheses.	Hypothetical-deductive, confirmatory
Primary data	Data gathered by the researcher for the current project.	
Secondary data	Use of existing data gathered by other people/organisations for other purposes.	
Self-reported	Subjects' own accounts of activity/behaviour.	
Observed	Researcher's observation of subjects' activity/ behaviour.	Unobtrusive
Validity	The research accurately identifies/measures what is intended.	
Reliability	Repetition of the research would produce similar findings.	
Trustworthiness	Trust which can be placed in qualitative research.	

Figure 2.2 Terminology: approaches/dimensions/issues

- *Ontology* refers to the nature of reality assumed by the researcher – in the positivist paradigm (see below) the researcher assumes that the 'real world' being studied is as seen by the researcher, while in interpretive and similar approaches the researcher's perspective is not privileged: emphasis is placed on the varying views and realities as perceived by the people being studied.

- *Epistemology* refers to the relationship between the researcher and the phenomenon being studied – again the distinction is most sharply drawn between the positivist and interpretive stance, with the former seeking to adopt an objective, distanced stance, while the interpretive researcher is more subjective and engaged with the subjects of the study.

- *Methodology* refers to the ways by which knowledge and understanding are established: research methods. For example, the method used in the classic positivist approach is the controlled experiment (as discussed below), which is possible only in certain contexts. The quantitative and qualitative divide, as discussed below, also offers distinctive methodologies. Ideally the choice of method in a study should be closely influenced by the ontological and epistemological perspectives used.

Positivist, post-positivist, interpretive and critical approaches/paradigms

The positivism, post-positivism and interpretive and critical approaches refer to *paradigms* in the social sciences, which are ways of looking at the theoretical/research world.

- *Positivism* is a framework of research, similar to that adopted by the natural scientist, in which the researcher sees the phenomena to be studied from the outside, with behaviour to be explained on the basis of data and observations objectively gathered by the researcher, using theories and models developed by the researcher. The classic positivist approach uses the *hypothetical–deductive* model, a deductive process (as discussed below), to test a pre-established hypothesis. If successful, this results in the establishment of 'laws' – for example, Newton's laws of motion. Many commentators in the social sciences are highly suspicious of such attempts to translate natural science approaches into the social world, arguing that it is inappropriate to draw conclusions about the causes and motivations of human behaviour on the basis of the type of evidence used in the natural sciences. Giddens (1974: 2) pointed out that in the social sciences by the 1970s the term 'positivist' had almost become a term of abuse.

- *Post-positivism* is distinguished from the classic positivist approach by some writers (e.g. Guba and Lincoln, 2005) as an approach in which hypotheses found to be consistent with the data are deemed to be 'not falsified'; researchers do not claim to have discovered the 'truth' but to have established *probable* theories or laws which are useful until such time as they are supplanted by new theories/laws which provide a fuller or more comprehensive explanation of the available data.

- *Interpretive* approaches to research place reliance on people providing their own explanations of their situation or behaviour. The interpretive researcher tries to 'get inside' the minds of subjects and see the world from their point of view. This of course suggests a more flexible approach to data collection, usually involving qualitative methods and generally an inductive approach. A number of variations exist within this category, as indicated in the 'Associated terms' column in Figure 2.2, and these are discussed in Chapter 9.

- *Critical* approaches to research are influenced by particular sets of beliefs or values which are critical of the status quo in society: common examples are neo-Marxist perspectives, which are critical of the capitalist system, and various feminist perspectives, which are critical of the economic, social and political inequality between men and women in society. There are numerous other perspectives which researchers may adopt or causes with which they may be associated; for example, much research in the arts domain is predicated on the assumption that the arts are a 'good thing' and should be supported by the community. Critical researchers reject the notion of 'objectivity' (as discussed below) but will generally make their own values explicit in the conduct and reporting of their research. They would argue that the so-called 'objectivity' often claimed for or attributed to certain research approaches, notably the positivistic approach, is invalid because if researchers are not critical of the status quo then their values are, by implication, supportive or tolerant of it. Other terms used for research shaped by such commitments are: *standpoint* research (Hartsock, 1999), particularly related to feminism; *emancipatory* research (Antonio, 1989), which is committed to emancipation of society from oppressive forces; and *transformative* research, which is seen as a 'metaphysical umbrella' (Mertens, 2009: 13) for a number of areas of research which are committed to transforming society to achieve social justice in areas such as gender, race, class and disability.

Along with parallel debates on quantitative and qualitative research, there is much debate in the arts and events studies on the relative merits, suitability and appropriateness of the above alternative approaches to research. However, since arts and events researchers are generally all using a combination of theory and empirical evidence to draw conclusions about phenomena, the question arises as to how great the underlying, as opposed to surface, differences are between these approaches. Lee (1989) has explored this issue and, using the terms 'subjectivist' and 'objectivist', argues that a subjectivist case study in organisation studies has similarities to the classic scientific experiment, which is usually seen as positivist and quantitative.

Descriptive, explanatory and evaluative research

In Chapter 1 the differences between descriptive, explanatory and evaluative research were discussed and it is appropriate to raise the typology again here.

- *Descriptive* research aims to describe, as far as possible, what is. The focus is not on explanation. Another term that might be used here is *exploratory*, although exploratory research could also extend to attempts at explanation.
- *Explaining* the patterns in observed or reported data usually involves establishing that one phenomenon is caused by another, and the aim of research is to identify these causal relationships. For example, where descriptive research might show that an annual arts event is losing participants, explanatory research would seek to establish whether this was caused by, for example, competition from other events or changing local demographics. Explanation can often provide the basis for *prediction*.
- *Evaluative* research seeks to assess the success of policy or management action – for example, the effects of a marketing campaign.

These issues raise the question of *causality*: whether A or B is the cause. Labovitz and Hagedorn (1971: 4) state that there are 'at least four widely accepted scientific criteria for establishing causality. These criteria are association, time priority, nonspurious relation and rationale'.

- *Association* is a 'necessary condition for a causal relation' – that is, A and B must be associated in some way, for example A increases when B decreases.

  There are two characteristics of an association that generally strengthen the conclusion that one variable is at least a partial cause of another. The first is magnitude, which refers to the size or strength of the association. The second is consistency. If the relation persists from one study to the next under a variety of conditions, confidence in the causal nature of the relation is increased (Labovitz and Hagedorn, 1971: 5).

- *Time priority* means that for A to be the cause of B, A must take place before B.

- *Nonspurious relationships* are defined as associations between two variables that 'cannot be explained by a third variable' (Labovitz and Hagedorn, 1971: 9). This means that it must be established that there is no third factor, C, that is affecting both A and B.

- *Rationale* means that statistical or other evidence is not enough. The conclusion that A causes B is not justified simply on the basis of an observed relation; it should be supported by some plausible, theoretical or logical explanation to suggest how it happens.

These matters are taken up again in Chapter 3 and in Part III.

Qualitative and quantitative research

Much arts and events research involves the collection, analysis and presentation of statistical information. Sometimes the information is innately quantitative – for example, the numbers of people attending cultural events in a year, the amount of money spent on such attendances or the average income of a group of people. Sometimes the information is qualitative in nature but is presented in quantitative form – for instance, numerical scores obtained by asking people to indicate levels of satisfaction with different services, where the scores range from 1, 'very satisfied', to 5, 'very dissatisfied'.

The *quantitative* approach to research involves numerical data. It relies on numerical evidence to draw conclusions or to test hypotheses. To be sure of the reliability of the results it is often necessary to study relatively large numbers of people and to use computers to analyse the data. The data can be derived from questionnaire surveys, from observation involving counts or measurements, or from administrative sources, such as ticket sales data from a cultural facility.

There can be said to be three approaches to quantitative research:

A *Hypothetical-deductive:* quantitative research conforms to the hypothetical-deductive model discussed under positivism above. Invariably statistical methods and tests, such as the chi-square tests, t-tests, analysis of variance, correlation or regression outlined in Chapter 17, are used. This model is implicit in many discussions of quantitative methods.

B *Statistical:* quantitative research makes use of statistical methods but is not necessarily hypothetical-deductive. It can be descriptive, exploratory and/or deductive.

C *Inductive:* quantitative research is based on numerical data, but makes little or no use of statistical tests: its most sophisticated statistical measure is usually the percentage and sometimes means/averages. This type of quantitative research is more common in policy-related arts and events research. This type of research is more informal than type B or type A and is closer in approach to qualitative methods.

The *qualitative* approach to research is generally not concerned with numbers but typically with information in the form of words, conveyed orally or in writing. In addition to words, it may involve images and sounds. Definitions offered in the literature often go beyond this minimalist definition to include types of methods which are often associated with qualitative research but, arguably, are not exclusive to the approach. Thus, for example, Denzin and Lincoln (2005: 3) include in their definition the proposition that qualitative research practices 'transform the world', when clearly any type of research *may* seek to achieve this. Similarly, they state that qualitative research involves a 'naturalistic' (see below) approach, when clearly qualitative methods may be deployed in non-naturalistic settings (e.g. a laboratory) and quantitative research may take place in 'naturalistic' settings (e.g. quantitative measurement of audiences).

Qualitative research methods generally make it possible to gather a relatively large amount of information about the research subjects, which may be individuals, groups, places/ facilities, genres, events or organisations. But the collection and analysis processes typically place a practical limit on the number of subjects which can be included. The qualitative approach involves obtaining a full and rounded account and understanding of the behaviour, attitudes and/or situation of a few subjects, as opposed to the more limited amount of information that might be obtained in a quantitative study of a large sample of subjects. Therefore no claim is made that the sample studied in a qualitative study is representative of a larger population, so that the findings cannot be generalised to the wider population or community, although this principle is often breached.

The methods used to gather qualitative information include observation, informal and in-depth interviewing, participant observation and analysis of texts. Research studying groups of people using non-quantitative, anthropological approaches is referred to as *ethnographic research* or *ethnographic fieldwork*. Such methods were initially developed by anthropologists, but have been adapted by sociologists for use in their work on contemporary communities and organisations.

The question of the differences between, and respective merits of, quantitative and qualitative methods is one of the most discussed methodological issues in social research. The discussion is invariably led by proponents of qualitative methods who generally portray themselves as pioneering a novel approach in the face of opposition from proponents of 'traditional' quantitative methods. While the debate between protagonists of qualitative and quantitative research can become somewhat partisan, it is now widely accepted that the two approaches complement one another. Leading proponents of qualitative methods Egon Guba and Yvonna Lincoln (1998: 195) have stated: 'From our perspective, both qualitative and quantitative methods may be appropriate with any research paradigm'.

Quantitative research is often based on initial qualitative work and it is possible that the two approaches are moving closer together in one respect, as computers are now being used to analyse qualitative data, as outlined in Chapter 15.

While there is a tendency for positivist and post-positivist research to be associated with quantitative research methods and for interpretive/critical/constructivist researchers to use qualitative methods, to suggest that this must always be the case is, as Bryman (1984) puts it, to confuse method with epistemology. As outlined in Chapter 5, the principle followed in this book is that methods to be used in a particular research situation should be determined on the basis of the nature of the research question/issue, not on the basis of some prior commitment to particular methodologies.

Pragmatism

This principle is reflected in the idea of *pragmatism*. As an approach to research, pragmatism emerged in philosophy at the beginning of the twentieth century and involved the proposition that the criterion for valid knowledge should not be based on theoretical or logical rigour alone but also on experience in the real world and practical usefulness in addressing real-world problems. In the social sciences it has come to refer to an approach to research that is not committed, a priori, to either the post-positivist or interpretive paradigm but may combine them in different parts of the same research exercise. For example, a project might involve a survey of cultural participation with quantified results, but also some in-depth interviews with participants and non-participants, which adds complexity to the notion of 'participation', even challenging the definition used in the survey. That the approach may involve the use of quantitative and/or qualitative methods has also led to the use of the term 'mixed methods' to describe it.

Another related term is *bricolage,* a French word referring to the work of a handyman/woman who is multi-skilled and assembles a miscellany of tools and materials ('bits and pieces') to do the job in hand.

Participatory research

Typically, the researcher takes total responsibility for the design, conduct and reporting of the research. Some researchers, however, work in fields where the subjects of the research may be involved in directing the research in a cooperative manner. This can happen in exploratory research in relatively informal environments, such as community groups, but also in open-ended, diagnostic research involving organisations. The approach overlaps with the concept of action research, in which the research is part of a process for bringing about change with which the researcher is actively involved. Action research is discussed further in Chapter 5.

Research and arts practice

Arts practitioners are often involved in researching how they develop and produce work and where this work may reside or resonate within the field of arts history or how it contributes to a critique of received practice. This often takes the form of non-text research (visual or performing) and relationships between different strands of arts practice. This endeavour is often self-reflective and is a dialogistic way of advancing individual or sometimes group artistic practice (Biggs and Karlsson, 2010; Strand, 1998). The knowledge and skills involved draw on arts/creative practice and are beyond the social and policy science related scope of this book, but sources are indicated in the Resources section at the end of the chapter.

In a different vein, community cultural practitioners can question the status quo of social conditions through engaging types of communities in producing arts products. This involves artists working alongside communities (such as youth at risk, survivors of domestic violence) to identify and give voice to issues through creative products which act as documentation for the group. However, how such practice actually changes attitudes or social conditions has been the subject of debate and further research (Matarasso, 1997, 2003; Merli, 2002).

Theoretical and applied research

Theoretical research seeks to draw conclusions about the phenomena being studied which can be applied to that class of phenomena as a whole, not just to the cases or subjects included in the study. Indeed, some theoretical research is non-empirical (see below), so it does not involve the direct study of cases or subjects, but relies on the existing research literature and local analysis.

Applied research, however, is less universal in its scope: it does not necessarily seek to create wholly new knowledge about the world but to apply existing theoretical knowledge to particular problems or issues. Such problems or issues may arise in particular policy, planning or management situations. Policy studies, planning and management are themselves fields of study that have developed a body of theory. Because they are related to areas of practice they can be seen as *applied disciplines*. In these fields, therefore, there can be such a thing as *applied theory*. The rational–comprehensive model of management portrayed in Figure 1.5 is an example of a context for considering the difference between theoretical and applied research: research that might seek to develop or elaborate the model in general would be theoretical, whereas research that simply used the model as a framework for examining a problem in a particular group, activity or organisation would be called applied. In some discussions of this dimension the term 'pure' is used rather than 'theoretical'.

Reflexivity

A reflexive approach to research involves explicit consideration of the relationship between the researcher and the researched. Davies (1997:3) points out that all research involves a degree of reflexivity. Thus, for example, in small particle physics the very act of measurement can be achieved only by the researcher causing physical interference with the particle being measured and this becomes the focus of the research methodology. In questionnaire-based research, interaction between the researcher and the respondent is in the form of the asking of questions: different wording of the questions and the manner in which they are posed affect the answers given. Reflexivity is most often considered in the context of qualitative research and the deeper the involvement of the researcher with the research subjects, the more relevant it becomes, the most extreme being participant observation. Thus reflexivity may be related to physical relationships, to culture or power, or to a variety of forms of social interaction. In social research, reflexivity is sometimes referred to as intersubjectivity (Glancy, 1993).

In methodologies closer to the classic scientific model, the aim is generally to minimise the impact of the researcher on the research subjects and description of measures taken to achieve this is confined to the 'methods' section of the research report, although it may be revisited in the conclusions, particularly if the results are less than clear-cut and might be improved in future by changes in the research design. But in interpretive studies involving methods such as participant observation, discussion of the relationship between the researcher and the researched can be a major part of the analysis and reporting process.

Empirical and non-empirical research

The dichotomy here should probably be between purely empirical research, if such a thing exists, and purely theoretical research. Empirical research involves the collection and/or analysis of data, which may be quantitative or qualitative, primary or secondary. The research is informed by observations or information from the 'real world'. It is, however, rare for any research project to be exclusively empirical – it is usually informed by some sort of theory or conceptual framework (see Chapter 3), however implicit.

It is possible for the researcher to become carried away with data and their analysis and to forget the theory which should make them meaningful. The disparaging term *mindless empiricism* is sometimes used to describe such a situation. Similarly, theoretical research with no reference to information about the 'real world', however contested the description of that might be, is likely to be of limited value. Typically – and ideally – theoretical and empirical research coexist and enhance each other; indeed, most research projects have complementary theoretical and empirical components.

A review of the contents of one or two editions of the main arts or events journals will reveal the existence of both sorts of research – and the contributions that each can make. While the empirical studies provide some of the building blocks of a great deal of research and knowledge, non-empirical contributions are needed to review and refine ideas and to place the empirical work in context. A book like this inevitably devotes more space to empirical methods, because they involve more explicit, technical processes which can be described and taught. It cannot be too strongly stressed, however, that a good review of the literature or a thoughtful piece of writing arising from deep, insightful, inspirational thinking about a subject can be worth a thousand unthinking surveys or experiments.

Induction and deduction

Induction and deduction refer to alternative approaches to explanation in research. It has been noted that research involves *finding out* and *explaining*. Finding out might be called the 'what?' of research. Explaining might be called the 'how?' and the 'why?' of research.

Finding out involves description and gathering of information. Explaining involves attempting to understand that information: it goes beyond the descriptive. Appropriate research methods can facilitate both these processes. Description and explanation can be seen as part of a circular model of research, as illustrated in Figure 2.3.

The research process can work in two ways:

- *Deductive:* The process starts at point A1 and moves via observation/description (B) to analysis/testing (C) which confirms or disproves the hypothesis (D1). The process is deductive: it involves deduction, where the process is based on prior logical reasoning and available evidence from observation or the research literature resulting in a hypothesis to be tested.

- *Inductive:* The process may begin with a question, at point A2, or it may begin with observation/description, at point B in the figure; it then moves from analysis (C) to answering, or failing to answer, the question. The process is inductive: the explanation is induced from the data, the data come first and the explanation later.

The concept of a hypothesis arises in the deductive process. A hypothesis is a proposition about how something might work or behave – an explanation that may or may not be supported by data, or possibly by more detailed or rigorous argument. A hypothesis may be suggested from informal observation and experience of the researcher or from examination of the existing research literature. As we see in Chapter 3, not all research projects involve the use of hypotheses, which are associated with the classic positivistic or hypothetical-deductive model as discussed above.

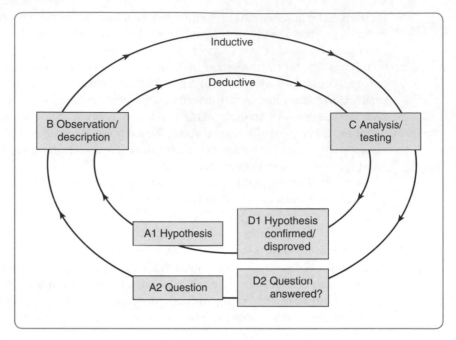

Figure 2.3 Circular model of the research process

The terms *theory* or *model* could also be included at point D1: when more elaborate hypotheses or a number of inter-related hypotheses are involved, the term theory or model may be used. A theory or model can be similar to a hypothesis, in being propositional, or it may have been subjected to empirical validation – that is testing against data. A research project may involve a single circuit or a number of circuits of the process, possibly in both directions. Theory and models can also arise out of the inductive process if, for example, the question was a 'why?' question.

Case study 2.1 illustrates the concepts of induction and deduction using an example of the relative popularity of two cultural activities.

In practice, data are rarely collected without at least an informal explanatory model in mind – otherwise how would the researcher know what data to collect? As Charmaz (2005: 509) puts it: 'No qualitative method rests on pure induction'. So there is always an element of deduction in any research. And it is not possible to develop hypotheses and theories without at least some initial information on the topic in hand, however informally obtained, so there is always an element of induction. Thus most research is partly inductive and partly deductive.

There is a tendency, particularly among writers on qualitative methods, to associate quantitative methods with a deductive approach and qualitative methods with inductive approaches. But quantitative research can be, and often is, inductive. For example:

● *Factor analysis*, as discussed in Chapter 17, is a highly quantitative data-manipulation technique that seeks to identify a manageable number of meaningful 'factors' from a large number of variables, such as might be generated from a questionnaire. The technique can be used as an *exploratory* (i.e. inductive) tool, to discover what, if any, factors might exist in the data, and as a *confirmatory* (i.e. deductive) tool, to confirm the existence of hypothesised factors.

CASE STUDY 2.1

Cinema attendance vs museum attendance – inductive and deductive approaches

The relative popularity of cinema attendance and museum attendance could be studied using an inductive or deductive approach to research and explanation.

A Inductive

A descriptive survey shows that more people attend the cinema than attend a museum. This is just a piece of information; we cannot explain why this is so without additional information and analysis. If the research also reveals that it costs more to visit a museum than to go to the cinema then we could offer the explanation that relative popularity is related to price.

However, qualitative information from the survey might also indicate that more people consider the cinema to offer a more enjoyable experience than a museum. This suggests that for many people the cinema is intrinsically more attractive than museums and its popularity is not related to price but to intrinsic enjoyment.

The research might indicate that there are more cinemas than museums in the particular community being studied, suggesting that if there were more museums available, then museums would be more popular – implying that popularity is related to availability of facilities.

In this example, a series of possible explanations is being *induced* from the data. In its most fully developed form the explanation amounts to a theory. In this case a theory of cultural participation might be developed relating levels of participation to costs of participation,

perceived intrinsic attractiveness/enjoyableness, supply of facilities and so on.

B Deductive

On the basis of existing literature and theory on leisure activities generally, the following two hypotheses are put forward:

H$_1$ If activity A is more expensive to participate in than activity B, then activity B will be more popular than activity A.

H$_2$ If more facilities are available for activity B than for activity A, then activity B will be more popular than activity A.

To test these hypotheses, a research project is designed to collect information on:

a. the levels of participation in the two activities – cinema attendance and museum attendance

b. the costs of participating in the two activities

c. the availability of facilities for the two activities in the study area.

The two hypotheses would then be tested using the data collected. The data collection and outcomes are limited by the hypotheses put forward. In this example the idea of 'intrinsic motivation', which featured in the inductive approach, was not identified because it did not arise in the hypothesising: the research is guided from the beginning by the initial hypotheses. The process is deductive.

- *Structural equation modelling* (SEM), as discussed in Chapter 17, is also a highly quantitative technique. In his book on the technique, Rex Kline notes that computer programs used to analyse data for SEM require the researcher to provide in advance specifications of the model to be tested, and observes:

  These *a priori* specifications reflect the researcher's hypotheses, and in total they make up the model to be evaluated in the analysis. In this sense SEM could be viewed as confirmatory [i.e. *deductive*]. That is, the model is given at the beginning of the analysis, and one of the main questions to be answered is whether it is supported by the data. But, as often happens in SEM, the data may be inconsistent with the model, which means that the researcher must either abandon the model or modify the hypotheses on which it is based. The former option is rather drastic. In practice, researchers more often opt for the second choice, which means the analysis now has a more exploratory [i.e. *inductive*] nature as revised models are tested with the same data.

  (Kline, 2005: 10)

Whether hypotheses or theories containing the explanation are put forward at the start of a research project or arise as a result of exploratory data analysis, they represent the key creative part of the research process. Data collection and analysis can be fairly mechanical, but interpretation of data and the development of hypotheses and explanations require at least creativity, and at best inspiration.

Experimental and naturalistic methods

The experiment is the classic scientific research method: the popular image of the scientist is someone in a white coat in a laboratory, conducting experiments. In the experimental method of research the scientist aims to control the environment of the subject of the research and measure the effects of controlled change. Knowledge based on the experimental method progresses on the basis that, in a controlled experimental situation, any change in A must have been brought about by a change in B because everything except A and B have been held constant. The experimental researcher therefore aims to produce conditions such that the research will fulfil the requirements for causality discussed above.

In the world of human beings, with which the social scientist deals, there is much less scope for experiment than in the world of inanimate objects or animals with which natural scientists deal. However, some situations do exist where experimentation with human beings in the field of the arts and events can take place. For example, it is possible to experiment with:

- variations in the design of a programme to teach the playing of a musical instrument;
- involving willing subjects in game-playing or decision-making tasks under different conditions, or responding to 'stimuli', such as photographs or videos;
- management situations, for instance varying prices or advertising strategies in relation to arts events.

Many areas of interest to the arts and events researcher are not susceptible to controlled experiment, however. For example, the researcher interested in the effect of income levels on cultural participation rates cannot take a group of people and vary their incomes in order to study the effects on their participation behaviour – it would be difficult to find people on executive salaries willing voluntarily to spend a year living on a student grant in the interests of research! Furthermore, unlike the natural scientist experimenting with rats, it is not possible to find two groups of humans identical in every respect except for their level of income. Even more fundamentally, it is of course not possible to vary people's social class or race. In order to study these phenomena it is necessary to use *non-experimental* methods; that is, it is necessary to study differences between people as they exist in society.

So, for example, in order to study the effects of income on cultural participation patterns it is necessary to gather information on the behaviour patterns of a range of people with different levels of income. But people differ in all sorts of ways, some of which may be related to their level of income and some not. For example, two people with identical income levels can differ markedly in terms of their personalities, their family situation, their education, and so on. So, in comparing the behaviour of two groups of people, it is difficult to be sure which differences arise as a result of income differences and which as a result of other differences. The results of the research are therefore likely to be less clear-cut than in the case of the controlled experiment.

One term used for studying people in their normal environment, that is, not in a laboratory, is *naturalistic*. In a fully naturalistic study the researcher would be as unobtrusive as possible so as not to interfere in any way with the normal behaviour of the research subjects. Unlike the laboratory experiment, where as many variables as possible are controlled, the naturalistic researcher would be taking a *holistic* or *systematic* view, in which all relevant known and unknown variables are in operation simultaneously. As Lincoln and Guba (1985: 8) put it, in naturalistic research: 'First, no manipulation on the part of the inquirer is implied and, second, the inquirer imposes no *a priori* units on the outcome'.

Some observational methods seek to achieve this, but interviews of various types may begin to interfere with the normal or 'natural' behaviour of the subject (although the asking of a question can be seen as a sort of loosely controlled experiment). Interviews that take place in a subject's home or at an arts venue or event site are more naturalistic than a focus group session in the office of a market research company, which is closer to the experimental end of the experimental–naturalistic continuum. For some types of naturalistic research project, quite extensive interaction may be required between the researcher and the subjects being researched in order to gain an understanding of behaviour in the subject's normal/natural environment.

The experimental method is dealt with in Chapter 11. The survey and qualitative methods discussed in Chapters 7–10 can all be seen as naturalistic but varying in their degrees of naturalism.

Objectivity and subjectivity

As indicated in Chapter 1 and in the discussion of the experimental method above, the classical stance of the researcher in the natural science research model is as an objective observer. Experiments are set up to prove or disprove a hypothesis. If the data from the experiment are consistent with the hypothesis, the latter is accepted as reflecting the real world until such time as new evidence emerges that is inconsistent with the hypothesis, which is then rejected or modified. In practice, absolute objectivity is impossible since the researcher's selection of one research topic rather than any one of a thousand others suggests a value position: the researcher's choice implies that the selected topic is, in some way, more important than the others. If the research has been funded from a trust or government grant-giving body the application will invariably have been required to demonstrate the 'social benefits' of the research. When moving into the social science area it becomes even more difficult to maintain the classic objective stance; thus much research on the arts and events is conducted because the researcher is convinced of the value of the arts and events to society as a whole or to particular groups within society. Nevertheless, researchers typically seek to be as objective as possible and to report honestly on the results of empirical enquiry, as discussed in Chapter 4.

Primary and secondary data

In planning a research project it is advisable to consider whether it is necessary to go to the expense of collecting new information (primary data, where the researcher is the first user) or whether existing data (secondary data, where the researcher is the secondary user) will do the job. Sometimes existing information is in the form of research already completed on the topic or a related topic; sometimes it arises from non-research sources, such as administration. A fundamental part of any research project is therefore to scour the existing published – and unpublished – sources of information for related research. Existing research might not obviate the need for the originally proposed research, but it may provide interesting ideas and points of comparison with the proposed research.

Even if the research project is to be based mainly on new information it will usually be necessary also to make use of other, existing, information – such as official government statistics or financial records from an event, facility or service. Such information is generally referred to as *secondary data*, as opposed to the *primary data*, which is the new data to be collected in the proposed research. The topic of secondary data is dealt with in Chapter 7.

Self-reported and observed data

The best, and often the only, sources of information about people's cultural behaviour or attitudes are individuals' own reports about themselves. Much arts and events research therefore involves asking people about their past activity, attitudes and aspirations, by means of an interviewer-administered or respondent-completed questionnaire (Chapter 10) or by means of informal, in-depth, semi-structured or unstructured interview (Chapter 9). In some cases information can be gathered from written sources, such as diaries, letters or biographies.

There are some disadvantages to this approach, mainly that the researcher is never sure just how honest or accurate people are in responding to questions. In some instances people may deliberately or unwittingly distort or 'bend' the truth – for instance in understating the amount of alcohol they drink or overstating the amount of involvement they have with cultural events. In other instances they may have problems of recall – for example in remembering just when they last visited an art museum. In biomedical research, which relies a great deal on subjects/patients accurately reporting such things as symptoms and behaviour, the study of the design and practice of such data collection has come to be referred to as the 'science of self-report' (Stone and Turkkan, 2000).

For some types of information an alternative to relying on self-report is for the researcher to observe behaviour. For instance, to find out how people move around a gallery it would probably be better to observe them than to try to ask them about it. Sometimes people leave behind evidence of their behaviour – for instance the most popular exhibits in a museum are likely to be those where the floor is most worn. Generally these techniques are referred to as *observational* or *unobtrusive* techniques and are dealt with in Chapter 8. Clearly observation does not provide direct information on motives, attitudes and aspirations or past behaviour.

Validity, reliability and trustworthiness

The quality of research and the trust which can be placed in it depends on the methods used and the care with which they have been deployed. Two dimensions are generally considered in this context: validity and reliability.

Validity is the extent to which the information presented in the research truly reflects the phenomena which the researcher claims it reflects.

- *External validity* refers to generalisability or representativeness: to what extent can the results be generalised to a population wider than the particular sample used in the study? This will depend on how the members of the sample are selected, as discussed in Chapter 13.

- *Internal validity* refers to how accurately the characteristics of the phenomena being studied are represented by the variables used and the data collected – sometimes referred to as measurement or instrument (e.g. questionnaire) validity – and the extent to which the study identifies and measures all the relevant variables.

Arts and events research is fraught with difficulties in this area, mainly because empirical research is largely concerned with people's behaviour and with their attitudes, and for information on these the researcher is, in the main, reliant on people's own reports in the form of responses to questionnaire-based interviews and other forms of interview. These instruments are subject to a number of imperfections, which means that the validity of the data can rarely be as certain as in the natural sciences. For example, data on the number of people who have participated in an activity at least once over the last year (a common type of measure used in the arts and events research) covers a wide range of different types of involvement, from the person who participates for two or three times a month to the person who had an unplanned engagement with the activity just once when they were on holiday. So the question of what is a participant can be complex. More detailed questioning to capture such complexity can be costly to undertake on a large scale and can try the patience of interviewees, thus increasing the risk that responses will be inaccurate or incomplete.

Reliability is the extent to which research findings would be the same if the research were to be repeated at a later date or with a different sample of subjects. Again it can be seen that the model is taken from the natural sciences where, if experimental conditions are appropriately controlled, a replication of an experiment should produce identical results wherever and whenever it is conducted. This is rarely the case in the social sciences, because they deal with human beings in differing and ever-changing social situations. While a single person's report of his or her behaviour may be accurate, when it is aggregated with information from other people, it presents a snap-shot picture of a group of people, which is subject to change over time, as the composition of the group changes, or as some members of the group change their patterns of behaviour. Further, identical questions asked of people in different locations, even within the same country or region, are likely to produce different results, because of the varying social and physical environment. This means that the social scientist, including the arts and events researcher, must be very cautious when making general, theoretical statements on the basis of empirical research. While measures can be taken to ensure a degree of generalisability, strictly speaking, any research findings relate only to the subjects involved, at the time and place the research was carried out.

There is a considerable literature on validity and reliability, particularly related to experimental research and the use of scales (see Chapter 5); sources are indicated in the Resources section at the end of the chapter.

It has been noted that the use of validity and reliability as criteria for assessing the quality of research arose from the positivist tradition and that they are therefore not always fully appropriate for non-positivist research approaches. In qualitative research in particular, the concepts of trustworthiness and authenticity have been introduced by Lincoln and Guba (1985) to replace validity and reliability.

- Trustworthiness has four components: credibility (paralleling internal validity), transferability (external validity), dependability (reliability) and confirmability (objectivity).

- Authenticity includes fairness and ontological, educative, catalytic and tactical authenticity.

Because qualitative studies do not follow a regimented process, a detailed explanation of the research process is advisable. As Henderson (2006: 231) has put it: 'A thorough reporting of the process and the results of qualitative data collection and analysis is the key to justifying and assuring that trustworthiness exists in the study'.

Summary

The aim of this chapter is to provide an introduction to the disciplinary context and traditions of arts and events research and to introduce some of the general dimensions and concepts associated with social science research. It begins with a brief overview of the contributions of individual disciplines to arts and events research, covering sociology and cultural studies, economics, psychology/social psychology, history and anthropology, and political science. The review indicates that most of the disciplines contributing to this area of research now make use of a wide variety of research methods. The second half of the chapter covers a range of generic social science concepts and issues that arise in the literature and with which the arts and events researcher should be familiar. They are ontology, epistemology and methodology; positivist, post-positivist, interpretive and critical approaches; descriptive, explanatory and evaluative research as discussed in Chapter 1; qualitative and quantitative research; theoretical and applied research; empirical and non-empirical research; induction and deduction; experimental and non-experimental research; primary and secondary data; self-reported and observed data; and validity and reliability.

TEST QUESTIONS

1. What are the basic differences between theoretical and applied research?
2. What are the basic differences between empirical and non-empirical research?
3. What are the basic differences between the inductive and deductive approaches to research?
4. What are the basic differences between descriptive and explanatory research?
5. What are the basic differences between the positivist and the interpretive approach to research?
6. What are the basic differences between experimental and non-experimental research?
7. What is the basic difference between primary and secondary data?
8. What is the basic difference between self-reported and observed data?
9. What are the basic differences between qualitative and quantitative research?
10. What are validity and reliability?

EXERCISES

1. Examine any issue of an arts and events studies-related journal and classify the articles into disciplinary areas. Contrast the key questions which each article is addressing.
2. Using the same journal issue as in exercise 1, determine whether the articles are: a) empirical or non-empirical; b) deductive or inductive; c) positivist or interpretive.
3. Select an issue of a relevant journal at two-yearly intervals over 10 or 12 years and summarise the apparent change over time in the topics addressed and methods used in the articles.

Resources

- Action research: general: Greenwood and Levin (2007); and the arts: Finley (2005); see also Chapter 5.

- *Bricolage*: Kincheloe (2001) – see also mixed methods, pragmatism, eclecticism.

- Disciplines and the arts and events studies – arts administration/management: Ebewo and Sirayi (2009), Pick and Anderton (1996: 39–51); events studies: Getz (2012: as a field of study: 5–7; in relation to disciplines: 71–185); event tourism: Getz (2008).

- Economics:
  - arts/culture: Towse (2003)
  - evaluation of events: Dwyer *et al.* (2010: 405–456)

- Eclecticism: Hammersley (1996) – see also *bricolage*, mixed methods, pragmatism.

- Emancipatory theory: Antonio (1989).

- Ethnography – in a museum: Noy (2011); cultural tourism: Fox *et al.* (2010).

- Experimental method: see Chapter 11, Resources section.

- History – events: Falassi (1967), Getz (2012: 131–135); arts policy: UK: Evans (2001: 19–44), Pick and Anderton (1996: 1–15); USA: Ivey (2008), Straight (1979); Australia: Stevenson (2000), Radbourne and Fraser (1996); social impact of the arts: Belfiore and Bennett (2010: 13–39).

- Mixed methods: Creswell (2009), Howe (1988), Mertens (2009), Teddlie and Tashakkori (2009), Tashakkori and Creswell (2007), Tashakkori and Teddlie (2003) – see also pragmatism, *bricolage*, eclecticism.

- Observation: in a museum: Noy (2011).

- Participatory research – general: Greenwood and Levin (2007), Heron and Reason (1997), Patton (1988); in the arts: Finley (2005).

- Positivism: Chiaravalloti and Piber (2011).

- Pragmatism – general: Greenwood and Levin (2007: 9–11, 59–63, 71–73), Howe (1988), Patton (1988); in museum-related research: Falk (2011: 150) – see also mixed methods, *bricolage*, eclecticism.

- Qualitative versus quantitative research: Allwood (2012), Borman *et al.* (1986), Bryman (1984), Bryman and Bell (2003: Chapters 21, 22), Hammersley (1996), Howe (1988), Krenz and Sax (1986), Platt (1986).

- Reflexivity: Davies (1997); in researching a museum: Noy (2011).

- Research and arts practice: Biggs and Karlsson (2010), Kershaw and Nicholson (2011), Simmons and Holbrook (2013), Smith and Dean (2009), Strand (1998).

- Standpoint research: Hartsock (1999), Lather (1986).

- The science of self-report: Stone and Turkkan (2000).

- Transformative paradigm: Mertens (2009), Mertens *et al.* (2007).

- Trustworthiness: Lincoln and Guba (1985), Guba and Lincoln (1998).

- Validity/reliability: Burns (1994: 206–228).

References

Allwood, C. M. (2012) The distinction between qualitative and quantitative research methods is problematic. *Quality and Quantity*, 46(5), 1417–1429.

Antonio, R. J. (1989) The normative foundations of emancipatory theory: evolutionary versus pragmatic perspectives. *American Journal of Sociology*, 94(4), 721–748.

Belfiore, E. and Bennett, O. (2010) *The Social Impact of the Arts: An Intellectual History*. Basingstoke: Palgrave Macmillan.

Biggs, M. and Karlsson, H. (eds) (2010) *The Routledge Companion to Research in the Arts*. London: Routledge.

Borman, K. M., LeCompte, M. D. and Goetz, J. P. (1986) Ethnographic and qualitative research design and why it doesn't work. *American Behavioral Scientist*, 30(1), 42–57.

Bryman, A. (1984) The debate about quantitative and qualitative research: a question of method or epistemology? *British Journal of Sociology*, 35(1), 75–92.

Bryman, A. and Bell, E. (2003) Breaking down the quantitative/qualitative divide, and Combining quantitative and qualitative research. *Business Research Methods*. Oxford: Oxford University Press, Chapters 21–22, pp. 465–494.

Burns, R. B. (1994) *Introduction to Research Methods*, Second Edition. Melbourne: Longman Cheshire.

Charmaz, K. (2005) Grounded theory in the 21st century. In N. K. Denzin and Y. S. Lincoln (eds), *Handbook of Qualitative Research*, Third Edition. Thousand Oaks, CA: Sage, pp. 507–535.

Chiaravalloti, F. and Piber, M. (2011) Ethical implications of methodological settings in arts management research: the case of performance evaluation. *Journal of Arts Management, Law and Society*, 41(3), 240–266.

Creswell, J. W. (2009) *Research Design: Qualitative, Quantitative and Mixed Methods Approaches*, Third Edition. Thousand Oaks, CA: Sage.

Davies, C. (1997) *Reflexive Ethnography: A Guide to Researching Selves and Others*. London: Routledge.

Denzin, N. K. and Lincoln, Y. S. (eds) (2005) *Handbook of Qualitative Research*, Third Edition. Thousand Oaks, CA: Sage.

Dwyer, L., Forsyth, P. and Dwyer, W. (2010) Economic evaluation of special events. *Tourism Economics and Policy*. Bristol: Channel View Publications, Chapter 11, pp. 405–456.

Ebewo, P. and Sirayi, M. (2009) The concept of arts/cultural management: a critical reflection. *Journal of Arts Management, Law and Society*, 38(4), 281–295.

Evans, G. (2001) *Cultural Planning: An Urban Renaissance?* London: Routledge.

Falassi, A. (ed.) (1967) *Time out of Time: Essays on the Festival*. Albuquerque, NM: University of New Mexico Press.

Falk, J. H. (2011) Contextualizing Falk's identity-related visitor motivation model. *Visitor Studies*, 14(2), 141–157.

Finley, S. (2005) Arts-based inquiry: performing revolutionary pedagogy. In N. K. Denzin and Y. S. Lincoln (eds), *Handbook of Qualitative Research*, Third Edition. Thousand Oaks, CA: Sage, pp. 681–694.

Fox, D., Edwards, J. and Wilkes, K. (2010) Employing the grand tour approach to aid understanding of garden visiting. In G. Richards and W. Munsters (eds) *Cultural Tourism Research Methods*. Wallingford: CABI, pp. 75–86.

Getz, D. (2008) Event tourism: definition, evolution and research. *Tourism Management*, 29(4), 403–428.

Getz, D. (2012) *Event Studies: Theory, Research and Policy for Planned Events*, Second Edition. London: Routledge.

Giddens, A. (ed.) (1974) *Positivism and Sociology*. London: Heinemann.

Glancy, M. (1993) Achieving intersubjectivity: the process of becoming the subject in leisure research. *Leisure Studies*, 12(1), 45–60.

Greenwood, D. J. and Levin, M. (2007) *Introduction to Action Research: Social Research for Social Change*, Second Edition. Thousand Oaks, CA: Sage.

Guba, E. G. and Lincoln, Y. S. (1998) Competing paradigms in qualitative research. In N. K. Denzin and Y. S. Lincoln (eds), *The Landscape of Qualitative Research: Theories and Issues*. Thousand Oaks, CA: Sage, pp. 195–220.

Guba, E. G. and Lincoln, Y. S. (2005) Paradigmatic controversies, contradictions and emerging confluences. In N. K. Denzin and Y. S. Lincoln (eds), *Handbook of Qualitative Research*, Third Edition. Thousand Oaks, CA: Sage, pp. 191–216.

Hammersley, M. (1996) The relationship between qualitative and quantitative research: paradigm loyalty versus methodological eclecticism. In J. T. E. Richardson (ed.), *Handbook of Qualitative Research Methods for Psychology and the Social Sciences*. Leicester: BPS Books, pp. 159–174.

Hartsock, N. (1999) *The Feminist Standpoint Revisited, and Other Essays*. New York: Basic Books.

Henderson, K. A. (2006) *Dimensions of Choice: A Qualitative Approach to Recreation, Parks, and Leisure Research*, Second Edition. State College, PA: Venture.

Heron, J. and Reason, P. (1997) A participatory inquiry paradigm. *Qualitative Inquiry*, 3(3), 274–294.

Howe, K. R. (1988) Against the quantitative–qualitative incompatibility thesis: or dogmas die hard. *Educational Researcher*, 17(8), 10–16.

Ivey, B. (2008) *Arts Inc.: How Greed and Neglect Have Destroyed Our Cultural Rights*. Berkeley, CA: University of California Press.

Kershaw, B. and Nicholson, H. (eds) (2011) *Research Methods in Theatre and Performance*. Edinburgh: Edinburgh University Press.

Kincheloe, J. L. (2001) Describing the bricolage: conceptualizing a new rigor in qualitative research. *Qualitative Inquiry*, 7(6), 679–692.

Kline, R. B. (2005) *Principles and Practice of Structural Equation Modeling*, Second Edition. New York: Guilford Press.

Krenz, C. and Sax, G. (1986) What quantitative research is and why it doesn't work. *American Behavioral Scientist*, 30(1), 58–69.

Labovitz, S. and Hagedorn, R. (1971) *Introduction to Social Research*. New York: McGraw-Hill.

Lather, P. (1986) Issues of validity in openly ideological research: between a rock and a soft place. *Interchange*, 17(4), 63–84.

Lee, A. S. (1989) Case studies as natural experiments. *Human Relations*, 42(2), 117–137.

Lincoln, Y. and Guba, E. G. (1985) *Naturalistic Inquiry*. Beverly Hills, CA: Sage.

Matarasso, F. (1997) *Use or Ornament? The Social Impact of Participation in the Arts*. Stroud: Comedia.

Matarasso, F. (2003) Smoke and mirrors: a response to Paola Merli's 'Evaluating the Social Impact of Participation in Arts Activities'. *International Journal of Cultural Policy*, 9(3), 337–346.

Merli, P. (2002) Evaluating the social impact of participating in arts activities. *International Journal of Cultural Policy*, 8(1), 107–118.

Mertens, D. M. (2009) *Transformative Research and Evaluation*. New York: Guilford Press.

Mertens, D. M., Fraser, J. and Heimlich, J. E. (2007) M or F? Gender, identity, and the transformative research paradigm. *Museums and Social Issues*, 3(1), 81–92.

Noy, C. (2011) The aesthetics of qualitative (re)search: performing ethnography at a heritage museum. *Qualitative Inquiry*, 17(10), 917–929.

Patton, M. (1988) Paradigms and pragmatism. In D. Fetterman (ed.), *Qualitative Approaches to Evaluation in Educational Research*. Newbury Park, CA: Sage, pp. 116–137.

Pick, J. and Anderton, M. (1996) *Arts Administration*. London: E. and F. N. Spon.

Platt, J. (1986) Functionalism and the survey: the relation of theory and method. *Sociological Review*, 34(3), 501–536.

Radbourne, J. and Fraser, M. (1996) *Arts Management: A Practical Guide*. St Leonards, NSW: Allen and Unwin.

Simmons, B. and Holbrook, A. (2013) From rupture to resonance: uncertainty and scholarship in fine art research degrees. *Arts and Humanities in Higher Education*, 12(2–3), 204–221.

Smith, H. and Dean, R. T. (eds) (2009) *Practice-led Research, Research-led Practice in the Creative Arts*. Edinburgh: Edinburgh University Press.

Stevenson, D. (2000) Art and Organisation: *Making Australian Cultural Policy*. St Lucia, Qld: University of Queensland Press.

Stone, A. A. and Turkkan, J. S. (2000) *The Science of Self-report: Implications for Research and Practice*. Mahwah, NJ: Lawrence Erlbaum.

Straight, M. (1979) *Twigs for an Eagle's Nest: Government and the Arts: 1965–1978*. New York: Devon Press.

Strand, D. (1998) *Research in the Creative Arts*. Canberra: Department of Employment, Education, Training and Youth Affairs.

Tashakkori, A. and Creswell, J. W. (2007) Exploring the nature of research questions in mixed methods research. *Journal of Mixed Methods Research*, 1(3), 207–211.

Tashakkori, A. and Teddlie, C. (eds) (2003) *Handbook of Mixed Methods in Social and Behavioral Research*. Thousand Oaks, CA: Sage.

Teddlie, C. and Tashakkori, A. (eds) (2009) *Foundations of Mixed Methods Research: Integrating Quantitative and Qualitative Approaches in the Social and Behavioral Sciences*. Thousand Oaks, CA: Sage.

Towse, R. (ed.) (2003) *A Handbook of Cultural Economics*. Cheltenham: Edward Elgar.

Chapter 3

Starting out: research plans and proposals

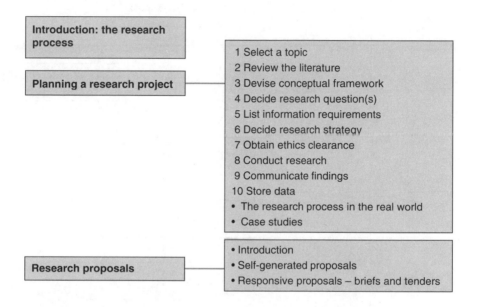

Introduction: the research process

Planning a research project

1 Select a topic
2 Review the literature
3 Devise conceptual framework
4 Decide research question(s)
5 List information requirements
6 Decide research strategy
7 Obtain ethics clearance
8 Conduct research
9 Communicate findings
10 Store data
• The research process in the real world
• Case studies

Research proposals

• Introduction
• Self-generated proposals
• Responsive proposals – briefs and tenders

Introduction

The research process
This chapter examines:

- stages in the planning of research projects;
- the formulation and presentation of research proposals and tenders.

Planning a research project

A research plan or proposal must summarise how a research project is to be conducted in its entirety; consequently preparation of a plan or proposal involves examination of the whole research process from beginning to end. In this chapter, therefore, a certain amount of cross-referencing is required to later chapters, where particular elements of the process are dealt with in detail.

The research process can be envisaged in a number of ways, but for the purposes of discussion in this chapter it is divided into ten main elements, as shown in Figure 3.1. The enormous variety of approaches to research means that all research projects do not follow precisely the sequence as set out in the figure. In particular, the first four elements depicted – selecting the topic, reviewing the literature, devising a conceptual framework and deciding the key research questions – rarely happen in the direct, linear way that the numbered

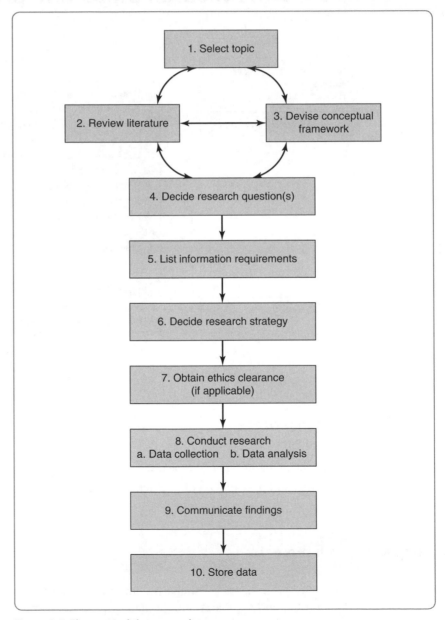

Figure 3.1 Elements of the research process

sequence implies. Indeed, in the case of grounded theory research, as discussed in Chapter 9, it is even argued that any literature review should be conducted after data collection and at least initial analysis have taken place, so that it does not overly influence the latter process (Charmaz, 2006: 6). There is generally a great deal of 'to-ing and fro-ing' between the elements. Hence, in Figure 3.1, these elements are depicted on a circle, implying that a number of circuits may be necessary before proceeding to element 5. To illustrate the process in operation, case studies are presented in summary at the end of this section. Each of the ten elements in Figure 3.1 is discussed in turn below.

1 Select a topic

How do research topics arise? They may come from a range of sources, including the researcher's personal interests, reading research literature, a policy or management problem, an issue of social concern, a popular or media issue, published research agendas and/or brainstorming, which may draw on a number of the above sources. Examples of topics arising from these sources are shown in Figure 3.2.

Personal interest

Personal interest can give rise to a research project in a number of ways. For example, the researcher may be personally involved in a particular cultural activity or event or may be a member of a particular social group, based on gender, ethnicity or occupation, and so be

Source of topic	Examples of topics
Personal interest (usually combined with one or more of the next five sources)	● A particular art form with which the researcher is involved, e.g.: 　○ Trends in participation, participants' motivations/ satisfactions. 　○ A particular cultural event – history, impact. 　○ A particular professional group – its ethos, history and future.
The literature	● Does Csikszentmihalyi's (1990) idea of 'flow' apply to participation in the creative arts? ● How do different theories of management apply in arts and event management?
Policy/management	● Why are visits to a particular museum declining? ● What market segments should be used to develop a strategy for promoting a cultural festival? ● What are the cultural provision needs of a community?
Social	● The impact of increasingly privatised lifestyles on social capital. ● The arts in remote communities.
Popular/media	● The social, economic and environmental impact of a major event on a host community. ● Is public money spent on the arts justified?
Published research agendas	● Listing of research topics by organisations or academics.
Brainstorming	● Conduct a 'brainstorm' session on any of the above topics/sources – a means of exploring the potential of all of the above.
Opportunism	● Government-collected cultural participation data provide the opportunity to undertake some demand forecasting. ● Becoming a volunteer in a cultural or sporting event offers an opportunity to conduct research on the event.

Figure 3.2 Examples of research topics from different sources

personally aware of certain pertinent issues or problems. Using personal interest as a focus for research has advantages and disadvantages. The advantage lies in the knowledge of the phenomenon that the researcher already has, the possibility of access to key individuals and information sources, and the high level of motivation that is likely to be brought to the research. The disadvantage is that the researcher may be unduly biased and may not be able to view the situation 'objectively'; familiarity with the subject of the research may result in too much being taken for granted so that the researcher cannot 'see the wood for the trees'.

While a particular personal interest in the research topic may be referred to in writing up a research project – generally in a foreword or preface rather than in the main body of the report – it is often not mentioned in formal reports of research, such as journal articles. For some types of qualitative or 'standpoint' research, however, as discussed in Chapter 2, the researcher's personal relationship with the subjects of the research may be an important aspect of the methodology.

Personal interest may be a component in the process of selecting a research topic but does not alone generally provide a sufficient rationale or focus for a research project; it is necessary to develop additional criteria for selection of a specific topic from among the other sources discussed below.

The research literature

The research literature is the most common source of topics for academic research. A researchable topic derived from reading of the literature can take a variety of forms. It may arise from an informal scanning of the literature, which stimulates a spark of interest in a topic, or it may arise from a more critical and focused reading. Much reported research is very specific to time and place, so that even a widely accepted theory might merit further testing and exploration. Thus it may be that a certain theory or theoretical proposition has never been tested empirically, or further empirical testing is justified for a variety of reasons, as set out in Figure 3.3.

Reason	The theories'/propositions'/ observations' history	Examples
Geographical	May have been tested in only one country/region	– Theory established using US data could be tested in another country. – Behaviour patterns of urban residents – are they replicated in rural areas?
Social	May have been established on the basis of the experience of one social group only	– Theory based on men's experience – does it apply to women? – Theory tested on middle-class subjects – does it apply to working-class people?
Temporal	May be out of date	– Theory on youth culture established in the 1980s – is it still valid?
Contextual	May have been established in fields other than arts/events	– Foucault's (1979) theories on power are based on studies in a hospital – are they relevant in the arts?
Methodological	May have been tested using only one methodology	– Conclusions from a qualitative study could be tested quantitatively and vice versa (e.g. Atkinson, 2011).
Disciplinary	May have been researched in the context of only one discipline	– How does social inequality (sociology) in cultural participation play out in spatial terms (geography)?

Figure 3.3 Reasons for re-visiting theories/propositions/observations from the literature

Clearly, therefore, identifying a topic from the literature requires a special, *questioning, exploratory* approach to reading research literature: the aim is not to identify just what the literature says but also what it does not say or the basis for assertions made or conclusions reached. The process of critically reviewing the literature is discussed further below under element 2 of the research process, and in Chapter 6. If the research literature is to be the main source of ideas for a research topic then the first two elements of the research process, selecting a topic and reviewing the literature, are effectively combined.

A policy or management issue/problem

Policy or management topics are often specified by an organisation, but students or academics interested in policy or management issues can also identify such topics. For example, cultural participation and event evaluation research is conducted not only by, and at the behest of, government and other organisations but also by academics. The difference between industry-sponsored and academically initiated research is that:

- academically initiated research results will often be made public, will generally be presented so as to highlight their more general implications rather than the particular application to the facility or programme being studied, and will be concerned as much with the methodology of the study as with its substantive findings;
- industry-sponsored research results may often not be made public, the wider implications of the research might not be examined and the methodology, while it must be sound, will often not be of particular interest to the sponsoring organisation.

In some cases academics involved with one or more industry-sponsored projects, the results of which have been reported to the sponsoring organisation, may publish academic articles highlighting particular features for a wider readership.

Research sponsored by government bodies lies somewhere in between these two situations: the results of the research may be very specific but will often not be confidential.

It is common for an organisation requiring research on a particular policy or management topic to outline its requirements in a brief or set of terms of reference for a funded research or consultancy project. Research organisations – usually consultants – are then invited to respond in the form of a competitive tender to conduct the project. This type of procedure has its own set of practices and conventions, as discussed later in the chapter under *Responsive proposals – briefs and tenders*.

Social concern

Social concern – of the researcher and/or sections of society at large – can give rise to a wide range of research topics. For example, concern for certain deprived or neglected groups in society, such as at-risk youth, can lead to research on the cultural needs or behaviour of members of such groups. Concern for the environment can lead to research on the environmental impact of major events in sensitive areas, for example car rallies or music festivals in natural areas. Often such research is closely related to policy or management issues, but the research may have a more limited role, seeking to highlight problems rather than necessarily devising solutions.

Popular/media

A popular issue can inspire research that seeks to explore popular beliefs or conceptions, especially where it is suspected that these may be inaccurate or contestable. 'Popular' usually means 'as portrayed in the media'. For example, this might be seen as the motivation for much research on media portrayals of such phenomena as controversial artworks or photography (Marr, 2008) or major controversial developments, such as building expensive new national museums/galleries/theatres or facilities to stage global events.

Published research agendas

From time to time public agencies, professional bodies or individual academics publish 'research agendas', based on an assessment, often made by a committee, of the research needs of a field of study. The Resources section includes a list of examples of such publications. Often the aim of the body initiating the agenda is to implement the published research agenda itself, but in other cases the idea is for researchers in the field generally – including students – to respond by adopting topics in the agenda for their own research. Thus, the (USA) National Endowment for the Arts (2012: 6) states that its research agenda document 'proposes a way for the nation's cultural researchers, arts practitioners, policy-makers, and the general public to view, analyse and discuss the arts as a dynamic, complex system'. Students looking for research topics know that if their topic is selected from such a published agenda, or can be located within its conceptual framework, then there will be at least a few people 'out there' who will be interested in the results.

Brainstorming

Brainstorming involves a group of two or more people bouncing ideas off one another in pursuit of inspiration or solutions to a problem. Typically this might be done with the aid of a whiteboard or flip chart to write down ideas as they emerge. It can be seen as a separate source of ideas for a research topic or a way of refining ideas from any or all of the other sources discussed.

Opportunism

Sometimes an idea for research is prompted for opportunistic reasons: for example, a data source or access to a cultural facility becoming available. Various government surveys and other data collected for policy and administrative purposes and used for limited and internal policy-related or administrative purposes often present opportunities for secondary analysis, and this is discussed further in Chapter 7. Membership of an organisation or a visit to a cultural facility or event provides the opportunity for participant observation and the availability of organisational or personal archives may lead to historical research. In all these cases, as well as considering the nature and quality of the available data, one or more of the above rationales have to be brought into play to establish whether conducting a project using the data can be justified.

Selecting the topic

What makes a viable research topic? There is no single, or simple, answer to this question. In general it is not the topic itself that is good or bad but the way the research is conceptualised (see element 3 of the research process) and how the research question or questions are framed (element 4). A key question is whether the topic has already been researched by someone else – hence the need for a review of the literature, as discussed in element 2. But even when a topic has already been researched there is invariably scope for further research – sometimes this is pointed out by the original researcher in concluding comments.

Thus the first four elements of the research process – select topic, review literature, conceptualise, define research questions – form an iterative, often untidy, process, which is invariably difficult and challenging and sometimes frustrating. But it is essential to get this stage right or the rest of the research effort may be wasted.

The purpose of research

The purposes of a research project can shape the choice of topic and the subsequent research design. Three types of purpose are discussed here: knowledge for its own sake, ideological/political purposes and policy/management purposes. Their key features are summarised in Figure 3.4. These purposes or motivations for research are often not explicitly stated in research reports but are generally implicit. They affect the choice of topic and the overall shaping of the research process.

Knowledge for its own sake

The classic purpose of research is to 'add to knowledge' for its own sake, or for the general good as judged by the researcher. Some researchers continue to be driven by this goal in all or some of their research and work in an institutional environment where it can be pursued. Much unfunded research undertaken by academics in their own time is of this nature. But even in such a 'pure' situation, other, less noble, although not necessarily illegitimate, purposes may be involved – for example personal career advancement.

Ideological/political

Many academic researchers are motivated in whole or in part by an ideological, political or values agenda. It could be said that all researchers are so motivated to a certain extent, and in certain areas of the social sciences this is a valid point. Thus, many social scientists might be described as *reformist*, in that they are motivated by a general desire for a more equitable or just society and their research will tend to be at least consistent with such a goal, if not centrally concerned with it. For example, much arts research is concerned with equality and inequality of access to cultural opportunities. Similarly, environmental protection and sustainability is often an implicit or explicit concern.

Type of purpose/motivation	Features
Pursue knowledge for its own sake	Academic/scientific criteria – but may combine with others below
Ideologically driven:	
– Conservative	– defence/acceptance of the status quo
– Reformist	
– social-democratic	– a more egalitarian society
– environmental	– sustainability
– Radical/critical	
– neo-liberal	– defence/extension of the market
– neo-Marxist	– demonstration of class conflict/exploitation
– radical-feminist	– demonstration of patriarchy/women's oppression
– anti-globalist	– demonstrate undesirable features of global market trends
Policy/management:	
– Critical	– Critiques current policy/management – may reflect one or more radical/critical stances above
– Instrumental	– Accepts, at least by implication, the broad philosophy or organisational milieu in which the study is taking place

Figure 3.4 Purposes of research

If none of these concerns is apparent, but the research is dealing with social issues, the implicit stance may be taken as *conservative* – implying contentment with the political, social and/or economic status quo. In contrast, some researchers are guided by one or more of a number of ideological positions that seek fundamental change in society and might be described as *radical* or *critical*. In Chapter 2 the concept of standpoint research was noted. On the right of the political spectrum is radical 'New Right' thinking, which endorses market processes and seeks their extension and might be termed *neo-liberal*. There is relatively little research in the arts and events field with this outlook, although it is implicit in some research concerned with the use of culture and events as a vehicle for economic development.

By contrast, there are researchers who, in the words of Lincoln (2005: 165), are 'committed to seeing social science used for democratic and liberalizing social purposes'. Researchers on the left with, for example, neo-Marxist views, are often explicit about the political purpose of research. Thus, for example, Lenskyj (2008: 6), in her book on the Olympic Games, states that her 'radical approach' is 'not neutral' and that she approaches the topic 'from a social justice and equity perspective, in order to develop an analysis of interlocking systems of oppression, particularly classism, racism, and sexism, and their impacts on disadvantaged populations in Olympic bid and host cities'. There has been persistent and widespread controversy on policy-related research that appears to view the arts as instrumental rather than of intrinsic value (e.g. Ratiu, 2009). In these instances the stance taken by a researcher may be seen as ideological or political. For example, Bereson's (2005) analysis of arts policies in Australia reveal what she believes to be unwelcome instrumental goals overlaying the intrinsic worth of the arts. Others see researching the instrumental nature of the arts (economic and social benefits) as ensuring sustainable investment (e.g. Holden, 2006). Other sources on these topics are indicated in the Resources section.

Policy/management

The purpose of policy- or management-related research seems obvious enough: to address policy or management problems. But the stance adopted can vary and can be affected by the ideological positions outlined above. Some research might be seen as *critical*, in that it steps outside the policy or management milieu of the public- or private-sector organisations being studied and adopts a reformist or, as in the examples above, leftist/critical stance when it critiques processes such as privatisation or 'managerialism' or seeks to demonstrate the inequitable outcomes of certain policies or management practices. Research that seeks to make management systems more efficient or profitable and generally accepts the broad philosophical stance of the organisational milieu being studied can be seen as *functional*.

2 Review the literature

Introduction

The process of reviewing the existing research literature is sufficiently important for a complete chapter to be devoted to it in this book (Chapter 6). 'Reviewing the literature' is a somewhat academic term referring to the process of identifying and engaging with previously published research relevant to the topic of interest. The process can play a number of roles, as listed in Figure 3.5 and discussed further in Chapter 6.

In many cases the review undertaken in the early stages of the research has to be seen as a preliminary or interim literature review only, since time does not always permit a thorough literature review to be completed at the start of a project. Part of the research programme

- Entire basis of the research
- Source of ideas on topics for research
- Source of information on research already done by others
- Source of methodological or theoretical ideas
- Basis of comparison
- Source of information that is an integral/supportive part of the research

Figure 3.5 Roles of the literature in research

itself may then be to explore the literature further. Having investigated the literature as thoroughly as possible, it is usually necessary to proceed with the research project in the hope that all relevant material has been identified. Exploration of the literature will generally continue for the duration of the project. Researchers always run the risk of coming across some previous – or contemporaneous – publication that will negate or upstage their work just as they are about to complete it. But that is part of the excitement of research. In fact, unlike the situation in the natural sciences, the risk of this happening in the arts and events field is minimal, since research in this area can rarely be replicated exactly. In the natural sciences, research carried out in, say, California can reproduce exactly the findings of research carried out in, say, London. In arts and events research, however, this is rarely the case – a set of research procedures carried out in relation to individuals or organisations in California could be expected to produce very different results from identical procedures carried out in London – or even San Francisco – simply because arts and events research is involved with unique people in varying social settings.

Published and unpublished research

Where possible, attempts should be made to explore not just published research – the literature – but also unpublished and on-going research. This process is very much hit and miss. Knowing what research is on-going or knowing of completed but unpublished research usually depends on having access to informal networks, although some research organisations produce registers of on-going research projects. Once a topic of interest has been identified it is often clear, from the literature, where the major centres for such research are located and to discover, from direct approaches or from websites, annual reports or newsletters, what research is currently being conducted at those centres. This process can be particularly important if the topic is a 'fashionable' one. In such cases the communication networks are usually very active, which eases the process. In this respect papers from conferences and seminars are usually better sources of information on current research than books and journals, since the latter have long gestation periods, so that the research reported in them is generally based on work carried out two or more years prior to publication.

What discipline?

In an academic context, especially for undergraduate or graduate projects, it is helpful to consider what discipline(s) the project relates to. In some cases this is obvious because the project is linked to a particular disciplinary field – for example, marketing. In other cases the project is a capstone exercise in a degree course which may draw on one or more of any of the subjects studied in the course. Often, the fact that a topic does not have an obvious disciplinary label results in student researchers failing to draw on available disciplinary theories and frameworks and failing to take the opportunity to demonstrate the knowledge they have gained during the course of their studies. For example, if the research topic is to do with the subject of theatre, searching library catalogues and databases using the keyword 'theatre' will undoubtedly produce a certain amount of useful material. But consideration of whether the focus of the study is to be on theatre management, theatre marketing, the social context of theatre or the motivations or training regimes of actors or directors opens up the possibility of applying generic theories and relating the research to comparable studies of other phenomena in the area of management, planning, sociology, psychology and education, respectively. An important question to ask is, therefore: what disciplinary field(s) is this research related to? What theories and ideas can be drawn from the literature in this discipline or these disciplines?

Outcomes

As discussed in Chapter 6, a review of the literature should be concluded with a summary giving an overview of the field, its substantive and methodological merits and deficiencies or gaps, and an indication of how such conclusions are related to the research task at hand.

3 Devise conceptual framework

The idea of a conceptual framework

The development of a conceptual framework is arguably the most important part of any research project and also the most difficult. And it is the element which is the weakest in many research projects. A conceptual framework involves concepts involved in a study and the hypothesised relationships between them.

In this discussion the term 'conceptual framework' has been used to cover a wide range of research situations. Thus, such a term can be used in applied research when the framework adopted might relate to such activities as evaluation, planning or marketing. In such cases, ideas for conceptual frameworks may readily be found in the evaluation, planning or marketing literature. When the research is more academically orientated, the term 'theoretical framework' might equally well be used. Miles and Huberman, in their book on *Qualitative Data Analysis*, describe conceptual frameworks as follows:

> A conceptual framework explains, either graphically or in narrative form, the main things to be studied – the key factors, constructs or variables – and the presumed relationships among them. Frameworks can be rudimentary or elaborate, theory-driven or commonsensical, descriptive or causal.

(Miles and Huberman, 1994: 18)

Different types of research – descriptive, explanatory or evaluative, as discussed in Chapter 1 – tend to call for different styles of conceptual framework. Descriptive research rarely requires an elaborate conceptual framework, but clear definitions of the concepts involved are necessary. In some cases this can nevertheless be a considerable undertaking – for example, if the descriptive task is concerned with levels of cultural participation, considerable thought will need to be given to the question of just how this is to be measured (see Chapter 7). Both explanatory and evaluative research call for well-developed conceptual frameworks which form the basis for the explanatory or evaluative work required from the research.

One reaction to this discussion of conceptual frameworks is to observe that the approach seems inconsistent with the inductive approach, as discussed in Chapter 2, in which theory is derived from the data rather than data being used to test pre-existing theory. In particular, it seems inconsistent with apparently more open-ended approaches such as grounded theory and informal, flexible approaches used in qualitative research. However, as Miles and Huberman (1994) indicate, conceptual frameworks are just as vital for qualitative research as for quantitative – arguably more so. In the context of qualitative research, Henderson uses the term 'working hypothesis' to indicate that an initial framework may lack detail and may be subject to change as the research unfolds:

> A researcher conducting an inductive qualitative study should have a broad research question, conceptual framework, or working hypothesis in mind when beginning a project and, subsequently, as data collection begins … however, a researcher must be willing to let the working hypothesis metamorphose as the study progresses.
>
> (Henderson, 2006: 79)

In fact, a conceptual framework need not be a straitjacket: it can be a flexible, evolving device. As discussed in Chapter 8, in qualitative research, theory development and data collection and analysis are often intertwined, rather than being sequential. But the researcher rarely starts with a blank conceptual framework – there is usually some sort of rudimentary framework drawn from the literature or other sources. At the minimum there will be an initial list of relevant concepts with which the researcher is concerned and without which it is difficult to know what questions to ask or what issues to explore. In some cases the researcher may start with a framework from the literature which is seen as unsatisfactory in some way: the aim of the research is then not to validate the framework but to do the opposite and replace it with an improved – and possibly very different – model. The conceptual framework drawn up at the beginning of the research project can be seen as the 'first draft'. As data gathering and analysis proceed, further drafts emerge, incorporating new insights arising from the research. The developing conceptual framework becomes the focus of the research process. As Miles and Huberman (1994: 298) put it: 'Many qualitative analysts would not start with a conceptual framework, but rather aim to end up with one'.

The concepts identified and the framework within which they are set determine the whole course of the study. In exploring the conceptual framework for the study the researcher is asking: What's going on here? What processes are at work or likely to be at work? Sometimes the framework is developed from individual reflection or 'brainstorming' and sometimes it arises from the literature; indeed, an existing framework from the literature might well be adopted for application in a new situation. Where a number of areas of literature have been reviewed to provide the basis for the research, the skill is to draw together the theoretical ideas into a common framework – even if the aim is to show the incompatibility between two or more perspectives. Such links of course should be clearly and fully explained in the exposition of the framework.

Devising a conceptual framework

The development of a conceptual framework can be thought of as involving four elements, as depicted in Figure 3.6. The element 'Identification of concepts' should, perhaps, be the starting point, but this is rarely the case: the tendency is to think about relationships first, and then identify and define the concepts involved as this becomes necessary. In fact, the exercise is generally iterative – that is, it involves going backwards and forwards, or round and round, between the various elements until a satisfactory solution is reached. The four elements are discussed in turn below.

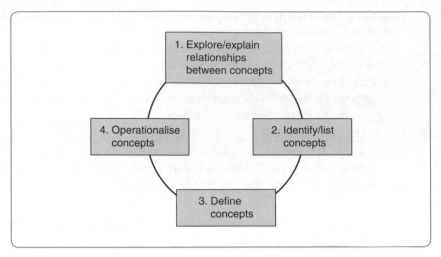

Figure 3.6 Development of a conceptual framework

1 Explore/explain the relationships

Relationships may represent power relationships, culturally influencing factors (e.g. role models), money or information flows, or simply a time-related sequence of elements in a temporal process. The postulated relationships correspond to the theory – however tentative – that underpins the conceptual framework. Explaining a conceptual framework may be a lengthy and complex process, especially when links with the literature are involved. The example in Figure 3.7 is very simple. It shows how the ideas develop from a simple statement (Stage A) to a more complex statement or series of statements (Stage C) as the ideas develop. In the example, the statements are expressed in the form of hypotheses; they could alternatively be expressed as questions, for example: 'To what extent is the decision influenced by income?'

One aid to the development of a conceptual framework is to use the device of a *concept map*, sometimes referred to as a mental map or relevance tree. While some concept maps are more self-evident than others, a concept map is only an optional aid – a full narrative discussion and explanation always form the core of the conceptual framework; a concept map merely illustrates or summarises the discussion. Concept mapping can be seen as a form of

Stage	Statements/hypotheses (concepts are in italics)
A	*Participation* in a cultural activity arises as a result of an individual (or group/household/family) decision-making process.
B	Whether or not a person participates could depend on a variety of *events and circumstances*, for example: – the *availability of and access to facilities* may be good or bad; – *advertising, promotion, reviews* may vary in quantity and influence; – the *cost* of participation may be high or low; – a *chance event*, such as meeting up with a group of friends or seeing an artist on television, may trigger the desire to *participate*.
C	Whether or not individuals participate will also depend on their *characteristics*, such as: – *age/gender* – *income* – *personality* – *education* – *past experience* in participating in that or similar experiences.

Figure 3.7 Exploration of relationships between concepts – example

visual 'brainstorming' and can be done alone or as part of a group exercise. The idea is to write down all the concepts that appear to be relevant to a topic, in any order in which they come to mind. This can be done on one or more pieces of paper, Post-it Notes, a board or flip chart, or on a computer screen using suitable software (for example, in Word, go to 'Insert' and insert a 'Text Box': right-click for menus to produce a variety of shapes and colours). Then begin to group the concepts and indicate linkages between them. This is likely to involve a process of trial and error. Figure 3.8 illustrates diagrammatically the framework described verbally in Figure 3.7. Three versions of the concept map correspond to the three stages in Figure 3.7.

The concept map, then, depicts *concepts* – usually depicted in boxes or circles – and the *relationships* between concepts, which are usually represented by lines connecting the concepts, with or without directional arrows. Different types of concept might be represented by different shaped boxes and different types of relationship by different types or colour of line. The concepts and their relationships are explained in the accompanying text (Figure 3.7). The key relationships identified at stages A, B and C in the process are labelled accordingly.

2 Identify/list concepts

Concepts are general representations of the phenomena to be studied – the 'building blocks' of a study. Concepts emerge in the discussion of relationships and the concept mapping process: here we formally identify, recognise and list them. They might involve types of individuals (e.g. manager, audience member), groups of individuals (e.g. band, community) or

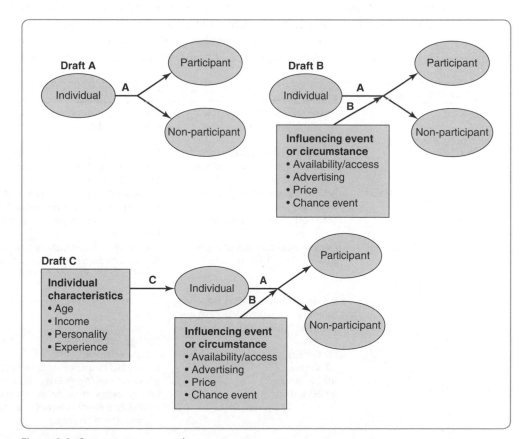

Figure 3.8 Concept map example

organisations (e.g. company, government) or their characteristics or actions. The first column of Figure 3.9 lists the concepts encountered in Figures 3.7 and 3.8.

3 Define concepts

Concepts must be clearly defined for research purposes. Dictionary definitions or definitions from the research literature may be used, but it is often necessary to be selective or adaptive. Column 2 of Figure 3.9 includes suggested definitions for the concepts listed there. Definitions might be very rudimentary in the early stages of the exercise and become more detailed and complex with time: as we talk about 'X' we have to clarify exactly what we mean by 'X'.

4 Operationalise concepts

The terminology used to describe the process of *operationalisation* depends on whether a concept is quantitative or qualitative in nature or in its treatment:

- quantitative: operationalisation involves deciding how the concept might be measured;
- qualitative: operationalisation process involves deciding how the concept might be identified, described or assessed when conducting qualitative research, such as in-depth interviews.

Examples of operationalisation of concepts are shown in column 3 of Figure 3.9. Most of the concepts listed lend themselves to quantification and measurement, at least in part, but concepts 2a, 2b and 2d have qualitative characteristics and could be treated either way. The question of measurement is discussed more fully in Part II of the book, particularly in Chapter 7.

To some extent operationalisation involves thinking ahead as to how information about a concept might be gathered in practice: it is an indication of the practical implications of the

Concept (see Figure 3.7)	Definition	Operationalisation
1 *Participant*	Person who engages in a public cultural activity.	Attending a cultural venue or event outside the home at least once in the preceding year.
2 *Influencing event or circumstance*		
(a) Availability/access	Preferred type of facility at an affordable price available in home community.	Range of facility within 30 minutes' travel time at or below various 'bench-mark' costs, e.g. £5, £10, £25 a head.
(b) Advertising/ promotion/ reviews	Advertising/promotion/reviews to which individual is exposed.	Individual's recall of a specified list of advertisements/promotions/reviews in last 3 months
(c) Cost	Total cost of cultural experience.	Costs of visit: a. per season (if applicable); b. per visit.
(d) Chance event/ viewing	Unplanned occurrence or media viewing that affects decision to participate.	Events which individual claims affected recent decisions to participate: experience, advice from friend/relative, item read or seen in the media.
3 *Individual characteristics*		
	Individual attributes (that influence cultural participation decisions), for example:	
	(a) Age	(a) Age last birthday
	(b) Gender	(b) Male/female
	(c) Income	(c) Annual household income before tax
	(d) Personality	(d) Results of Myers-Briggs type indicator
	(e) Education	(e) Secondary, technical or university education
	(f) Past cultural experience	(f) Public cultural activities undertaken in last year (from checklist)

Figure 3.9 Examples of concepts – definition and operationalisation

definition. Often arbitrary or pragmatic choices have to be made in order to operationalise the project. For example, should 'public cultural participation' involve 'regular' participation to be counted as 'participation' or is 'at least once a year' adequate? These decisions may be arbitrary or based on the need to gather data that are comparable to other, existing data, for example national survey data.

Models

A conceptual framework might also be called a *model*, particularly when the research is quantitative in nature. For example, the relationship between cultural participation and a person's social and economic circumstances could be expressed in quantitative modelling terms, as shown in Figure 3.10. A participation survey would identify various groups with different levels of participation and income, and statistical analysis could be used to 'calibrate' the equation, that is find values for the 'parameters' a and b, so that the level of participation of a particular group could be predicted once the average income of that group was known. In Figure 3.10 hypothetical parameters of 0.2 and 0.31 are presented to illustrate the approach and an example is given of how such an equation might be used to estimate or predict participation frequency of groups with given income levels, now or in the future. The technicalities of the statistical process are not pursued further here but are touched on again in Chapter 17, when the technique of regression is discussed. More complex models could be developed, including such concepts as age, education level, the price of participation and so on.

Figure 3.11 presents an example of a conceptual framework for a market research study and Figure 3.12 presents one for a customer service quality study.

4 Decide research question(s)

Research question, problem or hypothesis?

The focus of a research project might be expressed as a question, a problem or a hypothesis.

● A question requires an answer.

● A problem requires a solution.

● A hypothesis is expressed as a statement, which must be shown to be 'true' (consistent with the evidence) or 'false' (not consistent with the evidence).

The differences and relationships between the question-based approach and the hypothesis-based approach are illustrated in Figure 3.13, which uses the problem of declining visitor numbers at a cultural facility as an example. Two versions are offered – A being the simple version and B the more complex version – involving exploration of a range of possible answers in the question form and testing a range of hypotheses in the hypothesis form. In each case the left-hand column uses the question form and the right-hand column uses the hypothesis form.

Conceptual framework/theory	The average frequency of cultural participation of a particular group is positively related to the group's average level of income
Concepts/variables	C = frequency of cultural participation per year N = annual income in £000s
Relationship/equation	C = a + bN
Example of calibrated equation (value of a and b found from survey-based research)	C = 0.2 + 0.31 N
Use of the equation for prediction (assume N = £30k)	C = 0.2 + 0.31 × 30 = 0.2 + 9.3 = 9.5 times a year

Figure 3.10 Conceptual framework as quantifiable model

Aim: to assess the size and nature of the market for a potential new cultural facility/service/event.

Strategy (concepts are indicated in italic):
1. obtain information on the general level of *demand* for this type of *facility/service/event* in the community at large, and the *market profile* of users of existing similar facilities, using national or regional data;
2. estimate the *current level of demand and future level of demand* for this type of facility/service/event in the specified *market area*, based on demand;
3. assess *existing provision* of this type of facility/service/event in the locality and the likely *market share* which it might attract;
4. conduct a consumer study of *quality* of existing provision to guide developers on the design of the proposed new facility.

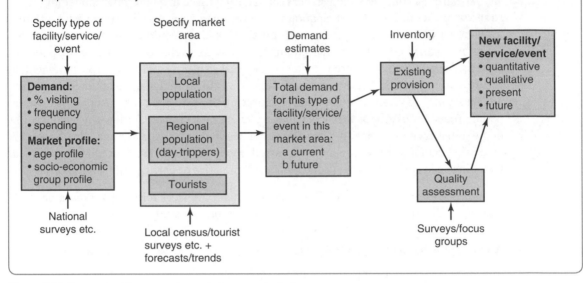

Figure 3.11 Conceptual framework: market research study

Aim: To assess customers' satisfaction with a cultural facility/service or event.

Strategy (concepts in italic): Use the SERVQUAL approach to customer service quality measurement (see Parasuraman *et al.*, 1985; Williams, 1998), which compares customers' *expectations* concerning various *attributes of service quality* with customers' assessment of actual *performance* of the service in regard to those attributes. The *difference* or *disconfirmation* between the two assessments provides information for managers on areas of service quality which require *management action*.

Identify service quality attributes from literature/focus groups or survey.

Customer survey

Service quality attributes:
a.
b.
c.
Etc.

A. Customer expectations – scores on a, b, c etc.

B. Customer performance assessment: scores on a, b, c etc.

Disconfirmation: Compute differences between A scores and B scores

Identify areas for management action

Figure 3.12 Conceptual framework: customer service quality study

Research question format	Hypothesis format
A Simple version	
1. Pose research question: Why have visit levels at venue X declined in the last two years?	1. State hypothesis: Visit levels declined in the last two years at venue X because of the attraction of newer, better-value venues.
2. Conduct research.	2. Conduct research.
3. Answer: Because of the attraction of newer, better-value venues.	3. Result: Consistent with the evidence.
B More detailed version	
1. Pose research question: Why have visit levels at venue X declined in the last two years?	1. Develop hypotheses: Brainstorm/review literature/make enquiries as to range of possible reasons for decline in attendance.
2. Develop research strategy: Brainstorm/review literature/make enquiries as to range of possible reasons for decline in visits. Compile list of possible reasons: (a) attraction of newer, better-value venues (b) declining income in local catchment (c) boom in competing activities (d) decline in quality of the venue (e) increase in prices.	2. Formulate/state hypotheses: Visit levels have declined because of: (a) attraction of newer, better-value venues (b) declining disposable income in local catchment (c) boom in competing activities (d) decline in quality of the venue, or (e) increase in prices … or a combination of the above.
3. Conduct research: Collect evidence/data to discover which reasons are plausible.	3. Conduct research: Collect evidence/data and test all five hypotheses.
4. Answer: Because of the attraction of newer, better-value venues.	4. Results: a. consistent with evidence; b–e. not consistent with evidence.

Figure 3.13 Research question vs hypothesis format

The hypothesis format is more common in the natural sciences while the research question format is more common in the social sciences. The latter lends itself to descriptive and inductive research, while the former is more appropriate for explanatory and deductive research, as discussed in Chapter 2. For most of the book the research question format is assumed, but the hypothesis format is integral to certain forms of statistical analysis and so is discussed in more detail and used in Chapter 17.

Specific starting point

In some cases the research topic selected by the researcher is quite specific from the beginning and is initially expressed in the form of a question: the subsequent literature review and the conceptual framework are then the processes by which this specific issue is analysed and placed in the context of existing knowledge. This is demonstrated in the example used in Figure 3.13 on declining visit numbers at a site.

Decision-making models

The conceptual framework can involve decision-making models, that is, the research is designed to explore the causal factors and processes involved in people's decisions to engage in an activity or visit a venue, in order to discover how others might be persuaded to participate or visit. The literature review in such a case would involve a review of similar existing models and of existing research on the various factors that influence people to choose an activity or visit a venue or event.

Area of interest

In other cases the topic is initially quite vague: it is an 'area of interest' without a specific focus. In such cases the literature review and the process of developing a conceptual framework help to focus the topic and determine what exactly should be researched. The aim is to focus the research on one or more specific questions which can be answered by the research. This is inevitably an iterative process; a question that looks simple and answerable, once subject to thought, reading and analysis, often develops into many questions which become conceptually too demanding to deal with in one project or cannot be managed in the time and with the resources available. In such a situation a smaller part of the problem must be isolated for research. This does not mean that the complex 'big picture' must always be ignored – there is always a case, when writing up a research project, for setting it in its wider context and explaining how and why the particular focus was adopted.

Research questions or objectives?

Often research projects have a set of practical objectives but these should not be confused with research questions. Nor should objectives be confused with the list of tasks necessary to conduct the research – as discussed under 'Decide research strategy' below. Thus, for example, to say that the purpose of this research is 'to conduct a survey of a group of clients' is to confuse ends with means. The survey, in this case, is being conducted for a purpose, to answer the research question(s), not as an end in itself. Of course, stylistically, a research question can be embedded in an objective; thus it is possible to say that 'the objective of this research is to answer the following question: Why are attendances falling?'

The one possible exception to this rule is the sort of research project aimed at establishing a database for a range of possible future uses. For example, the national statistics office of most countries conducts the population census every five or ten years as a service to a multitude of people who use the data for a wide range of purposes (see Chapter 7) – so 'conducting a census of the population' could be said to be the objective of the research project. But even in this case, most of the possible future uses are known: the project assumes at least a prior range of policy-orientated research questions, related to trends in ageing, educational needs, health matters and so on. Few arts or events researchers find themselves in this sort of 'open-ended' data-collection situation: data should generally not be collected for their own sake or in the hope that they 'might come in useful'.

Primary and secondary questions

In most situations the idea of a combination of primary and secondary or subsidiary questions is helpful. The subsidiary questions are necessary steps towards answering the primary question. For example, in Figure 3.11 a number of unknowns are indicated which could be turned into subsidiary research questions. Thus in Figure 3.11 the 'market profile' could be translated into the subsidiary question: 'What is the profile of existing visitors to this type of attraction?' Compiling an inventory of existing competing local attractions pre-supposes the subsidiary question: 'What are the existing competing local attractions for the proposed development?'

5 List information requirements

The research question(s) and the conceptual framework should give rise to a list of information requirements. In some cases these are quite clear and the likely sources of information are straightforward. For example, in the case of the market research study in Figure 3.11 each of the concepts suggests the need for data to determine its nature or to measure it. This is illustrated in Figure 3.14, which indicates the information needs for the market research study. It also suggests some likely sources for this information. But some types of information can be obtained from a variety of sources, so the sourcing decision is a separate issue and is

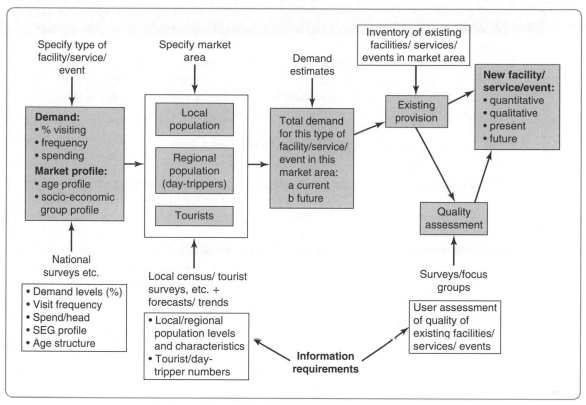

Figure 3.14 Information needs for the market research study

(a) Identify project elements/stages.
(b) Decide information-gathering techniques to be used.
(c) Decide data-analysis techniques to be used.
(d) Decide budget.
(e) Draw up timetable.

Figure 3.15 Research strategy components

discussed further below. The information needs are indicated in abbreviated form only in Figure 3.14 – for example, a 'market profile' for a particular type of attraction could involve more than just age and socio-economic group. This is clearly linked to the idea of 'operation-alising' concepts, as discussed above.

6 Decide research strategy

Development of a research strategy involves making decisions on a number of aspects of the research process, as listed in Figure 3.14.

(a) Project elements/stages

Often a research project will involve a number of different elements, or 'sub-projects' – for example, gathering of primary and secondary data or gathering data in different locations or in different time periods. This is clearly illustrated in the project shown in Figure 3.15, where there is an initial 'sub-project' to establish the nature of the market generally, a second sub-project to assess the nature and scale of the local market base, then a third sub-project to estimate demand for the proposed venue in relation to existing facilities. A project may involve detailed design of stages one at a time, particularly when one part is dependent on the findings from another. For example, stage 1 might involve some fieldwork in a particular location and, depending on the outcomes, stage 2 might involve more in-depth work in the same location or conducting work in a second location.

(b) Information-gathering techniques to be used

It is at this stage that alternative information-gathering techniques are considered. While the operationalisation of concepts and the identification of information-needs processes may already have indicated certain types of information sources, it is here that the detail is determined. For each item in the list of information needs, a range of sources may be possible. Judgement is required to determine just what techniques to use, particularly in the light of time and resources available, or likely to be made available.

A further review of the literature can be valuable at this stage, concentrating particularly on techniques used by previous researchers, and asking such questions as whether their chosen methods were shown to be limiting or even misguided and whether lessons can be learned from past errors.

The range of information-gathering methods most likely to be considered at this stage is covered in the following chapters:

- utilisation of existing information, including published and unpublished research and secondary data (Chapters 6 and 7);
- observation (Chapter 8);
- qualitative methods, including ethnographic methods, participant observation, informal and in-depth interviews, group interviews or focus groups (Chapter 9);
- questionnaire-based surveys, including household face-to-face surveys, street surveys, telephone surveys, user/site surveys, postal surveys (Chapter 10);
- experimental methods (Chapter 11);
- the case study approach (Chapter 12).

These individual techniques are not discussed further here since they are covered in general terms in Chapter 4 and in detail in subsequent chapters.

Where the process of information gathering involves going out into the field – for instance, to conduct interviews or to undertake observation – the planning of fieldwork needs to be considered. In the case of experimental research, the proposed programme of experiments would be considered here, including consideration of location. If the proposed research does not involve primary data collection then this will not be a consideration. Where extensive data collection is involved, the organisation of fieldwork may be complex, involving recruitment and training of field staff (e.g. interviewers or observers), obtaining of permissions, including ethics committee clearance in universities (as discussed in Chapter 4), and organisation of data processing and analysis.

(c) Approach to data analysis

Data analysis may be simple and straightforward and may follow fairly logically from the type of information-collection technique to be used. This is particularly the case when the research

Item*	Cost, £
Printing of questionnaires (500)	250
Interviewers (2 × 60 hrs @ £17 hr, gross)	2040
Data preparation (75 hrs @ £17 hr, gross)	1275
Travel to site (research and interviewers)	1500
Total	5065

Figure 3.16 Example research budget

* NB: the salary of the main researcher is not included

is descriptive in nature. In some cases, however, the analysis of data may be complex and particular thought needs to be given to the time and the skills required to undertake the analysis. Consideration must be given to the format of the data which will be collected and just how its analysis will answer the research questions posed. The planned analysis procedures have implications for data collection. Where qualitative data are to be collected, for example using in-depth interviews, thought must be given as to how the results of the interviews will be analysed. Details of analysis methods that are appropriate and possible for different data-collection techniques are discussed in subsequent chapters in Part 2 of the book, but it must be borne in mind that when planning a project, full consideration should be given to the time and resources required not only for the collection of data but also for its analysis, as discussed in Part 3.

(d) Budget and (e) Timetable

In some situations, key aspects of the research budget and timetable are fixed. For example, students generally have only their own labour available and no other resources and may be required to submit a report by a specified date. Research consultants usually have an upper budgetary limit and a fixed completion date. In other situations, for example when seeking a grant for research from a grant-giving body, or permission to conduct an 'in-house' project, the proposer of the research is called upon to recommend both budget and timetable. Whatever the situation, the task is never easy, since there is rarely enough time or money available to conduct the ideal research project, so compromises invariably have to be made. An example of a research budget is presented in Figure 3.16.

The research strategy and timetable can be represented in various graphical formats – examples are shown in Figures 3.17 and 3.18.

7 Obtain ethics clearance

Ethical behaviour is important in research, as in any other field of human activity. Certain ethical considerations, concerned with matters such as plagiarism and honesty in reporting of results, arise in all research, but additional issues appear when the research involves human subjects, in both the biological and the social sciences. The principles underlying 'research ethics' are universal – they concern things such as honesty and respect for the rights of individuals.

Professional groups, such as market researchers, have established explicit 'codes of ethics' to which members are obliged to adhere. Universities have codes of ethics enforced by ethics committees. Typically, undergraduate and graduate projects are covered by a generic code of behaviour, but research proposals for theses and funded research by academics that involve humans or animals must be individually submitted for approval by the university ethics committee before the research can proceed. The issue of research ethics is considered in more detail in Chapter 4.

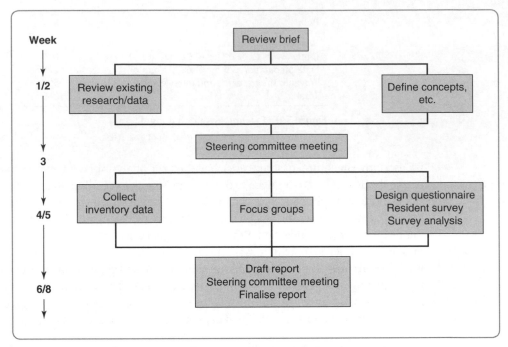

Figure 3.17 Research programme: diagrammatic representation

Week:	1	2	3	4	5	6	7	8
Review literature	▨	▨	▨					
Secondary data analysis			▨	▨	▨			
Conduct survey				▨	▨			
Analyse survey						▨		
Focus groups			▨					
Meetings with clients	X			X		X		X
Write up report				▨			▨	▨

Figure 3.18 Research project timetable

8 Conduct research

Element 8 of the research process is divided into two components: a. data collection and b. data analysis. These two components have not been presented as two sequential elements because in some research approaches, particularly qualitative methods, they are often intertwined; in other cases there are multiple data-collection/analysis tasks in a single research project, with some being contingent on the results of others.

Actually conducting the research is what the rest of the book is about, so it is not discussed in detail here. However, it cannot be stressed enough that good research will rarely result if care is not taken over the preparatory processes discussed in this chapter. In a more positive vein, good preparation can ease the rest of the research process considerably. Often, inexperienced researchers move too rapidly from stage 1, selecting the topic, to stage 8, conducting the research. This can result in the collection of data of doubtful use and the researcher being challenged to make sense of information that has been laboriously collected but does not fit into any framework. If the above process is followed then every item of information collected should have a purpose, since it will have been collected to answer specific questions or test specific hypotheses. This does not mean, of course, that the unexpected will not happen and 'serendipitous' findings may not arise, nor is it intended to ignore methodologies in which the framework, strategy, data-collection/analysis relationships are iterative in nature: it is intended to ensure that the core intellectual structure of the research is 'front of mind'.

It might be thought that inductive research, 'grounded theory' and various forms of qualitative research require less preparation, but in practice this is rarely the case. As discussed in Chapter 9, in qualitative research it is certainly true that there is often a more fluid, evolutionary structure to the research design, but a sound preparatory base is still vital.

9 Communicate findings

The question of writing up of research results is not discussed in detail here because the whole of the final chapter of the book is devoted to the topic. Unlike the conduct of the empirical components of research, which inexperienced researchers invariably rush into too quickly, beginning the writing up of results is often delayed too long, so that insufficient time is left to complete it satisfactorily. An outline of the research process, as presented here, can itself be part of the problem, in that it implies that the writing-up process comes right at the end. In fact, the writing of a research report can commence almost as soon as the project begins, since all the early stages, such as the review of the literature and the development of the conceptual framework, can be written up as the project progresses.

10 Store data

Data, in the form of questionnaires, images and audio and video tapes/disks, in various hardcopy and electronic formats, must be securely stored while a project is being carried out and for a period of time after its conclusion. Particular ethical and legal issues arise in the case of personally identifiable data and these are discussed in Chapter 4. These matters are generally affected by legislation relating to privacy and rights of access to personal records. Some data may also be subject to freedom of information laws.

Research organisations, such as universities, generally have policies on the minimum length of time for which hard-copy and electronic copies of materials such as questionnaires and experimental observations must be stored after completion of research projects, typically five years. Given the length of time sometimes taken for results to be published, this is seen as a necessary precaution in case errors are detected in published results and may need to be checked back to original data sources – for example, errors can arise from miscoding of questionnaires or in transferring of data from notes or other sources into electronic form. Given that researchers may move on from institutions before the minimum storage time period elapses, it is clearly necessary for institutions to have organised archiving and disposal systems.

Of course, the ease of electronic storage means that this form of the data will generally be stored indefinitely. Re-analysis of data at a later stage and replication of research for comparative purposes often arises. Indeed, in some fields of research the lodging of data in an appropriate format on an accessible website is becoming a pre-requisite of publication, as discussed in Chapter 4. In the case of longitudinal research, as discussed in Chapter 5, this is intrinsic to the method. This means that the data as stored should be easily accessible and readable by the original researcher and possibly others.

The research process in the real world

As noted in the introduction, the research process rarely proceeds in the ordered way depicted in Figure 3.1 and in the above discussion. The ten-element process is an idealised framework that underpins the actual process. It is also the sort of process that has to be outlined

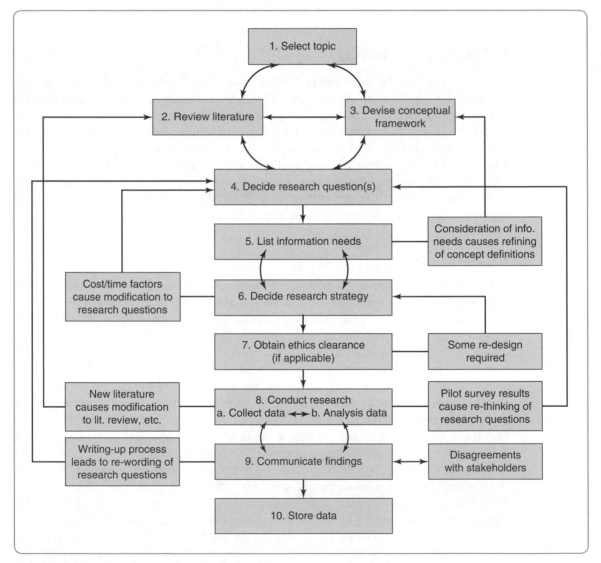

Figure 3.19 The research process in the real world

when planning the allocation of time in a project and when seeking funding. The idea that the process might not be entirely uni-directional is indicated by the fact that the first four elements are shown as connected in a circular process. Figure 3.19 shows some additional examples of iterative components of the process, and additional events that might occur during the course of research cause revisions of any element. In some more inductive research processes iteration between the data and the research questions and conceptual framework is intrinsic to the approach and this can be conveyed verbally and diagrammatically in research proposals. This is particularly the case with qualitative methods, as discussed in Chapter 9.

Case study

A case study is presented here to demonstrate the first six elements of the research process shown in Figure 3.1 in a somewhat abbreviated form. Using the terms introduced in Chapter 1, the case study envisages an explanatory approach to research with evaluative features and arises from a hypothetical management problem – it seeks to find an explanation for a decline in the number of visits to a museum.

CASE STUDY 3.1

Facility use: research design process

This case study outlines the sequence of six elements in the research process which lead up to the preparation of a responsive research proposal. The outline is presented in a summary form to illustrate the process.

1 Select topic

The topic has been presented by the management of a museum. While attendances from tourists have been rising, attendances by members of the local community have been declining over a number of years and the management would like to know why.

2 Summary of literature review relevant to museum visitation

The literature to be reviewed covers museums and leisure/tourism facility management generally. There is an extensive research literature on museum visitors and part of the proposed research will therefore involve a detailed examination of this literature. At this planning stage three sources have been drawn on to provide a starting point for the study. The first two suggest that the decline could be related to trends in the general community, while the third suggests that the problem may lie with the management of the facility.

- Fenn *et al.* (2004: 42) show that gallery and museum users are overwhelmingly drawn from the more highly educated, higher-income social groups.

- Rojek (2000: 22–24), suggests that the phenomenon of 'fast leisure' might be a characteristic of the postmodern age.

- The literature on customer service and service quality offers ideas on how to research the problem of declining attendances. The SERVQUAL model has been applied in arts contexts, including art galleries, museums and theatres (Williams, 1998), as discussed in Figure 3.15, and relates customers' expectations concerning aspects of their experience with a product or service to their actual experience.

3 Conceptual framework/theoretical discussion: models of facility visitation

The three literature resources examined above can be said to reflect different, but possibly complementary, models of leisure facility visiting/demand.

Model 1 – Social class, etc. and demand: segmentation. The socio-economic characteristics of the catchment of a real population may have changed over recent years, resulting in a decline in numbers in the groups from which museum visitors are traditionally drawn. This suggests a simple model of changing visitor demand, based on the proposition that the changing level of visitor demand is determined by

Case study 3.1 (*continued*)

changes in the size of target demographic demand segments between the current time period and some earlier time.

Model 2 – Perceived time-squeeze: fast leisure: Whether or not there have been changes in the size of the target demographic segments, Rojek's 'fast leisure' phenomenon could also be at work. Although it is difficult to assess this, if people feel that they are rushed, perhaps because of longer paid working hours and more demanding domestic commitments, this may affect their leisure behaviour and they may be able to articulate this change in a survey response.

Model 3 – Service quality. The SERVQUAL model relates visitors' expectations concerning aspects of a visit to the actual experience. It involves initial identification of key service dimensions (KSDs), which are seen as critical to management and visitors. Discrepancies between expectations and experience on the various KSDs – the pattern of disconfirmation – provide a guide to management on where action may be necessary. Current users may be first-time visitors or regular visitors who are tolerant of poor-quality aspects of their visit, so lapsed visitors may be of more interest.

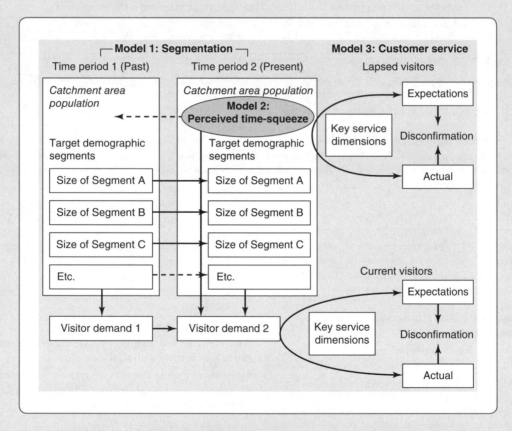

Figure 3.20 Facility use study: conceptual framework

A concept map summarising the above discussion is presented in Figure 3.20.

Figure 3.21 presents definitions of the concepts involved in the conceptual framework and indications as to how they might be operationalised.

4 Decide research questions

The primary research question and the subsidiary research questions arising from the conceptual framework are presented in Figure 3.22.

Case study 3.1 (*continued*)

Concept*	Definition	Operationalisation*	Research question no.
Catchment area	Geographical area from which most visitors are drawn	Area where **70% of visitors live**	a.
Target demographic segments (TDS)	Demographic/socio-economic groups living in the catchment area and most likely to visit museums	– Segment A: **Managerial/professional group** – Segment B: **35–44 age group**	b., c.
Visitor demand	Current number of visits to the museum	Number of **visits in a calendar year** (see Figure 10.10 for alternative measures of leisure)	c.
Perceived time-squeeze	Individual's subjective feeling of being pressed for time	ABS method: Individual response to question as to whether person **feels 'pressed for time'** – Always/ often, Sometimes, Rarely/never	d., e.
Key service dimensions (KSD)	Those aspects of a service or visit considered important by visitors and/or management	List of key service dimensions **determined by focus groups** with visitors and management	f.
Lapsed visitors	Persons who have visited the museum but no longer do so	Lapsed visitors = persons who last visited the museum **more than 12 months ago** but live within the catchment area	h.
Visitor expectations re KSD	The level of service/quality of experience visitors expect to find in regard to KSD	Response, using **Likert scales**, in regard to statements on the importance/expectations of each KSD	g., h.
Visitor actual experience	Level of satisfaction with the KSD	Response, using **Likert scales**, in regard to satisfaction with each KSD	g., h.
Disconfirmation	Discrepancy between expectations and actual experience re KSD	Difference between **expectation and satisfaction scores** for each KSD	g., h.

Figure 3.21 Facility use study: concepts, definitions and operationalisation

* Items in bold are key operationalisation decisions

Primary question	Why are attendances at the museum falling?
Subsidiary questions	
General	(a) What is the catchment area of the facility from which most visitors are drawn?
Model 1	(b) What are the target demographic segments (TDS) which are attracted to museums/this museum?
	(c) What was the relationship between visitor demand and population in the TDS living in the catchment area in time period 1 and time period 2?
Model 2	(d) Are people in the TDS living in the catchment area feeling 'time-squeezed'?
	(e) If the answer to d. is 'yes', is this likely to be affecting museum visiting?
Model 3	(f) What are the key service dimensions (KSD) for the museum?
	(g) What are *current* visitors' expectations, actual experience and disconfirmation with regard to the KSD?
	(h) What are *lapsed* visitors' expectations, actual experience and disconfirmation with regard to the KSD?

Figure 3.22 Facility use study: research questions

Case study 3.1 (*continued*)

5 List information needs: what do we need to know?

Information needed to answer each of the subsidiary questions is listed in Figure 3.23 together with possible sources for the information.

6 Decide research strategy: studying the market

From the above process a number of elements of a possible research strategy emerge, as indicated in Figure 3.24. The feasibility of such a strategy will need to be evaluated in relation to available time and resources.

Item	Information required	Likely sources
(a) Catchment area	Data on where visitors to the museum travel from – 70% cut-off.	User survey (new survey or museum's past survey if available).
(b) Target demographic segments (TDS)	Data on demographic/socio-economic groups with high museum visit rates – for this museum (if available) or museums in general.	ABS report No. 4114.0 or museum's past survey if available.
(c) Change in period 1 to 2 in: – TDS population numbers in catchment area – visitor demand at museum	For period 1 and period 2: – catchment area TDS numbers – annual visit numbers.	– Population census – Museum's own data.
(d) Catchment area TDS and time-squeeze	Information on subjective feelings of catchment area TDS members.	Survey of catchment area TDS.
(e) Time-squeeze effects on museum visiting	Information on museum visiting patterns of catchment area TDS members.	Survey of catchment area TDS.
(f) List of key service dimensions (KSD)	Information on customers' and managers' views on important aspects of a museum visit.	Focus groups of customers and managers.
(g) Current visitors' evaluation of expectations and actual experience re KSD	Current visitors' scores on KSD expectation and actual experience scales.	User survey.
(h) Lapsed visitors' evaluation of expectations and actual experience re KSD	Lapsed visitors' scores on KSD expectation and actual experience scales.	Catchment area social survey.

Figure 3.23 Facility use study: information needs and likely sources

Data-collection method	Subjects	Purpose
Focus groups	Managers and users	Establish KSD
On-site questionnaire-based survey	Current visitors	Establish catchment area of the facility Establish target demographic groups (TDG) Model 3: collect SERVQUAL data
Secondary data: population census	Catchment area population	Establish size of TDGs in catchment area – years 1, 2
Household survey	Catchment area population	Model 2: to establish extent of perceived time-squeeze Model 3: collect SERVQUAL data from lapsed users

Figure 3.24 Facility use study: research strategy

Research proposals

Introduction

Research proposals of two broad kinds are discussed here:

- *self-generated* – proposals of the sort prepared by students seeking approval for research for a project or thesis on a topic of their own choosing, or by academics seeking funds for a research project of their own devising;

- *responsive* – proposals prepared by consultants responding to research briefs prepared by potential clients, sometimes simulated in the teaching environment with student projects being conducted for real or hypothetical client organisations.

Planners and managers seeking 'in-house' resources to conduct research fall somewhere between the two.

In each case the proposal is a written document, which may also be supported by an oral presentation, and which must be convincing to the person or people who will decide whether the research should go ahead. The writers of a research proposal are faced with the difficult task of convincing the decision makers of:

- the value of the research;
- the soundness of the proposed approach;
- the valuable and original insights which they will bring to the project; and
- their personal capability to conduct the research.

In some cases the decision makers will be experts in the field, while in other cases they may be non-experts, so care must be taken to ensure that the proposal is understandable to all concerned. Clarity of expression and succinctness are often the key qualities required in these situations.

Self-generated research proposals

Academic research proposals, for student theses/projects or for academics seeking funding, must not only describe what research is to be done and how but also provide a rationale for the choice of topic. This may be in part related to the declared research strategy and areas of strength of the host organisation. The topic and its treatment must be seen to be appropriate, in terms of scale and complexity, to the particular level of project involved, be it an undergraduate project, a PhD thesis or a funded project involving a team of researchers over a number of years.

In general the academic research proposal must cover the material dealt with in this chapter. In some cases considerable work will already have been completed before the proposal is submitted. This could apply in the case of a PhD proposal, which might be based on as much as a year of preparatory work, or a proposal from an experienced academic who has been working in a particular field for a number of years. In such cases, the proposal may present considerable completed work on elements 1 to 6 of the research process. The funding being sought may be required only to conduct the fieldwork part of the research and write up the results – elements 7 to 10 of the process. In other cases little more than the selection of the topic may have been completed and the proposal outlines a programme of funding to undertake elements 2 to 10 of the process.

Item	Element of Figure 3.1	Chapter
1 Background and justification for selection of topic	1	3
2 (Preliminary) review of the literature	2	3
3 Conceptual/theoretical framework/theoretical discussion	3	3
4 Statement of research questions or hypotheses	4	3
5 Outline of data/information requirements and research strategy	5, 6	3
6 Details of information-collection methods: structured by the research strategy but including:	6	
– outline of any additional literature to be reviewed		6
– summary of any secondary data sources to be used		7
– outline of empirical tasks to be conducted – qualitative and/or quantitative, including, as appropriate:		7–12
– sample/subject selection methods (Chapter 13)		13
– justification of sample sizes		13
– measures to ensure quality		7–12
7 Consideration of ethical implications	7	4
8 Details of data analysis methods	6	9, 11,12, 14–17
9 Timetable or work/tasks (Section 6e above)	6d	3
10 Budget, where applicable, including costing of each element/stage/task	6	3
11 Report/thesis chapter outline or indication of number and type of publications	9	18
12 Other resources, researcher skills/experience/'track record' (necessary when seeking funds)	6d	3

Figure 3.25 Research proposal checklist: self-generated research

Some proposals contain a preliminary review of the literature with a proposal to undertake more as part of the project. Some proposals are very clear about the conceptual framework to be used, while in other cases only speculative ideas are presented. While bearing in mind, therefore, that there can be substantial differences between proposals of various types, the checklist in Figure 3.25 is offered as a guide to the contents of a proposal and indicates links with elements of the research process and chapters in the book.

Responsive proposals – briefs and tenders

Context

A brief is an outline of the research an organisation wishes to have undertaken. Consultants who would like to be considered for the project must submit a written, costed proposal or *tender*. Usually briefs are prepared by an organisation with a view to a number of consultants competing to obtain the contract. In some cases potential consultants are first asked, possibly through an advertisement, to indicate their *expression of interest* in the project. This will involve a short statement of the consultants' capabilities, their track record of previous consultancies and the qualifications and experience of staff available. In some cases public bodies maintain a register of accredited consultants with interests and capabilities, who may be invited to tender for particular projects. In the light of such statements of interest or information in the register, a shortlist of consultants is sent the full brief and invited to submit a detailed proposal. In very large projects some financial compensation may be provided to shortlisted candidates to cover the costs of the work taken to prepare a more detailed tender.

The successful tender is not usually selected on the basis of price alone (the budget is in any case often a fixed sum indicated in the brief) but on the quality of the submitted proposal and the track record of the consultants.

Briefs vary in the amount of detail they provide. Sometimes they are very detailed, leaving little scope for consultants to express any individuality in their proposals. In other cases they are limited and leave a great deal of scope to consultants to indicate proposed methods and approaches. Client organisations experienced in commissioning research can produce briefs that are clear and 'ready to roll'. In other situations potential tenderers may find it necessary to clarify the client's meanings and intentions. For example, a client might ask for a study of the 'cultural needs' of a community, in which case it would be necessary to clarify the client's view of the term 'culture', such as whether it includes various forms of commercial entertainment. If a client asks for the 'effectiveness' of a programme to be assessed it may be necessary to clarify whether a statement of objectives or a list of performance criteria for the programme already exists, or whether that must be developed as part of the project.

Paradoxically, problems can arise when client organisations are over-specific about aspects of their requirements but vague about other aspects. For example, an organisation may ask for an 'audience survey' or 'visitor survey' to be conducted. It is not easy to decide what should be included in such a survey without information on the management or policy issues which the resultant data are intended to address. Is the organisation concerned about declining attendances? Does it want to change its 'marketing mix'? Is it concerned about the particular mix of clientele being attracted? Is it concerned about future trends in demand? It would be preferable in such a situation for the client to indicate the nature of the management issue and leave the tenderer to suggest the most suitable research approach to adopt, which might or might not include a survey.

Sometimes there is a hidden agenda which the potential researcher would do well to become familiar with before embarking on the research. For example, research can sometimes be used as a means to defuse or delay difficult management decisions in an organisation. An example would be where a venue is suffering declining attendances because of poor maintenance of facilities and poor staff attitudes to visitors; this is very clear to anyone who walks in the door, but the management decides to commission a 'market study', in the hope that the answer to their problem can be found 'out there' in the market when in fact the problem is very much 'in here' and their money might be better spent on improving maintenance and staff training than on research.

A situation where the client's requirements may seem vague is when the research is not related to immediate policy needs but to possible future needs or simply to satisfy curiosity. For example, a manager of a venue or event might commission a visitor survey (perhaps because there is spare money in the current year's budget) without having any specific policy or management problems in mind. In that case the research will need to specify hypothetical or potential policy or management issues which could arise and match the data specifications to them.

Content

What should a proposal contain? The first and golden principle is that it should *address the brief*. It is likely that the brief will have been discussed at great length in the commissioning organisation; every aspect is likely to be of importance to some individual or section in the organisation, so *all* aspects should be addressed in the proposal. So if the brief lists, say, four

	Element of Fig. 3.1	Chapter
1 Brief summary of key aspects of the proposal, including any unique approach and particular skills/experience of the consultants		
2 Re-statement of the key aspects of the brief and interpretation/definition of key concepts		
3 Conceptual framework/theoretical discussion	3	3
4 Research strategy – methods/tasks	6	3
5 Details of information-collection methods – structured by the research strategy but including:	5, 6	
– outline of any additional literature to be reviewed	2	6
– summary of any secondary data sources to be used		7
– outline of fieldwork to be conducted – qualitative and/or quantitative		7–12
– sample/subject selection methods		13
– sample sizes and their justification		13
– measures to ensure quality		
6 Timetable of tasks, including interim reporting/meetings with clients/draft and final report submission	6	3
7 Budget: costing of each element/stage/task	6	3
8 Chapter outline of report and, if appropriate, details of other proposed reporting formats – e.g. interim reports, working papers, articles	9	18
9 Resources available, staff, track record		3

Figure 3.26 Research proposal checklist: responsive research

objectives, it would be advisable for the proposal to indicate clearly how each of the four objectives will be met. A proposal must therefore answer the following questions:

- What is to be done?
- How is to be done?
- When will it be done?
- What will it cost?
- Who will do it?

A typical responsive proposal might include elements as shown in Figure 3.26, with links shown to elements in the research process and chapters in the book.

Summary

This chapter covers the process of planning a research project and preparing a research proposal. It is structured around ten 'elements':

1. Selecting the topic.
2. Reviewing the literature.
3. Devising a conceptual framework.
4. Deciding the research questions.
5. Listing information needs.
6. Deciding a research strategy.
7. Obtaining ethics clearance (where relevant).
8. Conducting the research.

9. Reporting the findings.
10. Storing the data.

The term 'elements' is used rather than 'stages' or 'steps', since the ten elements do not always occur in the precise order indicated. In particular, the first elements listed take place in a variety of orders, often in an iterative process. The overview of the research process is followed by a discussion of research proposals – self-generated proposals, where the researcher initiates the research, and responsive proposals, which are prepared in response to a research brief from a commissioning organisation.

TEST QUESTIONS

1. In this chapter, it is suggested that a research topic might arise from eight different sources. What are the eight sources?
2. What is a concept?
3. What is meant by 'operationalisation' of a concept?
4. What is a conceptual framework?
5. What is the difference between a research question and a hypothesis?
6. What are the differences between a self-generated research proposal and a responsive research proposal and what implications do they have for the content of the two types of proposal?

EXERCISES

1. Select three articles from an issue of an arts/events journal and identify the basis of their choice of research topic.
2. Select any article from a copy of an arts/events journal and (a) identify the key concepts used in the article, and (b) draw a simple concept map to show how the concepts are related.
3. Draw a concept map for a possible research project on: (a) the effects of American culture in another country of your choice, (b) the effects of the ageing of the population on trends in cultural participation in Western countries, or (c) the impacts of special events on people's lives.
4. Write a case study, similar in structure and length to Case study 3.1, on a topic of your choice.

Resources

The best reading material for this chapter would be examples of successful research grant applications and proposals written in response to tenders. Completed research reports, whether academic or non-academic, vary in the amount of detail they provide about the development of the process.

● Approaches to events research: Getz (2012: 355–386).
● Conceptual frameworks:
   o general: Miles and Huberman (1994: 18–22), general and tourism-related: Pearce (2012: 28–49)

- after-school art programmes: Wright (2007)
- business investment in the arts: Comunian (2009)
- cultural tourism: Murphy and Boyle (2006)
- culture and sport engagement: CASE (2010: 84, 86)
- event marketing (sustainable): Tinnish and Mangal (2012)
- event satisfaction: Wysong *et al.* (2011)
- event volunteering: Baum (2007)
- event tourism: Getz (2008: 413; 2012: 5–7)
- festival volunteer retention: Love *et al.* (2012)
- festivals and regional development: Moscardo (2007)
- leisure participation: Brandenburg *et al.* (1982), Veal (1995)
- museums and consumer choice: Guintcheva and Passebois (2009)
- museum experience: Falk and Dierking (2013: 26–33)
- museum marketing by word of mouth: Hausmann (2012)
- museum policy: Ander *et al.* (2011)
- museums: new entrants: Burton (2007)
- organisational 'greening'/business events: Mair and Jago (2010)
- opera companies: Auvinen (2001) – see Case study 12.2
- service quality: Parasuraman *et al.* (1985)
- well-being effects of museum visiting: Ander *et al.* (2011)

- Importance–performance analysis: general: Veal (2010: Chapter 13); museums: Lin (2009).
- SERVQUAL: Parasuraman *et al.* (1985), Williams (1998).
- Instrumental vs intrinsic value of the arts: Bereson (2005), Craik (2007), Klamer (1996), Ratiu (2009), Throsby (2000).
- Logic model: Hulett (1997), Wright (2007), Wyatt Knowlton and Phillips (2012).
- Operationalisation of concepts: Richards (2010: 22–25).
- Purposes of research: Newman *et al.* (2003).
- Research strategies/agenda:
  - arts impact research (conceptual rather than detailed/specific): Belfiore and Bennett (2010)
  - arts, outdoor recreation, etc. in New Zealand: Cushman *et al.* (2010)
  - the arts as a system: National Endowment for the Arts (2012)
  - the arts and human development (across the life cycle): National Endowment for the Arts (2011)
  - events: Harris *et al.* (2000); Getz (2012: 378–384), Mair and Whitford (2013), Weed (2012)
  - event tourism: Getz (2008: 413–421)
  - museums as educational institutions: Falk and Dierking (1995)
  - performing arts entrepreneurship: Preece (2011) – although the title of this paper contains the expression 'towards a research agenda', it does not spell out a research agenda as such, but maps the field of study conceptually and in terms of issues which might be addressed
  - the challenges of developing a research agenda: Scullion and Garcia (2005)
- Sustainability and investment in the arts: Craik (2007), Heilbrun and Gray (2001).
- Topic selection: general: Howard and Sharp (1983: Chapter 2).

References

Ander, E., Thomson, L. and Noble, G. (2011) Generic well-being outcomes: towards a conceptual framework for well-being outcomes in museums. *Museum Management and Curatorship*, 26(3), 237–259.

Atkinson, W. (2011) The content and genesis of musical tastes: omnivorousness debunked, Bourdieu buttressed. *Poetics*, 39(2), 169–186.

Auvinen, T. (2001) Why is it difficult to manage an opera house? The artistic–economic dichotomy and its manifestations in the organizational structures of five opera companies. *Journal of Arts Management, Law and Society*, 30(4), 268–282.

Baum, T. (2007) Volunteers and mega sporting events: Developing a research framework. *International Journal of Event Management Research*, 3 (1), 29.

Belfiore, E. and Bennett, O. (2010) Beyond the 'toolkit approach': arts impact evaluation research and the realities of cultural policy-making. *Journal for Cultural Research,* 14(2), 121–142.

Bereson, R. (2005) Advance Australia – fair or foul? Observing Australian arts policies. *Journal of Arts Management Law and Society*, 35(1), 49–59.

Brandenburg, J., Greiner, W., Hamilton-Smith, E., Scholker, H., Senior, R. and Webb, J. (1982) A conceptual model of how people adopt recreation activities. *Leisure Studies*, 1(3), 263–276.

Burton, C. (2007) How a museum dies: the case of new entry failure of a Sydney museum. *Museum Management and Curatorship*, 22(2), 109–129.

Charmaz, K. (2006) *Constructing Grounded Theory*. London: Sage.

Comunian, R. (2009) Toward a new conceptual framework for business investments in the arts: some examples from Italy. *Journal of Arts Management, Law and Society*, 39(3), 200–220.

Craik, J. (2007) *Re-visioning Arts and Cultural Policy: Current Impasses and Future Direction*. Canberra: ANU Press.

Csikszentmihalyi, M. (1990) *Flow: The Psychology of Optimal Experience*. New York: Harper & Row.

Culture and Sport Evidence (CASE) Programme (2010) *Understanding the Drivers of Engagement in Culture and Sport: Technical Report*. London: Department for Culture, Media & Sport, available at: www.gov.uk/case-programme

Cushman, G., Gidlow, B. and Espiner, S. (2010) Developing a national leisure research strategy for New Zealand: arts, outdoor recreation, sport and community recreation. *Annals of Leisure Research*, 13(3), 352–375.

Falk, J. H. and Dierking, L. D. (1995) *Public Institutions for Personal Learning: Establishing a Research Agenda*. Washington, DC: American Association for Museums.

Falk, J. H. and Dierking, L. D. (2013) *The Museum Experience Revisited*. Walnut Creek, CA: Left Coast Press.

Fenn, C., Bridgwood, A. and Dust, K. (2004) *Arts in England 2003: Attendance, Participation and Attitudes*. London: Arts Council England.

Foucault, M. (1979) *Discipline and Punish*. Harmondsworth: Penguin.

Getz, D. (2008) Event tourism: definition, evolution and research. *Tourism Management*, 29(3), 403–428.

Getz, D. (2012) *Event Studies: Theory, Research and Policy for Planned Events,* Second Edition. London: Routledge.

Guintcheva, G. and Passebois, J. (2009) Exploring the place of museums in European leisure markets: an approach based on consumer values. *International Journal of Arts Management*, 11(2), 4–16.

Harris, R., Jago, L., Allen, J. and Huskens, M. (2000) Towards an Australian event research agenda: first steps. *Event Management*, 6(4), 213–221.

Hausmann, A. (2012) The importance of word of mouth for museums: an analytical framework. *International Journal of Arts Management*, 14(3), 32–43.

Heilbrun, J. and Gray, C. M. (2001) *The Economics of Art and Culture*, Second Edition. Cambridge: Cambridge University Press.

Henderson, K. A. (2006) Dimensions of Choice: A Qualitative Approach to Recreation, Parks, and Leisure Research, Second Edition. State College, PA: Venture.

Holden, J. (2006) Cultural Value and the Crisis of Legitimacy. London: Demos.

Howard, K. and Sharp, J. A. (1983) The Management of a Student Research Project. Aldershot: Gower.

Hulett, S. (1997) Program evaluation using logic models in arts programs for at-risk youth. Americans for the Arts Monographs, 1(6), 1–24.

Klamer, A. (ed.) (1996) The Value of Culture: On the Relationship between Economics and the Arts. Amsterdam: Amsterdam University Press.

Lenskyj, H. J. (2008) Olympic Industry Resistance. Albany, NY: State University of New York Press.

Lin, Y.-N. (2009) Importance–performance analysis of the Taipei Fine Arts Museum's services. Museum Management and Curatorship, 24(2), 105–121.

Lincoln, Y. (2005) Institutional review boards and methodological conservatism: the challenge to and from phenomenological paradigms. In N. K. Denzin and Y. S. Lincoln (eds), Handbook of Qualitative Research, Third Edition. Thousand Oaks, CA: Sage, pp. 165–190.

Love, G. W., Sherman, K. and Olding, R. (2012) Will they stay or won't they? A study of volunteer retention at film/music festivals in the southwest United States. Event Management, 16(4), 269–281.

Mair, J. and Jago, L. (2010) The development of a conceptual model of greening in the business events tourism sector. Journal of Sustainable Tourism, 18(1), 77–94.

Mair, J. and Whitford, M. (2013) An exploration of events research: event topics, themes and emerging trends. International Journal of Event and Festival Management, 4(1), 6–30.

Marr, D. (2008) The Henson Case. Sydney: Text Publishing.

Miles, M. B. and Huberman, A. M. (1994) Qualitative Data Analysis, Second Edition. Thousand Oaks, CA: Sage.

Moscardo, G. (2007) Analyzing the role of festivals and events in regional development. Event Management, 11(1–2), 23–32.

Murphy, C. and Boyle, E. (2006) Testing a conceptual model of cultural tourism development in the post-industrial city: a case study of Glasgow. Tourism and Hospitality Research, 6(2), 111–126.

National Endowment for the Arts (2011) The Arts and Human Development: Framing a National Research Agenda for the Arts, Lifelong Learning, and Individual Well-being. Washington, DC: National Endowment for the Arts.

National Endowment for the Arts (2012) How Art Works: The National Endowment for the Arts' Five-year Research Agenda, with a System Map and Measurement Model. Washington, DC: National Endowment for the Arts.

Newman, I., Ridenour, C. S., Newman, C. and DeMarco, G. M. P. (2003) A typology of research purposes and its relationship to mixed methods. In A. Tashakkori and C. Teddlie (eds), Handbook of Mixed Methods in Social and Behavioral Research. Thousand Oaks, CA: Sage, pp. 167–188.

Parasuraman, A., Zeithaml, V. A. and Berry, L. L. (1985) A conceptual model of service quality and implications for future research. Journal of Marketing, 49(4), 41–50.

Pearce, D. (2012) Frameworks for Tourism Research. Wallingford: CABI.

Preece, S. B. (2011) Performing arts entrepreneurship: toward a research agenda. Journal of Arts Management, Law and Society, 41(2), 103–120.

Ratiu, D.-L. (2009) Cultural policy and values: intrinsic versus instrumental? The case of Romania. Journal of Arts Management Law and Society, 39(1), 24–44.

Richards, G. (2010) The traditional quantitative approach. Surveying cultural tourists: lessons from the ATLAS Cultural Tourism Research Project. In G. Richards and W. Munsters (eds), Cultural Tourism Research Methods. Wallingford: CABI, pp. 13–32.

Rojek, C. (2000) Leisure and Culture. Basingstoke: Macmillan.

Sandell, R. (1998) Museums as agents of social inclusion. Museum Management and Curatorship, 17(4), 401–418.

Scullion, A. and Garcia, B. (2005) What is cultural policy research? *International Journal of Cultural Policy*, 11(2), 113–126.

Throsby, D. (2000) *Economics and Culture*. Cambridge: Cambridge University Press.

Tinnish, S. M. and Mangal, S. M. (2012) Sustainable event marketing in the MICE industry: a theoretical framework. *Journal of Convention and Event Tourism*, 13(3), 227–249.

Veal, A. J. (1995) Leisure studies: frameworks for analysis. In H. Ruskin and A. Sivan (eds), *Leisure Education: Towards the 21st Century*. Provo, UT: Brigham Young University Press, pp. 124–136.

Veal, A. J. (2010) *Leisure, Sport and Tourism: Politics Policy and Planning*, Third Edition. Wallingford: CABI.

Weed, M. (2012) Towards an interdisciplinary events research agenda across sport, tourism, leisure and health. In S. J. Page & J. Connell (eds), *The Routledge Handbook of Events*. London: Routledge, pp. 57–71.

Williams, C. (1998) Is the SERVQUAL model an appropriate management tool for measuring service delivery quality in the UK leisure industry? *Managing Leisure*, 3(2), 98–110.

Wright, R. (2007) A conceptual and methodological framework for designing and evaluating community-based after-school art programs. *International Journal of Cultural Policy*, 13(1), 124–132.

Wyatt Knowlton, L. and Phillips, C. C. (2012) *The Logic Model Guidebook: Better Strategies for Great Results*, Second Edition. Thousand Oaks, CA: Sage.

Wysong, S., Rothschild, P. and Beldona, S. (2011) Receiving a standing ovation for the event: a comprehensive model for measuring fan satisfaction with sports and entertainment events. *International Journal of Event Management Research*, 6(1), 1–9.

Chapter 4

Research ethics

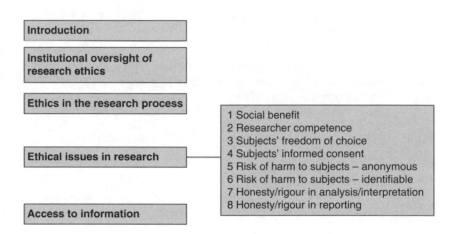

Introduction

Institutional oversight of research ethics

Ethics in the research process

Ethical issues in research

1 Social benefit
2 Researcher competence
3 Subjects' freedom of choice
4 Subjects' informed consent
5 Risk of harm to subjects – anonymous
6 Risk of harm to subjects – identifiable
7 Honesty/rigour in analysis/interpretation
8 Honesty/rigour in reporting

Access to information

Introduction

Ethical behaviour is important in research, as in any other field of human activity. Ethical considerations, such as plagiarism and honesty in reporting of results, arise in all research, but additional issues arise when the research involves human and animal subjects, in both the social and the biological sciences. Increasingly, ethical issues also arise in relation to research that may have an impact on the physical environment. The underlying principles of research ethics are universal: they concern things like honesty and respect for the rights of individuals and animals, and the integrity of eco-systems. The issue came to the fore at the end of the Second World War when details were revealed of horrific experiments which had been conducted on prisoners in the Nazi concentration camps, and certain medical experiments conducted in the United States in the 1960s and 1970s without the consent of the subjects (Loue, 2002). These events raised questions about not only the ethical conduct of research but also the use of findings from research conducted unethically. The result has been the establishment of international, national, professional and institutional codes of research ethics and their oversight by regulatory organisations.

An example of a code of research ethics is the document on the responsible conduct of research published in 2007 by a consortium of Australian organisations, which covered:

- honesty and integrity;
- respect for human research participants, animals and the environment;
- good stewardship of public resources used to conduct research;
- appropriate acknowledgement of the role of others in research;
- responsible communication of research results. (NHMRC *et al.*, 2007: 13).

In this chapter we consider:

- the institutional oversight of research ethics;
- ethics in the research process;
- ethical issues in research, including:
  - researcher competence
  - subjects' freedom to participate or not
  - informed consent
  - risk of harm to subjects
  - honesty/rigour in analysis, interpretation and reporting
  - authorship and acknowledgements
  - access to research information.

Before turning to these matters, some examples of ethics issues arising in arts/events research are presented in Case study 4.1.

CASE STUDY 4.1

Examples of ethical issues in arts and events research

A Museum attendance figures

The compilation of museum/gallery attendance figures may be seen as a management rather than a research activity, but such figures are often used in research, particularly applied research such as feasibility studies. Silberberg (2005) argues that if inaccurate attendance figures are used in such studies, the fault is partly that of the consultants/researchers for not questioning the basis of the figures provided by management. He suggests that figures are often exaggerated by such matters as:

- including website hits (which should obviously be counted, but listed separately from on-site visits);
- counting tickets sold rather than people when different parts of a facility have separate ticketing;
- counting restaurant-only visitors;
- counting conference visitors when the museum includes a conference facility;
- where admission is free (and visits are often counted by infra-red counters – see Chapter 8),

failing to discount for staff, volunteers and tradespeople.

Silberberg observes that managers are tempted to publish exaggerated figures for a variety of reasons, including:

- the desire to show that measures taken to increase attendance have been successful;
- the wish for new directors not to be seen to be responsible for reduced figures compared with those produced by their predecessors, so not bothering to correct faulty data-collecting practices;
- 'because others do it' – Silberberg estimates that 'well over half' of museum directors may inflate their figures.

B Performance evaluation

Conducting the research required to evaluate the performance of a cultural organisation raises ethical issues if the measurements used do not align with

Case study 4.1 (*continued*)

the performance criteria as assumed by key participants. Thus, for example, it would be unfair if an artist were to be commissioned to produce a work of a 'high artistic standard' but the result was evaluated entirely in terms of tickets sold. Chiaravalloti and Piber (2011) suggest that evaluations based on a positivist approach to research would be liable to ignore such a consideration because of the tendency to use performance criteria which are easily and 'objectively' measured. Conversely, a researcher working in the 'anti-positivist' tradition might be similarly at fault in relying entirely on assessment of subjective views of selected stakeholders. The authors suggest that the ethical requirement to align organisational performance assessment measures with the legitimate concerns of all relevant stakeholders is likely to be best achieved by adopting a pragmatic approach (see Chapter 3), which does not have an *a priori* commitment to a particular research paradigm. They examine the work of seven researchers who have reported on performance evaluation exercises of a number of arts organisations.

C Restitution of cultural heritage

An abiding ethical dilemma for museums has centred on collections and the provenance of artworks and artefacts, particularly after wars. The British Museum's Elgin Marbles, taken from the Parthenon, in Athens, are a celebrated case, with considerable debates as to whether they were legally acquired or stolen (Anderegg, 2004; Thompson, 2003). The return of human remains collected by museums, mainly in the nineteenth and early twentieth centuries, has continued to be an ethical impasse for some museums, particularly in the United Kingdom (Australian Government, Office for the Arts, 2011; Mitchell, 2012). The problems centre on the aim of museums to acquire,

conserve and protect collections for research/scholarship, education and display as opposed to the source society's right to own its own heritage. The issue has attracted the attention of the United Nations Educational, Scientific and Cultural Organization (UNESCO), which has established sets of principles and a conciliation process under its Intergovernmental Committee for Promoting the Return of Cultural Property to its Countries of Origin or its Restitution in Case of Illicit Appropriation (see www.unesco.org/new/en/culture/themes).

D Researchers, public-sector clients and 'spin'

Many researchers with an interest in the arts have been accustomed to adopting an independent, critical stance in their research, particularly in regard to public policy. Belfiore (2009) raises the problem of researchers accepting commissions from governments to conduct research to fit predetermined outcomes. The initial ethical issue arises in regard to researchers being tempted, even feeling compelled, to trade their principles in return for patronage and/or involvement in the policy process. A second ethical issue arises in regard to the use of the results. The example Belfiore gives involves the UK Labour government of 2008–2010 which, in the context of its policies for 'social inclusion', adopted an instrumental approach to the arts, justifying expenditure on the basis of assumed economic and social impacts. Even though available research provides little support for such claims, there is a tendency for politicians to ignore such difficulties and 'spin' the results or, as Belfiore puts it, to offer 'bullshit'.

A similar situation arises when politicians make unjustifiable claims regarding the impact of major sporting events, such as the Olympic Games, on grassroots sport participation in the host community (Veal *et al.*, 2012).

Institutional oversight of research ethics

Most universities now have their own codes of research ethics enforced by ethics committees or boards. Typically, undergraduate and graduate projects are covered by a generic code of behaviour, but research proposals for student theses and funded and unfunded research by academics which involve human or animal subjects must be individually submitted for approval by the university ethics committee.

Codes of research ethics have intrinsic value in protecting the rights of humans and animals involved in research, but they also serve a professional and organisational function. Researchers may be subject to litigation and can lose professional indemnity if they are not seen to have adhered to the appropriate code of ethics. A related consideration is the question of relationships with the public and the standing of organisations responsible for research within the community. Some practices may be ethical but still give offence, so the value of the data collected using such practices must be weighed against the ill-will that may be generated.

Some universities have established ethics committees to cover the whole of the university, although invariably with at least two committees, covering human- and animal-related research. In some cases committees are faculty or division-based. Typically the approval process involves the completion of an 'Application for Ethics Approval Form', which must provide full details of the rationale for the research, the methods to be used and qualifications of the researchers involved. The 'National Ethics Application Form' of the Australian National Health and Medical Research Council (NHMRC, nd), which is a model for the use of Australian research institutions, runs to more than 450 items of information.

When ethics committees are faculty/division-specific a researcher would expect committee members to be familiar with the research methods being used, but with university-wide committees there is a possibility that committee members might not be familiar with research methods being used by colleagues from very different disciplines, especially newer methods. This is believed by some to be the case with some qualitative methods which reflect a very different epistemology from the positivist approach of the natural sciences, as discussed in Chapter 2. This issue is argued by Lincoln (2005: 167), who notes 'increased scrutiny' from research committees in the United States 'largely in response to failures in biomedical research', but spilling over into the social sciences and resulting in 'multiple rereviews of faculty proposals for qualitative research projects and… rereviews and denials of proposed student research (particularly dissertation research) that utilise action research methods, research in the subjects' own settings (e.g. high schools), and/or research which is predominantly qualitative in nature'. This is just one example of the expression of unease about the growing significance of a formalised ethics bureaucracy in universities and the spread of their influence from natural sciences into social sciences, as expressed, for example, by Haggerty (2004).

Various professional groups outside of the academic world are also committed to codes of ethics, both for moral reasons and for self-interest, connected to the ethos and social standing of the professional. For example, market researchers and opinion pollsters depend on client, media and public accepting the validity of their findings. Official statisticians seek to maintain standards of objectivity and to resist tendencies for their political masters to incorporate them into policy advocacy roles. As Karttunen (2012: 143) puts it: 'In democratic societies, statistical offices aim to maintain a status comparable to that of an independent agency instead of a branch of government'. References to such groups are provided in the Resources section at the end of this chapter.

Ethics in the research process

Research ethics can be examined in regard to three dimensions: the nature of the ethical issue, the stage or component of the research process where the issues arise, and whether the research subject is anonymous or personally or organisationally identified.

Nature of the ethical issue

Most codes of ethics and ethical practice are based on the 'golden rule', which relates to all human conduct and is endorsed by most religions, that is, that you should treat others as you yourself would wish to be treated. More specifically, the general principles usually invoked in codes of research ethics are that:

● the research should be beneficial to society;
● researchers should be suitably qualified and/or supervised to conduct the research;
● subjects should take part freely;
● subjects should take part only on the basis of informed consent;
● no harm should befall the research subjects;
● data should be honestly and rigorously analysed, interpreted and reported.

Component of the research process where issues arise

These issues tend to arise in different stages/components of the research process, as summarised in Figure 4.1.

Ethical issue	Stage in the research process					
	Design/ organisation	Collection	Analysis/ interpretation	Storing data during project	Reporting	Storing data after project
1 Social benefit	●				●	
2 Researcher competence	●					
3 Subjects' freedom of choice		●				
4 Subjects' informed consent		●				
5 Risk of harm to subjects – anonymous		●				
6 Risk of harm to subjects – identifiable	●		●	●	●	●
7 Honesty/rigour in analysis/ interpretation			●			
8 Honesty/rigour in reporting					●	

Figure 4.1 Ethics in the research process

Anonymous versus personally/organisationally identifiable data

In much primary empirical arts and events research, for example on-site questionnaire-based surveys and most observational studies, data are collected and stored anonymously: the researcher never knows the names of the subjects, so names are not recorded in any form. However, in other cases the names and contact details of individual subjects are known to the researcher and may be recorded in hard copy or electronically as part of the data from the research.

Ethical issues in research

Here, we discuss in turn the issues listed in Figure 4.1.

1 Social benefit

Research on nuclear and chemical weaponry has given rise to the proposition that research should be supported only if its social benefits can be demonstrated. Such an assessment is, of course, subjective. Thus, during the Cold War, it was argued that, despite the obvious negative connotations and widespread opposition to research for the development of nuclear weapons, it could be defended on the grounds that peace was maintained as long as each side – the West and the communist bloc – matched the other's weapons, in terms of technological sophistication as well as quantity, so that neither side would risk attacking the other: the principal of mutually assured destruction (MAD). In contemporary arts and events research the issues are not as dramatic, but ethical concerns can arise in relation to impacts on host communities and funding sources: for example, should research funding be accepted from organisations sponsored by tobacco companies or by companies with questionable environmental practices? The most publicly visible form of research, the opinion poll, often evokes a certain cynicism among the public or in the mass media, expressed in the view that answers can be determined by manipulation of the format of the question. The most egregious example of this is the 'push poll' (see below).

Policy/practice-related research

Ethics issues can arise in policy-related research commissioned by government, commercial or non-profit organisations when such organisations see research as supporting their particular political/policy, interest-group or commercial actual or planned activities, as discussed in Case study 4.1 (point D). This has become a live issue in cultural policy research commissioned by governments to demonstrate the social and economic impacts of the arts and in major cultural and sport events research designed to justify public investment in major sport events. Not only can this result in research designed to produce the desired results, but it can result in policy making being based on possibly inappropriate instrumental factors rather than intrinsic factors.

Push polls

In 1995 the US National Council on Public Polls issued the following media release about:

> … a growing and thoroughly unethical political campaign technique, commonly called 'push polls', masquerading as legitimate political polling… . A 'push poll' is a telemarketing technique in which telephone calls are used to canvass vast numbers of potential voters, feeding them false and damaging 'information' about a candidate under the guise of taking a poll to see how this 'information' affects voter preferences. In fact, the intent is to 'push' the voters away from one candidate and toward the opposing candidate. This is clearly political telemarketing, using innuendo and, in many cases, clearly false information to influence voters; there is no intent to conduct research.
>
> These telemarketing techniques damage the electoral process in two ways. They injure candidates, often without revealing the source of the information. Also, the results of a 'push poll', if released, give a seriously flawed and biased picture of the political situation.
>
> (National Council on Public Polls, 1995)

Push polling typically takes place in marginal electorates where a successful telephone campaign can have a significant impact on the election outcome. A typical push poll question would be of the following format: 'Given that candidate X could increase income tax by 50 per cent, whereas candidate Y is committed to no increases in income tax, how does this affect your voting intentions?' The results of such a poll are of less interest than the planting of the false or misleading information about candidate X in the listener's mind.

Push polling occurs in the political realm and would rarely be relevant to arts and events-related research, but it highlights the ethical dimension of the use of the 'leading question', which is discussed further in Chapter 10.

2 Researcher competence

Research ethics guidelines require that those undertaking research have appropriate levels of training, qualifications and experience, including familiarisation with ethical issues. Occasionally cases in which unqualified individuals are found to have been practising as doctors and even surgeons attract media publicity. The community is shocked that unqualified people should be undertaking such important work and the individuals are duly prosecuted. Such cases represent the extreme of public ethical concern because of the level of risk of harm involved. But the issue of professional competence, while less clear-cut in other areas, is nevertheless applicable. In arts and events research a researcher who is not competent, through training and/or experience, to conduct research runs the risk of:

- wasting the resources of the funding organisation;
- wasting the time of subjects;
- abusing the goodwill of subjects;
- misleading the users of the research results; and/or
- damaging the reputation of the research organisation.

3 Free choice

It seems obvious that subjects should not be coerced to become involved in research projects, but there are some grey areas. Some of these are institutional and some are intrinsic to the design and nature of the research. These are summarised in Figure 4.2 and discussed below.

Captive groups

In universities, students are often used as subjects in research. In some places students are required to be available for a certain amount of experimental or survey work conducted by academic staff, and in some cases they receive study credit for this involvement.

Type	Description	Examples
Captive groups	Groups where the 'person in charge' approves the research.	Schools, workplaces, clubs
Children	Because of adult authority, children may not feel free to decline cooperation.	Children in any setting
Official surveys	Participation in key government surveys required by law.	Population census
Observation	People being observed in public places do not have any choice.	Pedestrian movement studies
Participant observation	Informants do not have choice if the participant observer is incognito.	Researcher engaging in a music scene

Figure 4.2 Free choice 'grey' areas

Although, invariably, students are able to opt out of such activities, there is moral pressure on them to conform and possibly fear of sanctions if they do not. Clearly it is unethical for academic staff or the university to allow such undue moral pressure to be brought to bear.

Other captive group cases involve classes of school children, staff of arts and event managing organisations, or medical patients, whose participation is agreed to by the person in charge. Again, while opting out may be possible, in practice it may be difficult and the subject may be, to all intents and purposes, coerced. As a consequence, education authorities generally place strict controls on research that may be carried using school children. Research in prisons and mental and other hospitals raises similar questions about genuine freedom of choice on the part of the subject.

Children

Research involving children raises particular ethical issues. At what age are children able to give informed consent to being involved in research? How does this relate to the rights and obligations of parents or carers? If children below a certain age are not deemed to be able to give consent on their own behalf, in what circumstances, if any, is it appropriate for carers to give consent on the child's behalf? Are there situations where the risk of physical or emotional harm is greater for children than for adults involved with similar research processes?

In general it is believed that particular care should be taken in conducting research involving children because they typically see adults – including researchers – as figures of authority. Thus they may be less likely than adults to exercise their right to non-cooperation. This is not only a human rights issue but can also raise validity issues if children see questions as some sort of performance test and/or feel a need to please the questioner by answering or behaving in certain ways.

Where institutions are involved, such as play centres or schools, those organisations will have their own guidelines, particularly in regard to the requirements for parental permission.

Often the issue is avoided by simply assuming that parents are able to represent children's views/interests – thus, for example, Maher *et al.* (2011), in a study of service quality in a children's museum, interviewed only adults.

Official surveys

The principle of freedom of choice is constantly infringed by governments: it is an offence, for example, not to complete the population census forms or to refuse cooperation with a number of other official surveys. In these cases, the 'social benefit' argument relating to the need for accurate and complete data is considered to outweigh the citizen's right to refuse to give information.

Observation

In the case of some types of research where large numbers of subjects are involved – for example, studies of traffic flows, pedestrian movements within a venue or crowd behaviour – choice on the part of individual subjects on whether or not to be part of the research is impossible. In many such observational research situations, if the subjects knew they were being observed they might well modify their behaviour and so invalidate the research. This consideration might apply in research on people's interpersonal behaviour in a venue and can involve situations where anti-social, and even illegal, behaviour may be involved.

Participant observation

The problem of freedom to participate arises in research using participant observation where, as discussed in Chapter 9, the researcher is a participant in the phenomenon being studied. The whole basis of such research may rely on the researcher being accepted and trusted by the group being investigated: this may not be forthcoming if it is known that the participant is a researcher. If the researcher does 'come clean', there is the risk – even the likelihood – of the subjects modifying their behaviour, thus invalidating the research. To what extent is it ethical for researchers to disguise their identity to the people they are interacting with and studying – in effect to lie about their identity? When researchers are involved with groups engaging in illegal and/or anti-social activities, for example, graffiti activity or some youth groups, where do the researchers' loyalties lie? In some research methodologies a different approach is adopted and fully informed interaction between researcher and subjects is embraced and becomes part of the analysed and reported research.

If it is accepted that research of this type is permissible, despite the lack of freedom of consent, then the issue of confidentiality in reporting, as discussed below, becomes even more critical.

4 Informed consent

In experimental research, where there is a risk, however remote, of physical harm to the subject (for example where allergies might be involved, or a risk of muscle strains, or even of heart attack), it is clearly necessary for the subject to be fully aware of the risks in order to be able to give their *informed consent* to participate. The level of risk of harm is a matter of judgement, and often only the researcher is fully aware of the extent of risk involved in any given research procedure. This raises the question of the extent to which the subject can ever be 'fully informed'. Subjects can never be as fully informed as the researcher and thus a judgement has to be made about what is reasonable.

In the traditional science laboratory setting, verbal and written explanations of the nature of the research are given to the potential subjects and they are asked to sign a document indicating their agreement to being involved in the research. A checklist regarding the sort of information that should be provided to potential participants is provided in Figure 4.3 and an example of a consent form is provided in Figure 4.4. The quasi-experimental arts/events research discussed in Chapter 11 may require this sort of consent procedure. In the case of a single, anonymous questionnaire-based survey, verbal consent is generally considered adequate, but if names are recorded and lengthy and/or repeated interviews or other types of activity are involved, then written consent is advisable.

A researcher could of course 'go through the motions' of following this procedure but abuse it by providing misleading information about the level of risk – itself an unethical practice. Hence the need for clear guidelines and monitoring of these matters.

In addition to risks of physical or mental harm, there may be a moral dimension. For example, some people may object to being involved in research being conducted for certain public, political or commercial organisations. So being informed also involves being informed about the purpose of the research and the nature of the sponsor or beneficiary.

In some cases the status of the researcher is ambivalent, for example when students engaged in a project as part of their learning process in a university course conduct the project on behalf of a real client organisation, or when part-time students conduct research for a

- Name of organisation conducting the research
- Purpose of the research
- Sponsoring/funding organisation if applicable
- Participants and how they are being selected
- What is required from participants
- Nature of involvement (experiments, interviews, focus groups, etc.)
- Time required for each session
- Number of sessions
- Time period over which sessions will take place
- Any risks to the participant
- Voluntary nature of participation
- Right of participant to refuse to answer any questions or withdraw at any stage without giving reasons
- Privacy and security of data
- Ways in which data will be used
- Contact details for research project supervisor

Figure 4.3 Information for research participants: checklist

University of XXX, Social Research Institute

Cultural needs research project

CONSENT FORM

I confirm that I have read and understood the research project information sheet for the 'Cultural needs research project' and have had any questions answered to my satisfaction. _____

I understand that my participation in the study is entirely voluntary and I may cease to take part at any time without giving reasons. _____

I agree to take part in the study as described in the information sheet. _____

I agree to interviews/discussion sessions being recorded. _____

I agree that anonymous quotations from interviews/discussions may be used in publications. _____

Name: _____ Date: _____

Signature: _____

Researcher's name: _____ Date: _____

Signature: _____

Figure 4.4 Example of a consent form

university assignment using as subjects their fellow employees in their workplace or conduct research on competitors. It is clearly unethical for students to identify themselves only as students and not to identify to their informants the organisation which will be the beneficiary of the research. Yet in some situations, it might be thought that a student rather than a professional identity could be helpful for the conduct of the project (e.g. Brown, 2011: 138).

Here again there are some grey areas. In some cases the research would be invalidated if subjects knew its purpose in detail. For example, responses could be affected if the subjects knew that a survey was being conducted to see how respondents reacted to interviewers of differing race or gender. In some attitudinal research, for example on potentially sensitive topics such as race or sex, it might be thought that responses would be affected if respondents were told too much about the research and therefore placed 'on their guard' to give 'correct' or 'acceptable' answers. Clearly, such deception raises ethical issues and judgements have to be made about whether the value of the research justifies the use of mild deception.

1. Interviewers should be identified with a badge including their given name and the name of the organisation involved (the host/client organisation or university).
2. Interviewers should be fully briefed about the project so that they can answer questions if asked.
3. If a respondent-completion ('handout') questionnaire is used, a brief description of the purpose of the project should be provided on the questionnaire (typically two or three lines so that it takes just a few seconds to read), with contact telephone numbers of supervisors for those requiring more information.
4. Interviewers approaching potential respondents should introduce themselves and seek cooperation using wording such as the following: 'We are conducting a survey of users of —, would you mind answering a few questions?'
5. Telephone numbers of supervisors should be available and can be given to respondents if required.
6. A short printed handout may be available with more information for those respondents who are interested.
7. Respondents should not be pressured if they refuse to answer a question or wish to terminate the interview at any time.

Figure 4.5 Ethics guidelines for anonymous questionnaire-based surveys

In some cases the provision of detailed information to informants, and obtaining their written consent, is neither practicable nor necessary. Thus the typical arts/events questionnaire-based survey:

- is anonymous;
- involves only a short interview (e.g. four or five minutes);
- involves fairly innocuous, non-personal questions;
- takes place at a facility/site with the agreement of the management or authorities.

In this type of situation most respondents tend not to be particularly interested in detailed explanations of the research. Most adults are familiar with the survey process and their main concern is that, if they are to take part, the interview should not take up too much of their time. Thus, potential respondents can become impatient with attempts to provide detailed explanations of the research and would prefer to 'get on with it'. Often questions about the purpose of the survey, if they arise at all, do so later during the interview process, when the respondent's interest has been stimulated. A suggested set of guidelines for such survey situations is provided in Figure 4.5.

5 Risk of harm to the subject

There may be a risk of harm to the subject in the collection of data, in its storage and handling or in publication. Such risks obviously need to be eliminated or minimised, for the sake of the subjects, the researcher and sponsoring organisations and, indeed, the whole research process.

Risk of harm in the data-collection process

The risk of harm in data collection arises particularly in medical/biological research, where a subject's physical health may be put at risk by an experimental procedure, for example, involving physical exertion. Assuming there is appropriate screening and selection of subjects, such as checking on health status, this risk should be minimised by appropriate briefing of subjects and clear explanation and implementation of informed consent procedures. This risk is, however, most unlikely in arts and events-related research.

Risks of harm can also arise in psychological research, where stress and distress can be caused, and in socio-psychological research, where inter-personal relationships could be damaged. Again, this is unlikely in arts/event research, but can arise in organisational research.

Anxiety during the data-collection process may arise if the subject has concerns about how the data are to be used. This may relate to themselves and their own privacy, which relates to data storage, handling and publication, as discussed below. The potential harm if privacy is breached could vary from mild embarrassment to disruption of relationships with friends, colleagues or employers, or to loss of reputation and/or position. Concerns may also relate to moral principles, for example the use of data by certain types of corporation or governments, which relates to the 'fully informed' issue discussed above. In this case the potential harm is the affront to the subject's moral principles. Both concerns relate to the right of the subject to refuse to answer questions and/or withdraw from the process at any stage.

Risk of harm in data storage and handling

Data storage and handling involve not only hard-copy materials, such as questionnaires and records of experimental results, but also digital material, such as audio and video recordings, transcripts and coded data files. Typically, hard-copy data may be kept for several years as the project progresses and the publication process unfolds, and for a minimum period of time after the completion of the project specified by research organisations, usually about five years. Digital data today are likely to be stored indefinitely. The term 'handling' is used as well as storage because, while data may be stored securely in a formal sense, there are issues about who has access to it at the various stages (e.g. coding, computerised data entry, transmission) and whether they are aware of and adhere to confidentiality commitments.

Hard-copy data should be protected by an appropriately secure form of storage and digital data by password-protected access.

The risk of harm to the subject due to the way data are stored and handled is affected by whether the information is provided entirely anonymously or the subject's name and/or contact details are known to the researcher and/or recorded. There are in-between situations, which can be termed *partial anonymity*. Three such situations are discussed in turn below.

● *Anonymous subjects*: Even in an anonymous situation, informants may be reluctant to give certain types of information, such as income, to 'a complete stranger'. Where such sensitivity is encountered, the usual approach is to stress the voluntary and anonymous nature of the information-giving process, while respecting the respondent's right to refuse to provide certain types of information.

● *Partial anonymity*: Often research participants are not randomly drawn from the population but are members of a community or organisation. While the community or organisation may not be named in the publication, as discussed below, it may be named in the stored data, and it is possible that individuals or groups could be identified by their position – e.g. president, secretary, director, manager, curator, head teacher. Participants may therefore have concerns about the security of the data, particularly if they have revealed information about themselves or expressed views about others which they would like to be kept confidential. Much digital information is anonymous because of use of identification numbers rather than names, but somewhere there will be a list linking names and identification numbers, so the security and confidentiality of that list become important. In addition to written information, observational research may involve photography and video material, which may invade people's privacy if they are recognised, even in the most innocent-seeming activities.

- *Identified subjects*: Privacy is a valued right in Western society and such rights are generally enshrined in laws, which vary in detail between jurisdictions. People can be offended and suffer stress if their affairs are made public or divulged to certain third parties. There is therefore an obligation on the researcher to ensure confidentiality of any personally identifiable data which have been collected.

Situations where personally identifiable data inevitably arise and the nature of the confidential material are summarised in Figure 4.6, together with suggested means to reduce risk. Some routine methods for maintaining individuals' privacy, such as keeping lists of names separate from actual data and use of pseudonyms, are indicated, but these measures may not always prevent research subjects from being offended in ways discussed further below. An important principle, but one that is difficult to prescribe in detail, is that the researcher should be aware of research subjects' sensitivities, whether they be personal, professional, cultural or organisational.

In some research projects the naming of individuals is inevitably involved – for example, where the number of subjects is small and they are key figures associated with particular high-profile organisations or communities. Indeed, in some research it may be important to 'name names'. Where interviews are conducted with such individuals, care must be taken to adopt the journalist's practice of checking whether information is being given 'on the record' or 'off the record'. Thus, in interviews, particularly where sensitive matters arise, it is wise to ask named informants whether they are prepared to be quoted.

In reporting results, the use of false names or numbers to identify individuals, organisations, events, places and communities is the obvious solution. However, this is not always sufficient. The use of false names may protect identities from the world at large, but for those 'in the know', the places and the people involved in the research project may be all too easily identifiable – the partial anonymity situation discussed above. Particular care should be taken when dealing with members of close-knit communities: the researcher should be aware of cultural and inter-personal sensitivities within such communities. Such issues are further highlighted in certain types of qualitative research where the research methodology involves gaining the trust and confidence of research subjects. It would be unethical to betray such trust and confidence.

Occasionally this issue can be carelessly exacerbated by the author's own list of 'acknowledgements' if it clearly identifies people, organisations and places.

When data are confidential, measures must be taken to protect that confidentiality through ensuring the security of the raw data, such as interview tapes/transcripts/questionnaires. Specific freedom of information and privacy laws invariably cover the storage of and access to personally identifiable data, including allowing individuals access to their own records and the right to have inaccuracies corrected.

Data can be stored with code numbers or false names, with a key to the code numbers or names being kept securely in a place apart from the data.

Mail surveys are an in-between case. If returned questionnaires do not have any identification, then there is no way of identifying non-respondents in order to send reminders. Sending reminders to everyone is costly and an irritation to those who have already responded. One solution is to place an identifying number on the return envelope rather than on the questionnaire, with an assurance that the number will not be transferred to the questionnaire. In some situations a third party, such as a legal firm, is used to receive the questionnaires and pass them on to the researcher in anonymous form.

Research method	Who is identified?	Identifying information	Why identify?	Issues re storage or publication?	Methods to reduce risk
Postal surveys – quantitative	Sampled members of general public or of organisations	Names + addresses	Intrinsic to method	Storage	List of names and addresses kept separate from question-naires and destroyed at end of data collection.
Telephone surveys – quantitative	Sampled members of general public or of organisations	Telephone numbers	Intrinsic to method + quality control	Storage	List of names and addresses kept separate from question-naires and destroyed at end of data collection.
Online surveys	Individuals may be sampled via email lists.	Email address	May be sampling method	Storage	Use of commercial online survey company provides a buffer.
Big Data investigations (see Chapter 7)	Customers	Name + other data provided to corporate body	Intrinsic to method	Storage	Corporate body's own security system and privacy policies.
Interviews – qualitative – individuals	Private individuals	Name + possibly telephone no./ address	Intrinsic to method	Both	Use of pseudonyms; be aware of sensitivities.
Interviews – qualita-tive – individuals in organisational roles	Individuals in identifiable public offices (e.g. mayor) or corporate roles (e.g. managing director)	Names, positions, organisation/place/ contact details	Intrinsic to method	Both	Use pseudonyms for individu-als, place or organisation, but not always possible. Clarify 'on record' / 'off record'; be aware of sensitivities.
Interviews – qualitative – small groups	Members of small groups (e.g. a village, a club or a small business)	Names (possibly addresses, tel. nos.; surnames may not be involved)	Intrinsic to method	Both, but mainly publication	Use of pseudonyms for indi-viduals, group and place, but not always possible. Clarify 'on record' / 'off record'; be aware of sensitivities.
Ethnographic – variety of subjects and qualitative methods	Individuals, separately or as members of a group	Names (as above)	Intrinsic to method	Mainly publication	Use of pseudonyms, but issue may lie in betraying confidence/trust. Be aware of sensitivities
Longitudinal research: a. quantitative b. qualitative	Same subjects are contacted to be studied at intervals over a number of weeks, months, years	Names, addresses, tel. nos	Intrinsic to method	a. Storage b. Both	a. Keep names etc. separate from data. b. Storage: as for a. Publica-tion: use pseudonyms.

Figure 4.6 Personally identifiable data

Confidentiality issues often arise with regard to the relationship between the researcher and the organisation funding the research. In particular, if the funding organisation 'owns' the data, the researcher may wish to protect the confidentiality of informants by not passing on to the sponsoring organisation any information that could identify informants by name.

Risk of harm in publication

Many of the considerations discussed above in relation to data storage and handling also apply in the case of publication of results. Any undertaking given to individuals or organisations with regard to anonymity should be respected and steps should be taken to avoid inadvertent breaches of confidentiality. Typically, such issues do not arise at the publication stage with individuals in quantitative research, particularly if they were anonymous from the start. But if the subjects were drawn from a particular geographical community or an organisation, unintended embarrassment could arise. General readers would not be able to make the identification, or would not be concerned even if they could. People in the academic or policy community familiar with the research may be able to make the identification, as might interested residents or members of the organisation. So the researcher must be prepared, in ethical terms, for the possibility of such identification and take this into account when writing the research report.

6 Honesty/rigour in analysis, interpretation and reporting

The falsification of research results is clearly unethical. There have been some notorious cases in the natural sciences where experimental results have been falsified.

A common practice in quantitative research is to exclude 'outliers' from the analysis. Thus, for example, if a survey of cultural participation found that all respondents participated three times a week or less except for two who participated ten times a week, these two might be termed outliers and excluded from the analysis because they would distort averages. This is generally seen as ethical as long as it is stated in the research report that it has taken place. The same principle could apply in qualitative research, of course, although identifying an outlier would be a more complex task.

Researchers are concerned about reporting 'negative findings' or non-findings. This typically does not arise with descriptive research, where what is, is, or in evaluative research, where the performance of the programme/organisation is as found. The difficulty arises with explanatory research when no apparent 'explanation' is found. But negative findings are of interest and use if the research has been carefully designed. Thus, if the interest is in the effect on variable X of 15 different independent variables and none of them is found to have a significant influence, then this would generally be of interest, in that it suggests that other variables must be at work. In the case of qualitative research, of course, the fact that the 15 variables are not influential in one study does not preclude them from being influential in another study, since the findings would not be generalisable.

Ethical issues arise when claims are made that cannot be supported by the available data. This sometimes arises when data are used by managers or politicians not directly involved with the research, but some researchers can also become consciously or inadvertently caught up in the process when advocacy on behalf of their field of interest is involved. This phenomenon is discussed by Eisner (1998) in relation to the claimed influence of arts education on general educational performance, and Crompton (1995) in relation to the claimed benefits of events.

In some cases, negative findings are the result of a limited sample size: there may be an effect, but the small sample size makes it impossible to be confident about it – it is statistically insignificant, as discussed in Chapter 17. With a larger sample, a small but significant relationship may have been found. But such findings may be relevant for later studies when considering required sample sizes and may be taken into account in systematic reviews of research, or meta-analyses (see Chapter 5), which aggregates the findings of many similar studies. This may seem like purely practical rather than ethical matters, but, arguably, there is an ethical obligation to report all the findings of research that might contribute to the development of knowledge.

7 Honesty/rigour in reporting

Authorship

A clear ethical principle is that all those involved with a research project should receive appropriate acknowledgement of their contribution in any publication. Acknowledgement of funding sources, named informants or collaborators, and anonymous research subjects may be made in a footnote or in a preface or acknowledgements section. Difficulties can arise in the case of claims for joint authorship, especially in academic research where careers are dependent on such matters. A judgement has to be made as to whether a research assistant, who may be a research student, has simply undertaken routine work for payment or whether he or she has contributed intellectually to the research.

Typically, in team research situations, the name of the leader of the team, or 'principal investigator', is placed first in the list of authors, but where the leadership is shared, names may appear in alphabetical order or may be rotated in different publications in a research programme.

Plagiarism

Plagiarism – the use of others' data or ideas without due acknowledgement and, where appropriate, permission – is clearly unethical and is also covered by copyright and intellectual property laws.

Use and abuse of research results in policy/practice

The policy/practice dimension discussed under 'Social benefit' also arises here. If research findings do not provide the support the commissioning, governmental or other body seeks, it may 'cherry pick' or misrepresent the results, ignore the research or seek to actively suppress it. While the unethical conduct in this instance is being committed by the commissioning body, it has implications for the researchers, whether they are employed by the organisation or are private or academic consultants. The issue arises as to whether to go public in some way.

Access to research information

Some of the controversies surrounding climate research in recent years have highlighted the issue of rights of access to research information. We have already referred to individuals' rights of access to personal information about them held by public and other corporate bodies, as covered by freedom of information and privacy legislation. But such legislation also covers the public rights of access to information held by public bodies, for example on decision-making processes, a right which is regularly pursued by journalists. While the provisions of legislation vary between jurisdictions, the common principle is that information held by public bodies is not secret unless publication would threaten individual privacy, commercial property rights or national security, or the costs of compiling information and making it publicly available would be prohibitive. In theory, such provisions apply to research data gathered with the support of public funds and/or held by public research institutions and have implications for the way research data-sets are stored and the length of time for which they are kept. As noted above, since most research data in the social sciences are held in digital form, their storage is, for the most part, potentially indefinite.

It might be thought that if the results of research have been published, there should be no further interest in the raw data, but as Montford (2010: 134, 379–383) and Mann (2012) discuss in the case of climate research, in the natural sciences *replication* is a key criterion in assessing validity. Yet as data-sets become increasingly complex and expensive to compile, the only way of checking and replicating some types of published research is through access to authors' original data. Some scientific journals are therefore requiring public (website) archiving of data-sets and of the computer code used to analyse them as a condition of publication.

Summary

This chapter considers the ethical and legal dimensions of conducting research. It is noted that in universities and other research organisations the responsible and ethical conduct of research is regulated by codes of conduct and ethics committees. In this chapter we consider mainly issues arising in research involving human subjects. In the biological and physical sciences, consideration is also given to involvement with animals and, increasingly, environmental dimensions.

Ethical considerations arise in all components of the research process, including design, data collection, data storage and handling, analysis and interpretation and publication. A number of questions must be answered satisfactorily for a research project to be judged to be ethical. Is the research likely to be of social benefit? Are the researchers involved competent to conduct the research? Are the subjects involved participating voluntarily, without compulsion? Are the individuals taking part fully informed about the purposes and nature of the research – have they given 'informed consent'? Is the risk of harm to subjects at an acceptably low level? Has the analysis and interpretation of data and reporting of the results been undertaken honestly and rigorously? Have all those involved been suitably acknowledged or, where appropriate, included among the authors?

TEST QUESTIONS

1. What are the main ethical issues that arise in research?
2. What is 'informed consent' and what measures must be taken to ensure it?
3. What are the 'grey areas' where participation in research may not be voluntary?
4. What are the main possible sources of harm to participants in social science research?
5. What is plagiarism?

EXERCISES

1. In interviews with 15-year-olds on arts and events activities, a few of the respondents let you know that they take illegal drugs and indicate indirectly who supplies them. Do you tell anyone or maintain confidentiality? Do you include the finding, anonymously, in your research report?

2. Read Christensen's (1980) critique of Moeller *et al.* (1980a) and the response of Moeller *et al.* (1980b) and discuss, including how the issues might play out in an arts/events context.

3. Summarise either Eisner (1998) or Crompton (1995) and assess the extent to which the comments in the paper are applicable in your own community.

Resources

Websites

Research ethics guidelines:

- Market Research Society (UK): www.mrs.org.uk/standards/codeconduct.htm
- UNESCO regarding restitution of cultural property: www.unnesco.org/new/en/culture/themes
- Social Research Association (UK): www.the-sra.org.uk/documents/pdfs/ethics02.pdf
- NHMRC/ARC/Universities Australia guidelines: www.nhmrc.gov.au/_files_nhmrc/file/publications/synopses/r39.pdf
- University of Technology, Sydney: for undergraduate and postgraduate students: www.gsu.uts.edu.au/policies/hrecguide.html

Publications

- General: Haggerty (2004), Israel and Hay (2006), Loue (2002); in sport and leisure: Tomlinson and Felming (1997).
- Autobiographical research: Jones *et al.* (2006).
- Ethics guidelines: business research: Saunders *et al.* (2009: 183–204).
- Ethics committees and qualitative research: Lincoln (2005).
- Research ethics:
  - arts management: Chiaravalloti and Piber (2011)
  - leisure: Fleming and Jordan (2006)
  - official statisticians, professional integrity: Karttunen (2012)
  - policy-related research – politicians versus researchers: cultural policy: Belfiore (2009), major sport events: Veal *et al.* (2012)
  - social media in museums: Wong (2011)
  - survey research example: Moeller *et al.* (1980a, 1980b), Christensen (1980)
  - Research involving children: protocols: Blair (2000); examples: Debenedetti *et al.* (2009), Dockett *et al.* (2011); arts-based methods: Driessnack and Furukawa (2012)
  - Restitution of cultural heritage: Anderegg (2004), Thompson (2003)

References

Anderegg, S. (2004) The repatriation of the Elgin Marbles. *TED Case Studies*, No. 732, available at: www1. american.edu/ted/greekmarbles.htm

Australian Government, Office for the Arts (2011) *Australian Government Policy on Indigenous Repatriation*. Canberra: Australian Government.

Belfiore, E. (2009) On bullshit in cultural policy practice and research: notes from the British case. *International Journal of Cultural Policy*, 15(3), 343–359.

Blair, J. (2000) Assessing protocols for child interviews. In A.A. Stone and J.S. Turken (eds), *The Science of Self-report: Implications for Research and Practice*. Mahwah, NJ: Lawrence Erlbaum, pp. 161–174.

Brown, P. (2011) Us and them. Who benefits from experimental exhibition making? *Museum Management and Curatorship*, 26(2), 129–148.

Chiaravalloti, F. and Piber, M. (2011) Ethical implications of methodological settings in arts management research: the case of performance evaluation. *Journal of Arts Management, Law and Society*, 41(3), 240–266.

Christensen, J. E. (1980) A second look at the informal interview. *Journal of Leisure Research*, 12 (2), 183–186.

Crompton, J. L. (1995) Economic impact analysis of sports facilities and events: eleven sources of misapplication. *Journal of Sport Management*, 9(1), 14–35.

Debenedetti, S., Caro, F. and Krebs, A. (2009) 'I'd rather play than look at statues': the experience of children with art works and interactive devices at an art exhibition. *International Journal of Arts Management*, 11(3), 46–86.

Dockett, S., Main, S. and Kelly, L. (2011) Consulting young children: experiences in a museum. *Visitor Studies*, 14(1), 13–33.

Driessnack, M. and Furukawa, R. (2012) Arts-based data collection techniques used in child research. *Journal for Specialists in Pediatric Nursing*, 17(1), 3–9.

Eisner, E. W. (1998) Does experience in the arts boost academic achievement? *Art Education*, 51(1), 7–15.

Fleming, S. and Jordan, F. (eds) (2006) *Ethical Issues in Leisure Research*. LSA Publication 90, Eastbourne: Leisure Studies Association.

Haggerty, K. D. (2004) Ethics creep: governing social science research in the name of ethics. *Qualitative Sociology*, 27(4), 391–414.

Israel, M. and Hay, I. (2006) *Research Ethics for Social Scientists*. Los Angeles: Sage.

Jones, R. L., Potrac, P., Haleem, H. and Cushion, C. (2006) Exposure by association: anonymity and integrity in autobiographical research. In S. Fleming and F. Jordan (eds), *Ethical Issues in Leisure Research*. LSA Publication 90, Eastbourne: Leisure Studies Association, pp. 45–62.

Karttunen, S. (2012) Cultural policy indicators: reflections on the role of official statisticians in the politics of data collection. *Cultural Trends*, 21(2), 133–147.

Lincoln, Y. (2005) Institutional review boards and methodological conservatism: the challenge to and from phenomenological paradigms. In N. K. Denzin and Y. S. Lincoln (eds), *Handbook of Qualitative Research*, Third Edition. Thousand Oaks, CA: Sage, pp. 165–190.

Loue, S. (2002) *Textbook of Research Ethics: Theory and Practice*. New York: Kluwer.

Maher, J. K., Clark, J. and Gambill Motley, D. (2011) Measuring museum service quality: relationship to visitor membership: the case of a children's museum. *International Journal of Arts Management*, 13(2), 29–42.

Mann, M. E. (2012) *The Hockey Stick and the Climate Wars: Dispatches from the Front Lines*. New York: Columbia University Press.

Mitchell, S. (2012) Return Aboriginal sacred objects. *Australian Geographic*, 21 December, retrieved from: www.australiangeographic.com.au/journal/should-museums-hold-aborigina-sacred-objects.htm

Moeller, G. H. *et al.* (1980a) The informal interview as a technique for recreation research. *Journal of Leisure Research*, 12(2), 174–182.

Moeller, G. H. *et al.* (1980b) A response to 'A second look at the informal interview'. *Journal of Leisure Research*, 12(2), 187–188.

Montford, A. W. (2010) *The Hockey Stick Illusion: Climategate and the Corruption of Science*. London: Stacey International.

National Council on Public Polls (1995) *Push Polls*. Press release, 25 May, Clifton, NJ: NCPP, available at: www.ncpp.org/?q=node/41

National Health and Medical Research Council (NHMRC) (nd) *National Ethics Application Form*. Canberra: NHMRC, available at: www.neaf.gov.au/default.aspx

National Health and Medical Research Council (NHMRC)/Australian Research Council (ARC) and Universities Australia (2007) *Australian Code for the Responsible Conduct of Research*. Canberra: Australian Government (website, see above).

Saunders, M., Lewis, P. and Thornhill, A. (2009) *Research Methods for Business Students*, Fifth Edition. Harlow: Financial Times-Prentice Hall.

Silberberg, T. (2005) The importance of accuracy in attendance reporting. *International Journal of Arts Management*, 8(1), 4–7.

Thompson, J. (2003) Cultural property, restitution and value. *Journal of Applied Philosophy*, 20(3), 251–262.

Tomlinson, A. and Fleming, S. (eds) (1997) *Ethics, Sport and Leisure*. Aachen, Germany: Meyer and Meyer Verlag.

Veal, A. J., Toohey, K. and Frawley, S. (2012) The sport participation legacy of the Sydney 2000 Olympic Games and other international sporting events hosted in Australia. *Journal of Policy Research in Tourism, Leisure and Events*, 4(2), 155–184.

Wong, A. S. (2011) Ethical issues of social media in museums: a case study. *Museum Management and Curatorship*, 26(2), 97–112.

Chapter 5

The range of research methods

Introduction

Horses for courses

In this chapter the range of alternative research methods and criteria for their use are examined in broad terms, as an introduction to the methods and techniques to be covered in more detail in subsequent chapters. The chapter has four main sections:

- *major methods*: a range of major methods used in arts/events research, including the roles of scholarship, 'just thinking', the use of the research literature, secondary data, observation, particular qualitative methods and questionnaire-based surveys;

- *subsidiary and cross-cutting methods*: approaches and techniques which are subsidiary to one or more of the major methods, in that they are a variation on or an application of the major methods or cut across a number of the major methods;

- *multiple methods*: including triangulation and of the case-study method;

- *policy and management-related research-based techniques*; and

- *choice of method*: the process of selecting a research method for a particular purpose.

Choosing appropriate research methods is clearly vital. In this book we espouse the principle that every technique has its place; the important thing is for researchers to be aware of the limitations of any particular method and to take these into account when reporting research results. A horses for courses approach is adopted; techniques are not intrinsically good or bad, but are considered to be appropriate or inappropriate for the task at hand. This aligns with the pragmatic approach to research discussed in Chapter 3. Further, it is maintained that it is not a question of good or bad techniques that should be considered but good or bad *use* of techniques.

The major research methods

The range of major methods to be examined is listed in Figure 5.1. The methods are discussed in turn below.

Introduction – horses for courses	• Scholarship

The range of major research methods	• Scholarship • Just thinking • Existing sources – using the literature • Existing sources – secondary data • Observation • Qualitative methods • Questionnaire-based surveys • Experimental method • Case study method

Subsidiary, cross-cutting and multiple techniques/methods	• Action research • Big data • Conjoint analysis • Coupon surveys/conversion studies • Delphi technique • Diary methods • Discourse analysis • En route/intercept/cordon surveys • Experience sampling method (SEM) • Historical research • Longitudinal methods • Mapping techniques • Media reader/viewer/listener surveys • Meta-analysis • Multiple correspondence analysis/Latent class analysis • Netnography • Network analysis • Panel studies • Perceptual mapping • Projective techniques • Psychographic/lifestyle studies • Q methodology • Quantitative modelling • Repertory grid, laddering • Scales • Time-use surveys • Visitor conversation research • Web-based research

Multiple methods	• Triangulation • Counting heads

Policy/management-related research-based techniques	

Choosing methods	• The research question or hypothesis • Previous research • Data availability/access • Resources • Time and timing • Validity, reliability and generalisability • Ethics • Uses/users of the findings

Method	Brief description
Scholarship	Being well read about a topic and thinking deeply and creatively about it.
Just thinking	The thinking part of scholarship.
Existing sources – using the literature/systematic reviews	Identifying, summarising and evaluating the research literature – part of all research but can be the sole method used in a project.
Existing sources – secondary data	Re-use of data originally collected by another organisation for other purposes.
Observation	Direct looking at behaviour, or use of still or video cameras.
Qualitative methods	Range of methods where the data gathered are in the form of words, as opposed to quantitative methods, where data are in the form of numbers.
Questionnaire-based surveys	Methods using a formal, printed schedule of questions to gather data – the main quantitative method in arts/events research.
Experimental method	The researcher controls the environment of the phenomenon being studied, holding all variables constant except those that are the focus of the research.
Case study	The focus of the research is on one or a small number of cases, and typically a number of data-gathering and analysis methods are used.

Figure 5.1 The range of major research methods

Scholarship

Although the dividing line between scholarship and research can be difficult to draw, it is useful to consider the differences between the two. Scholarship involves being well informed about a subject and also thinking critically and creatively about a subject and the accumulated knowledge on it. Scholarship therefore involves knowing the literature, but also being able to synthesise it, analyse it and critically appraise it. Scholarship is traditionally practised in the role of teacher, but when the results of scholarship are published they effectively become a contribution to research.

Research involves the generation of new knowledge. Traditionally this has been thought of as involving the gathering and presentation of new data – empirical research – but clearly this is not a necessary condition for a contribution to be considered research. New insights, critical or innovative ways of looking at old issues, or the identification of new issues or questions – the fruits of scholarship – are also contributions to knowledge. Indeed, the development of a new framework or *paradigm* for looking at a field can be far more significant than a minor piece of empirical work using an outmoded paradigm.

Just thinking

There is no substitute for thinking! Creative, informed thinking about a topic can be the only process involved in the development and presentation of a piece of research, although it will usually also involve consideration of the literature, as discussed below.

But even when data collection is involved, the difference between an acceptable piece of research and an exceptional or significant piece of research is usually the quality of the creative thought that has gone into it. The researcher needs to be creative in:

- identifying and posing the initial questions or issues for investigation;
- conceptualising the research and developing a research strategy;
- analysing data; and
- interpreting and presenting the findings.

Texts on research methods, such as this, can provide a guide to mechanical processes, but creative thought must come from within the individual researcher – in the same way that the basics of drawing can be taught but art comes from within the individual artist.

Existing sources – using the literature/systematic reviews

There is virtually no research that would not benefit from some reference to the existing literature and for most research such reference is essential. It is possible for a research project to consist only of a review of the literature: in comparatively new areas of study, such as arts/events, especially when they are multi-disciplinary as arts/events research invariable is, there is a great need for the consolidation of existing knowledge that can come from good literature reviews. In the science area, a systematic review of research on a specific topic is seen as a research method in its own right; this is discussed further in Chapter 6.

The review of the literature often plays a key role in the formulation of research projects; it indicates the state of knowledge on a topic and is a source of, or stimulant for, ideas, both substantive and methodological.

A review of the literature can be important even when it uncovers no literature on the topic of interest. To establish that no research has been conducted on a particular topic or a particular aspect of a topic, especially when the topic is considered to be of some importance to the field, can be a research finding of some significance in its own right. The literature review process is discussed in detail in Chapter 6.

Existing sources – secondary data

Clearly, if information is already available that will answer the research questions posed, it would be wasteful of resources to collect new information for the purpose. As discussed in Chapter 7, large quantities of information, including sales figures and visitor numbers, income and expenditure, staffing, accident reports, crime reports, and travel and cultural participation data, are collected and stored by government and other organisations as routine functions of policy making, management and evaluation. Such data are referred to as *secondary* data, because their primary use is administrative and research is only a secondary use. Even when such data are not ideal for the research at hand, they can often provide answers to some questions more quickly and at less cost than the collection of new data.

Secondary data need not be quantitative. Historians, for example, use diaries, official documents, records or newspaper reports as sources – such sources may be seen as secondary, since they were not initially produced for research purposes, but for historians some of them are described as primary sources. In policy research such documents as the annual reports or minutes of meetings of organisations might be utilised.

In some cases data have been collected for research as opposed to administrative purposes but may not have been fully analysed, or they may have been analysed in only one particular way for a particular purpose, or even not analysed at all. Secondary analysis, or re-analysis, of research data is a potentially fruitful, but widely neglected, activity.

Observation

The technique of observation, discussed in Chapter 8, has the advantage of being unobtrusive – indeed, the techniques involved are sometimes referred to as *unobtrusive* techniques (Kellehear, 1993). Unobtrusive techniques involve gathering information about people's behaviour without their knowledge. While in some instances this may raise ethical questions (see Chapter 4), it clearly has certain advantages over techniques where subjects are aware of the researcher's presence and may therefore modify their behaviour, or where reliance must be placed on subjects' recall and description of their behaviour, which can be inaccurate or distorted.

Observation may be the only possible technique to use in certain situations, for example when researching illicit activity which people may be reluctant to talk about, or when researching the behaviour of children (their play patterns, for instance) who may be too young to interview.

Observation is capable of presenting a perspective on a situation that is not apparent even to the individuals involved. For example, the users of a crowded part of a venue or site may not be aware of the uncrowded areas available to them – the uneven pattern of use of the site can be assessed only by observation.

Observation is therefore an appropriate technique to use when knowledge of the presence of the researcher is likely to lead to unacceptable modification of subjects' behaviour, and when mass patterns of behaviour not apparent to individual subjects are of interest.

Qualitative methods

As discussed in Chapter 2, qualitative methods stand in contrast to quantitative methods. The main difference between the two techniques is that quantitative methods involve numbers – quantities – whereas qualitative methods rely on words, and sometimes images, as the unit of analysis. In the case of qualitative techniques, the information collected does not generally lend itself to statistical analysis and conclusions are not based on such analysis.

In consequence there is a tendency for qualitative techniques to involve the gathering of large amounts of relatively detailed information about relatively few cases (people, organisations, events, programmes, venues) and for quantitative techniques to involve the gathering of relatively small amounts of data on relatively large numbers of cases. It should be emphasised, however, that this is just a *tendency*. It is possible, for example, for a quantitative research project to involve the collection of, say, 500 items of data on only 20 people and for a qualitative research project to involve the collection of relatively little information on, say, 200 people. Conversely, some surveys designed to collect quantitative data can involve questionnaires many pages long, which take an hour or more to administer and can collect hundreds of items of data from each respondent. The difference in the two approaches lies in the nature of information collected and the way it is analysed.

In what situations are qualitative techniques used? They tend to be used when one or more of the following situations apply:

- when the focus of the research is on meanings and attitudes (although these can also be studied quantitatively);
- when the situation calls for exploratory theory-building rather than the testing of theory;
- when the researcher accepts that the concepts, terms and issues must be defined by the subjects themselves and not by the researcher in advance;
- when interaction between members of a group is of interest.

Qualitative techniques are not appropriate when the aim of the research is to make general statements about large populations, especially if such statements call for quantification.

Data-collection methods	Alternative names/variations	Description
In-depth interviews	Informal, semi-structured or unstructured interviews	One-on-one interviews with small numbers of individuals, interviewed at length, possibly on more than one occasion, typically using a checklist of topics rather than a formal questionnaire.
Focus groups	Group interviews	Discussions with groups of people (typically 6–12) led by a facilitator.
Observation	Unobtrusive techniques	The phenomenon of interest is examined by the naked eye or by use of still or video camera.
Participant observation		The researcher becomes a participant in the phenomenon being studied.
Biographical methods	Auto-ethnography, memory work	Research subjects are invited to provide their own accounts of events, etc., in written or recorded oral form.
Analysis of texts	Content analysis,* hermeneutics	Analysis and interpretation of the content of published or unpublished texts. May also involve audio-visual materials (images, TV, film, music, radio).
Ethnography	Field research (in anthropology)	Studying groups of people using a mixture of the above methods.
Netnography	–	Ethnographical research on users of the internet.

Figure 5.2 Qualitative data-collection methods

* Can also be quantitative

Figure 5.2 summarises a range of qualitative data-collection methods and these are discussed in more detail in Chapter 9.

Questionnaire-based surveys

A questionnaire is a printed or electronic list of questions. In a questionnaire-based survey the same questionnaire is used to interview a sample of respondents. The term questionnaire-based survey is used because such surveys can take two formats:

- *interview format*, in which an interviewer, in a face-to-face situation or via telephone, reads out the questions from the questionnaire and records the answers;

- *respondent-completion format*, in which the respondent reads the questions and writes answers on the questionnaire or on-screen, and no interviewer is involved.

In many discussions of research methods in the literature 'questionnaires' and 'interviews' are presented as alternatives; this is clearly misleading, since interviews may be conducted using a questionnaire. A more accurate distinction would be made between questionnaires and informal, in-depth or unstructured interviews.

Questionnaire-based surveys are popular in arts and events research, partly because the basic mechanics are relatively easily understood and mastered, but also because so much arts/events research calls for the sorts of general, quantified statements referred to above. Thus, for example, governments want to know how many people engage in cultural activities generally or visit particular types of cultural venue; managers of cultural facilities and of events want to know what proportion of customers are dissatisfied with a service; and marketers want to know how many people are in a particular market segment. All these examples come from practical policy/management situations, which emphasises that most of the resources for survey research come from the public or private sector of the cultural/ events industries. Academic papers are often a secondary spin-off from research that has been sponsored for such specific, practical purposes.

Unlike qualitative techniques, where the researcher can begin data collection in a tentative way, return to the subjects for additional information and gradually build the data and concepts and explanation, questionnaire-based surveys require researchers to be specific about their data requirements from the beginning, since they must be committed irrevocably to a questionnaire.

A further key feature of questionnaire-based surveys is that they depend on respondents' own accounts of their behaviour, attitudes or intentions. In some situations – for example, in the study of 'deviant' behaviour or in the study of activities which are socially approved (e.g. cultural activities) or disapproved of (e.g. smoking or drinking) – this can raise some questions about the validity of the approach, since accuracy and honesty of responses may be called into question.

Questionnaire-based surveys are used when quantified information is required concerning a specific population and when individuals' own accounts of their behaviour and/ or attitudes are acceptable as a source of information. Questionnaire surveys nevertheless may be used to gather qualitative as well as quantitative data by the inclusion of open-ended questions, as discussed in Chapter 10 – although this is not a view shared by all researchers (see, for example, Dupuis (1999: 45)).

Questionnaire surveys can be divided into six types, as shown in Figure 5.3 and considered in more detail in Chapters 10 and 16.

Experimental method

The experimental method is the traditional approach of the natural sciences, although 'quasi-experimental' studies are widely used in policy-related areas, as discussed in Chapter 11. The method involves the researcher controlling the environment in order to study the effects of specified variables, typically in a laboratory setting. The principles of the method were discussed in Chapter 2 and are addressed in more detail in Chapter 11.

Type	Alternative name	Description
Household survey	Community survey or social survey	People are selected on the basis of where they live and are interviewed in their home.
Street survey	Quota or intercept survey	People are selected by stopping them in the street, in shopping malls, etc.
Telephone survey	–	Interviews are conducted by telephone.
Online survey	Web-based survey	Respondents complete screen-based questionnaire online.
Mail survey	Postal survey	Questionnaires are sent and returned by mail.
Site or user survey	Visitor survey, customer survey, intercept survey	Visitors at a cultural facility or an event are surveyed on-site.
Captive group survey	–	Members of groups such as classes of school children, members of a club or employees of an organisation are surveyed.

Figure 5.3 Types of questionnaire-based survey

Case study method

A case study involves the study of an example – a case – of the phenomenon being researched. The aim is to seek to understand the phenomenon by studying single examples. Cases can consist of individuals, groups of individuals, communities, organisations or whole countries. Invariably multiple methods are used, including historical/documentary research, the use of secondary data, interviews and, in the case of communities, questionnaire-based or qualitative surveys. The case study method and its use in arts/events research is discussed further in Chapter 12.

Subsidiary/cross-cutting techniques

The somewhat inelegant term 'subsidiary and cross-cutting' is used to describe a number of techniques that are subsidiary to one or more of the major methods discussed above, in that they are a variation on or an application of the major method (e.g. the Delphi technique, which uses questionnaires) or cut across a number of major methods (e.g. action research, which can use any or all of the major methods). The techniques discussed here are listed in Figure 5.4 and discussed in turn below. The brief descriptions presented here do not provide a basis for implementing the various techniques, but they indicate their general nature and possibilities. Guides to further information are provided in the Resources section at the end of the chapter. It should be noted that the emphasis here is on forms of data collection or combined collection and analysis processes. Particular forms of data *analysis* are presented in Part 3 of the book.

Action research

The common image of research is as a detached process reporting objectively on what is discovered. When a researcher is personally committed to the topic under investigation, whether that be self-interest-related, such as the fortunes of a company, or a social cause, like saving the environment, efforts are still generally made to abide by the rules of science, for ethical reasons or because of the general belief that sound research is more likely to be effective in supporting a cause. Nevertheless, some types of research can be deliberately designed to involve the researcher more directly in the topic of study and are intended to be overtly part of the process of bringing about change – such research is termed 'action research'. Typically, action research is also distinguished by being conducted on behalf of, and in association with, one or more organisations, or a group of stakeholders. Indeed, some definitions envisage the action research process as happening within a corporate organisation, with the researcher 'embedded' in the organisation for the duration of the project.

The action research process shown in Figure 5.5 indicates that researchers are involved in the 'action' stages of the process as well as the research stage and there may be various feedback loops in the process as research is conducted to assist the campaign for change and to evaluate outcomes.

There are similarities with the conventional management research process within an organisation, where step 3 is an internal resource allocation and implementation process. It can also be seen as a quasi-experimental process. Action research is not constrained as to

115

Technique	Brief description
Subsidiary and cross-cutting techniques/methods	
Action research	Research committed to social outcomes, typically involving collaboration with a client organisation.
Big data	Analysis of very large electronic/digital data-sets: for example, organisations with a large customer base can analyse data from electronic records of customer activity to reveal patterns of behaviour of use in marketing.
Conjoint analysis/Discrete choice analysis	A process for studying people's choice processes by asking people to express preferences for hypothetical products with different combinations of attributes.
Content analysis	Quantitative study of printed/written documents or static/moving images (see also 'qualitative methods').
Coupon surveys/conversion studies	Analysis of returns from 'special offer', 'two for the price of one', etc. vouchers/ advertisements.
Delphi technique	Process in which a sample of experts responds to questions about future events in repeated rounds, ideally to achieve consensus.
Diary methods	see Time-use surveys.
Discourse analysis	Examination of the ways in which language is used in the treatment of a topic, typically in social/political contexts and/or in the popular and/or academic print and other communications media.
En route/intercept/cordon surveys	Survey conducted with visitors entering, leaving or travelling to or from a site/destination.
Experience sampling method (ESM)	Subjects are 'beeped' or contacted electronically several times a day to record activities/ feelings, etc. as they go about day-to-day activities.
Historical research	Research on past events.
Longitudinal studies	The same sample of subjects is surveyed repeatedly, typically over a number of years.
Mapping techniques	Subjects provide graphic representation of components of a problem/issue/ experience, sometimes collaborative.
Media reader/viewer/ listener surveys	Media report on surveys which readers/listeners have been invited to take part in, typically online or via automated phone-in.
Meta-analysis	Examination and summary of a number of studies on the same topic, typically with a key outcome measure such as a correlation coefficient.
Multiple correspondence analysis/latent class analysis	Analytical techniques used to group subjects on the basis of comparable behaviour patterns, tastes and socio-demographic (lifestyle) characteristics.
Netnography	Research using the internet as data source and/or subject.
Network analysis	Study of links between individuals and/or organisations involved in an activity.
Panel studies	A sample of individuals recruited to a 'panel' who may take part in several surveys over a period of time.
Perceptual mapping	See Mapping techniques.
Projective techniques	Subjects are asked to respond to hypothetical scenarios.
Psychographic/lifestyle studies	Research that gathers data on a wide range of attitudes, values and socio-demographic characteristics and analyses them to determine distinctive psychographic/lifestyle groups or market segments.
Q methodology	Process in which subjects rank scale items depicted on cards.
Quantitative modelling	Quantitative method in which relationships between two or more variables are assessed statistically.
Repertory grid, laddering	Pairs of contrasting descriptors for the phenomenon being studied are elicited from respondents to form *constructs*, and scores on the constructs are analysed to form a perceptual picture. 'Laddering' pursues questions on importance of aspects of an experience to produce a hierarchy of values/motivations.
Scales	Development and use of batteries of 'stimulus items' (statements/ questions, features, etc.) to be responded to via Likert-type scales.

Figure 5.4 Subsidiary, cross-cutting and multiple techniques/methods

Technique	Brief description
Time-use surveys	Surveys in which respondents complete a detailed 1–2-day diary of activities.
Visitor conversation research	In informal spaces (e.g. museums), selected visitors wear microphones so that their discussion of exhibits can be recorded and analysed.
Web-based research	Research on, or using, the internet – see also Netnography above.
Multiple methods	
Triangulation	Two or more methods used to focus on the same phenomenon, providing confirmation or differing insights.
Counting heads	A management task involving various research approaches, needed in situations where usage/visitor numbers are not available from ticket sales.

Figure 5.4 (*continued*)

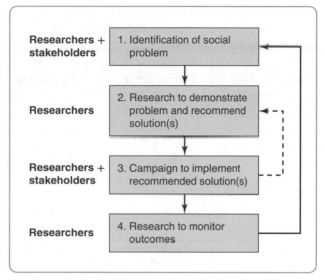

Figure 5.5 Action research process

methods or techniques. There is a tendency to see it as a form of qualitative research, but as Greenwood and Levin state in their introductory text on the subject:

> It is wrong to think of action research as 'qualitative' research, yet a great many conventional researchers and far too many action researchers make this error. … An action research process must use qualitative, quantitative and/or mixed-method techniques wherever and whenever the conditions and subject an action research team deals with require.
>
> (Greenwood and Levin, 2007: 98)

Action research is less usual in the arts/events context than in some areas of social policy, such as housing or ethnic affairs.

Big data

'Big data' is a form of secondary data analysis using large electronic/digital data-sets. Thus, for example, commercial or public organisations with a large customer base, often running into millions, can make use of the data which has accumulated from online and other electronic purchasing records to discover patterns of behaviour and socio-demographic, geographic and temporal relationships that may be of use in marketing (see Case Study 14.5).

One of the market phenomena identified by this research activity is the 'long tail': the observation, which applies particularly to cultural products such as books and recorded music, that, while bestsellers and blockbusters attract most of the publicity, the bulk of the market is accounted for by hundreds or thousands of titles that sell very few copies, and may even be only marginally economic. Thus, for example, Anderson (2011: 121) notes that in 2004, the 420 books which sold over 100,000 copies each in the USA accounted for 100 million sales, but the 1.1 million titles selling 1,000 copies or less each accounted for 230 million sales. Centralised online sales through organisations such as Amazon can result in the compilation and exploitation of data patterns of book purchases. Without knowing why thousands of purchasers of book A often also purchase book B, they can use this information to recommend book B to new purchasers of book A (Mayer-Schönberger and Cukier, 2013: 56). The 15 million books scanned and stored by Google Books have been used to examine cultural trends as revealed by the changing content of books published over a period of time. Michel *et al.* (2011) refer to this sort of analysis as 'culturomics'. Public arts agencies also have customer data and websites but whether they have the awareness or capacity to take advantage of this resource is debatable, as explored in a report by Lilley and Moore (2013).

Big data practices are relatively new and heighten concerns about the privacy implications of the personal data that corporations hold on individuals, raising ethics issues when used for research.

Conjoint analysis

Conjoint analysis is a methodology used to explore people's decision-making processes, such as choosing a film to see, a book to buy or a cultural venue or event to visit. In particular, it seeks to discover how various features of products are evaluated by the consumer and how this evaluation influences choices. One way of doing this would be to examine people's actual selections against the attributes of a range of existing products, and there is research that adopts this approach, but it is a complex and, in terms of data collection, possibly an expensive process. Furthermore, such research would be constrained by existing products and their features and would not include people for whom existing choices are not attractive and have therefore been rejected.

In conjoint analysis subjects are asked to express their preferences among a range of hypothetical products with varying combinations of features. The more distinct features are considered and the more levels or categories exist for each feature, the more combinations there will be for consideration. For example, four features, each with four levels/categories, produces 256 ($4 \times 4 \times 4 \times 4$) different combinations. Selecting combinations for inclusion in a study and analysing the results is the complex mathematical task undertaken by conjoint analysis. The detail is beyond the scope of this book, but further reading is indicated in the Resources section at the end of the chapter and the approach is discussed again in Chapter 11 under the heading of 'Discrete choice experiments'.

Content analysis

In some fields of inquiry the focus of research is textual – for example, the content of organisations' annual reports, politicians' speeches or the coverage of the arts or a major event in the media. The analysis and interpretation of the content of published or unpublished texts is referred to as *content analysis*, often when the analysis is quantitative, or *hermeneutics*, when the analysis is of a more qualitative nature. The technique has not traditionally been widely used in arts/event studies, but with the development of postmodernism and the widening of the scope of text to include a wide variety of cultural products such as company documents, advertising material, websites, letters and social media communications, the approach is attracting increasing attention. Some examples of quantitative studies are listed in the Resources section and qualitative approaches are discussed in Chapter 9.

Coupon surveys/conversion studies

In marketing research use can be made of information from the responses of the public to advertising coupons – that is where the public is invited in an advertisement or other communication to write or telephone for information on a product. The data can be used in research to indicate the level of interest in the product on offer (compared with other products or with the same product in previous periods) and also to show the geographical spread of the interested public. The question then arises as to the extent to which people who respond to such advertising actually become customers. Thus conversion studies are designed to examine the extent to which enquirers convert to become customers (Woodside and Ronkanen, 1994). A more contemporary use of the term 'conversion rate' refers to the rate at which hits on retail websites convert into sales.

Delphi technique

The Delphi technique (named after the classical Greek 'Delphic oracle') is a procedure involving the gathering and analysing of information from a panel of experts on future trends in a particular field of interest. The experts in the field (e.g. theatre, events) complete a questionnaire indicating their views on the likelihood of certain developments taking place in future. These views are then collated and circulated to panel members for further comment, a process that might be repeated a number of times before the final results are collated. The technique is used in some areas of business and technological forecasting, but no published accounts of its use in the arts/events context have been identified. In this book the technique is not examined explicitly, but to some extent it involves questionnaire design and analysis, as covered in Chapters 10 and 16. Literature on the technique is indicated in the Resources section.

Discourse analysis

Discourse analysis is research on the use of language in relation to a topic/issue in popular and/or academic texts and other communications media. The way language is used, consciously or unconsciously, in relation to a phenomenon shapes popular and official conceptualisations of that phenomenon. For example, the public view of the arts is likely to be affected if the term is invariably accompanied by the descriptor 'elite' or 'taxpayer-funded'. The conscious adoption of one term rather than another – for example 'rave' rather than 'dance' – signals an intent on the part of the users. In the organisational context, the process is the stock-in-trade of public relations practitioners or 'spin merchants'. Research on this dimension of human interaction typically involves analysis of media and official broadcast and print material on a topic over a period of time – for example, Jaimangal-Jones's (2012) examination of the media coverage of dance music events.

En route/intercept/cordon surveys

En route surveys (Hurst, 1994) arise in tourism research and so are likely to be relevant to arts/events only in the context of cultural and event tourism. Such surveys, typically for official planning-related purposes, may be conducted in aeroplanes, at airports or while travelling by car (when travellers are waved into lay-bys by police for survey purposes). In this book this type of survey, which invariably involves a questionnaire, is considered to be a special case of site or user surveys, as discussed in Chapter 9. Since respondents are 'intercepted' at or near a destination, site or attraction, the term intercept survey is sometimes used, and if all approaches to the destination, site or attraction are covered, the term cordon survey may be used.

Experience sampling method (ESM)

The ESM was pioneered by Mihaly Csikszentmihalyi and his colleagues at the University of Chicago in 1977 (Csikszentmihalyi and Larson, 1977) and can be seen as a development of the time-budget survey/diary method. Alternative names for the technique are ecological momentary assessment (EMA) (Smyth and Stone, 2003) and ambulatory assessment.

An ESM study typically takes place over a few days, during which, on about eight occasions each day, study participants are alerted by some electronic device – a pager in the early examples, later by watches programmed to 'beep' at certain times and most recently by mobile phone. When alerted, or as soon as practically possible thereafter, the study participant completes a short questionnaire in a booklet that the participant carries at all times, or, in recent versions, responds to questions via text message. Information is gathered on activities being undertaken, where and with whom, and attitudes and feelings. The method has the advantage of recording activities and feelings in real time and in the subject's 'natural' environment, rather than relying on recall at a later date in a different environment. While the amount of information that can be elicited in any one episode is limited, the cumulative amount of information gathered, together with any information included in a preliminary conventional questionnaire, can be substantial.

The research approach made possible by ESM has been characterised as *idiographic*, based on the Greek word *idios*, meaning specific to an individual (Conner *et al.*, 2009). This is in contrast to *nomothetic* research, based on the Greek word *nomos*, meaning law, which seeks to establish general scientific laws of behaviour based on studies of a number of individuals. However, unlike qualitative research, which is often idiographic, ESM is generally quantitative in nature since it gathers data from individuals on repeated occasions.

Further developments in this type of electronically aided research are:

● the Electronically Activated Recorder (EAR) in which the subject wears a small microphone and recording device which is automatically activated for short periods (for example for 30 seconds, 12 times per hour), thus providing a record of the environments the subject experiences and conversational interaction with people – this has been used in psychological research to track social interaction (Mehl *et al.*, 2001) but there are no known examples in the arts/events field;

● digital tracking using Global Positioning Systems, discussed in Chapter 8. The details of the method are not pursued further in this book, but references to examples of its use, generally and in arts/events, are provided in the Resources section.

Historical research

History is, of course, a major discipline with its own approaches to research. Historical research arises in the arts/events environment in at least two contexts: biographical research, discussed as a qualitative approach in Chapter 8, and in case study research, discussed in Chapter 11. It can also be seen as a form of secondary data analysis, since historians are invariably dependent on documents contemporary to a period, which were originally compiled for other purposes. As a discipline, history is part of the humanities, although in the context of arts/events research it clearly extends into the social sciences when history is presented as a partial explanation for contemporary phenomena, for example in research on significant events, such as the Olympic Games, or significant institutions, such as arts councils.

A major preoccupation of scholars in the arts is the topic of public policy, notably state subsidies and promotion of the arts, and the history of this phenomenon in various countries is often the focus of research, as indicated in the Resources section. Compared with the social science literature, in historical literature there is a tendency for the question of method to be played down or taken for granted. While historical accounts are generally conducted in a scholarly manner, with detailed reference to sources, just how the source material has been used and analysed is not always clear: thus there is rarely a 'methods' section in historically based articles. Historical methods are not pursued in this book, but some sources/examples are indicated in the Resources section.

Longitudinal studies

Longitudinal studies involve surveying the same sample of individuals periodically over a number of years (Young *et al.*, 1991). Such studies are expensive, of course, because of the need to keep track of the sample members over the years, and the need to have a large enough sample at the beginning to allow for the inevitable attrition to the sample over time. They are, however, ideal for studying social change and the combined effects of social change and ageing.

Media reader/viewer/listener surveys

Newspapers, magazines and radio and television stations often run opinion poll-type surveys among their readers, viewers or listeners, often web-based. At the local level the public's views on an issue may be canvassed by the inclusion of some form in a newspaper, which readers may fill in and return, and radio and television stations often run 'phone-in' polls on topical issues. The results of these exercises have entertainment value, but should not generally be taken seriously. This is mainly because there is no way of knowing whether either the original population (the readers/listeners/viewers who happen to read, hear or view the item) or the sample of respondents are representative of the population as a whole. In most cases they are decidedly unrepresentative, in that the audiences and readership of particular media outlets tend to have particular socio-economic characteristics and only those with pronounced views, one way or the other, are likely to become involved in the survey process.

One of the largest examples is the 2011 web-based Great British Class Survey, run by the BBC, which attracted a sample of 166,000, of whom 70 per cent were in the professional and managerial occupational classes, compared with a traditionally conducted, demographically representative version of the survey which had a more accurate 29 per cent in those classes and was used to weight the main survey results (Savage *et al.*, 2013: 224). These exercises should not, of course, be confused with surveys sponsored by the media but conducted by reputable survey companies, such as Newspoll or AC Nielsen.

Meta-analysis

Meta-analysis – or systematic reviewing – combines features of a literature review and secondary data analysis and typically involves a quantitative appraisal of the findings of a number of research projects on the same topic. The technique is suitable for the sort of research where findings are directly comparable from one study to another – for example, when the key findings are expressed in terms of correlation and regression coefficients between particular variables (see Chapter 17). In a meta-analysis, the reported findings of a large number of individual research projects in the same area provide the basis for further exploration and analysis of the area. Typically, because many studies are involved and must be compared on a common basis, only relatively simple relationships can be examined. Examples of meta-analysis in the arts/events area are given in the Resources section.

A less formal approach to cross-project appraisal is the consensus study in which a group of researchers reviews the accumulated research on a topic and seeks to reach a consensus on the state of knowledge, the most well known of these in recent years being the reviews of the United Nations Intergovernmental Panel on Climate Change (2007). Meta-analysis is discussed further in Chapter 6.

Multiple classification analysis/latent class analysis

Multiple classification analysis (MCA) and latent class analysis are analytical techniques used to group subjects on the basis of comparable behaviour patterns, tastes and socio-demographic (lifestyle) characteristics. They are similar to cluster and factor analysis (see Chapter 17), but do not require quantitative variables. They have been used extensively in analysis of cultural participation patterns and their relationship to class and lifestyle, most notable in the work of Bourdieu (1984). Examples are listed in the Resources section and they are discussed further in Chapter 17.

Netnography

The internet, and social networks in particular, are increasingly significant as means of communication. They are therefore key potential sources of information about people's attitudes, values, tastes and behaviour which are of interest to marketers and social and cultural researchers. A set of practices and associated literature has grown up in this area, referred to as *netnography* or *virtual research*. Sources are indicated in the Resources section.

Network analysis

Many human activities operate through networks involving nodes and links between them, including transport systems, electricity supply systems and telecommunications. A science has developed around this idea and has been used to optimise the design of networks. Figure 5.6 shows a simple network represented in analogue and digital format, with the numbers indicating the size of the flows between the nodes (e.g. traffic flows, financial flows, communication). Analysis can be confined to graphical format and can involve qualitative approaches, but it is clear that this situation lends itself to mathematical analysis, which is

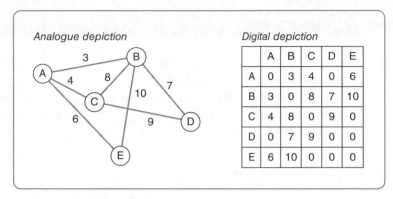

Figure 5.6 A simple network

not pursued here. In terms of data collection, the method involves the identification of the relevant nodes (organisations, destinations) in the system and measuring the extent of links between them. The approach has similarities to the notion of *sociometry* as used in psycho-therapy and education research (see Dayton, 2005; Oppenheim, 2000: 254–259).

Major arts/events, particularly multi-component events such as arts festivals or the Olympic Games, clearly involve networks, including the major sponsoring organisations, individual event organisers and numerous organisations in the host community (Wäsche and Woll, 2010). Everyday arts/events activities also involve networks, among individuals and groups. The phenomenon of the social networking website is the latest manifestation of this and indeed, when network analysis is applied at the individual and small-group level, it is referred to as *social network analysis*. Surveys of leisure facility and service users over many years have illustrated the importance of friendship networks when they have discovered that word of mouth is a far more significant source of information for most people than any form of advertising. Social network analysis is not common in the arts/events area specifically, but has been explored in the event management context by Sallent *et al.* (2011) and in the general leisure context by Stokowski (1994; Stokowski and Lee, 1991).

Panel studies

Market research companies often maintain panels of individuals for some of their surveys. Panels are made up of a representative cross-section of the public who agree to be on call for a series of surveys over a period of time. Often some financial reward is paid to panel members, but this cost is offset by the savings in not having to select and contact new samples of respondents for every survey. While managing such panels presents particular challenges, the range of survey methods which can be used with panels – telephone, web-based, mail or face-to-face interview – is the same as for normal one-off samples. Panel studies can therefore be seen as a particular form of household questionnaire survey.

Perceptual mapping

One of the issues in arts/events planning and marketing is the extent to which the public are well informed about available facilities and services. This is partly related to information coming through the media, formal marketing activities and personal networks, but can also relate to people's spatial perception of the neighbourhood, city or region in which they live.

For example, people are likely to be familiar with their immediate neighbourhood and the route to their place of work or education, but are likely to be less familiar with areas on the other side of town. This can apply particularly to people without cars, notably young people and the elderly. Information on people's 'perceptual space' can be elicited by inviting them to draw 'perceptual maps' of their city.

The idea of spatial perception and mapping can be extended to mental processes, so that the process becomes similar to the development of conceptual frameworks, concept maps and culture maps, as discussed in Chapters 3 and 14.

Projective techniques

Projective techniques might be termed 'what if?' techniques, in that they involve subjects responding to hypothetical – projected – situations. For example, subjects might be asked to indicate how they might spend a particular sum of money if given a free choice, or how they might spend additional leisure time if it were made available, or they might be invited to respond to photographs of particular facilities. While the technique can become elaborate and specialised, in this book it is considered to be an extension of questionnaire-based surveys and possibly of focus-group interviews – the discrete choice experiment technique discussed in Chapter 11 is an example of its use.

Psychographic/lifestyle research

Psychographic research, as discussed in Chapter 2, involves gathering data on a wide range of attitudes and socio-demographic characteristics of people and analysing the data to establish groupings or market segments with common characteristics, typically using statistical techniques such as factor and cluster analysis (discussed in Chapter 17). A number of commercial market research or survey/consultant organisations offer psychographic/lifestyle systems to clients to classify survey respondents into segments seen as more meaningful than those based on the usual age, gender and social class.

- The VALS (Values, Attitudes and Lifestyles) typology, developed in the United States, classifies people into nine segments, as shown in Figure 5.7. This system has been widely used in market research.

- The ACORN (A Classification of Residential Neighbourhoods) was developed in Britain by the commercial survey company CACI and is based on socio-demographic data from census collection areas (see Chapter 7), so since it does not contain attitude data it must be classified as a lifestyle rather than a psychographic system. It has five segments divided into 17 sub-segments, as shown in Figure 5.7, and has been used in leisure research, notably in the annual Active People Survey, as discussed in Chapter 7.

Q methodology

Q methodology was developed in the 1930s by physicist/psychologist William Stephenson to examine people's subjective opinions of phenomena. It involves five steps:

1. Definition of the 'concourse', the scope of the phenomenon to be studied – typically in the form of a set of attitude statements (see Chapter 10), but sometimes verbal or photographic descriptions.

VALS*	ACORN†	
1 Survivor 2 Sustainer 3 Belonger	1 Wealth achievers	A Wealthy executives B Affluent greys (older people) C Flourishing (well-off) families
4 Emulator 5 Achiever 6 I-Am-Me	2 Urban prosperity	D Prosperous professionals E Educated urbanites (young urban professionals) F Aspiring singles (mainly urban area students)
7 Experiential 8 Socially Conscious 9 Integrated	3 Comfortably off	G Starting out (young couples) H Secure families I Settled suburbia (older couples in suburbs) J Prudent pensioners
	4 Moderate means	K Asian communities L Post-industrial families (older skilled) M Blue-collar roots (manual workers)
	5 Hard-pressed	N Struggling (low-income) families O Burdened singles (elderly and single parents) P High-rise hardship Q Inner-city adversity

Figure 5.7 Examples of psychographic/lifestyle categories

*Values, Attitudes and Lifestyles: Strategic Business Insights (2009).
†A Classification of Residential Neighbourhoods: CACI Ltd (2006).
Examples of the use of psychographic/lifestyle segmentation in the arts/events sector are listed in the Resources section.

2. Development of the 'Q-sample' or 'Q-set' of stimulus items – typically a set of cards, each containing one of the statements/labels/photographs.

3. Selection of the 'person-sample', 'P-sample' or 'P-set' – the sample of individuals to be involved in the study.

4. Q-sorting – individuals sort the cards into piles arranged along a spectrum, for example from strongly agree to strongly disagree, scored as in a Likert scale (see Chapter 10). Subjects are required to arrange cards on a template in the shape of a bell-shaped 'normal curve' (as shown in Figure 17.1a).

5. Analysis and interpretation – this involves factor analysis of the data (see Chapter 17) to discover themes.

Computer software packages, such as 'PQ Method', are available to analyse the data.

Quantitative modelling

The techniques discussed in this chapter tend to be distinguished primarily by their data-collection procedures and in some cases also by their data-analysis procedures. Quantitative modelling is distinguished by an approach to theory and data analysis: the data used are quantitative but may have been collected by one or more of a variety of methods (e.g. observation, questionnaires, documentary records, experiment). The idea of quantitative modelling is discussed briefly in Chapter 3, where it is noted that hypotheses concerning the relationships between variables may be expressed and tested in the form of models/equations. This approach to research is considered further in Chapter 17, particularly in connection with the analysis procedures of linear and multiple regression.

Friendly					Threatening
Cool					Uncool
Expensive					Cheap
Etc.					

Figure 5.8 Repertory grid: example

Repertory grid

The repertory grid technique was developed by psychologist George Kelly in the 1950s and is used from time to time in arts/events research. It can be seen as a formalisation and quantification of the conceptual form of perceptual mapping. Research subjects are asked to indicate a range of qualities of the phenomenon being studied and then the opposite of that quality – for example friendly–threatening; cool–uncool; expensive–cheap. A number of these bipolar constructs are elicited (typically up to about 20) and presented in a grid, as shown in Figure 5.8. Subjects then indicate on the grid where the study object fits on each construct, for example for the first construct, whether it is closer to the friendly end or the threatening end. This information can be scored and analysed using graphic and/or statistical analyses such as factor analysis (see Chapter 17) at the individual level and/or collectively.

Scales

A scale is a numerical index used to measure concepts that are generally not intrinsically quantitative. Typically subjects are asked to respond to questions on a number of factors using rating scales and the scores are combined to produce a scale or index of the phenomenon of interest. In Chapter 10 the development and use of customised scales in questionnaires is discussed, but it is quite common for researchers to make use of standardised scales that have been developed by others. The advantage of the use of existing scales is that researchers are not continually 'reinventing the wheel' by devising their own measure of a particular phenomenon. Widely used scales have generally been subject to considerable testing to ensure validity – that is, they measure what they are intended to measure. Further, the use of common measures facilitates comparability between studies. The disadvantage is, of course, that any fault in the scale validity may be replicated across many studies and a fixed scale may not fully reflect different socio-economic environments or change over time.

The use of such scales is widespread, particularly in psychology and related disciplines, the most well known being personality indicators, such as the Myers–Briggs personality scale. The *Marketing Scales Handbook*, published in a number of volumes by the American Marketing Association (Bruner and Hensel, 1992), lists hundreds of scales used in marketing research, most relating to generic topics, such as consumer motivation and attitudes, but others relating to specific settings. A selection of relevance to arts/events is listed in Figure 5.9.

Time-use surveys

There is a long tradition of investigating people's allocation of time between such categories as paid work, domestic work, sleep and leisure, including arts/events (Pentland *et al.*, 1999; Szalai, 1972). Some of the early studies were sponsored by radio broadcasting organisations interested in learning about listening habits – for example, those sponsored by the BBC in Britain in the 1930s (Harvey and Pentland, 1999: 5–6). Such studies involve survey respondents keeping a detailed diary of activity, typically for one or two days.

Listed in Bruner *et al. (2001)*
Involvement (televised soccer match) (217)
Pressure to be thin (259)
Quality of service (stadium) (285)
Satisfaction (with health club) (307)
Sensation seeking (323)
Service quality (health club) (345)
Other examples
Arts Audience Experience Index: Radbourne *et al.* (2010)
Festival quality: Tkaczynski *et al.* (2010)
Festival social impact: Woosnam *et al.* (2013)
Heritage: service quality: Frochot *et al.* (2000)
Life Satisfaction Index: Neugarten *et al.* (1961)
Locus of Control Scale: Levenson (1974)
Museum service quality: Raajpoot *et al.* (2010)
Personality of performing arts venues: Ouellet *et al.* (2008)

Figure 5.9 Scales for arts/events-related topics

Time-use surveys are conducted periodically in most economically developed countries and inform discussion on such issues as mass media use and work–life balance. While a continuous one-day diary is the most common, shorter and intermittent periods can also be used, as illustrated by the ESM discussed above. One arts-related project involved people recording diary-type accounts of information-seeking activity during the course of a day (Elsweiler *et al.*, 2011). Examples of studies, which invariably include data on arts/events, are provided in the Resources section. Time-use or time-budget research is basically a special case of the household survey and some reference is made to it in that context in Chapter 10.

Visitor conversation research

In the context of the museum as a learning institution, researchers have sought to explore the extent to which visitors are engaging and absorbing the educational message by inviting selected visitors to wear microphones so that their within-group discussions can be recorded and analysed. The technique typically involves interviews before and/or following the visit and researchers track the subjects' route and stopping points so that the audio-recording can be linked with appropriate exhibits.

Web-based research

Since the internet, and the social network phenomenon in particular, are increasingly significant as means of communication, they have become potential sources of information about people's attitudes, values, tastes and behaviour. A set of practices and associated literature has grown up in this area, referred to as netnography or virtual research, noted above. Research on websites themselves and on their users can also be quantitative. Sources and examples are indicated in the Resources section.

Multiple methods

We have discussed mixed-methods research above, in which two or more distinct methods are used in a single project, based on the requirements of the various components of the project.

Here we discuss research methods which themselves involve the use of more than one technique. Two multi-method situations are discussed here: triangulation and counting heads. The case study method is also a multi-method approach, but is considered a primary method in this book, so is discussed separately above and in Chapter 12.

Triangulation

Triangulation gets its name from the land-surveying method of fixing the position of an object by measuring it from two different positions, with the object of study being the third point of the triangle. In research, the triangulation method involves the use of more than one research approach in a single study to gain a broader or more complete understanding of the issues being investigated. The methods used are often complementary in that the weaknesses of one approach are complemented by the strengths of another. Triangulation often utilises both qualitative and quantitative approaches in the same study. Duffy (1987: 131) has identified four different ways that triangulation can be used in research, namely:

- analysing data in more than one way;
- using more than one sampling strategy;
- using different interviewers, observers and analysts in the one study;
- using more than one methodology to gather data.

If triangulation methods are to be used in a study, the approaches taken will depend on the imagination and the experience of the researcher. However, it is important that the research question is clearly focused and not confused by the methodology adopted, and that the methods are chosen in accordance with their relevance to the topic. In particular, the rationale for using triangulation should be outlined in reporting the research. The possible weaknesses of one method and the ways in which the additional method has been used to overcome such a weakness should be explained. This is clearly relevant to the issue of validity and reliability discussed in Chapter 2.

Often triangulation is claimed in a study because more than one data source and/or analytical method has been used to address different aspects of the research question, or even different research questions. However, it is when the different data/methods address the same question that true triangulation can be said to have occurred. Figure 5.10 presents an example where four data-collection methods are used to address two research questions. A research report on a project where triangulation is claimed should therefore compare and contrast the findings from the multiple methods. Whether the multiple methods produce similar or different findings should then be an issue for discussion.

Counting heads

In virtually all arts/events management/policy contexts there is a requirement for information on visitor numbers for planning and management purposes. This calls for what is colloquially referred to as 'counting heads' or, in seated venues, counting 'bums on seats'. In many cases the required information is generated automatically by the ticket sales process. But there are also situations where ticket numbers are not available, for example free outdoor events and situations where bookings are made on behalf of a club. In these cases a variety of data-collection methods may be available from which one or more may be selected. The methods/sources can be divided into administrative, survey-based and direct counts.

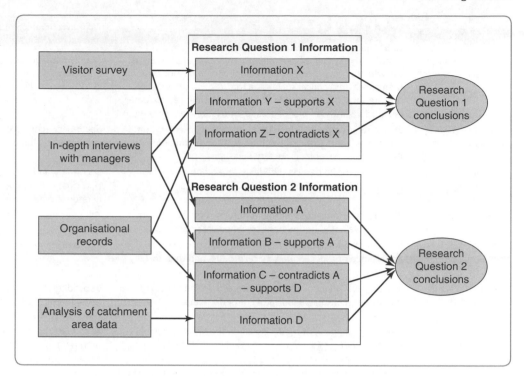

Figure 5.10 Triangulation

Thus, assembling data concerning one venue or event involves consideration of methods addressed in a number of the chapters in Part 2, particularly Chapters 7, 8 and 10. This issue is addressed initially in Chapter 7, and information provided in Figures 7.2 and 7.3 is cross-referenced in Chapters 8 and 10.

Policy/management-related research-based techniques

All of the above approaches and concepts are academically-based. While all of these also apply in various ways to research conducted in policy or management contexts, the latter have given rise to a range of research approaches, which are listed in Figure 5.11, with brief descriptions and an indication of the main data-collection methods used in their conduct. They are not discussed in detail, but examples arise from time to time in the Resources sections of later chapters.

Choosing methods

The process of choosing appropriate methods for a research task is part of the whole process of planning and designing a research project, as discussed in Chapter 3. There are a number of considerations to bear in mind. These are listed in Figure 5.12 and are discussed in turn below:

Approach/ technique	Description	Main data-collection and/or analysis methods
Balanced scorecard analysis	A structured system of performance measures applied across the whole of an organisation, beginning with mission/vision, then specifying 'critical success factors' (CSFs), then metrics for four facets for each CSF: financial performance, customer perspective, internal processes and innovation and learning.	Mainly management-generated data from the organisation, but could also involve survey results.
Cost–benefit analysis	Evaluation of a project (building, programme, organisation, service) by comparison of the total costs and total benefits using, where possible, monetary measures.	Secondary economic data and surveys of customers.
Demand forecasting	Estimating future participation levels, based on a variety of assumptions and using a variety of techniques.	Secondary and survey-based participation, demographic and economic data.
Evidence-based policy	The idea that public/government policies should be based on, and evaluated on the basis of, empirical evidence.	All, but often mainly quantitative.
Importance-performance analysis	Service/product users/visitors are asked to scale the importance of aspects of a service/product and then to scale the actual performance experienced.	Customer surveys.
Key performance indicators (KPIs)	The success/failure of policies is assessed on the basis of a number of measurable indicators of performance.	Secondary data (e.g. sales, attendances, profit) or survey-based (e.g. customer satisfaction).
Logic model	Rational management model based on the sequence: initial conditions, needs, problems, resources; action; outcomes; impacts.	Secondary/management-generated data, possibly surveys.
Market segmentation	Actual and potential customers for a product or service are grouped into 'segments' on the basis of product preferences and socio-demographic characteristics.	Mostly customer surveys, also use of customer purchasing patterns.
Performance evaluation	Assessment of the success or failure of an organisation, unit or programme on the basis of outcomes compared with stated objectives, often using KPIs.	As for KPIs.
Resource auditing/ mapping	Compiling a register/inventory of existing or potential resources (e.g. cultural or heritage resources) of an area, for public information or as input to a policy process. See 'mapping' above.	Use of secondary sources, documents, internet, observation, organisational survey.
SERVQUAL	Short for 'service quality': similar to importance-performance analysis, but users compare service quality expectations with actual quality experienced.	Customer surveys.

Figure 5.11 Policy/management-related research approaches/techniques

- the research question or hypothesis;
- previous research;
- data availability/access;
- resources;
- time and timing;
- validity, reliability, trustworthiness;
- generalisability;
- ethics;
- uses/users of the findings.

Figure 5.12 Considerations in selecting a research method

The research question or hypothesis

Much of the decision on how to research a topic is bound up in the basic research question or hypothesis. As discussed in Chapter 3, the research question can take a variety of forms, but generally it will point the researcher in the direction of certain data sources – for example, in relation to participants, employees, customers or organisations. Certain types of data also suggest certain types of analysis.

Previous research

If the proposed research is closely keyed into the literature and previous research, then the methods used in earlier research are likely to influence the choice of methods. The aim may be to replicate the methodology used in previous studies to achieve comparability, to improve on the methods used, or to deliberately adopt a contrasting methodology that may be capable of revealing new insights.

Data availability/access

In some cases an obvious existing source of data presents itself and may even have prompted the research in the first place – termed *opportunistic research* in Chapter 2. For example:

● a set of archives of an organisation can provide the basis for historical research;

● official survey-based data which have been published but only superficially analysed could be analysed in more depth;

● access to a sample of people, such as the workforce or customer base of a company, members of a club or members of an informal interest group can be seen as a research opportunity too good to miss.

In other cases lack of access shapes the research – for example, ethical or practical issues may preclude some research on children, so data may have to be gathered from parents.

Resources

Clearly the resources of staff and money will have a major effect on the type and scale of the research to be conducted.

Time and timing

Time and timing is always a limitation. Most research projects have a time limit. Timing in relation to external events or routines is also often a factor: for example, research using the current year's attendance data must be completed quickly if it is to be used to influence next year's strategic planning, while empirical research on events is constrained by their timing.

Validity, reliability, trustworthiness and generalisability

Validity, reliability, trustworthiness and generalisability are key considerations in all research. As discussed in Chapter 2:

● *validity* is the extent to which the data collected truly reflect the phenomenon being studied;

● *reliability* is the extent to which research findings would be the same if the research were to be repeated at a later date, or with a different sample of subjects;

- *trustworthiness* is sometimes used in place of the above in qualitative research;
- *generalisability* refers to the extent to which the results of the research findings apply to other subjects, other groups and other conditions: the extent to which this is required as an outcome of the research will influence the choice of method.

Ethics

Ethical issues also limit choices of research method. Reference has already been made to ethical issues surrounding research on children; further examples of ethical issues are discussed in Chapter 4.

Uses/users of the findings

The uses and users of the research are often taken for granted, but they are an important factor in shaping research. If substantial investment or changes in practice will depend on the results of the research, then a more extensive and thorough project will be required than if the research is used only to generate ideas for further exploration. When life and death issues are at stake – for example in medical research on the effects of a treatment for a disease – much more precision is needed in the results than if, for example, a company merely wishes to know the socio-economic characteristics of its customers for marketing purposes.

Summary

This chapter complements Chapter 3 in setting out in brief the range of research methods available to the arts/events researcher. It reinforces the message of Chapter 3, that research methods should ideally be selected on the basis of their suitability to answer the research questions posed, not on the basis of some prior preference for a particular method. Initially the 'major' research methods are reviewed, namely:

- scholarship;
- 'just thinking';
- the use of existing information – the literature and secondary data;
- observation;
- qualitative methods;
- questionnaire-based surveys;
- case study method;
- experimental method.

The first two are included to emphasise that research is not just about deploying techniques but also involves being well informed about the field and thinking about the problems and issues being researched in theoretical and practical terms. The other major methods foreshadow subsequent chapters, which deal with them in detail.

The middle section of the chapter briefly introduces a number of approaches and techniques that are subsidiary to one or more of the major methods, in that they are a variation on or an application of the major method, or cut across a number of the major methods. The approaches and techniques covered are:

- action research;
- big data;
- conjoint analysis;
- content analysis;
- coupon surveys/conversion studies;
- Delphi technique;
- experience sampling method;
- en route/intercept surveys;
- historical research;
- longitudinal studies;
- media reader/viewer/listener surveys;
- meta-analysis;

- netnography;
- network analysis;
- panel studies;
- perceptual mapping;
- projective techniques;
- psychographic/lifestyle research;
- Q methodology;
- quantitative modelling;
- repertory grid;
- scales;
- time-use surveys;
- visitor conversation analysis.

Consideration is also given to multiple methods, with a discussion of the concepts of triangulation and counting heads. The chapter also briefly refers to a range of policy- and management-related research-based techniques.

Finally, factors to be considered in selecting research methods are examined.

TEST QUESTIONS

1. What is 'scholarship'?
2. Define each of the following:
    (a) Action research
    (b) Big data
    (c) Conjoint analysis
    (d) Content analysis
    (e) Coupon surveys/conversion studies
    (f) The Delphi technique
    (g) Discourse analysis
    (h) En route/intercept surveys
    (i) Experience sampling method (ESM)
    (j) Historical research
    (k) Longitudinal studies
    (l) Media reader/viewer/listener surveys
    (m) Meta-analysis

    (n) Netnography
    (o) Network analysis
    (p) Panel studies
    (q) Perceptual mapping
    (r) Projective techniques
    (s) Psychographic/lifestyle research
    (t) Q methodology
    (u) Quantitative modelling
    (v) Repertory grid
    (w) Scales
    (x) Time-use surveys
    (y) Visitor conversation analysis

3. What is triangulation and why is it used in research?
4. What does counting heads involve?

EXERCISES

Exercises involving the major methods and subsidiary and cross-cutting methods arise in the subsequent chapters.

Resources

Websites

● Experience sampling method: Society for Ambulatory Assessment: www.ambulatory-assessment.org; software sites:

  ○ www.experience-sampling.org
  ○ http://myexperience.sourceforge.net
  ○ www.cfs.purdue.edu/mfri/pages/PMAT/

● Meta-analysis: the Cochrane Collaboration: www.cochrane.org

● Q methodology: www.qmethod.org/about.php

● Time use:

  ○ Centre for Time Use Research, USA: www.timeuse.org
  ○ International Association for Time Use Research: www.iatur.org

Publications

Topic/method	References
Major methods	See Resources sections of Chapters 6–12
Action research	Greenwood and Levin (2007), McNiff and Whitehead (2002), Reason and Bradbury (2001), Tzibazi (2013), Rydzik et al. (2013)
Balanced scorecard analysis	Weinstein and Bukovinsky (2009)
Big data	Boyd and Crawford (2012), Anderson (2011), Clifton (2012), Hjorth-Andersen (2007), Mayer-Schönberger and Cukier (2013), Michel et al. (2011)
Conjoint analysis	Caldwell and Coshall (2003), Cosper and Kinsley (1984), Willis and Snowball (2009); see also Discrete Choice Analysis, Chapter 11
Correspondence analysis	See: Multiple correspondence analysis
Counting heads	Gartner and Hunt (1988); see Chapter 8
Cultural mapping	See Mapping
Delphi technique	General: Hsu and Sandford (2007), Landeta (2006)
Diary methods	See time-use studies and Bolger, Davis and Rafael (2003)
Discourse analysis	Gee (2010), Frohman (1994); dance events: Jaimangal-Jones (2012); critical discourse analysis: Locke (2004)
En route surveys	Gartner and Hunt (1988), Hurst (1994)
Experience sampling method (ESM)	Connor et al. (2009), Csikszentmihalyi and Larson (1977), Hektner, Schmidt and Csikszentmihalyi (2006)
Historical research	Australian cultural policy: Stevenson (2000); Edinburgh Festival: Bruce (1975); museums: Bennett (1995)
SERVQUAL and Importance-performance analysis	General: Martilla and James (1977); Parasuraman et al. (1985), Veal (2010: Ch. 13); arts venues: Williams (1998); festivals: Baker and Draper (2013); Tkaczynski and Stokes (2010); museums: Carmen de Rojas and Carmen Camarero (2006); Lin (2009)

Laddering	General/marketing: Reynolds and Gutman (1988), Saaka, Sidon and Blake (2004) Museums in the leisure market: Guintcheva and Passebois (2009) Museum visiting: Jensen-Verbeke and Van Rokem (1996)
Latent class analysis	Cultural tourism: Burke *et al*. (2010), Van der Ark and Richards (2006), Van Rees *et al*. (1999)
Logic model	Hulett (1997), Wright (2007), Wyatt Knowlton and Phillips (2012); on case study method: Yin (2014: 155–163)
Longitudinal studies	Social sciences: Young *et al*. (1991); cultural participation: Konlaan *et al*. (2000)
Mapping	Cultural mapping: Evans and Foord (2008: 78–90), Lee and Gilmore (2012), British Council (2010) Creative industries: Higgs and Cunningham (2008) Mind mapping: Buzan (1994), Crowe and Sheppard (2012) Visitor behaviour: Nurse Rainbolt *et al*. (2012) Visitor meaning: Brown (2011), Stylianou-Lambert (2009)
Mental maps	See Mapping
Meta-analysis	General: Card (2011), Glass, McGaw and Smith (1981) Cultural heritage: Noonan (2003)
Methodological debate	Bryman (1984), Bryman and Bell (2003: 465–478), Dupuis (1999), Borman *et al*. (1986), Krenz and Sax (1986)
Mixed methods	Creswell (2009), Howe (1988), Mertens (2009), Teddlie and Tashakori (2009), Tashakkori and Creswell (2007), Tashakkori and Teddlie (2003); UK cultural participation patterns: Bennett *et al*. (2009); cultural tourism: Collins *et al*. (2010)
Multiple correspondence analysis (MCA)	Bennett *et al*. (2009), Bourdieu (1984), Coulangeon (2013), Nantel and Colbert (1992), Roose *et al*. (2012)
Netnography	General: Kozinets (2009); Marketing: Xun and Reynolds (2010); Cultural preferences: Lewis *et al*. (2008); TV watching/cultures: Elsweiler *et al*. (2011), Kozinets (1997); Pop music concert attendance: Beaven and Laws (2007), Perkins (2012); Twitter and marketing: Asur and Huberman (2010)
Network analysis	Amateur artists: Bendle and Patterson (2008); Event management: Sallent *et al*. (2011); Cultural preferences: Lewis *et al*. (2008); Cultural tourism: Binkhorst *et al*. (2010); Design industry: Joel (2009); Facebook, use of: Miller (2011); Women's cultural participation: Kane (2004); Leisure: Stokowski (1994); Sociometry: Oppenheim (2000: 254–255)
Observation	See Chapter 8 Resources
Panel surveys	Kasprzyk *et al*. (1989), Rose (2000)
Participant observation	See Chapters 9 and 15 Resources
People meters	Barnes and Thompson (1994); other audience research media: Patriarche *et al*. (2014)
Perceptual mapping	See Mapping
Projective techniques	Semeonoff (1976), Oppenheim (1992: Chapter 12), Bekkers (2010)
Psychographic/lifestyle research	General: Strategic Business Insights (2009), CACI Ltd (2006); arts, Australia: Australia Council (2010)
Q methodology	Principles: McKeown and Thomas (1988)
Qualitative methods	See Chapters 9 and 15 References
Quantitative modelling	Demand for arts centres: Radbourne (2001) Music events: Hand (2009)

Topic/method	References
Questionnaire-based surveys	General: Platt (1986); see Chapter 10; examples of national surveys: see Chapter 7
Repertory grid	General: Kelly (1955); arts examples: Caldwell and Coshall (2002), Rayment (2000) – see also laddering
Scales	See Figure 5.9
Segmentation	Cultural heritage (cathedral) visitors: Francis *et al*. (2010) Cultural tourists: Dolnicar (2002); Event visitors (airshow): Warnick *et al*. (2011); Museum visitors: Hooper-Greenhill (1995); Music festival visitors: Bowen and Daniels (2005); Performing arts audiences: Nevin and Cavusgil (1987); Theatre: Guillon (2011); Zoo visitors and general: Dawson and Jensen (2011)
Surveys	See Questionnaire-based surveys
Textual analysis	General: Altheide (2000), Prior (2003), music events: Jaimangal-Jones (2012)
Time-use studies	General: Szalai (1972), Pentland *et al*. (1999); Arts-related: Elsweiler *et al*. (2011); Leisure: Zuzanek and Veal (1998)
Triangulation	Bryman and Bell (2003: 482–484), Duffy (1987), Findahl *et al*. (2014), Puczko *et al*. (2010); more advanced/critical discussion: Blaikie (1991)
Visitor conversation research	A number of examples in: Leinhardt, Crowley and Knutson (2002)
Web-based research	See Netnography

References

Altheide, D. L. (2000) Tracking discourse and qualitative document analysis. *Poetics*, 27(3), 287–299.

Anderson, C. (2011) *The Long Tail: How Endless Choice is Creating Unlimited Demand,* Revised Edition. New York: Random House.

Asur, S. and Huberman, B. A. (2010) *Predicting the Future with Social Media*. On-line paper, Palo Alto, CA: Hewlett-Packard, available at: www.hpl.hp.com/research/scl/papers/socialmedia/socialmedia.pdf

Australia Council (2010) *More than Bums on Seats – Australian Participation in the Arts*. Sydney: Australia Council, available at: www.australiacouncil.gov.au

Baker, K. L., and Draper, J. (2013) Importance-performance analysis of the attributes of a cultural festival. *Journal of Convention and Event Tourism*, 14(1), 104–123.

Barnes, B. E., and Tompson, L. M. (1994) Power to the people (meter): audience measurement technology and media specialization. In J. S. Ettema & D. C. Whitney (eds), *Audiencemaking* Thousand Oaks, CA: Sage, pp. 75–94.

Beaven, Z. and Laws, C. (2007) 'Never let me down again': loyal customer attitudes towards ticket distribution channels for live music events: a netnographic exploration of the US leg of the Depeche Mode 2005–2006 world tour. *Managing Leisure*, 12(2), 120–142.

Bekkers, R. (2010) Who gives what when? A scenario study of intentions to give time and money. *Social Science Research*, 39(4), 369–381.

Bendle, L. J. and Patterson, I. (2008) Network density, centrality and communication in a serious leisure social world. *Annals of Leisure Research*, 11(1–2), 1–19.

Bennett, T. (1995) *The Birth of the Museum: History, Theory, Politics*. London: Routledge.

Bennett, T., Savage, M., Silva, E., Warde, A., Gayo-Cal, M. and Wright, D. (2009) *Culture, Class, Distinction*. London: Routledge.

Binkhorst, E., Den Dekker, T. and Melkert, M. (2010) Blurring boundaries in cultural tourism research. In G. Richards and W. Munsters (eds), *Cultural Tourism Research Methods*. Wallingford: CABI, pp. 41–51.

Blaikie, N. (1991) A critique of the use of triangulation in social research. *Quality and Quantity*, 25(2), 115–136.

Bolger, N., Davis, A., & Rafael, E. (2003) Diary methods: capturing life as it is lived. *Annual Review of Psychology*, 54(4), 579–616.

Borman, K. M., LeCompte, M. D. and Goetz, J. P. (1986) Ethnographic and qualitative research design and why it doesn't work. *American Behavioral Scientist*, 30(1), 42–57.

Bourdieu, P. (1984) *Distinction: A Social Critique of the Judgement of Taste*. London: Routledge and Kegan Paul.

Bowen, H. E. and Daniels, M. (2005) Does music matter? Motivations for attending a music festival. *Event Management*, 9(2), 155–164.

Boyd, D., and Crawford, K. (2012) Critical questions for big data: provocations for a cultural, technological, and scholarly phenomenon. *Information, Communication & Society*, 15(5), 662–679.

British Council (2010) *Mapping the Creative Industries: A Toolkit*. London: British Council.

Brown, P. (2011) Us and them: who benefits from experimental exhibition making? *Museum Management and Curatorship*, 26(2), 129–148.

Bruce, G. (1975) *Festival in the North: the Story of the Edinburgh Festival*. London: Robert Hale.

Bruner, G. C. and Hensel, P. J. (1992) *Marketing Scales Handbook: A Compilation of Multi-Item Measures*. Chicago, IL: American Marketing Association.

Bruner, G. C., James, K. E. and Hensel, P. J. (2001) *Marketing Scales Handbook: A Compilation of Multi-Item Measures, Volume III*. Chicago, IL: American Marketing Association.

Bryman, A. (1984) The debate about quantitative and qualitative research: a question of method or epistemology? *British Journal of Sociology*, 35(1), 75–92.

Bryman, A. and Bell, E. (2003) Breaking down the quantitative/qualitative divide, and Combining quantitative and qualitative research. Chapters 21–22 of *Business Research Methods*. Oxford: Oxford University Press, pp. 465–494.

Burke, P., Burton, C., Huybers, T., Islam. M., Louviere, J., & Wise, C, (2010) Museum visitation: a scale adjusted latent class model. *Tourism Analysis*, 15(1), 47–165.

Buzan, T. (1994) *The Mind Map Book: How to Use Radiant Thinking to Maximise your Brain's Untapped Potential*. New York: Dutton.

CACI Ltd (2006) *ACORN User Guide*. London: CACI Ltd, available at: www.caci.co.uk/financialacorn.aspx

Caldwell, N. and Coshall, J. (2002) Measuring brand associations for museums and galleries using repertory grid analysis. *Management Decision*, 40(4), 383–392.

Caldwell, N., & Coshall, J. (2003) Tourists' preference structures for London's Tate Modern gallery: the implications for strategic marketing. *Journal of Travel and Tourism Marketing*, 14(2), 23–45.

Card, N. A. (2011) *Applied Meta-Analysis for Social Science Research*. New York: Guilford Press.

Carmen de Rojas, M. del, & Carmen Camarero, M. del (2006) Experience and satisfactions of visitors to museums and cultural exhibitions. *International Review on Public and Non-Profit Marketing*, 3(1), 49–65.

Clifton, B. (2012) *Advanced Web Metrics with Google Analytics*, 3rd edn. Indianapolis, IN: John Wiley.

Collins, J., Darcy, S. and Jordan, K. (2010) Multi-method research on ethnic cultural tourism in Australia. In G. Richards and W. Munsters (eds), *Cultural Tourism Research Methods*. Wallingford: CABI, pp. 87–103.

Connor, T. S., Tennen, H., Fleeson, W. and Barrett, L. F. (2009) Experience sampling methods: a modern idiographic approach to personality research. *Social and Personality Psychology*, 3(3), 292–313.

Cosper, R. and Kinsley, B. L. (1984) An application of conjoint analysis to leisure research: cultural preferences in Canada. *Journal of Leisure Research*, 16(3), 224–233.

Coulangeon, P. (2013) Changing policies, challenging theories and persisting inequalities: social disparities in cultural participation in France from 1981 to 2008. *Poetics*, 41(2), 177–209.

Creswell, J. W. (2009) *Research Design: Qualitative, Quantitative and Mixed Methods Approaches,* Third Edition. Thousand Oaks, CA: Sage.

Crowe, M. and Sheppard, L. (2012) Mind mapping research methods. *Quality and Quantity*, 46(6), 1493–1504.

Csikszentmihalyi, M. and Larson, R. (1977) The ecology of adolescent activity and experience. *Journal of Youth and Adolescence*, 6(3), 281–294.

Dawson, E. and Jensen, E. (2011) Towards a contextual turn in visitor studies: evaluating visitor segmentation and identity-related motivations. *Visitor Studies*, 14(2), 127–140.

Dayton, T. (2005) *The Living Stage: A Step-by-step Guide to Psychodrama, Sociometry and Experiential Group Therapy*. Deerfield Beach, FL: Health Communication Books.

Dolnicar, S. (2002) Activity-based market sub-segmentation of cultural tourists. *Journal of Hospitality and Tourism Management*, 9(2), 94–105.

Duffy, M. E. (1987) Methodological triangulation: a vehicle for merging qualitative and quantitative research methods. *IMAGE: Journal of Nursing Scholarship*, 19(1), 130–133.

Dupuis, S. (1999) Naked truths: towards a reflexive methodology in leisure research. *Leisure Sciences*, 21(1), 43–64.

Elsweiler, D., Wilson, M. L. and Lunn, B. K. (2011) Understanding casual-leisure information behaviour. In A. Spink and J. Heinström (eds), *New Directions in Information Behaviour*. London: Emerald, pp. 211–241.

Evans, G. and Foord, J. (2008) Cultural mapping and sustainable communities: planning for the arts revisited. *Cultural Trends*, 17(2), 65–96.

Findahl, O., Lagerstedt, C., & Aurelius, A. (2014) Triangulation as a way to validate and deepen knowledge about user behavior. In Patriarche, G., Bilandzic, H., Jenson, J. L., & Jurisic, J. (eds), *Audience Research Methodologies*. London: Routledge, pp. 54–72.

Francis, L. J., Mansfield, S., Williams, E. and Village, A. (2010) Applying psychological type theory to cathedral visitors: a case study of two cathedrals in England and Wales. *Visitor Studies*, 13(2), 175–186.

Frochot, I., & Hughes, H. (2000) HISTOQUAL: The development of a historic houses assessment scale. *Tourism Management*, 21(2), 157–167.

Frohman, B. (1994) Discourse analysis as a research method in library and information science. *Library and Information Science Research*, 16(2), 119–131.

Gartner, W. and Hunt, J. D. (1988) A method to collect detailed tourist flow information. *Annals of Tourism Research*, 15(1), 159–172.

Gee, J. P. (2010) *An Introduction to Discourse Analysis*. London: Routledge.

Glass, G. V., McGaw, B. and Smith, M. L. (1981) *Meta-Analysis in Social Research*. Beverly Hills, CA: Sage.

Greenwood, D. J. and Levin, M. (2007) *Introduction to Action Research*. Thousand Oaks, CA: Sage.

Greenwood, D. J., and Levin, M. (2005) Reform of the social sciences, and universities through action research. N. K. Denzin & Y. S. Lincoln (Eds), *Handbook of Qualitative Research*, 3rd edn. Thousand Oaks, CA: Sage, pp. 43–64.

Guillon, O. (2011) Loyalty behaviours and segmentation of performing arts audiences: the case of Théâtre de l'Athénée in Paris. *International Journal of Arts Management*, 14(1), 32–44.

Guintcheva, G. and Passebois, J. (2009) Exploring the place of museums in European leisure markets: an approach based on consumer values. *International Journal of Arts Management*, 11(2), 4–16.

Hand, C. (2009) Modelling patterns of attendance at performing arts events: the case of music in the United Kingdom. *Creative Industries Journal*, 2(3), 259–271.

Harvey, A. S. and Pentland, W. E. (1999) Time use research. In W. E. Pentland, A. S. Harvey, M. Powell Lawton and M. A. McColl (eds), *Time Use Research in the Social Sciences*. New York: Kluwer/Plenum, pp. 3–18.

Hektner, J. M., Schmidt, J. A. and Csikszentmihayli, M. (eds) (2006) *Experience Sampling Method: Measuring the Quality of Everyday Life*. Thousand Oaks, CA: Sage.

Higgs, P. and Cunningham, S. (2008) Creative industries mapping: where have we come from and where are we going? *Creative Industries Journal*, 1(1), 7–30.

Hjorth-Andersen, C. (2007) Chris Anderson, 'The Long Tail: How Endless Choice is Creating Unlimited Demand': the new economics of culture and commerce. *Journal of Cultural Economics*, 31(3), 235–237.

Hooper-Greenhill, E. (1995) Audience – a curatorial dilemma. In S. Pearce (ed.) *Art in Museums*. London: Athlone, pp. 143–163.

Howe, K. R. (1988) Against the quantitative–qualitative incompatibility thesis: or dogmas die hard. *Educational Researcher*, 17(8), 10–16.

Hsu, C.-C. and Sandford, B. A. (2007) The Delphi technique: making sense of consensus. *Practical Assessment, Research and Evaluation*, 12(10), 1–8.

Hulett, S. (1997) Program evaluation using logic models in arts programs for at-risk youth. *Americans for the Arts Monographs*, 1(6), 1–24.

Hurst, F. (1994) En route surveys. In J. R. B. Ritchie and C. R. Goeldner (eds), *Travel, Tourism and Hospitality Research*, Second Edition. New York: John Wiley, pp. 453–472.

Jaimangal-Jones, D. (2012) More than worlds: analyzing the media discourses surrounding dance music events. *Event Management*, 16(3), 305–318.

Jansen-Verbeke, M. and Van Rekom, J. (1996) Scanning museum visitors. *Annals of Tourism Research*, 23(2), 364–375.

Joel, S. (2009) A social network analysis approach to a social model of the creative industries: design subsector. *Creative Industries Journal*, 2(2), 191–201.

Kane, D. (2004) A network approach to the puzzle of women's cultural participation. *Poetics*, 32(2), 105–127.

Kasprzyk, D., Duncan, G., Kalton, G. and Singh, M. P. (1989) *Panel Surveys*. New York: John Wiley and Sons.

Kellehear, A. (1993) *The Unobtrusive Researcher: A Guide to Methods*. Sydney: Allen and Unwin.

Kelly, G. A. (1955) *The Psychology of Personal Constructs*. New York: Norton.

Konlaan, B. B., Bygren, L. O., and Johansson, S-E. (2000) Visiting cinema, concerts, museums or art exhibitions as determinant of survival. *Scandinavian Journal of Public Health*, 28(2), 174–178.

Kozinets, R. V. (1997) 'I want to believe'. A netnography of 'The X-Philes' subculture of consumption. *Advances in Consumer Research*, 24(1), 470–475.

Kozinets, R. V. (2009) *Netnography: Doing Ethnographic Research Online*. London: Sage.

Krenz, C. and Sax, G. (1986) What quantitative research is and why it doesn't work. *American Behavioral Scientist*, 30(1), 58–69.

Landeta, J. (2006) Current validity of the Delphi method in social sciences. *Technological Forecasting and Social Change*, 73(5), 467–482.

Lee, D. and Gilmore, A. (2012) Mapping cultural assets and evaluating significance: theory, methodology and practice. *Cultural Trends*, 21(1), 3–28.

Leinhardt, G., Crowley, K. and Knutson, K. (eds) (2002) *Learning Conversations in Museums*. Mahwah, NJ: Lawrence Erlbaum Associates.

Levenson, H. (1974) Activism and powerful others: distinction within the concept of internal–external control. *Journal of Psychology and Aging*, 1 (1), 117–126.

Lewis, K., Kaugman, J. and Gonzalez, M. (2008) Tastes, ties and time: a new social network dataset using Facebook.com. *Social Networks*, 30(3), 330–342.

Lilley, A., and Moore, P. (2013) *Counting What Counts: What Big Data can do for the Cultural Sector*. London: Magic Lantern consultancy, available at: www.magiclantern.co.uk.

Lin, Y-N. (2009) Importance-performance analysis of the Taipei Fin Arts Museum's services. *Museum Management and Curatorship*, 24(2), 105–121.

Locke, T. (2004) *Critical Discourse Analysis*. London: Continuum.

Martilla, J. A., and James, J. C. (1977). Importance-performance analysis. *Journal of Marketing*, 41(1), 77–79.

Mayer-Schönberger, V. and Cukier, K. (2013) *Big Data: A Revolution that Will Transform How We Live, Work and Think*. London: John Murray.

McKeown, B. and Thomas, D. (1988) *Q Methodology*. Newbury Park, CA: Sage.

McNiff, J. and Whitehead, J. (2002) *Action Research: Principles and Practice*. London: Routledge/Falmer.

Mehl, M. R., Pennebaker, J. W., Crow, D. M., Dabbs, J. and Price, J. H. (2001) The Electronically Activated Recorder (EAR): a device for sampling naturalistic daily activities and conversations. *Behavior Research Methods, Instruments, and Computers*, 33(4), 517–523.

Mertens, D. M. (2009) *Transformative Research and Evaluation*. New York: Guilford Press.

Michel, J.-B., Shen, Y. K. and Aiden, A. P. (2011) Quantitative analysis of culture using millions of digitized books. *Science*, 331, Jan, 14, 176–182.

Miller, D. (2011) *Tales from Facebook*. Cambridge: Polity.

Nantel, J. A. and Colbert, F. (1992) Positioning cultural arts product in the market. *Journal of Cultural Economics*, 16(2), 63–71.

Neugarten, P. L., Havighurst, R. J. and Tobin, S. S. (1961) The measurement of life satisfaction. *Journal of Gerontology*, 16(1), 134–143.

Nevin, J. R. and Cavusgil, S. T. (1987) Audience segments for the performing arts. In J. H. Donnelly and W. R. George (eds), *Marketing of Services*. Chicago, IL: American Marketing Association, pp. 126–128.

Noonan, D. S. (2003) Contingent valuation and cultural resources: a meta-analytic review of the literature. *Journal of Cultural Economics*, 27(2), 159–176.

Nurse Rainbolt, G., Benfield, J. A. and Loomis, R. J. (2012) Visitor self-report behavior mapping as a tool for recording exhibition circulation. *Visitor Studies*, 15(2), 203–216.

Oppenheim, A. N. (2000) *Questionnaire Design, Interviewing and Attitude Measurement: New Edition*. London: Pinter.

Ouellet, J.-F., Savard, M.-A. and Colbert, F. (2008) The personality of performing arts venues: development of a measurement scale. *International Journal of Arts Management*, 10(3), 49–59.

Patriarche, G., Bilandzic, H., Jenson, J. L., and Jurisic, J. (eds) (2014) *Audience Research Methodologies: Between Innovation and Consolidation*. London: Routledge.

Pentland, W. E., Harvey, A. S., Powell Lawton, M. and McColl, M. A. (eds) (1999) *Time Use Research in the Social Sciences*. New York: Kluwer/Plenum.

Perkins, A. (2012) How devoted are you? An examination of online music fan behaviour. *Annals of Leisure Research*, 15(4), 354–365.

Platt, J. (1986) Functionalism and the survey: the relation of theory and method. *Sociological Review*, 34(3), 501–536.

Prior, L. (2003) *Using Documents in Social Research*. London: Sage.

Puczko, L., Bard, E. and Fuzi, J. (2010) Methodological triangulation: the study of visitor behaviour at the Hungarian Open Air Museum. In G. Richards and W. Munsters (eds), *Cultural Tourism Research Methods*. Wallingford: CABI, pp. 61–74.

Raajpoot, N., Koh, K. and Jackson, A. (2010) Developing a scale to measure service quality: an exploratory study. *International Journal of Arts Management*, 12(3), 54–69.

Radbourne, J. (2001) Full House Theory: a new theory for assessing demand for arts centres. *Journal of Arts Management, Law and Society*, 30(4), 254–267.

Radbourne, J., Glow, H. and Johanson, K. (2010) Measuring the intrinsic benefits of arts attendance. *Cultural Trends*, 19(4), 307–324.

Rayment, T. (2000) Art teachers' views of national curriculum art: a repertory grid analysis. *Educational Studies*, 26(2), 165–176.

Reason, P. and Bradbury, H. (eds) (2001) *Handbook of Action Research: Participative Inquiry and Practice*. London: Sage.

Reynolds, T. J. and Gutman, J. (1988) Laddering theory, method, analysis and interpretation. *Journal of Advertising Research*, 70(1), 11–15.

Roose, H., Van Eijck, K. and Lievens, J. (2012) Culture of distinction or culture of openness? Using a social space approach to analyze the social structuring of lifestyles. *Poetics*, 40(4), 491–513.

Rose, D. (ed.) (2000) *Researching Social and Economic Change: The Uses of Household Panel Studies*. London: Routledge.

Rudd, A. and Johnson, R. B. (2010) A call for more mixed methods in sport management research. *Sport Management Review*, 13(1), 14–24.

Saaka, A., Sidon, C. and Blake, B. F. (2004) *Laddering: A 'How to do it' Manual – With a Note of Caution*. Research Reports in Consumer Behavior: Methodology Series. Cleveland, OH: Cleveland State University, available at: http://academic.csuohio.edu:8080/cbrsch/home.html

Sallent, O., Palau, R. and Guia, J. (2011) Exploring the legacy of sport events on sport tourism networks. *European Sport Management Quarterly*, 11(4), 397–421.

Savage, M., Devine, F. and Cunningham, N. (2013) A new model of social class? Findings from the BBC's Great British Class Survey experiment. *Sociology*, 47(2), 219–250.

Semeneoff, B. (1976) *Projective Techniques*. London: John Wiley and Sons.

Smyth, J. M. and Stone, A. A. (2003) Ecological momentary assessment research in behavioral medicine. *Journal of Happiness Studies*, 4(1), 35–52.

Stevenson, D. (2000) *Art and Organisation: Making Australian Cultural Policy*. St Lucia, Qld: University of Queensland Press.

Stokowski, P. A. (1994) *Leisure in Society: A Network Structural Perspective*. London: Mansell.

Stokowski, P. A. and Lee, R. G. (1991) The influence of social network ties on recreation and leisure: an exploratory study. *Journal of Leisure Research*, 23(2), 95–113.

Strategic Business Insights (2009) The VALS Survey. Menlo Park, CA: Strategic Business Insights, available at: www.strategicbusinessinsights.com/vals/presurvey.shtml

Stylianou-Lambert, T. (2009) Perceiving the art museum. *Museum Management and Curatorship*, 24(2), 139–158.

Szalai, A. (ed.) (1972) *The Use of Time: Daily Activities of Urban and Suburban Populations in Twelve Countries*. The Hague: Mouton.

Tashakkori, A. and Creswell, J. W. (2007) Exploring the nature of research questions in mixed methods research. *Journal of Mixed Methods Research*, 1(3), 207–211.

Tashakkori, A. and Teddlie, C. (eds) (2003) *Handbook of Mixed Methods in Social and Behavioral Research*. Thousand Oaks, CA: Sage.

Teddlie, C. and Tashakkori, A. (eds) (2009) *Foundations of Mixed Methods Research: Integrating Quantitative and Qualitative Approaches in the Social and Behavioral Sciences*. Thousand Oaks, CA: Sage.

Tkaczynski, A. and Stokes, R. (2010) FESTPERF: a service quality measurement scale for festivals. *Event Management*, 14(1), 69–82.

Tzibazi, V. (2013) Participatory action research with young people in museums. *Museum Management and Curatorship*, 28(2), 153–171.

United Nations Intergovernmental Panel on Climate Change (UNIPCC) (2007) Climate Change 2007: Synthesis Report. Geneva: UNIPCC, available at: www.ipcc.ch

Van der Ark, L. A. and Richards, G. (2006) Attractiveness of cultural activities in European cities: a latent class analysis. *Tourism Management*, 27(6), 1408–1413.

Van Rees, K., Vermunt, J. and Verboord, M. (1999) Cultural classification under discussion: latent class analysis of highbrow and lowbrow reading. *Poetics*, 26(3), 349–365.

Veal, A. J. (2010) *Leisure, Sport and Tourism: Politics Policy and Planning*, 3rd edn. Wallingford, UK: CABI.

Warnick, R. B., Bojanic, D. C., Mathur, A. and Ninan, D. (2011) Segmenting event attendees based on travel distance, frequency of attendance, and involvement measures: a cluster segmentation technique. *Event Management*, 15(1), 77–90.

Wäsche, H. and Woll, A. (2010) Regional sports tourism networks: a conceptual framework. *Journal of Sport and Tourism*, 15(3), 191–214.

Weinstein, L. and Bukovinsky, D. (2009) Use of the Balanced Scorecard and performance metrics to achieve operational and strategic alignment in arts and culture not-for-profits. *International Journal of Arts Management*, 11(2), 42–55.

Williams, C. (1998) Is the SERVQUAL model an appropriate management tool for measuring service delivery quality in the UK leisure industry? *Managing Leisure*, 3(2), 98–110.

Willis, K. G. and Snowball, J. D. (2009) Investigating how the attributes of live theatre productions influence consumption choices using conjoint analysis: the example of the National Arts Festival, South Africa. *Journal of Cultural Economics*, 33(2), 166–183.

Woodside, A. G. and Ronkainen, I. A. (1994) Improving advertising conversion studies. In J. R. B. Ritchie and C. R. Goeldner (eds) *Travel, Tourism and Hospitality Research,* Second Edition. New York: John Wiley, pp. 481–487.

Woosnam, K. M., Van Winkle, C. M. and An, S. (2013) Confirming the festival social impact attitude scale in the context of a rural Texas cultural festival. *Event Management*, 17(3), 257–270.

Wright, R. (2007) A conceptual and methodological framework for designing and evaluating community-based after-school art programs. *International Journal of Cultural Policy*, 13(1), 124–132.

Wyatt Knowlton, L. and Phillips, C. C. (2012) *The Logic Model Guidebook: Better Strategies for Great Results*, Second Edition. Thousand Oaks, CA: Sage.

Xun, J. and Reynolds, J. (2010) Applying netnography to market research: the case of the online forum. *Journal of Targeting, Measurement and Analysis for Marketing,* 18(1), 17–31.

Yin, R. K. (2014) *Case Study Research: Design and Methods,* Fifth Edition. Thousand Oaks, CA: Sage.

Young, C. H., Savola, K. L. and Phelps, E. (1991) *Inventory of Longitudinal Studies in the Social Sciences*. Newbury Park, CA: Sage.

Zuzanek, J. and Veal, A. J. (eds) (1998) Time pressure, stress, leisure participation and well-being. Special issue of *Loisir et Société (Society and Leisure)*, 21(2).

Chapter 6

Reviewing the literature

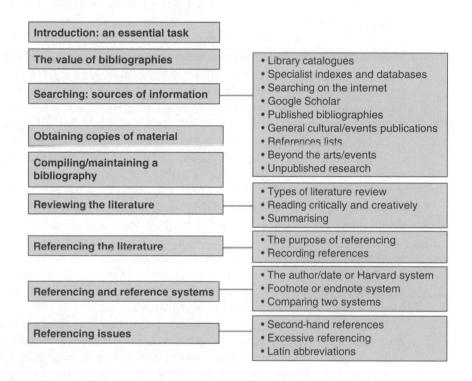

Introduction: an essential task	
The value of bibliographies	
Searching: sources of information	• Library catalogues • Specialist indexes and databases • Searching on the internet • Google Scholar • Published bibliographies • General cultural/events publications • References lists • Beyond the arts/events • Unpublished research
Obtaining copies of material	
Compiling/maintaining a bibliography	
Reviewing the literature	• Types of literature review • Reading critically and creatively • Summarising
Referencing the literature	• The purpose of referencing • Recording references
Referencing and reference systems	• The author/date or Harvard system • Footnote or endnote system • Comparing two systems
Referencing issues	• Second-hand references • Excessive referencing • Latin abbreviations

Introduction

An essential task

The aim of this chapter is to explain the importance, for any research project, of reviewing previous research and being aware of existing writing – the literature – on a topic. In addition, the chapter indicates general sources of information on arts/events studies literature, sets out the mechanics of compiling bibliographies and recording bibliographical references, and considers the process of reviewing the literature for research purposes.

Reviewing existing research or writing on a topic is a vital step in the research process. The field of arts/events studies comprises relatively new areas of academic enquiry which are wide-ranging and multi-disciplinary in nature. Research funding is not so plentiful in the field that we

- The entire basis of the research.
- Source of ideas on topics for research.
- Source of substantive information on research already done by others.
- Source of methodological or theoretical ideas.
- Source of confirmation and/or comparison between your research and that of others.
- Source of information that is an integral or supportive part of the research – for example, statistical data on the study area population.

Figure 6.1 The roles of the literature in research

can afford to ignore research that has already been completed by others. As discussed briefly in Chapters 3 and 5, the literature can serve a number of functions, as indicated in Figure 6.1.

The aim of research of an academic nature is to add to the body of human knowledge. In most societies that body of knowledge is generally in written form – the literature. To presume to add to the body of knowledge it is necessary to be familiar with what knowledge already exists and to indicate precisely how the proposed or completed research relates to it. In research of a consultancy or policy nature, where the primary aim is not to add to knowledge but to use research to assist directly in the solution of policy, planning or management problems, a familiarity with existing knowledge in the area is still vital. Much time and valuable resources can be wasted in 're-inventing the wheel' to devise suitable methodologies to conduct a project, or in conducting projects with inadequate methodologies, when reference to existing work could provide information on tried-and-tested approaches.

The fifth bullet point in Figure 6.1 draws attention to confirmatory or comparative engagement with the literature, which is particularly applicable in the case of the grounded theory approach to research. As noted in Chapter 3, in this case the practice is often to conduct fieldwork and a certain amount of data analysis or interpretation before conducting any substantial literature review. In such a situation, the researcher discovers whether the literature confirms or contradicts the research conducted so far or compares and contrasts the research conducted, and the conclusions drawn, with the literature, in an iterative manner. This process can, however, arise in any sort of research. Even when a research project is initiated with a substantial initial literature review, unexpected findings, or simply the detail of the findings, may give rise to further examination of the literature.

Identifying relevant literature is often a demanding task. It involves a careful search for information on relevant published and, if necessary, unpublished work; obtaining copies of relevant items and reading and them; making a list of useful items to form a bibliography; and assessing and summarising aspects which are salient for the research proposal or the research report in hand.

The value of bibliographies

This chapter focuses on reviewing the literature in relation to the planning of research projects, but the development of a bibliography can be a useful end in itself. It might be thought that modern electronic search methods have made the compilation and publication of bibliographies on specific topics obsolete, but this is not the case. While electronic databases are continually developing, they are still incomplete, especially with regard to:

- older published material;
- 'ephemeral' material, such as conference papers and reports and working papers not published by mainstream publishers;

- chapters from edited collections of papers;
- relevant content not mentioned in abstracts or key words.

More importantly, electronic databases do not provide an *evaluation* of material: they do not always distinguish between a substantial research paper and a lightweight commentary with no original content. Further, not all databases are full-text, so electronic systems will be able to identify items only on the basis of their titles or, in some cases, key words and abstracts. A database may not indicate, for example, whether a report on 'the arts' includes data on a specific sector, such as dance, or how broadly 'the arts' is defined. A great deal of useful work can therefore still be done in compiling bibliographies on specific topics, thus helping to consolidate the 'state of the art' and saving other researchers a great deal of time and trouble in searching for material.

Examples of published bibliographies in the arts/events area are listed in the Resources section at the end of the chapter and considerable scope exists for the development of similar bibliographies on other topics.

A bibliography can be just a list of references, or it can be extended by the inclusion of key words and abstracts or by some form of classification, for example by methodology. Further analysis and commentary on content takes us into the realm of the literature review, the systematic review and meta-analysis, which are discussed separately below.

Searching: sources of information

Where can the researcher look for information on existing published research on a topic? In this section a number of sources are examined, as listed in Figure 6.2.

Library catalogues

Modern libraries have computerised catalogues which are accessible via terminals within the library and also from remote locations via the internet. These online catalogues include information on:

- the library's physical holdings;
- online materials, including online versions of journals, e-books and bibliographical databases and statistical database sites such as national governmental statistical offices;
- in some cases, access to other university and public library catalogues.

Many of the online materials are, like lending rights, available only to registered library members, such as students or academic staff.

- Library catalogues
- Specialist indexes and databases
- Searching the internet
- Google Scholar
- Published bibliographies
- General arts/events studies books
- Reference lists
- Beyond arts/events

Figure 6.2 Sources of information

Searches can be made on the basis of the titles of publications or using key words assigned to them by the library. This can be very helpful as a starting point in establishing a bibliography. But it is only a starting point, particularly for the researcher with a specialist interest.

If search words such as *theatre* or *events* are used, the typical computerised catalogue will produce an enormous number of references, running to thousands, and far too many to be manageable. But if more specialised terms, such as *theatre visits* or *event visits*, are entered, the catalogue will produce few references, sometimes none at all. Whether a large or small number of references are produced, a proportion will be of a 'popular' nature, concerned with, for example, biographies of theatre producers or picture souvenir books of the Olympic Games, although some databases will distinguish between refereed academic journals and other sources. 'Popular' material may be of interest to some researchers, but will be of little use if the researcher is interested in such aspects as patterns of visitation to the theatre or to major events.

A library catalogue cannot indicate, for instance, whether a general report on 'culture' includes all forms of culture. And of course the catalogue will not necessarily identify publications which, while they deal with one topic, provide a suitable methodology for studying other topics. Such material can be identified only by actually reading – or at least perusing – original texts.

Catalogues of a library's physical holdings do not contain references to individual articles in journals, individual chapters in books which are collections of readings, or individual papers in collections of conference papers. But integrated within library online catalogues is access to internet sources provided by specialist organisations, such as EBSCO, Project MUSE, Informaworld and Ingenta, and online services provided by journal publishers.

Specialist indexes and databases

Specialist indexes and databases are online resources generally accessed via subscribing libraries. In the general social science area is the ISI Web of Knowledge (formerly Social Sciences Citation Index), which is a comprehensive listing of papers from thousands of social science journals, cross-referenced by author and subject. In addition, items of literature referred to by authors in papers are themselves listed and cross-referenced, so that further writings of any cited author can be followed up. The advantage of using this type of database is that they ensure a level of reliability by dealing mainly with peer-reviewed material, as discussed later in this chapter. It is too early for databases to have been specifically developed for the events sector, but examples in the arts area include:

- Arts & Entertainment Management (AEM) (Informit: 1982–2000)
- Art full text (H.W. Wilson) (EBSCO)
- Artstor (images)
- Project MUSE (humanities and social science journals and e-books).

Searching on the internet

Direct searching on the internet using a search engine such as Google is second nature to computer users. Such searches are clearly effective when searching for organisational websites but are a rather blunt tool for searching for published material compared with the specialist sources discussed above. Detailed searches, for example of the full title of an article, will generally provide publication information on the item but will typically not provide full access.

Extreme caution should be exercised in using internet sources. Thus, for example, while Wikipedia can be a useful source, its anonymous nature and frequent lack of source references are such that it should be used only as a route to other, more fully authenticated sources.

Google Scholar

The Google Scholar website stores bibliographical information related to authors. It does not contain a complete bibliography for the individuals listed, just those items that have been referenced – or 'cited' – by other authors. It therefore has a similar structure to the ISI Web of Knowledge mentioned above. For example, entering the name of the well-known events studies author Donald Getz produces a long list of his publications, arranged in order of number of citations. The first is his book, *Event Management and Event Tourism* (2005), which, in April 2013, had received 1,195 citations. Clicking on the book title provides details of the book and clicking on the citation number brings up a list of the 1,195 publications in which the book has been cited. This is an effective way of identifying other publications on the broad topic of event management. The database can also be searched using key words.

Published bibliographies

Reference has already been made to the value of bibliographies on particular topics. Libraries usually have a separate section for bibliographies and it may be worth browsing in that section, especially when the topic of interest is interdisciplinary. While many bibliographies have been published in hard-copy form over the years (see Resources section for examples), the trend recently has been to publish these resources online.

General arts/events publications

The researcher should be aware of publications which contain information on specific activities or aspects of arts/events. For example, Chapter 6 discusses national arts/events participation surveys which contain information on numerous cultural/events activities and a number of background items such as age and income. They are therefore a source of basic statistical information on many topics of interest.

General introductory books on arts/events may have something to say on the topic of interest or may provide leads to other sources of information via the index and bibliography. In addition, specialist encyclopaedias typically include bibliographic references. Some examples are:

- *Cultural Planning* (Evans, 2001);
- *Handbook of Cultural Economics* (Towse, 2003);
- *Creative Industries* (Hartley, 2005);
- *The Routledge Handbook of Events* (Page and Connell, 2012);
- *Event Studies: Theory, Research and Policy for Planned Events* (Getz, 2012);
- *Events Management* (Bowdin *et al.*, 2011);
- *Encyclopedia of the Modern Olympic Movement* (Findling and Pelle, 2004).

Searching through such texts, using the contents pages or the index, can be a somewhat 'hit and miss' process, but can often be rewarded with leads which could not be gained in any other way. Even scanning through the contents pages of key journals may produce relevant material which would not be identified by conventional searches.

Reference lists

Most importantly, the lists of references in the books and articles identified in initial searches will often lead to useful material. Researchers interested in a particular topic should be constantly on the alert for sources of material on that topic in anything they are reading. Sometimes key items are encountered when they are least expected. The researcher should become a 'sniffer dog', obsessed with 'sniffing out' anything of relevance to the topic of interest. In a real-world research situation this process of identifying as much literature as possible can take months or even years. While a major effort should be made to identify material at the beginning of any research process, it will also be an on-going exercise, throughout the course of the project.

Beyond arts/events

Lateral thinking is also an aid to the literature search task. The most useful information is not always found in the most obvious places. Arts/events studies is an interdisciplinary area of study, not a discipline in its own right – it does not have a set of research methods and theories uniquely its own. Much is to be gained from looking outside the immediate area of arts/events studies. For example, if the research involves measurement of attitudes then certain psychological literature will be of interest; if the research involves the study of arts or events markets then general marketing journals may be useful sources; and if the research involves the arts/events activities of older people then gerontology journals should be consulted.

Unpublished research

Where possible, attempts should be made to explore not just published research – the literature – but also unpublished and on-going research. This process is very much hit and miss. Knowing what research is on-going or knowing of completed but unpublished research usually depends on having access to informal networks, although some organisations produce registers of on-going research projects, typically on their websites. Once a topic of interest has been identified it is often clear, from the literature, where the major centres for such research are located and to discover, from direct approaches or from websites, annual reports or newsletters, what research is being conducted at those centres. This process can be particularly important if the topic is a 'fashionable' one. However, in such cases the communication networks are usually active, which eases the process. In this respect papers from conferences and seminars are usually better sources of information on current research than books and journals, since the latter have long gestation periods – the research reported in them is generally based on work carried out two or more years prior to publication. Some key websites are listed in the Resources section.

Obtaining copies of material

If material is not available in a particular library, in hard copy or online, it can often be obtained through the inter-library loan service. This is a system through which loans of materials can be made between one library and another. In the case of older journal articles not available online, the service usually involves the provision of a digital copy. In theory any item published in a particular country should be available through this system since it is connected with national copyright libraries – such as the British Lending Library in Boston Spa or the National Library in Australia – where a copy of all published items must be lodged by law. Practices vary from library to library, but in academic libraries the service is often available to postgraduate students while undergraduate students may gain access only through a member of academic staff.

For researchers working in metropolitan areas the other obvious source of material is specialist libraries, particularly of government agencies. In metropolitan areas and some other regions there is often a cooperative arrangement between municipal reference libraries such that particular libraries adopt particular specialist areas, so it can be useful to discover which municipal library service specialises in arts/events.

Compiling and maintaining a bibliography

What should be done with the material once it has been identified? First, a record should be made of everything that appears to be of relevance. The researcher is strongly advised to start a file of every item of literature used. This can be of use not only for the current research project but also for future reference – a personal bibliography can be built up over the years. Such record keeping can be done using cards, but is best done on a computer, using a word-processor or a database program, which can also store key words. This has the attraction that when there is a need to compile a bibliography on another topic in future, a start can be made from your personal bibliography by getting the computer to copy designated items into a new file. In this way the researcher only ever needs to type out a reference once. Bibliographic computer packages, such as Endnote and Pro-Cite, store reference material in a standard format, but will automatically compile bibliographies in appropriate formats to meet the requirements of different report styles and the specifications of different academic journals.

It takes only seconds to record full details of a reference when it is first identified. If this practice is adopted, hours of time and effort can be saved in not having to chase up details at a later date. Not only should the details be recorded accurately, as set out below, but a note should be made on the database about the availability of the material – for example, the library catalogue reference, or the fact that the item is not in the library, or that a photocopy or digital copy has been taken. Needless to say, storage of downloaded material on the researcher's computer should be organised in a suitable way and backed up.

Reviewing the literature

Reviewing the literature on a topic can be one of the most rewarding research tasks – and one of the most frustrating. It requires a range of skills and qualities, including patience, persistence, insight and lateral thinking.

Types of literature review

The review of the literature can play a number of roles in a research project, as outlined above, and this leads to a number of approaches to conducting a review, as listed in Figure 6.3.

- Inclusive bibliography
- Inclusive/evaluative/systematic reviews, meta-analysis
- Exploratory
- Instrumental
- Content analysis/hermeneutics

Figure 6.3 Types of literature review

Inclusive bibliography

The inclusive approach to reviewing the literature seeks to identify everything that has been written on a particular topic. The compilation of such a bibliography may be a significant achievement in itself, independent of any research project with which it may be connected. It becomes a resource to be drawn on by others in the future. Such a bibliography does not amount to a 'review' of the literature if there is no accompanying commentary, although classification of entries into categories (e.g. books, articles, government reports), time periods, methodology or sub-topics can be seen as the beginning of such a process. In some cases bibliographies merely list the reference details; in other instances they include abstracts of the contents, in which case they are referred to as *annotated* bibliographies. A number of examples of comprehensive bibliographies are listed in the Resources section.

Inclusive/evaluative/systematic reviews

The inclusive/evaluative approach or systematic review takes the inclusive approach a stage further by providing a commentary on the literature in terms of its coverage and its contribution to knowledge and understanding of the topic. When this type of exercise is undertaken by a panel of researchers appointed by a governmental or other organisation, it may be referred to as a 'consensus study'. The most well-known study of this type in recent years has been the series of reports by the United Nations Intergovernmental Panel on Climate Change, which evaluated the results of thousands of scientific publications to draw conclusions regarding climate change and its causes (UNIPCC, 2013).

An even more formalised quantitative approach to analysing the literature is known as meta-analysis and involves a systematic, quantitative appraisal of the findings of a number of research projects focused on the same topic. The technique is suitable for the sort of research where findings are directly comparable from one study to another – for example when the key research findings are expressed in terms of correlation or regression coefficients (see Chapter 17). In this approach the reported findings of the research themselves become the subject of research and the number of reported projects can become so large that it is necessary to sample from them in the same way that individuals are sampled for empirical research. The meta-analysis approach is discussed in more detail below.

Exploratory review

The exploratory approach is more focused and seeks to discover existing research that might throw light on a specific research question or issue. This is very much the classic literature review which is the norm for academic research and best fits the model of the research process outlined in Chapter 3. Comprehensiveness is not as important as the focus on the particular question or issue. The skill in conducting such a review lies in keeping the question or issue in sight, while 'interrogating' the literature for ideas and insights that may help shape the research. The reviewer needs to be open to useful new ideas, but must not be side-tracked into areas which stray too far from the question or issue of interest.

Instrumental review

An example of the instrumental approach is the brief review in Case Study 3.1. Here the research is concerned with management issues and the literature is used as a source of suitable ideas on how the research might be tackled.

Content analysis and hermeneutics

Content analysis and hermeneutics are techniques which involve detailed analysis of the contents of a certain body of literature or other documentary source as texts. The texts might be, for example, novels, media coverage of a topic, politicians' speeches or the contents of advertising. Content analysis tends to be quantitative, involving, for example, counting the number of occurrences of certain phrases. Hermeneutics tends to be qualitative in nature, the term being borrowed from the traditional approach to analysis and interpretation of religious texts. The essence of this approach is discussed in Chapter 8, in relation to the analysis of in-depth interview transcripts.

Reading critically and creatively

Reviewing the literature for research purposes involves reading the literature in a certain way. It necessitates being concerned as much with the methodological aspects of the research (which are not always well reported) as the substantive content. That is, it involves being concerned with *how* the conclusions are arrived at as well as with the conclusions themselves. It involves being critical – questioning rather than accepting what is being read. The task is as much to ascertain what is not known as it is to determine what is known. This is different from reading for other purposes, such as some essay writing, when a particular substantive critical issue may be being explored but the research basis or overall scope of the literature being discussed may not be an issue.

As material is being read, a number of questions might be asked, as set out in Figure 6.4. The questions relate to both individual items and to the body of literature as a whole.

It can be helpful to be conscious of the appropriate way in which the contents of an item of literature should be reported. A number of styles of reporting are used, including:

- Smith believes/thinks/is of the opinion…
- Smith argues…

(a) *Individual items*
- What is the (empirical) basis of this research?
- How does the research relate to other research writings on the topic?
- What theoretical framework is being used?
- What geographical area does the research refer to?
- What social group(s) does the research refer to?
- When was the research carried out and is it likely still to be empirically valid?

(b) *In relation to the literature as a whole*
- What is the range of research that has been conducted?
- What methods have generally been used and what methods have been neglected?
- What, in summary, does the existing research tell us?
- What, in summary, does the existing research not tell us?
- What contradictions are there in the literature – either recognised or unrecognised by the authors concerned?
- What are the deficiencies in the existing research, in substantive or methodological terms?

Figure 6.4 Questions to ask when reviewing the literature

- Smith establishes…
- Smith observes…
- Smith speculates…
- Smith puts forward the possibility that…
- Smith concludes…

An author's opinion or beliefs may be important if the author is someone who deals in opinions and beliefs, such as a politician or cleric, but we generally expect more than just statements of belief from academic literature. An academic may be influenced by particular ideological or religious beliefs – for example, a well-known theorist in the field of leisure, Josef Pieper, author of *Leisure, the Basis of Culture* (1952/1999), was a Catholic priest and this is not irrelevant to his work, but if his work had been merely a statement of faith it would not have been as influential as it has been in the development of leisure theory. A review of the literature should convey accurately the basis of the material presented, whether it be opinion, the result of argument or presentation of empirical evidence, informal observation or speculation.

The type of literature being summarised is therefore important: newspaper and popular and professional magazine articles are not subject to the same checks and balances as academic journal articles; and reports emanating from arts/events organisations or from politically motivated organisations cannot always be relied on to tell 'the truth, the whole truth and nothing but the truth'. Of course, such material may appear in a literature review, but its status and the way it is reported and interpreted should be treated with caution and subtlety.

Care should be taken when referring to textbooks, such as this one, which, while they may contain some original contributions from the author, will mostly contain summaries of the state of knowledge in a field, with some material attributed to specific sources and some not. Generally, in a research report, particularly a thesis, original scholarly sources rather than textbooks should be referred to where possible.

As regards the substantive content of the literature, a major challenge for a reviewer is to find a framework to classify and analyse it. In the case of an inclusive review, literature might be classified:

- chronologically;
- by geographical origin; or
- by discipline.

For other types of review, themes or issues are likely to be more important. Reviewing the literature in this way can be similar to the development of a conceptual framework for a research project, as discussed in Chapter 3. Some sort of diagrammatic, concept map, approach, as indicated in Figure 6.5, may be helpful. Such a diagram might be devised before starting a review, or may be developed, inductively, as the review progresses.

Summarising

A review of the literature in a research report should draw conclusions and implications for the proposed research programme. It is advisable to complete a review by presenting a summary that addresses the second set of questions in Figure 6.4. This summary should

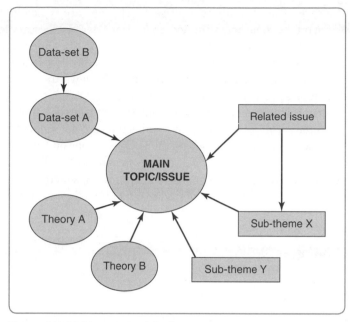

Figure 6.5 Making sense of the literature

lead logically to the research project in hand. It should make clear to the reader just how the proposed research relates to the existing body of literature – whether it is seeking to:

● add to the body of knowledge in a unique way;
● fill a gap in knowledge;
● update existing knowledge;
● correct or contradict some aspect of existing knowledge; or
● use ideas from the literature as a source of ideas or comparison.

When a large amount of literature with similar format is being reviewed it may be helpful to summarise it in a tabular quasi-meta-analytical form, using headings such as: geographical area covered, sample size, independent variables used, year of survey.

Meta-analysis/interpretation/evaluation/review

Meta-analysis and related approaches regard the literature review process as a project in its own right, with research publications being treated rather like observations in an empirical study. The alternative formats for this type of project are as follows:

● meta-analysis – research projects under review have common format with quantitative outcomes, which are aggregated;
● meta-interpretation – meta-analysis for qualitative research;
● meta-evaluation – focus of the review is on methodology used in projects;
● meta-review – a review of other reviews of varying types.

In the case of meta-analysis, precise conclusions are typically drawn about the field of research on the topic being studied, so it is considered necessary to detail the steps taken to identify the literature included in the evaluation, in the same way that the process of selecting a sample of human subjects for a study would be described. Formal meta-analysis is not common in the arts/events field but systematic reviews are becoming increasingly common, and examples are listed in the Resources section.

A version of meta-analysis for qualitative research has been put forward, referred to as *meta-interpretation*. This process is 'iterative rather than pre-determined' and rather than being based on statistical findings it is based on the interpretations of data in the original studies (Weed, 2005). *Meta-evaluation* may refer to a meta-analysis of evaluation studies, such as those that might evaluate policy interventions, or it may refer to a meta-analysis that concentrates on the methods and rigour of a range of studies rather than their substantive findings (Weed, 2008).

Referencing the literature

The purpose of referencing

What is the purpose of referencing? First, referencing is evidence of the writer's scholarship: it indicates that the particular research report is related to the existing body of knowledge. This is not only of importance to teachers marking student assignments or theses, it is part and parcel of the development of knowledge. Second, references enable readers of the research report to check sources – either to verify the writer's interpretation of previous research or to follow up their own particular areas of interest.

Recording references

A number of standard or conventional formats exist for recording references to the literature. The conventions have been established by leading academic organisations and publishers. Guides are produced by organisations such as the American Psychological Association (2009) and Oxford University Press (2012). The formats presented here do not conform to any one standard approach but offer a style which, if followed consistently, would be acceptable in most academic contexts. In what follows, the word *text* refers to the main body of the research report or article. It should be noted that if bibliographic management systems such as Endnote and Pro-Cite are used, references can be formatted in a variety of styles and automatically changed to suit publication requirements.

The general format recommended for recording references is shown in Figure 6.6. In some systems the date is put at the end, but when using the author/date or Harvard system, as discussed below, the date should follow the author name as indicated.

- *A book or report*:
  Author(s), Initials (Year) *Title of Book or Report in Italic*. Place of publication: Publisher.
- *An article from a periodical (journal/magazine/newspaper)*:
  Author(s), Initials (Year) Title of article. *Title of Periodical in Italic*, Volume number (Issue number), Page numbers.

Figure 6.6 Standard/generic reference formats

1	A book	Getz, D. (2012) *Event Studies: Theory, Research and Policy for Planned Events*, Second Edition. London: Routledge.
2	An edited book	Towse, R. (ed.) (2003) *A Handbook of Cultural Economics*. Cheltenham, UK: Edward Elgar.
3	A chapter from an edited book	Goldstone, L. (2003) Cultural statistics. In R. Towse (ed.), *A Handbook of Cultural Economics* (pp. 177–182). Cheltenham, UK: Edward Elgar.
4	A published conference report	Allen, J., Harris, R., Jago, L. K., and Veal, A. J. (eds) (2000) Events Beyond 2000*: Setting the Agenda, Proceedings of a Conference on Event Evaluation, Research and Education, Sydney, July 2000*. Sydney: Australian Centre for Event Management, University of Technology, Sydney.
5	A published conference paper	Getz, D. (2000) Developing a research agenda for the event management field. In J. Allen, R. Harris, L. K. Jago and A. J. Veal, A. J. (eds) *Events Beyond 2000: Setting the Agenda, Proceedings of a Conference on Event Evaluation, Research and Education, Sydney, July 2000* (pp. 9–20). Sydney: Australian Centre for Event Management, University of Technology, Sydney.
6	A government agency report, authored and published by the same agency	Australia Council (2010) *More than Bums on Seats – Australian Participation in the Arts*. Sydney: Australia Council, available at: www.australiacouncil.gov.au.
7	A journal article	Bennett, O. (2004) The torn halves of cultural policy research. *International Journal of Cultural Policy*, 10(2), 237–248.
8	A newspaper article with named author	Fenton, J. (2004) Down with this access pottiness. *The Guardian*, 29 May, p. 12.
9	An internet source	Veal, A. J. (2012) *The Olympic Games: A Bibliography*. Sydney: Business School, University of Technology, Sydney, Online Bibliography 5, available at: www.olympic.uts.edu.au/downloads/olympic_bib_update2.pdf (Accessed May 2014)

Figure 6.7 Examples of reference formats

Note that the part of the reference which is in *italic* is the title that would be found in a library catalogue, that is, the name of the periodical, not the title of the article, and the title of the book, not the title of a chapter.

Note that the publisher of a book is not the same as the printer of the book (in the case of this book, the publisher is Pearson, but the *printer* is Ashford Colour (see p. iv). References do not need to refer to the printer. And note that it is not necessary to refer to the publisher in the case of periodicals.

Some examples of reference formats are set out in Figure 6.7 to illustrate the principles.

Particular note should be made that, in the book chapter example, the main reference is to the chapter author(s), not to the book editor(s).

Internet references are becoming increasingly common. One of the problems with this medium is that some sources disappear or their website address (URL) change over time, so that it is difficult for the reader to follow them up. For individual publications it is often advisable to give the index or 'list of publications' address rather than the often long and complex address of the individual publication. The general principle to be followed is that an internet reference should include all the details which would normally apply to hard copy items, *plus* the website URL *and* the date accessed. The geographical place of publication is not always clear from the website, but can generally be found with a little effort. If accessing a journal article via the internet, it is not necessary to give the website address unless the journal is known to be published only electronically. Published style guides are available for referencing in relation to this medium, for example, *The Columbia Guide to Online Style* (Walker and Taylor, 1998).

Some guidelines suggest that newspaper articles should be referenced with the title of the article rather than, as here, with the author. The important point to note is that, once a style is adopted, it should be consistent throughout the report.

Referencing and referencing systems

There are two commonly used referencing systems: the author/date system, sometimes referred to as the Harvard system, and the footnote or endnote system. These two systems are discussed below.

The author/date or Harvard system

Basic features

In the author/date, or Harvard, system, references to an item of literature are made in the text using the author's name and the year of the publication, as in this book. At the end of the paper or report, references are listed in alphabetical order. In books, the list of references may be at the end of each chapter, as in this book, or at the end of the whole book. A sentence in a report using this system might look something like this:

> Researchers have examined museum visitors from a number of perspectives, including, for example, the educational perspective of Davis (2011), the economic perspective of Ashworth and Johnson (1996) and the personal identity perspective of Falk and Dierking (2013).

Note that authors' initials are not used in these references (unless there are two authors with the same surname). A more informal style can be used by including an author's first, or given, name, which can be appropriate when mentioning an author for the first time, and especially for particularly significant authors.

At the end of the report a list of references is provided, arranged in alphabetical order, as follows:

References

Ashworth, J. and Johnson, P. (1996) Sources of 'value for money' for museum visitors: some survey evidence. *Journal of Cultural Economics*, 20(1), 67–83.

Davis, J. A. (2011) Putting museum studies to work. *Museum Management and Curatorship*, 26(5), 459–479.

Falk, J. and Dierking, L. D. (2013) *The Museum Experience Revisited*. Walnut Creek, CA: Left Coast Press.

Style variation

The style of presentation can be varied. For example, the above statement could be made drawing less explicit attention to specific authors:

> Researchers have examined museum visitors from a number of perspectives, including, for example, education, economics and personal identity (Davis, 2011; Ashworth and Johnson,1996; Falk and Dierking, 2013).

Specifics and quotations

When referring to specific points from an item of literature, rather than making a general reference to the whole item, as above, page references should be given to the specific point of interest. This is particularly important when referring to a specific point from a substantial publication like a book. Thus, while reference to the general contents of Falk and Dierking's book can be made as above, a specific reference would be made as follows:

> Falk and Dierking (2013: 26) examine the museum experience from the personal, socio-cultural and physical contexts.

Page references should also be given when *quoting* directly from a source:

> They nevertheless observe that these should be considered together since 'the whole is greater than the sum of the parts' (Falk and Dierking, 2013: 26).

A longer quotation (of 2–3 lines or longer) would be indented in the page and handled like this:

> In their discussion of these three contexts, Falk and Dierking note:

> Although we can separate and discuss these contexts as more or less distinct entities, in reality they always interact and connect with each other. The whole that we call the museum experience can only be understood when all the pieces are considered together the whole is greater than the sum of the parts. (Falk and Dierking, 2013: 26)

Advantages and disadvantages

The author/date system is an academic style. Its disadvantage is therefore that referencing is very 'up-front', even obtrusive, in the text. It is not an appropriate style for some practically orientated reports, particularly where the readership is not academic. Large numbers of references using this style tend to clutter the text and make it difficult to read. The system also has the disadvantage that it does not incorporate footnotes (at the foot of the page) or endnotes (at the end of the chapter or report). However, one view is that footnotes and endnotes are undesirable anyway – that if something is worth saying it is worth saying in the text. If notes and asides are nevertheless considered necessary it is possible to establish a footnote system for this purpose in addition to using the author/date system for references to the literature only. This becomes somewhat complex, of course. If a number of footnotes/endnotes are considered necessary then it is probably best to use the footnote/endnote style for everything, as discussed below.

The advantages of the author/date system are that it saves the effort of keeping track of footnote or endnote numbers; it indicates the date of publication to the reader; the details of any one item of literature have to be written out only once; and it results in a tidy, alphabetical list of references at the end of the document or chapter.

Footnote or endnote system

Basic features

The footnote style involves the use of numbered references in the text and a list of corresponding numbered references at the foot of the page, at the end of each chapter or at the end of the report. The term *footnote* originates from the time when the notes were invariably printed at the foot of each page, and this can be seen in older books. However, this came to be viewed as too complex to organise and too expensive to set up for printing, so it was generally abandoned in favour of providing a list of notes at the end of each chapter or at the end of the book. Consequently endnotes are now more common. Ironically, the advent of word processing has meant that the placing of footnotes at the bottom of the page can now be done automatically by computer. Most word-processing packages offer this feature, automatically making space for the appropriate number of footnotes on each page and keeping track of their numbering and so on. Book publishers have, however, generally adhered to the practice of placing the notes all together at the end of the chapter or book.

The actual number reference in the text can be given in brackets (1) or as a superscript:[1] Using the footnote system, the paragraph given above appears as follows:

> Researchers have examined museum visitors from a number of perspectives, including, for example, the educational perspective of Davis,[1] the economic perspective of Ashworth and Johnson[2] and the personal identity perspective of Falk and Dierking.[3]

The list of notes at the end of the report appear in the numerical order in which they appear in the text:

Notes
1. Davis, J. A. (2011) Putting museum studies to work. *Museum Management and Curatorship*, 26(5), 459–479; Ashworth, J. and Johnson, P. (1996) Sources of 'value for money' for museum visitors: some survey evidence. *Journal of Cultural Economics*, 20(1), 67–83; Falk, J. and Dierking, L. D. (2013) *The Museum Experience Revisited*. Walnut Creek, CA: Left Coast Press.

It can be seen that this format is less obtrusive in the text than the author/date system. In fact, it can be made even less obtrusive by using only one footnote, as follows:

> Researchers have examined museum visitors from a number of perspectives, including, for example, educational, economic and the personal identity perspective.[1]

At the end of the report the reference list then appears as follows:

Notes
1. Davis, J. A. (2011) Putting museum studies to work. *Museum Management and Curatorship*, 26(5), 459–479.
2. Ashworth, J. and Johnson, P. (1996) Sources of 'value for money' for museum visitors: some survey evidence. *Journal of Cultural Economics*, 20(1), 67–83.
3. Falk, J. and Dierking, L. D. (2013) *The Museum Experience Revisited*. Walnut Creek, CA: Left Coast Press.

Multiple references

It should never be necessary to write a reference out in full more than once in a document. Additional references to a work already cited can be made using *op. cit.* or references back to previous footnotes. For example, the above paragraph of text might be followed by:

> The research reported on by Falk and Dierking was spread over a quarter of a century.[2]

The footnote would then say:

> 2. Falk and Dierking, *op. cit.*   OR   2. See footnote 1.

Specifics, quotations

Page references for specific references or quotations are given in the footnote rather than the text. So the Falk and Dierking quotation given above would look like this:

> They nevertheless observe that these should be considered together since 'the whole is greater than the sum of the parts'.[1]

> 1. Falk, J., & Dierking, L. D. (2013) *The Museum Experience Revisited*. Walnut Creek, CA: Left Coast Press, p. 26.

A longer quotation (of about three lines or longer) would be indented in the page and handled like this:

> In their discussion of these three contexts, Falk and Dierking note:
>
> > Although we can separate and discuss these contexts as more or less distinct entities, in reality they always interact and connect with each other. The whole that we call the museum experience can only be understood when all the pieces are considered together: the whole is greater than the sum of the parts.[1]

The footnote would then say:

1. Falk, J. and Dierking, L. D. (2013) *The Museum Experience Revisited*. Walnut Creek, CA: Left Coast Press.

Further quotations from the same work might have footnotes as follows:

1. Falk and Dierking, *op. cit.* p. 26.

Advantages and disadvantages of the footnote/endnote system

One of the advantages of the footnote system is that it is less obtrusive than the author/date system and it can accommodate authors' notes in addition to references to the literature, as discussed above. A disadvantage of the system is that it does not result in a tidy, alphabetical list of references. This diminishes the convenience of the report as a source of literature references for the reader. Some writers therefore resort to producing a bibliography in addition to the list of references, resulting in extra work and space. Keeping track of footnotes or endnotes and their numbering in a long report is much less of a disadvantage than it used to be, since this can now be taken care of by the computer.

Comparing two systems

The features, advantages and disadvantages of the two systems, author/date and footnote/endnote, are summarised in Figure 6.8.

One way of combining the advantages of both systems is for the list of notes in a footnote/endnote system to consist of author/date references and then to provide an alphabetical list of references at the end of the report. So the list of footnotes for the above paragraph would then appear as follows:

Feature	Harvard/Author/date	Footnote/Endnote
Reference in text	Author (date)	Number, e.g.: 1
Reference format	Author (date) *Title*. Publishing details	1. Author *Title*. Publishing details, date
Reference list format	Alphabetical list at end of report	Numbered list at: – foot of pages, or – end of chapters, or – end of report
Advantages	– alphabetical bibliography – easy to use – date of publication conveyed in text	unobtrusive in text can add other notes/comments
Disadvantages	– obtrusive in text – can't add notes	– can be difficult to use without computer – no alphabetical bibliography

Figure 6.8 Reference systems: features, advantages, disadvantages

Notes

1. Davis (2011)
2. Ashworth and Johnson (1996)
3. Falk and Dierking (2013)

An alphabetical bibliography would then follow which would be the same as for the author/date system. This approach is particularly useful when making several references to the same document.

Referencing issues

Second-hand references

Occasionally you make a reference to an item which you yourself have not read directly but which is referred to in another document you have read. This can be called a second-hand reference. It is misleading, somewhat unethical, and risky, to give a full reference to the original if you have not read it directly yourself. The reference should be given to the second-hand source, not to the original. For example:

> Kerlinger characterises research as 'systematic, controlled, empirical, and critical investigation of hypothetical propositions about the presumed relations among natural phenomena' (quoted in Iso-Ahola, 1980: 48).

In this instance the writer has not read Kerlinger in the original but is relying on Iso-Ahola's quotation from Kerlinger. The Kerlinger source is not listed in the references; only the Iso-Ahola reference is listed. It is ethical to treat the second-hand reference this way and it is also safe, since any inaccuracy in the quotation then rests with the second-hand source.

In academic research reports – journal articles and theses – second-hand references should be avoided and every effort made to access and refer to the original source.

Excessive referencing

A certain amount of judgement must be exercised when a large number of references are made to a single source. It becomes tiresome when reference is made repeatedly to the same source on every other line of a report. One way to avoid this is to be up-front about the fact that a large section of your literature review is based on a single source. For example, if you are summarising Falk and Dierking's work on the museum experience, rather than have large numbers of formal references to Falk and Dierking cluttering up the text it may be preferable to create a separate section of the report and announce it as follows:

> *The Work of Falk and Dierking*
> This section of the review summarises Falk and Dierking's (2013) work on the museum experience.

Subsequently, formal references need be given only when using specific quotations.

Latin abbreviations

A number of Latin abbreviations are used in referencing.

If there are more than two authors of a work, the first author's name and *et al.* may be used in text references, but all authors should be listed in the bibliography: *et al.* stands for the Latin *et alia*, meaning 'and the others', and is generally presented in italic, although some publishers are now abandoning this practice.

op. cit.   stands for the Latin *opere citato*, meaning 'in the work cited'.

ibid.   In the footnote system, if reference is made to the same work in consecutive footnotes, the abbreviation *ibid.* is sometimes used, short for *ibidem*, meaning 'the same'.

Summary

This chapter provides an overview of the process of reviewing the literature, as a research tool in its own right and as an essential element of any research project. It is noted that a literature review can have a number of purposes and can take a number of forms, ranging from being the entire basis of a research project to being the source of ideas and methods for conducting a research project. The mechanics of searching for relevant literature are examined, including library catalogues, published bibliographies and indexes and electronic sources. The process of reviewing the literature is examined, addressing the sorts of questions that should be asked when conducting such a review for research purposes. Finally, the chapter reviews the process of referencing the literature, examining the characteristics and advantages and disadvantages of the author/date or Harvard system and the footnote or endnote system.

TEST QUESTIONS

1. What are the potential uses of the literature review in research?
2. Name three different sources of bibliographical information and their advantages and limitations.
3. What is the difference between conducting a literature review for the purpose of writing an essay compared with providing the context for a research project?
4. What are the advantages and disadvantages of the author/date referencing system compared with the footnote/endnote system?
5. What is a second-hand reference?

EXERCISES

1. Compile an inclusive bibliography on a topic of your choice, using the sources outlined in this chapter.
2. Choose a research topic and:
   (a) investigate the literature using a library computerised catalogue and any other electronic database available to you;
   (b) explore the literature via literary sources, such as reference lists and indexes in general textbooks, journal contents and lists of references in articles;
   (c) compare the nature and extent of the bibliography arising from the two sources.

Resources

Websites

CASE (Culture and Sport Evidence Programme) Impacts Database: a bibliographical compendium of studies on the impact of arts engagement/investment: www.gov.uk/case-programme

Publications

Examples of bibliographies: Events: Mair and Whitford (2013); the Olympic Games: Veal (2012)
Content analysis: art museum annual reports: Rentschler (2002: 78, 96–103).

Literature reviews:

- Systematic reviews methodology: Littell *et al.* (2008); including qualitative research: Thomas *et al.* (2004); see journal: *Research Synthesis Methods*.
- Examples of literature reviews:
  - art, design and environment and mental health: Daykin *et al.* (2008)
  - arts-based research with children: Driessnack and Furukawa (2012)
  - arts/cultural management research: Perez-Cabanero and Cuadrado-Garcia (2011)
  - attendance/public participation in performing arts: Seaman (2006)
  - creative activity and mental health: Leckey (2011)
  - cultural policy: Selwood (2002)
  - events journal literature: Kim *et al.* (2013)
  - exotic dance: Wahab *et al.* (2011)
  - heavy metal music: Brown (2011)
  - impact of museums and libraries: Wavell *et al.* (2002)
  - lifestyle as a concept: Veal (1993)
  - measuring the economic/social impact of the arts: Reeves (2002)
  - museology: Rounds (2001)
  - museum visitor studies: Kirchberg and Trondle (2012)
  - music and relief of depression: Chan *et al.* (2011)
  - performing arts and adolescent health: Daykin *et al.* (2008)
  - singing and health: Clift *et al.* (2008)

Meta-analysis/interpretation/evaluation:

- meta-analysis: generally: Glass *et al.* (1981), Littell *et al.* (2008);
- study and academic performance: Winner and Cooper (2000);
- survey response rates: Cook *et al.* (2000);
- valuation of cultural resources: Noonan (2003).

Style manuals:

- American Psychological Association (APA) (2009) and www.apastyle.org
- Australia: DCITA (2002);
- UK: Oxford University Press (2012);
- Electronic/digital style manual: Walker and Taylor (1998); APA guidelines at: www.apastyle.org/elecref.html

References

American Psychological Association (APA) (2009) *Concise Rules of APA Style,* Sixth Edition. Washington, DC: APA.

Bowdin, G., Allen, J., O'Toole, W., Harris, R. and McDonnell, I. *Events Management,* Third Edition. London: Routledge.

Brown, A. R. (2011) Heavy genealogy: mapping currents, contraflows and conflicts of the emergent field of metal studies, 1978–2010. *Journal for Cultural Research*, 15(3), 213–242.

Chan, M. F., Wong, Z. Y. and Thayala, N. V. (2011) The effectiveness of music listening in reducing depressive symptoms in adults: a systematic review. *Complementary Therapies in Medicine*, 19(6), 332–348.

Clift, S., Hancox, G., Staricoff, R. and Whitmore, C. (2008) *Singing and Health: Summary of a Systematic Mapping and Review of Non-Clinical Research*. Canterbury: Sidney De Haan Research Centre for Arts and Health, Canterbury Christchurch University.

Cook, C., Heath, F. and Thompson, R. L. (2000) A meta-analysis of response rates in web- or internet-based surveys. *Educational and Psychological Measurement*, 60(6), 821–836.

Daykin, N., Byrne, E., Soteriou, T. and O'Connor, S. (2008) The impact of art, design and environment in mental healthcare: a systematic review of the literature. *Journal of the Royal Society for the Promotion of Health*, 128(2), 85–94.

Daykin, N., Orme, J., Evans, D. and Salmon, D. (2008) The impact of participation in performing arts on adolescent health and behaviour: a systematic review of the literature. *Journal of Health Psychology*, 13(2), 251–264.

DCITA (2002) *Style Manual for Authors, Editors and Printers*. Brisbane: John Wiley.

Driessnack, M. and Furukawa, R. (2012) Arts-based data collection techniques used in child research. *Journal for Specialists in Pediatric Nursing*, 17(1), 3–9.

Evans, G. (2001) *Cultural Planning: An Urban Renaissance?* London: Routledge.

Findling, J. E. and Pelle, K. D. (eds) (2004) *Encyclopedia of the Modern Olympic Movement*. Westport, CT: Greenwood Press.

Getz, D. (2012) *Event Studies; Theory, Research and Policy for Planned Events*, Second Edition. London: Routledge.

Glass, G. V., McGaw, B. and Smith, M. L. (1981) *Meta-Analysis in Social Research*. Beverly Hills, CA: Sage.

Hartley, J. (ed.) (2005) *Creative Industries*. Oxford: Blackwell.

Kim, J., Boo, S. and Kim, Y. (2013) Patterns and trends in event tourism study topics over 30 years. *International Journal of Event and Festival Management*, 4(1), 66–83.

Kirchberg, V. and Trondle, M. (2012) Experiencing exhibitions: a review of studies on visitor experiences in museums. *Curator: the Museum Journal*, 55(4), 435–452.

Leckey, J. (2011) The therapeutic effectiveness of creative activities on mental well-being: a systematic review of the literature. *Journal of Psychiatric and Mental Health Nursing*, 18(6), 501–509.

Littell, J. H., Corcoran, J. and Pillai, V. (2008) *Systematic Reviews and Meta-Analysis*. New York: Oxford University Press.

Mair, J. and Whitford, M. (2013) An exploration of events research: event topics, themes and emerging trends. *International Journal of Event and Festival Management*, 4(1), 6–30.

Noonan, D. S. (2003) Contingent valuation and cultural resources: a meta-analytic review of the literature. *Journal of Cultural Economics*, 27(2), 159–176.

Oxford University Press (2012) *New Oxford Style Manual*. Oxford: OUP.

Page, S. J. and Connell, J. (eds) (2012) *The Routledge Handbook of Events*. London: Routledge.

Perez-Cabanero, C. and Cuadrado-Garcia, M. (2011) Evolution of arts and cultural management research over the first ten AIMC conferences (1991–2009). *International Journal of Arts Management*, 13(3), 56–68.

Pieper, J. (1952/1999) *Leisure, the Basis of Culture*. Indianapolis, IN: Liberty Fund.

Reeves, M. (2002) *Measuring the Economic and Social Impact of the Arts: a Review*. London: Arts Council England.

Rentschler, R. (2002) *The Entrepreneurial Arts Leader: Cultural Policy, Change and Reinvention*. Brisbane: University of Queensland Press.

Rounds, J. (2001) Is there a core literature in museology? *Curator*, 44(2), 194–206.

Seaman, B. A. (2006) Attendance and public participation in the performing arts: a review of the empirical literature. In V. A. Ginsburgh and D. Throsby (eds), *Handbook of the Economics of Art and Culture*. Amsterdam: Elsevier, pp. 415–472. (Also available as Working Paper at: http://aysps.gsu.edu/publications/2006/index.htm

Selwood, S. (2002) The politics of data collection: gathering, analysing and using data about the subsidised cultural sector in England. *Cultural Trends*, 12(47), 13–73.

Thomas, J., Harden, A. and Oakley, A. (2004) Integrating qualitative research with trials in systematic reviews. *British Medical Journal*, 328(7446), 1010–1012.

Towse, R. (ed.) (2003) *A Handbook of Cultural Economics*. Cheltenham: Edward Elgar.

United Nations Intergovernmental Panel on Climate Change (UNIPCC) (2013) *Climate Change 2013: The Physical Science Basis*. Geneva: UNIPCC, available at: <www.ipcc.ch>

Veal, A. J. (1993) The concept of lifestyle: a review. *Leisure Studies*, 12(4), 233–252.

Veal, A. J. (2012) *The Olympic Games: A Bibliography*. Business School, University of Technology, Sydney, Online Bibliography 5, available at: www.olympic.uts.edu.au/downloads/olympic_bib_update2.pdf

Wahab, S., Baker, L. M., Smith, J. M., Cooper, K. and Lerum, K. (2011) Exotic dance research: a review of the literature from 1970 to 2008. *Sexuality and Culture*, 15(1), 56–79.

Walker, J. R. and Taylor, T. (1998) *The Columbia Guide to Online Style*. New York: Columbia University Press.

Wavell, C., Baxter, G., Johnson, I. and William, D. (2002) *Impact Evaluation of Museums, Archives and Libraries: Available Evidence Project*. Aberdeen: Aberdeen Business School, Robert Gordon University, available at: https://www4.rgu.ac.uk/files/imreport.pdf

Weed, M. (2005) Research synthesis in sport management: dealing with 'chaos in the brickyard'. *European Sport Management Quarterly*, 5(1), 77–90.

Weed, M. (2008) Sports tourism research 2000–2004: a systematic review of knowledge and a meta-evaluation of methods. In M. Weed (ed.) *Sport and Tourism: A Reader*. London: Routledge, pp. 90–112.

Winner, E. and Cooper, M. (2000) Mute those claims: no evidence (yet) for a causal link between arts study and academic achievement. *Journal of Aesthetic Education*, 34(3–4), 11–75.

PART 2

Data collection

This section is concerned with six forms of data collection and the process of sampling, which is relevant to all empirical methods. The chapters are: 7 Secondary data sources and measurement; 8 Observation; 9 Qualitative methods: introduction and data collection; 10 Questionnaire surveys: typology, design and coding; 11 Experimental research; 12 The case study method; and 13 Sampling: quantitative and qualitative. Specific chapters on data analysis are provided in Part 3 for secondary data, qualitative methods and questionnaire surveys.

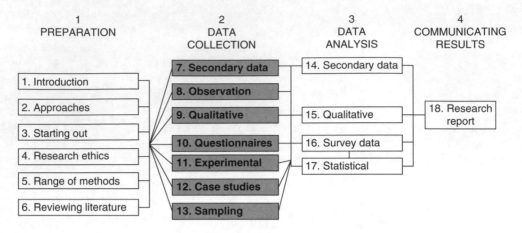

Chapter 7

Secondary data sources and measurement

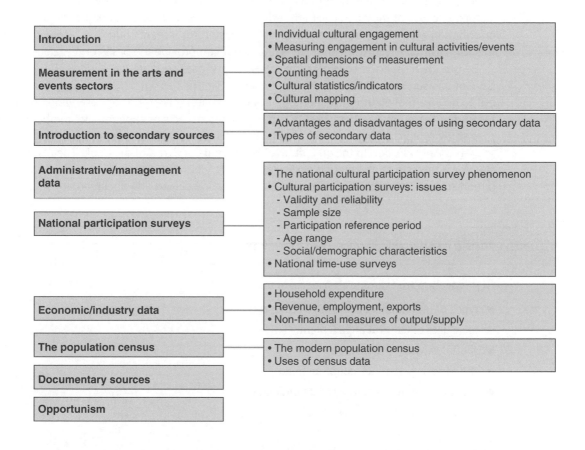

Introduction		• Individual cultural engagement • Measuring engagement in cultural activities/events • Spatial dimensions of measurement • Counting heads • Cultural statistics/indicators • Cultural mapping
Measurement in the arts and events sectors		
Introduction to secondary sources		• Advantages and disadvantages of using secondary data • Types of secondary data

Administrative/management data		• The national cultural participation survey phenomenon
		• Cultural participation surveys: issues
		  - Validity and reliability
		  - Sample size
		  - Participation reference period
		  - Age range
		  - Social/demographic characteristics
		• National time-use surveys

National participation surveys		
Economic/industry data		• Household expenditure • Revenue, employment, exports • Non-financial measures of output/supply
The population census		• The modern population census • Uses of census data
Documentary sources		
Opportunism		

Introduction

In this chapter we consider the use of existing sources of data/information – secondary data – as opposed to the collection of new information – primary data – which is the subject of most of the rest of the book. The chapter examines mainly published statistical sources, such as the census and national and arts/events participation surveys and other sources, such as archives and management data.

A considerable amount of data on arts/events are collected on a regular basis at substantial cost, particularly by government agencies. Often the immediate policy requirements of the data are quite limited – for example, to announce a figure on the number of participants in cultural activity in a country. However, in a sector where research funds are limited, it would seem unwise for the research community to waste such resources by failing to extract all possible potential from them. This requires careful consideration of ways in which available data might be used, and often calls for a quasi-inductive approach to research, posing the question: what can these data tell us?

One aspect of the use of secondary information has already been touched on in Chapter 6 in relation to the use of the literature. In searching the literature the researcher may come across references to statistical or other data which are open to alternative analyses and interpretations or which may not have been fully analysed or exploited by their original collectors, because of their particular interests or limitations on time or money. In other cases, information may exist that was not originally collected for research purposes – for example, the administrative records of an organisation – but can provide the basis for research.

Before giving specific consideration to secondary data sources, we address the general issue of measurement in the arts and events sector. This relates not only to secondary sources but to any form of quantitative method, including quantitative forms of observation (Chapter 8), the design of questionnaires (Chapter 10) and aspects of experimental methods and case study research (Chapters 11 and 12). The initial section of the chapter can therefore be seen as an introduction to the quantitative components of Part 2 of the book. The rest of the chapter is then structured around particular secondary data sources, namely national participation surveys, economic/industry data, the population census and documentary sources.

Measurement in the arts and events sectors

In this section we examine six aspects of measurement:

- types of individual cultural engagement;
- measures of cultural engagement;
- spatial aspects of measurement;
- the generic activity of 'counting heads';
- the idea of cultural statistics and indicators;
- the process of cultural mapping.

Individual cultural engagement

Engagement with the arts varies along a spectrum from the full-time professional at one end, via the amateur and the committed, enthusiastic consumer to the most casual and occasional, mediated audience member or consumer at the other. Various organisations and researchers have addressed this issue, but there is no consensus in the field as to how the range of types of engagement should be identified or the terminology to use. Thus, for example, the Australia Council (2010) divides participation into *creative* and *receptive* types. In research for the Endowment for the Arts (USA) (Novak-Leonard and Brown, 2011) the term 'creation' is also used, but the receptive activity is divided into 'attendance' and 'media-based'.

Production/ consumption	Type of economic involvement	Mode of engagement	Examples
Production/ creative	P1 Professional	Full-time	Actor, musician, artist, writer, manager, producer, teacher
		Part-time	As above, but part-time, often teacher
	P2 Volunteer	Unpaid	Volunteer museum guide or event marshal
	P3 Creative leisure	Amateur	Amateur performer, blogger
		Hobbyist	Painting for pleasure, digital creator
Consumption/ receptive	C1 Audience member	Committed live	Regular (subscriber) concert-goer
		Casual live	Occasional concert/gig attendee
		Mediated (digital)	Watch on TV/DVD, listen on radio, MP3, etc., online/digital
	C2 Consumer/ collector	Committed	Serious: record collector, book reader, etc.
		Occasional	Casual: record collector, book reader, etc.

Figure 7.1 Typology of individual cultural engagement

Drawing on these and other sources, a conceptual typology is represented in Figure 7.1, defined along three dimensions: the traditional production/consumption dimension, type of economic involvement and mode of engagement.

This is not a fully developed and tested typology, but is offered as a contribution to the development of measurement in the field, since each category points to a mode of measurement. There is considerable overlap between the part-time professional category and the creative and volunteer participants, with the latter categories often being seen as a route to professional status. Individuals can, of course, be involved with culture in more than one category, at one period of their lives, or in different periods. It should be noted that there is some resemblance to Robert Stebbins' (1992, 2007) *serious/casual leisure* perspective, with categories P2 and P3 being forms of serious leisure and items C1 and C2 forms of casual leisure.

Measuring engagement in cultural activity/events

Figure 7.2 presents a more practically oriented five-fold typology of ways in which cultural engagement can be measured and the relationships between the measures. The measures can be applied to each of the five types of engagement shown in Figure 7.1. Because professional engagement is so distinctive, different terminology is used, so details are presented separately in Part 2 of Figure 7.2. When formalised and routinised, such measures can be seen as *indicators*, an idea that is discussed further below.

In regard to Part 1 of the table:

A The percentage *participation rate* is the most commonly used measure in cultural policy and planning research: it indicates the proportion of the whole population, or of particular social groups, participating. This is particularly salient because of the public policy emphasis on equity and access. Participation includes consumption, both public (e.g. going to a concert) and private (e.g. listening to the radio or recorded music).

B The *number of participants* is equal to the participation rate multiplied by the population. This means that if the population is rising, the number of participants can be rising even if the participation *rate* is falling.

Measure	Definition	Relationships	Example
1 Non-professional			
A Participation rate	The proportion of a defined population that engages in an activity in a given period of time.		6% of the adult population of community X go to a cultural event at least once a month.
B Number of participants	Number of people in a defined community who engage in an activity in a given period of time.	A × population or C ÷ frequency of visit	20,000 people in community X go to a cultural event at least once a month.
C Volume of activity (visits)	The number of times members of a defined community engage in an activity or visit a venue in a specified time period.	B × visits per time period	There are 2 million visits to cultural events by community X residents in a year.
D Time	Amount of time devoted to all cultural activity by an individual or a community, over a specified period – or time spent on specific activity.	C × time per visit	The average retired person devotes 0.75 hours to cultural activity per day.
E Expenditure	The amount of money spent per individual or a defined community on cultural goods or services over a specified time period.	C × spend per visit	Consumer expenditure on cultural activities in Britain is more than £50 billion a year.
F Intensity/quality	Emotional/temporal/cognitive commitment to engagement with the activity.	A or B × measure of commitment	30% of theatre-goers are members of subscriber lists.
2 Professional engagement			
A Employment rate	% of overall labour force in arts/events + unemployment rate (e.g. among artists).	–	x% of the UK labour force are in the creative industries.
B Number of jobs	Number of people employed in a sector (usually full-time equivalents).	–	1.5 million jobs in the creative industries in UK.
C Volume of activity	Days worked (not generally used).	B × average days worked	x million days worked in creative industries in UK.
D Time	Average or total hours worked (not generally used).	C × hours per day	y million hours worked in creative industries in UK.
E Economic value	Average income, or total wages bill, sales, value added, government expenditure.	D × wage rate	Creative industries contribute £36 billion to UK economy.
F Intensity/quality	Information on qualifications/skills.		x% of creative workers have degrees.

Figure 7.2 Measures/indicators of engagement in cultural activities/events

C The *volume of activity* is equal to the number of participants multiplied by frequency of participation and is one of the measures of significant interest to venue and event managers because it corresponds to the number of tickets sold. This introduces the issue of the nature of the area or 'community' to which the measurements apply, and this is discussed further below.

D *Time* spent on an activity is relevant in the cultural policy context because cultural activities/events compete among themselves and with non-cultural activities for a share of people's relatively fixed leisure time.

E *Expenditure* per visit and in total is, of course, the key measure for the private sector, and increasingly so in the public sector.

F *Intensity* refers to the emotional, and sometimes physical, commitment to engagement with the activity. This might be partly reflected in allocation of time (item D) and money (item E), but also refers to the type of involvement, such as membership of and leadership in organisations (e.g. 'friends of' groups, amateur enthusiasts groups), the time-span of the individual's involvement and peer esteem. This type of measure has not been used extensively in the arts/event research, but in leisure studies the idea of 'serious' leisure (Stebbins, 2007) captures some of it, and in physical activity it is partly captured by physical energy expenditure. In those arts sectors with educational aims (e.g. museums/heritage), intensity might be seen as the extent to which visitors/audiences absorb, retain and value the educational messages on offer.

Part 2 of Figure 7.2 relates to professional involvement with the cultural or creative industries. While equivalent measures can be envisaged for all six categories, the most common is the number of jobs (typically expressed as 'full-time equivalents') and measures of sales, wages or incomes that are related to economic impact. These aspects are followed up in the economic section of the chapter.

Spatial dimensions of measurement

The definitions and examples in Figure 7.2 refer to time periods and to unspecified study areas or 'communities', since all social research is temporally and geographically specific. The time dimension is discussed further at various points in the chapter; here we consider the spatial dimension. Communities can vary from the local, such as a neighbourhood, via villages, towns, cities, regions/states/provinces to nations and international regions, such as the European Union or South-East Asia. Measures of engagement for a community at any one of these levels can refer to residents of the community and to visitors from outside the community – tourists. This is illustrated visually in Figure 7.3. It should be borne in mind that some research methodologies, such as ticket sales at venues, include both residents and tourists, while others, such as resident surveys, include only one category.

Counting heads

As noted in Chapter 5, a key aspect of arts/events policy making, planning and management is the identification of levels of use – 'counting heads' or, to use the terminology adopted in regard to audiences and spectators, counting 'bums on seats'. Figure 7.4 shows a variety of sources of information on arts/events participant/visitor numbers divided into three sections: administrative/secondary sources, questionnaire-based surveys and direct/

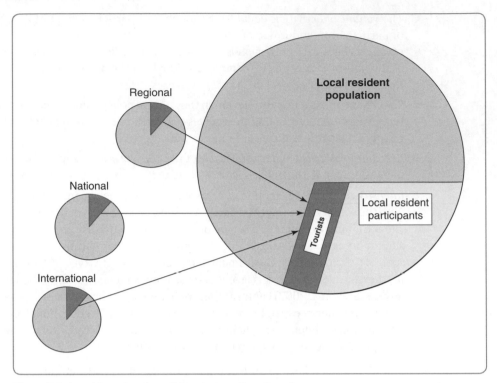

Figure 7.3 Local/non-local participants in culture/events

observational counts. The inclusion of questionnaire-based surveys and observation means that the figure clearly includes more than just secondary data, but the full range of sources/methods is presented here to make the point that none of these methods should be considered in isolation; indeed, for many estimation purposes, data from different sources must be combined. Observation-based counts and survey methods are discussed in Chapters 8 and 10 where further reference is made to Figure 7.4.

Depending on how much information is gathered in the process, counting heads can provide the basis for much more than presentation of numbers. It can facilitate examination, explanation and extrapolation of trends in usage, performance levels (e.g. costs or income per visit), market reach and social/economic impact. The process of analysing these various forms of data and using them to estimate visitor numbers is addressed in Chapter 14.

Cultural statistics/indicators

At least since the 1970s, there have been national and international efforts to develop the collection and dissemination of cultural statistics on a rationalised basis. Development of these systems has taken place under the auspices of organisations such as UNESCO and the Council of Europe and has involved:

- consideration of classification systems for cultural activities and occupations;
- examination of the data requirements of various stakeholders in the cultural industries;
- the planning of social survey programmes, as discussed below;
- international liaison to achieve cross-national comparability.

Method/type	Data available	Additional data required to estimate numbers
Administrative – facility-based		
1 Individual ticket sales	Ticket sales per time period/event	–
2 Bookings data	Facility bookings per time period/event	Group size (may be by sample observation)
3 Season ticket/annual pass sales	Annual/season ticket sales	No. of visits per time period per ticket (by user survey)
4 Membership records/surveys	Member numbers + *if* member visits are automatically recorded: visits per time period per event	If data not collected automatically: member survey: for frequency data
5 Parking ticket sales data	Parking ticket sales per time period per event	Vehicle occupancy (by sample observation)
Questionnaire-based surveys (see Chapter 10)		
6 Resident survey	% participating in activity and/or visiting particular venues/events by type, average frequency per time period	Resident population (from census)
7 On-site visitor interview surveys	% commuters, neighbours*	–
On-site visitor counts (see Chapter 8)		
Automatic counters		
8 Automatic vehicle counters	Number of vehicles per time period	Vehicle occupancy (by sample observations)
9 Automatic pedestrian counters	Number of persons per time period	
10 Video/time-lapse cameras/ aerial photography	Number of persons/vehicles/craft present – sampled times, gives person/vehicle/craft-hours gives person-vehicle hours	For vehicles/craft: vehicle occupancy For all: average length of stay (by survey)
Visual/manual counts		
11 Entrance or exit flows	Number of visitors per time period	–
12 Spot counts of numbers present	Number of persons present – sampled times, gives person-hours	Average length of stay (by survey)

* *Commuters* and *neighbours* live in other administrative areas and use facilities in the local area: the former work in the local area and use local facilities from their workplace while the latter use local facilities from their home.

Figure 7.4 Counting heads in arts/events settings: sources and methods

This has resulted in a number of reports of enquiries and conferences as well as academic commentary, as indicated in the Resources section at the end of the chapter. In an international review of current practice conducted for the United States, Mark Schuster noted the range of institution-based and other approaches to organising this process in various countries, as shown in Figure 7.5.

One of the major outputs from this activity is the *2009 UNESCO Framework for Cultural Statistics*, which is an updated version of a framework first devised in 1986. It is based on a five-component 'culture cycle', as shown in Figure 7.6. The first four, shaded, components refer to the production dimensions of culture. The interconnections between components in the centre indicate that any components may interact with any other and in some cases certain components may be missed out, or at least may be informal – for example, an artist selling an artwork direct to a customer.

The framework is made up of *domains*, comprising 'industries, activities and practices', which may appear in any parts of the cycle. The domains are divided into 'cultural', 'related' and 'transversal', as shown in Figure 7.7. Within this domains framework, hundreds of industry sub-sectors and occupations are identified and listed, drawing from existing general international classification systems, such as the International Standard Industrial Classification (ISIC) and the International Standard Classification of Occupations (ISCO). Since these generic systems

Type of arrangement	Examples (details in Resources section)
Institution-based	
Research division of a government cultural funding agency	Arts Council England, Australia Council
National statistics agency	Office for National Statistics (UK), Australian Bureau of Statistics
Independent non-profit research institute	Boekmanstichting, Netherlands
Government-designated university-based research centre	Creative Industries Innovation Centre (University of Technology, Sydney), Centre for Creative Industries (Queensland University of Technology)
Private consulting firm	International Intelligence on Culture
Cultural observatories	Numerous – see IFACC, Resources section
Non-institution-based	
Networks	Cultural Information and Research Centres Liaison in Europe (CIRCLE) (1984–2007)
Programme models	Harmonised European Time Use Survey; Council of Europe Compendium Project
Journals/periodicals	Cultural Trends, CultureLink

Figure 7.5 Models of national statistics gathering/dissemination arrangements
Summarised from Schuster (2002: 6–11).

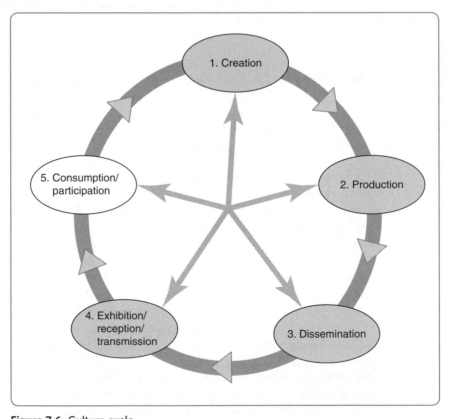

Figure 7.6 Culture cycle
Source: adapted from UNESCO (2009: 20)

	CULTURAL DOMAINS					RELATED DOMAINS	
A Cultural and natural heritage	B Performance and celebration	C Visual arts and crafts	D Books and press	E Audio and interactive media	F Design and creative services	G Tourism	H Sports and recreation
			Intangible cultural heritage*				
			Education and training*				
			Archiving and preserving*				
			Equipment and supporting materials*				

*Transversal domain

Figure 7.7 Framework for cultural statistics domains

Source: Abbreviated version of UNESCO (2009: Figure 2).

are typically used by national statistical agencies, this provides a guide for researchers in the cultural sector to draw on national sources – such as labour market surveys – to compile relevant data and also to design primary data-collection exercises to mesh with official data sources. This, in turn, should, in the long term, provide the basis for international comparisons.

Regarding the consumption/participation component of the culture cycle, it is noted that individual consumption of goods and services is generally associated with the payment of money, so this can be classified using the same industrial/occupational system. However, participation in cultural activities also includes non-traded items – for example, writing a poem, attending a free concert, cultural blogging or watching free-to-air television. Such activity is generally researched by participation or time-use surveys, as discussed later in this chapter. The UNESCO document does not explore activity-classification systems for participation surveys, as discussed below, but does reproduce a United Nations-approved activity-coding system (International Classification of Activities for Time-Use Statistics (ICATUS)) for time-use surveys.

One form of the outcomes of the rationalist drive to develop statistical systems is the phenomenon of *cultural indicators*. These are a version of the key performance indicators discussed in Chapter 3 (Figure 3.13), which are designed to summarise the performance of an organisation or programme in a few measures, usually of a statistical nature, enabling the performance to be compared with national or international industry-wide benchmarks and/ or with performance in previous periods or as set in management targets. Such a move to embrace managerialism is not without its critics in the cultural sector: Schuster (1997: 254), for example, speaks of 'antipathy, if not outright opposition, to the use of performance indicators in the arts and culture', while Madden (2005a: 217) notes that statistics are 'sometimes vilified in the arts'. Nevertheless, the trend seems to be unstoppable.

Even more ambitious is the idea of combining a number of indicators to form a single index, the most well-known general example being the United Nations Human Development Index, which is based on almost 50 national indicators, none of them explicitly cultural (UNDP, 2013). In the cultural context a National Arts Index drawing on 76 individual indicators was developed in 1998 in the United States and is published annually (Kushner and Cohen, 2011, 2012).

Cultural mapping

The desire for a rationalised approach to gathering and disseminating data on cultural activity finds expression in the development of the idea of cultural mapping, which involves compiling a comprehensive picture of cultural industries and activities in a given area.

The process is portrayed in some contexts as a practical tool for planning and policy making, in that it can form a baseline or starting point for the development of a cultural plan, akin to the position statements or audits developed in other sectors and discussed in Chapter 1. In other contexts it is viewed as an advocacy tool to demonstrate the significance of the cultural or creative industries sector to government and society at large, a practice that dates back to at least the 1980s (Casey *et al.*, 1996; Myerscough, 1988). Mercer (2005) argues that the cultural sector should aim to replicate the achievements of the environment sector which, over recent decades, has transformed the status of the environment from a separate entity to something that is seen as permeating all aspects of life and that must therefore be taken into account in all planning, design, development and management processes.

While some of the data sources used in cultural mapping can be seen as primary in nature (e.g. participation surveys), in the cultural mapping process they are often secondary, that is, succinct summaries of data previously collected.

While cultural mapping is seen as particularly appropriate at the local (state/province, county, municipality) level, the term can also be used to describe data compilations at the national level, the most well-known example being the *Cultural Mapping Document* published by the Department of Culture, Media and Sport (2001). While it does not use the term 'cultural mapping', the Arts and Cultural Indicators Project of the Urban Institute (Washington, DC), is a cultural mapping project, focused particularly on ranking cities on the basis of their 'cultural vitality' (Jackson *et al.*, 2006).

The term 'mapping' is not used in an exclusively geographical sense; physical mapping of data may or may not be involved. For example, while the DCMS *Cultural Mapping Document* provides some data broken down into regions, no physical maps are presented. Incorporation of spatial information into databases and their display and analysis are, however, being facilitated by the development of relevant computer software (Gibson *et al.*, 2010).

Some cultural maps are an end in themselves: they record information about an area's current and historical cultural resources and make it available in printed form or online for the use of residents, visitors and scholars. Key features of some are that they are collaborative in compilation and interactive in use (Evans and Foord, 2008: 79).

A number of toolkits providing guidelines for the conduct of cultural mapping have been published (see Resources section). These are typically concerned with the process of assembling, organising and presenting information, but do not extend to providing advice on how the information might be used in the policy-making/planning process, as Evans and Foord (2008: 79) observe. The latter indicate the extent of the data that might be included in a local mapping exercise, as set out in Figure 7.8. The range of information is substantial and includes dynamic elements such as 'growth drivers', so any exercise fully following this pattern would clearly be pointing towards the production of a plan rather than just a compilation of facts.

The Urban Institute project divides indicators into three domains and four tiers. The domains are:

- *presence*, which refers to the availability of mainly institutional opportunities for participation;
- *participation*, which refers to the non-professional aspects of engagement listed in Figure 7.2; and
- *support*, which refers to public and philanthropic/non-profit expenditure and working artists, and can be seen as the financial/economic expression of phenomena included in the other two domains (Jackson *et al.*, 2006: 14).

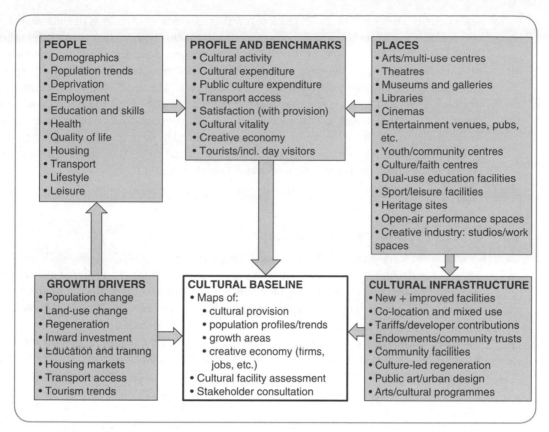

Figure 7.8 Populating a cultural map

Source: modified version of Evans and Foord (2008: 80), Figure 2

The four tiers are pragmatically related to the availability of data, with Tier 1 being publicly, freely and regularly available, nationally generated quantitative data, while Tier 4 refers to intermittent and relatively inaccessible, locally generated qualitative data (Jackson *et al.*, 2006: 35). Pragmatism is inevitable if organisations are to put cultural mapping into operation straight away, and this is evident in the seven indicators presented in the Urban Institute report for the larger United States metropolitan areas:

● number of arts establishments per thousand population;

● employment in arts establishments as a percentage of all employment;

● number of arts non-profit organisations per 1,000 population;

● non-profit community celebrations, festivals, fairs and parades per 1,000 population;

● non-profit arts organisation expenditure per capita;

● level of governmental, non-governmental and individual financial contributions to non-profit arts organisation per capita;

● artist jobs as a percentage of all jobs.

The emphasis on non-profit data results from the regular data-collection work of the National Center for Charitable Statistics, while the lack of financial data on public-sector and commercial organisations and lack of any participation data reflects the absence of any comparable centralised data-collection mechanism for this type of data at the sub-national level. For data at Tiers 2–4, the Urban Institute report provides only case-study examples.

Cultural mapping is therefore a work in progress. One development from this type of comprehensive data-compilation activity is to undertake the analytical and computer programming work to create a satellite account, which is a sub-set of the national accounts specifically for that industry. This means that annual economic data on the industry can be assembled routinely from the national accounts produced by the national treasury. A number of countries have begun to produce such accounts for the cultural or creative industries in recent years, and sources are indicated in the Resources section.

Introduction to secondary data sources

As with the literature, secondary data can play a variety of roles in a research project, from being the whole basis of the research to being a vital or incidental point of comparison. But to be seen as a research method in its own right, the use of secondary data should contribute significantly to answering research questions or testing hypotheses.

Some secondary data are available in a very 'raw' form – for example, organisational membership data – and in such cases the dividing line between primary and secondary data becomes blurred. In other cases the data are highly processed, for example the already published results of national surveys conducted by national agencies. However, in such cases the data may still require considerable additional processing to be useful for the research purpose at hand, and data from different sources may need to be combined in various ways. In some cases the data available in published documents are in a format that is not adequate for the purpose and fresh analysis of the raw data is required – for example, involving accessing computer files of survey data for re-analysis. In this chapter we address just the sources of data; data analysis is addressed in Chapter 14. Before considering specific forms of secondary data, we examine the advantages and disadvantages of using such data and present a typology of secondary data types.

Advantages and disadvantages of using secondary data

Some advantages and disadvantages of using secondary data are listed in Figure 7.9. As with the other techniques/approaches considered in this part of the book, different advantages and disadvantages will come into play depending on the real-world circumstances of the proposed research and the intrinsic nature of the research task. The key message here is that, in the process of selecting methods and data sources, as discussed in Chapter 3, all advantages and disadvantages should be given due consideration.

Types of secondary data

Six main types/sources of secondary data are listed in Figure 7.10 and discussed in the rest of the chapter. The inclusion of national cultural/events surveys might seem incongruous, since they are questionnaire-based surveys and so it might be thought that they should be discussed in Chapter 10. But the class of survey discussed here is the large-scale survey, typically conducted on an annual or periodic basis by a national government body so they

Advantages

- Timing – data may be instantly available.
- Cost – cost of collecting new data avoided.
- Experience – the 'trial and error' experience of those who collected the original data can be exploited.
- Scale – secondary data may be based on larger samples than would otherwise be possible.
- Serendipity – inductive process of data analysis may yield serendipitous findings, which may not have arisen with primary, purpose-designed data collection.

Disadvantages

- Timing – available data may be out of date.
- Design – secondary data have been designed for another purpose, so may not be ideal for current project.
- Analysis limitations – if access to the raw data for re-analysis is not possible, opportunities for analysis/manipulation of the data for the current project may be limited.

Figure 7.9 Advantages and disadvantages of using secondary data

- Administrative/management data
- National culture/events participation surveys
- Economic surveys
- The Census of Population
- Documentary sources
- Opportunism

Figure 7.10 Types of secondary data

take on the characteristics of 'official statistics'. The government departments and agencies that commission them can be seen as the primary users, but they are also used by a variety of other organisations and individuals, including industry bodies and firms, other levels of government, consultants and academics. Where appropriate, reference is made to specific examples in Britain and Australia.

Administrative/management data

Most arts/events organisations generate routine data which can be of use for research purposes and many have management information systems specifically designed to produce data upon which assessments of the performance of the organisation are based. Examples of such data, which may be available on an hourly, daily, weekly, monthly, seasonal or annual basis, are listed in Figure 7.11. It is usually advisable to explore fully the nature, extent and availability of such data, and their potential utilisation, before embarking on fresh data collection. For example, in Case study 3.1 in Chapter 3, the manager of a facility is concerned about declining levels of visits. Before initiating expensive procedures, such as surveys, to investigate the causes it would be advisable to study the available visitor data to determine, for example, whether the decline was across all services, and whether it was taking place at all times or only at certain times of the day, week, season or year.

Numerous agencies are involved in collection of management data for their own administrative purposes, and in many cases the information is available in summary form in their annual reports (particularly if they are public bodies) and sometimes on their websites. But generally the data made public are presented in only summary form and the detail remains

---

- Visitor/user/customer numbers (in various categories)
- Visitor/user/customer expenditure levels/patterns
- Visitor/user/customer characteristics
- Bookings and facility utilisation
- Customer enquiries via various media
- Customer complaints via various media
- Membership numbers and details, where applicable
- Results of past visitor/customer surveys
- Expenditure of the organisation (under various headings)
- Staff turnover/absenteeism, etc.
- Information assembled for strategic/marketing plans

Figure 7.11 Management data

unpublished. Collation of such information, for example as input to a local plan, therefore becomes a research project in its own right. If information across a number of sectors is required at national level, even in summary form, that also often requires considerable effort. Some limited examples of such national collations are listed in the Resources section.

Most customer data is now held in digital form and this provides a basis for research that can feed into policy making and marketing. The complex utilisation of such large data resources is referred to as 'big data' analysis. This involves 'mining' or 'drilling down' into customer data to understand trends and patterns of consumption related to seasonal, demographic and geographical factors, as noted in Chapter 3.

National cultural/events participation surveys

The national cultural survey phenomenon

Arts/events participation surveys are the main source of information, not only on overall levels of participation but also on differences in participation between various groups in the community, such as the young and the old, men and women, and different occupational and income groups. Any arts/events researcher or professional should therefore be familiar with such key data sources.

In most developed countries surveys of cultural participation are conducted by government departments or agencies, and sometimes academic bodies or independent centres, on a regular or occasional basis since at least the 1980s. Each country has tended to adopt different design principles, particularly in the way 'participation' is defined, as discussed below, so that the findings between countries are generally not comparable, although in recent years surveys conducted for the European Commission have begun to correct this for EU member countries. Despite the challenge of comparability, a number of publications have, over the years, sought to bring together data and commentaries on cultural participation from a number of national surveys. Some of these are listed in Figure 7.12.

The first three are print publications but the Council of Europe example is an on-going, annual, web-based project, drawing together information on national cultural policies, but also including participation data. These composite publications reveal that a number of countries conduct cultural/event participation surveys, some on a regular basis, such as once every year or every five years, and some irregularly. In Figure 7.13, details are provided for major examples of such surveys in Europe, Britain, the USA and Australia.

	Hantrais and Kamphorst (1987)	Cushman et al. (2005)	Schuster (1995)	Council of Europe (ongoing)*
Australia	–	•	–	–
Austria	–	–	•	–
Bulgaria	–	–	–	•
Canada	•	•	•	•
Croatia	–	–	–	•
Cyprus	–	–	–	–
Czechoslovakia	•	–	–	–
Denmark	–	–	•	–
Estonia	–	–	–	•
Finland	–	•	•	–
France	•	•	•	–
Germany	–	•	•	•
Great Britain/UK	•	•	•	–
Greece	–	–	–	•
Hong Kong	–	•	–	–
Hungary	•	–	–	•
Ireland	–	–	•	–
Israel	–	•	–	–
Italy	–	–	–	•
Japan	–	•	–	–
Lithuania	–	–	–	•
Netherlands	•	•	•	–
New Zealand	–	•	–	–
Poland	–	•	–	•
Portugal	–	–	•	•
Russia	–	•	–	•
Serbia	–	–	–	•
Slovenia	–	–	–	•
Spain	–	•	•	–
Sweden	–	–	•	–
Switzerland	–	–	–	•
Ukraine	–	–	–	•
USA	•	•	•	–

* Details: see Resources section websites

Figure 7.12 National cultural participation surveys: composite international publications

The following comments can be made on the surveys listed in Figure 7.13:

- There are no separate national surveys of participation in special events. Attendance at special events is included, of course, particularly for the performing arts, but is not specifically identified. Indeed, the Australian Bureau of Statistics includes 'events' in the title of its main survey (7), but does not specifically identify special events. The USA survey (6), however, includes 'performing arts festivals' as a separate activity.
- For the most part, the data refer to participation as a member of a live audience, the exceptions being:
  - the Arts in England survey (4), which also includes watching on TV/DVD and actively taking part, for example painting or being a member of a band or theatre group;
  - the USA survey (6), which includes 'personally performing or creating art';
  - the Australian *More than Bums on Seats* survey (8), which includes 'creative' (active) participation and 'receptive' participation (i.e. as audience member).

181

Country/survey	Organisation/ref.	Details†	Activities covered
Europe (27 countries)			
1 European Cultural Values survey	European Commission (2007)	a. 2007 b. 26,000 c. 15+ d. Year	Ballet/dance/opera, cinema, theatre, sport event, concert, library, historic monuments, etc., museum/gallery, culture on TV/radio, read book.
Britain			
2 Taking Part Survey	DCMS (see ONS, 2012)	a. Annual, 2005– b. 28,000 c. 16+ (11–15)* d. Year	Historic environments, museums, galleries, libraries, archives, arts events, active sport, gambling, broadcasting.
3 Target Group Index	BMRB/Arts Council England (2010)	a. Annual b. 25,000 c. 15+ d. Year	Theatre: plays, opera, ballet; contemporary dance; concerts: classical, jazz, other; art galleries/exhibitions; cinema.
4 Arts in England	Office for National Statistics (Fenn et al., 2004)	a. 2001, 2003 b. 6000 c. 16+ d. 4 weeks, year	Combined arts (carnivals, street arts, circus, cultural festivals); reading fiction, etc.; writing; watching live, watching on TV/DVD and participated in: dance, theatre, music; viewed/made visual arts.
5 Active People Survey	Sport England (see ACE, nd)	a. 2008–10§ b. 190,000 c. 16+ d. Year	Watch TV, friends/family, music, shopping, read, restaurants, day visits, internet use, sport/exercise, gardening, cinema, pubs/bars/clubs, theatre/concerts, DIY, historic sites, museums/galleries, computer games, arts/crafts, play instrument, other.
USA			
6 Survey of Public Participation in the Arts	National Endowment for the Arts (2009)	a. 10-yearly b. 18,400 c. 18+ d. Year	Music (5 categories), performing arts festivals (1), drama (2), dance (2), art exhibitions (2), parks and historic sites, literature. Attending as audience and personally performing.
Australia			
7 Attendances at Selected Cultural Venues and Events	Australian Bureau of Statistics (2010)	a. 5-yearly b. 14,000 c. 15+ d. Year	Art galleries, museums, zoos, botanical gardens, libraries, classical concerts, pop concerts, theatre, dance, musicals/opera, other performing arts, cinema.
8 More than Bums on Seats: Australian Participation in the Arts	Australia Council (2010)	a. 2010 b. 3,000 c. 15+ d. Year	Creative and receptive participation in: visual arts and crafts, theatre and dance, music, creative writing/reading.
9 Children's Participation in Cultural Leisure Activities	Australian Bureau of Statistics (2013a)	a. 3-yearly b. 7,000 c. 5–14 d. Year	Participation in organised cultural activities (singing, dancing, drama, play musical instrument) and attendance at cultural venues/events (library, museum/gallery, performing arts).

DCMS = Department of Culture, Media and Sport, BMRB = British Market Research Bureau.

† a. year of conduct, b. sample size, c. age range of sample, d. participation reference period.

§ Active People survey continues beyond 2010 for sport only.

* Limited sampling and questions for 11–15 year olds.

Figure 7.13 National cultural participation survey details

- The large sample size (190,000) of the Active People Survey (5) is to provide a minimum sample size of 500 for every local council area in England and Wales (there is a separate survey for Scotland). This was linked to the 1997–2010 Labour government's national–local planning/management/funding process, which also included the arts – hence the inclusion of the latter in a Sports Council-sponsored survey. However, the specific planning process was discontinued by the incoming Conservative/Liberal Democrat coalition government in 2010 and the arts questions were dropped (although Sport England continued the survey for sport participation using its National Lottery funds).

Cultural participation surveys: issues

National cultural participation surveys are the main source of information available to researchers on overall participation levels in a range of cultural activities. However, a number of issues, discussed below, arise in the use of these important databases, including:

- questions of validity and reliability;
- sample size;
- the participation reference period;
- the age range of the population covered;
- the range of activities included;
- availability of information on the social characteristics of respondents.

Validity and reliability

National cultural participation surveys suffer from the limitation of all interview surveys in that they are dependent on respondents' own reports of their patterns of participation. How sure can we be, therefore, that the resultant data are accurate? We cannot be absolutely certain, as discussed in Chapter 10; however, a number of features of these surveys lend credence to their reliability and value as sources of data:

- national government statistical organisations, and the commercial polling organisations sometimes involved, have a strong reputation for quality and professionalism in their work and are guided by codes of ethics (Karttunen, 2012);
- the surveys are typically based on large sample sizes;
- the fact that there has been little dramatic variation in the findings of the various surveys over the years is reassuring. Erratic and unexplainable fluctuations in reported levels of participation would have led to suspicions that the surveys were unreliable, but this has generally not happened.

Some commentators have questioned the validity of participation surveys, conducting experiments that show there is a tendency for respondents to exaggerate levels of participation substantially. Studies have shown this for physical recreation surveys (Chase and Godbey, 1983; Chase and Harada, 1984). For some groups, some activities and some surveys there may also be under-reporting of levels of activity (Boothby, 1987). There are no known examples for the cultural sector, but a study of 'landmark events' has demonstrated the problem of accurate recall of events over long time periods (Gaskell *et al.*, 2000). While national survey data, especially when sponsored by governments, have the imprimatur of being 'official statistics', they are subject to all the limitations of questionnaire-based surveys, as discussed in Chapter 10.

Sample size

It is generally the case that the larger the sample size, the more reliable and precise are the survey findings, as discussed in Chapter 13. The surveys listed in Figure 7.13 have samples of several thousand and are therefore subject to only minimal 'statistical error' (a term explained in Chapter 13). While for many arts/events activities covered in the surveys the proportion of the population participating may be small, even 5 per cent of the adult population can represent large numbers of people, for example in Britain this is around 2 million people.

Participation reference period

The level of participation in an activity depends substantially on the 'reference period' used, that is, the period of time to which the participation relates. Thus, for example, the proportion of the population who have been to a concert in the last 24 hours would be quite small, the proportion who have done so in the last month would be higher, while the proportion who have ever been to a concert would be almost 100 per cent. This phenomenon is illustrated by the 2003 Arts in England survey data in Figure 7.14, which shows, for a number of arts/events activities, the proportion of the population who participated at least once in the year prior to interview compared with the proportion who had participated in the last four weeks. It can be seen that in each case the second measure results in a substantially lower participation rate.

The one-year reference period is becoming the international norm (Cushman *et al.*, 2005: 284). This practice has the advantage of covering participation in all seasons of the year in one survey and including relatively infrequent participants. However, it has the disadvantage of introducing possible inaccuracies in respondents' recall of their activities over such a long time period. Use of a shorter reference period has the advantage of increased accuracy of recall, but the disadvantage that any seasonal variation must be covered by interviewing at a number of different times of the year.

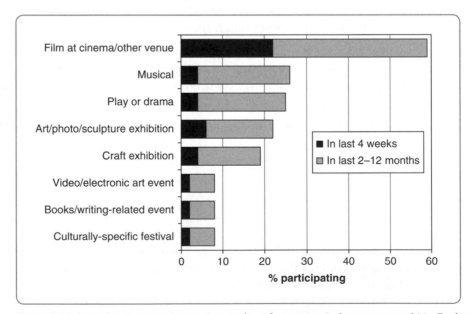

Figure 7.14 Participation rates in arts/events by reference period, persons aged 16+ England, 2003

Source: Arts in England 2003 survey: Fenn (2004), adapted from Table 2.1, p. 29

Age range

Social surveys are generally restricted in terms of age range covered. Some include respondents as young as 12 years, while some cover only those aged 18 and over and others stipulate upper age limits. The surveys presented in Figure 7.13 mostly cover people aged 15 or 16 and over. The reasons for not interviewing young children are three-fold:

1. It may be difficult to obtain accurate information from very young children.

2. It may be considered ethically unacceptable to subject children to the sort of questioning that adults can freely choose to face or not (see Chapter 4).

3. There is a question as to when children are considered to engage in their own independent arts/events activities as opposed to being under the control of parents.

Some surveys present data on children from 'proxy' interviews, in which questions about children's activities are answered by parents: an example is the Australian Bureau of Statistics (2013a) survey of children's participation in culture and sport activities. By contrast, the British Taking Part Survey includes some data from direct interviews with children, but this is limited to those aged 11–15 years.

A lower age limit in the mid-teens has effects on the results, in that for some activities – for example, going to the cinema or pop concerts – teenagers may be a significant proportion of total participants. For other activities – for example, opera-going – the lower age limit may be less important because young people do not form a significant proportion of participants. When using data from arts/events participation surveys, particularly when seeking to compare results from different surveys, it is therefore important to bear in mind the age range covered.

Social/demographic characteristics

In addition to the basic information on participation, national surveys generally include a wide range of background information on the people interviewed, including such variables as gender, occupation, age, education level reached, income, size of family or household unit and ethnicity or country of birth. This information can be used to examine levels of participation by different social groups from either an equity or a marketing point of view, and can also be used to predict demand, as future changes in the underlying socio-demographic structure of the community are likely to affect patterns of demand; this is explored in Chapter 14.

National time-use surveys

Time-use, or time-budget, research became a significant focus of international social research with the conduct of the UNESCO-funded *Multinational Comparative Time-Budget Research Project* in the 1960s (Szalai, 1972). In Britain, such surveys were conducted as long ago as the 1930s when the BBC used them to explore the public's patterns of use of broadcast media, while in Australia they date back to the 1970s. In recent years, time-use surveys have been of particular interest because of the belief that people are becoming increasingly time-pressured. The most recent UK time-use surveys which permit analysis of trends in time use were conducted in 2001 and 2005. UK time-use surveys are conducted in association with 14 other European countries under the auspices of the Harmonised European Time Use Survey, which makes data available online (see Resources section). The most recent in Australia were the 1997 and 2006 surveys conducted by the Australian Bureau of Statistics.

Time-use surveys ask respondents to keep a diary of their activities for one or two days, so they cover all aspects of time use, including arts/events, and are a key source of information

Table 7.1 Time use, Britain and Australia*

Activity	Hours per week, people aged 15+	
	Britain, 2005	Australia, 2006
Sleep	57.2	59.7
TV/video/radio/music	18.3	16.1
Entertainment/cultural	0.6	0.5
Sport/physical recreation	1.2	2.2
Other leisure	21.6	15.7
Paid work	19.8	24.1
Personal care	14.7	17.0
Domestic work/childcare	22.3	22.7
Travel and other	12.3	10.0
Total	168.0	168.0

*NB: some differences between Britain and Australia may be due to differences in activity definitions and some to differing age structure.

Sources: Britain: Office for National Statistics (2006); Australia: ABS (2006)

for cultural studies. Compared with the participation surveys discussed above, the reference period for a time-use survey is effectively one or two days. This overcomes the problem of recall accuracy involved in surveys which use longer recall periods, resulting in more reliable data, but drastically reduces the proportion of sample respondents engaging in any one type of activity. Apart from activities in which large numbers of people engage on most days, notably watching television and listening to the radio, time-use surveys are not ideal for studying individual arts/events activities; they are used to examine broad categories of time use, as shown in Table 7.1. It shows that, in both Britain and Australia, time spent on out-of-home entertainment and culture is, on average, just about half an hour per week. It should, however, be noted that some of the differences in time allocation between the two countries may be a reflection of the difference in age-structure, since the average age of the Australia population is lower than that of Britain.

Economic/industry data

Household expenditure

In most developed countries surveys of household expenditure are conducted on a regular basis. In Britain the *Expenditure and Food Survey* is conducted annually, while the Australian equivalent, the *Household Expenditure Survey*, is conducted every five years (see Resources section). These surveys collect information from a substantial sample of families on their weekly expenditure on scores of items, many of which relate to cultural activity. The main purposes of the surveys are to provide input into calculation of the consumer price index, since the prices of goods/services must be weighted by their importance in household budgets. Figure 7.15 indicates the cultural expenditure items covered in these surveys.

Most of the consumption items actually have mixed uses or purposes, for example computers and transport. In some cases there is information from other sources which may help – for instance, travel surveys indicate that about 30 per cent of travel is for leisure purposes and there are surveys indicating the amount of internet use for various purposes. Since the number of households in a country, state or city is known from the population census, it is possible to use the information to estimate expenditure for the whole country, state or city. The household expenditure surveys also provide information on household size, so expenditure per head can

Telephone charges†
Internet charges†
TV, video, etc.
TV licence (UK)
Home computer equipment†
Blank and pre-recorded media†
Photographic, optical equipment
Books, newspapers, magazines†
Cinema, theatre and museums, etc. admission charges
Other cultural fees and charges
Transport†

† Items only partially cultural

Figure 7.15 Household expenditure: cultural items

be estimated. Information is also provided on expenditure for households with different income levels – typically divided into deciles (ten income categories) or quintiles (five categories).

Revenue, employment, exports

Assessing the scale of the cultural/creative/events industries is a key aspect of the cultural mapping process and of studies of economic potential and impact. The work done on cultural statistics/indicators, as discussed earlier in the chapter, has been important in laying the groundwork for this type of exercise, but it remains difficult because of the diverse and fragmented nature of the sector and problems of definition, particularly if the term *creative industries/occupations* is used. Many organisations that are not part of the cultural sector nevertheless employ significant numbers of creative staff – for example, design staff in the manufacturing sector or art teachers in schools. Conversely, cultural organisations employ non-creative staff – for example, security, box-office and building maintenance staff in a theatre. These challenges are worked through in various cultural mapping exercises, as discussed above.

The three categories of industry information – revenue, exports and employment – are discussed together because they are the focus of the DCMS (2001) *Cultural Mapping Document*, which has become the main source of cultural industry information in Britain over the last decade (Clark, 2009). Table 7.2 lists the 13 industry sectors used in the document, and the overall figures for revenue, employment and exports as at 2001. Data sources include specialist surveys of industry by the Office for National Statistics and customs and excise records. One curious omission is the museums/galleries sector. It is notable that the events sector is not separately identified. If it were to be included, it would include the performing arts sector, but also sports events and exhibitions and conferences which are not included in the DCMS's definition of 'culture'.

Non-financial measures of output/supply

Non-financial measures of industries are as varied as the industries themselves – indeed, more so, since many industries have more than one product and individual products themselves often have a number of measurable characteristics. Thus, for example, non-monetary measures of the output of a theatre include audience numbers, number of shows, numbers of productions of various types and international productions. Some examples from the DCMS document are listed in Figure 7.16, the sources being from industry periodicals, consultant reports and formal audience measurement processes.

Table 7.2 Cultural industry sectors and revenue, employment and exports (UK, 2001)

Industry/sector	Revenue £bn	Employment '000s	Exports £bn
Advertising	3.0	93	0.8
Architecture	1.7	21	0.1
Arts and antiques market	3.5	37	0.6
Crafts	0.4	24	0.1
Design	26.7	76	1.0
Designer fashion	0.6	12	0.3
Film and video	3.6	45	0.7
Interactive leisure software	1.0	21	0.5
Music	4.6	122	1.3
Performing arts	0.5	74	0.1
Publishing	18.5	141	1.7
Software and computer services	36.4	555	2.8
Television and radio	12.1	102	0.4
Total	**112.6**	**1,323**	10.4

Source: DCMS (2001: 10–12)

Industry sector	Measure	Source
Advertising	Agency winners at Cannes International Advertising Festival	*Variety, Lions Daily*
Film and video	Titles produced (annual)	*BFI Handbook, Screen Digest*
Music	Number of concerts by venue capacity	*NMC/KPMG*
Performing arts	Performances by major companies	*SOLT Box Office Data Report, TMA Audience Data*
Publishing	Book-buying and newspaper readership by region	*Book Sales Yearbook, TGI/ BMRB*
Television/radio	TV station audience share	*RAJAR*

Figure 7.16 Examples of non-financial measures of output/supply

Source: Compiled from DCMS (2001)

The population census

Historical sources indicate that the taking of a census of the whole population, for taxation and other purposes, is a long-standing practice of governments dating back at least to the Roman Empire. A well-known example is the *Domesday Book*, compiled by William the Conqueror for the whole of England in the eleventh century.

The modern population census

The population census is an important source of information and any aspiring cultural manager or researcher should be fully aware of its content and potential. A complete census of the population is taken in Britain by the Office for National Statistics (ONS) every ten years; the latest was 2011, and before that 1991, 1981 and so on back to 1801. It is, however, likely that the 2011 census will be the last, as other forms of data may provide a cheaper means of assembling the required data (the 2011 census cost almost £500 million to conduct and analyse). Details of discussions on the future of the British census can be found under 'Beyond 2011' on the ONS website (see Resources section). Finland has already abandoned complete censuses, finding that the required data are already available through governmental administrative records (Karttunen, 2001). In Australia, because the population is growing relatively rapidly, a census is conducted every five years. It is a statutory requirement for householders (and hoteliers, hospital managers, boarding school principals and prison governors) to fill out a census form on 'census night', indicating the number of people, including visitors, staying in the building, and their age, gender, occupation and so on. Some people escape the net, for instance illegal immigrants and people sleeping rough, but efforts are even made to contact as many of the latter as possible on census night, so generally the information is believed to be reliable and comprehensive.

Data from the census are available at a number of geographical levels, from national down to the level of enumeration districts (EDs) (collection districts (CDs) in Australia), as indicated in Figure 7.17. EDs are small areas, with populations of around 250 to 500, which a single census collection officer deals with. By adding together data from a few EDs, a cultural facility or event manager can obtain data on the demographic characteristics of the population of the catchment area of the facility. An enormous amount of information is available on each of these areas, as listed in Figure 7.18.

Britain	Australia
National	National
Regions	State
Counties	Postal codes
Local government areas	Local government areas
Parliamentary constituencies	State and federal parliament electorates
Enumeration districts (EDs)	Collection districts (CDs)

Figure 7.17 Census data: geographical levels of availability

Resident population

- Number of males/females
- Number/proportion in 5-year age groups (and single years for under 20s)
- Numbers of people:
    - with different religions
    - by country of birth
    - speaking different languages
    - by country of birth of parents
- Numbers of families/households:
    - of different sizes
    - with different numbers of dependent children
    - that are single-parent families
    - with various numbers of vehicles
- Numbers of people:
    - who left school at various ages
    - with different educational/technical qualifications
    - in different occupational groups
    - by working hours
    - unemployed
    - living in different types of dwelling

Figure 7.18 Census data available

Uses of census data

It can be seen that none of the census information is concerned directly with cultural activity, so why should the census be of interest to the arts/events researcher? Among the uses, which are explored further in Chapter 14, are:

● planning cultural facilities/events and conducting feasibility studies – provision of socio-demographic information;

● area management/marketing – information on the local community;

● facility performance evaluation – measurement of market penetration;

● market segmentation – based on socio-economic and spatial residential patterns.

Documentary sources

Documentary sources lie somewhere between literature and management/administrative data as an information source for research. Typical examples are listed in Figure 7.19. In many cases these sources are wholly or partially available online, so 'digital sources' could be seen increasingly as a more appropriate categorisation. Many of these sources are important for historical research, either for a primarily historical research project or as background for a project with a contemporary focus. The dividing line between primary and secondary data becomes blurred here, since such sources are seen as primary resources for historians and media studies researchers. There is also a blurring of the boundaries between qualitative and quantitative analysis. Approaches to analysing such data are therefore addressed in Chapter 15.

● Minutes of committee/council/board meetings
● Correspondence of an organisation or an individual
● Archives (may include both of the above and other papers)
● Popular literature, such as novels, magazines
● Newspapers, particularly coverage of specific topics and/or particular aspects, such as editorials, advertising or correspondence columns
● Brochures and advertising material
● Visitor feedback (e.g. in visitor books, digital feedback, social media)
● Diaries

Figure 7.19 Documentary sources

Opportunism

Secondary data often give rise to what might be called opportunistic research, as discussed in Chapter 3. This applies to many of the government-sponsored surveys discussed above: data exist and have been used by the collecting agency only for limited purposes, or in internal policy-making processes which are not in the public domain, so a researcher sees this as an unexploited opportunity for research. An example is the exploration of the usefulness of data on the performing arts in Britain and the USA by Feist (1998). Further examples are explored in Chapter 14.

Summary

This chapter is concerned with sources of secondary data, that is, data which have been collected by others for their own purposes but which might be utilised for current research purposes. There are potential cost- and time-saving advantages to such a strategy and even an ethical dimension, which suggests that scarce resources should not be expended on new data collection if suitable data already exist. The chapter reviews a number of sources of secondary data commonly used in cultural research, namely national cultural participation surveys, economic/industry data, the population census, documentary data and documentary sources. Analysis of such data is discussed in Chapter 14.

TEST QUESTIONS

1. What are the advantages and disadvantages of secondary data analysis?
2. What is cultural mapping and what are its aims?
3. What are some of the issues to be considered when using data from cultural participation surveys?
4. What are the names of the main cultural participation surveys conducted in your country?
5. The chapter lists nine sources of 'management data'. What are they?
6. The chapter lists seven types of 'documentary' source. What are they?

EXERCISES

No exercises are offered for this chapter, but exercises using secondary data are presented in Chapter 14.

Resources

Websites

(All URLs correct as at August 2013)

International

- Global Leisure Survey (guide to national leisure/cultural participation sources): www.leisuresources.net
- Council of Europe cultural policies/data: www.culturalpolicies.net/web/index.php
- Eurostat: http://epp.eurostat.ec.europa.eu/portal/page/portal/eurostat/home
- Harmonised European Time Use Survey: https://www.h2.scb.se/tus/tus
- International Federation of Arts Councils and Culture Agencies (IFACCA): www.ifacca.org

UK

- National statistics agency: Office for National Statistics: www.ons.gov.uk
- Arts participation: Arts Council England: www.artscouncil.org.uk/what-we-do/research-and-data/arts-audiences/
- CASE (Culture and Sport Evidence) programme (DCMS): summaries of Taking Part Survey and other data: www.gov.uk/case-programme#case-database
- Population census: www.statistics.gov.uk – click on 'Population' for past census results and search on 'Beyond 2011' for discussions on future alternatives.
- Scotland: Scottish Household Survey 'Culture and Sport Module': www.scotland.gov.uk/Topics/Statistics/16002/PublicationCulture
- Taking Part Survey: www.gov.uk/government/publications/taking-part-the-national-survey-of-culture-leisure-and-sport-adult-and-child-report-2011–12

Australia

- Attendances at cultural venues/events: Australian Bureau of Statistics (ABS): www.abs.gov.au
- Australia Council: www.australiacouncil.gov.au
- Cultural Ministers' Council: www.cmc.gov.au
- National statistics agency: Australian Bureau of Statistics: National Centre for Culture and Recreation Statistics: attendance at cultural venues/events, household expenditure survey, population census: www.abs.gov.au
- ARC Centre of Excellence for Creative Industries and Innovation: http://cci.edu.au/
- Creative Industries Innovation Centre: www.enterpriseconnect.gov.au/industrysupport/creativeindustries

USA

- Americans for the Arts: National Arts Index: www.artsindexusa.org/national-arts-index
- National Endowment for the Arts: www.nea.gov
- Cultural Policy and Arts National Data Archive: CPANDA: www.cpanda.org

Other

- Boekmanstichting, Netherlands: www.boekman.nl/en
- Cultural Information and Research Centres Liaison in Europe (CIRCLE), operated 1984–2007, but website still available (August 2013): www.circle-network.org
- Harmonised European Time Use Survey: https://www.h2.scb.se/tus/tus/
- International (London-based) consultancy: http://internationalintelligenceonculture.org
- International Federation of Arts Councils and Culture Agencies (IFACCA): http://ifacca.org/

Publications

- Measurement: types of engagement in culture: Australia Council (2010), Novak-Leonard and Brown (2009).

- Cultural indicators – see cultural statistics.
- Cultural mapping: Evans and Foord (2008: 78–90), Higgs and Cunningham (2008), Lee and Gilmore (2012), Mercer (2005), Bakhshi *et al.* (2013)
  - o Toolkits: British Council (2010), Creative City Network (2010)
  - o Spatial aspects: Gibson *et al.* (2010)
  - o Employment statistics: Higgs and Cunningham (2008)
  - o Examples: DCMS (2001), KEA European Affairs (2006), Lee and Gilmore (2012)
- Cultural participation surveys – as in Figure 7.13
  - o Australia: ABS (2010, 2013a), Australia Council (2010)
  - o Britain/England/UK: see Arts Council England and CASE websites above, ONS (2012), Arts Council England (2010, nd), Fenn *et al.* (2004)
  - o Europe: European Commission (2007), Eurostat (2011)
  - o USA: National Endowment for the Arts (2009)
- Cultural participation surveys – other
  - o Australia: Cultural Ministers Council (2008), Veal (2003)
  - o England: Bunting *et al.* (2008), Keaney (2008); CASE (Culture and Sport Evidence) programme: Cooper (2012), O'Brien (2012), Skelton *et al.* (2002)
  - o France: Coulangeon (2013)
  - o Scotland: McCall and Playford (2012)
  - o USA: DiMaggio and Mukhtar (2004), Pettit (2000)
  - o Global: Hantrais and Kamphorst (1987), Cushman *et al.* (2005)
  - o Europe: European Commission (2007), Eurostat (2011)
- Cultural statistics/indicators: Ferres *et al.* (2010), Karttunen (2012), Kushner and Cohen (2011), Madden (2005a), O'Brien (2012), Schuster (1997), Turbide and Laurin (2009), Zorloni (2010).
- Documentary sources: Altheide (2000), Kellehear (1993).
- Economic data:
  - o economic significance of the arts: Centre for Economics and Business Research (2013) Gordon and Beilby-Orrin (2007), KEA European Affairs (2006)
  - o employment: Clark (2009), Gibson *et al.* (2002)
  - o employment and expenditure, Europe: Eurostat (2011)
  - o satellite accounts: DCMS (2011), ABS (2013)
  - o UK local government data: CIPFA (annual)
- Facility use: Overskaug *et al.* (2010); local facility use data (including cultural facilities: costs, income), UK: Chartered Institute of Public Finance and Accountancy (CIPFA) (annual).
- International comparisons of arts data: Gordon and Beilby-Orrin (2007), Feist (1998), IFACCA (2002), Madden (2004).
- Networks: Madden (2005b).
- Performance indicators: see cultural statistics/indicators.
- Reliability of cultural surveys: Chase and Godbey (1983), Chase and Harada (1984), Cushman and Veal (1993).

- Satellite accounts – see economic data.
- Survey data: Keaney (2008); in Scotland: McCall and Playford (2012).
- Time-use surveys: Pentland *et al.* (1999)
  - International Classification of Activities for Time-Use Statistics (ICATUS): UN (2005)
  - Harmonised European Time Use Survey: https://www.h2.scb.se/tus/tus/
- Use of ticket/admissions data: museums: Davidson and Sibley (2011), Overskaug *et al.* (2010); theatre: Willis *et al.* (2012).
- Visitor feedback: Chen (2012).

References

Altheide, D. L. (2000) Tracking discourse and qualitative document analysis. *Poetics*, 27(3), 287–299.

Arts Council England (ACE) (2010) *Arts attendance in England and Great Britain, 2009/10 Estimates from the Target Group Index Survey*. London: Arts Council England.

Arts Council England (ACE) (nd) *Active People Survey*. London: ACE, available at: www.artscouncil.org.uk/what-we-do/research-and-data/arts-audiences/active-people-survey/

Australia Council (2010) *More than Bums on Seats: Australian Participation in the Arts*. Sydney: Australia Council.

Australian Bureau of Statistics (ABS) (2006) *How Australians Use Their Time, 2006* (Cat. No. 4153.0). Canberra: ABS.

Australian Bureau of Statistics (ABS) (2010) *Attendance at Selected Cultural Venues and Events* (Cat. No. 4114.0). Canberra: ABS.

Australian Bureau of Statistics (ABS) (2007) *Work in Selected Culture and Leisure Activities* (Cat. No. 6281.0). Canberra: ABS.

Australian Bureau of Statistics (ABS) (2013a) *Children's Participation in Cultural and Leisure Activities* (Cat. No. 49010DO001). Canberra: ABS, available on-line only, at: www.abs.gov.au

Australian Bureau of Statistics (ABS) (2013b) *Discussion Paper: Cultural and Creative Activity Satellite Accounts, Australia* (Cat. No. 5271.0.55.001). Canberra: ABS, available at: www.abs.gov.au

Bakhshi, H., Freeman, A. and Higgs, P. (2013) *A Dynamic Mapping of the UK's Creative Industries*. London: Nesta (National Endowment for Science, Technology and the Arts), available at www.nesta.org.uk

BMRB/Arts Council England (2010) *Arts Attendance in England and Great Britain, 1994/1995 – 2009/2010: Estimates from the Target Group Index Survey*. London: Arts Council England, available at: www.artscouncil.org.uk/what-we-do/research-and-data/arts-audiences/

Boothby, J. (1987) Self-reported participation rates: further comment. *Leisure Studies*, 6(1), 99–104.

British Council (2010) *Mapping the Creative Industries: A Toolkit*. London: British Council.

Bunting, C., Chan, T. W., Goldthorpe, J., Keaney, E. and Oskala, A. (2008) *From Indifference to Enthusiasm: Patterns of Arts Attendance in England*. London: Arts Council England, available at: www.artscouncil.org.uk

Casey, B., Dunlop, R. and Selwood, S. (1996) *Culture as Commodity? The Economics of the Arts and Built Heritage in the UK*. London: Policy Studies Institute.

Centre for Economics and Business Research (2013) *The Contribution of the Arts and Culture to the National Economy*. London: Arts Council England and National Museum Directors' Council.

Chartered Institute of Public Finance and Accountancy (CIPFA) (annual) *Culture, Sport and Recreation Statistics*. London: CIPFA.

Chase, D. R. and Godbey, G. C. (1983) The accuracy of self-reported participation rates. *Leisure Studies*, 2(2), 231–236.

Chase, D. and Harada, M. (1984) Response error in self-reported recreation participation. *Journal of Leisure Research*, 16(4), 322–329.

Chen, C.-L. (2012) Representing and interpreting traumatic history: a study of visitor comment books at the Hiroshima Peace Memorial Museum. *Museum Management and Curatorship*, 27(4), 375–392.

Clark, D. (2009) Crunching creativity: an attempt to measure creative employment. *Creative Industries Journal*, 2(3), 217–230.

Cooper, A. (2012) The drivers, impact and value of CASE: a short history from the inside. *Cultural Trends*, 21(4), 281–289.

Coulangeon, P. (2013) Changing policies, challenging theories and persisting inequalities: social disparities in cultural participation in France from 1981 to 2008. *Poetics*, 41(2), 177–209.

Creative City Network (2010) *Cultural Mapping Toolkit.* Vancouver, BC: Creative Cities Network/Legacies Now.

Cultural Ministers Council (2008) *Vital Signs: Cultural Indicators for Australia.* Canberra: Cultural Ministers Council, available at: www.culturaldata.gov.au/publications/statistics-working-group/cultural_participation

Cushman, G. and Veal, A. J. (1993) The new generation of leisure surveys – implications for research on everyday life. *Leisure and Society*, 16(1), 211–220.

Cushman, G., Veal, A. J. and Zuzanek, J. (eds) (2005) *Free Time and Leisure Participation: International Perspectives.* Wallingford: CABI Publishing.

Davidson, L. and Sibley, P. (2011) Audiences at the 'new' museum: visitor commitment, diversity and leisure at the Museum of New Zealand Te Papa Tongarewa. *Visitor Studies*, 14(2), 176–194.

Department of Culture, Media and Sport (2001) *Cultural Mapping Document.* London: DCMS.

Department of Culture, Media and Sport (2013) *Creative Industries Economic Estimates: Full Statistical Release.* London: DCMS.

DiMaggio, P. and Mukhtar, T. (2004) Arts participation as cultural capital in the United States, 1982–2002: signs of decline? *Poetics*, 32(2), 169–194.

European Commission (2007) *European Cultural Values: Special Eurobarometer 278.* Brussels: European Commission, available at: http://ec.europa.eu/public_opinion/archives/eb_special_en.htm

Eurostat (2011) *Cultural Statistics. Eurostat Pocketbook.* Brussels: European Commission, available at: http://epp.eurostat.ec.europa.eu

Evans, G. and Foord, J. (2008) Cultural mapping and sustainable communities: planning for the arts revisited. *Cultural Trends*, 17(2), 65–96.

Feist, A. (1998) Comparing the performing arts in Britain, the US and Germany: making the most of secondary data. *Cultural Trends*, 8(31), 29–47.

Fenn, C., Bridgwood, A. and Dust, K. (2004) *Arts in England 2003: Attendance, Participation and Attitudes, Research Report 37.* London: Arts Council England.

Ferres, K., Adair, D. and Jones, R. (2010) Cultural indicators: assessing the state of the arts in Australia. *Cultural Trends*, 19(4), 261–272.

Gaskell, G. D., Wright, D. B. and O'Muirheartaigh, C. A. (2000) Telescoping of landmark events: implications for survey research. *Public Opinion Quarterly*, 64(1), 77–89.

Gibson, C., Brennan-Horley, C. and Warren, A. (2010) Geographic information technologies for cultural research: cultural mapping and the prospects of colliding epistemologies. *Cultural Trends*, 19(4), 325–348.

Gibson, C., Murphy, P. and Freestone, R. (2002) Employment and socio-spatial relations in Australia's cultural economy. *Australian Geographer*, 33(2), 173–189.

Gordon, J. C. and Beilby-Orrin, H. (2007) *International Measurement of the Economic and Social Importance of Culture.* Paris: Organisation for Economic Co-operation and Development (OECD), available at: www.oecd.org/std/na/37257281.pdf

Hantrais, L. and Kamphorst, T. J. (eds) (1987) *Trends in the Arts: A Multinational Perspective.* Amersfoot, Netherlands: Giordano Bruno.

Higgs, P. and Cunningham, S. (2008) Creative industries mapping: where have we come from and where are we going? *Creative Industries Journal*, 1(1), 7–30.

International Federation of Arts Councils and Culture Agencies (IFACCA) (2002) *International Comparisons of Arts Participation Data*. Sydney: IFACCA (see website above).

Jackson, M. R., Kabwasa-Green, F. and Herranz, J. (2006) *Cultural Vitality in Communities: Interpretation and Indicators*. Washington, DC: Urban Institute, available at: www.urba.org

Karttunen, S. (2001) How to make use of census data in status-of-the-artist studies: advantages and shortcomings of the Finnish register-based census. *Poetics*, 28(4), 273–290.

Karttunen, S. (2012) Cultural policy indicators: reflections on the role of official statisticians in the politics of data collection. *Cultural Trends*, 21(2), 133–147.

KEA European Affairs (2006) *The Economy of Culture in Europe: Study Prepared for the European Commission*. Brussels: European Commission, available at: http://ec.europa.eu/culture/key-documents/doc873_en.htm

Keaney, E. (2008) Understanding arts audiences: existing data and what it tells us. *Cultural Trends*, 17(2), 97–113.

Kellehear, A. (1993) *The Unobtrusive Researcher: A Guide to Methods*. Sydney: Allen and Unwin.

Kushner, R. J. and Cohen, R. (2011) Measuring national-level cultural capacity with the National Arts Index. *International Journal of Arts Management*, 13(3), 20–40.

Kushner, R. J. and Cohen, R. (2012) *National Arts Index 2012: An Annual Measure of the Vitality of the Arts and Culture in the United States: 1998–2010*. Washington, DC: Americans for the Arts, available at: www.artsindexusa.org/national-arts-index

Lee, D. and Gilmore, A. (2012) Mapping cultural assets and evaluating significance: theory, methodology and practice. *Cultural Trends*, 21(1), 3–28.

Madden, C. (2004) *Making Cross-country Comparisons of Cultural Statistics: Problems and Solutions*. Sydney: Australia Council and IFACCA (available at Australia Council website – see above).

Madden, C. (2005a) Indicators for arts and cultural policy: a global perspective. *Cultural Trends*, 14(3), 217–247.

Madden, C. (2005b) International networks and arts policy research. *International Journal of Cultural Policy*, 11(2), 129–143.

McCall, V. and Playford, C. (2012) Culture and the Scottish Household Survey. *Cultural Trends*, 21(2), 149–172.

Mercer, C. (2005) From indicators to governance to mainstream: tools for cultural policy and citizenship. In C. Andrew and M. Gattinger (eds) *Accounting for Culture: Thinking Through Cultural Citizenship*. Ottawa: University of Ottawa Press, pp. 9–20.

Myerscough, J. (1988) *The Economic Importance of the Arts*. London: Policy Studies Institute.

National Endowment for the Arts (2009) *2008 Survey of Public Participation in the Arts*. Washington DC: NEA.

Novak-Leonard, J. L. and Brown, A. S. (2011) *Beyond Attendance: A Multi-Modal Under-standing of Arts Participation*. Washington, DC: National Endowment for the Arts.

O'Brien, D. (2012) The Culture and Sport Evidence programme: new forms of evidence and new questions for cultural policy (special issue editorial). *Cultural Trends*, 21(4), 275–280.

Office for National Statistics (2006) *Time Use Survey, 2005*. London: ONS, available at: www.ons.gov.uk

Office for National Statistics (ONS) (2012) *Taking Part: The National Survey of Culture, Leisure and Sport Adult and Child Report 2011/12*. London: ONS.

Overskaug, K., Holt, G., Hagen, K. G., Noess, A. and Steffensen, M. (2010) An analysis of visitation patterns at the Museum of Natural History and Archaeology, Trondheim, Norway, from 1954 to 2006. *Visitor Studies*, 13(1), 107–117.

Pentland, W. E., Harvey, A. S., Powell Lawton, M. and McColl, M. A. (eds) (1999) *Time Use Research in the Social Sciences*. New York: Kluwer/Plenum.

Pettit, B. (2000) Resources for studying public participation in and attitudes towards the arts. *Poetics*, 27(4), 351–395.

Schuster, J. M. (1995) The public's interest in the art museum's public. In S. Pearce (ed.) *Arts in Museums (New Research in Museum Studies, Vol. V)*. London: Athlone.

Schuster, J. M. (1997) The performance of performance indicators in the arts. *Nonprofit Management and Leadership*, 7(3), 253–269.

Schuster, J. M. (2002) *Informing Cultural Policy: The Research and Information Infrastructure*. New Brunswick, NJ: Center for Urban Policy Research, Rutgers, State University of New Jersey.

Skelton, A., Bridgwood, A. and Duckworth, K. (2002) *Arts in England: Attendance, Participation and Attitudes in 2001*. London: Arts Council of England.

Stebbins, R. A. (1992) *Amateurs, Professionals and Serious Leisure*. Montreal: McGill-Queen's University Press.

Stebbins, R. A. (2007) *Serious Leisure: A Perspective for Our Time*. New Brunswick, NJ: Transaction Publishers.

Szalai, A. (ed.) (1972) *The Use of Time: Daily Activities of Urban and Suburban Populations in Twelve Countries*. The Hague: Mouton.

Turbide, J. and Laurin, C. (2009) Performance measurement in the arts sector: the case of the performing arts. *International Journal of Arts Management*, 11(2), 56–70.

United Nations (2005) *A Guide to Producing Statistics on Time Use: Measuring Paid and Unpaid Work*. New York: Department of Economic and Social Affairs Statistics Division, United Nations.

United Nations Education, Scientific and Cultural Organisation (UNESCO) (2009) *Framework for Cultural Statistics*. Paris: UNESCO.

United Nations Human Development Programme (UNDP) (2013) *Human Development Report 2013*. New York: UNDP, available at: http://hdr.undp.org

Veal, A. J. (2003) Tracking change: leisure participation and policy in Australia, 1985–2002. *Annals of Leisure Research*, 6(3), 245–277.

Veal, A. J. (2010) *Leisure, Sport and Tourism: Politics, Policy and Planning*. Wallingford: CABI Publishing.

Willis, K. G., Snowball, J. D. and Wymer, C. (2012) A count data travel cost model of theatre demand using aggregate theatre booking data. *Journal of Cultural Economics*, 36(2), 91–112.

Zorloni, A. (2010) Managing performance indicators in visual art museums. *Museum Management and Curatorship*, 25(2), 167–180.

Chapter 8

Observation

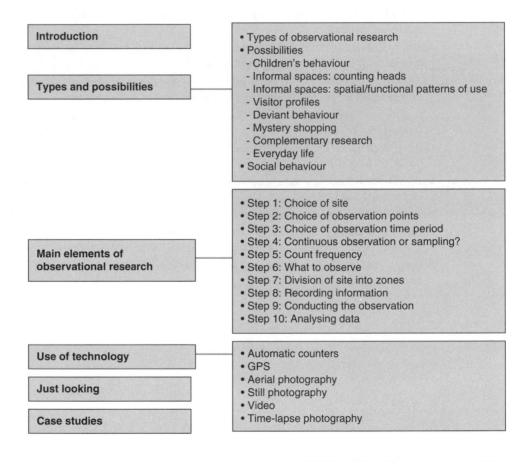

Introduction	• Types of observational research
	• Possibilities
	  - Children's behaviour
	  - Informal spaces: counting heads
	  - Informal spaces: spatial/functional patterns of use
	  - Visitor profiles
	  - Deviant behaviour
	  - Mystery shopping
	  - Complementary research
	  - Everyday life
	• Social behaviour

Types and possibilities	

Main elements of observational research	• Step 1: Choice of site • Step 2: Choice of observation points • Step 3: Choice of observation time period • Step 4: Continuous observation or sampling? • Step 5: Count frequency • Step 6: What to observe • Step 7: Division of site into zones • Step 8: Recording information • Step 9: Conducting the observation • Step 10: Analysing data

Use of technology	• Automatic counters • GPS • Aerial photography • Still photography • Video • Time-lapse photography
Just looking	
Case studies	

Introduction

The aim of this chapter is to draw attention to the importance of *looking* in research and to introduce some of the specific approaches of observational methods. It examines situations in which observation is particularly appropriate and outlines the main steps to be taken in designing and conducting an observation-based project. Observation is a neglected technique in social research; nevertheless, while it is rarely possible to base the whole of a project on observation, the technique has a vital role to play, formally or informally, in most research strategies. Typically, observation is one of a number of techniques that may be used in a study, especially when 'head counting' is concerned, as indicated in Figure 7.4.

The chapter is located in Part 2 of the book which is concerned with data collection, but there is no corresponding separate data-analysis chapter in Part 3. This is because, in the case of quantitative observation, data can readily be analysed using simple spreadsheet collation, calculation and graphics, as indicated in Chapter 16. In the case of qualitative observation, the field notes to be analysed are similar to any other field notes or interview transcripts, so are covered by the discussion of qualitative data analysis in Chapter 15. Nevertheless, some case studies, including analysis, are included in the chapter to demonstrate the outcomes of observational research.

Sometimes observational research is referred to as *unobtrusive methods*, since often there is generally no involvement with the observed subjects, who may not even be aware that they are being observed. But the term 'unobtrusive methods' is also used in relation to documentary sources, such as the media, organisational records and diaries (see Kellehear, 1993); in this book these sources are dealt with in the chapters on secondary data and qualitative methods. In this chapter we concentrate on direct visual engagement with cultural/ events activity and sites.

The chapter comprises three main sections:

- an overview of type of observational research and possible situations where observational methods might be used;
- a step-by-step examination of the typical observational research process;
- the use of technology.

Types and possibilities

Types of observational research: quantitative and qualitative

Observation involves *looking*. It can take a number of forms, as indicated in Figure 8.1. Of importance here is that observational research can be quantitative, qualitative or a combination of both. There is also overlap with experimental methods (Chapter 11) and with participant observation (Chapter 9).

Structured or systematic observation	Observation process subject to formal rules about what should be observed, how often, etc. – results typically recorded on forms and analysed quantitatively. Equivalent to the formal questionnaire-based survey in survey research.
Unstructured/ naturalistic/qualitative observation	No formal rules established; relatively informal recording or analysis procedures. Observer seeks to describe the phenomenon of interest and develop explanations and understandings in the process. Observational equivalent of the informal, in-depth interview.
Quasi-experimental observation	Researcher intervenes to change the environment and observes what happens – for example, changing the layout of an exhibit. May be structured or unstructured.
Participant observation	The researcher is a participant in the milieu being studied – for example, a drama group or major event – rather than a separate, 'objective' researcher. May involve any of the above forms of observation. Discussed in Chapter 9.

Figure 8.1 Types of observational research

▊ Possibilities

A number of types of situation where observation is possible, appropriate or necessary can be identified, as listed in Figure 8.2. These situations are discussed in turn below.

- Children's behaviour
- Informal culture/event areas
  - visit numbers – counting heads
  - spatial/functional patterns of use: crowd behaviour
- Visitor profiles
- Deviant behaviour
- Mystery shopping
- Complementary research
- Everyday life
- Social behaviour

Figure 8.2 Situations for observational research

Children's behaviour

There is some research which can only be tackled by means of observation. One example is children's behaviour. Such research is concerned with issues including:

- extent to which behaviour is physically active or passive;

- patterns of behaviour in different environments;

- the types of exhibit or equipment children of different ages prefer and the variation in time spent per exhibit;

- whether patterns of behaviour of boys differ from those of girls or whether children of different ethnic backgrounds behave differently;

- whether behaviour is affected by accompanying adults.

It is unlikely that questions on these matters could be fully answered by interviewing children, particularly very young children. The obvious approach is to *observe* children and record their behaviour.

Informal areas/facilities

The most obvious cultural environment in which visitor behaviour is informal is the museum or gallery, since visitors generally have the freedom to come and go and move around at will – the exception being 'blockbuster' exhibitions where visitor numbers are very high, timed ticketing may be involved and visitors can be channelled along a pre-determined route with little opportunity to deviate or retrace their steps. Other examples of informal sites include fairs, multi-venue events with free entry and multi-stage music festivals. However, the bulk of published observational research in this field has taken place in museums, as indicated in the Resources section.

Visit numbers/counting heads at informal sites: One of the features of many informal sites is that no entrance fee is charged. This applies to many museums, galleries, libraries and some heritage sites, and to the free components of some arts festivals. Estimating visitor numbers for these situations is therefore a form of observational research. Some built facilities, notably libraries, have used automatic turnstiles which provide visitor counts, but this is not appropriate for many venues. In museums and galleries, security/reception staff have traditionally counted visitors with a manual 'clicker' device, but this is, of course, subject to human error. Automated infra-red devices can now be used and these are discussed further below.

Where the bulk of users arrive at a facility by private car and a charge is made for parking, indications of variations or trends in use levels may be provided by parking income, but this does not account for non-vehicular use and in some cases (e.g. heritage sites) parking charges do not apply outside of certain hours, or there may be season permit holders who are not recorded every time they enter. To account for all vehicular use it may be possible to install automatic vehicle counters to count the number of vehicles entering and leaving the site, as discussed later in the chapter. Vehicle counts, however, provide information on the number of vehicles using a site but not the number of people. To obtain estimates of the numbers of people it is necessary to supplement the vehicle counts by direct observation for a period of time to ascertain the average number of people in vehicles and, at some sites, to estimate the numbers arriving by foot or bicycle, who may not be recorded by the mechanical counting device.

Spatial/functional patterns of use of informal sites: Observation is useful not only for gathering data on the number of users of a site but also for studying the way people make use of a site. This is particularly important in relation to the design and layout of exhibits and spaces, and their capacity. For example, if a gallery has certain exhibits which attract more attention than others, consideration will need to be given to the amount of space around the exhibit and between it and adjacent exhibits.

The extent to which people make use of written information, accompanying exhibits or provided in printed materials can be ascertained by observation, as can the use of recent innovations such as personal audio guides. *Visitor conversation research*, as discussed in Chapter 5, involves a combination of audio recording of selected visitors' discussion of exhibits together with observation.

Buildings and open spaces for public use are often designed with little or no consideration as to how people will actually use them, or on the basis of untested assumptions about how they will be used. In reality it is often found that people do not actually behave as anticipated by the designers and some spaces are under-used while others are overcrowded, or spaces are not actually used for the activities for which they were designed or equipped. How people move around a space is likely to be affected by its design, so that different designs/layouts can be more or less successful in achieving the aims of the facility. These issues can be addressed through observation, both informally and through systematic observational research. An example is presented in Case study 8.1.

Visitor profiles

Questionnaire-based site surveys are the typical means for researching demographic and group composition data which combine to provide a *visitor* or *user profile*. However, depending on the design of the questionnaire, and given that questionnaires in such situations are invariably quite brief, the information collected can miss vital features of the characteristics of the users of a site which can be identified by observation. For example, two venues could have identical user age/gender/group size profiles but, because of the different types of

CASE STUDY 8.1

Movement patterns in a museum

In a book chapter reviewing a number of issues related to visitors to museums and visitor centres, Pearce (1988: 90–113) at one point discusses the implications of visitors' decision to turn either to the right on entering a museum and proceeding in an anti-clockwise direction, or to the left and proceeding in a clockwise direction.

Research in the Telecom Museum in Victoria, Australia, as shown in Figure 8.3, showed that the pattern of attention paid to the exhibits, as measured by the proportion of visitors who stopped to view each exhibit, differed for the two groups of visitors. In particular, those who went anti-clockwise had a higher level of attention throughout the exhibition (33.9% viewing

per exhibit on average compared with 28.5% for the clockwise group). This, it is argued, was likely to be due to the fact that they immediately encountered interactive exhibits, whereas those who went clockwise first encountered non-interactive exhibits.

The methodology used, individual visual tracking of visitors, is clearly simple, but possibly time-consuming, depending on how long visitors stayed and the extent to which more than one group could be studied at the same time. But it clearly produced data likely to be of interest to, and readily understood and interpreted by, managers. In this particular case the data analysis is simple: all that is required is for the data to be collected and suitably displayed.

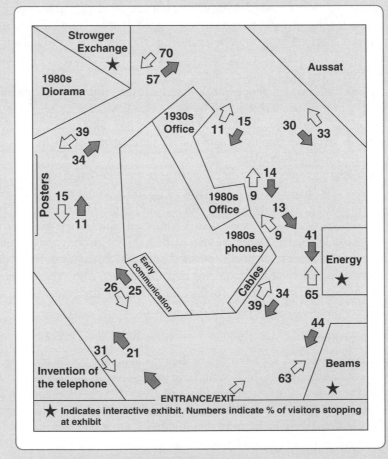

Figure 8.3 Visitor movement patterns in a museum

programme or exhibits offered, could attract very different crowds, in terms of fashion, life-style and behaviour. Even at a single venue an overall profile based on averages and percent-ages may hide the fact that it is used by a number of distinct user groups.

Questionnaire-based profiles may also miss distinctive usage patterns. For example, a museum survey may indicate that there are x% mothers with young children, or single elderly users, but fail to pick up the fact that these groups attend at particular times and meet and socialise at the museum cafe. Of course, a questionnaire survey could pick up these features if it included appropriate questions and if the sample was large enough and the analysis sophisticated enough, but this is not always the case. In addition to being a research approach in its own right, observational research can be used as a preliminary process to identify features of the user profile so that appropriate questions can be included in a questionnaire.

Deviant behaviour

The notion of *deviant* behaviour is a contested one, with one person's 'deviance' being another person's 'acceptable' or even 'creative' behaviour. The term covers such activities as the use of illicit recreational drugs, rowdy crowd behaviour or other forms of 'rule breaking' in public settings. Deviant behaviour is a situation where observation is likely to be more fruitful than interviews. People are unlikely to tell an interviewer about their litter-dropping habits or their beer can-throwing habits at a football match. Finding out about such things requires observation – usually of a covert nature! This, of course, raises ethical issues, such as people's rights to privacy, as discussed in Chapter 4.

In relation to formal cultural venues, the phenomenon of 'deviance' makes an appear-ance from time to time when controversy arises in relation to literary, visual or dramatic art works or song lyrics which some people find confrontational, and in relation to forgery and copyright infringements, but this concerns venue managers and artists rather than the audiences, so research on such topics is not typically based on observational methods of the sort discussed here. There is, however, a body of relevant literature in event studies, includ-ing research on the behaviour of sports fans, and the historical and contemporary view of the carnival, where normal behavioural norms are breached, in a form of sanctioned, but temporally and spatially limited, deviance (see Resources section).

Mystery shopping

Mystery shopping is a potentially fruitful use of observation which is under-exploited in the cultural sector. It involves a researcher playing the role of user/visitor/customer/audience member as a method of obtaining information on the quality of the experience enjoyed by users of a venue or service. The mystery shopper is required to make use of the facilities or services on offer on an incognito basis. The researcher has a checklist of features to observe – such as cleanliness, information availability and clarity, staff performance – and makes a report after using the facilities or services. Such an approach draws on the expertise of the observer to assess quality of service and to record details, for example related to safety, which might not be noticed by routine users. The approach is, of course, not unlike that of the incognito art, film or restaurant critic.

Again, ethical and industrial relations issues may arise in such a study because of the ele-ment of deception involved in a researcher playing the part of a customer, typically on behalf of management; however, it is also argued that it can be used as a positive staff development tool (Bernstein, 2007: 148). Market research companies now offer mystery shopping to their clients as a service along with more traditional research approaches. A rare published example of the approach being used in the culture/events sector is Munsters' (2010) account of its use as part of a 'cultural destination experience audit' in an historic city.

Complementary research

Observation can provide essential quantitative or qualitative complements to other research methods.

Quantitative complementarity. Observation involving counts of users can be a necessary complement to interview surveys to correct for variation in sampling rates. For instance, in a venue such as a museum or gallery, two interviewers, working at a steady rate, may be able to interview virtually all users (100 per cent) in the less busy periods in the early morning but manage to interview only a small proportion of the users (say 5 per cent) during the busy lunch hour and afternoon periods. The final sample would therefore, in this case, over-represent early-morning users and under-represent midday and afternoon users. If these two groups have different characteristics, the differential rate of sampling would be likely to have a biasing effect on, for example, the overall balance of views expressed by the users. Observational counts of the hourly levels of use can provide data to give an appropriate *weight* to the midday and afternoon users at the analysis stage. The process of weighting is described in more detail in Chapter 16.

Qualitative complementarity. Informal observation may provide complementary material for any study focused on a particular location or type of location in order to set the research in context and provide some 'local colour'. Observation can also be part of a mixed-method project, as in the cultural tourism example referred to above (Munsters, 2010), in which the observational exercise was one of three methods used, the others being a questionnaire-based survey of cultural tourists and in-depth interviews with service providers.

Everyday life

The idea of simply observing *everyday life* as an approach to studying a society is associated with Britain's Mass Observation anthropological study of the British way of life in the 1930s and 1940s and with the work of Irving Goffman (1959), which was concerned with the ways individuals use space and interact in public and private places. One aspect of culture that has become part of everyday life is watching television and there are early ethnographic studies of families watching television, such as the work of Morley (1986) and Hobson (1982), which showed that people's consumption of this medium was not as passive as had been assumed.

Social behaviour

Observation has been used in sociological research to develop ideas and theories about social behaviour in specific milieux. The research of Fiske (1983) and Grant (1984) on the use of beaches, Marsh and his colleagues (1978) on football fans, and Goulding and Saren (2007) on the 'Goth' sub-culture are examples of this approach. These researchers use an interactive, inductive process to build explanations of social behaviour from what they observe. Very often a key feature of such studies is the way the researchers seek to contrast what they have observed with what has apparently been observed – or assumed to be taking place – by others, particularly those with influence or authority, such as officials, police and the media. Observational research can challenge existing stereotypical interpretations of events.

Main elements of observational research

Observation seems to be essentially a simple research method with little 'technique' to consider. However, as with any research method, careful thought must go into design, conduct and analysis stages of a project. In structured observation what is mainly required from the researcher is precision, painstaking attention to detail, and patience. In unstructured observation the same skills and attributes are required but, in addition, there is a need for a creative 'eye' which can perceive the significance and potential meanings of what is being observed and relate these to the research question. The main tasks in planning and conducting an observational project are as set out in Figure 8.4.

As with the 'elements of the research process' outlined in Chapter 3, it is difficult to produce a list of steps to cover all eventualities. In particular, if the approach is unstructured rather than structured, then a number of the steps discussed here, particularly those concerning counting, may be redundant. In what follows, it is assumed that:

- the *site* is a building or identifiable outdoor area, usually enclosed, in which some event is taking place or exhibits or heritage are on display;

- a *zone* may refer to a room in a building, an individual exhibit or a display point, such as a stage in a multi-stage music event, or a recognisable area within a multi-function site, such as the refreshment or camping area.

Step 1: Choice of site(s)

In the case of a provider-organisation's in-house or consultancy research, the site(s) to be studied may be fixed, but where there is an element of choice some time should be devoted to inspecting and choosing sites that will offer the appropriate behaviour but also provide suitable conditions for observation and/or will be representative of the range of types to be studied – a type of sampling process.

Step 2: Choice of observation point(s)

Some sites can be observed in their entirety from one spot. In other cases a circuit of viewing points must be devised, related to particular zones. For structured observation – for example, involving counting the number of people present or passing a point over a period of time – it may be vital to conduct the observation from the same point(s) in every study period, but for

---

1. Choice of site(s)
2. Choice of observation point(s)
3. Choice of observation time period(s)
4. Continuous observation or sampling?
5. Number and length of sampling periods
6. Deciding what to observe
7. Division of site into zones
8. Determination of information-recording method
9. Conducting the observation
10. Analysing/interpreting data

Figure 8.4 Steps in an observation project

unstructured observation this may not be a consideration; indeed, exploring and observing from different locations within a site may be desirable.

When unstructured but intensive observation of people's behaviour is involved, it may be necessary to choose observation points that are unobtrusive in order to avoid attracting attention, particularly in a confined space with relatively few people. This is related to the method of recording observations, as discussed in Step 8, since some types of formal recording are more obvious than others.

In some cases the observer unobtrusively follows individuals or groups around a museum/gallery or exhibition.

Step 3: Choice of observation time period(s)

The choice of time period may be important because of variations in use of a venue, by time of the year, day of the week, time of day or weather conditions, according to external social factors such as public holidays, or internal factors, such as the type of programme/exhibition – and hence of patron – offered on particular days. Observation to cover all time periods may be very demanding in terms of resources, so some form of sampling of time periods will usually be necessary.

Step 4: Continuous observation or sampling?

Decisions on whether to undertake continuous observation or to sample different time periods will depend on the resources available and the nature of the site and the overall design of the project. The issue is particularly important if one of the aims of the research is to obtain an accurate estimate of the number of visitors to the site, when the terminology used to refer to the two approaches is *continuous counts* versus *spot counts*. For example, resources may not be available to cover the opening hours of a venue for a whole year – except using automatic mechanical devices. A sampling approach must be adopted in most observation projects. Having decided to sample, it is of course necessary to decide how often to do this. This is discussed further under Step 5.

If counting is being undertaken there is also a decision to be made as to whether to count the number of people entering or leaving the site during specified time periods or the number of people present at particular points in time. Counting the number of people present is a *spot count*. Counting the number of people entering or leaving over a period of time generally constitutes continuous counting, but if the time periods are relatively short – for example, half an hour or an hour – then the results can be seen as a form of spot count. Counting the number of people present at particular points in time is generally less resource-intensive since it can often be done by one person and can provide information on the spatial use of the venue at the same time. Thus one person, at specified times, makes a circuit of the site and records the numbers of people present in designated zones (see Step 7).

When unstructured observation is being undertaken it is more likely that continuous observation will be adopted since the aim will generally be to observe the dynamics of events and behaviour at the site. However, the question of when to undertake such observation in order to cover all aspects of site use still needs careful consideration.

Step 5: Count frequency

When the study involves counts of users, how often should the counts be undertaken? This will depend to a large extent on the rate of change in the level of use of the venue. For example,

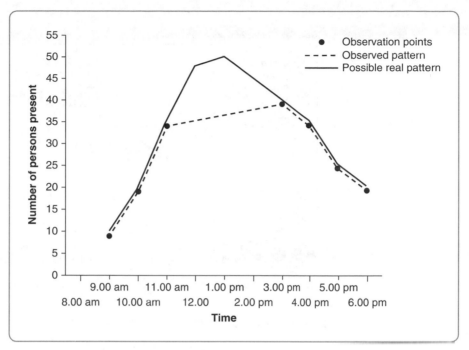

Figure 8.5 Counts of site use

the four counts in Figure 8.5 are clearly insufficient since, if the broken line is the pattern of use observed in a research project, but the unbroken line is the true pattern, the research would have inaccurately represented the true situation. There is little advice to overcome this problem, except to sample frequently at the beginning of a project until the basic patterns of peaks and troughs in usage have been established; subsequently it may be possible to sample less often.

Step 6: What to observe

One approach to observing the spatial behaviour of visitors within a site is to record numbers of users present in different zones, as indicated in Figure 8.6. In a museum or gallery the zones might be rooms and/or individual exhibits. In addition to observing numbers of people and their positions, it is possible to observe and record different types of activity or inactivity. Chiozzi and Andreotti (2001) describe a study in which visitors' signs of fatigue were recorded – for example, statements of tiredness made to companions, yawning or taking opportunities to sit. It is also possible, to a limited extent and depending on the scale of the observation exercise, to record visitor characteristics. For example, men and women could be separately identified and it is possible to distinguish between children and adults and to distinguish senior citizens, although, if a number of people are involved as counters, care will need to be taken over consistency of the dividing line between such categories as child, teenager, young adult, adult and elderly person. It is also possible, again with care, to observe the size of parties using a site, especially if they are observed arriving or leaving at a car park.

These additional items of information would of course complicate the recording sheet and symbols would be necessary to record the different types of person on a map. Care needs to be taken not to make the data collection so complicated that it becomes too difficult for the observers to observe and collect and leads to inaccuracies. This is one of those situations

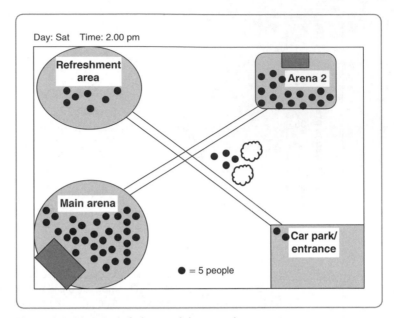

Figure 8.6 Mapping of observed data: outdoor event

where it is necessary to consider carefully *why* the data are being collected and not to get carried away with data collection for its own sake.

The objectives of the research could involve considerably more than just recording visitor numbers. More complex research, for example studying the interactions of participants in the use of a facility, may require an entirely different research strategy, since 'hanging around' with or without a clipboard or notebook may not be acceptable, depending on the level of crowding and the layout of the site. Participant observation, including the use of interviewing, may be one solution, depending on the aims of the project. These specific techniques are discussed in Chapters 9 and 10 respectively.

Car registration numbers can be a useful source of information. First, they can provide information on where people have travelled from. Second, number plates can be used to trace the movement of vehicles within some areas – for instance, within a national park or cultural tourist destination region with a number of stopping points.

Step 7: Division of site into zones

Most sites naturally fall into appropriate zones, as in Figure 8.6, but decisions may have to be made on boundaries and, in the case of a large-scale site, such as a museum, on a sample of zones/exhibits to include.

Step 8: Recording information

Figure 8.7 provides an example of counting sheets for recording usage information.

The data collected using such a form are ideal for storage, manipulation and presentation in graphic form using a spreadsheet computer program as discussed in Step 10. Space is also provided for comments. In the case of unstructured observation, the 'comments' section could be much more extensive, perhaps requiring a separate sheet for each facility.

Site	Observer	Date	Start time	Finish time

	Exhibit A	Exhibit B	Exhibit C	Exhibit D	Exhibit E	Exhibit F
Adults						
Children						
Organised group						
Comments						

Figure 8.7 Observation recording sheet: counts

Step 9: Conducting the observation

In the case of a structured observational project, if the project has been well planned then actually carrying it out should be straightforward. The main danger in a major project involving a lot of counting can be boredom for the research staff, leading to inaccuracies in observing and recording data. It is therefore advisable to vary the work of those involved, with, where appropriate, data collectors being involved in alternate spells of behavioural observation and counting and, where possible, being switched between sites. Counting can be done manually or using a hand-held mechanical counter.

In the case of unstructured observational projects, more demands are placed on the observer. Such a project is, in effect, a visual form of the qualitative type of research discussed in the next chapter. The observer is required to observe and describe what is going on at the site, but must also engage directly with the research questions of the project in order to determine what to observe and what aspects of the observed scene should be described and recorded and at least begin the process of explanation.

Step 10: Analysing data

In some cases of structured observation, the visual presentations of the sort shown in Figures 8.5 and 8.6 constitute the analysis. In other cases data must be analysed and processed to present useable results. These processes are discussed in Chapter 14.

Use of technology

A number of technologies are available which can assist or replace the human eye in observational research. These are listed in Figure 8.8 and discussed in turn below.

- Automatic counters
- Global Positioning Systems (GPS)
- Aerial photography
- Still photography and video
- Time-lapse photography

Figure 8.8 Observational technology

Automatic counters

Automatic counters are available for counting vehicles and pedestrians. Vehicle counters are based on one of four technologies:

- induction loop buried under the roadway: creates a magnetic field which detects vehicles passing through it – this option is relatively permanent and expensive due to installation costs;
- pressure pad or tube: vehicles passing over the pad or tube complete an electrical circuit – this is cheaper than an induction loop but has a limited life due to wear and tear;
- infra-red beam: the vehicle is recorded when it breaks the beam – the cheapest option;
- CCTV (closed circuit television): software can be used to analyse the images and count vehicles passing in view of the camera.

In each case, the device is attached to computerised equipment which can produce a variety of reports for users, for example, hourly, daily, weekly, monthly or annual counts and trend analysis. The technologies can generally detect vehicles of different types/sizes, for example, motorcycles, passenger vehicles, heavy vehicles.

Infra-red beams and CCTV can also be used to count pedestrian movements. But because pedestrians do not necessarily cross the beam one at a time, the counters may have to be calibrated using some direct observational data collected for a sample period. For example, direct visual counts may reveal that, in a certain location, a count of 100 on the automatic counter may represent, say, 120 individuals.

Cyclists sometimes use roadways, where they may be picked up by traffic counters, or they may use exclusive cycle ways, where infra-red devices can be used. Where they share paths with pedestrians, the mix of pedestrians and cyclists would need to be determined by calibration based on direct observation as discussed above.

One of the disadvantages of these devices is their fixed nature: one device can monitor only one route or pathway. Locating a device at every point or site entrance of interest may be expensive and moving them around on a roster may be costly. Again, calibration using a period of direct visual counts may be the solution. For example, if direct counts revealed that the main entrance to a site typically accounted for half of all visits, the counts from an automatic counter located at that entrance would be sufficient, with the results being doubled to provide an estimate of total visits.

Global Positioning Systems (GPS)

Global Positioning Systems, based on satellite technology, can be used to track people's spatial movements and this can clearly be applied in cultural/events contexts. Participants can wear devices that record the route they take, distance they travel and time taken, and this information can be transmitted to a base computer or downloaded at the end of a session. The technology has begun to be used to study cultural tourists' patterns of movement in areas such as historic cities, as indicated in the Resources section.

Aerial photography

The use of aerial photography is well developed in geography and geology, where a whole sub-discipline of *remote sensing* has developed using a variety of techniques. It can also be effective in events research. Where large areas are concerned, such as a multi-event complex (e.g. Olympic Games stadia or arts festival sites), or where access is difficult and use of the site is scattered, for example in some natural heritage areas, aerial photography may be the only way of obtaining estimates of levels and patterns of use. Needless to say, high-quality equipment is needed for such work.

Still photography and video

The value of ordinary, land-based photography as an adjunct to direct observation should not be overlooked. Cheap digital equipment and computer software for editing still photography and video have made the incorporation of visual material into research increasingly easy. The level of crowding of a venue, its nature, atmosphere and usage patterns can be conveyed to the reader of a report with the aid of photographs. Particular problems, for instance of congestion or design faults, can be conveyed better visually than verbally – a picture speaks a thousand words. A 'photo-essay' can be composed around a number of themes or messages to convey simple research findings. Photographs can be used with research subjects as a projective technique (see Chapter 5), one approach being to invite subjects to select from a supply of photographs to create a collage representing their image of a place (e.g. Gonzalez Fernandez et al., 2010).

Video can be used to record patterns of site use. As noted in relation to automatic counters and CCTV, some software can now analyse digital images. The medium can provide a useful illustration of 'before' and 'after' situations, to illustrate the nature of problems on a site and the effect of measures to ameliorate the problems – for example congestion, erosion or littering.

A distinct tradition of 'visual research' has emerged in social research, which is based largely on photography and has its own journal, *Visual Sociology*, and a growing literature in the cultural area (see Resources section).

Time-lapse photography

Time-lapse photography lies somewhere between still photography and video. A time-lapse camera can be set up to take pictures of a scene automatically, say every ten seconds or every minute. The resultant sequence of pictures can then be projected as a film or video to show the speeded-up pattern of use of the area viewed. This is the technique used in wildlife documentaries that show a plant apparently growing before your eyes, but it can also be used to show the changing pattern of use of a facility or site.

Just looking

Finally, we should not forget just how important it is to use our eyes in research, even if the research project does not involve systematic observational data collection. Familiarity with a cultural activity or site helps in the design of a good research project and aids in interpreting data. Many studies have been based just on informal, but careful, observation.

All useful information is not in the form of numbers. Careful observation of what is happening in a particular situation, at a particular facility or type of facility or event or among a particular group of people can be a more appropriate research approach in some circumstances than the use of questionnaires or even informal interviews. The good researcher is all eyes.

Case studies

CASE STUDY 8.2

Children's behaviour

In a study located within the Pompidou Centre in Paris, Debenedetti *et al*. (2009) set out to examine the interaction of children with exhibits in the *Face-to-Face* exhibition, which had been specifically designed for children aged 5–12 years old. It comprised 63 representations of the human head, 'drawn, sculpted, filmed or photographed, frontal or profile, of varying forms and materials', and including numerous interactive devices. In addition to interviews with children and respondent-completion questionnaires completed by adults, the study included 60 direct observations of child–adult dyads, from their entry to the exhibition to their exit. Among the findings of the observation was:

- only 20 per cent of the children followed the designed theme-related grouping and sequencing of the exhibits;

- on average each child engaged with 64 per cent of the interactive devices, but with only 29 per cent of the art works;

- the average time spent with individual art works was 12 seconds, but with individual interactive devices it was 104 seconds.

Clearly, such information could only have been collected by observational methods.

CASE STUDY 8.3

Observation studies of museum visitor behaviour

- We have already noted the use of observation in a museum setting in Case study 8.1, which is concerned with circulation patterns in a museum.

- A further observational case study also dealing with the attention museum visitors pay to exhibit labels can be found in Chapter 11: Case study 11.1.

Signage and reading in a major art museum

Jeanneret *et al*. (2010), in their study 'Written signage and reading practices of the public in a fine arts museum', set out to test the accepted wisdom that only a small proportion of visitors to art museums read the various forms of textual information on offer. They used qualitative methods, including direct observation and evaluation of the signage in the museum, and observation of, and interviews with, groups of visitors. They discovered the way that organised and non-organised groups of visitors made use not only of signage but also of the museum guide/plan, print material acquired in the museum and brought with them, and various audio sources. It was found that groups behaved in a variety of ways, with individuals often taking on the role of reading/listening to and interpreting information to other members of the group.

The study shows the complexity and variety of ways in which people make use of information from a variety of media.

Summary

This chapter is concerned with the neglected technique of observation – *looking* – as a tool for research in cultural and events studies. It is noted that observation can be formalised or structured, involving counting of numbers of users and strict time and space sampling methods, or it can be informal or unstructured. In general, observation is non-intrusive in the study site. Participant observation is a further type of observational research, but is dealt with in Chapter 9. Observational research spans the quantitative/qualitative methodological spectrum and can therefore involve both quantitative and qualitative analysis methods. In the chapter a number of cultural/events situations are described in which observation methods might be used, including children's play; the usage of informal areas where no entrance fee is required and capacity and use patterns are not constrained by factors such as formal seating or booking systems; spatial and functional patterns of use of sites; user profiles; studying deviant behaviour; mystery shopping; research that is complementary to research conducted using other methods; everyday life; and social behaviour.

The chapter outlines the observational research process in ten steps: 1. choice of study site(s); 2. choice of observation point(s); 3. choice of observation time period(s); 4. deciding on continuous observation or sampling; 5. deciding on the number and length of sampling periods; 6. deciding what to observe; 7. division of the study site(s) into zones; 8. recording observational information; 9. conducting the observation; and 10. analysing data (followed up in Chapter 14). Finally, brief consideration is given to various technological aids, including automatic counters, GPS devices, and still, video and time-lapse cameras, and this is followed by some case studies of observational research in the arts/events field.

TEST QUESTIONS

1. Four types of observational research are identified at the beginning of the chapter. What are they?
2. Eight situations are described where observation is a suitable, and sometimes the *most* suitable form of research. Name three of these situations and explain in each case why observation is a suitable research method.
3. What is the difference between spot counting and continuous counting?
4. In what forms can data from observational research be presented?
5. How can observational research findings assist in regard to weighting of survey data?

EXERCISES

1. Select an informal cultural venue or event site and position yourself in an unobtrusive location but where you can see what is going on. Over a period of half an hour to an hour, record what happens. Write a report on how the area is used, who it is used by, how many people use it, what conflicts there are, if any, between different groups of users, and how the design of the area aids or hinders the activity which people engage in on the site.

2. Establish a counting system to record the number of people present at a cultural venue or event site at hourly intervals during the course of its opening hours. Estimate the number of visitor-hours at the site for the day.

3. In relation to exercise 2: conduct interviews with three or four visitors each hour and ask them how long they have stayed, or expect to stay, at the site. Establish the average length of stay and, using this information and the data from exercise 2, estimate the number of people visiting the site in the course of the day.

4. Use photographs or video to create a visual image of a venue or event that might be used as a prompt for research interviews to explore people's attitudes towards the venue/event.

5. Choose one of the arts/events journals and identify a study that uses observation exclusively and one that uses observation as part of a mixed-methods approach. Identify what is observed, how it is observed and how the results are analysed and presented.

Resources

- General/methodological: Kellehear (1993), Adler and Adler (1994); at events/festivals: Seaton (1997).
- Automated vehicle/pedestrian counters: Green Space (1998).
- Children: Debenedetti *et al.* (2009), Tuckey (1992); and families: Sterry and Beaumont (2006).
- Deviant behaviour: carnival: Ravenscroft and Matteucci (2003); sport fans: Marsh *et al.* (1978), Cunneen and Lynch (1988), Cunneen *et al.* (1989).
- Exhibition planning/design: Screven (1990).
- GPS: cultural tourism: Edwards *et al.* (2010), Shoval and Isaacson (2007); events: Brown and Hutton (2013).
- Mixed methods, including observation: festival: Mackellar (2009).
- Mystery shopping: general: Dawson and Hillier (1995); in cultural tourism: Munsters (2010).
- Photography: English (1988); visitor-employed photography in museum: Puczko *et al.* (2010); cultural tourism: Willson and McIntosh (2010), Gonzalez Fernandez *et al.* (2010).
- Qualitative observation: Lofland and Lofland (1984).
- Studies using observation:
  - general: Birenbaum and Sagarin (1978)
  - museums: Bitgood *et al.* (1988), Chiozzi and Andreotti (2001), Debenedetti *et al.* (2009), Imamoglu and Yilmazsoy (2011), Jeanneret *et al.* (2010), Noy (2011), Nurse Rainbolt *et al.* (2012), Pearce (1988), Ross *et al.* (2012); children's behaviour: Dockett *et al.*, (2011), Tuckey (1992)
  - beaches as cultural phenomena: Fiske (1983), Grant (1984)
  - football fans: Marsh *et al.* (1978)
  - Goth sub-culture: Goulding and Saren (2007)
- Television audiences: Hobson (1982), Morley (1986).
- Structured versus unstructured observation: Bryman and Bell (2003).
- Video: in cultural tourism: Rakic (2010).

References

Adler, P. A. and Adler, P. (1994) Observational techniques. In N. K. Denzin and Y. S. Lincoln (eds) *Handbook of Qualitative Research*. Thousand Oaks, CA: Sage, pp. 377–392.

Bernstein, J. S. (2007) *Arts Marketing Insights*. San Francisco, CA: John Wiley and Sons.

Birenbaum, A. and Sagarin, E. (eds) (1973) *People in Places: The Sociology of the Familiar*. London: Nelson.

Bitgood, S., Patterson, D. and Benefield, A. (1988) Exhibit design and visitor behaviour. *Environment and Behaviour*, 20(4), 474–491.

Brown, S. and Hutton, A. (2013) Developments in real-time evaluation of audience behaviour at planned events. *International Journals of Event and Festival Management*, 4(1), 43–55.

Bryman, A. and Bell, E. (2003) Breaking down the quantitative/qualitative divide, and Combining quantitative and qualitative research. Chapters 21–22 of: *Business Research Methods*. Oxford: Oxford University Press, pp. 465–494.

Chiozzi, G. and Andreotti, L. (2001) Behavior vs. time: understanding how visitors utilize the Milan Natural History Museum. *Curator*, 44(2), 153–165.

Cunneen, C. and Lynch, R. (1988) The social meaning of conflict in riots at the Australian Grand Prix motorcycle races. *Leisure Studies*, 7(1), 1–20.

Cunneen, C., Findlay, M., Lynch, R. and Tupper, V. (1989) *Dynamics of Collective Conflict: Riots at the Bathurst Bike Races*. North Ryde, NSW: Law Book Co.

Dawson, J. and Hillier, J. (1995) Competitor mystery shopping: methodological considerations and implications for the MRS Code of Conduct. *Journal of the Market Research Society*, 37(4), 417–443.

Debenedetti, S., Caro, F. and Krebs, A. (2009) 'I'd rather play than look at statues.' The experiences of children with art works and interactive devices at an art exhibition. *International Journal of Arts Management*, 11(3), 46–58.

Dockett, S., Main, S. and Kelly, L. (2011) Consulting young children: experiences from a museum. *Visitor Studies*, 13(1), 13–33.

Edwards, D., Dickson, T., Griffin, T. and Hayllar, B. (2010) Tracking the urban visitor: methods for examining tourists' spatial behaviour and visual representations. In G. Richards and W. Munsters (eds) *Cultural Tourism Research Methods*. Wallingford: CABI, pp. 104–114.

English, F. W. (1988) The utility of the camera in qualitative inquiry. *Educational Researcher*, 17(May), 8–15.

Fiske, J. (1983) Surfalism and sandiotics: the beach in Oz popular culture. *Australian Journal of Cultural Studies*, 1(2), 120–149.

Goffman, I. (1959) *The Presentation of Self in Everyday Life*. Garden City: Doubleday/Anchor.

Gonzalez Fernandez, A. M., Rodriguez Santos, M. and Cervantes Blanco, M. (2010) Measuring the image of a cultural tourism destination through the collage technique. In G. Richards and W. Munsters (eds) *Cultural Tourism Research Methods*. Wallingford: CABI, pp. 156–172.

Goulding, C. and Saren, M. (2007) 'Gothic' entrepreneurs: a study of the subcultural commodification process. In B. Cova, R. V. Kozinets and A. Shankar (eds) *Consumer Tribes*. Oxford: Butterworth-Heinemann, pp. 227–242.

Grant, D. (1984) Another look at the beach. *Australian Journal of Cultural Studies*, 2(2), 131–138.

Green Space (1998) *A Guide to Automated Methods for Counting Visitors to Parks and Green Spaces*. Reading: Green Space, available at: www.green-space.org.uk

Hobson, D. (1982) *Crossroads: The Drama of a Soap Opera*. London: Methuen.

Imamoglu, C. and Yilmazsoy, A. C. (2011) Gender and locality-related differences in circulation behavior in a museum setting. *Museum Management and Curatorship*, 15(2), 203–216.

Jeanneret, Y., Depoux, A., Luckerhoff, J., Vitabo, V. and Jacobi, D. (2010) Written signage and reading practices of the public in a fine arts museum. *Museum Management and Curatorship*, 25(1), 53–67.

Kellehear, A. (1993) *The Unobtrusive Researcher: A Guide to Methods*. Sydney: Allen and Unwin.

Lofland, J. and Lofland, L. H. (1984) *Analyzing Social Settings: A Guide to Qualitative Observation and Analysis*, Second Edition. Belmont, CA: Wadsworth.

Mackellar, J. (2009) An examination of serious leisure participants at the Australian Wintersun Festival. *Leisure Studies*, 28(1), 85–104.

Marsh, P., Rosser, E. and Harré, R. (1978) *The Rules of Disorder*. London: Routledge.

Morley, D. (1986) *Family Televisions: Cultural Power and Domestic Leisure*. London: Comedia.

Munsters, W. (2010) The cultural destination experience audit applied to the tourist-historic city. In G. Richards and W. Munsters (eds) *Cultural Tourism Research Methods*. Wallingford: CABI, pp. 52–60.

Noy, C. (2011) The aesthetics of qualitative (re)search: performing ethnography at a heritage museum. *Qualitative Inquiry*, 17(10), 917–929.

Nurse Rainbolt, G., Benfield, J. A. and Loomis, R. J. (2012) Visitor self-report behavior mapping as a tool for recording exhibition circulation. *Visitor Studies*, 15(2), 203–216.

Pearce, P. L. (1988) *The Ulysses Factor: Evaluating Visitors in Tourist Settings*. New York: Springer-Verlag.

Puczko, L., Bard, E. and Fuzi, J. (2010) Methodological triangulation: the study of visitor behaviour at the Hungarian Open Air Museum. In G. Richards and W. Munsters (eds) *Cultural Tourism Research Methods*. Wallingford: CABI, pp. 61–74.

Rakic, T. (2010) *Tales from the field: vide*o and its potential for creating cultural toursim knowledge. In G. Richards and W. Munsters (eds) *Cultural Tourism Research Methods*. Wallingford: CABI, pp. 129–140.

Ravenscroft, N. and Matteucci, X. (2003) The festival as carnivalesque: social governance and control at Pamplona's San Fermin Fiesta. *Culture and Communication*, 4(1), 1–15.

Ross, S. R., Melber, L. M., Gillespie, K. L. and Lukas, K. E. (2012) The impact of a modern, naturalistic exhibit design on visitor behavior: a cross-facility comparison. *Visitor Studies*, 15(1), 3–15.

Screven, C. G. (1990) Uses of evaluation before, during and after exhibit design. *ILVS Review*, 1(2), 36–66.

Seaton, A. V. (1997) Unobtrusive observational measures as a quality extension of visitor surveys at festivals and events: mass observation revisited. *Journal of Travel Research*, 35(4), 25–30.

Shoval, N. and Isaacson, M. (2007) Tracking tourists in the digital age. *Annals of Tourism Research*, 34(1), 141–159.

Sterry, P. and Beaumont, E. (2006) Methods for studying family visitors in art museums: a cross-disciplinary review of current research. *Museum Management and Curatorship*, 21(2), 222–239.

Tuckey, C. J. (1992) Schoolchildren's reactions to an interactive science center. *Curator*, 35(1), 28–38.

Van der Zande, A. N. (1985) Distribution patterns of visitors in large areas: a problem of measurement and analysis. *Leisure Studies*, 4(1), 85–100.

Visual Sociology (2012) Olympic Games: special issue, 10(1–2).

Willson, G., and McIntosh, A. (2010) Using photo-based interviews to reveal the significance of heritage buildings to cultural tourism experiences. In G. Richards and W. Munsters (eds) *Cultural Tourism Research Methods*. Wallingford: CABI, pp. 141–155.

Chapter 9

Qualitative methods: introduction and data collection

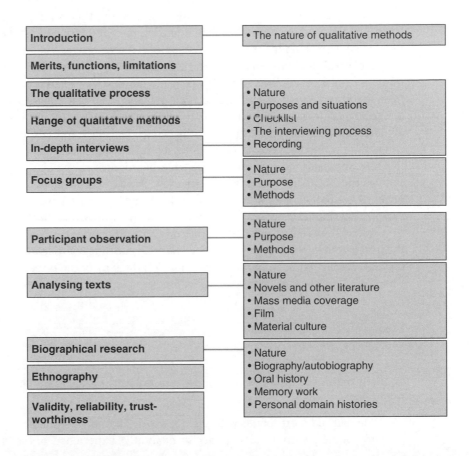

Introduction	• The nature of qualitative methods
Merits, functions, limitations	
The qualitative process	• Nature
	• Purposes and situations
Range of qualitative methods	• Checklist
	• The interviewing process
In-depth interviews	• Recording
Focus groups	• Nature
	• Purpose
	• Methods
Participant observation	• Nature
	• Purpose
	• Methods
Analysing texts	• Nature
	• Novels and other literature
	• Mass media coverage
	• Film
	• Material culture
Biographical research	• Nature
	• Biography/autobiography
Ethnography	• Oral history
	• Memory work
Validity, reliability, trust-worthiness	• Personal domain histories

Introduction

This chapter addresses methods of research that involve the collection and analysis of *qualitative* information using the media of words, images or sounds, as distinct from numbers as used in quantitative methods. The chapter discusses the nature and advantages of qualitative methods, their role in research and the range of specific methods available, including in-depth interviews, group interviews/focus groups, participant observation, biographical methods and ethnographic approaches. The qualitative analysis of the content of *texts* is also discussed.

For most qualitative research projects data collection, analysis and interpretation are inter-mingled, rather than being functionally and temporally separated as is generally the case in quantitative methods. Nevertheless, distinct data-collection and analysis processes can be identified. Analysis procedures tend to have common characteristics across the range of qualitative data-collection methods, so qualitative data *analysis* is discussed in Part II of the book, in Chapter 15.

The nature of qualitative methods

The term *qualitative* is used to describe research methods and techniques that use and give rise to qualitative rather than quantitative information, that is information in the form of words, images and sounds rather than numbers. In general, the qualitative approach tends to collect a large amount of detailed (sometimes referred to as 'rich or 'thick') information about relatively few cases or subjects rather than the more limited information about a large number of cases or subjects which is typical of quantitative research. It is possible, however, to envisage qualitative research that actually deals with large numbers of cases. For example, a research project on arts audiences, involving observation and participation in audience activity, could involve information relating, collectively, to tens of thousands of people.

Qualitative methods can be used for pragmatic reasons, in situations where formal, quanti-fied research is not necessary or is not possible, but there are also theoretical grounds for using such methods. Qualitative research is generally based on the belief that the people personally involved in a particular (cultural/event) situation are best placed to describe and explain their experiences, motivations and world view in their own words, and that they should be allowed to speak without the intermediary of the researcher and without being overly constrained by the framework imposed by the researcher. Some argue that a particular qualitative epistemol-ogy necessarily implies a particular ontology on the part of the researcher, but, as noted in Chapter 2, this idea has been challenged, for example by Bryman (1984).

Merits, functions, limitations

Some of the merits of qualitative methods in the arts/events research context include the following:

1. The method corresponds with the nature of the phenomenon being studied – that is, involvement with the arts/events is a qualitative experience for the individual.

2. The method brings people into the research and can study them 'in the round'. By con-trast, quantitative methods tend to be very impersonal – real people with names and unique personalities do not generally feature.

3. The results of qualitative research are more understandable to people who are not statistically trained.

4. The method is better able to encompass personal change over time – by contrast, much quantitative research tends to look only at current or recent behaviour as related to

current social, economic and environmental circumstances, ignoring the fact that most people's behaviour is heavily influenced by their life history and experience.

5. Arts/events activity involves a great deal of face-to-face interaction between people – involving symbols, gestures, etc. – and qualitative research is well suited to investigating this.

6. Qualitative techniques are better at providing an understanding of people's needs and aspirations, although some researchers in the psychological field in particular might disagree with this proposition (Kelly, 1980).

In this book it has been argued that different methods are not inherently good or bad, just more or less appropriate for the task at hand. Thus, to some extent, the above comments relate to particular types of research with particular purposes. For example, qualitative methods would clearly be most appropriate if the focus of interest is the qualitative experience of culture, personal arts/events engagement histories, the use of symbols, gestures, etc. in arts/events contexts, and/or communicating with a readership without statistical training.

Peterson (1994), speaking from a market researcher's perspective, lists the potential uses of qualitative research as:

1. to develop hypotheses concerning relevant behaviour and attitudes;

2. to identify the full range of issues, views and attitudes that should be pursued in larger-scale research;

3. to suggest methods for quantitative enquiry – for example, in terms of deciding who should be included in interview surveys;

4. to identify language used to address relevant issues (thus avoiding the use of jargon in questionnaires);

5. to understand how a buying decision is made – questionnaire surveys are not very good at exploring processes;

6. to develop new product, service or marketing strategy ideas – the free play of attitudes and opinions can be a rich source of ideas for the marketer;

7. to provide an initial screening of new product, service or strategy ideas;

8. to learn how communications are received – what is understood and how – particularly related to advertising.

On the grounds that qualitative methods are often used for certain purposes or in certain contexts, there is a tendency to associate them definitively with such purposes and contexts. For example, Hastie and Glotova (2012: 310) declare that 'qualitative research is, by definition, exploratory', while quantitative research is 'essentially conclusive'. However, while it may often be the case that qualitative research is used for exploratory purposes and quantitative research is used to reach conclusions by testing theories, this is not always so. As indicated in Chapter 14, quantitative secondary data analysis can be exploratory, while the frequently exploratory nature of experimental research is discussed in Chapter 11.

While partisan proponents of qualitative methods are vigorous in promoting their virtues, like all methods they also have their limitations. For example, Miles and Huberman, in their book *Qualitative Data Analysis*, note the substantial increase in the prevalence of qualitative research in the social sciences but caution:

> In the flurry of this activity, we should be mindful of some pervasive issues that have not gone away. These issues include the labour-intensiveness (and extensiveness over months or years)

of [qualitative] data collection, frequent data overload, the distinct possibility of researcher bias, the time demands of processing and coding data, the adequacy of sampling when only a few cases can be managed, the generalisability of findings, the credibility and quality of conclusions, and their utility in the world of policy and action.

(Miles and Huberman, 1994: 2)

The qualitative research process

Qualitative methods generally require, and enable, a more flexible, although no less rigorous, approach to overall research design and conduct than other approaches. Most quantitative research tends to be *sequential* in nature; the components of research as set out in Chapter 3 tend to be distinct and follow in a pre-planned sequence. This is inevitable because of the nature of the typical quantitative core primary data-collection task. Much qualitative research involves a more fluid relationship between the various elements of the research – an approach that might be called *recursive*. In this approach hypothesis formation evolves as the research progresses, data analysis and collection take place concurrently, and writing is also often evolutionary and on-going, rather than a separate process which takes place at the end of the project. The two approaches are represented diagrammatically in Figure 9.1.

Although the sequential and recursive models are presented here in the context of a contrast between quantitative and qualitative methods, in fact both quantitative and qualitative methods can involve sequential and recursive approaches. Thus, it is possible for an essentially quantitative study to involve a variety of data sources and a number of small-scale studies, which build on one another in an iterative way. It is also possible for an essentially qualitative study to be conducted on a large scale, with a single data source – for example, a nation-wide study of managers of arts venues or festivals, involving fairly standardised in-depth interviews.

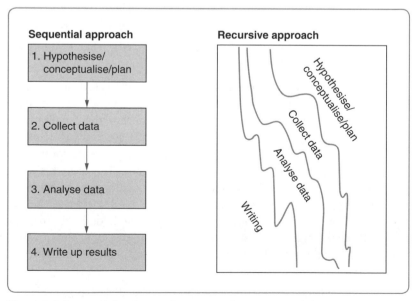

Figure 9.1 Sequential and recursive approaches to research

An important philosophical perspective in the analysis of qualitative data is the concept of *grounded theory* developed by sociologists Glaser and Strauss (1967). Grounded theory is concerned with the generation of theory from research, as opposed to research that tests *a priori* theory. It is therefore, in the terms discussed in Chapter 2, inductive rather than deductive. In this paradigm, theories and models should be grounded in real empirical observations rather than being governed by traditional methodologies and theories. In the generation of theory the researcher approaches the data with no pre-formed notions in mind, instead seeking to uncover patterns and contradictions through close examination of the data. To achieve this the researcher needs to be familiar with the data, the subjects and the cultural context of the research. The process is a complex and personal one. This is discussed further in Chapter 15.

One way in which qualitative research has been characterised is by referring to the researcher as 'research instrument', in contrast to, for example, the survey method where the research instrument is a questionnaire.

The range of qualitative methods – introduction

Qualitative techniques commonly used in arts/events research and discussed in more detail in this chapter include in-depth interviews, group interviews or focus groups, participant observation, textual analysis, biographical methods and ethnography. The basic characteristics of these approaches are summarised in Figure 9.2.

As indicated above, while data collection and data analysis are, in practice, often difficult to separate in qualitative research, the discussions of individual methods below concentrate on data collection. Guides to further reading for each method are provided in the Resources section.

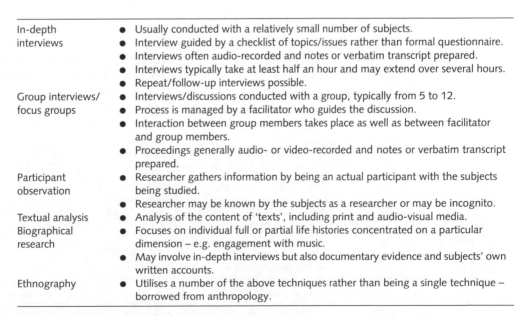

In-depth interviews	● Usually conducted with a relatively small number of subjects.
	● Interview guided by a checklist of topics/issues rather than formal questionnaire.
	● Interviews often audio-recorded and notes or verbatim transcript prepared.
	● Interviews typically take at least half an hour and may extend over several hours.
	● Repeat/follow-up interviews possible.
Group interviews/ focus groups	● Interviews/discussions conducted with a group, typically from 5 to 12.
	● Process is managed by a facilitator who guides the discussion.
	● Interaction between group members takes place as well as between facilitator and group members.
	● Proceedings generally audio- or video-recorded and notes or verbatim transcript prepared.
Participant observation	● Researcher gathers information by being an actual participant with the subjects being studied.
	● Researcher may be known by the subjects as a researcher or may be incognito.
Textual analysis	● Analysis of the content of 'texts', including print and audio-visual media.
Biographical research	● Focuses on individual full or partial life histories concentrated on a particular dimension – e.g. engagement with music.
	● May involve in-depth interviews but also documentary evidence and subjects' own written accounts.
Ethnography	● Utilises a number of the above techniques rather than being a single technique – borrowed from anthropology.

Figure 9.2 Qualitative methods: summary

In-depth interviews

Nature

An in-depth interview, sometimes referred to as semi-structured, is characterised by its length, depth and structure.

- *Length:* In-depth interviews tend to be much longer than questionnaire-based interviews, typically taking at least 30 minutes and sometimes several hours. The method may involve interviewing people more than once.

- *Depth:* As the name implies, the in-depth interview seeks to probe more deeply than is possible with a questionnaire-based interview. Rather than just asking a question, recording a simple answer and moving on, the in-depth interviewer typically encourages respondents to talk, poses supplementary questions and asks respondents to explain their answers.

- *Structure:* The in-depth interview is therefore less formally structured than a questionnaire-based interview. While the latter are typically seen as being structured, in-depth interviews are seen as semi-structured or unstructured, as discussed further below. As a result, every interview in a qualitative study, although dealing with the same issues, will be different.

Arguably, interviews in general can be said to span part of a spectrum related to the extent to which the questions and their wording are fully prescribed in advance or not prescribed at all and the extent to which responses are pre-coded or open-ended. This is illustrated in Figure 9.3, which shows that questionnaire-based and in-depth interviews overlap in the middle of the spectrum.

Purposes and situations

In-depth interviews tend to be used in three situations:

1. The subjects of the research are relatively few in number so a questionnaire-based, quantitative style of research would be inappropriate.

2. The information likely to be obtained from each subject is expected to vary considerably, and in complex ways. An example would be interviews with the management staff of an arts organisation event or participants in an activity with varying backgrounds and motivations. Each of the interviews would be different and would be a 'story' in its

Interview type	Question format	Responses	Interviewer–interviewee interaction
Structured	Prescribed by questionnaire	Pre-coded and open-ended	Formal, consistent
Structured + semi-structured elements	Prescribed by questionnaire + supplementary	Open-ended	Mostly formal, consistent
Semi-structured	Checklist: question format not prescribed	Open-ended	Conversational, variable
Unstructured	Only the broad topic area is prescribed	Open-ended	Free-flowing conversational, variable

Figure 9.3 Questions, responses and interview types

own right. In reporting the research it would be the unique nature and structure of each of these accounts that would be of interest – data on 'what percentage of respondents said what' would not be relevant.

3. A topic is to be explored as a preliminary stage in planning a larger study, possibly a quantitative study, such as a questionnaire-based survey.

Checklist

Rather than a formal questionnaire the 'instrument' used for semi-structured in-depth interviews is often a *checklist* of topics to be raised, although a few key pre-determined, prescribed questions may be included. For example, a formal questionnaire might ask a question: 'Which of the following cultural events have you ever taken part in in the last year?' The informal interview checklist might simply include the words 'recent events'. The interviewer would shape the question according to the circumstances of a particular interview. If the interviewer is interested, for example, in the influence of childhood exposure to the arts on adult participation patterns, in some interviews it may be necessary to ask a specific question such as: 'What cultural venues and events were you taken to as a child?' In other interviews, in response to the interviewer's initial question, the interviewee might talk at length and volunteer detailed, unprompted information on childhood visits. It is then not necessary to ask the separate question. Thus in-depth interviews vary from interview to interview; they take on a life of their own.

The skill on the part of the interviewer is to ensure that all relevant topics are covered – even though they may be covered in different orders and in different ways in different interviews. This, however, assumes that the list of relevant topics is known from the beginning and is already covered by the checklist. In practice the qualitative research allows the range of topics – and hence the content of the checklist – to evolve during the research process. New topics may emerge from interviewees themselves, leading to on-going modification of the checklist.

The design of the checklist should nevertheless be as methodical as the design of a formal questionnaire – in particular, the items to be included on the checklist should be based on the conceptual framework for the study and the resultant list of data needs, whether this be detailed or general in nature, as discussed in Chapter 3. An example of a checklist is presented in Figure 9.4. The example given is in the form of a fairly terse list of topics. An alternative would be to include fully worded questions to initiate discussion of various topics, as would appear in a questionnaire; this may be advisable when a number of interviewers are involved – examples of this format can be seen in Charmaz (2006: 30–31). The problem with fully worded questions is that actually turning to the clipboard and reading out lengthy questions can interrupt the flow and informality of the interview. The more detailed the checklist, the more the interview would be described as *semi-structured*. If only a brief checklist is used, or even none at all, the interview would be described as *unstructured*.

The interviewing process

Conducting a successful in-depth interview could be said to require the skills of a good investigative journalist. As Dean and his colleagues put it:

> Many people feel that a newspaper reporter is a far cry from a social scientist. Yet many of the data of social science today are gathered by interviewing and observation techniques that resemble those of a skilled newspaper [reporter]… at work on the study of, say, a union strike or a political convention. It makes little sense for us to belittle these less rigorous methods as

This is part of a checklist devised in connection with a study of people's participation in and attitudes towards the arts/cultural events.

CURRENT ARTS/CULTURAL ACTIVITY EXPLORE EACH ONE – COMPARE	How often? Active or audience? Why? Key events? Where? – Home/away from home Who with? Meaning/importance Type of involvement
ACTIVITIES WOULD LIKE TO DO MEANING OF 'CULTURE' TO YOU MEANING OF 'THE ARTS' TO YOU	What prevents you?
CONSTRAINTS:	Home/family commitments Work – time/colleagues Money/costs Availability Car/transport Knowledge
PAST CULTURAL ACTIVITY WHY CHANGES?	At school At college/univ. With family
FACILITIES	Locally Favourite City Use/non-use – why? REGION ACCESS
HOME-BASED	Reading/books Music
PERSONALITY LIKES/DISLIKES	Skills/knowledge Aspirations

Figure 9.4 Example of a checklist for in-depth interviewing

'unscientific'. We will do better to study them and the techniques they involve so that we can make better use of them in producing scientific information.

(Dean *et al.*, quoted in McCall and Simmons, 1969:1)

There are two approaches to conducting an in-depth interview: standardised and informal or unstructured.

Standardised approach

The standardised approach is one in which the emphasis in 'semi-structured' is on the 'structured' dimension and where elements of the traditional scientific approach are replicated. The interaction between researcher and subject is, as far as possible, similar for all subjects. So prescribed questions are used, although the interviewer also improvises, depending on the flow of the interview. In this case, an important skill in interviewing is to avoid becoming so taken up in the conversational style of the interview that the interviewee is 'led' by the interviewer. The interviewer avoids agreeing – or disagreeing – with the interviewee or suggesting answers. This is more difficult than it sounds because in normal conversation we tend to make friendly noises and contribute to the discussion. In this situation the interviewer is torn between the need to maintain a friendly, conversational atmosphere and the desire not to influence the interviewee's responses. Some of the carefully planned sequencing of questions that is built into formal questionnaires must be achieved by the interviewer being sensitive and quick thinking. For example, having discovered that the respondent does not attend cultural events, the interviewer should not lead the respondent by saying: 'Is this because it is too expensive?' Rather, the interviewee should be asked a more open question, such as: 'Why is that?' If the interviewee does not mention cost, but cost is of particular interest in the study, then the respondent might be asked a question such as: 'What about seat prices?' But this would be only *after* the interviewee has given his or her own unprompted reasons for not attending.

An important skill in interviewing of this sort is not to be afraid of silence. Some questions puzzle respondents and they need time to think. The interviewer does not have to fill the space with noise under the guise of 'helping' the interviewee; the interviewee is allowed time to ponder. The initiative can be left with the respondent to ask for an explanation if a question is unclear. While it is pleasant to engender a conversational atmosphere in these situations, the semi-structured interview is in fact different from a conversation. The interviewer is meant to listen and encourage the respondent to talk – not to engage in debate.

Informal or unstructured approach

Some researchers favour a more informal or unstructured approach. Dupuis (1999), for example, sees the semi-structured approach as inappropriately seeking to reflect the positivist paradigm in qualitative research. She argues that using qualitative methods involves full interaction with research informants, so interviewers should be free to engage in a relatively free-flowing two-way conversation with interviewees. But she makes the further point that, if this is to happen, much more detail about this aspect of the research process should be reported in research accounts than is usually the case. Thus, for example, information gained by means of a full two-way conversation and exchange of views with an extrovert and loquacious interviewee is arguably different in nature from information gained from interviews where the interviewee is more reserved.

Distinction between standardised and informal approaches

The distinction between the standardised and informal interview approaches can be seen as corresponding to the phenomenographic and phenomenological approach to research (Ryan, 2000: 125). In the former, researchers adopt a minimalist approach to intervention in the interview and subsequently analyse and interpret the output – typically in the form of a transcript – in the same way that any text would be analysed. In the latter, researchers/interviewers are more active in eliciting responses to assist them in understanding an interviewee's world view during the course of the interview.

Whyte (1982) provides a sort of hierarchy in interviewer responses which vary in their degree of intervention in the interview, seeing this as the interviewer exercising varying degrees of control over the interview. Beginning with the least intrusive style of intervention, Whyte's list is as shown in Figure 9.5. It should be noted that, except for the sixth of these responses, the interviewer is essentially drawing on what the subject has already said and is inviting her or him to expand on it.

1 'Uh-huh'	A non-verbal response that merely indicates that the interviewer is still listening and interested.
2 'That's interesting'	Encourages the subject to keep talking or expand on the current topic.
3 Reflection	Repeating the last statement as a question – e.g. 'So you don't like classical music?'
4 Probe	Inviting explanations of statements – e.g. 'Why don't you like classical music?'
5 Back tracking	Remembering something the subject said earlier and inviting further information – e.g. 'Let's go back to what you were saying about your school days'.
6 New topic	Initiating a new topic – e.g. 'Can we talk about other cultural activities – what about museums?'

Figure 9.5 Interviewing interventions – Whyte (1982)

Recording

Sound or video recording of in-depth interviews is common, although in some cases it might be felt that such a procedure could inhibit respondents. If recording is not possible then notes must be taken during the interview or immediately afterwards. There can be great value in producing complete verbatim (word-for-word) transcripts of interviews from recordings. This is a laborious process – one hour of interview taking as much as six hours to transcribe manually – but there are now online services that use voice-recognition technology to transcribe digitised recordings automatically. Transcripts can be used to analyse the results of interviews in a more methodical and complete manner than is possible with notes, including the use of computer software, as discussed in Chapter 15.

Focus groups

Nature

The idea of interviewing groups of people together rather than individually is becoming increasingly popular in market and community research. In this technique the interviewer becomes the facilitator, convenor or discussion leader rather than an interviewer as such. The aim of the process is much the same as in an in-depth interview, but in this case the participants interact with each other as well as with the researcher/facilitator.

Purposes

The technique can be used:

- when a particular group is important in a study but is so small in number that members of the group would not be adequately represented in a general community questionnaire-based survey – for example, members of minority ethnic groups or people with disabilities;

- when the interaction/discussion process itself is of interest – for example, in testing reactions to a proposed new product, or when investigating team behaviour;

- as an alternative to the in-depth interview, when it may not be practical to arrange for individual in-depth interviews but people are willing to be interviewed as a group – for example, some youth groups or members of some ethnic communities.

Methods

A group will usually comprise between five and twelve participants. They may be chosen from a 'panel' of people who make themselves available to market researchers for this sort of exercise, or they may be chosen because they are members of a particular group of interest to the research, such as members of a theatre group or local residents in a particular area. The members of the group may or may not be known to one another.

The usual procedure is to record the discussion and for the researcher to produce a written summary from the recording.

Many of the same considerations apply here as in the in-depth interview situation: the process is informal but the facilitator still has a role in guiding the discussion and ensuring that all the aspects of the topic are covered. In addition, in the group interview, the facilitator has the task of ensuring that everyone in the group has their say and that the discussion is not dominated by one or two vociferous members of the group.

Participant observation

Nature

In participant observation the researcher becomes a participant in the social process being studied. The classic study of this type is Whyte's *Street Corner Society* (1955), in which the researcher spent several years living with an inner-city US Italian community. Studies of individual cultural organisations, events or groups can be conducted by members of the organisation or group or by volunteers or audience participants in the event. Traditionally the process has involved considerable interaction of the researcher with the people being researched, and personal involvement of the researcher in a group provides an ideal environment for studying a cultural activity or the organisation of an event over an extended period of time.

Purposes

In many cases some sort of participant observation is the only way of researching particular phenomena – for instance, it would be difficult to study what really goes on in a drug sub-culture, some youth sub-cultures or a close-knit group such as a choir or work team using a questionnaire and clipboard. Becoming part of the group and immersion in its activities is the obvious way of studying the group.

Methods

Participant observation raises a number of practical/tactical challenges, and sometimes ethical challenges, as discussed in Chapter 4. For example, in some cases actually gaining admittance to the social setting of interest may be difficult, especially where close-knit groups are involved. Having gained admittance to the setting, the question arises for the researcher as to whether to pose as a typical member of the group, to adopt a plausible disguise or persona (e.g. a 'journalist' or 'writer') or to admit to being a researcher.

Selection of informants is an issue to be addressed by the participant observer in the same way that sampling must be considered by the survey researcher. The members of the study group who are most friendly and talkative may be the easiest to communicate with, but may give a biased picture of the views and behaviour of the group as a whole.

There are practical problems to be faced over how to record information. When the researcher's identity as a researcher has not been revealed, the taking of notes in real time or the use of a recorder may be impossible. Even when the researcher has identified herself as such, or has assumed a plausible identity, the use of such devices may interfere with the sort of natural relationship the researcher is trying to establish. The taking of regular and detailed notes is, however, the basic data-recording method. This may be supplemented by photographs and even video and recordings in some instances.

Analysing texts

Nature

The analysis of texts, such as plays and novels, is the very basis of some disciplines in the humanities, such as literature, media studies and cultural studies. However, researchers interested in social, management and policy issues related to 'cultural products' and their production, consumption and impact have also come to see texts as a useful source of insights. The term *text* is now used to embrace not just printed material but also pictures, posters, recorded music, film and television and the internet. Indeed, virtually any cultural product can, in the jargon, be read as text.

It is not proposed to outline analysis techniques in detail in this book, since approaches are varied, including the qualitative, literary 'reading' of texts, the interpretation of texts, sometimes referred to as *hermeneutics*, and the highly quantified form of analysis known as *content analysis*. The approach here is, rather, to introduce some examples of work in this area.

Mass media coverage

Media coverage of selected topics can be studied quantitatively by measuring the column centimetres devoted to the topic in newspapers or the time devoted to the topic on television. Examples are the studies by:

- Zillmann and Voderer (2000): a collection of studies of audience involvement in types of television programme, video games and music videos;
- Jackson and McPhail (1989): a collection of papers on the television coverage of the Olympic Games.

Film

- Rojek (1993) provides an analysis of Disney films and their role in contemporary culture, in his paper 'Disney culture'.

Internet

- Clavio and Eagleman (2011) examine gender and images in arts/events blogs.

Material culture

- Hodder (1994), in his paper on 'The interpretation of documents and material culture', devotes relatively little space to documents, but concentrates on the idea of studying 'material culture' or artefacts. Among the latter he includes dress fashions, national flags and the archaeological study of garbage.
- Examples of the direct study of cultural products in the research literature are studies of:
  - the theme parks of the Disney Corporation (Rojek, 1993; Klugman *et al*, 1995);
  - postcards (Cohen, 1993);

- American musicals (Dyer, 1993);
- heavy metal rock music (Straw, 1993).

Biographical research

Nature

Biographical research covers a range of techniques involving researching all or a substantial part of the lives of individuals or groups of individuals. The most common example of such research is the conventional biography or autobiography, but the biographical approach includes a number of other research approaches and outputs, including oral history, memory work and personal domain histories. Detailed guidance on the conduct of biographical research is not given in this book, but a brief overview of the field is given here and sources of further information in the Resource section.

Biography/autobiography/personal narrative

There are many published accounts of lives of business leaders which, while often read for entertainment, also provide insight into how business and business leaders operate. Perhaps the most well known is the autobiography of Lee Iacocca (1984), the CEO of Chrysler during a turbulent period. Examples of biographies that go beyond the telling of a personal story to relate the subject's life to wider social and cultural issues include Bryman's (1995) account of Walt Disney and his company, Rojck's (2004) study of Frank Sinatra and his broader study *Celebrity* (Rojek, 2001).

Oral history

Oral history involves tape-recording witness accounts of events and typically storing the tapes and/or a transcription of them in an archive as a source for research. While such accounts range more widely than the interviewees' own lives, they are nevertheless personal accounts. Perlis (1994) discusses this approach in relation to music.

Memory work

Memory work is a structured way of eliciting subjects' memories of events; it can be seen as a focus group aided by individual writing. Participants are asked to write a short account of an experience related to the research topic – for example, bullying in the workplace or successful selling. The written accounts are read aloud in focus group settings and discussed, and may be followed up with further writing and/or interviewing (Onyx and Small, 2001).

Personal domain histories

In the 1980s, a technique termed 'personal leisure histories' was developed by Hedges (1986) to study the ways in which significant changes in life circumstances (marriage, birth of a child, change of job, health issues, etc.) impacted on patterns of leisure, including cultural participation. This idea can be widened to focus on any domain of an individual's life, hence the use of the term 'personal domain histories'.

Ethnography

The ethnographic style of research is not one technique but an approach drawing on a variety of techniques. Traditionally, ethnography has been the research methodology of anthropologists studying non-industrial communities. Generally, it seeks to see the world through the eyes of those being researched, allowing them to speak for themselves, often through extensive direct quotations in the research report. The aim is often to debunk conventional, establishment, 'common sense' views of 'social problems', 'deviants', sexual and ethnic stereotypes, and so on. The approach is particularly associated with 'cultural studies', for example of youth sub-cultures and ethnic groups.

Ethnography can be seen as a 'mixed method' approach, as discussed in Chapter 5. In the qualitative research context, a term used for mixed methods is *bricolage*, a French word referring to craft-workers who are able to 'make do' with whatever materials or tools are at hand, as in quilt-making. The practitioner is then known as a *bricoleur* (Denzin and Lincoln, 2006: 4–6).

Validity and reliability, trustworthiness

The issues of validity – the extent to which research accurately represents what it is intended to represent – and reliability – the extent to which research is replicable – were discussed in Chapter 2, and it was noted there that some researchers prefer to use the term *trustworthiness* when discussing qualitative methods.

Internal validity is concerned with the processes by which information is gathered from the subjects of the study. A case could be made that information collected by qualitative methods has a greater chance of being internally valid than information gathered by means of, for example, a short questionnaire, since, in the qualitative data-collection situation, more time and effort are generally taken to collect any one piece of information. Thus the exchange between interviewer and interviewee in an in-depth interview or the discussion in a focus group should increase the likelihood of interviewer/facilitator and interviewee/participants understanding each other. Verbatim records also help in this process.

External validity is concerned with the applicability of the findings beyond the subjects of the research. Typically, no claim of formal generalisability is made on the basis of qualitative study but, as noted in Chapter 2, this strict rule is often implicitly ignored. It is noted in Chapter 13 that efforts are often made to select samples of subjects for qualitative research that have some semblance of representativeness, at least in terms of the qualitative diversity of the population being studied. It would be strange if researchers conducting qualitative research projects did not believe that there were some implications beyond the limited sample of subjects studied. Thus, the belief is generally that what has been found is true of some people among the population from which the study subjects were drawn, but the extent cannot be quantified. In theoretical terms, if the findings of qualitative research are inconsistent with existing theory, it at least establishes that the theory is not universally valid. Furthermore, theoretical propositions arising from qualitative research may be more widely applicable.

Unlike the physical sciences, exact replicability of qualitative social research findings is basically impossible. However, accumulation of similar, or logically consistent, findings from a wide range of studies lends strength to the findings, not in a statistical sense but in terms of the robustness of the findings in different settings. There is a parallel in quantitative meta-analyses, where it can be argued that similar, but statistically insignificant, findings from a number of studies may be given some cumulative support if the level of significance of individual studies was affected by sample sizes.

Thus, while qualitative research cannot offer the formally rigorous tests of validity and reliability of quantitative research, the issues can be discussed, and some form of assessment of trustworthiness can be arrived at.

Early qualitative research

There is a tendency to think of the use of qualitative methods as being quite a recent development in the social sciences, including in the area of arts/events research, but this is not entirely correct. Case study 9.1 is included to demonstrate that there were some examples dating back to the 1940s.

CASE STUDY 9.1

Early qualitative research: *English Life and Leisure*

In the earliest large-scale British study of leisure, including cultural activities, *English Life and Leisure*, published in 1951, the authors describe their research method as follows:

> In making our study of contemporary life in England and Wales, we concluded that, besides the usual and obvious methods of approaching the subject, we needed some means of letting a substantial number of men and women, of all ages and social classes, speak for themselves, in the hope that, as they told their individual stories, we should build up a living picture of English life and leisure. For such a purpose as we had in mind, formal interviewing, or the use of questionnaires, would have been useless, for many of the matters about which we desired information are intensely personal, and in any case we were interested more in behaviour than in such opinions as could be elicited by answers to short, set questions. We therefore decided to build up our picture of what people are like by a system of indirect interviewing. This method consists of making an acquaintance of an individual – the excuses for doing so are immaterial – and developing the acquaintance until his or her confidence is gained and information required can be obtained in ordinary conversation, without the person concerned ever knowing that there has been an interview or that any specific information was being sought. Such a method is laborious but effective.
>
> (Rowntree and Lavers, 1951: xii)

Apart from likely ethics committee concerns about 'informed consent' on the part of interviewees, such an explanation would not look out of place in a twentieth-century account of the rationale for use of qualitative methods. The first 121 pages of *English Life and Leisure* consist of individual 'case histories' of 220 (103 female, 117 male) of the almost 1,000 people interviewed in 11 cities. These vary from just a few lines to almost a page in length and, although anonymous, are often remarkably candid. The scope of the interviews and case histories is indicated by the titles of the following 12 summary chapters:

- Commercialized gambling
- Drink
- Smoking
- Sexual promiscuity
- How honest is Britain?
- The cinema
- The stage
- Broadcasting [radio]
- Reading habits
- Adult education
- Religion.

➡

Case study 9.1 (*continued*)

Half of the chapters include one or two small tables based on the survey respondents, but most of the discussion is qualitative in nature, including frequent short quotations from interviews.

Also of note is that the report includes an early example analysis of cultural 'texts', in this case films. In a distinctive indicator of the times, the authors say:

> When we started our investigations early in 1946 neither of us knew much about the cinema. We were not in any way hostile to it, but it so happened that preoccupation with other matters had prevented both of us from paying other than very infrequent visits to cinemas. We decided, however, that we must be in a position to write from first-hand knowledge, and one of us... has accordingly during the course of our investigations visited 125 cinemas of all types in London [and 10 other cities]. After every visit a careful analysis was made of the principal film shown, and our remarks in this section are based on these analyses.
>
> (Rowntree and Lavers, 1951: 232–33)

The section includes summary details of seven of the films, the researcher's assessment of the 'desirability' of the 125 films viewed and a discussion of the censorship system. Desirability is assessed in a way that is unlikely to be seen in a contemporary study, using a five-category scale:

- broadly of cultural or educational value;
- reasonable entertainment but nothing more;
- harmless but inane;
- glorifying false values;
- really objectionable.

Summary

This chapter introduces the role of qualitative approaches in arts and events research. One of the basic assumptions of qualitative research is that reality is socially and subjectively constructed rather than objectively determined. In this perspective researchers are seen as part of the research process, seeking to uncover meanings and an understanding of the issues they are researching. In general, qualitative research involves the collection of a large amount of 'rich' information concerning relatively few people or organisations rather than the more limited information from a large number of people or organisations common in quantitative methods.

Qualitative methods generally require a more flexible, recursive approach to overall research design and conduct in contrast to the more linear, sequential approach used in most quantitative research. Hypothesis formation evolves as the research progresses; data collection and analysis typically take place concurrently and writing is also often an evolutionary process, rather than a separate process that happens at the end of the project.

There is a range of qualitative methods available to the researcher, including in-depth interviews, group interviews, focus groups, participant observation, textual analysis, biographical methods and ethnographic methods. The chapter outlines the nature and techniques involved in using each of these methods.

Validity and reliability of qualitative methods cannot be assessed using the rigorous, quantified tests of quantitative methods, but the issues can be addressed and assessed to give an assessment of what some have termed *trustworthiness*.

TEST QUESTIONS

1. Outline some of the merits of qualitative data.
2. Explain the difference between sequential and recursive approaches to research.
3. Outline Whyte's levels of interviewer intervention in an in-depth/informal interview.
4. In-depth interviews involve an interviewer: what is the equivalent in a focus group?
5. Name three types of biographical research.

EXERCISES

1. Use the checklist in Figure 9.4 to interview a willing friend or colleague. Assess your performance as an interviewer.
2. If you are studying with others, arrange yourselves into groups of five or six and organise a focus-group interview, with one person as facilitator, choosing a topic of mutual interest, such as 'Art for social benefit or art for art's sake?' or 'Events for the community or the economy?' Take turns in acting as convenor and assess each other's skills as convenor.

Resources

- Qualitative methods:
  - in social science: Lofland and Lofland (1984), Burgess (1982), Denzin and Lincoln (1994, 2006), Silverman (1993)
  - arts/events research: Fox *et al.* (2014)
  - internet/blog-based: Chenail (2011)

- Qualitative/quantitative issues: Bryman (1984).
- Autoethnography: TV watching: Uotinen (2010).
- Biography/autobiography/personal narrative: Atkinson (1998), Bertaux (1981), Roberts (2002); personal domain histories: Hedges (1986); personal narratives: White and Hede (2008).
- Content analysis: Altheide (2000).
- Ethnography: museum setting: Noy (2011).
- Examples of qualitative research in the arts/events field:
  - art museum visitors: in-depth interviews: Stylianou-Lambert (2009), Jagger *et al.* (2012)
  - ethnography, museum: Noy (2011)
  - multi-media and social media-based study of a music festival: Flinn and Frew (2013)
  - oral history, music: Perlis (1994)
  - participant observation, music: Eastman (2012)
  - text analysis: music events: Jaimangal-Jones (2012)

- Focus groups: general: Calder (1977), Greenbaum (1998, 2000), Krueger (1988), Morgan (1993), Reynolds and Johnson (1978), Stewart and Shamdasani (1990); museums: Combs (1999); TV audiences: Roscoe *et al.* (1995).

- Grounded theory: in general: Glaser and Strauss (1967), Strauss and Corbin (1994); Charmaz (2006).

- Informal/in-depth interviews: Dunne (1995); festivals: Jaeger and Mykletun (2013).

- Media consumption: Zillman and Voderer (2000).

- Memory work: Onyx and Small (2001).

- Participant observation: events: Mackellar (2013).

- Text/documents: Prior (2003).

References

Altheide, D. L. (2000) Tracking discourse and qualitative document analysis. *Poetics*, 27(3), 287–299.

Atkinson, R. (1998) *The Life Story Interview*. London: Sage.

Bertaux, D. (ed.) (1981) *Biography and Society*. London: Sage.

Bryman, A. (1984) The debate about quantitative and qualitative research: a question of method or epistemology? *British Journal of Sociology*, 35(1), 75–92.

Bryman, A. (1995) *Disney and his Worlds*. London: Routledge.

Burgess, R. G. (ed.) (1982) *Field Research: A Sourcebook and Field Manual*. London: Allen and Unwin.

Calder, B. (1977) Focus groups and the nature of qualitative marketing research. *Journal of Marketing Research*, 14(Aug), 353–364.

Charmaz, K. (2006) *Constructing Grounded Theory*. London: Sage.

Chenail, R. J. (2011) Qualitative researchers in the blogosphere: using blogs as diaries and data. *The Qualitative Report,* 16(1), 249–254.

Clavio, G. and Eagleman, A. N. (2011) Gender and sexually suggestive images in sports blogs. *Journal of Sport Management*, 7(4), 295–304.

Cohen, E. (1993) The study of touristic images of native people: mitigating the stereotype of a stereotype. In D. G. Pearce and R. W. Butler (eds), *Tourism Research: Critiques and Challenges*. London: Routledge, pp. 36–69.

Combs, A. A. (1999) Why do they come? Listening to visitors at a decorative arts museum. *Curator*, 42(3), 186–197.

Denzin, N. K. and Lincoln, Y. S. (eds) (1994) *Handbook of Qualitative Research*. Thousand Oaks, CA: Sage.

Denzin, N. K. and Lincoln, Y. S. (eds) (2006) *Handbook of Qualitative Research*, Third Edition. Thousand Oaks, CA: Sage.

Dunne, S. (1995) *Interviewing Techniques for Writers and Researchers*. London: A. and C. Black.

Dupuis, S. (1999) Naked truths: towards a reflexive methodology in leisure research. *Leisure Sciences*, 21(1), 43–64.

Dyer, R. (1993) Entertainment and utopia. In S. During (ed.), *The Cultural Studies Reader*. London: Routledge, pp. 271–283.

Eastman, J. T. (2012) Rebel manhood: the hegemonic masculinity of the Southern rock music revival. *Journal of Contemporary Ethnography*, 41(2), 189–219.

Flinn, J. and Frew, M. (2014) Glastonbury: managing the mystification of festivity. *Leisure Studies*, 33(4), 418–433.

Fox, D., Gouthro, M. B. and Brackstone, J. (2014) *Doing Events Research*. London: Routledge.

Glaser, B. and Strauss, A. L. (1967) *The Discovery of Grounded Theory: Strategies for Qualitative Research*, Chicago, IL: Aldine.

Greenbaum, T. L. (1998) *The Handbook for Focus Group Research*, Second Edition. Thousand Oaks, CA: Sage.

Greenbaum, T. L. (2000) *Moderating Focus Groups: A Practical Guide for Group Facilitation*. Thousand Oaks, CA: Sage.

Hastie, P. and Glotova, O. (2012) Analysing qualitative data. In K. Armour and D. Macdonald (eds), *Research Methods in Physical Education and Youth Sport London*. Routledge, pp. 309–320.

Hedges, B. (1986) *Personal Leisure Histories*. London: Sports Council/Economic and Social Research Council.

Hodder, I. (1994) The interpretation of documents and material culture. In N. K. Denzin and Y. S. Lincoln (eds), *Handbook of Qualitative Research*. Thousand Oaks, CA: Sage, pp. 393–402.

Iacocca, L. A. (1984) *Iacocca: An Autobiography*. Toronto: Bantam Books.

Jackson, R. and McPhail, T. (eds) (1989) *The Olympic Movement and the Mass Media: Past, Present and Future Issues*. International Conference Proceedings, University of Calgary, Calgary, BC: Hurford Enterprises.

Jaeger, K. and Mykletun, R. J. (2013) Festivals, identities and belonging. *Event Management*, 17(3), 213–226.

Jagger, S. L., Dubek, M. M. and Pedretti, E. (2012) 'It's a personal thing': visitors' response to Body Worlds. *Museum Management and Curatorship*, 27(4), 357–374.

Jaimangal-Jones, D. (2012) More than worlds: analyzing the media discourses surrounding dance music events. *Event Management*, 16(3), 305–318.

Kelly, J. R. (1980) Leisure and quality: beyond the quantitative barrier in research. In T. L. Goodale and P. A. Witt (eds), *Recreation and Leisure: Issues in an Era of Change*. State College, PA: Venture, pp. 300–314.

Klugman, K., Kuenz, J., Waldrop, S. and Willis, S. (1995) *Inside the Mouse: The Project on Disney*. Durham, NC: Duke University Press.

Krueger, R. A. (1988) *Focus Groups: A Practical Guide for Applied Research*. Newbury Park, CA: Sage.

Lofland, J. and Lofland, L. H. (1984) *Analyzing Social Settings: A Guide to Qualitative Observation and Analysis*, Second Edition. Belmont, CA: Wadsworth.

Mackellar, J. (2013) Participant observation at events: theory, practice and potential. *International Journal of Event and Festival Management*, 4(1), 56–65.

McCall, G. J. and Simmons, J. L. (eds) (1969) *Issues in Participant Observation*. Reading, MA: Addison-Wesley.

Miles, M. B. and Huberman, A. M. (1994) *Qualitative Data Analysis*, Second Edition. Thousand Oaks, CA: Sage.

Morgan, D. L. (ed.) (1993) *Successful Focus Groups: Advancing the State of the Art*. Newbury Park, CA: Sage.

Noy, C. (2011) The aesthetics of qualitative (re)search: performing ethnography at a heritage museum. *Qualitative Inquiry*, 17(10), 917–929.

Onyx, J. and Small, J. (2001) Memory-work: the method. *Qualitative Inquiry*, 7(6), 773–786.

Perlis, V. (1994) Oral history and music. *Journal of American History*, 81(2), 610–619.

Peterson, K. I. (1994) Qualitative research methods for the travel and tourism industry. In J. R. B. Ritchie and C. R. Goeldner (eds), *Travel, Tourism and Hospitality Research*, Second Edition. New York: John Wiley, pp. 487–492.

Prior, L. (2003) *Using Documents in Social Research*. London: Sage.

Reynolds, F. and Johnson, D. (1978) Validity of focus group findings. *Journal of Advertising Research*, 19(1), 3–24.

Roberts, B. (2002) *Biographical Research*. Buckingham: Open University Press.

Rojek, C. (1993) Disney culture. *Leisure Studies*, 12(2), 121–136.

Rojek, C. (2001) *Celebrity*. London: Reaktion.

Rojek, C. (2004) *Frank Sinatra*. Cambridge: Polity.

Roscoe, J., Marshall, H. and Gleeson, K. (1995) The television audience: a reconsideration of the taken-for-granted terms 'active', 'social' and 'critical'. *European Journal of Communication*, 10(1), 87–108.

Rowntree, B. S. and Lavers, G. R. (1951) *English Life and Leisure: A Social Study*. London: Longmans, Green and Co.

Ryan, C. (2000) Tourist experiences, phenomenographic analysis, post-positivism and neural network software. *International Journal of Tourism Research*, 2(1), 119–131.

Silverman, D. (1993) *Interpreting Qualitative Data: Methods for Analysing Talk, Text and Interaction*. London: Sage.

Stewart, D. W. and Shamdasani, P. N. (1990) *Focus Groups: Theory and Practice*. Newbury Park, CA: Sage.

Strauss, A. and Corbin, J. (1994) Grounded theory methodology. In N. K. Denzin and Y. S Lincoln (eds), *Handbook of Qualitative Research*. Thousand Oaks, CA: Sage, pp. 273–285.

Straw, W. (1993) Characterising rock music culture: the case of heavy metal. In S. During (ed.), *The Cultural Studies Reader*. London: Routledge, pp. 368–381.

Stylianou-Lambert, T. (2009) Perceiving the art museum. *Museum Management and Curatorship*, 24(2), 139–158.

Uotinen, J. (2010) Digital television and the machine that goes 'Ping!': autoethnography as a method for cultural studies of technology. *Journal for Cultural Research*, 14(2), 161–175.

White, T. R. and Hede, A.-M. (2008) Using narrative inquiry to explore the impact of art on individuals. *Journal of Arts Management, Law and Society*, 38(1), 19–36.

Whyte, W. F. (1955) *Street Corner Society*. Chicago, IL: University of Chicago Press.

Whyte, W. F. (1982) Interviewing in field research. In R. G. Burgess (ed.), *Field Research: A Sourcebook and Field Manual*. London: Allen and Unwin, pp. 111–122.

Zillman, D. and Voderer, P. (eds) (2000) *Media Entertainment: The Psychology of its Appeal*. New York: Routledge.

Chapter 10

Questionnaire surveys: typology, design and coding

Introduction	• Definitions and terminology • Roles, Merits, Limitations • Interviewer-completion or respondent-completion • Types of questionnaire survey
The household survey	• Nature, Conduct, Omnibus, Time use surveys, National surveys
The street survey	• Nature, Conduct, Quota sampling
The telephone survey	• Nature, Conduct, Representativeness/response, national surveys
The mail survey	• Nature, Low response rates, Mail/visitor survey combos
E-surveys	• Nature, Conduct, Advantages and disadvantages
Visitor/on-site surveys	• Nature, Conduct, Uses of visitor surveys, Visitor/mail combos
Captive group surveys	• Nature, Conduct
Questionnaire design	• Intro., General, Example questionnaire, Types of info., Activity, Characteristics, Attitudes, Market segments, Ordering and layout
Coding	• Pre-coded and Open-ended questions, Recoding coded info.
Validity	• Threats to validity, Checking validity
Conducting surveys	• Planning fieldwork arrangements, Conducting a pilot survey

Introduction

This chapter presents an overview of the types of questionnaire surveys and an introduction to questionnaire design. Questionnaire surveys involve the gathering of information from individuals using a formally designed *questionnaire* or *interview schedule* and are arguably the most commonly used technique in arts/events research.

The first part of the chapter discusses the merits of questionnaire methods and the distinction between the interviewer-completion and respondent-completion modes, followed by an overview of the characteristics of the various forms of questionnaire survey: the household questionnaire survey, the street survey, the telephone survey, the postal or mail survey, e-surveys, visitors, on-site or user surveys, and captive group surveys.

The second half of the chapter considers the factors to be taken into account in designing questionnaires. First, the relationships between research problems and information require-ments are examined. This is followed by consideration of the types of information typically included in arts/events-related questionnaires, the wording of questions, coding of ques-tionnaires for computer analysis, the ordering and layout of questions, and the problem of validity. Finally, some consideration is given to the process of conducting surveys, including pilot surveys.

Definitions and terminology

A questionnaire can be defined as 'a written/printed or computer-based schedule of ques-tions and a *pro forma* for recording answers to the questions'. It is therefore both a means of eliciting information from respondents and a medium for recording answers.

The term *questionnaire survey* or *questionnaire-based survey* is used deliberately in this chapter to emphasise that the words *survey* and *questionnaire* mean two different things. There is a tendency in common parlance – and unfortunately in some research literature – to use the terms survey and questionnaire synonymously. For example, researchers have been known to make statements such as '1,000 surveys were distributed'. This is not so: only *one* survey was involved – 1,000 *questionnaires* were distributed. To make clear the distinction between the two terms:

- a questionnaire is a written/printed or computer-based schedule of questions;
- a survey is the *process* of designing and conducting a study involving the gathering of information from a number of subjects.

A 'survey' does not always include a questionnaire; thus, for example, a study could involve a visual survey of crowding at a venue or a documentary survey of the contents of organisa-tions' annual reports.

Alternative terms for the word questionnaire are 'research instrument' or 'survey instru-ment', which reference the science laboratory context. In addition 'survey form', 'question schedule' or 'interview schedule' are sometimes used.

Roles

Questionnaire surveys are used when a specified range of information is required from individuals or organisations. The most common form involves a representative sample of a defined population of individuals or organisations, although in some cases the whole popu-lation is included, as in a national census of the population. In both cases the aim is to make statements about the characteristics of the population on the basis of the data from the sur-vey, typically in the form of percentages, averages, relationships and trends. Where a sample is involved, therefore, the sampling process is critical (see Chapter 13).

Questionnaire-based surveys are generally used to collect responses to questions which have a limited number of possible answers, for example a person's gender or educational level, but some questions can be open-ended, with an unspecified range of answers, such as an open question on motivation for participation, or a visitor's complaints or suggestions regarding the management of a venue, programme or event.

Questionnaire-based surveys can play a role in the task of estimating the number of visits to venues or events where visitor numbers are not automatically gathered by administrative means, such as the sale of tickets. Examples include some museums, cultural tourism destinations and free events, and venues/events/destinations where car-borne visitors are significant. In this process information on visitor numbers may be gathered administratively (ticket sales, bookings), by direct counts/observation or wholly or in part by questionnaire-based survey (see Figure 7.2).

Merits

Compared with the qualitative techniques, questionnaire surveys usually involve quantification – the presentation of results in numerical terms. This has implications for the way the data are collected, analysed and interpreted. The merits and qualities of questionnaire surveys which can make them useful in arts/events-related research are set out below.

- Arts activities and events are often mass phenomena, requiring major involvement from governmental, non-profit and/or commercial organisations, which rely on quantified information for significant aspects of their decision making. Questionnaire surveys are an ideal means of providing some of this information.

- While absolute objectivity is impossible, questionnaire methods provide a transparent set of research procedures such that the way information was collected and how it was analysed or interpreted is clear for all to see, although, it must be said, journal articles reporting on the results vary in the amount of methodological detail provided. Questionnaire survey data, which are invariably available in digital form, can often be re-analysed by others if they wish to extend the research or provide an alternative interpretation (see Chapter 7).

- Quantification can provide relatively complex information in a succinct, easily understandable form, including graphics.

- Methods such as longitudinal surveys and annually repeated surveys provide the opportunity to study change over time, using comparable methodology.

- Arts/events encompass a wide range of activities, with a range of characteristics, such as frequency, duration and degree of organisation, expenditure, location, level of enjoyment and aspirations. Questionnaires are a good means of ensuring that a complete picture of people's patterns of cultural or event-related participation is obtained.

- While qualitative methods are ideal for exploring attitudes, values, motivations, meanings and perceptions on an individual basis, questionnaire methods provide the means to gather and record simple information on such matters among a substantial sample of the population, thus indicating not only that certain attitudes, values, etc. exist but how widespread they are in a given population.

Comparison of this list of merits/qualities with similar lists referring to other methodological approaches (e.g. for qualitative methods in Chapter 9) reinforces the view that each method has its merits and appropriate uses – the 'horses for courses' idea. Questionnaire surveys

Organisation	Topic	Questionnaire survey	Qualitative methods	Secondary data
Arts venue/ events management	How to increase number of visitors	• Visitor survey on what types of people use which services and when. • Community survey on socio-demographic characteristics of visitors vs non-visitors and perceptions of venue/event.	• Observation and/or focus groups on experience of visiting the venue/event – quality, atmosphere, service.	• Analysis of ticket sales and capacity utilisation data re relative popularity of different venues/events.
Arts Commission	Data for strategic cultural tourism plan	• Intercept survey of visitors to the area on accommodation used, sites/events visited, expenditure patterns and socio-demographic characteristics of visitors from different origins.	• In-depth interviews or focus groups with visitors on quality of visitor experience. • Focus groups with residents on attitudes towards tourists and tourist development.	• Arrival and departure data (if national or regional study).
Individual researcher	The role of culture in family life	• Household survey on participation of family members in cultural activities by household type and socio-demographic characteristics.	• In-depth interviews on meanings and importance of culture in individual and family lifestyles.	• Analysis of individual vs family ticket sales to events/venues.

Figure 10.1 The use of questionnaire surveys compared with other methods: examples

have a role to play when the research questions indicate the need for fairly structured data and generally when data are required from samples which are explicitly representative of a defined wider population. Examples of the role of questionnaire surveys versus other methods are shown in Figure 10.1.

Limitations

Questionnaire-based surveys have a number of limitations, related to the fact that they are based on self-reported data and generally on samples.

Self-reported data

Questionnaire surveys rely on information from respondents. The accuracy of what respondents say depends on their powers of recall, on their honesty and, fundamentally, on the format of the questions included in the questionnaire. There has been relatively little research on the validity or accuracy of questionnaire data in arts/events studies, but some examples from other sectors are indicated in the Resources sections. Problems of validity and accuracy arise from a number of sources, including exaggeration and under-reporting, accuracy of recall and sensitivity.

● *Exaggeration/under-reporting:* Some research has suggested that respondents exaggerate levels of participation in some activities and under-report others. This may be conscious or unconscious and may be for reasons of prestige or lack of it – what Oppenheim (2000: 138) calls 'social desirability bias' – or a desire to be positive and friendly towards the interviewer, at least in a face-to-face situation. For example, if the interview is about cultural activity, respondents may exaggerate their interest in and involvement in such activity in order to appear in a positive light or just to be helpful and positive. It has been suggested that some people may not have any considered views on a topic but they answer questions anyway, to be polite and helpful or to 'show themselves in a good light by giving the answer they judge to be the most noble one' (Bourdieu and Darbell, 1997: 5).

- *Accuracy of recall:* Mistakes can be made in recalling events at all or in estimating frequency: for example, if someone claims to take part in an activity twice a month, is that equivalent to 24 times a year? The actual level of participation across the year is likely to be affected by such factors as illness, weather, public holidays and family and work emergencies. Even if the question attempts to avoid this problem by asking respondents the actual number of occasions on which they have participated in a given time period, respondents may, in their own minds, be working from the 'twice a month' notion and still over-estimate. Where alternative sources of information, such as reservation records, are available it is possible to check the accuracy of questionnaire-based information. Studies of this phenomenon suggest substantial overestimation in some leisure activities and in recalling events (see Resources section). It might be thought that the problem of accurate recall is particularly characteristic of arts/event-based activity, which may be seen by some as less significant in people's lives than other domains such as work or family, but Loftus *et al.* (1990) indicate that the problem also arises in the health domain.

- *Sensitivity:* Sensitive topics can also give rise to under- or over-estimation or non-response. In some cases these are generic, for example income (discussed further below); in other cases they are specific to the research area, for example drug use.

These matters suggest the need for careful questionnaire design and cross-checking/triangulation where possible, and for the researcher and the user of research results to always bear in mind the nature and source of the data and not fall into the trap of believing that because information is presented in numerical form and is based on large numbers, it represents immutable 'truth'.

Samples

Questionnaire surveys usually, but not always, involve only a proportion, or *sample*, of the population in which the researcher is interested. For example, national surveys (see Chapter 7) are typically based on samples of only a few thousand to represent tens of millions of people. How such samples are chosen, how the size of the sample is decided and the implications of relying on a sample to represent a population are discussed in Chapter 13.

Interviewer-completion or respondent-completion?

Questionnaire surveys can take one of two forms:

- *Interviewer-completed:* The questionnaire provides the script for an interview; an interviewer reads out the questions to the respondent and records the respondent's answers on the questionnaire – the classic 'clipboard' situation, where the method may be referred

	Interviewer-completion	Respondent-completion
Advantages	More accuracy.	Cheaper.
	Higher response rates.	Quicker.
	Fuller and more complete answers.	Relatively anonymous.
	Design does not have to be so 'user-friendly'.	
Disadvantages	Higher cost.	Patchy response.
	Less anonymity.	Incomplete response.
		Risk of frivolous responses.
		More care needed in design.

Figure 10.2 Interviewer-completion compared with respondent-completion

to as *face-to-face interviewing*. When telephone surveys are involved, the interviewer may record answers on a computer and this is also increasingly possible in face-to-face situations using portable devices.

● *Respondent-completed,* often referred to as *self-completion:* Respondents read and fill out the questionnaire for themselves, on paper or online.

Each approach has its particular advantages and disadvantages, as summarised in Figure 10.2.

Interviewer-completion is more expensive in terms of interviewers' time (which usually has to be paid for) but the use of an interviewer usually ensures a more complete response and more accurate recording. Respondent-completion can be cheaper and quicker but often results in low response rates, which can introduce bias into the results because those who choose not to respond, are unable to respond or to respond fully, perhaps because of language or literacy difficulties, may differ from those who do respond.

When designing a questionnaire for respondent-completion, greater care must be taken with layout and presentation since it must be read and completed by 'untrained' people. In terms of design, respondent-completion questionnaires should ideally consist primarily of *closed* questions – that is, questions that can be answered by ticking boxes. *Open-ended questions* – where respondents have to write out their answers – should generally be avoided in such a situation, since they invariably achieve only a low response. For example, in an interview, respondents will often give expansive answers to questions such as 'Do you have any comments to make on the overall management of this venue?' but they will not as readily write down such answers in a respondent-completion questionnaire.

There may, however, be cases when respondent-completion is to be preferred, or is the only practicable approach – for example, when the people to be surveyed are widely scattered geographically, which would make face-to-face interviews impossibly expensive, so a mail or postal survey, which intrinsically involves respondent-completion, is an obvious choice; or when it is felt that, on sensitive matters, respondents might prefer the anonymity of the respondent-completed questionnaire. Some of the issues connected with respondent-completion questionnaires are discussed more fully in the section on mail surveys.

It should be noted that some commentators, in discussions of research methods, draw a distinction between 'interview methods' and 'questionnaire methods'; this is clearly misleading because, while the respondent-completed questionnaire-based survey does not involve an interview, the interviewer-completed questionnaire-based survey does involve an interview. So some 'questionnaire methods' involve an interview. What such comments are invariably referring to is a distinction between questionnaire-based methods and *in-depth* or *semi-structured* interviews (see Chapter 9).

Type	Interviewer or respondent completion	Cost	Sample	Possible length of questionnaire	Response rate
Household					
Standard	Either	Expensive	Whole population	Long	High
Time-use	Respondent	Expensive	Whole population	Long	High
Omnibus	Either	Medium per client	Whole population	Long	High
Street	Interviewer	Medium	Most of population	Short	Medium
Telephone	Interviewer	Medium	People with land-line telephone	Short	High but falling
Mail	Respondent	Cheap	General or special	Varies	Low
E-survey	Respondent	Cheap	People accessible via email/internet	Medium	Medium
On-site	Either	Medium	Site users only	Medium	High
Captive	Respondent	Cheap	Captive group only	Medium	High

Figure 10.3 Types of questionnaire survey: characteristics

Types of questionnaire survey

Questionnaire surveys can be divided into seven types: household surveys, street surveys, telephone surveys, mail surveys, e-surveys, user/on-site/visitor surveys and captive group surveys. Each of these is discussed in more detail below and some of their basic characteristics are summarised in Figure 10.3.

The household questionnaire survey

Nature

A significant amount of quantified data on arts/events participation is derived from household questionnaire surveys. While academics draw on the data extensively, the majority of such surveys are commissioned by government and commercial arts/events organisations for policy or marketing purposes. The advantage of household surveys is that they are generally representative of the community – the samples drawn tend to include all age groups, above a certain minimum age, and all occupational groups. They also generally represent a complete geographical area – a whole country, a state or region, a local government area or a neighbourhood. Household surveys are therefore designed to provide representative information on the reported arts/events behaviour, characteristics and/or opinions of the community as a whole or a particular group drawn from the whole community – for example, the older population aged 65 and over, or young people aged 15–24.

While some household arts/events surveys are specialised, many are broad-ranging in their coverage; that is, they tend to ask, among other things, about participation in a wide range of cultural activities. This facilitates exploration of a wide range of issues that other types of survey cannot so readily tackle.

Conduct

Normally household questionnaire surveys are interviewer-completed. However, it is possible for a questionnaire to be left at a respondent's home for respondent-completion and later collection, in which case the field-worker then has the responsibility of checking that questionnaires have been fully completed and perhaps conducting an interview in those situations where respondents have been unable to fill in the questionnaire, because they have been too busy, have forgotten, or have lost the questionnaire, or because of literacy or language problems or infirmity.

Being home-based, this sort of survey can involve quite lengthy questionnaires and interviews. By contrast, in the street, at an arts facility or event, or over the telephone, it can be difficult to conduct a lengthy interview. General arts/events participation surveys involve a complex questionnaire that is difficult to administer 'on the run'. With the home-based interview it is usually possible to pursue issues at greater length than is possible in other settings. An interview lasting 45 minutes is not out of the question and 20–30 minutes is quite common.

A variation on the standard household questionnaire interview survey is to combine interviewer-completed and respondent-completed elements: the interviewer conducts an interview with one member of the household about the household itself – how many people live there, whether the dwelling is owned or rented, perhaps information on cultural items (books, musical instruments, etc.) in the home, or anything to do with the household as a whole. Then an individual questionnaire is left for one or more members of the household to complete, concerning their cultural activity. The interviewer calls back later to collect these individual questionnaires.

The potential length of interviews, the problems of contacting representative samples and, on occasions, the wide geographical spread of the study area mean that household surveys are usually the most expensive to conduct, per interview. Costs in the order of £25 or £30 per interview are typical, depending on the amount of analysis included in the price. When samples of several thousands are involved, the costs can therefore be substantial.

Omnibus surveys

While considering household surveys, mention should be made of the *omnibus survey*. This type of survey is conducted by a market research or survey organisation with various questions included in the questionnaire on behalf of different clients. The main costs of conducting the survey, which lie in sampling and contacting respondents, are therefore shared by a number of clients. The cost of collecting fairly standard demographic and socio-economic information – such as age, gender, family structure, occupation and income – is also shared among the clients. With regular omnibus surveys many of the procedures, such as sampling and data processing, have become routinised, and interviewers are in place throughout the country already trained and familiar with the type of questionnaire and the requirements of the market research company – these factors can reduce costs significantly.

The British *General Lifestyle Survey* (formerly *General Household Survey*) is an omnibus survey of 20,000 people run by the Office for National Statistics, the clients being government departments and agencies. A similar *General Social Survey* is conducted by the Australian Bureau of Statistics (see Chapter 7).

Although discussed here as a sub-category of household surveys, omnibus surveys may also be conducted using other formats, notably telephone and e-surveys.

Time-use surveys

Time-use, or time-budget, surveys are designed to collect information about people's use of time. Such information is generally collected as the main or subsidiary part of a household survey. In addition to answering a questionnaire, respondents complete a diary, typically covering a period of one or two days. Respondents are asked to record their waking hours' activities in a time-use diary, including starting and stopping times, together with information on where the activity was done, with whom, and possibly whether the respondent considered it to be paid work, domestic work or leisure. Information on secondary activities is also generally gathered, for example listening to music while doing housework. The early examples of such studies in the UK were conducted on behalf of the BBC to establish radio-listening patterns.

Coding and analysis of time-use data presents a considerable challenge, since hundreds of different activities must be given a code and information processed for, say, 60 or 70 quarter-hour periods each day. Detailed treatment of this highly complex and specialised field of research is not pursued here. The results are, however, of significance in cultural research and policy making, and relevant literature and online sources are indicated in the Resources section (and see Chapter 14).

National surveys

National arts/events participation surveys, typically conducted by government statistical agencies, are large-scale household or telephone surveys. While their main use is for national policy purposes, they are also used as secondary sources of data (Chapter 7) in comparison with regional or local surveys conducted by state/provincial governments or local councils, the aim being to establish whether, on some participation measure, the regional or local community is above or below the national average. If such comparisons are to be made, it follows that the local survey must be conducted in a similar way and the comparison questions in the questionnaire must be identically worded. This clearly places a constraint on design but, apart from the ability to make comparisons, it also has the advantage that the question format has been thoroughly tested.

The street survey

Nature

The street survey involves a relatively short questionnaire and is conducted, as the name implies, on the street – usually a shopping street or business area – or in squares or shopping malls, where a cross-section of the community might be expected to be found. The method can also be used to interview tourists to an area, including cultural tourists, in which case the survey would be conducted at locations where such tourists are known to congregate, such as in the environs of relevant cultural attractions or near tourist accommodation areas, or transport locations, such as airports or bus stations. In the cultural tourism case the survey could also be seen as having some of the characteristics of the visitor, on-site or user survey, as discussed below.

Conduct

Stopping people in the street or similar environments for an interview places certain limitations on the interview process. First, the interview cannot generally be as long as one conducted at someone's home, especially when the interviewee is in a hurry. Of course, there are some household interviews that are very short because the interviewee is in a hurry or is a reluctant respondent and there are street interviews that are lengthy because the respondent has plenty of time. As a general rule, however, the street interview must be shorter. Both in the home and street interview situation, before committing themselves to an interview, potential respondents invariably ask: 'How long will it take?' In the home-based situation, a reply of '15–20 minutes' is generally acceptable, but in the street situation anything more than '5 minutes' would generally lead to a marked reduction in the proportion of people prepared to cooperate. The range of topics/issues/activities that can be covered in a street interview is therefore restricted and this must be taken into account in designing the questionnaire.

The second limitation of the street survey is the challenge of contacting a representative sample of the population. Certain types of people might not frequent shopping areas at all, or only infrequently – for instance, people who are housebound for various reasons or those who have other people to do their shopping. Such individuals might be of particular importance in some studies, so their omission can significantly compromise the results. There is little that can be done to overcome this problem; it has to be accepted as a limitation of the method. The other side of this coin is that certain groups will be over-represented in shopping streets – notably full-time home/child carers, the retired and the unemployed in suburban shopping areas, or office workers in business areas. It might also be the case that certain areas are frequented more by, for example, young people than old people or by men rather than women, so any sample would be representative of the users of the area, but not of the local population or visitor population as a whole. One approach to overcoming some of these problems is quota sampling.

Quota sampling

The technique of *quota sampling* involves the interviewer being given a pre-determined quota of different types of people to interview – for example, by age, sex, occupation. The proportions in each category in the target population must be known in advance, for instance by reference to the Population Census (see Chapter 7). In some cases there may be relevant information, for example arrivals and departure data give information on proportions of visitors from various countries that could be used to determine quotas in a cultural tourism survey. When the survey is complete, if the sample is still not representative with regard to the key characteristics, further adjustments can be achieved through the process of *weighting* (see Chapter 13). Where background information on the population is not known, it is not possible to use the quota sampling method to achieve representativeness.

The telephone survey

Nature

The telephone survey is particularly popular with political pollsters because of its speed and the ease with which a widespread sample of the community can be contacted. It is also used extensively in market and academic research for the same reasons.

An obvious limitation of the technique is that it excludes people without land-line telephones. These include people in mobile phone-only households, discussed below, or some low-income groups and some mobile sections of the population. In the case of relatively simple surveys such as political opinion polls, where the researcher has access to previous results from both telephone and face-to-face interviews, this problem may be overcome by the use of a correction factor – for instance, it might be known that inclusion of non-land-line telephone subscribers always adds x per cent to the Labour vote. In certain kinds of market research the absence of the poorer parts of the community from the survey may be unimportant because they do not form a significant part of the market, but for much public policy and academic research, this can be a significant limitation.

An increasingly significant problem is the case of households that do not have land-line telephones, relying only on mobile phones, which are not listed in publicly available directories. This involves mainly young people, who are an important target of much survey work. Again, it may be possible to correct for this statistically if the characteristics of this group are known. Mobile phone numbers can be contacted randomly when the range of numbers used for domestic, as opposed to business, subscribers is made available to survey organisations by telephone companies (telcos). However, unlike land-line telephones, mobile numbers are not geographically linked, unless the telcos also provide this information. This means that local area Population Census data cannot be used to gross up and/or weight the results. These issues are an on-going focus of discussion within the survey/opinion poll industry.

Conduct

Length of interview can be a limitation of telephone surveys – but not as serious as in the case of street interviews; telephone interviews of 10 or 15 minutes are acceptable.

The technique has its own unique set of problems in relation to sampling. Generally the numbers to be called are selected at random from the telephone directory. Market research companies generally use Computer Assisted Telephone Interviewing (CATI), involving equipment and software that automatically dials random telephone numbers from a digital database. CATI systems also enable the interviewer to key answers directly into a computer, thus dispensing with the printed questionnaire. This speeds up the analysis process considerably and cuts down the possibility of error in transcribing results from printed questionnaire to computer. It also explains how the results of overnight political opinion polls can be published in newspapers the next morning.

If a representative cross-section of the community is to be included then it is necessary for telephone surveys to be conducted in the evenings and/or at weekends if those who have paid day-time jobs are to be included.

A limitation of the telephone interview is that respondents cannot be shown such things as lists or images, for example of activities or attitude dimensions. For long lists, of more than six or seven items, reading them out can become tedious.

It can be argued that telephones have an advantage over face-to-face interviews in that respondents may feel they are more anonymous and may therefore be more forthcoming in their opinions. But it could also be argued that the face-to-face interview has other advantages in terms of eye contact and body language, which enable the skilled interviewer to conduct a better interview than is possible over the telephone.

The main advantage of the telephone survey is that it is quick and relatively cheap to conduct. However, in some countries there is growing reluctance on the part of the public to cooperate with telephone surveys, resulting in the need to make numerous calls to contact cooperative respondents, thus raising the costs and raising questions about representativeness. The solution being adopted in market research is the use of online methods, discussed below,

Representativeness and response levels

An increasing number of problems arise in the conduct of telephone surveys, including consumer-related, technological, legal and social factors.

Reference has already been made to problems caused by the consumer shift to mobile phone technology – unlike land-line telephones, mobile phone numbers are not publicly listed and geographically identifiable and people who rely entirely on mobile phones are not a cross-section of the whole community, so continued reliance on land-line telephones for surveys can result in biased samples. In developing countries the history is unfolding differently since the mobile phone has arrived in advance of universal access to land-line telephones.

Technological devices used to control and manage telephone access also present difficulties in contacting survey respondents, including user ID and answer machines/voice mail. Added to this, privacy legislation enables telephone subscribers to deny access for tele-marketing, although bona-fide social research calls are generally exempt.

In addition to consumer and technological change, surveyors note an increasing tendency for members of the public to refuse to cooperate with telephone surveys. Thus, one American organisation reports that, once contact is made using standard survey techniques, while 58 per cent of those contacted agreed to an interview in 1997, this had fallen to 38 per cent by 2003, although these figures were higher (at 74 per cent and 59 per cent respectively) when more rigorous techniques, including call-backs, were used (Pew Research Center, 2004).

The result of these changes is increased costs for telephone surveys as well as greater concerns about representativeness, leading to a trend towards e-surveys, as discussed below. Market research companies using telephone and e-survey methods seek to overcome the challenges of sampling problems by maintaining a representative 'panel' of respondents, who agree to respond to a number of survey requests, typically for a fee, as discussed in Chapter 5.

National surveys

The comments about national surveys, made in relation to household surveys above, also apply to national telephone surveys.

The mail survey

Nature

There are certain situations where the mail or postal method is the only practical survey technique to use. The most common example is where members or customers of some national organisation are to be surveyed. The costs of conducting face-to-face interviews with even a sample of the members or customers would be substantial – a mail survey is the obvious solution. The mail survey has the advantage that a large sample can be included. In the case of a membership organisation, there may be advantages in surveying the whole membership, even though this may not be necessary in statistical terms. However, it can be very helpful in

1. The interest of the respondent in the survey topic.
2. The length of the questionnaire.
3. Questionnaire design/presentation/complexity.
4. Style, content and authorship of the accompanying letter.
5. Provision of a reply-paid envelope.
6. Rewards for responding.
7. Number and timing of reminders/follow-ups.

Figure 10.4 Factors affecting mail survey response

terms of the internal politics of the organisation for all members to be given the opportunity to participate in the survey and to 'have their say'.

The problem of low response rates

The most notorious problem of postal surveys is low response rates. In many cases as few as 25–30 per cent of those sent a questionnaire bother to reply and when surveys are poorly conceived and designed the response rate can fall to 3–4 per cent. Surveys with only 30 per cent response rates are regularly reported in the research literature, but questions must be raised as to their validity when 70 per cent of the target sample is not represented.

What affects the response rate in mail surveys? Seven different factors can be identified, as listed in Figure 10.4. The various factors and measures listed are discussed in turn below.

1 Interest of the respondent in the survey topic

A survey of a local community about a proposal to route a six-lane motorway through the neighbourhood would probably result in a high response rate, but a survey of the same community on general patterns of arts/events participation would probably result in a low response rate. Variation among the population in the level of interest in the topic can result in a biased (that is, unrepresentative) response. For example, a survey on cultural provision might evoke a high response rate among those interested in cultural activity and a low response rate among those not interested – giving a false impression of community enthusiasm for cultural provision. To some extent this can be corrected by weighting if the bias corresponds with certain known characteristics of the population (see Chapter 13). For example, if there was a high response rate from young people and a low response rate from older people, information from the Population Census on the actual proportions of different age groups in the community could be used to weight the results.

2 Length of the questionnaire

It might be expected that a long questionnaire would discourage potential respondents. It can, however, be argued that other factors, such as the topic and the presentation of the questionnaire, are more important than its length – that is, if the topic is interesting to the respondent and is well presented then the questionnaire length and the time taken to complete it may be less of an issue.

3 Questionnaire design/presentation/complexity

More care must be taken in design and physical presentation with any respondent-completed questionnaire. Typesetting, colour coding of pages, graphics and so on may be necessary. Cultural participation surveys can involve long lists of activities that can make a questionnaire look complicated and demanding to complete, but suitable design can ameliorate this impression.

4 The accompanying letter

The letter from the sponsor or researcher that accompanies the questionnaire may have an influence on people's willingness to respond. Does it give a good reason for the survey? Is it from someone, or the type of organisation, the potential respondent trusts or respects?

5 Postage-paid reply envelope

It is usual to include a postage-paid envelope for the return of the questionnaire. Some believe that an envelope with a real stamp on it will produce a better response rate than a business reply-paid envelope. Providing reply envelopes with real stamps is more expensive because, apart from the time spent in sticking stamps on envelopes, stamps are effectively wasted on those who do not respond.

6 Rewards

The question of rewards or incentives for taking part in a survey can arise in relation to any sort of survey but it is a device used most often in mail surveys. One approach is to send every respondent some small reward, such as a voucher for a firm's or agency's product or service, or even money (see James and Bolstein, 1990). A more common approach is to enter all respondents in a draw for a prize. Even a fairly costly prize may be money well spent if it results in a substantial increase in the response rate, and when considered in relation to the cost of the alternative methods, such as a household survey involving face-to-face interviews. It could be argued, however, that the introduction of rewards causes certain people to respond for the wrong reasons and that it introduces a potential source of bias in responses. It might also be considered that the inclusion of a prize or reward 'lowers the tone' of the survey and places it in the same category as other, commercial, junk mail that comes through people's letter boxes every day.

7 Reminders/follow-ups

Sensible reminder and follow-up procedures are perhaps the most significant tool available to the researcher to secure a high response level. They can include postcard/email/phone reminders, supplying a second copy of the questionnaire and offering a telephone interview, indicated in the sequence suggested in Figure 10.5. Dillman *et al.* (2009) have conducted experiments with the offer of a telephone interview and note that this clearly increases the response rate but may provide different responses from the standard mail survey – this may be seen as a strength (a sort of triangulation) or a weakness.

An example of the effects of follow-ups can be seen in Figure 10.6, which relates to a mail survey of residents' recreational use of a water area. It can be seen that the level of responses peaked after only 3 days and looked likely to cease after about 16 days, which would have given a potential response rate of just 40 per cent. The surges in responses following the

Day	Attachments		Comment
1	Initial mail-out	Questionnaire	–
8	Postcard reminder	–	Email or telephone might be used if available and resources permit.
15	Letter reminder	Copy of questionnaire	Copy of questionnaire is enclosed 'in case the original has been mislaid'. Email might be used. Offer of telephone interview.
22	Final postcard reminder	–	As above, email or phone might be used and offer of telephone interview.

Figure 10.5 Mail survey follow-ups

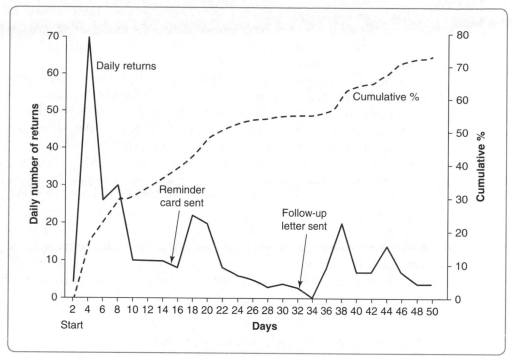

Figure 10.6 Mail survey response pattern

sending of the postcard and the second copy of the questionnaire can be seen and the net result was a 75 per cent response rate, which is very good for this type of survey. The need for follow-ups must be considered when budgeting for a postal survey, since postage and printing costs are often the most significant item in such budgets.

The sending out of reminders means that it must be possible to identify returned questionnaires, so that reminders are not sent to those who have already replied. This means that questionnaires or envelopes must have an identifying number that can be matched with the mailing list. Some respondents resent this potential breach of confidentiality but it cannot be avoided if only non-respondents are to be followed up. The confidentiality issue may be overcome if the identifying number is place on the reply envelope rather than the questionnaire itself. A further possibility is for the replies to be sent to a 'neutral' party, such as a lawyer or accountant. However, there is often a further advantage to being able to identify responses in general terms: known information on respondents can be used to check the representativeness of the response. For instance, the questionnaire may not include respondents' addresses, but the geographical spread of the response can be examined if the identity of the responses is known, and any necessary weighting can be carried out.

It has been shown that sending final reminders with a personalised letter and sending it via certified/registered mail can significantly increase the response rate compared with non-personalised letters and ordinary mail (Gitelson and Drogin, 1992).

How much is enough?

What level of response is acceptable? One answer would be to say that an adequate response has been achieved if the characteristics of non-respondents and the responses they would have given are not significantly different from those of respondents. But how do you know the characteristics and responses of non-respondents? In some cases the researcher has access to some limited information on non-respondents – for example their geographical location and other information that might be held on the database from which addresses were drawn. This can be used to make comparisons.

One approach that covers both characteristics and question responses is to compare early responders with later responders – if there is no difference this may indicate that further pursuit of non-responders is not necessary. It would, of course, be helpful to the research community if results of such examinations were publicly available so that conclusions could be drawn as to whether there is a general response rate at which further response patterns stabilise, whether there is no such rate or whether it is variable. Bennett (2005) compared early respondents' characteristics with those of later respondents and also sent a short, single-question questionnaire to a sample of non-respondents to discover their reasons for not reply-ing. Just a few researchers have conducted experiments on this question and some examples are summarised in Case study 11.3 (Gitelson and Drogin, 1992; Hammitt and McDonald, 1982). The Gitelson and Drogin (1992) study was a user/site/visitor and mail survey combo (described below). Since both the respondents and non-respondents to the mail survey had been interviewed on-site, it was possible to compare the characteristics of the two groups using information from the on-site survey questionnaires.

Mail and user/site/visitor survey combos

A common practice is to conduct a brief face-to-face interview at a venue or event and ask respondents to complete a mail survey (or e-survey) questionnaire on their return home. This shortens the time taken to conduct the on-site interview but also means that respondents can give views about the venue or event when their visit has been completed in its entirety. In some cases the mail-back questionnaire may be provided following the on-site interview; in other cases addresses (or email addresses) may be obtained and the questionnaire mailed out. Of course, the mail or e-survey part of the exercise will be subject to the problems of non-response discussed under mail surveys.

Discussing/analysing non-response

However conscientious the researcher may be in making efforts to maximise the response rate in a mail survey, there will still be a certain level of non-response. In analysing and writing up results this issue should be addressed and consideration given to the extent to which there is any reason to believe, or even evidence to show, that the non-respondents may be different from the respondents, suggesting the possibility of the sample being biased.

E-surveys

Nature and conduct

E-surveys, or electronic, web-based or online surveys, are conducted via the internet. Stand-ard 'hard-copy' mail has been the traditional medium for mail surveys and is still popular, but costs, speed and response rates, as discussed above, are increasingly seen as drawbacks

Type	Request	Questionnaire	Completion	Return
Hybrid email/mail	Email	Attached text file	Manual on hard copy	Traditional mail
Hybrid email	Email	Attached text file	Word-processor/ spreadsheet	Email + attached text file
Fully electronic				
Ad hoc	Email	Online, interactive	Online	Online submission
Panel	Panel member via email	Online, interactive	Online	Online submission

Figure 10.7 Types of e-survey

of the method. Similarly, the growing problems of traditional telephone surveys have been outlined above. The result has been increasing use of the electronic or e-survey. A number of formats exist, as summarised in Figure 10.7, ranging from simply using an email to transmit a traditional questionnaire, to a fully electronic, online format.

The first version simply uses email to replace the sending-out process. The second version uses email to send out and return, and uses a word processor and/or spreadsheet rather than hard copy, but the questionnaire is still in traditional format. In the electronic versions the whole process takes place online and the questionnaire has become interactive. The questionnaire simplifies completion for the respondent so that when 'filter' questions are involved, which require the respondent to skip certain questions and jump to a particular section of the questionnaire, this takes place automatically. The last type of e-survey involves a semi-permanent representative panel of respondents maintained by a survey company, as discussed in Chapter 5.

Commercial survey organisations offer e-survey services to researchers in which the customer/researcher specifies the questions to be included, then asks survey participants to access the organisation's website to take part in the survey. The customer/researcher can download the results on demand. Examples are SurveyMonkey, Zoomerang and Cool Surveys.

Many corporate organisations with an online customer base, such as banks and theatres, from time to time invite their customers to take part in an online questionnaire survey to obtain customer feedback on service quality. Similarly, while hotels still invite guests to complete a hard-copy feedback questionnaire at the end of their stay, it is now common for guests to receive an invitation to participate in an online survey via email some time after their return home.

An e-survey may be combined with a user/site/visitor survey in a similar way to the 'mail and user/site visitor survey combo' discussed above.

Advantages and disadvantages

The advantages of e-surveys to the researcher are the low cost and the speed with which they may be conducted. The fully electronic versions are designed to be user-friendly, as noted above. With appropriate software, including commercial online survey services, simple, standardised results can be obtained by the researcher instantaneously.

The disadvantage of the e-survey is that it is confined to those with access to the internet. As more and more households have internet access (typically 75 per cent or more in developed countries), this is less of a problem, but the elderly and less well-off continue to be under-represented. As with mobile telephone numbers, email addresses are not publicly listed, so it is difficult to use the e-survey to contact a representative sample of the population as a whole (see Chapter 13).

While the sending of reminders is cheap, the problem of low response may still be a problem for some surveys because they may be seen as part of the increasing volume of 'junk mail' received via email.

Visitor/user/on-site/surveys

Nature

The terms *visitor*, *user*, *on-site* or *site* survey are used to refer to surveys that take place at venues or events. *On-site* and *site survey* tend to be used in the context of outdoor studies, *user survey* in the context of indoor facilities, and *visitor survey* for cultural venues and tourists. The term visitor survey is utilised in this section to cover all these situations.

The visitor survey is the most common type of survey used by managers of arts venues and events. In general this is a more controlled setting than the street survey; interviewers are seen by respondents to be part of the management of the facility or event and usually it is possible to interview visitors at a convenient time when they are not in a rush, as they may be in the street or shopping centre.

Conduct

Visitor surveys can be conducted by interviewer or by respondent-completion. Unless carefully supervised, respondent-completion methods can lead to a poor standard in the completion of questionnaires and a low response level. And as with all low response levels this can be a source of serious bias in that those who reply may not be representative of the visitors as a whole.

The usual respondent-completion survey involves handing visitors a questionnaire on their arrival at the site and collecting them on their departure, or conducting the whole procedure upon departure. Where suitable breaks take place during a visitor's stay, for example during intervals at cultural events, interviewing may take place at this time. Where respondent-completion is thought to be desirable or necessary, sufficient staff should be employed to check all visitors leaving the site, to ask for the completed questionnaires, to provide replacements for questionnaires which have been mislaid, and to assist in completing questionnaires, including completion by interview if necessary. Leaving a pile of questionnaires with a busy receptionist to hand out and collect rarely works well.

Conducting visitor surveys by interview is generally preferable to respondent-completion for the reasons discussed earlier in this chapter. The use of interviewers obviously has a cost disadvantage but, depending on the length of the interview, costs per interview are usually comparatively low. Typically a visitor-survey interview will take about five minutes, but in some longer-stay facilities, such as a cultural precinct or an all-day event, significantly longer interviews are possible. Given the need to check through completed questionnaires, the gaps in visitor traffic and the need for interviewers to take breaks, it is reasonable to expect interviewers in such situations to complete about six interviews in an hour. Such estimates are of course necessary when considering project budgets and timetables.

The survey methods considered so far have been fairly multi-purpose – they could be used for market research for a range of products or services, by public agencies for a variety of policy-orientated purposes, or for academic research, which may or may not be policy or management orientated. Visitor surveys are more specific. The most common use of such surveys is for policy, planning or management purposes. They are the type of survey with which readers of this book are most likely to be involved; they are the most convenient for students to 'cut their teeth' on; and they are the most common surveys for individual managers to become involved in. For these reasons the uses of visitor surveys are considered in some detail below.

The uses of visitor surveys

What can visitor surveys be used for? Four topics are discussed briefly below: catchment area, visitor socio-demographic profile, visitor opinions and researching non-visitors.

Catchment area

What is the *catchment* or *market* area of the venue or event? That is, what geographical area do most of the visitors come from? Knowing this can be valuable in terms of marketing policy. Management can concentrate on its existing catchment area and focus its advertising and marketing accordingly, or it can take conscious a decision to use marketing to attempt to extend its catchment area. But in order to adopt either of these approaches it is first necessary to establish the current catchment area. In some cases this information is already available from membership records, but this does not always reflect the pattern of actual use, so in most cases it can be discovered only by means of a survey, that is, by asking visitors where they live or where they have travelled from, which can be their home of a place of work/education, or a hotel/motel in the case of tourists.

Visitor socio-demographic profile

What is the socio-economic/demographic profile of the venue/event visitors? It might be thought that a management capable of observation would be able to make this assessment without the need for a survey. This depends on the type of venue/event, the extent to which management is in continuous contact with visitors and the variability of the visitor profile. For example, the management of a single-purpose venue, such as a small theatre with a contemporary programme, might be well informed on this because of the range of drama offered and the nature of the subscriber list. But managers of large multi-purpose arts centres or directors of large, multi-component events, while they may have an impression of the different types of visitor groups, will be less informed, or even mis-informed, about the detail.

Profile information can be used in a number of ways. As with data on catchment area, it can be used to consolidate or extend the market. Very often the commercial operator will opt to consolidate – to focus on particular client groups and maximise the market share of those groups, by appropriate advertising, pricing and product development. In the case of a public-sector facility the remit is usually to attract as wide a cross-section of the community as possible, so the data would be used to highlight those sections of the community not being catered for and therefore requiring marketing, pricing or product development attention. More broadly, a public agency responsible for a range of types of venue could use data from a number of surveys to check whether the community is being appropriately provided for by all its facilities/events taken together.

Visitor opinions

What are the opinions of visitors about the design, accessibility and service quality of the venue/event? Such opinion data are invariably collected in visitor surveys and are usually of great interest to managers, but the interpretation of the data is not without its difficulties. If management is looking for pertinent criticisms, current visitors may be the wrong group to consult. Those who are most critical are likely to be no longer using the venue. Those using the venue may be reluctant to be critical because it undermines their situation – if the place is so poor, why are they visiting it? Furthermore, those who are prepared to be critical may not be the sorts of clients for whom the venue and its offerings are designed.

In some situations people have little choice of facility so criticisms are perhaps more easily interpreted. For example, comments about the quality of a local cinema can be particularly pertinent when it is the only cinema in the town.

When opinion data have been collected it is often difficult to know precisely what to do with the results. Very often the largest group of visitors have no complaint or suggestion to make – either because they cannot be bothered to think of anything in the interview situation or because, as mentioned above, the more critical users no longer visit. Often the most common complaint is raised by only as few as 10 per cent of visitors. If this is the most common complaint, then logically something ought to be done about it by the management – but it could also be said that 90 per cent of the visitors are not concerned about that issue, so perhaps there is no need to do anything about it! Very often, therefore, management can use survey results to suit their preferences. If they want to do something about X, they can say that X was complained about by more visitors than anything else; if they want to do nothing about X, they can say that 90 per cent of visitors are satisfied with X the way it is.

Managers mostly want to enhance and maximise the quality of the experience enjoyed by their visitors and so seek information on levels of satisfaction with specific features of the venue/event or with the overall experience of the visit. Thus, visitors can be asked to rate features or the visit as a whole using a scale such as: very good/good/fair/poor/very poor or very satisfied/satisfied/dissatisfied/very dissatisfied – as examined in relation to questionnaire design below. The results of such evaluations can be used to examine trends over time, to compare one group of visitors with another or one facility or programme with another, or to compare expectations with the actual experience, as in the 'importance-performance technique' (see Case study 3.1). This is, of course, a feature of evaluative research (see Chapters 1 and 2).

Non-visitors

Visitor surveys by definition involve only current visitors to a venue/event. This is often cited as a limitation of such surveys, the implication being that non-visitors may be of more interest than visitors if the aim of management and policy makers is to increase the number of visits or visitors. However, caution should be exercised in moving to consider conducting research on non-visitors. For a start the number of non-visitors is usually very large – in a city of a million population, a facility that has 5,000 visitors has 995,000 non-visitors! In a country with a population of 50 million, a museum that attracts 1 million visitors a year has 49 million non-visitors, and if management is interested in international visitors, they have around 6 billion non-visitors. The idea that all non-visitors are potential visitors, and should therefore be researched, is somewhat naive.

The visitor survey can, however, help in focusing any research which is to be conducted on non-visitors. For example, in the case of a local arts facility or event, the visitor survey defines the catchment area and unless there is some reason for believing that the catchment area can or should be extended, the non-visitors to be studied are those who live within that area. Similarly, the visitor profile indicates the type of person currently using the facility, and again, unless there is a conscious decision to attempt to change that profile, the non-visitors to be studied are the ones with that profile living within the defined catchment area. Importantly, comparison between the visitor profile and the profile of the population of the catchment area, as revealed by Population Census data (see Chapter 7), can be used to estimate the numbers and characteristics of non-visitors in the area. Thus, visitor surveys can reveal something about non-visitors.

Visitor/user/site survey and mail/e-survey combo

In the discussion of mail surveys above, the idea of a 'mail and visitor/user/site survey combo' is discussed, in which a short, face-to-face, on-site interview is followed by a request to the respondent to complete a mail survey or e-survey questionnaire on their return home.

Captive group surveys

Nature

The *captive group survey* is not generally referred to in other research methods texts. It refers to the situation where the people to be included in the survey comprise the membership of some group where access can be negotiated *en bloc*. Such groups include children in schools, adult education groups in classes, clubs of various kinds at their gatherings and groups of employees at their workplace – although all have their various unique characteristics. The practice of groups being 'volunteered' for research in this way does of course raise ethical issues (see Chapter 4).

Conduct

A roomful of cooperative people can provide a number of respondent-completed questionnaires very quickly. Respondent-completion is less problematic in captive group situations than in less controlled situations because it is possible to take the group through the questionnaire question by question and therefore ensure good standards of completion.

The most common example of a captive group is school children, since the easiest way to contact young people under school-leaving age is via schools. The method may, however, appear simpler than it is in practice. Research on children for education purposes has become so common that education authorities are cautious about permitting access to children for surveys. Very often permission for any survey work must be obtained from the central education authority – the permission of the class teacher or headteacher is not sufficient.

The use of tertiary students for psychologically orientated research is common and in some cases academic credit is given for such involvement.

While the most economical use of this technique involves using a respondent-completed questionnaire, interview methods can also be employed. The essential feature is that access to members of the group is facilitated by their membership of that group and the fact that they are gathered together in one place at one time. It is important to be aware of the criteria for membership of the group and to compare those with the requirements of the research. In some cases an apparent match can be misleading. For example, attendees at a retired people's club meeting do not include all retired people – it excludes 'non-joiners' and the house-bound. While schools include all young people, care must be taken over their catchment areas, compared with the study area of the research, and with the mix of public-sector and private schools.

Questionnaire design

Introduction – research problems and information requirements

The important principle in designing questionnaires is to take it slowly and carefully and to remember why the research is being done. Very often researchers move too quickly into 'questionnaire design mode' and begin listing all the things 'it would be interesting to ask'. In many organisations a draft questionnaire is circulated for comment and everyone in the organisation joins in. The process begins to resemble Christmas tree decorating – nobody must be left out and everybody must be allowed to contribute their favourite bauble. This is not the best way to proceed.

The decision to conduct a questionnaire survey should itself be the culmination of a careful process of thought and discussion, involving, as discussed in Chapter 3, consideration of all possible methods, not just surveys. The concepts and variables involved, and the relationships to be investigated, possibly in the form of hypotheses, theories, models or evaluative frameworks, should be clear and should guide the questionnaire design process, as illustrated in Figure 10.8. It is not advisable to begin with a list of questions to be included in the questionnaire; the starting point should ideally be an examination of the management, planning, policy or theoretical questions to be addressed, followed by the drawing up of a list of information required to address the problems (see Chapter 3 as elements 1–5 of the research process). Element 6 in the research design process, deciding the research strategy, involves determining which, if any, of the listed information requirements should be met by means of a questionnaire survey and which should be met by other methods. Questions should be included in the questionnaire only if they relate to requirements listed in element 5. This means that every question included must be linked back to the research questions.

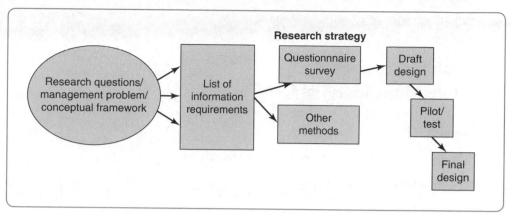

Figure 10.8 Questionnaire design process

In designing a questionnaire, the researcher should of course have sought out as much previous research on the topic or related topics as possible. This can have an effect on the overall design of a project. More specifically, if it is decided that the study in hand should have points of comparison with earlier studies, data will need to be collected on a similar basis to those in the earlier studies. Questionnaires from previous studies therefore become part of the input into the questionnaire design process.

Example questionnaires

Before considering questionnaire design in more detail, some examples of short questionnaires are presented in Case study 10.1, including typical questions used in household and visitor surveys, with interviewer-completed and respondent-completed examples:

- *Example A: site/street survey*: a questionnaire used to assess students' attitudes to cultural programmes on campus – it is labelled as a site/street survey since, as it would be administered to students on-campus, it partly resembles a visitor or site survey, but since not all students may make use of the services being examined, it resembles a survey conducted in a street or shopping centre. It is presented as respondent-completed, but completion would probably best be conducted 'under supervision' – that is completed and handed back to a survey worker at the time, rather than being handed out for later return, which would inevitably produce a low response rate. If the cooperation of the university authorities is obtained so that the questionnaire is handed out and completed in class time, it becomes a 'captive group' survey.

- *Example B: household survey:* an interviewer-completed questionnaire for a household survey on cultural activity.

- *Example C: site survey:* an interviewer-completed questionnaire for a visitor survey at an event.

Annotations in the margins of these example questionnaires indicate the type of question involved, as discussed later in the chapter. These examples cannot, of course, cover all situations, but they give a wide range of questions and appropriate formats.

Example questionnaires
A. Visitor/street survey: respondent-completed

Campus Entertainment Survey 2012 | Office Use
| # ____
| qno

1. Which of the following best describes your current situation?

         Full-time student with no regular paid work $\square_1$
         Full-time student with some regular paid work $\square_2$ | __status
         Part-time student with full-time job $\square_3$
         Part-time student - other $\square_4$

2. Which of the following university cultural/entertainment venues/events have you used in the last 4 weeks?

         Movie club $\square_1$ | __ movie
         Memorial theatre $\square_1$ | __ drama
         Rock/pop band gig $\square_1$ | __ rock
         Sunday jazz in the Lake Bar $\square_1$ | __ jazz

3. In thinking about using the entertainment services provided on campus, what are the most important considerations for you? Please rank the items below in terms of their importance to you. Rank them from 1 for the most important to 5 for the least important.

                           Rank
         Free or cheap access   ____ | __ cheap
         Convenient times   ____ | __ hours
         Quality of programmes   ____ | __ qual
         Opportunities to socialise/meet people   ____ | __ meet
         Available time   ____ | __ time

4. Approximately how much do you spend in an average two-week period on entertainment on and off campus?

         £ ____ | __ spend

5. Please indicate the importance of the following to you in relation to on-campus entertainment

	Very important	Important	Not at all important	
Relaxation opportunities	$\square_3$	$\square_2$	$\square_1$	__ relax
Social interaction	$\square_3$	$\square_2$	$\square_1$	__ social
E\Meaningful experience	$\square_3$	$\square_2$	$\square_1$	__ meaning

6. What suggestions would you make for improving campus entertainment?

_____ | __ sug1
| __ sug2
| __ sug3

_____

7. You are: Male $\square_1$ Female $\square_2$ | __ gend

8. Your age last birthday was: ___ years | __ age

Case study 10.1 (*continued*)

B: Household survey – interviewer-completed

Respondent No	**Arts Festival Survey**	_____#
	Introductory remarks: We are from St Anthony's College and we are conducting a survey of visitors to the arts festival. Would you mind answering a few questions? It will take 5 minutes and the results will be kept confidential.	

Pre-coded, factual	1. Is this your first visit to the arts festival? Yes 1 – go to Q. 3 No 2 – go to Q.2	_____ Q1
Open-ended, factual, numerical	2. How many times have you been to the festival before? Number of times: ___	_____Q2
Open-ended, factual	3. Where do you live? Local ☐₁ Non-local _____	_____Q3
	4. What were the main activities you engaged in on your visit?	_____Q4

Multiple response with open-ended option	a. Saturday folk concert 1	e. Art exhibition 1	a ___ b ___
	b. Sunday jazz concert 1	f. Street parade 1	c ___ d ___
	c. Saturday market 1	g. Other (please state below) 1	e ___ f ___
	d. Sunday market 1	_____	g ___

5. To what extent do you agree with the following statements?

Likert scale		Agree strongly	Agree	Neither	Disagree	Disagree strongly	
	The festival is good for the town	1	2	3	4	5	____
	The festival should be expanded	1	2	3	4	5	____

6. Can you tell me which of the following age-groups you fall into?

Pre-coded with showcard factual	Under 15 A 15–19 B 20–29 C 30–59 D 60+ E	____Q6

7. Which of the following best describes your current situation?

Pre-coded with showcard factual	In full-time paid work A In part-time paid work B In full-time education C Full-time home/child care D Retired E Looking for work F Other G	____Q7

Pre-coded, factual, observed	THANK YOU FOR YOUR HELP 8. Observe gender: Male 1 Female 2	____Q8

Case study 10.1 (*continued*)

C: Site survey – interviewer-completed

The survey is being carried out for the local council to find out what visitors to the arts centre think of the centre, and what changes they would like to see. A total of 200 visitors users of the centre are interviewed at the only entrance, in batches of 10, at different days of the week, at different times of the day.

Ramsey Street Arts Centre Survey _____
Excuse me: we are carrying out a survey for the council to find out what people think about the centre.
Could you spare a few minutes to answer a few questions?

1. How often do you visit this centre?

	Every day	1
Simple	Several times a week	2
pre-coded	Once a week	3
	Every 2 or 3 weeks	4
	Once a month	5
	Less often	6
	First visit	7

2. Where have you travelled from today?

Simple	Home	1
pre-coded,	Work	2
factual	School/college/univ.	3
	Other	4

3. What suburb is that in?

Open-ended, factual

_____

4. How long did it take you to get here?

Simple	5 minutes or less	1
pre-coded	6–15 minutes	2
factual	16–30 minutes	3
	31 minutes or more	4

5. What activity are you doing here?

Simple	Theatre	1
pre-coded	Pottery class	2
factual	Other class	3
	Gallery visit	4
	Cafe only	5
	Other	6

6. What do you like most about the centre?   Open-ended, opinion factual

_____

7. What do you like least about the centre?   Open-ended, opinion

_____

8. Looking at the card, where would you place this centre, in relation to others you know?   Attitude statement with show-card

A. Way below average	**1**
B. Below average	**2**
C. Average	**3**
D. Above average	**4**
E. Well above average	**5**

9. Can you tell me which of these age-groups you fall into?   Pre-coded factual with showcard

Under 15	**A**
15–19	**B**
20–29	**C**
30–9	**D**
60+	**E**

10. How many people are there in your group here today, including your self?   Open-ended, factual, numerical

Alone	1
Two	2
3–4	3
5 or more	4

THANK YOU FOR YOUR HELP

Observe: Male 1   Pre-coded, factual, observe
          Female 2

General design issues

Wording of questions

In wording the questions for a questionnaire the researcher should:

- avoid jargon;
- simplify wherever possible;
- avoid ambiguity;

Principle	Bad example	Improved version
Use simple language	What is your frequency of utilisation of cultural facilities?	How often do you visit the following: museums _____ art galleries _____ public libraries _____ cinemas _____
Avoid ambiguity	Do you engage in public cultural activities very often?	Have you participated in any of the following arts/events within the last four weeks? (show list)
Avoid leading questions	Are you against the proposed bid to host the Olympic Games?	What is your opinion on the proposed bid to host the Olympic Games: are you for it, against it or not concerned?
Ask just one question at a time	Do you use the local arts centre, and if so what do you think of its facilities?	1 Do you use the local arts centre? Yes/No 2 What do you think of the facilities in the centre?

Figure 10.9 Question wording: examples of good and bad practice

---

Open-ended

What is the main constraint on your ability to study?

Pre-coded/closed

Which of the following/items listed on the card is the main constraint on your ability to study? (show card if interviewer-completed)

    A My job   ☐$_1$
    B Timetabling   ☐$_2$
    C Child care   ☐$_3$
    D Spouse/partner   ☐$_4$
    E Money   ☐$_5$
    F Energy   ☐$_6$
    G Other _____ ☐$_7$
    Card shown to respondent:

Figure 10.10 Open-ended vs pre-coded questions: example

- avoid leading questions;
- ask only one question at a time (i.e. avoid multi-purpose questions).

Examples of good and bad practice in question wording are given in Figure 10.9.

Pre-coded vs open-ended questions

As illustrated in Figure 10.10, an open-ended question is one where the interviewer asks a question without any prompting of the range of answers to be expected and writes down the respondent's reply verbatim. In a respondent-completed questionnaire a line or space is left for respondents to write their answers. A closed or pre-coded question is one where the respondent is offered a range of answers to choose from, either verbally or from a show card or, in the case of a respondent-completed questionnaire, having the range of answers set out in the questionnaire and (usually) being asked to tick one or more boxes.

In the open-ended case there is no prior list; in the closed/pre-coded case there is a list which is shown to the respondent. A third possibility, in an interviewer-administered survey, is a combination of the two, where the question is asked in an open-ended manner, no card is shown to the respondent, but the answer is recorded by the interviewer ticking the appropriate box on a pre-coded list on the questionnaire. If the answer does not fit any of the items on the list it is written in an 'other' category and may be given a code at the analysis stage.

Advantages and disadvantages

The advantage of the open-ended question is that the respondent's answer is not unduly influenced by the interviewer or by the question wording and the verbatim replies from

Question: Do you have any complaints about this (beach/picnic) area?

(Site survey in a natural heritage area (a beachside national park with boating and camping facilities. Number of responses in brackets)

Sand bars (22)	Uncontrolled boats (23)
Parking (5)	Jet skis (39)
Wild car driving (1)	Surveys (1)
Lack of beach area (1)	Should be kept for locals (1)
Too few shops (1)	Seaweed (3)
Too few picnic tables (4)	Need showers (1)
No timber for barbecue (2)	Administration of national park (1)
Need more picnic space (3)	Maintenance and policing of park (1)
Need boat hire facilities (1)	Trucks on beach (2)
Need active recreation facilities (1)	Anglers (1)
Litter/pollution (74)	Crowds/tourists (26)
Urban sprawl (1)	Having to pay entry fee (6)
Need wharf fishing access (1)	Houses along waterfront (2)
Lack of info. on walking trails (1)	Unpleasant smell (drain) (2)
Not enough facilities (3)	Sales people (1)
Slow barbecues (2)	Need electric barbecues (1)
Uncontrolled camping (1)	Dogs (21)
Lack/poor toilets (9)	No access to coast (1)
Amenities too far from camp site (1)	Park rangers not operating in interest of the public (1)
Too much development (4)	Behaviour of others (20)
(Speed) boats (44)	Access – long indirect road (1)
Need more trees for shade (1)	Need more shops (2)
Yobbos drinking beer on beach (1)	Navigation marks unclear (1)
Spear fishermen (1)	Need more taps (1)
Water skiers (2)	Need more swings (1)
Against nudism (3)	No first-aid facilities (1)
Loud music (1)	Need powered caravan sites (1)
Dumped cars (1)	Allow dogs (1)
Traffic (1)	Private beach areas (1)
Poor roads (1)	Lack of restaurant (1)
Sand flies (1)	Need rain shelters (1)
More barbecues (1)	Can't spear fish (1)
Shells/oysters (1)	No road shoulders for cyclists (1)
Need outdoor cafes (1)	Remove rocks from swim areas (1)
Need more food places (1)	Dangerous boat ramp pollutant activities (1)
Water too shallow (1)	

Figure 10.11 Example of range of replies resulting from an open-ended question
Source: Robertson and Veal (1987).

respondents can provide a rich source of varied material that might have been hidden by categories on a pre-coded list. Figure 10.11 gives an example of the range of responses that can result from a single open-ended question.

Pre-coded groups are often used when asking respondents about quantified information, such as age, income, expenditure, because of convenience and saving any embarrassment respondents may have about divulging precise figures. However, there is an advantage in using the open-ended format for such data, that is in obtaining actual figures rather than group codes, in that recording the actual number permits the flexible option of grouping categories in alternative ways when carrying out the analysis. It also enables averages and other measures to be calculated and facilitates a range of statistical analysis not possible with grouped data. The actual figure is therefore often more useful for analysis purposes.

Open-ended questions have two major disadvantages. First, the analysis of verbatim answers to qualitative questions for computer analysis is laborious and may result in a final set of categories which is of no more value than a well-constructed pre-coded list. In the case of the answers in Figure 10.11, for example, for detailed analysis it may be necessary to group the answers into, say, six groups – this would be time-consuming and would involve a certain amount of judgement in grouping individual answers, which can be a source of errors. This process is discussed in more detail under Coding below. Often, therefore, an open-ended question is used in a pilot survey (see below), the results from which are then used to devise a coded list of categories for the main survey.

The second disadvantage of the open-ended approach is that, in the case of respondent-completed questionnaires, response rates to such questions can be very low: people are often too lazy or too busy to write out free-form answers and may have literacy or language problems. When to use open-ended or closed questions is therefore a matter of judgement.

Types of information

Generally the information to be gathered from questionnaire surveys can be divided into four groups:

1. Activities/events/place   What?
2. Type of engagement/involvement   How?
3. Respondent characteristics   Who?
4. Attitudes/motivations   Why?

Figure 10.12 lists some of the more common types of information collected under these four headings. The items are of course necessarily general in nature and do not cover all the specialised types of information that can be collected by questionnaire surveys. Some of these items require more intrusive questions than others – for example, income – and some can be difficult to ascertain accurately – for example, occupation or details of expenditure while on a cultural tourism trip. Therefore they are not all equally suitable for all survey situations.

Activities/event/place questions

People's patterns of activity are at the core of arts/events research and the procedure for measuring these patterns is far from simple. A variety of possible measures is indicated in Figure 7.1, including the participation rate, the number of participants, the volume of activity or visits, time and money spent and intensity of activity. In any study, consideration must be given as to which types of measure are required to address the research question.

For some research purposes it is only necessary to know that a person has engaged in a generic activity – for example, 'visited a museum'. In other cases it is necessary to know the geographical location, or 'place', of the activity – for example, 'visited a museum within/outside the local government area' – or the precise facility – for example, 'visited X museum'. Geographical location is obviously important for most tourism-related research. In other cases it is not just the generic activity or the place that is of interest but also the specific organised event – for example, '2012 summer concert in the park'.

Devising questions to gather information on activities in arts/events participation surveys presents six main issues:

- operationalising the term 'arts' or 'culture' or 'event';
- whether to use an open-ended or pre-coded format;

Visitor/site surveys	Household/telephone/postal surveys
1 *Activities/events/place*	
● Activities while at the venue/event (location known)	● Activities/participation –
● Frequency of visit to this venue/event	o what
● Time spent at venue/event	o type/mode of involvement (see Fig. 7.1)
● Expenditure per head – amounts/purposes	o when
● Travel-related information	o how often
o Trip origin (where travelled from)	o time and money spent
o Trip purpose	● Where? – Visiting particular venues/sites/events
o Home address	● Who with?
o Travel mode	● Travel mode to out-of-home activities
o Travel time	● Expenditure on activities
● Accommodation type used, where applicable	● Past activities (personal cultural/event histories)
● Visits to (other) attractions/facilities/events	● Planned future activities
	● Consumption activity (e.g. book, music, video purchase/ downloading)
	● Media use
2 *Type of engagement/involvement (see Fig. 7.1)*	● Professional
For most visitor/site surveys the type	● Creative leisure
of involvement is clear from the interview/	● Volunteer
distribution context.	● Audience/fan
	● Consumer/fan
3 *Respondent characteristics – all survey types*	
● Age	● Marital/family status
● Gender	● Household type/family size
● Economic status (paid work, retired, etc.)	● Life cycle
● Occupation/social class (own or 'head of household')	● Ethnic group/country of birth
● Employment history	● Residential location/trip origin
● Income (own or household)	● Mobility – driving licence, access to private transport
● Education/qualifications	● Party/group size/type (site/visitor surveys)
4 *Attitude/motivation information – examples*	
● Reasons for choice of venue/site/area	● Arts/events preferences/tastes (e.g. music, art genres)
● Meaning/importance/values	● Evaluation of services/facilities available
● Satisfaction/evaluation of services/experience	● Psychological meaning of activities, satisfactions
● Comments on facility/venue	● Reactions to development/provision proposals
● Future intentions/hopes	● Values – re environment, quality, elitism, etc.

Figure 10.12 Range of information in arts/events questionnaires

- the reference period for participation;
- cultural/event tourism issues;
- media use;
- intensity.

Operationalisation

The scope of the terms arts, culture and event should be clear from very early in the planning of a research project; it is, after all, part of the process of defining and operationalising concepts, as discussed in Chapter 3. For example, if the term 'culture' is to be used, its definition and/or scope will need to be made clear to the respondent through the introductory remarks and the wording of questions.

Open-ended or pre-coded format

An open-ended format question simply asks respondents to list the arts/events activity they have engaged in over a specified period. Without any prompting of the range of activities intended to be included, respondents might have difficulty in recalling all their activity, and in any case may not understand the full scope of the field of interest, despite the definition provided. Giving people checklists of activities to choose from may be unwieldy, but it ensures that all respondents consider the same range of options. The disadvantage of such a checklist is that the length of the list may be daunting to some respondents, particularly the less literate, and activities later in the list may be under-represented. In the case of an interviewer-completed questionnaire the main problem may be the time it takes to read out the list and the problem of patience and tedium which it may entail, so a show-card may be used; of course, this is not possible with telephone interviews. In the case of arts and events, activity groups can be asked about separately, for example, home-based activity, performing arts, visual arts.

In local surveys or surveys focused on specific policy areas, it is often important to explore the use of specific, named arts facilities or events using a variety of approaches to measuring use. In the case of visitor/site surveys asking about activities is usually straightforward, since the range of possible activities is limited to those available on the site. It is usual to ask people what activities they plan to engage in or have engaged in during their visit. Use of specific facilities, such as for refreshments, is also generally explored.

Reference period

The participation reference period for recalling activities crucially affects the survey findings. This is noted in Table 7.1, which shows that the effect of the length of reference period varies for different activities. It should also be noted that a reference time period shorter than a year may necessitate conducting the survey at different times of the year in order to take account of seasonal variation in types and levels of participation.

Cultural/event tourism

In the case of household questionnaire surveys concerned with cultural tourism, the activity question covers trips taken away from the home area over a specified time period in regard to cultural attractions or events. As with local arts/events activities, a major consideration is the recall time period. For major holidays a one-year recall period is not out of the question, but for short breaks, asking about trips during that length of time may lead to inaccuracies in recall, so a shorter time period of, say, three months is often adopted. This means that a survey must be conducted at different times of the year to capture seasonal variation.

A second time period issue concerns the definition of tourist 'trip'. The definition used in a survey may follow an accepted definition of tourism, for example a trip involving a stay away from home of one night or more. However, in some local tourism studies day trips may also be of interest and may involve a minimum distance travelled to distinguish them from local trips.

In addition to indicating trips taken, household cultural tourism questionnaires generally include questions on the trip destination, activities at the destination (active or passive/spectator), length of stay, travel mode and type of accommodation used. Tourism and events-related surveys are usually particularly concerned with economic matters, so questions on the cost of the trip and on expenditure in various categories are often included.

For visitor surveys in a cultural tourism context, the activity questions asked of tourists may be similar to those asked of locals but the reference period will of course be the period of their stay in the destination.

Media use

Questionnaires often include questions on media use because this may be the focus of interest of the study or because such information can be useful when considering advertising policy. Obtaining accurate information in this area would require a considerable number of questions on frequency of reading/viewing/listening and, in the case of electronic media, the type of broadcast programmes or websites favoured. When the research is concerned with small-scale local facilities or services, television advertising is generally out of the question because of cost, so information on television watching may not be gathered. Similar considerations may apply to magazine and national newspaper reading. For many surveys, therefore, two questions are involved (show-cards with lists of publications would usually be used):

- What (local) newspapers do you read regularly, that is at least weekly?
- What (local) radio stations do you listen to regularly, that is at least twice a week?

Intensity

The intensity of involvement with an activity may be reflected in frequency of visit information, but other measures include membership of organisations and type of engagement – for example, going on a specialist programmed cultural tour, as opposed to visiting some cultural sites as part of a multi-activity holiday trip. For some activities, such as dance, standards reached in performance may be relevant.

Respondent characteristics

Age

Any examination of arts/events participation data will show the importance of age in differentiating patterns of behaviour and attitudes; it is therefore one of the data items most commonly included in questionnaires. The main decision to be made is whether to use pre-coded groups or ask for respondents' actual age. The advantages and disadvantages of the two approaches are discussed above, under pre-coded vs open-ended questions. If using pre-coded groups, it is important to ensure that there are no overlapping age categories. For example, in the following it would not be clear into which group a 14 year-old respondent would fall.

> A 0–14
> B 14–19

Note that to ensure comparability with Population Census data, age groups should be specified as: 15–19, 20–24, 25–29, etc., not 16–20, 21–25, 26–30, etc.

In some studies there may be a case for dividing younger respondents into smaller age groups while maintaining the ability to reassemble them into the standard five-year groups for some analysis purposes. Thus, for example, the 15–19 year group might be divided into two groups, 15–17 and 18–19, since the latter age group tends to have considerably more behavioural freedom than younger age groups, including living away from home and, in many countries, access to licensed premises.

Gender

There are marked differences between male and female cultural participation patterns, so this is clearly a significant variable. Only specialised surveys explore beyond the simple male/female distinction to identify gay, lesbian, transgender categories.

Economic status
- In full-time paid work
- In part-time paid work
- Full-time with home or child care
- In full-time education
- Retired
- Unemployed/looking for paid employment
- Other

Market research occupation/socio-economic groups (SEG) classification

AB Managerial, administrative, professional (at senior or intermediate level)
C1 Supervisory or clerical (i.e. white collar) and junior managerial, administrative or professional
C2 Skilled manual
DE Semi-skilled, unskilled and casual workers and those entirely dependent on state pensions

National Statistics, Socio-Economic Classification (NS-SEC)[†]
- Employers (large organisations) and senior managers
- Higher professionals
- Lower managerial and professional
- Intermediate (e.g. clerks, secretaries, computer operators)
- Small employers and own-account non-professional
- Supervisors, craft and related
- Semi-routine (e.g. cooks, bus drivers, hairdressers, shop assistants)
- Routine (e.g. waiters, cleaners, couriers)
- Never worked, long-term unemployed

† The NS-SEC system was adopted by the UK Office for National Statistics in 1998 (Roberts, 2011: 20). Earlier editions of this book have used pre-1998 systems.

Figure 10.13 Economic status, occupational and socio-economic groupings

Economic status/occupation/socio-economic group/class

A person's economic and occupational situation clearly impinges on arts/events behaviour, mainly due to related levels of income and education. Information on such matters is important for marketing and planning and also in relation to public policy concerns with equity. Economic status is a person's situation vis-à-vis the formal economy, as listed in Figure 10.13.

Occupation typically denotes a person's type of paid work, so it is generally asked only of those identified from the economic status question as being in paid work. In contemporary developed economies, only about half the population is engaged in the paid workforce. Others (e.g. unemployed, retired, full-time carers) are sometimes asked what their last paid job was or what the occupation of the 'main breadwinner' of the household is. Such questions can become complex, however, because of situations such as full-time students living with parents or independently, single parents living on social security and so on. For those in paid work the sorts of question asked are:

- What is your occupation?
- What sort of work do you do?
- Which of the groups on this card best describes your occupation?

Sufficient information should be obtained to enable respondents to be classified into an appropriate occupational category.

Market researchers and official bodies, such as the Office for National Statistics, tend to use slightly different classifications, as shown in Figure 10.13. Such groupings, along with economic status, are often referred to as a person's *socio-economic group* or SEG. This is closely related to the idea of class or social class. Space does not permit a discussion of this complex concept here, but sources are given in the Resources section.

Because people can be vague in response to an open-ended question on occupation it is wise to include a supplementary question to draw out a full description – for example, 'office worker', 'engineer' or 'self-employed' are not adequate answers because they can cover such a wide variety of grades of occupation. A supplementary question could be: 'What sort of work is that?' Additional questions might be asked to be absolutely sure of the respondent's occupation. Such questions would check on the industry involved and the number of staff supervised by the respondent. In a household survey it may be possible to pursue these matters, but in other situations, such as site surveys, it would generally seem inappropriate because it would appear too intrusive.

There is considerable debate among sociologists concerning the concept of *class*, based on an individual's relationship to the economy, in a Marxian sense, and the Weberian concept of *status*, which is based on the *honour* accorded to an individual or group, which is determined substantially on non-economic factors. The use of 'socio-economic status' to some extent confuses these two concepts. There is a body of conflicting research that has sought to determine whether patterns of cultural participation are related to class or status. Sources are indicated in the Resources section.

Income

A typical wording of a question on income would be:

- What is your personal gross income from all sources before taxes?

or

- Which of the groups on the card does your personal gross income from all sources fall into?

Gross income is normally asked for, since it can be too complicated to gather information on income net of taxes and other deductions. Since there is often a major difference between gross and net income, this makes the variable a somewhat imprecise one. A further problem with income as a variable is that personal income is not a particularly useful variable for those who are not income recipients or who are not the main income recipients of the household. This can be overcome if all members of the household are being interviewed or if the respondent is asked about the 'main income earner' in the household. However, many teenage children, for example, do not know their parents' income and it might be seen as improper to ask them. Income is a sensitive issue and, in view of the limitations discussed above, is often excluded in site or visitor surveys.

Marital status

Since legal marital status fails to indicate the domestic situation of increasing numbers of people, the usefulness of this variable is declining. In terms of arts/events behaviour, whether or not a person has responsibility for children is likely to be a more important variable. Usual categories for marital status are:

- married
- single – never married
- widowed/divorced/separated.

Respondents who are not formally married but living in a *de facto* relationship can then decide for themselves how they want to be classified, or a separate category can be created.

(a) *Household type – household survey*
Question format: *Can you please tell me who lives here?*

Person	Relationship to respondent	Gender M/F	Age	Occupation
1	Respondent			
2				
3				
4				
5				

Household type classification based on the above information:

  A. Single parent and 1 dependent child
  B. Single parent and 2 or more dependent children
  C. Couple and 1 dependent child
  D. Couple and 2 or more dependent children
  E. Couple, no children
  F. Related adults only
  G. Unrelated adults only
  H. Single person
  I. Other

(b) *Visitor groups – visitor/site survey*
Question format:

  a. *How many people are there in this group, including yourself?* ___
  b. *How many children aged under 5 are there in the group?* ___
  c. *How many children age between 5 and 15 are there?* ___
  d. *How many people aged 60 or over are there?* ___

Group classification based on the above information:
  A. Youngest member aged 0–4
  B. Youngest member aged 5–15
  C. Lone adult
  D. Two adults (under 60)
  E. Older couple (60 and over)
  F. 3–5 adults
  G. 6+ adults

Figure 10.14 Household type and visitor group type

Household type and group type and size

Household type is a useful variable for many studies but, except in the household interview situation, the data may be difficult to collect because a number of items of information are required. In a household interview it is possible to ask, 'Who lives here?' A simplified version would be to just ask about the number of children of various ages in the household. Classifying the information into 'household type' must be done subsequently. Typical categories are set out in Figure 10.14a.

In the case of visitor/site surveys it is more usual to ask about the size of the party or group and its composition – for example, how many children and adults of various ages are present. Clearly such information is important for planning, marketing, managing and programming facilities and events. A typical categorisation of groups is shown in Figure 10.14b. It should be noted, however, that 'size of group' is not the same as 'vehicle occupancy', since some larger groups may arrive in several vehicles. So if the latter information is required for traffic-management purposes, it must be asked separately.

271

A	Child/young single – dependent (on parents)
B	Young single – independent
C	Young married/partnered – no children
D	Parent – dependent children
E	Parent – children now independent
F	Retired – up to 70
G	Retired – over 70

Figure 10.15 Life-cycle stages

Life-cycle

Some researchers have argued that individual variables, such as age and marital status, are not good predictors of cultural behaviour; rather, we should examine the composite variable *life-cycle*. As with household type, a person's stage in the life-cycle is not based on a single question but built up from a number of items of information, including age, economic status and marital/family status. A possible classification is set out in Figure 10.15. *Lifestyle* (see Chapter 2) is a further development of this idea but generally involves collection of a considerable amount of additional data.

Ethnic group

Ethnic group is often included in questionnaires because ethnically based cultures influence patterns of behaviour and consumption and also because of policy concerns for equity between social groups. Everyone belongs to an ethnic group – that is, a social group that shares religious, language and other cultural values and practices and experiences, including arts/events involvement – whether that be a majority or a minority ethnic group in a given society. Ethnicity therefore becomes important in cultural policy, planning and management, particularly as regards minority groups whose needs may not be met by mainstream facilities and services.

A common approach to ethnicity in the past was to ask the respondent's country of birth since, in many countries, most minority ethnic groups were migrant groups. But this of course does not identify members of ethnic minority groups not born overseas. Own and parents' place of birth identifies the first and second generation of migrant groups but not third and subsequent generations. Country of birth has therefore become less and less useful as an indicator of ethnic group membership in many countries. Observation is a solution for some but is not reliable for many groups. The solution is to ask people what ethnic group they consider they belong to. While this may cause offence to some, it is the most satisfactory approach overall.

Residential location/trip origin

Where a person lives can be a significant determinant of access to arts facilities and events and is a reflection of socio-economic position and related patterns of consumption. Residential location and trip origin are also the basis of catchment area analysis for individual facilities. The situation varies depending on the survey type:

● Household survey: The residential location is already known by the interviewer and some sort of code – for street, suburb, local government area, county, as appropriate – can be recorded on the questionnaire.

● Street survey: Home location is not always required, but if it is, a broad category, such as suburb, is usually adequate.

● Visitor/site surveys: If an aim of the survey is to study the catchment area of the facility, it will be necessary to ask people where they live and/or where they have travelled from. How much detail is required? This depends on the nature of the venue. For local venues with small

Type of dwelling	Tenure
Separate house	Owned outright
Semi-detached house	Being purchased
Terrace house	Rented
Flat/maisonette	Other
Caravan, houseboat	
Other	

Figure 10.16 Housing information

catchment areas it may be necessary to know the street (but not the number of the dwelling). For less local urban facilities the suburb is sufficient. For countryside/tourist facilities the town/city of residence will be required. For overseas visitors the country is usually adequate information, although there may be interest in where they are staying within the destination.

In Case study 14.3 an example is given of the use of home-location data to show the catchment area of a facility. In that example the information came from membership records, but it could equally well arise from a visitor survey.

Market research firms often record full addresses and/or telephone numbers of survey respondents in order to undertake subsequent quality checks on interviewers, to ensure that the respondents have in fact been interviewed.

Housing information

Information on the type of dwelling in which respondents live is usually collected in household surveys because it can easily be gathered by observation. Rather than dwelling type, it is more likely that home contents – books, artworks, internet access – will have an effect on cultural activity, but whether or not people own their own home is an important socio-economic variable. Typical categories for these items of information are shown in Figure 10.16.

Transport

Because mobility is such an important factor in cultural behaviour, questionnaires often include questions on ownership of and access to vehicles. People are sometimes asked if they possess a current driver's licence. In the case of visitor/site surveys, the mode of transport used to travel to the site, and vehicle occupancy as discussed under household/groups above, is often sought. If people claim to have used two or more modes of transport to reach a site, the various modes can all be recorded or respondents can be asked to indicate the one on which they travelled the furthest.

Attitude/opinion questions

Attitudes and opinions are more complex aspects of questionnaire design. A range of techniques exists to explore people's opinions and attitudes, as listed in Figure 10.17. The first three formats – direct, open-ended questions, checklists and ranking – are straightforward, but the other formats merit some comment.

Likert scales

Scaling techniques are sometimes known as 'Likert scales' after the psychologist Rensis Likert, who developed their use and analysis. In this technique respondents are asked to indicate their agreement or disagreement with a proposition or the importance they attach to a factor,

a. Open-ended/direct: What attracted you to apply for this course?

_____

b. Checklist: Of the items on the card, which was the most important to you in applying for this course?

> A. Good reputation
> B. Easy access
> C. Curriculum
> D. Level of fees
> E. Easy parking

c. Ranking: Please rank the items on the card in terms of their importance to you in choosing a course. Please rank them 1 for the most important to 5 for the least important.

	Rank
A. Good reputation	___
B. Easy access	___
C. Curriculum	___
D. Level of fees	___
E. Easy parking	___

d. Likert scales: Looking at the items on the card, please say how important each was to you in deciding to visit this area; was it: Very important, Quite important, Not very important or Not at all important?

	Very important	Quite important	Not very important	Not at all important
Good reputation	$\square_1$	$\square_2$	$\square_3$	$\square_4$
Easy access	$\square_1$	$\square_2$	$\square_3$	$\square_4$
Curriculum	$\square_1$	$\square_2$	$\square_3$	$\square_4$
Level of fees	$\square_1$	$\square_2$	$\square_3$	$\square_4$
Easy parking	$\square_1$	$\square_2$	$\square_3$	$\square_4$

e. Attitude statements: Please read the statements below and indicate your level of agreement or disagreement with them by ticking the appropriate box.

	Agree Strongly	Agree	No opinion	Disagree	Disagree strongly
The learning experience is more important than the qualification in education	$\square_1$	$\square_2$	$\square_3$	$\square_4$	$\square_5$
Graduate course fees are too high	$\square_1$	$\square_2$	$\square_3$	$\square_4$	$\square_5$

f. Semantic differential: Please look at the list below and tick the line to indicate where you think this course falls in relation to each factor listed.

Difficult	|___|___|___|___|	Easy
Irrelevant	|___|___|___|___|	Relevant
Professional	|___|___|___|___|	Unprofessional
Dull	|___|___|___|___|	Interesting

Figure 10.17 Opinion or attitude question formats

using a standard set of responses. One of the advantages of this approach is that the responses can be quantified.

Responses to both Likert scale questions and attitude statements, discussed below, can be scored, as indicated by the numerals beside the boxes in Figure 10.17. For example, 'agree strongly' could be given a score of 5, 'agree' a score of 4, and so on, to 'disagree strongly' with a score of 1. Scores can then be averaged across a number of respondents. So, for example, a group of people who mostly either 'agree' or 'agree strongly' with a statement would produce an average score between 4 and 5, whereas a group who 'disagree' or 'disagree strongly' would produce a low score, between 1 and 2. Such scores enable the strength of agreement with different statements to be compared, and the opinions of different groups of people to be compared.

Ranking

Asking respondents to rank items in order of importance is a relatively straightforward process, provided the list is not too long: more than five or six items could test respondents' patience. Again, the responses can be quantified – for example, in the form of average ranks.

Attitude statements

Attitude statements are a means of exploring respondents' attitudes towards a wide range of issues, including questions of a philosophical or political nature. Respondents are shown a series of statements and asked to indicate, using a scale, the extent to which they agree or disagree with them. Scoring or attitude statement is discussed under Likert scales above.

Semantic differential

The semantic differential method involves offering respondents pairs of contrasting descriptors and asking them to indicate how the facility, place or service being studied relates to the descriptors. This technique is suitable for a respondent-completion questionnaire, since the respondent is required to place a tick on each line. Each space/box can be coded as in a Likert scale. It would be difficult to replicate this exactly in an interview situation with no visual prompts, such as in a telephone survey; the effect would be to reduce the possible answers to three: close to one end, close to the other end and in the middle. The choice of pairs of words used in a semantic differential list should arise from the research context and theory.

Repertory grid

A further development of this approach is the *repertory grid* technique (see Chapter 5). In this case, the pairs of words – called *personal constructs* – are developed by the respondent. This technique is not explored further here, but references are given in the Resources section.

Market segments

Market segmentation or lifestyle studies (introduced in Chapter 1) involve classifying survey respondents according to a mix of activity, socio-demographic and attitude variables. All the necessary data items for this have therefore been discussed above. Actually determining market segments or lifestyle groupings is then an analytical task (see Chapter 17 under Cluster and factor analysis).

Ordering of questions and layout of questionnaires

Here we discuss introductory remarks, question order and layout.

Introductory remarks

Should a questionnaire include introductory remarks, for example explaining the purpose of the survey and asking for the respondent's assistance? This depends on the context:

● *Mail survey:* Introductory material is generally included in the covering letter.

● *Other forms of respondent-completion questionnaire:* A short note at the beginning of the questionnaire is advisable, although field-workers handing out questionnaires will usually provide the necessary introduction and explanation.

● *Interviewer-administered questionnaires:* The remarks can be printed on the top of each questionnaire or can be included in the interviewers' written instructions. In practice, interviewers are unlikely to approach potential interviewees and actually read from a script. When seeking cooperation of a potential interviewee it is usually necessary to maintain eye contact, so interviewers must know in advance what they want to say.

   ○ *Household surveys:* Potential interviewees may require a considerable amount of information and proof of identity from the interviewer before agreeing to be interviewed.

   ○ *Visitor/site survey interviews:* respondents are generally more interested in knowing how long the interview will take and what sort of questions they will be asked – so only minimal opening remarks are necessary. For example, for a site survey the introduction could be as brief as: 'Excuse me, we are conducting a survey of visitors to the festival; would you mind answering a few questions?'

It is usually necessary for interviewers to indicate what organisation they represent, and this can be reinforced by an identity badge. Market research or consultancy companies often instruct interviewers to indicate only that they represent the company and not the client who commissioned the research. This can ensure that unbiased opinions are obtained, although in some cases it can raise ethical considerations if it is felt that respondents have a right to know what organisation will be using the information gathered.

One function of opening remarks can be to assure the respondent of confidentiality. In the case of visitor/site surveys, where names and addresses are not generally collected, confidentiality is easy to maintain. In the case of household and some mail surveys, respondents can be identified, so assurances are generally necessary. The issue of confidentiality, including practical means of ensuring it, is an ethical issue (see Chapter 4).

Question order

It is important that an interview based on a questionnaire flows in a logical and comfortable manner. A number of principles should be borne in mind:

1. Start with easy questions.

2. Start with 'relevant' questions – for example, if the respondent has been told that the survey is about cultural activity, begin with some questions about cultural activity.

3. Personal questions, dealing with such things as age or income, are generally best left to near the end: while they do not generally cause problems, and respondents need not answer those personal questions if they object, they are less likely to cause offence if asked later in the interview when a rapport has been established between interviewer and respondent. Similar principles apply in relation to respondent-completion questionnaires. It is sometimes suggested that this is an unethical practice, in that people might not agree to cooperate if they were to know in advance that personal questions would

be asked. But since in arts/events surveys the personal information is rarely deeply personal, and respondents can and do decline to answer such questions, the practice is widely seen as acceptable.

Layout

- *General:* A questionnaire should be laid out and printed in such a way that the person who must read it – whether interviewer or interviewee – can follow all the instructions easily and answer all the questions that are meant to be answered. In the case of respondent-completion questionnaires extra care must be taken with layout because it can be difficult to rectify faults once the survey process is under way. Clarity of layout and the overall impression given by the questionnaire can be all-important in obtaining a good response. Mail surveys, where the researcher does not have direct contact with the respondent, are the most demanding. A professionally laid-out, typeset and printed questionnaire will pay dividends in terms of response rate and accuracy and completeness of responses.

- *Filtering:* Layout becomes particularly important when a questionnaire contains filters – that is, when answers to certain questions determine which subsequent questions must be answered. An example, with alternative ways of dealing with layout, is shown in Figure 10.18.

- *Length:* A professionally laid-out and typeset format can reduce the number of pages considerably, which may increase the response rate if the perceived length of the questionnaire is a factor. Even where interviewers are used, there are advantages in keeping the questionnaire as compact as possible for ease of handling. A two-column format, as used in Case study 10.1C, is worth exploring and can be easily achieved with word-processing packages.

- *Tick boxes and codes:* The questionnaire shown in Case study 10.1A is designed for respondent-completion and therefore involves boxes for the respondent to tick. Boxes can, however, be laborious to type and lay out, so where an interviewer is being used, as in examples B and C, the interviewer can easily circle codes.

- *Office use column:* The 'office use' column is not always necessary in interviewer-administered questionnaires, but is included in examples B and C for exposition purposes. This type of layout can be used for respondent-completion in some situations – for example, in certain 'captive group' situations or where respondents are known to be highly literate and are unlikely to be deterred by the apparent technicalities of the layout.

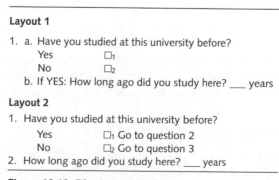

Figure 10.18 Filtering: examples

Coding

Most questionnaire survey data are now analysed by computer. This means that the information in the questionnaire must be coded – that is, converted into, generally numerical, codes and organised in a systematic, 'machine-readable' manner. Different procedures apply to pre-coded and open-ended questions and these are discussed in turn below.

Pre-coded questions

The principle for coding of pre-coded questions is illustrated in many of the questions in the example questionnaires in Case study 10.1A, which should be mostly self-explanatory. In question 1 the codes are as shown beside the boxes: only one answer is possible, so only one code is recorded as the answer to this question. Where the answer is already numerical, there is no need to code the answer because the numerical answer can be handled by the computer. For example, in question 4 actual expenditure is asked for, which is a number and does not require coding.

Scaled answers, as in Likert scales and attitude statements, readily lend themselves to coding, as shown by the numerals in the examples given in questions 5 and 6 and in Figure 10.17. In the case of the semantic differential, each of the sections of the response line can be numbered, say 1–4, so that answers can be given a numerical code, depending on where the respondent marks the line.

Open-ended questions

In the case of completely open-ended questions quite an elaborate procedure must be followed to devise a coding system. As already suggested, the answers to open-ended questions can be copied from the questionnaires and presented in a report 'raw', as in Figure 10.11. If this is all that is required from the open-ended questions then there is no point in spending the considerable labour necessary to code the information for computer analysis: the computer will merely reproduce what can be more easily achieved manually.

Computer analysis comes into its own if it is intended to analyse the results in more detail – for example, comparing the responses of two or more age groups. If such comparisons are to be made it will usually be difficult to do so with, say, 50 or 60 different response groups to compare, especially if many of the responses are given by only one or two respondents. The aim then is to devise a coding system that groups the responses into a manageable number of categories.

If a large sample is involved, it is advisable that the coding system be devised using a pilot survey, so that open-ended questions become pre-coded, but if this is not considered desirable then a representative sub-sample of the responses, say 50 or 100, might be used for the purpose. All responses are written down, noting the number of occurrences of each answer as in Figure 10.19. Then individual codes are given for the most frequent responses and the others are grouped into meaningful categories, as indicated. This is a matter of judgement. The aim is to not leave too many responses in the 'other' category.

Recording coded information

Computer analysis is conducted using the coded information from a questionnaire. This is best illustrated by an example – a completed questionnaire from Case study 10.1A is set out in Figure 10.20.

Answers from 25 respondents to the question: 'What suggestions would you make for improving campus entertainment?'

Uncoded answers	Suggested coding system code	
More events available ///	Comments on programmes	1
Upgrade social facilities ////	Comments on timing	2
More weekday events //	Comments on facilities	3
More lunchtime events /	Comments on costs	4
More evening events //	Comments on organisation	5
More first-run movies /	Other	6
More old/silent movies ///		
Better class of band ///		
Free transport from city //		
Keep out non-students //		
Better audience accommodation ///		
Lower entry costs ////		
Better air-conditioning ////		
Better control of facility users //		
Upgrade wi-fi access ////		

Figure 10.19 Coding open-ended questions: example

In the 'office use' column, spaces are provided into which the codes from the answers can be written. The 'variable names' in the office column – qno, status, movie, etc. – are explained in more detail in Chapter 16.

Questionnaire number, in the 'office use' column, is an identifier so that a link can be made between data in the computer and actual questionnaires – the example questionnaire is number 001.

- Question 1 – only one answer/code can be given.

- Question 2 – respondents can tick up to four boxes.

- Question 3 – five ranks must be recorded.

- Question 4 – asks for an actual number and this will be transferred into the computer without coding.

- Question 5 – consists of three Likert-scale items.

- Question 6 – an open-ended question. It is envisaged that some respondents might give more than one answer, so spaces have been reserved for three answers (although in the example, only one has been given). The answers have a coding system (devised as discussed above) as follows:

Comments on range of programmes	1
Comments on timing	· 2
Comments on facilities	3
Comments on costs	4
Comments on organisation	5
Other	6

The data from this particular completed questionnaire therefore become a single row of numbers, as shown in the first row of Figure 10.21, which shows how data from 15 completed questionnaires would look. How such a set of data may be analysed by computer is discussed in Chapter 16.

Campus Entertainment Survey 2012

| Office Use
| # _001_
| qno

1. Which of the following best describes your current situation?

       Full-time student with no regular paid work   ☐ 1

       Full-time student with some regular paid work   ☑ 2 | _2_ status

       Part-time student with full-time job   ☐ 3

       Part-time student – other   ☐ 4

2. Which of the following university cultural/entertainment venues/events have you used in the last four weeks?

       Movie club   ☑ 1 | _1_ movie

       Memorial theatre   ☑ 1 | _1_ drama

       Rock/pop band gig   ☐ 1 | ___ rock

       Sunday jazz in the Lake Bar   ☐ 1 | ___ jazz

3. In thinking about using the entertainment services provided on campus, what are the most important considerations for you? Please rank the items below in terms of their importance to you. Rank them from 1 for the most important to 5 for the least important.

                                   Rank

       Free or cheap access   _1_ | _1_ cheap

       Convenient times   _4_ | _4_ hours

       Quality of programmes   _2_ | _2_ qual

       Opportunities to socialise/meet people   _3_ | _3_ meet

       Available time   _5_ | _5_ time

4. Approximately how much do you spend in any two-week period on entertainment on and off campus?

       £ _100_ | 100 spend

5. Please indicate the importance of the following to you in relation to campus entertainment activities

	Very important	Important	Not at all Important	
Relaxation opportunities	☑ 3	☐ 2	☐ 1	_3_ relax
Social interaction	☑ 3	☐ 2	☐ 1	_3_ social
Meaningful experience	☐ 3	☐ 2	☑ 1	_1_ meaning

6. What suggestions would you make for improving campus entertainment?

       Provide a better standard of band | _1_ sug1

                                      | ___ sug2

                                      | ___ sug3

7. You are: Male ☑ 1   Female ☐ 2 | _1_ gend

8. Your age last birthday was: _18_ years | _18_ age

Figure 10.20 Completed questionnaire

qno	status	movie	drama	rock	jazz	cheap	hours	qual	meet	time	spend	relax	social	meaning	sug1	sug2	sug3	gend	age
1	2	1	1	0	0	1	4	2	3	5	100	3	3	1	1			1	18
2	2	1	1	1	0	1	4	2	3	5	50	2	3	1	2	1		1	19
3	3	1	0	0	0	2	5	1	3	4	250	2	2	2	3	4		2	19
4	4	0	0	0	0	2	3	1	4	5	25	3	2	2	1	2	4	1	22
5	3	1	0	0	1	1	4	3	2	5	55	3	3	1				2	24
6	3	1	1	1	0	2	4	1	3	5	40	2	3	1	2			2	20
7	2	1	0	0	0	3	2	1	4	5	150	2	3	2	3	5		2	20
8	2	1	0	1	0	3	4	2	1	5	250	1	2	2	4			1	21
9	4	0	1	0	0	1	5	2	3	4	300	2	3	2				1	21
10	3	1	1	0	0	2	3	1	5	4	100	1	2	1	1	1		2	21
11	3	1	1	0	1	2	3	1	4	5	75	2	2	1	2	3		2	19
12	2	1	0	1	0	1	4	3	2	5	50	2	3	1				1	22
13	1	1	0	1	0	1	5	2	3	4	55	2	3	2	1	2		2	21
14	3	1	1	0	0	2	4	1	3	5	75	3	3	2	4			2	20
15	1	1	1	0	0	3	2	1	5	4	150	3	3	1	1	2	5	1	20

Figure 10.21 Data from 15 questionnaires

Validity of questionnaire-based data

◼ Threats to validity

Questionnaires are designed to gather information from individuals about their behaviour, characteristics and attitudes. Whether or not they achieve this adequately depends on a number of possible threats to validity. Some of these are summarised in Figure 10.22.

The principles of questionnaire design discussed above, and the principles of sampling (see Chapter 13), are designed to minimise threats to validity. To some extent the researcher must simply live with the limitations of the survey method and hope that inaccuracies are not significant and that some of them cancel each other out. There are, however, some measures which can be taken to check on the presence of this type of problem.

◼ Checking validity

Some aspects of validity can be checked. The possibility of random or systematic error in responses may be checked by the use of dummy questions or answer categories, semi-disguised duplication of questions, comparing time periods, and referring to an alternative data source, where one exists. These possibilities are discussed in turn below.

Threat	Nature
Non-response	Non-respondents may be significantly different from respondents, thus resulting in a biased sample.
Questionnaire design: lack of clarity	Leading questions, ambiguity, etc. result in inaccurate data.
Accuracy of recall	Respondents vary in their ability to recall activity or its timing/nature, especially over long time periods.
Desire to impress	People have a natural desire to impress others, to give a good report of themselves, resulting in exaggeration of good points and down-playing of bad points.
Privacy concerns/sensitivity	People may be reluctant to provide information at all on private/sensitive matters, or may provide incomplete or inaccurate information.
Communication	Respondents may have difficulty with the language of the questionnaire.
Interviewee patience/fatigue	Interviews perceived to be excessively long or uninteresting may lead to incomplete responses.
Physical context	If interview or questionnaire completion takes place in a distracting environment, inaccuracies or incompleteness may result.
Authenticity of opinions	Respondents may be asked their opinions about matters to which they have not given much, or any, serious thought (Bourdieu, 1978).
Interviewer-administered	
Interviewer–respondent rapport	Particularly good or poor interviewer–respondent rapport may affect the accuracy and completeness of responses.
Communication	Respondent or interviewer may have difficulty in understanding the other's accent.
Interviewer consistency	If interviewer does not consistently follow instructions, or different interviewers interpret instructions differently, inaccuracies may result.
Respondent-completed	Respondents have difficulty in understanding questions or, in the case of
Literacy	open-ended questions, in writing answers.
Non-completion	For a variety of reasons, some questions are not answered.

Figure 10.22 Questionnaire surveys: threats to validity

Dummy questions or answer categories

In a survey of managers in Britain in the early 1980s respondents were asked to indicate, from a list, what books and reports they had heard of and read. Included in the list was one plausible but non-existent title. A significant proportion of respondents indicated that they had heard of the publication and a small proportion claimed to have read it. Such a response does not necessarily mean that respondents were lying – they may simply have been confused about the titles of particular publications. But it does provide cautionary information to the researcher on the degree of error in responses to such questions, since it suggests that responses to the genuine titles may also include a certain amount of inaccuracy. For example, if 2 per cent of respondents claim to have heard of the non-existent publication, this could suggest that all answers are subject to an error of plus or minus about 2 per cent.

Semi-disguised duplication of questions

A similar approach is to include two or more questions in different parts of the questionnaire that essentially ask the same thing. For example, an early question could ask respondents to rank a list of activities or events in order of preference, then later in the questionnaire, in the context of asking some detailed questions, respondents could be asked to indicate their favourite activity or event. In the analysis, the responses could be tested for consistency.

Rather than detecting error, it is possible that this approach can discover that the interview or questionnaire completion experience itself has caused respondents to change their opinion, because it causes them to think through in detail something which they previously might have considered only superficially. At the beginning of the interviews in an Australian survey of gambling behaviour and attitudes towards a proposed casino development, Grichting and Caltabiano (1986) asked: 'What do you think about the casino coming to the town? Are you for it or against it?' At the end of the interview they asked: 'Taking everything you have said into consideration, what do you think now about the casino coming to the town? Are you for it or against it?' It was found that about 'one in six respondents changed their attitude toward the casino during the course of the interview'.

Comparing time periods

Bachman and O'Malley (1981) used data from a survey of marijuana and alcohol use among senior high-school students to explore apparent inconsistencies in reported use levels in the last month and in the last year. Except for seasonal activities, it might be expected that use levels in the last month would be about one-twelfth of use levels for the whole year. However, it was found that use levels reported for the last month were very much higher than one-twelfth of the one-year figure, suggesting that either the one-month figures were exaggerated or the one-year figures were under-reported.

Use of an alternative data source

Managers of venues typically keep records of spectator attendances that could be compared with estimates derived from survey research.

Two studies conducted at the University of Pennsylvania by David Chase and colleagues compared questionnaire survey results on estimated numbers of visits to local leisure venues with club sign-in records. In the first study (Chase and Godbey, 1983) it was found that more than 75 per cent of respondents overestimated their visits and in over two-fifths of cases the error was greater than 100 per cent. The second, larger-scale, study (Chase and Harada, 1984) confirmed the general picture, with survey respondents' estimate of previous season visits averaging 30, while the club records indicated that the actual frequency was 17. While the studies referred to swimming and tennis clubs, there is no reason to presume that similar results would not apply to cultural activity.

Taking account of validity problems

There is no indication in the research and policy literature that those organisations and researchers conducting and using questionnaire survey results in the arts/events area take into account the above findings on validity problems. These discussions refer only to recall of factual information, but questions may also arise in regard to the validity of responses to questions on opinion, attitudes and aspirations, a topic discussed by Bourdieu (1978). There does not seem to be much interest in exploring these problems among the research community. Some of the issues have, however, been addressed by researchers in the medical sector, as the volume of papers edited by Stone *et al.* (2000) demonstrates.

Conducting questionnaire surveys

Planning fieldwork arrangements

The scale and complexity of the data-collection, or fieldwork, process in survey research can obviously vary enormously. At one extreme the process is largely a matter of personal organisation on the part of the researcher; at the other extreme a staff of hundreds may need to be recruited, trained and supervised. Fieldwork must be organised in any empirical study involving primary data collection, but because of the popularity of the survey method and the likelihood that it will involve organisation of individuals other than the single researchers, some attention is given to the task in this chapter. Some of the items that need to be considered are listed in Figure 10.23 and brief notes are presented below.

(a) Seek permissions

It is important to remember that permission is often needed to interview in public places because of local bye-laws. Many areas that are thought of as 'public', such as shopping centres and public squares, are in fact the responsibility of some public or private organisation. Permission must be sought from these organisations to conduct fieldwork. It is also good practice to inform the local police if interviewing is being conducted in public places, in case of complaints or queries from the public.

(a) Seek permissions – to visit venues/sites, obtain records, etc.
(b) Obtain lists for sampling – e.g. voter lists.
(c) Arrange printing – of questionnaires, etc.
(d) Check insurance issues.
(e) Prepare written instructions for interviewers.
(f) Recruit interviewers and supervisors.
(g) Prepare identity badges/letters for interviewers.
(h) Train interviewers and supervisors.
(i) Obtain quotations for any fieldwork to be conducted by other organisations.
(j) Appoint and train data coders/processors.

Figure 10.23 Fieldwork planning tasks

(b) Obtain lists

Obtaining lists, such as voter or membership lists, for sampling may seem routine, but often apparently straightforward tasks can involve delays, or the material may not be quite in the form anticipated and it takes time to process. Often research projects are conducted on tight schedules and delays of a few days can be crucial. Therefore the earlier these routine tasks are tackled, the better.

(c) Arrange printing

Printing sounds straightforward, but the in-house print shop has busy periods when it may not be possible to obtain a quick job turnaround. Checking on printing procedures and turnaround times at an early stage is therefore advisable.

(d) Check insurance

When conducting fieldwork away from a normal place of work, insurance issues may arise, including public liability and workers' compensation for interviewers. In the case of educational institutions, staff and students are normally covered as long as they are engaged in legitimate university/college activities, but these matters should be checked with a competent legal authority in the organisation.

(e) Prepare written instructions for interviewers

Provision of written instructions for interviewers is advisable and may cover:

- detailed comments on questionnaires and/or other instruments;
- instructions in relation to checking of completed questionnaires, etc. for legibility and completeness;
- instructions on returning questionnaires, etc.;
- dress and behaviour codes;
- relevant information on ethical issues, such as confidentiality and interviewees' rights;
- roster details;
- 'wet weather' instructions, if relevant;
- instructions on what to do in the case of 'difficult' interviewees, etc.;
- details of time-sheets, payment, etc.;
- contact telephone numbers.

A note on questionnaire-based interviewing is appropriate here. The general approach to interviewing when using a questionnaire is that the interviewer should be instructed to adhere precisely to the wording on the questionnaire. If the respondent does not understand the question, the question should simply be repeated exactly as before; if the respondent still does not understand then the interviewer should move on to the next question. If this procedure is to be adhered to, the importance of question wording and the testing of such wording in one or more pilot surveys is clear.

The above procedure is clearly important in relation to attitude questions. Any word of explanation or elaboration from the interviewer could influence, and therefore bias, the response. In relation to factual questions, however, it may be less important – a word of explanation from the interviewer may be acceptable if it results in obtaining accurate information.

(f) Recruit interviewers and supervisors

Where paid interviewers, supervisors or other fieldworkers are to be used it will be necessary to go through the normal procedures for employing part-time staff. Advice from the organisation's human resources unit, or someone familiar with their procedures, will need to be sought.

(g) Prepare identity badges/letters

If working in a public or semi-public place, fieldworkers should be clearly identified. A badge with the institutional logo and the fieldworker's given name is advisable. A letter from the research supervisor indicating that the fieldworker is engaged in legitimate research activity for the organisation may also be helpful.

(h) Training

The length of training will vary with the complexity of the fieldwork and the experience of the fieldwork staff. Paid fieldworkers should be paid for the training session(s), and this should be budgeted for. A two- or three-hour session is usually sufficient, but more may be necessary for a complex project. It is advisable for interviewers to practise interviews on each other and report back on any difficulties.

(i) Obtain quotations

In some cases certain aspects of the project, such as data processing, may be undertaken by other organisations. Obtaining detailed quotations on price as early as possible is clearly advisable.

(j) Appoint and train data processors

In some cases the coding, editing and processing of data for computer analysis is a significant task in its own right, requiring staff to be recruited. Recruitment and training procedures will need to be followed as for fieldworkers.

Conducting a pilot survey

Pilot surveys are small-scale 'trial runs' of a larger survey. Pilot surveys relate particularly to questionnaire surveys, but can in fact relate to trying out any type of research procedure. It is always advisable to carry out one or more pilot surveys before embarking on the main data-collection exercise. The purposes of pilot surveys are summarised in Figure 10.24.

(a)	Test questionnaire wording.
(b)	Test question sequencing.
(c)	Test questionnaire layout.
(d)	Code open-ended questions.
(e)	Gain familiarity with respondents.
(f)	Test fieldwork arrangements/logistics.
(g)	Train and test fieldworkers.
(h)	Estimate response rate.
(i)	Estimate interview time.
(j)	Test analysis procedures.

Figure 10.24 Pilot survey purposes

Clearly the pilot can be used to test all aspects of the survey, not just question wording. Item e. 'familiarity with respondents' refers to the role of the pilot survey in alerting the researcher to any characteristics, idiosyncrasies or sensitivities of the respondent group with which he or she may not have been familiar previously. Such matters can affect the design and conduct of the main survey components. Items h and i, concerned with the response rate and length of interview, can be most important in providing information to fine-tune the survey process. For example, it may be necessary to shorten the questionnaire and/or vary the number of field staff so that the project keeps on schedule and within budget.

In principle some of the pilot interviews should be carried out by the researcher in charge, or at least by some experienced interviewers, since the interviewers will be required to report back on the pilot survey experience and contribute to discussions on any revisions to the questionnaire or fieldwork arrangements that might subsequently be made. The de-briefing session following the pilot survey is important and should take place as soon as possible after the completion of the exercise, so that the details are fresh in the interviewers' minds.

Summary

This chapter provides an introduction to questionnaire surveys, arguably the most commonly used data-collection vehicle in arts/events research. The merits of questionnaire surveys are discussed, including the ability to quantify the results, transparency of procedures, succinctness in data presentation, the ability to study change over time, comprehensive coverage of complex phenomena and generalisability to the whole population. The second part of the chapter is devoted to discussing the features of seven different forms of the questionnaire survey: household surveys, street surveys, telephone surveys, mail surveys, e-surveys, visitor/on-site surveys and captive group surveys. The third part of the chapter considers questionnaire design and coding. Finally, the chapter considers fieldwork arrangements for questionnaire surveys, including the conduct of pilot surveys.

TEST QUESTIONS

1. What are the merits of questionnaire surveys?

2. Seven types of questionnaire survey are discussed in the chapter: list three of these and outline their characteristics in terms of: respondent or interviewer completion; cost; nature of the sample; possible length of questionnaire; and likely response rate.

3. What type of survey methodology would you use to conduct for a sample of 500 of the following:

   (a) Visitors to a multi-venue cultural festival.

   (b) Museum volunteers.

   (c) The users of an arts centre.

   (d) Visitors to the cultural precinct of a city.

   (e) People visiting a country to attend a major international cultural or sport event.

   (f) People who are not attendees at performing arts venues.

(g) Members of a theatre group.

(h) Amateur musicians in a city.

(i) People aged 14 and over living in a local council area.

(j) Young people aged 11–13 living in a local council area.

4. What is quota sampling?

5. What measures might be used to increase response rates in mail surveys?

6. What principles should be followed for wording questions in questionnaires?

7. What is the difference between pre-coded and open-ended questions and what are the advantages and disadvantages of the two formats?

EXERCISES

1. Design a questionnaire in relation to one of the studies discussed in Case study 3.1, limiting the questionnaire to ten questions only.

2. Design a survey question on people's attitudes towards commercial sponsorship of the arts, using three alternative question formats.

3. If you are a member of a class/tutorial group, invite members of the group to complete the questionnaire in Case study 10.1A and devise a coding system for the answers to the open-ended question based on the answers obtained.

4. Locate a published research report or thesis which includes a questionnaire survey and contains a copy of the questionnaire used (usually in an appendix, see Resources section) and provide a critique of the questionnaire design.

Resources

Websites

Time-budget diaries/time-use surveys:

- Australian Bureau of Statistics: 2006 time-use survey: www.abs.gov.au
- UK Office for National Statistics: 2005 Time use Survey: www.statistics.gov.uk
- Harmonised European Time Use Survey: www.h2.scb.se/tus/tus/default.htm
- Centre for Time Use Research, University of Oxford: www.timeuse.org/

Publications

- Attitude measurement: Oppenheim (2000, Chapter 11).
- Captive group surveys: see children.
- Children: Dockett et al. (2011), Martin et al. (2012).
- Class versus status and cultural participation: Chan (2010); Chan and Goldthorpe (2007); summary: Veal (2013).
- Cultural tourism surveys: Richards (2010); the (USA) General Social Survey cultural module: Marsden and Swingle (1994).

- E-surveys: Dillman *et al.* (2009), Parsons (2007).
- Life-cycle: Rapoport and Rapoport (1975).
- Mail surveys: Dillman *et al.* (2009); incentives/rewards: James and Bolstein (1990).
- National household surveys of cultural participation: see Resources section in Chapter 7.
- Opinions: Bourdieu (1978).
- Questionnaires – examples of studies which include copies of the questionnaire used:
  - art and health programmes: Health Development Agency (2000: 38–69)
  - art gallery visitors: Bennett and Frow (1991: 63–70)
  - Australian 'Everyday Cultures' project: Bennett *et al.* (1999: 272–289)
  - cultural landscapes: Collins *et al.* (2010: 99–103)
  - cultural tourism: ATLAS on-site survey: Richards (2010: 28–32)
  - cultural values and participation: European Commission (2007: 91–107)
  - event visitors: Bowdin *et al.* (2011); economic: Jago and Dwyer (2006: 47–49)
  - museum visitors: Bourdieu and Darbell (1997: 119–125)
  - participation in the arts: England: Fenn *et al.* (2004: 96–108); USA: National Endowment for the Arts (2009: 89–93); Australia: Australia Council (2009: 3–23)
  - public attitudes towards the arts: McDonnell (1995: 28–30)
- Questionnaire design generally: Oppenheim (2000); life-cycle: Rapoport and Rapoport (1975); class: Giddens (1993: 211–250); opinions on the arts: Filicko (1996).
- Repertory grid technique/personal constructs: Kelly (1955).
- Semantic differential: aesthetics: Levy (1980: 39, 46).
- Sensitive questions/topics: Schaeffer (2000).
- Spatial/place dimensions: Widdop and Cutts (2012).
- Surveys generally: limitations regarding opinions: Bourdieu (1978).
- Telephone surveys: Lavrakas (1993), Lepkowski *et al.* (2008); mobile phone problem: Link and Lai (2011).
- Time-budget diaries/time-use surveys: Szalai (1972), Australian Bureau of Statistics (2007), Gershuny (2000), Pentland *et al.* (1999).
- Validity: exaggerated/unreliable, etc. responses to questionnaires: Bachman and O'Malley (1981), Chase and Godbey (1983), Chase and Harada (1984), Grichting and Caltabiano (1986), Loftus *et al.* (1990), Oppenheim (2000: 138–139); remembering events: Gaskell *et al.* (2000); opinions: Bourdieu (1978).
- Web-based surveys: see e-surveys.

References

Australian Bureau of Statistics (ABS) (2007) *How Australians Use Their Time, 2006* (Cat. No. 4153.0). Canberra: ABS.

Australia Council (2009) *More than Bums on Seats: Australian Participation in the Arts: Technical Appendices*. Sydney: Australia Council.

Bachman, J. G. and O'Malley, P. M. (1981) When four months equal a year: inconsistencies in student reports of drug use. *Public Opinion Quarterly*, 45(4), 536–548.

Bennett, R. (2005) Factors encouraging competitive myopia in the performing arts sector: an empirical investigation. *Services Industry Journal*, 25(3), 391–401.

Bennett, T. Emmison, M. and Frow, J. (1999) *Accounting for Tastes: Australian Everyday Cultures*. Cambridge: Cambridge University Press.

Bennett, T. and Frow, J. (1991) *Art Galleries: Who Goes?* Sydney: Australia Council.

Bourdieu, P. (1978) Public opinion does not exist. In A. Mattelart and S. Siegelaub (eds), *Communication and Class Struggle 1. Capitalism, Imperialism*. New York: International General, pp. 124–130.

Bourdieu, P. and Darbell, A. (1997) *The Love of Art*. Cambridge: Polity Press (first published in France, 1969).

Bowdin, G., Allen, J., O'Toole, W., Harris, R. and McDonnell, I. (2011) *Events Management*, Third Edition. London: Routledge.

Chan, T. W. (ed.) (2010) *Social Status and Cultural Consumption*. Cambridge: Cambridge University Press.

Chan, T. W. and Goldthorpe, J. H. (2007) Class and status: the conceptual distinction and its empirical relevance. *American Sociological Review*, 72(4), 512–532.

Chase, D. R. and Godbey, G. C. (1983) The accuracy of self-reported participation rates. *Leisure Studies*, 2(2), 231–236.

Chase, D. and Harada, M. (1984) Response error in self-reported recreation participation. *Journal of Leisure Research*, 16(4), 322–329.

Collins, J., Darcy, S. and Jordan, K. (2010) Multi-method research on ethnic cultural tourism in Australia. In G. Richards and W. Munsters (eds) *Cultural Tourism Research Methods*. Wallingford: CABI, pp. 87–103.

Dillman, D. A., Smyth, J. D. and Christian, L. M. (2009) *Internet, Mail, and Mixed-Mode Surveys: The Tailored Design Method*, Third Edition. New York: Wiley.

Dockett, S., Main, S. and Kelly, L. (2011) Consulting young children: experiences in a museum. *Visitor Studies*, 14(1), 13–33.

European Commission (2007) *European Cultural Values: Special Eurobarometer 278*. Brussels: European Commission, available at: http://ec.europa.eu/public_opinion/archives/eb_special_en.htm

Fenn, C., Bridgwood, A. and Dust, K. (2004) *Arts in England 2003: Attendance, Participation and Attitudes, Research Report 37*. London: Arts Council England.

Filicko, T. (1996) In what spirit do Americans cultivate the arts? *Journal of Arts Management, Law and Society*, 26(3), 221–246.

Gaskell, G. D., Wright, D. B. and O'Muircheartaich, C. A. (2000) Telescoping of landmark events: implications for survey research. *Public Opinion Quarterly*, 64(1), 77–89.

Gershuny, J. (2000) *Changing Times: Work and Leisure in Postindustrial Society*. Oxford: Oxford University Press.

Giddens, A. (1993) *Sociology*. Cambridge: Polity Press.

Gitelson, R. J. and Drogin, E. B. (1992) An experiment on the efficacy of a certified final mailing. *Journal of Leisure Research*, 24(1), 72–78.

Gratton, C. (2005) Great Britain. In G. Cushman, A. J. Veal and J. Zuzanek (eds), *Free Time and Leisure Participation: International Perspectives*, Wallingford: CABI Publishing, pp. 109–126.

Grichting, W. L. and Caltabiano, M. L. (1986) Amount and direction of bias in survey interviewing. *Australian Psychologist*, 21(1), 69–78.

Hammitt, W. E. and McDonald, C. D. (1982) Response bias and the need for extensive mail questionnaire follow-ups among selected recreation samples. *Journal of Leisure Research*, 14(3), 207–216.

Health Development Agency (2000) *Art for Health: A Review of Good Practice in Community-Based Arts Projects and Initiatives Which Impact on Health and Wellbeing*. London: HDA.

Jago, L. and Dwyer, L. (2006) *Economic Evaluation of Special Events: A Practitioner's Guide*. Gold Coast, Australia: Sustainable Tourism Cooperative Research Centre, available at www.crctourism.com.au

James, J. M. and Bolstein, R. (1990) The effect of monetary incentives and follow-up mailings on the response rate and response quality in mail surveys. *Public Opinion Quarterly*, 54(3), 346–361.

Kelly, G. A. (1955) *The Psychology of Personal Constructs*. New York: Norton.

Lavrakas, P. K. (1993) *Telephone Survey Methods: Sampling, Selection and Supervision*, Second Edition. Newbury Park, CA: Sage.

Lepkowski, J. M., Tucker, C., Brick, J. M. and de Leeuw, E. (eds) (2008) *Advances in Telephone Survey Methodology*. New York: John Wiley.

Levy, S. J. (1980) Arts consumers and aesthetic attributes. In M. P. Mokwa, W. M. Dawson and E. A. Prieve (eds) *Marketing the Arts*. New York: Praeger, pp. 29–46.

Link, M. W. and Lai, J. W. (2011) Cell-phone-only households and problems of differential non-response using an address-based sampling design. *Public Opinion Quarterly*, 75(4), 613–655.

Loftus, E. F., Klinger, M. R., Smith, K. D. and Fiedler, J. (1990) A tale of two questions: benefits of asking more than one question. *Public Opinion Quarterly*, 54(3), 330–345.

Marsden, P. V. and Swingle, J. F. (1994) Conceptualizing and measuring culture in values, strategies, and symbols. *Poetics*, 22(3), 269–289.

Martin, A. J., Anderson, M. and Adams, R.-J. (2012) What determines young people's engagement with performing arts events? *Leisure Sciences*, 34(3), 314–331.

McDonnell, J. S. (1995) *Public Attitudes to the Arts, 1994*. Sydney: Australia Council.

National Endowment for the Arts (2009) *2008 Survey of Public Participation in the Arts*. Washington, DC: NEA.

Oppenheim, A. N. (2000) *Questionnaire Design, Interviewing and Attitude Measurement*, New Edition. London: Continuum.

Parsons, C. (2007) Web-based surveys: best practices based on the research literature. *Visitor Studies*, 10(1), 13–33.

Pentland, W. E., Harvey, A. S., Lawton, M. P. and McColl, M. A. (eds) (1999) *Time Use Research in the Social Sciences*. New York: Kluwer/Plenum.

Pew Research Centre for the People and the Press (2004) *Polls Face Growing Resistance, But Still Representative, Survey Experiment Shows*. Washington, DC: Pew Research Center, available at: http://people-press.org/report/211/

Rapoport, R. and Rapoport, R. N. (1975) *Leisure and the Family Life Cycle*. London: Routledge.

Richards, G. (2010) The traditional quantitative approach. Surveying cultural tourists: lessons from the ATLAS Cultural Tourism Research Project. In G. Richards and W. Munsters (eds), *Cultural Tourism Research Methods* (pp. 13–32). Wallingford: CABI.

Roberts, K. (2011) *Class in Contemporary Britain*, Second Edition. Basingstoke: Palgrave Macmillan.

Robertson, R. W. and Veal, A. J. (1987) *Port Hacking Visitor Use Study*. Sydney: Centre for Leisure and Tourism Studies, University of Technology, Sydney.

Schaeffer, N. C. (2000) Asking questions about threatening topics: a selective overview. In A. A. Stone and J. S. Turken (eds), *The Science of Self-report: Implications for Research and Practice*. Mahwah, NJ: Lawrence Erlbaum, pp. 105–122.

Stone, A. A., Turkkan, J. S., Bachrach, C. A., Jobe, J. B., Kurtzman, H. S. and Cain, V. S. (2000) *The Science of Self-report: Implications for Research and Practice*. Mahwah, NJ: Lawrence Erlbaum.

Szalai, A. (ed.) (1972) *The Use of Time: Daily Activities of Urban and Suburban Populations in Twelve Countries*. The Hague: Mouton.

Veal, A. J. (2013) Lifestyle and leisure theory. In T. Blackshaw (ed.), *Handbook of Leisure Studies*. London: Routledge, pp. 266–279.

Widdop, P. and Cutts, D. (2012) Impact of place on museum participation. *Cultural Trends*, 21(1), 47–66.

Chapter 11

Experimental research

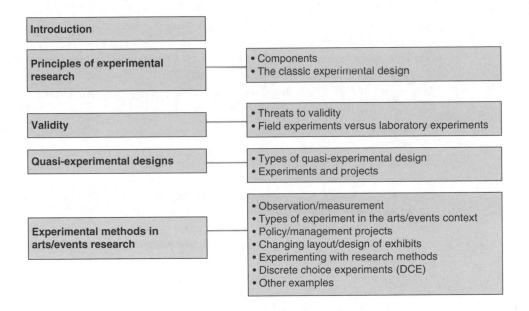

Introduction

Principles of experimental research — • Components
• The classic experimental design

Validity — • Threats to validity
• Field experiments versus laboratory experiments

Quasi-experimental designs — • Types of quasi-experimental design
• Experiments and projects

Experimental methods in arts/events research — • Observation/measurement
• Types of experiment in the arts/events context
• Policy/management projects
• Changing layout/design of exhibits
• Experimenting with research methods
• Discrete choice experiments (DCE)
• Other examples

Introduction

The essence of the experiment is that the researcher aims to control all the relevant variables in the research environment. Selected variables related to the subjects or objects of the research are manipulated while others are held constant and the effects on subjects/objects are then measured. The experimental approach is closely associated with the positivist paradigm and is consistent with the classic scientific model of testing hypotheses and seeking to establish cause-and-effect relationships and it is also the methodology that seeks to capture the principles of causality (see Chapter 2).

Use of the experimental method is generally thought of as rare in arts/events research, but when consideration is given to the full range of experimental and quasi-experimental methods available, and the diversity of disciplinary contributions to the field, the body of experimental research is found to be quite substantial. The second part of the chapter therefore examines the use of experimental methods in a range of arts/events research contexts.

This chapter is located in Part 2 of the book, which is concerned with data collection, while data analysis is addressed in Part 3. In the case of experimental methods, however, there is no corresponding separate analysis chapter in Part 3. This is because, in experimental methods in the arts/events context, data are often collected via questionnaire, so a major part of the methodology is covered in Chapters 10 and 16. Furthermore, for projects in which data are gathered by means of observation, the analysis of observations from subjects/cases is analogous to analysis of answers to questions (see Chapter 8), so the data file from an experimental study can be analysed in the same way as the data file from a questionnaire survey.

The first part of the chapter explores, in turn, the principles of experimental research, the issue of validity and quasi-experimental designs.

Principles of experimental research

Components

The essence of the experiment is that, ideally, the researcher controls all the relevant variables in the research environment. Selected variables are manipulated while others are held constant and the effects on subjects are then measured. In the terminology of experimental study the researcher is concerned with a dependent variable, an independent or treatment variable, a treatment group and a control group. There may be one or more of each of these components in any one study.

- *Dependent variable:* The dependent variable is a measurable outcome of the experiment. For example, participation in an arts/event activity and level of satisfaction with a service could be dependent variables.

- *Independent variable:* The independent variable or *treatment variable* represents a quality or characteristic that is varied or manipulated during the experiment. Some examples of independent variables are provision of information/education or incentives, a changed design or layout of an exhibit, or a change in marketing activity. The independent or treatment variable is manipulated during the experiment to examine its effect on the dependent variable.

- *Treatment or experimental group:* The group of participants or subjects exposed to the treatment is referred to as the treatment or experimental group.

- *Control group:* In order to take account of the possible effects of other environmental variables on the outcome of the experiment, the researcher often uses a control group that is not subject to the treatment. The attributes of the control group may be matched with the attributes of the experimental or treatment group so that the two groups are as similar as possible or subjects may be randomly assigned to the two groups.

The classic experimental design

The classic or true design for experimental research – the pre-test/post-test control group design – is summarised in Figure 11.1 and involves six steps:

1. *Selection of subjects* from a population (sampling).
2. *Random allocation* of subjects to two groups: R_t, the treatment group, and R_c, the control group.

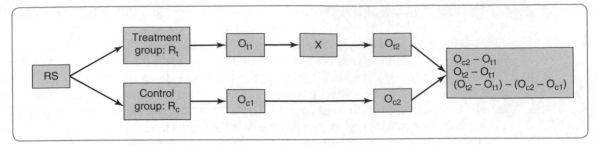

Figure 11.1 Classic experimental design

3. *Pre-test observation*: Subjects in both groups are measured with respect to the dependent variable (O_{t1} and O_{c1}).

4. *Experimental treatment*, X, is applied to the treatment group, but not to the control group.

5. *Post-test observation*: Subjects in both groups are measured again with respect to the dependent variable (O_{t2} and O_{c2}).

6. *Examination of effects*: For the experimental treatment to be judged positive:
   - there should be no significant difference between O_{t1} and O_{c1};
   - there should be a significant difference between ($O_{t2} - O_{t1}$) and ($O_{c2} - O_{c1}$).

In step 6 the calculations are typically based on mean scores for each measurement for each group. The concept of significant difference is discussed in Chapter 17.

Validity

The aim of the classic design is to ensure, as far as possible, the *validity* of the research findings. Validity refers to the extent to which the information collected in a research study truly reflects the phenomenon being studied. There is generally a trade-off to be made between research validity and practicality and cost. While perfection is impossible, researchers should be aware of *threats to validity* and take these into account in the design of the experiment.

Threats to validity

Threats to the validity of experimental research fall into two main groups: *internal*, in which design components are compromised, and *external*, which relate to the application of the findings to the population to which the results are intended to apply. Some of these threats are summarised in Figure 11.2.

In Figure 11.2, reference is made to the 'Hawthorne effect', in which being part of a study affects people's behaviour. This was demonstrated many years ago in a study in the Hawthorne Plant of the Western Electric Company in the USA, which investigated the relationship between productivity and the brightness of lighting in the factory. As expected, productivity increased as illumination was increased. However, productivity also rose as brightness was decreased. It was concluded that it was the attention the workers were receiving as a result of the study rather than the lighting level itself that was affecting production.

Internal validity	Aspects of the experimental design that raise doubts as to whether change in dependent variable can be attributed entirely to the independent variable/ treatment.
Maturation	Change occurs in study subject during the study period – e.g. fatigue.
History	Change in the external environment affects the study – e.g. weather conditions.
Testing	The test/observation process itself may affect subjects – e.g. asking questions raises awareness of, and therefore changes, behaviour.
Instrumentation	Inconsistency or unreliability in the measuring instruments or observation procedures during a study – e.g. change in the way a questionnaire is designed.
Selection bias	Treatment group and control group have significantly different characteristics – e.g. one group markedly older than the other.
Mortality	Attrition of subjects from a study – likely to happen if treatment process is spread over a long period of time.
External validity	Extent to which results may be generalised beyond the study subjects and setting.
Reactive effects of testing	Tests/observation may sensitise subjects and affect behaviour responses, which would not happen in 'real life' – e.g. subjects wish to impress the researchers.
Effects of selection	Subjects may not be representative of wider population – e.g. when experiments conducted with tertiary students or city-centre dwellers. The very fact of involvement with a study may cause subjects to behave differently from people generally – the 'Hawthorne effect'.

Figure 11.2 Threats to validity of experiments

Field experiments versus laboratory experiments

There is a trade-off between field experiments (experiments in naturalistic settings) and laboratory experiments in relation to external and internal validity. In the case of social or psychological arts/event research, the equivalent of a 'laboratory' is often an office, meeting room or classroom where data are elicited from subjects. In general, field experiments undertaken in typical arts/event settings have greater external validity than laboratory-based experiments, but experimentation involves the researcher intervening to change something and if the subjects of the research are aware of this, there is an immediate loss of 'naturalness' and the subjects may therefore not behave in a normal way. Furthermore, there is always a chance of other uncontrollable, and unmeasured, external factors intervening to affect behaviour. Laboratory-based experiments, meanwhile, tend to have greater internal reliability than field experiments because the researcher has more control over extraneous variables in a laboratory.

The decision on 'laboratory' or naturalistic experimentation should be made only after careful consideration of the threats to internal and external validity described above, and consideration of the objectives of the research. The 'obvious' approach may not in fact be ideal. For example, it might seem obvious that it would be appropriate to gather data from arts/events participants at an arts facility or event, but if the interest is in general patterns of cultural behaviour, it might be best to avoid the possibility of subjects being over-influenced by any immediate facility or environmental experience.

Quasi-experimental designs

Types of quasi-experimental design

In a natural science experiment, the subjects will be identical specimens or samples of organic or inorganic matter, or laboratory animals that are as near as possible identical, and are treated identically except for the experimental treatment. This is not possible in the sorts of

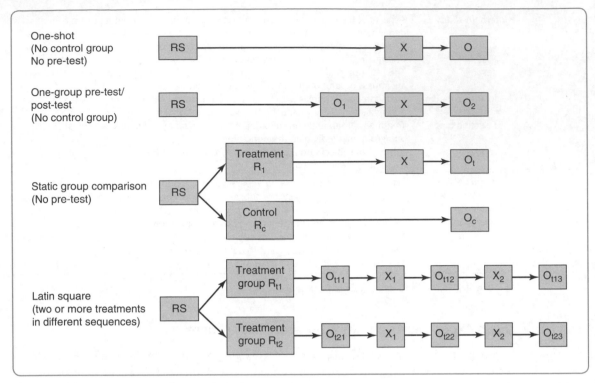

Figure 11.3 Quasi-experimental research designs

social or organisational contexts with which arts/events research is involved. In such contexts, therefore, compromises must be made with the classic model and *quasi-experimental* designs must be devised.

Four common quasi-experimental designs are shown in Figure 11.3. Some designs simplify the classic model, for example by dispensing with a control group or the pre-test stage, while others complicate it, for example by adding treatments. They are often used where time, cost and practicality are important considerations, but there is sometimes a loss of validity associated with each design. The four designs are:

- the one-shot design;
- the one group pre-test/post-test design;
- the static group design;
- the Latin square.

Experiments and projects

There is a tendency in some references to the experimental method to equate 'experiment' with 'research project'. But typically a research project will comprise a series of experiments. In order to conduct an individual experiment it is necessary to define the relevant dependent and independent/treatment variables. However, a project can comprise a number of experiments and the programme of experiments may evolve during the course of the project. Imagine a medical scientist searching for a drug to treat a virus: a number of possibilities may be explored before a successful treatment is discovered. This may take a number of experiments, even a number of projects. Thus, an experimental project may be much more exploratory, even inductive, than the formal hypothetical–deductive model of the single experiment.

Experimental methods in arts/event research

Observation/measurement

As noted above, *observation* is the term often used in the natural sciences to refer to the act of *measurement*. Figure 7.2 lists a number of measures or indicators of engagement with the arts/events which come into play in the examples of experimental research discussed below.

Types of experiment in the arts/events context

Experiments involve research in a controlled environment in which the researcher is able to vary the conditions of the environment for research purposes. Opportunities for this are limited in arts/event contexts, but some are listed in Figure 11.4 and discussed in turn below.

Policy/management experimental projects

Conducting experiments, often called *pilot projects*, *pilot programmes* or *trials*, is popular in the government sector, partly for the overt reason that it is wise to test the effectiveness of policies on a small scale before implementing them on a wide scale, but also because, to be somewhat cynical, they are much cheaper than a full-scale policy roll-out and can delay having to make a decision on such a roll-out. Invariably such projects include an evaluation component, although this is not always adequately resourced or rigorously conducted.

In some cases the declared policy-related experimentation is to increase levels of participation in arts/events activities. However, invariably the rationale behind the policy to boost participation is related to other policy areas, notably economic development, and in Britain, under the New Labour government (1997–2010), 'social inclusion' – the notion that all groups should enjoy the rights of citizenship, including engagement with social and cultural activity. In these cases, the criteria for the success of a project are not just participation itself but the resultant hoped-for improvements in the economy or social inclusion of the participants. The experimental model is therefore as shown in Figure 11.5. Two forms of measurements/observations are made, relating to *participation* and *social policy* criteria, and the 'control' is often, in effect, the community at large, for example the general level of arts/events participation in the whole population.

Policy/management pilot/trial projects	Innovations in policy or management practice are tested by experimental or pilot projects and outcomes evaluated using a variety of methods.
Changing layout/design of exhibits	Exhibitors can experiment with various aspects of exhibitions, including physical layout, signage and lighting, and monitor visitor responses.
Experimenting with research methods	Testing of innovative or alternative research methods or techniques, usually in the same setting, with the same subjects or split samples.
Discrete choice experiments (DCE)	Consumption or activity choice processes are studied by presenting subjects with hypothetical product descriptions with differing combinations of features and asking them to express their preferences.
Other examples	Action research; qualitative methods; physical models.

Figure 11.4 Types and contexts of experiments in arts/events research

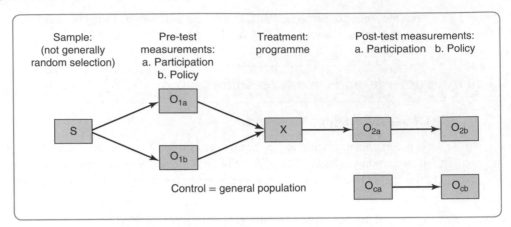

Figure 11.5 Experimental model of policy projects

The research aspect of these projects is experimental, but in terms of the types of research discussed in Chapter 1, it can be seen as *evaluative*. The aim of the research is to assess the extent to which the projects have achieved the policy objectives set for them. This takes us into the complex realm of the interface between research and policy/management, which it is not possible to explore in detail here but for which additional sources are indicated in the Resources section. This type of project can also be linked with the phenomenon of cultural indicators (see Chapter 7), which can be used to evaluate policy outcomes at governmental level or the performance of individual departments or facilities. Some of the same issues – what to measure, how to measure it, the validity of the measures available and how much weight to give to various measures – arise, but on a different scale.

A number of reviews of this type of quasi-experimental project have been undertaken. One of these, *Use or Ornament? The Social Impact of Participation in the Arts,* by François Matarasso (1997) of the UK think tank Comedia, should be mentioned because of its effect on the debate on the impact of the arts in the UK. It will not be discussed in detail here, however, for a number of reasons. The report refers to 60 diverse arts-based projects which were 'looked at closely' and 30 others 'involved more peripherally'; just 17 are described individually, eight in a single paragraph and nine in a single sentence. So it is not possible to examine individual projects and their goals, methods and outcomes. However, the report is of general interest from a methodological point of view because, some years after its publication, it attracted methodological criticism (Belfiore, 2002; Merli, 2002). Matarasso's (2003) subsequent vigorous defence of the report is of interest because he rejects the rigour of the traditional scientific method in favour of an approach 'informed by practice' (see Chapter 1).

A second UK review document, *Count Me In: The Dimensions of Social Inclusion through Culture and Sport* (Centre for Leisure and Sport Research, 2002), is also notable because it was specifically commissioned by the Department for Culture, Media & Sport to assess the extent to which arts- and sport-based projects – most of which could be seen as experimental in nature – could play a part in implementing the New Labour government's overall policy of social inclusion. The review includes only 14 projects (10 arts/culture-based), so more information is given on individual projects, but still only one or two pages. Again, the projects are evaluated collectively, not individually, and it is clear that individual projects are not generally subject to the sort of rigorous evaluation generally expected in an evidence-based policy regime. This is similar to the situation in the sport domain where most of the projects reviewed by Coalter (2007) and Collins (2003) did not have the resources, or often the motivation, to engage in any sort of systematic evaluation, so their contribution to the move towards evidence-based policy was generally limited.

Part of the social inclusion agenda includes consideration of well-being, including health. This may operate in aiding in the relief of stress in everyday life and also in clinical and care settings, for example with visual and aural arts aiding recovery from illness and being used therapeutically for rehabilitation and in care of dementia patients (Health Development Agency, 2000). Some have expressed doubt that such programmes can be evaluated with the same rigour as clinical programmes (e.g. Baum, 2001) and a report on 16 case studies of art/ health projects in the UK stated:

> The majority of projects do not carry out evaluation, as they seldom have the money, time or inclination to do so. Evaluation according to health criteria is infrequent. Furthermore, there is a fear of evaluation – that it may be reductionist, and may set uncomfortable precedents in justifying art in terms of social usefulness. Inevitably, respondents suspect that evaluation will be linked to funding.
>
> (Health Development Agency, 2000: 26)

However, it has been argued that if proponents are seeking funding from the medical budget, then there is little choice but to adopt rigorous medical evaluation practices (Hamilton *et al.*, 2003).

Many special events can also be seen as partly experimental in a policy sense. This certainly applies to new events which the organisers hope will be repeated on an annual basis. Host communities, typically in the form of a local, state/provincial or national government, will invariably require some sort of evaluation before agreeing to continue to provide financial support into the future, and this requirement can be repeated in subsequent years. Even one-off events, such as being designated the European Cultural Capital for a year, may be seen by the host city as a starting point for a future programme of cultural events, so that evaluation is required (e.g. see Hitters, 2000). One of the features of the professionalisation of event management, from the 1980s onwards, has been the commitment to evaluation. Typically, such evaluative research focuses on the impact on, and economic benefits generated for, the host community (Jago and Dwyer, 2006). In experimental terms, therefore, the 'subjects' are the population and businesses of the host community and the 'treatment' is the holding of the event – although, for large-scale events, the treatment period may last during several years of preparations, including the construction of major infrastructure. This idea is reflected in the International Olympic Committee's *Olympic Games Impact* (OGI) system, which requires cities hosting the Games to gather data on 150 indicators for an eleven-year period from two years before the announcement of the winning bid to two years after the hosting of the Games (Toohey and Veal, 2007: 74–75), giving a series of seven pre-test observations and two post-test observations. This requirement was introduced for the Beijing 2008 Games, but no host city has yet published a complete report, although some interim reports have been compiled for London 2012 (University of East London, 2013).

Changing layout/design of exhibits

In Case study 8.1 we saw an example of research demonstrating the effects of layout on the pattern of visitors' viewing of exhibits. In this example, visitors who moved in an anti-clockwise direction around a museum exhibition were immediately exposed to interactive displays and the attention they then paid to the museum exhibits overall was shown to be greater than that of visitors who went in a clockwise direction and encountered the interactive displays at the end of their visit. In experimental terms this study can be seen as the *pre-test observation* only. The measure used is 'volume of activity' (item 1C in Figure 7.2), but it should be noted that the measure relates not to the number of visitors to the museum but to the proportion who actually stop to view individual exhibits, so it has an element of the intensity measure (item 1F). If the experiment were to be continued to the *treatment* stage this would involve changing the layout/signage of the exhibition. The *post-test observation* would then be to repeat the observation counts of the original study. A positive result would be indicated by an overall increase in the proportion of visitors viewing each exhibit.

Bitgood (2006) considers the question of visitor circulation more broadly, suggesting that people's circulation patterns may be dictated by a tendency to minimise effort – for example, being reluctant to double back or to cross over from one side of a room or pathway to another. Most of the research on this topic seems to involve passive observation, as reported in Case study 8.1, but two involving active 'treatment' are described in Case study 11.1.

CASE STUDY 11.1

Exhibit layout and labels

A Exhibit layout

Falk (1993) reported an example of an experimental project in the National Museum of Natural History (USA) involving a special exhibit with about a dozen displays and two video presentations. In the *pre-test observation* visitor behaviour was first observed with the exhibit arranged in a 'structured' layout, with an entrance area with small 'taster' exhibits and video displays, followed by a set route through the exhibits (rather like progressing through an IKEA store). After a period, the exhibit was reconfigured into an 'unstructured' layout (the *treatment*), in which there was no set route and visitors were able to roam freely among the exhibits.

For each layout, observers visually tracked about 150 visitors from point of entry to exit, recording time spent in the exhibit area and displays viewed (*post-test observation*). It was found that average time spent in the exhibit was about the same for the two layouts, but that in the formal layout a large proportion did not venture beyond the initial entrance area, so that the average number of displays viewed was substantially less than in the informal layout. Furthermore, in the informal layout there was less viewing of the videos.

Since the exhibit had an educational function to do with eco-systems, a sample of visitors was interviewed to assess their understanding of the 'message' and it was found that, while there were some differences between the two groups, it was not substantial. Nevertheless, Falk concludes that layout does have a significant effect on visitor behaviour.

B Exhibit labels

Hirschi and Screven (1988) describe an experimental project conducted in the Milwaukee Public Museum. The aim was to see whether questions adjacent to exhibit labels would increase the amount of attention visitors paid to the labels. Five exhibits were selected for the study. In the *pre-test* observation, 20 randomly selected family groups were unobtrusively tracked and the times taken viewing the exhibits and reading the labels were recorded. The *treatment* was the attachment to each exhibit of a card containing a question, which could be answered from the information on the label (e.g. 'Do polar bears hibernate?'). The *post-test* observation repeated the pre-test procedure, tracking another 20 family groups. The time spent reading the labels rose dramatically, from less than 10 seconds in the pre-test, when many groups failed to read the labels at all, to almost 100 seconds. The non-reading time spent viewing exhibits also increased, from 122 seconds to 180 seconds.

▮ Experimenting with research methods

Experiments can also be undertaken on alternative research methods to see which methods work best. The experimental quality of the studies lies in going beyond what would be normal practice by using multiple methods, variations on methods or new methods in order to discover the effects of different research practices. Examples are presented in Case study 11.2.

CASE STUDY 11.2

Experimenting with research methods

A Mail survey monetary incentives

James and Bolstein (1990) conducted an experiment to test whether incentives to encourage response in mail surveys worked at all and, if so, whether the size of the incentive was a relevant factor. In a survey of cable television subscribers, the sample was divided into five groups: a control group with no incentive and four groups with cash incentives of $0.25, $0.50, $1 and $2 respectively (these sums would be about one-third higher at today's prices). Three follow-up reminders were sent and the effect on the response rate was as shown in Figure 11.6 (the $0.25 group was similar to the $0.50 group and is omitted from this figure).

It can be seen that the $0.50 group performed slightly worse than the control group, while both the $1 and $2 groups performed significantly better.

B Visitor circulation

Typically, visitor circulation patterns in cultural venues are monitored by unobtrusive observation of individual visitors, or small groups, as discussed above, or, more recently, by GPS devices.

Nurse Rainbolt *et al.* (2012) present a study that explores the possibility of museum visitors reporting on their own circulation patterns on a map. The core of the project involved two samples of visitors. In one sample, groups of visitors were asked, as they entered the building, to fill in their route on a blank map/plan of the museum and its rooms and main exhibits during their visit and return the map on exit. A second sample represented the conventional approach, with groups not completing a map but being observed unobtrusively by a researcher who recorded a map of their routes.

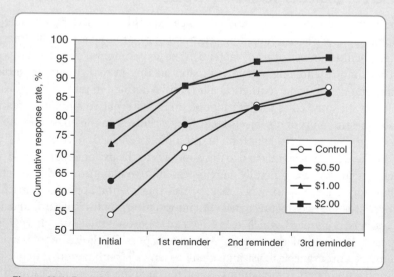

Figure 11.6 Experimenting with mail survey incentives

Source: Graphic created from James and Bolstein (1990: Table 1).

Case study 11.2 (*continued*)

The maps were analysed in terms of 'extensive-ness' (the amount of the museum covered) and detail (the amount of information about the route taken – direction, stopping points, etc.). It was found that the differences between the two sets of maps were not significant, indicating that visitors can accurately record their own routes. This is a much cheaper option than individual observation and/or would enable a much larger sample of users to be studied. However, it was found that self-mapping seemed to result in visitors spending more time in the museum, which may bias the research findings, but could be seen as a positive outcome in its own right.

C Assessing event-visitor expenditure

Irwin *et al.* (1996) compared two methods of collecting data from event visitors on their expenditure allocation patterns – a key data item in economic impact studies. Most studies ask people to estimate their allocations of expenditure to categories such as travel, accommodation, entry fees, food and souvenirs, by means of a questionnaire survey conducted during the event. This involves an element of estimation of expenditures not yet incurred at the time of completing the questionnaire, which is a possible source of error. The

researchers therefore decided to experiment with a real-time diary approach.

The research was conducted at two US National Collegiate Athletic Association championship events. From pre-booking data, one sample of attendees for each event was mailed diary forms and asked to keep a record of expenditures during the event and mail the completed forms back to the researchers after the event. Another sample was selected on-site during the event and asked to complete a questionnaire on estimated total expenditure patterns.

At both sites it was found that the on-site survey respondent estimated average expenditure was between 11 per cent and 23 per cent less than the diary-based estimates. The authors argue that the diary-based method is likely to be more accurate and therefore suggest that it should be used where possible, even though it is more costly to administer. In this case, the experiment concerns the measurement process rather than the substantive experiences or behaviour of the subjects, so the *treatment* is the administering of the measurement or observation method. In terms of the types of quasi-experimental design presented in Figure 11.3, therefore, the process comes close to the 'statics group comparison' model, with the conventional on-site questionnaire method being the control.

Discrete choice experiments (DCEs)

The aim of *stated choice* or *discrete choice* experiments (DCEs), or *conjoint analysis*, is to explore people's decision-making processes in regard to choice of alternative products, services, facilities or activities (Chapter 5). The 'experimental' feature of this approach is that, rather than researching people's decision making in real situations, subjects are asked to make choices among hypothetical alternatives defined in terms of various combinations of features. In some cases the information on the alternative bundles of features is presented via a questionnaire and subjects record their choices on the questionnaire, so the approach could be seen as a particular form of questionnaire-based survey.

Bekkers (2010) has referred to this approach as the use of *scenarios*, and points out that the fact that surveys are generally more representative in nature, and have larger samples than laboratory-based experiments, makes this experimental approach particularly valuable. In other cases subjects are presented with information on physical cards and asked to sort them in order of preference, which is, in effect, an experimental approach. Digital media may also be used. In most situations, the total number of possible choice bundles would be large and it would be unreasonable to ask individuals to rank all combinations, but one person could rank a limited number of combinations and all the combinations could be cycled through a sample of respondents and a mathematical procedure used to combine the results. The mathematics is therefore a key aspect of the method, but one which we are not able to explore here.

Two examples of DCEs in the arts/events field are summarised in Case study 11.3.

CASE STUDY 11.3

Discrete choice experiments: examples

A Cultural events

In an early example of a discrete choice experiment, but using the term *conjoint analysis*, Cosper and Kinsley (1984) present an analysis of preferences for different types of cultural festival, based on a survey of 6,000 people aged 15 years and above, conducted in 1978. Cultural events were classified in terms of four attributes – content, medium, quality and price – each with four possible values/categories, as shown in Figure 11.7; theoretically, this gives a total of 256 (4 × 4 × 4 × 4) combinations of attributes and values/categories.

In this study each respondent was presented with a selection of eight cards, each containing one of the combinations, and asked to rank them in order of preference. The analysis produced weights reflecting the respondents' mean preferences for the various attributes/values/categories, as shown in the preference columns in Figure 11.7. These weights are additive and can be used to assess the preference for any combinations of attribute and value/category. Thus, for example, a sporting event (0.2), shown on TV (0.34), with international/professional performers (0.14) and free of charge (0.03), would have a score of 0.71.

B Identifying attributes of choice in repeat museum visitation

Discrete choice experiments can be used to understand what matters to visitors in their decision making to visit a museum. One such study examined two major Sydney museums which were experiencing declining frequency of visitation with a view to providing guidance on how to improve repeat visitation levels (Burton *et al.*, 2009). Initial qualitative interviews with 40 museum visitors established the range of features of museum offerings that people would be likely to take into consideration when deciding on a visit. Analysis of the interview transcripts resulted in the inclusion in the study of five groups of features, covering opening hours, packages with other venues/attractions, packages related to transport/parking, incentives for frequent attendance and the level of standard entry fees. Each of these features could involve a number of settings. The aim of the study was to discover which combinations of feature settings would appeal most to visitors to each museum.

Museum visitors were invited to take part in an online survey which included eight scenarios, each consisting of two options with contrasting bundles of features. Respondents were asked to consider the benefits of each scenario and to reflect on which features mattered most overall to each respondent. An example of part of one of the scenarios is presented in Figure 11.8. A multinomial logit model was used to analyse the data to produce indicators of the relative importance in decision making of the sorts of factors listed (the technical details of such models are not considered in this book, but the type of model is discussed briefly in Chapter 17). It should be noted that this experiment did not model the whole decision-making process, since the intrinsic features of the museums, as compared with other leisure options, were not included, just those factors which museums could change in the short term and would be likely to influence repeat visitation.

Content category	Pref.	Medium category	Pref.	Quality category	Pref.	Price category	Pref.
Sports	0.20	Shown on TV	0.34	International/prof.	0.14	Free	0.03
Drama	0.19	Live	0.20	National/prof.	0.06	$3	−0.23
Classical music	−0.47	Recorded, audio	−0.25	Provincial/amateur	−0.14	$7	0.13
Popular music	0.08	On radio	−0.28	Local/amateur	−0.58	$5	0.06

Pref. = preference weights derived from the analysis.

Figure 11.7 Cultural events: attributes, values and preferences

Source: Summarised from Cosper and Kinsley (1984: 229).

Case study 11.3 (*continued*)

Attribute (extract)	Option A	Option B
Opening hours		
Summer	9.30 am – 7 pm	9.30 am – 6 pm
Winter	10 am – 6 pm	10 am – 5 pm
Packages with attractions		
Combined ticket to both museums	$40 per person	$40 per person
Combined ticket to museum + Sydney Aquarium	$50 per person	$40 per person
Packages with transport		
Combined museum + monorail ticket	$25 per person	$35 per person
Combined museum +2 hours' parking	$30 per person	–
Incentives		
More visits = reduced ticket price	–10% second visit	30% off all repeat visits
	–25% thereafter	
... Free membership of museum after:	2 visits in year	4 visits in year
Standard entry fee	Single adult: $20	Single adult: $10
	Children/concession: $10	Children/concession: $6
	Family $45	Family $25

Questions:

1. The museum can offer only one option at a time: which do you prefer?

   Option A _____   Option B _____   Neither _____

2. Suppose the museum could offer Option A only: would you be more likely to:

   Visit more often?
   Visit less often?
   Visit as you do now?

Figure 11.8 Example of museum choice scenario

Other examples of quasi-experimental research

Action research

Action research is research committed to social change and so can be said to have some features of an experimental design (see Chapter 5). The approach is depicted in Figure 5.5 as comprising four steps:

- steps 1 and 2, which identify and assess a social problem, can be seen as the pre-test observation, with selection of a treatment group implied;
- step 3, the campaign for and achievement of action, is the treatment;
- step 4, researching the results of the action, is the post-test observation.

One of the features of the experimental method is that the researcher controls the experimental process. In action research the researchers do not necessarily control the process but the philosophy is that they are involved with, and therefore seek to have an influence on, the process.

Qualitative methods

Much qualitative research is presented as distinct from the classic, positivist scientific experimental method. Paradoxically, however, some qualitative approaches, notably those in which the researcher engages actively with the subjects – such as some participant observation and non-standardised interviewing – have features of the experimental method. The researcher's involvement can be seen as paralleling the 'treatment' in an experiment, although, of course, it is not in a controlled environment.

Physical models

In a study concerned with public reactions to reuse of heritage buildings, Black (1990) arranged for 1:25 models to be made of four heritage buildings and photographed them in three situations: 'as is now'; with a 'small change'; and with 'large change' (indicating adaptation for commercial use as cafes/restaurants). A group of study participants were asked to scale the photographs on a range of features and the results were compared with a theoretical classification based on a limited number of physical characteristics. This type of research might now be conducted using computer graphics.

Screven (1990) considers the role of evaluative research at various stages in the development of an exhibition:

- planning stage: front-end evaluation – exploring existing visitors' views and reactions to ideas;
- design stage: formative evaluation – involvement of potential visitors in evaluating design options;
- construction/installation: no research;
- occupancy: summative evaluation – visitor levels, evaluation;
- remedial: remedial evaluation – possibly prompted by summative evaluation, research that leads to changes to the exhibit over time.

The relevant stage from an experimental perspective is the design stage. In discussing the role of research with the public, the role of 'mock-ups' of the exhibits is discussed. The preparation and evaluation of mock-ups can be seen as quasi-experimental.

Summary

Experimental methods are closely associated with the positivist paradigm and are consistent with the classic 'scientific' model of testing hypotheses and establishing cause-and-effect relationships. The essence of the experiment is that the researcher ideally controls all the relevant variables in the experiment. Selected variables are manipulated, while others are held constant and the effects on subjects are measured. Components of the experiment are the treatment or experimental group, the control group, the dependent variable and the independent or treatment variable. The independent or treatment variable is manipulated during the experiment to examine its effect on the dependent variable.

Typically, variables are measured before the treatment (pre-test) and after the treatment (post-test). Quasi-experimental designs vary this model by, for example, omitting a control group, omitting the pre-test or including more than one treatment group or treatment. Although experimental methods are usually associated with natural science and laboratories, it is possible to conduct some experiments in arts/events contexts. The main types of example discussed in the chapter are policy/management pilot/trial projects, changing layout/design of exhibits, experimenting with research methods and discrete choice experiments (DCE).

TEST QUESTIONS

1. What are the defining characteristics of the experimental method?
2. Outline two examples of quasi-experimental models and indicate how they deviate from the classic experimental model.
3. Give three examples of contexts where experimental methods have been used in arts/ events research.

EXERCISES

1. Outline a true experimental research design to test the hypothesis that engagement with the arts is good for people's health.
2. How could a cultural/events organisation set up an experiment to test the effectiveness of two forms of advertising? What elements of the 'classic' experimental design would need to be sacrificed? What type of quasi-experiment would this be?

Resources

Websites

Visitor Studies Association: www.visitorstudies.org/

Publications

- The classic work on experimental design for research is Campbell and Stanley (1972).
- Exhibition planning/design, testing mock-ups: Screven (1990).
- Inclusion/exclusion: Centre for Leisure and Sport Research (2002), Health Development Agency (2000), Stickley and Duncan (2007); sport: Collins (2003).
- Discrete choice experiments/stated choice method:
  - overview: Crouch and Louviere (2001), Louviere *et al.* (2000)
  - movie choice: Neelamegham and Jain (1999)
  - art gallery choice: Caldwell and Coshall (2003)
  - art gallery layouts: Kinghorn and Willis (2007)
  - festivals: Cosper and Kinsley (1984)
  - museums: Burton *et al.* 2009
  - music: Favaro and Frateschi (2007)
  - theatre productions: Grisolia and Willis (2011), Willis and Snowball (2009)
- Policy/management-related experiments: museum exhibits: Brown (2011); art education: Eisner (1998).
- Research on alternative research methods: Gitelson and Drogin (1992), Hammitt and McDonald (1982).

References

Baum, M. (2001) Evidence-based art? *Journal of the Royal Society of Medicine,* 94(3), 306–307.

Bekkers, R. (2010) Who gives what when? A scenario study of intentions to give time and money. *Social Science Research,* 39(4), 369–381.

Belfiore, E. (2002) Art as a means of alleviating social exclusion: does it really work? A critique of instrumental cultural policies and social impact studies in the UK. *International Journal of Cultural Policy,* 8(1), 91–106.

Bitgood, S. (2006) An analysis of visitor circulation: movement patterns and the general value principle. *Curator,* 49(4), 463–475.

Black, N. (1990) A model and methodology to assess changes to heritage buildings. *Journal of Tourism Studies,* 19(1), 15–23.

Brown, P. (2011) Us and them. Who benefits from experimental exhibition making? *Museum Management and Curatorship,* 26(2), 129–148.

Burton, C., Louviere, J. and Young, L. (2009) Retaining the visitor, enhancing the experience: identifying attributes of choice in repeat museum visitation. *International Journal of Nonprofit and Voluntary Sector Marketing,* 14(1), 21–34.

Caldwell, N. and Coshall, J. (2003) Tourists' preference structures for London's Tate Modern gallery: the implications for strategic marketing. *Journal of Travel and Tourism Marketing,* 14(2), 23–45.

Campbell, D. T. and Stanley, J. C. (1972) *Experimental and Quasi-Experimental Designs for Research.* Chicago, IL: Rand McNally.

Centre for Leisure & Sport Research (2002) *Count Me In: The Dimensions of Social Inclusion through Culture and Sport.* Report to the Department for Culture, Media and Sport, Leeds: Centre for Leisure and Sport Research, Leeds Metropolitan University, available at: www.leedsmet.ac.uk/ces/lssold/research/countmein.pdf

Coalter, F. (2007) *A Wider Social Role for Sport: Who's Keeping the Score?* London: Routledge.

Collins, M. F. (2003) *Sport and Social Exclusion.* London: Routledge.

Cosper, R. and Kinsley, B. L. (1984) An application of conjoint analysis to leisure research: cultural preferences in Canada. *Journal of Leisure Research,* 16(3), 224–233.

Crouch, G. I. and Louviere, J. J. (2001) A review of choice modelling research in tourism, hospitality and leisure. In J. A. Mazanec, G. I. Crouch, J. R. B. Ritchie and A. G. Woodside (eds), *Consumer Psychology of Tourism, Hospitality and Leisure, Vol. 2.* Wallingford: CABI Publishing, pp. 67–86.

Eisner, E. W. (1998) Does experience in the arts boost academic achievement? *Art Education,* 51(1), 7–15.

Falk, J. H. (1993) Assessing the impact of exhibit arrangement on visitor behavior and learning. *Curator,* 36(2), 133–146.

Favaro, D. and Frateschi, C. (2007) A discrete choice model of consumption of cultural goods: the case of music. *Journal of Cultural Economics,* 31(2), 205–234.

Gitelson, R. J. and Drogin, E. B. (1992) An experiment on the efficacy of a certified final mailing. *Journal of Leisure Research,* 24(1), 72–78.

Grisolia, J. M. and Willis, K. G. (2011) An evening at the theatre: using choice experiments to model preferences for theatres and theatrical productions. *Applied Economics,* 43(27), 3987–3998.

Hamilton, C., Hinks, S. and Petticrew, M. (2003) Arts for health: still searching for the Holy Grail. *Journal of Epidemiology and Community Health,* 57(6), 401–402.

Hammitt, W. E. and McDonald, C. D. (1982) Response bias and the need for extensive mail questionnaire follow-ups among selected recreation samples. *Journal of Leisure Research,* 14(3), 207–216.

Health Development Agency (2000) *Art for Health: A Review of Good Practice in Community-Based Arts Projects and Initiatives Which Impact on Health and Wellbeing.* London: HDA.

Hirschi, K. D. and Screven, C. G. (1988) Effects of questions on visitor reading behavior. *ILVS Review,* 1(1), 50–61.

Hitters, E. (2000) The social and political construction of a European Cultural Capital: Rotterdam 2001. *International Journal of Cultural Policy*, 6(2), 183–199.

Irwin, R. L., Wang, P. and Sutton, W. A. (1996) Comparative analysis of diaries and projected spending to assess patron expenditure behavior at short-term sporting events. *Festival Management and Event Tourism*, 4(1), 29–37.

Jago, L. and Dwyer, L. (2006) *Economic Evaluation of Special Events: A Practitioner's Guide*. Gold Coast, Australia: Sustainable Tourism Cooperative Research Centre, available at www.crctourism.com.au

James, J. M. and Bolstein, R. (1990) The effect of monetary incentives and follow-up mailings on the response rate and response quality in mail surveys. *Public Opinion Quarterly*, 54(3), 346–361.

Kinghorn, N. and Willis, K. (2007) Estimating visitor preferences for different art gallery layouts using a choice experiment. *Museum Management and Curatorship*, 22(1), 43–58.

Louviere, J. J., Hensher, D. A. and Swait, J. D. (2000) *Stated Choice Methods: Analysis and Applications*. Cambridge: Cambridge University Press.

Matarasso, F. (1997) *Use or Ornament? The Social Impact of Participation in the Arts*. London: Comedia.

Matarasso, F. (2003) Smoke and mirrors: a response to Paola Merli's 'Evaluating the social impact of participation in arts activities'. *International Journal of Cultural Policy*, 9(3), 337–346.

Merli, P. (2002) Evaluating the social impact of participation in arts activities: a critical review of François Matarasso's *Use or Ornament? International Journal of Cultural Policy*, 8(1), 107–118.

Neelamegham, R. and Jain, D. (1999) Consumer choice process for experience goods: an econometric model and analysis. *Journal of Marketing Research*, 36(3), 373–386.

Nurse Rainbolt, G., Benfield, J. A. and Loomis, R. J. (2012) Visitor self-report behavior mapping as a tool for recording exhibition circulation. *Visitor Studies*, 15(2), 203–216.

Screven, C. G. (1990) Uses of evaluation before, during and after exhibit design. *ILVS Review*, 1(2), 36–66.

Stickley, T. and Duncan, K. (2007) Art in Mind: implementation of a community arts initiative to promote mental health. *Journal of Public Mental Health*, 6(4), 24–32.

Toohey, K. and Veal, A. J. (2007) *The Olympic Games: A Social Science Perspective*. Wallingford: CABI.

University of East London (2013) *Olympic Games Impact Study: London 2012: Games-time Report*. London: Centre for Geo-Information Studies, University of East London.

Willis, K. G. and Snowball, J. D. (2009) Investigating how the attributes of live theatre productions influence consumption choices using conjoint analysis: the example of the National Arts Festival, South Africa. *Journal of Cultural Economics*, 33(2), 167–183.

Chapter 12

The case study method

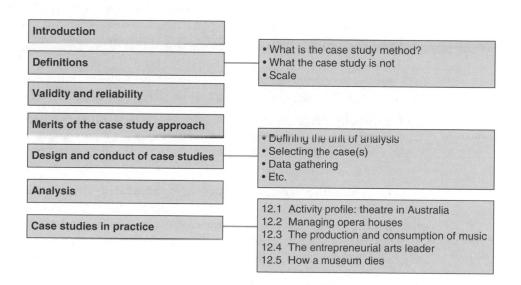

Introduction

Definitions
- What is the case study method?
- What the case study is not
- Scale

Validity and reliability

Merits of the case study approach

Design and conduct of case studies
- Defining the unit of analysis
- Selecting the case(s)
- Data gathering
- Etc.

Analysis

Case studies in practice

12.1 Activity profile: theatre in Australia
12.2 Managing opera houses
12.3 The production and consumption of music
12.4 The entrepreneurial arts leader
12.5 How a museum dies

Introduction

A case study involves the study of an individual example – a case – of the phenomenon being researched. The aim is to seek to understand the phenomenon by studying one or more single examples. To some extent all social research is a case study at some level, since all research is geographically and temporally unique. Thus, for example, a survey of 500 visitors to a particular cultural venue can be seen as a case study of the use of that venue, and even a nation-wide survey of the cultural activities of thousands of people in a Western country carried out in 2012 could be viewed, in one sense, as a case study of the activities of the population of one affluent country in the early twenty-first century.

The case study *research method* should be distinguished from other uses of the concept of cases, including in the law, where it refers to an individual crime, arrest and trial, and is often important in setting precedents, and in medicine, where cases refer to individual patients. In both these examples, the case – either live or as a written record – becomes a vehicle for teaching and in the business sector this is its exclusive use, the most well-known example being the Harvard Business School cases (Harvard Business School, nd).

Definitions

What is the case study method?

Gerring (2007:19–20) defines a *case* as 'a spatially delimited phenomenon (a unit) observed at a single point in time or over some period of time' and a *case study* as 'the intensive study of a single case'. He goes on to observe:

> Case study research may incorporate several cases, that is, multiple case studies. However, at a certain point it will no longer be possible to investigate those cases so intensively. At the point where the emphasis of a study shifts from the individual case to a sample of cases, we shall say that a study is *cross-case*. Evidently the distinction between case study and cross-case study is a matter of degree. The fewer cases there are, and the more intensively they are studied, the more the work merits the appellation 'case study'. … All empirical work may be classified as either case study (comprising one or a few cases) or cross-case study (involving many cases).
>
> (Gerring, 2007:20)

Thus, there is a continuum between the case study method and cross-case research rather than a sharp line of separation. Gerring goes on to express a hope that his book:

> will contribute to breaking down the rather artificial boundaries that have separated these genres within the social sciences. Properly constituted, there is no reason that case study results cannot be synthesized with results gained from cross-case analysis, and vice versa.
>
> (Gerring, 2007: 13).

There are no rules about the detail with which a case study should be conducted or communicated. For example, a whole book or thesis might be dedicated to a single case study – for example, case studies of events have appeared singly as book-length studies (e.g. Cashman and Darcy, 2008), as single articles (e.g. Garcia, 2001) or as several case studies in a single article (e.g. Williams and Bowdin, 2007).

What the case study method is not

The fact that research projects using the case study method typically involve only one or a few cases suggests some similarity with qualitative research methods and in some texts the case study method is subsumed under 'qualitative methods' (e.g. Finn *et al.*, 2000: 81) but, as leading authority Robert Yin states:

> The case study method is not just a form of 'qualitative research', even though some have recognised the case study as being among the array of qualitative research choices… . The use of a mix of quantitative and qualitative evidence… are but two of the ways that case study research goes beyond being a type of qualitative research.
>
> (Yin, 2014:19)

In fact, the use of a variety of types of data and analysis can be said to be a key feature of the case study method.

Some commentators (for example, Zikmund, 1997: 108) have implied that the case study method is used only for 'exploratory' purposes but this is not the only possible purpose: as Yin (2014: 7) asserts: 'Case study research is far from being only an exploratory strategy'. Indeed, case studies can be used at all stages of research, from exploratory to theory development (George and Bennett, 2005) and theory testing, as discussed below (see Figure 12. 2). Thus,

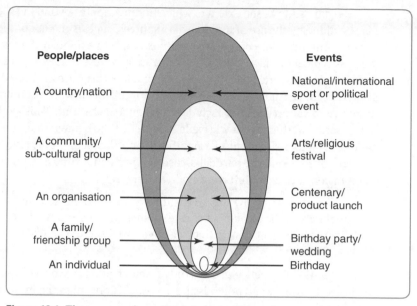

Figure 12.1 The case study method: demographic and geographic levels

they can be the basis of substantive research projects in their own right, as the case studies summarised later in the chapter demonstrate.

Scale

Cases can consist of individuals, communities (villages, islands, cities), whole countries, organisations and companies, places and projects or events. These demographic and geographic dimensions are illustrated in Figure 12.1.

A case study of an individual or small group, such as a theatre company, can involve a range of qualitative and quantitative methods. As we move up in scale the range of methods increases, both in terms of primary and secondary sources, including, for example, the use of information on a site and its environment and history, and the social and demographic characteristics of the population of a community or country. Thus, the sheer variety of types of data and data analysis would offer a 'rich' description of the *case* – the site or the country and its people. Furthermore, a case study at one level (for example, of a community or an organisation) could involve a variety of quantitative and qualitative methods and data sources involving components at lower levels (for example, questionnaire surveys of residents or employees, or financial and membership data).

Validity and reliability

Arguably, the multiple methodologies and data sources used in the typical case study offer the possibility of achieving as high a level of internal validity as any single method discussed elsewhere in this book, since the limitations of one method or data source, as discussed in each of the previous five chapters, may be overcome by drawing on the qualities of another.

External validity – the extent to which findings apply beyond the specific case study – may also be aided by the use of multiple data sources, such as the use of secondary data from the wider population for comparative purposes and to establish the extent to which the case study is typical or unique – drawing on cross-case research as suggested by Gerring, above. In case study research, because only one or a few cases are examined, the method does not seek to produce findings that are generally or universally representative. Thus, a case study of an organisation does not include statements of the kind 'This explains the behaviour of organisation X, therefore it will explain or predict the behaviour of the 50,000 similar organisations in similar situations or a significant proportion of them'. However, if research has no implications beyond the particular case at a particular time and place, there would be little point in conducting it. Referring again to Gerring:

> To conduct a case study implies that one has also conducted cross-case analysis, or at least thought about the broader set of cases. Otherwise, it is impossible for an author to answer the defining question of all case study research: what is this a case *of*?
>
> (Gerring, 2007: 13)

The relationship between case study research and the world beyond the case itself can be mediated by theory and policy issues, so conclusions might be in the form:

- This explains the behaviour of organisation X, which is inconsistent with theoretically based expectations, suggesting the possible need for some modification to the theory.

Or:

- This explains the behaviour of organisation X, suggesting that other types of organisation might be examined to see whether the explanation applies more widely.

Thus, while case study research may not result in generalisations about a population, it can have valid things to say in relation to theory explanatory research, and in relation to policy in evaluative research. A number of scenarios can be envisaged in regard to theory and policy, as shown in Figure 12.2.

Type of research	Research purpose	Case study outcomes
Descriptive research	Identifying the characteristics of a particular phenomenon	Descriptions of and comparisons between phenomena, which may be used for education purposes or to inform corporate or public policy making and decision making or as input to other research.
Explanatory research	Testing a single existing theory	*Case study confirms applicability of theory in at least one setting or, alternatively, raises doubts as to applicability of theory and suggests modification or alternatives.*
	Testing alternative/competing theories	*Case study demonstrates that one theory works better than the other in a particular situation, or that neither works.*
	Develop theory where none exists	The case study can suggest *possible* theory and may, at least partially, test the theory empirically.
Evaluative research	Testing effectiveness of a single policy	Case study *confirms* effectiveness of the policy in at least one setting or, alternatively, *raises doubts* as to effectiveness of the policy and possibly suggests modification or alternatives.
	Testing alternative/competing policies	Case study demonstrates that one policy is more effective than the other in a particular situation, or that neither works.
	Establish need for policy measures	The case study outlines the current problems and their likely causes and suggests the need for policy action.

Figure 12.2 Case study research: theory and policy

Using the typology discussed in the first chapter of this book: in the case of explanatory research a case study can be used to test the applicability of an existing theory. This might occur in situations where a theoretical proposition has never been tested empirically or where it has not been tested in a particular context. Thus, for example, a proposition about motivation with regard to engagement with arts/events activity may have been tested in regard to performing arts but not visual arts or sport events. If the theory is found to be non-applicable in a particular case study situation, this does not necessarily 'disprove' it, but can raise doubts as to its universality.

In the case of policy-related *evaluative* research the corresponding research task would be to test the effectiveness of a policy or type of management practice. For example, while the impact of promotional/advertising policy could be examined by use of aggregate national statistics on customer/participant numbers, it could also be examined by means of a case study of the experience in one or two communities or neighbourhoods, particularly if the results of the national statistical analysis were unclear or indicated an apparent lack of impact.

Reliability, in the sense of exact replication of research, is virtually impossible in case study research, of course, but the accumulation of evidence from a number of case studies may build a consensus around the findings of a programme of case study research and other evidence.

Merits of the case study approach

The particular merits of the case study method can be summarised as follows.

- The ability to place people, organisations, events and experiences in their social and historical context.
- The ability to treat the subject of study as a whole, rather than abstracting a limited set of pre-selected features.
- Multiple methods – triangulation – are implicit and seen as a strength.
- The single or limited number of cases offers a manageable data-collection task when resources are limited.
- Flexibility in the data-collection strategy allows researchers to adapt a research strategy as the research proceeds.
- There is no necessity to generalise to a defined wider population.

Design and conduct of case studies

While the case study method offers flexibility, it does not absolve the researcher from undertaking the usual initial preparatory steps – specifying research questions, reviewing the literature, establishing a theoretical framework and determining data needs and sources (see Chapter 3). As in any research, it is important to plan ahead to avoid the problem of having collected a lot of data and not knowing what to do with it. While flexibility is possible in some research environments, it is rarely unlimited – for example, in some circumstances it may be possible to interview people, or ask them for data, a number of times as new issues emerge in the course of the research, but in other circumstances this may not be possible.

In addition to general guidance on the planning of research projects (see Chapter 3), three specific issues are discussed here: defining the unit of analysis, selection of cases and data gathering.

Defining the unit of analysis

While it might be a somewhat obvious point to make: it is necessary to be clear about the *unit of analysis* in case study research. For example, if the unit of analysis – the case – is a single facility owned by a large organisation, it is important to keep the analysis at the facility level. Thus, for example, the policies and practices of the parent organisation are inevitably relevant, but they are 'given' influences on the facility management, the research is not *about* the parent organisation. Conversely, data on individual staff of the facility will form part of the research, but only insofar as they contribute to an understanding of the operation of the facility as a unit.

Selecting the case(s)

Of key importance in the case study method is the selection of the case or cases. This is comparable to sampling in cross-case studies. Four types of case selection process can be considered:

- *Purposive:* Where multiple cases are involved, the selection of cases is likely to be purposive – for example, in selecting a range of organisations of similar or different sizes, in the same or different sectors, in comparable or contrasting geographical locations, or of similar or contrasting levels of profitability.

- *Illustrative:* Often the case(s) will be chosen deliberately to increase the likelihood of illustrating a particular proposition – for example, if the research is concerned with leadership success, then *successful* organisations with high-profile leaders may be chosen.

- *Typical/atypical:* The case may be chosen because it is believed to be typical of the phenomenon being studied, or it may be deliberately chosen as an extreme or atypical case. Thus, a study examining the secrets of success in a particular arts/event organisation might well select a particularly successful organisation or event for study – or failures, as in Hall's (1980) *Great Planning Disasters*.

- *Pragmatic/opportunistic:* In some cases the selection of cases may be pragmatic – for example, when the researcher has ready access to an organisation, possibly because he or she is a member or employee.

Whatever the rationale for the selection of a case or cases, it should be clearly articulated in the research report and the implications of the selection discussed.

Data gathering

A case study project generally uses a number of data sources and data-gathering techniques, including the use of documentary evidence, secondary data analysis, in-depth interviews, questionnaire surveys, observation, participant observation and experimental methods.

The process of selecting data sources and collection techniques is the same as in any other research process. The idea that different data sources might be used in the same project to address different research questions or aspects of research questions, as in triangulation, has already been discussed (Chapters 3 and 5) and it has been argued that all data collection should be linked to the research questions – even in cases where the research questions are being modified as the research progresses. When a number of disparate data types and sources are involved, two other issues should be borne in mind:

- *consistency of the unit of analysis* – if, for example, participation data are involved, it is important that the data relate to the same geographical unit, or if this is not possible, to be clear about any inconsistencies and their possible implications;

- *temporal consistency* – ideally, except when the focus of the research is on change over time, all data should relate to the same time period. This is related to the issue of the unit of analysis, since reorganisation – of, for example, a corporate body or administrative boundaries – can result in changes in the size, composition and functions of organisations over time.

Analysis

To the extent that the design of the case study, or parts of it, resembles that of more formalised research projects, with fixed research questions and corresponding data-collection and analysis procedures, the analysis process will tend to be deductive in nature; the data analysis will be designed to address the questions posed in advance. But a case study can involve qualitative methods with a recursive, more inductive format, as discussed in Chapter 15. Indeed, the flexibility of the whole case study approach suggests a more inductive approach. Thus the discovery, in the course of the research, of a previously unknown source of information might lead the researcher to ask the question: can these data add something to the research? While the new data source might help in addressing the existing research questions in unanticipated ways, it could also suggest whole new research questions.

Five main methods of analysis are outlined by Yin (2014: 142–167):

- *pattern matching:* relating the features of the case to what might be expected from some existing theory – for example, finding gender-related differences in the exercise of power;

- *explanation building:* often an iterative process whereby a logical/causal explanation of what is discovered is developed by to-and-fro referencing between theory/explanation and data – for example, discovering a failure to cope adequately with crises;

- *time-series analysis:* explanations are developed on the basis of observing patterns of change over time – for example, discovering a pattern of ageing in the audience profile;

- *logic models:* management/evaluation models based on the sequence: initial conditions, needs, problems, resources; action; outcomes; impacts – see Figure 5.11;

- *cross-case synthesis:* where multiple cases are involved, cross-case comparison may be involved, sometimes using quantitative methods.

George and Bennett (2005: 181–232) use the terms:

- *congruence method:* events or characteristics A and B occur together, in the same or different case studies, suggesting some sort of relationship (the equivalent of correlation in quantitative research) (similar to Yin's *cross-case synthesis*); and

● *process tracing:* seeking one or more possible causal explanations from within the case study material, for the observed concurrence of A and B (similar to Yin's *explanation building*).

In fact, since all forms of data may arise in a case study, all forms of analysis, as described in Part 3, are possible. It is the pulling together of the results of analyses of different sorts to form coherent conclusions that presents the challenge.

Case studies in practice

Five case studies of case studies conclude the chapter. They provide brief details on each study, but further details can be followed up in the references provided.

CASE STUDY 12.1

Activity profile: theatre attendance in Australia

In an *activity profile* the 'case' is the activity. This case study is an example of descriptive research which, as suggested in Figure 12.2, may be of use in education or corporate or public policy making and decision making and as an input to other research. The example presented here refers to theatre attendance. It is quite limited, drawing on a single source, the periodic Australian Bureau of Statistics surveys of *Attendance at Cultural Venues and Events* (see Chapter 7).

Figure 12.3 presents data on trends in Australian adult attendance at the theatre at least once in the course of a year and provides a lesson in data interpretation related to the issue of alternative measures discussed in Chapter 7 (Figure 7.2). Graph (a), of the number of persons attending, shows a steady increase between 1991 and 2010. But graph (b), of the percentage of the population attending, shows a static or declining trend. The explanation for the difference is

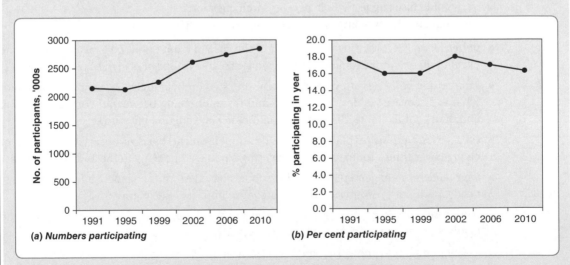

(a) *Numbers participating* (b) *Per cent participating*

Figure 12.3 Trends in theatre attendance, Australian adults 15+, 1991–2010
Source: Graphic compiled from data in ABS (2002, 2006, 2010).

the increase in the adult population of Australia, from 12.0 million to 17.5 million over the period. Thus, theatre operators may not have been aware of the fact that during this period they were attracting a static or declining proportion of the population.

Figure 12.4 presents information on the relationship between theatre attendance and household income, showing that members of households in the top fifth of income groups have a participation rate two and a half times that of the lowest two-fifths, although even among this high income group almost 75 per cent do not attend a theatre in the course of a year.

The ABS survey includes additional data on such matters as age, gender, household composition, country of birth, labour force status, education level, state/region of residence and frequency of attendance.

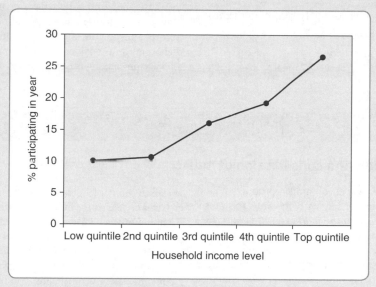

Figure 12.4 Theatre attendance by income, Australia, 2010

Source: Graphic compiled from data in ABS (2010: 17) NB. Income = 'equivalised gross household income', i.e. taking account of household size/composition; quintile = one fifth of households ranked by income level.

CASE STUDY 12.2

Managing opera houses

Auvinen's (2000, 2001) study of the management of European opera houses begins with the development of a theoretical framework informed by the work of Jürgen Habermas. This outlines the differences between the values, constraints and internal and external relationships of the artistic part of an opera house organisation and those of the financial and administrative part. This is termed the *artistic–economic* dichotomy. Set against the background of frequent, highly publicised financial crises in European opera house management over recent decades, it is hypothesised that it is the failure to adequately manage the relationships between the two parts of the dichotomy that causes the problems. The study involves five case studies: Deutsche Oper Berlin, English National Opera, Finnish National Opera, Glyndebourne Festival

Case study 12.2 (*continued*)

Opera and Opéra National de Paris. Information on each is presented in a separate chapter with ten common headings:

1. Organisational history and the legal status of the organisation.
2. Income structure.
3. Expenditure structure.
4. Personnel structure.
5. The opera house building (history, description).
6. Programming, pricing and audience figures.
7. Organisational structure.
8. Relationship with government/funding sources.
9. Artistic and financial planning and decision-making structure.
10. Summary.

Most of the information is derived from documentary/administrative sources within each organisation and from semi-structured interviews with key personnel. Focusing particularly on the organisational structures, the thesis shows how the artistic–economic dichotomy plays out in different settings and how the failure to accord appropriate authority to both parts of the dichotomy and consider their relationships to the overall decision-making process leads to difficulties.

CASE STUDY 12.3

The production and consumption of music

Peterson's (1994) paper on music production and consumption is concerned with the way the music industry's perception of the *market* during the second half of the twentieth century was often shown to be inaccurate as a result of advances in technology and research that revealed the true nature of actual music *audiences*. The paper contains a number of case studies – generally unsourced and in some cases, arguably, just illustrative examples – which demonstrate the flexibility of the approach. Among them are the following:

- An account of how, in 1991, when *Billboard* magazine started basing its ranking of record sales on the basis of actual sales data from a sample of retailers' cash tills, rather than reports from store managers, the more reliable data revealed the popularity of country and rap music and the fact that some country music singers were outselling major rock bands.

- Discussions of how radio stations and the mainstream recording industry classified and pigeonholed music genres, recordings and artistes to suit their own convenience and preconceptions, thereby effectively stifling rather than encouraging innovation (e.g. rap), which emerged through other means, such as musicians' live tours, dance clubs and independent radio.

- A summary of the research which has revealed that, rather than taste in music genres being related to class, as traditionally believed – for example, country music being associated with working-class groups and classical music with higher-status groups – social status seems to be related to a division between *omnivores*, who enjoy a wide variety of music genres, and *univores*, who enjoy only one genre.

CASE STUDY 12.4

The entrepreneurial arts leader

Ruth Rentschler (2002) investigated arts leaders' orientation towards creativity and entrepreneurship in Australia and New Zealand art museums. She adopted a multi-method approach, using content analysis of documents, in-depth interviews with arts leaders and a questionnaire survey of museum directors.

Case study 12.4 (*continued*)

Twelve arts organisations were chosen as case studies on the basis of various attributes such as whether the organisation was new or older, and well resourced or struggling, and involved interviews with staff and volunteers and content analysis of annual reports.

The research, originally conducted for a master's thesis, was set in the context of a literature-based review of the development of cultural policy in Australia and New Zealand since the 1950s. This resulted in a conceptual framework involving 12 identified elements of entrepreneurship in arts organisations and classification of arts leaders using a two-dimensional matrix covering the two conceptual dimensions of funding diversity and creative programming, as shown in Figure 12.5.

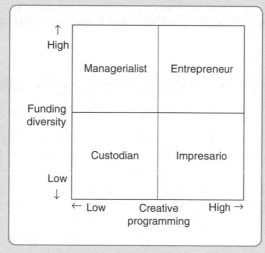

Figure 12.5 Role variance of arts leaders: Renstchler (conceptual framework)
Source: Rentschler (2002: 59).

The aim of the empirical work was to investigate the extent to which arts leaders/managers and the organisations for which they were responsible had moved, or were moving, away from the traditional 'custodian' role into the other roles indicated in the framework. Rentschler concluded that her study was more exploratory than confirmatory but suggested that the use of statistical analysis through the deployment of a questionnaire-based survey provided evidence for particular trends and validated the qualitative component of her research.

CASE STUDY 12.5

How a museum dies

A study of four cases of new entrant museums included examination of how a new museum failed (Burton, 2007). Under investigation was the *liability*, or risks, of new entry and how new entrants create value for a range of stakeholders in order to successfully 'capture' and 'exchange' value, which marks the survival of the new entrant museum.

The study highlights a number of factors on case selection: two museums were chosen on the basis of their historical comparability (size, national status, governance, established a decade apart, purpose-built); one was selected on the basis of its success in reinventing itself within the museum sector over a period of time, and the other on the basis that, while it had also

Case study 12.5 (*continued*)

reinvented itself, it did not survive in the museum sector. In this sense the selection basis was to look for similarities but also to identify what Denzin (1989) calls cases of 'regularity', 'irregularity' and 'deviancy'.

The research approach was qualitative, including analysis of documents (letters, policies, reports, annual reports, contemporary newspaper reports) and interviews with a range of stakeholders (politicians, museum directors, members of boards of directors, government arts administrators and professional museum

personnel). It was found that in both cases a disruptive event occurred in the early period of the museum's life cycle. Their chances of survival were either jeopardised or secured, depending on how the museum management team juggled the conflicting demands of their most powerful stakeholders, while maintaining adherence to their core mission. Although the research was limited to the museum sector the research threw additional light on the concept of new entry which had the potential to be extrapolated to other cultural institutions.

Summary

This chapter considers the case study method, which involves the study of a single case, or a small number of cases, on the phenomenon of interest, in contrast with other methods discussed in the book which generally involve *cross-case* methods. But cross-case research may be embedded in a case study – for example, a study of a single community or cultural tourist destination may involve a questionnaire-based survey of residents or visitors respectively. Thus, case studies often use multiple methods, including any or all of the other methods discussed in the book. The chapter examines tasks in the design and conduct of case studies, including definition of the unit of analysis and selection of cases. Five examples of contrasting arts/events case studies complete the chapter.

TEST QUESTIONS

1. Define case study research and cross-case research.
2. Discuss the external validity challenges involved in case study research.
3. What are the five approaches to selecting cases discussed in the chapter?
4. Five approaches to case study analysis have been suggested in the literature: name and describe these approaches.

EXERCISES

1. Consider a successful arts facility or event known to you and outline the elements that might be involved in setting up a case study to explore the reasons for its success.

2. Compile an activity profile, similar to that in Case study 12.1, using data on another activity and/or another country (possibly from sources identified in Chapter 7).

3. Read two of the example case studies listed in the Resources section below and identify the range of data sources used, methods of analysis and how the various types of information are drawn together to draw conclusions.

Resources

Websites

- Harvard Business School cases: http://hbsp.harvard.edu – search on terms such as arts, festival, Olympic Games.

Publications

- General texts: Bromley (1986), Burns (1994: 312–331), Byrne and Ragin (2009), Flyvbjerg (2006), George and Bennett (2005), Gerring (2007), Gomm *et al.* (2000), Simons (2009), Stake (1994, 1995), Thomas (2012), Yin (2014).

- Examples of case studies:

  o art gallery choice – Tate Modern: Caldwell and Coshall (2003)
  o arts and health/well-being: Health Development Agency (2000)
  o cultural tourism: Murphy and Boyle (2006), Richards (2001: eight case studies in Part 2)
  o events – media coverage: Green *et al.* (2003)
  o festivals: Avignon: Fabiani (2003); Budapest Spring Festival: Puczko and Ratz (2001); UK arts festivals: Williams and Bowdin (2007); Pamplona: Ravenscroft and Matteucci (2003)
  o heritage – living history: Tivers (2002)
  o Millennium Dome, London: McGuigan and Gilmore (2002)
  o museum: new entrant: Burton (2007)
  o music and education: Komel and Juznic (2010)
  o opera house (Sydney) building: Hall (1980: 138–151)
  o opera company management: Auvinen (2000, 2001)
  o organisations and companies – creative project management: Simon (2006)

- Misunderstandings about the case study method: Flyvbjerg (2006).

References

Australian Bureau of Statistics (ABS) (2002, 2006, 2010) *Attendance at Selected Cultural Venues and Events* (Cat. No. 4114.0). Canberra: ABS.

Auvinen, T. (2000) *Unmanageable Opera? The Artistic–Economic Dichotomy and its Manifestations in the Organisational Structures of Five Opera Organisations*. PhD thesis. London: City University, available at: www.creader.fi/sites/default/files/phd_thesis_tuomas_auvinen.pdf

Auvinen, T. (2001) Why is it difficult to manage an opera company? The artistic–economic dichotomy and its manifestation in the organizational structures of five opera companies. *Journal of Arts Management, Law and Society*, 30(4), 268–282.

Bromley, D. B. (1986) *The Case-Study Method in Psychology and Related Disciplines*. New York: John Wiley and Sons.

Burns, R. B. (1994) *Introduction to Research Methods*, Second Edition. Melbourne: Longman Cheshire.

Burton, C. (2007) How a museum dies: the case of new entry failure in a Sydney museum. *Museum Management and Curatorship*, 22(2), 109–129.

Byrne, D. and Ragin, C. C. (eds) (2009) *The Sage Handbook of Case-Based Methods*. London: Sage.

Caldwell, N. and Coshall, J. (2003) Tourists' preference structures for London's Tate Modern gallery: the implications for strategic marketing. *Journal of Travel and tourism Marketing*, 14(2), 23–45.

Cashman, R. and Darcy, S. (2008) *Benchmark Games: The Sydney 2000 Paralympic Games*. Sydney: Walla Walla Press.

Denzin, N. K. (1989) *The Research Act: A Theoretical Introduction to Sociological Methods*, Third Edition. New Jersey: Prentice Hall.

Fabiani, J.-L. (2003) The audience and its legend: a sociological analysis of the Avignon Festival. *Journal of Arts Management, Law and Society*, 32(4), 265–277.

Finn, M., Elliott-White, M. and Walton, M. (2000) *Tourism and Leisure Research Methods*. Harlow: Longman.

Flyvbjerg, B. (2006) Five misunderstandings about case-study research. *Qualitative Inquiry*, 12(2), 219–245.

Garcia, B. (2001) Enhancing sport marketing through cultural and arts programs: lessons from the Sydney 2000 Olympic Arts Festivals. *Sport Management Review*, 4(2), 193–209.

George, A. L. and Bennett, A. (2005) *Case Studies and Theory Development in the Social Sciences*. Cambridge, MA: MIT Press.

Gerring, J. (2007) *Case Study Research: Principles and Practices*. New York: Cambridge University Press.

Gomm, R., Hammersley, M. and Foster, P. (eds) (2000) *Case Study Method*. London: Sage.

Green, B. C., Costa, C. and Fitzgerald, M. (2003) Marketing the host city: analysing exposure generated by a sport event. *International Journal of Sports Marketing and Sponsorship*, 4(4), 335–353 (reprinted in M. Weed (ed.) (2008) *Sport and Tourism: A Reader*. London: Routledge, pp. 346–361).

Hall, P. (1980) *Great Planning Disasters*. London: Weidenfeld and Nicolson.

Harvard Business School (nd) *Harvard Business School Case Studies*. Cambridge, MA: Harvard University, available at: http://hbsp.harvard.edu

Health Development Agency (2000) *Art for Health: A Review of Good Practice in Community-Based Arts Projects and Initiatives Which Impact on Health and Wellbeing*. London: HDA.

Komel, I. and Juznic, P. (2010) A case study of the project: 'With Music to Knowledge'. *Annals of Leisure Research*, 13(1–2), 70–85.

McGuigan, J. and Gilmore, A. (2002) The Millennium Dome: sponsoring, meaning and visiting. *International Journal of Cultural Policy*, 8(1), 1–20.

Murphy, C. and Boyle, E. (2006) Testing a conceptual model of cultural tourism development in the post-industrial city: a case study of Glasgow. *Tourism and Hospitality Research*, 6(2), 111–126.

Peterson, R. A. (1994) Measured markets and unknown audiences: case studies from the production and consumption of music. In J. S. Ettema and D. C. Whitney (eds), *Audiencemaking: How the Media Create the Audience*. Thousand Oaks, CA: Sage, pp. 171–185.

Puczko, L. and Ratz, T. (2001) The Budapest Spring Festival: a festival for Hungarians? In G. Richards (ed.), *Cultural Attractions and European Tourism*. Wallingford: CABI Publishing, pp. 199–214.

Ravenscroft, N. and Matteucci, X. (2003) The festival as carnivalesque: social governance and control at Pamplona's San Fermin Fiesta. *Culture and Communication*, 4(1), 1–15.

Rentschler, R. (2002) *The Entrepreneurial Arts Leader: Cultural Policy, Change and Reinvention*. Brisbane: University of Queensland Press.

Richards, G. (ed.) (2001) *Cultural Attractions and European Tourism*. Wallingford: CABI Publishing.

Simon, L. (2006) Managing creative projects: an empirical synthesis of activities. *International Journal of Project Management*, 24(2), 116–126.

Simons, H. (2009) *Case Study Research in Practice*. London: Sage.

Stake, R. E. (1994) Case studies. In N. K. Denzin and Y. S. Lincoln (eds), *Handbook of Qualitative Research*. Thousand Oaks, CA: Sage, pp. 236–247.

Stake, R. E. (1995) *The Art of Case Study Research*. Thousand Oaks, CA: Sage.

Thomas, G. (2012) *How to Do Your Case Study: A Guide for Students and Researchers*. London: Sage.

Tivers, J. (2002) Performing heritage: the use of live 'actors' in heritage presentation. *Leisure Studies*, 21(3–4), 187–200.

Williams, M. and Bowdin, G. (2007) Festival evaluation: an exploration of seven UK arts festivals. *Managing Leisure*, 12(1–2), 187–203.

Yin, R. K. (2014) *Case Study Research: Design and Methods*, Fifth Edition. Thousand Oaks, CA: Sage.

Zikmund, W. G. (1997) *Business Research Methods*, Fifth Edition. Orlando, FL: Dryden Press.

Chapter 13

Sampling: quantitative and qualitative

Introduction

The idea of sampling

Samples and populations

Representativeness

- Sampling for household surveys
- Sampling for telephone surveys
- Sampling for visitor/site/user surveys
- Sampling for street surveys and quota sampling
- Sampling for mail surveys
- Sampling for e-surveys
- Sampling for complex events and destination studies
- Sampling and random assignment in experimental research

Sample size

Weighting

Sampling: qualitative research

1. Level of precision – confidence intervals
2. Detail of proposed analysis
3. Budget
4. Reporting sample size issues
5. Confidence intervals applied to population estimates
6. Sample size and small populations

Introduction

This chapter is an introduction to the principles of sampling subjects for study, which arises in most of the research techniques discussed in this book.

The idea of sampling

In most survey research and in some observational and qualitative research it is necessary to *sample*. Mainly because of costs, it is not usually possible to gather data from all the people, organisations or other entities that are the focus of the research. For example, if the aim of a research project is to study the cultural participation patterns of the adult population of a country, no one has the resources to conduct interviews with the millions of individuals who make up the adult population. The only time when the whole population of a country is interviewed is every five or ten years, when the government statistical agency conducts the official Census of Population – and the cost of collecting and analysing the data runs into tens of millions of pounds or dollars (see Chapter 7).

At a more modest level, it would be virtually impossible to conduct face-to-face interviews with all the users of a large venue, even in one event, since thousands of people might enter the site and leave in a short space of time. It might be possible to hand respondent-completion questionnaires to all visitors, but this approach has disadvantages in terms of quality and level of response (see Chapter 10). The usual procedure is to interview a sample – a proportion – of the users. We have noted that in observational research (see Chapter 8) involving counting of numbers of visitors at cultural/events sites, available resources typically dictate that the numbers entering the site or present at the site be counted on a sample of occasions rather than throughout the event.

Sampling has implications for the way data are collected, analysed and interpreted.

Samples and populations

One item of terminology should be clarified initially. The total category of subjects which is the focus of attention in a particular research project is known as the *population*. A *sample* is selected from the population. The use of the term population makes obvious sense when dealing with communities of people – for instance, when referring to the population of Britain or the population of London. But in social research the term also applies in other instances – for example, the visitors to a museum over the course of a year constitute the *population of museum visitors* and the totality of visitors to a festival constitute the *population of festival visitors*.

The term *population* can also be applied to non-human phenomena – for example, if a study of the art galleries of Europe indicated that there were 5,000 galleries in all, from which 50 were to be selected for study, then the 5,000 galleries can be referred to as the *population of galleries* and the 50 selected for study would be the *sample*. In some texts the word *universe* is used instead of population.

If a sample is to be selected for study then two questions arise:

1. What procedures must be followed to ensure that the sample is representative of the population?

2. How large should the sample be?

These two questions are related, since, other things being equal, the larger the sample, the more chance it has of being representative.

Representativeness

A sample that is not representative of the population is described as *biased*. The whole process of sample selection must be aimed at minimising bias in the sample. The researcher seeks to achieve representativeness and to minimise bias by adopting the principles of *random sampling*. This is not the most helpful term since it implies that the process is not methodical. This is far from the case – random does not mean haphazard. The meaning of random sampling is as follows:

In random sampling all members of the population have an equal chance of inclusion in the sample.

For example, if a sample of 1,000 people is to be selected from a population of 10,000 then every member of the population must have a 1 in 10 chance of being selected. In practice, most sampling methods involving human beings can only approximate this rule.

The problems of achieving random sampling vary with the type of survey and are discussed below in relation to the range of survey types discussed in Chapter 10. In addition, the challenges presented by complex, multi-site events are discussed, and sampling and random assignment in experimental research.

Sampling for household surveys

The problem of achieving randomness can be examined in the case of a household survey of the adult residents of a country. If the adult population of the country is, say, 40 million and we wish to interview a sample of 1,000, then every member of the adult population should have a 1 in 40,000 chance of being included in the sample. How would this be achieved? Ideally, there should be a complete list of all 40 million of the country's adults – their names should be written on slips of paper and placed in a revolving drum, physically or electronically, as in a Lottery draw, and 1,000 names should be drawn out. Each time a choice is made, everyone has a 1 in 40 million chance of selection – since this happens 1,000 times, each person in the population has a total of 1,000 in 40 million or 1 in 40,000 chance of selection.

This would be a laborious process. Surely a close approximation would be to forget the slips of paper and the drum and choose every 40,000th name on the list. But where should the starting point be? It should be some random point between 1 and 40,000. There are published 'tables of random numbers', which can also be produced from computers, which can be used for this purpose. Strictly speaking, the whole sample should be chosen using random numbers, since this would approximate most closely to the 'names in a drum' procedure.

In practice, however, such a list of the population being studied rarely exists. The nearest thing to it would be the electoral registers of all the electoral constituencies in the country. Electoral registers are fairly comprehensive because adults are required by law to register, but they are not perfect. Highly mobile/homeless people are often not included; many who live in multi-occupied premises are omitted. The physical task of selecting the names from such a list would be immense, but there is another disadvantage with this approach: if every 40,000th voter on the registers were selected, the sample would be scattered throughout the country. The cost of visiting every one of those selected for a face-to-face interview would be very high.

In practice, therefore, organisations conducting national surveys employ 'multi-stage' and 'clustered' sampling. Multi-stage means that sampling is not done directly but by stages. For example, if the country had, say, four states or regions, a proposed sample of 2,000 would be sub-divided in the same proportions as the populations of the regions. Within each region, local government areas would then be divided into country and urban and, say, four urban and two rural areas would be selected at random – with the intention of selecting appropriate sub-samples, of perhaps 25, 40 or 50 from each area. These sub-samples could be selected from electoral registers, or streets could be selected and individuals contacted by calling on, say, every fifth house in the street. In any one street interviewers might be instructed to interview, say, 10 or 15 people.

By interviewing 'clusters' of people in this way costs are minimised. But care must be taken not to reduce the number of clusters too much since then the full range of population and area types would not be included. Once a residence has been selected for interview, a procedure must be devised for selecting a respondent from the household members; this is discussed in relation to telephone surveys below.

Sampling for telephone surveys

We have already examined the traditional process for sampling for telephone surveys from public residential telephone directories and the move to computer-aided telephone interviewing (CATI) methods (see Chapter 10). Some of the emerging difficulties with this method, given the rise of mobile telephones (see Chapter 10), threaten the representativeness of samples. Insofar as the resultant bias is age-related, this can be corrected by weighting (see below), but if it reflects lifestyle differences, not much can be done about it. The printed or electronic telephone directory is close to the list of people on the electoral register, as discussed above, except that, since there is typically only one land-line telephone per house, the list effectively refers to households rather than individuals. As with household surveys, it is therefore necessary to use some procedure for selecting a respondent from among household members.

If, in face-to-face household surveys or telephone surveys, the interviewer were to interview the person who happened to answer the door or telephone, this could result in bias, depending on local customs as to who in the household is more likely to answer the door or the phone. There is, of course, invariably a lower age limit for the study, so persons under the prescribed age will not be selected.

A typical procedure to 'randomise' the process of choosing among eligible household members is to ask to interview the person whose birthday is nearest to the interview date.

Sampling for visitor/site/user surveys

Conditions at cultural/event sites or facilities vary enormously, depending on the type, size and design of the venue, the season, day of the week, the time of day or the weather. This discussion can therefore be in general terms only. To ensure randomness, and therefore representativeness, it is necessary for interviewers to adhere to strict rules. On-site interviewers operate in two ways:

1. ISUM: interviewer stationary, users mobile – for instance, when the interviewer is located near the entrance and visitors are interviewed as they enter or leave.

2. USIM: users stationary, interviewer mobile – for instance, when interviewing audiences or spectators at a seated venue.

In the ISUM case, the instructions for interviewers should be something like:

> When one interview is complete, check through the questionnaire for completeness and legibility. When you are ready with a new questionnaire, stop the next person to enter the gate. Stick strictly to this rule and do not select interviewees on any other basis.

The important thing is that interviewers should not avoid certain types of user by 'picking and choosing' whom to interview. Ideally, there should be some rule such as interviewing every fifth person to come through the entrance, but since users will enter at a sporadic rate and interviews will vary in length, this is rarely possible.

In the USIM case, the interviewer should be given a certain route to follow at the site and be instructed to interview, say, every fifth group they pass. Seated venues vary in design and formality. With theatres and concert halls, the interviewing will typically take place during intervals, in the circulation areas. The same may apply to sports venues, but for those sports with plenty of breaks in play, such as at cricket, it may also be possible to conduct interviewing in the seating areas.

Where interviewers are employed, the success of the process will depend on the training given to the interviewers and this could involve observation of them at work to ensure that they are following the rules.

Sampling in visitor surveys leads inevitably to variation in the proportion of users interviewed at different times of the day (see Chapter 10). Where users tend to stay for long periods – as in the case of some multi-site or outdoor festivals – this may not matter, but where people stay for shorter periods and where the type of user may vary during the course of the day or week, the sample will probably be unrepresentative – that is, biased. This should be corrected by weighting as indicated at the end of the chapter.

When surveys involve the handing out of questionnaires for respondent-completion – as may happen, for example, at a performing arts event – unless field staff are available to encourage their completion and return, respondents will be self-selected. Busy reception or box office staff can rarely be relied upon to do a thorough job in handing out and collecting in questionnaires, unless the survey is a management priority and therefore closely supervised. Normally a significant proportion of the population will fail to return the questionnaire, but it is unlikely that this self-selection process will be random. For example, people with difficulties in reading or writing, or those in a hurry, may fail to return their questionnaires. Those with 'something to say', whether positive or negative, are more likely to return their questionnaires than people who are apathetic or just content with the service, thus giving a misleading impression of the proportion of users who have strong opinions. So it can be seen that this type of 'uncontrolled' survey is at risk of introducing serious bias into the sample and should therefore be avoided if at all possible.

Sampling for street surveys and quota sampling

Although the technique of quota sampling can be used in other situations, it is most common in street surveys. The street survey is usually seen as a means of contacting a representative sample of the community but in fact it can also be seen as a sort of 'site survey', the site being, for example, the shopping area. As such, a survey involving a random sample of the users of the street would be representative of the users of the shopping area rather than of the community as a whole – in a suburban shopping centre, for example, it would have a high proportion of retired people or full-time home/child carers.

If the aim is to obtain a representative sample of the whole community, interviewers are given 'quotas' of people of different types to contact, the quotas being based on information about the community which is available from the population census. For example, if the census indicates that 12 per cent of the population is retired then interviewers would be required to include 12 retired people in every 100 interviewed. Once interviewers have filled their quota in certain age/gender groups, they are required to become more selective in whom they approach in order to fill the gaps in their quotas.

The quota method can, of course, be used only when background information on the target population is known, as with community surveys. In many surveys this information is not known so the strict following of random sampling procedures must be relied upon.

Sampling for mail surveys

The initial list of people to whom the questionnaire is sent in a mail survey may be the whole population or a sample. If a sample is selected it can usually be done completely randomly because the mailing list for the whole population is usually available.

The *respondents* to a mail survey form a sample, yet it is not randomly selected but self-selected. This introduces sources of bias similar to those in the uncontrolled self-completion site surveys discussed above. There is little that can be done about this except to make every effort to achieve a high response rate. In some cases information may be available on the population that can be used to weight the sample to correct for certain sources of bias at the analysis stage – for example, in the case of a national survey the sample could be weighted to correct for any geographical bias in response because the geographical distribution of the population would be known. If, for example, the survey is of an occupational association and the proportion of members in various grades is known from records, then this information can be used for weighting purposes. But ultimately, mail surveys suffer from an unknown and uncorrectable element of bias caused by non-response. All surveys experience non-response of course, but the problem is greater with mail surveys because the level of non-response is usually greater (see Chapter 10).

Sampling for e-surveys

Often, when a population, such as the workforce or membership of an organisation, is to be studied by means of an e-survey, a complete listing of email addresses is available. The sampling process then resembles that of the mail survey: the entire population may be included or a specified proportion, for example every fifth individual on the list. The challenges of non-response and representativeness are therefore the same as for mail surveys.

A common practice is for organisations, such as pressure groups or local councils, to place an online questionnaire on their website and invite people to respond – that is, to self-sample. The resultant sample cannot therefore be said to be representative even of visitors to the website, since only those with sufficient interest and/or time will be motivated to take part in the survey. The sample is certainly not, as is sometimes claimed, representative of the general public.

Sampling for complex events studies

Events with multiple ticketed and non-ticketed sites present particular challenges for the researcher, not least in the task of sampling. Typically, research is required to provide information on a number of matters, including the number of tourists and locals visiting the event as a whole, number of visitors and locals attending individual sites and events, and the socio-demographic profile, expenditure patterns and satisfactions/evaluations of the event by tourists and local participants. This information will be gathered by one or more of the methods discussed above, but most often through a form of site/visitor survey. The sampling task, then, involves considering the relevant protocols discussed above. In addition, secondary data sources, such as ticket sales records, will be drawn upon. The unique challenge, therefore, is not the sampling and data collection *per se* but combining data from different sources to provide estimates for the whole event, particularly when an event involves large non-ticketed components.

Sampling and random assignment in experimental research

Often experimental subjects are, in effect, a 'convenience' sample, as used in qualitative research, discussed at the end of the chapter. The group of students or members of an organisation are selected on the basis of convenient accessibility. In this case, the sample can at best be seen as likely to be representative of people in a similar situation – for example, 18–19-year-old arts or events management students at a major urban university, mostly from middle-class backgrounds. But, of course, university environments vary, so the students may have different lifestyles from such students at other universities. The question of representativeness, or otherwise, is often established when experiments are replicated in other environments, and results are consolidated in systematic reviews of the research literature (see Chapter 6).

A sampling-related task in experimental research arises in relation to the random assignment of subjects to the experimental and control groups (see Chapter 11). Typically, the overall sample is of manageable size, so a list of names is available. The truly random way of proceeding is to use random numbers. For example, if there are 234 individuals in the overall sample and the aim is to allocate half to the experimental group and half to the control group, the subjects should be numbered from 1 to 234 and 117 random numbers should be used to select the experimental group. In the past, tables of random numbers, often published as an appendix in statistics textbooks, were used to do this, but now 'random number generators' are available online (e.g. www.random.org). In the example, the online generator would be requested to produce 117 random numbers between 1 and 234.

Sample size

There is a popular misconception that the size of a sample should be decided on the basis of its relationship to the size of the population – for example, that a sample should be, say, 5 per cent or 10 per cent of the population. This is not so. What is important is the *absolute size* of the sample, regardless of the size of the population. For example, a sample size of 1,000 is equally valid, provided proper sampling procedures have been followed, whether it is a sample of the British adult population (50 million), the residents of London (population 7 million), the residents of Brighton (population 100,000) or the students of a university (population, say, 15,000).

It is worth repeating that it is the *absolute size of the sample* that is important, not its size relative to the population. This rule applies in all cases, except when the population itself is small – this exception and its implications are discussed later in the chapter.

On what criteria therefore should a sample size be determined? The criteria are basically threefold:

1. the required level of precision in the results;
2. the level of detail in the proposed analysis;
3. the available budget.

These issues are discussed in turn below. In addition, some comments are offered on:

4. reporting sample size issues;
5. application of confidence intervals to population estimates;
6. sample size for small populations.

1 Level of precision – confidence intervals

The idea of the level of precision can be explained as follows. The question to be posed is: to what extent do the findings from a sample precisely reflect the population from which it has been drawn? For example, if a survey was designed to investigate cinema-going and it was found that 50 per cent of a sample of 500 people had visited a cinema in the previous year, how sure can we be that this finding – this *statistic* – is true of the population as a whole? How sure can we be, having taken all appropriate measures to choose a representative sample, that it is, indeed, representative, and that the percentage of cinema-going in the population is not in fact, say, 70 per cent or 30 per cent?

This question is answered in terms of probabilities. If the true population value is around 50 per cent, then as long as random sampling procedures have been followed, the *probability* of drawing a sample which was so wrong that no one in the sample had been to a cinema would be remote – almost impossible, one might say. Yet the probability of coming up with, say, 48 per cent or 49 per cent, or 51 per cent or 52 per cent, would, one would think, be fairly high. The probability of coming up with 70 per cent or 30 per cent would be somewhere in between.

Statisticians have examined the likely pattern of distribution of all possible samples of various sizes drawn from populations of various sizes and established that, when a sample is randomly drawn, the *sample value* of a statistic has a certain probability of being within a certain range either side of the *population value* of the statistic. That range is plus or minus twice the 'standard error' of the statistic. The size of the standard error depends on the size of the sample and is unrelated to the size of the population. A properly drawn sample has a 95 per cent chance of producing a statistic with a value that is within two standard errors of the true, population, value, so, conversely, there is a 95 per cent chance that the true population value lies within two standard errors of the sample statistic. This means that, if 100 samples of the same size were drawn, in 95 cases we would expect the value of the statistic to be within two standard errors of the population value; we would expect it to be outside the range in 5 cases. Since we do not generally actually know the population value, we have to rely on this theoretical statement of probability about the likely accuracy of our finding: we have a 95 per cent chance of being approximately right and a 5 per cent chance of being wrong.

This 'two standard errors' range is referred to as the '95 per cent confidence interval' of a statistic. The relationship between standard errors and level of probability is a property of the 'normal curve' – a bell-shaped curve with certain mathematical properties – which we are not able to pursue here. The idea of a normal curve and 95 per cent confidence intervals is illustrated in Figure 13.1. The general idea of probabilities related to the properties of certain types of 'distribution' is pursued in more detail in Chapter 17.

Statisticians have drawn up tables that give the confidence intervals for various statistics for various sample sizes, as shown in Table 13.1. Down the side of the table are various sample sizes, ranging from 50 to 10,000. Across the top of the table are statistics one might find from a survey – for example, 20 per cent visit museums. The table shows 20 per cent together with 80 per cent because, if it is found that 20 per cent of the sample visit museums, then it

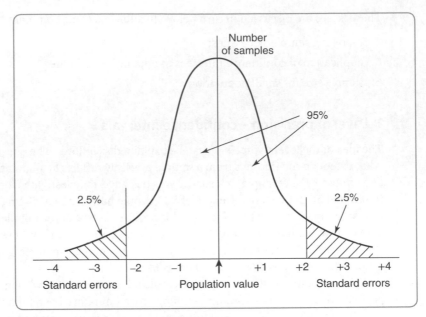

Figure 13.1 Normal curve and confidence intervals

Table 13.1 Confidence intervals related to sample size

Sample size	50%	40 or 60%	30 or 70%	20 or 80%	10 or 90%	5 or 95%	2 or 98%	1 or 99%
				Confidence intervals (±%)				
50	±13.9	±13.6	±12.7	±11.1	±8.3	*	*	*
80	±11.0	±10.7	±10.0	±8.8	±6.6	*	*	*
100	±9.8	±9.6	±9.0	±7.8	±5.9	±4.3	*	*
150	±8.0	±7.8	±7.3	±6.4	±4.8	±3.5	*	*
200	±6.9	±6.8	±6.3	±5.5	±4.2	±3.0	±1.9	*
250	±6.2	±6.1	±5.7	±5.0	±3.7	±2.7	±1.7	*
300	±5.7	±5.5	±5.2	±4.5	±3.4	±2.5	±1.6	*
400	±4.9	±4.8	±4.5	±3.9	±2.9	±2.1	±1.4	±1.0
500	±4.4	±4.3	±4.0	±3.5	±2.6	±1.9	±1.2	±0.9
750	±3.6	±3.5	±3.3	±2.9	±2.1	±1.6	±1.0	±0.7
1000	±3.1	±3.0	±2.8	±2.5	±1.9	±1.3	±0.9	±0.6
2000	±2.2	±2.1	±2.0	±1.7	±1.3	±1.0	±0.6	±0.4
4000	±1.5	±1.5	±1.4	±1.2	±0.9	±0.7	±0.4	±0.3
10,000	±1.0	±1.0	±0.9	±0.8	±0.6	±0.4	±0.3	±0.2

The top spanning header reads: **Percentages found from sample ('results')**

* Confidence interval greater than the percentage
Interpretation of table: for example, for a sample size of 400, a finding of 30% is subject to a confidence interval of ±4.5 (that is to say, we can be 95% certain that the population value lies in the range 25.5% to 34.5%). For formula to calculate confidence intervals see Appendix 13.1.

has also been found that 80 per cent *do not* visit museums. Any conclusion about the accuracy of the statistic 20 per cent also applies to the corresponding statistic 80 per cent. In the body of the table are the *confidence intervals*.

An example of how the table is interpreted is as follows. Suppose we have a sample size of 500 and we have a finding that 30 per cent of the sample have a certain characteristic – for example, have been to at least one festival in the previous year (so 70 per cent have *not* been to a festival). Reading off the table, for a sample size of 500, we find that a finding of 30 per cent (and 70 per cent) is subject to a confidence interval of plus or minus 4.0. So we can be fairly certain that the population value lies in the range 26.0 per cent to 34.0 per cent.

An important point should be noted about these confidence intervals: to halve the confidence interval it is necessary to quadruple the sample size. In the example above, a sample of 2,000 people (four times the original sample) would give a confidence interval of plus or minus 2.0 per cent (half the original confidence interval). The cost of increasing the precision of surveys by increasing the sample is therefore high.

Note that for smaller samples the confidence intervals become very large – for instance, for a sample of 50 the interval is plus or minus 13.9 per cent, meaning that a finding of 50 per cent can only be estimated to be within the range 36.1 per cent to 63.9 per cent. For some statistics, for the smaller sample sizes, the confidence intervals are not calculable because the total margin of error is larger than the original statistic.

It should be noted that these confidence intervals apply only for samples drawn using random sampling methods; other methods, such as multi-stage sampling, tend to produce larger confidence intervals, but the difference is generally small, so the matter is not pursued here.

The implications of the precision criterion for deciding sample size now become clear. A sample size of, say, 1,000 would give a confidence interval of plus or minus 3.1 per cent for a finding of 50 per cent. If that margin of error was not considered acceptable then a larger sample size would be necessary. Whether or not it is considered acceptable depends on the uses to which the data will be put and is related to the type of analysis to be done, as discussed below.

An alternative way of considering these relationships between sample size and confidence interval is presented in Table 13.2. This shows, in the body of the table, the necessary sample size to achieve a given confidence interval.

2 Detail of proposed analysis

The confidence intervals in Table 13.1 illustrate further the second criterion concerning the choice of sample size: the type of analysis to be undertaken. If many detailed comparisons

Table 13.2 Necessary sample sizes to achieve given confidence intervals

Conf. interval	Percentages found from sample ('results')						
	50%	40 or 60%	30 or 70%	20 or 80%	10 or 90%	5 or 95%	1 or 99%
	Minimum necessary sample size						
±1%	9,600	9,216	8,064	6,144	3,456	1,824	380
±2%	2,400	2,304	2,016	1,536	864	456	*
±3%	1,067	1,024	896	683	384	203	*
±4%	600	576	504	384	216	114	*
±5%	384	369	323	246	138	73	*
±6%	267	256	224	171	96	*	*
±7%	196	188	165	125	71	*	*
±8%	150	144	126	96	54	*	*
±9%	119	114	100	76	43	*	*
±10%	96	92	81	61	35	*	*

are to be made, especially concerning small proportions of the population, then the sample size may preclude meaningful analysis. For example, suppose a survey is conducted with a sample of 200 and it is found that 20 per cent of respondents preferred classical music, while 30 per cent preferred rock music. The 20 per cent is subject to a confidence interval of plus or minus 5.5 per cent and the 30 per cent is subject to a margin of plus or minus 6.3 per cent. Thus it is estimated that the proportions with the two preferences are as follows:

Classical: between 14.5 and 25.5%   Rock: between 23.7 and 36.3%

The confidence intervals overlap, so we cannot conclude that there is any 'significant' difference in the popularity of the two genres among this sample, despite a 10 per cent difference given by the survey. This is likely to be limiting in any analysis. However, if the sample were 500, the confidence intervals would be 3.5 per cent and 4.0 per cent respectively, giving estimates as follows:

Classical: between 16.5 and 23.5%   Rock: between 26.0 and 34.0%

In this case the confidence intervals do *not* overlap and we can be fairly certain that rock music *is* more popular than classical music.

The detail of the analysis, the extent of sub-division of the sample into sub-samples, and the acceptable level of precision will therefore determine the necessary size of the sample. By and large this has nothing to do with the overall size of the original population, although there is a likelihood that the larger the population, the greater its diversity and therefore the greater the need for sub-division into sub-samples.

3 Budget

A further point to be noted is that it could be positively wasteful to expend resources on a large sample when it can be shown to be unnecessary. For example, a sample of 10,000 gives estimates of statistics with a maximum confidence interval of ± 1 per cent. Such a survey could cost, say, £250,000 to conduct. To halve that confidence interval to ± 0.5 per cent would mean quadrupling the sample size to 40,000 at a cost of £1 million. There can be few situations where such expenditure would be justified for such a small return.

Ultimately, then, the limiting factor in determining sample size will be this third criterion, the resources available. Even if the available budget limits the sample size severely, it may be decided to go ahead and risk the possibility of an unrepresentative sample. If the sample is small, however, the detail of the analysis will need to be limited. If resources are so limited that the validity of quantitative research is questionable, it may be sensible to consider qualitative research, which may be more feasible. Alternatively, the proposed research can be seen as a 'pilot' exercise, with the emphasis on methodology, preparatory to a more adequately resourced full-scale study in future.

4 Reporting sample size issues

How should the issue of sample size and confidence intervals be referred to in the report on the research? In some scientific research, complex statistical tests are considered necessary in reporting statistical results from surveys. In much social science research, including arts/events research in particular, requirements are less rigorous. This is true to some extent in academic research, but is markedly so in the reporting of applied policy or management-related research. While it is necessary to be aware of the limitations imposed by the sample size and not to make comparisons which the data cannot support, explicit reference to such matters in the text of a consultancy report is rare. A great deal of statistical jargon is not generally required: the lay reader expects the researcher to do a good job and expert readers should be given enough information to check the analysis in the report for themselves. It is recommended that an appendix be included in reports indicating the size of the sampling errors. Appendix 13.1 gives a possible format.

In academic journals, the rules are somewhat different and there is an expectation that statistical tests (see Chapter 17) be 'up front'.

5 Confidence intervals applied to population estimates

The above comments are focused on confidence intervals applied to percentages derived from samples. Caution should be used when discussing *population estimates* based on sample surveys. In many cases the sample statistics are applied to the population as a whole to obtain estimates of, for example, total visits to a museum, when even more care should be taken. A hypothetical worked example is outlined in Table 13.3. It might be thought that because the survey finding of the proportion of the population visiting a museum (12 per cent) is subject to a confidence interval of ±2.0 per cent, this also applies to the estimated number of persons visiting and to the number of visits. But this is not so: both the number of persons and the number of visits are subject to a confidence interval of +16.7 per cent. To obtain a confidence interval of ±2.0 per cent of the number of persons/visits, that is to reduce it to an eighth of its current size, would require a sample size of at least 64,000.

6 Sample size and small populations

The above discussion of sample size assumes that the population is large – in fact, the statistical formulae used to calculate the confidence intervals are based on the assumption that the population is, in effect, infinite. The relationship between the size of confidence intervals and the size of the population becomes noticeable when the population size falls below about 50,000, as shown in Table 13.4. The table presents sample sizes necessary to produce 95 per cent confidence intervals of ±5 per cent and ±1 per cent for a sample finding of 50 per cent for different population sizes. Only the sample sizes for a 50 per cent finding

Table 13.3 Confidence intervals applied to visit numbers

Item	Source	Number
Population	Census	500,000
Sample	Household survey	1000
% visiting museum in a year	Household survey	12%
Percentage confidence interval	Table 13.1	±2.0%
Estimated number of persons	12% of 500,000	60,000
Conf. interval in terms of persons	±2% of 500,000	±10,000
Confidence interval as % of no. of persons	$(10,000/60,000) \times 100$	±16.7
Frequency of visit, times per year	Household survey	2.5
Estimated total visits	Calc.: $60,000 \times 2.5$	150,000
Confidence interval in terms of visits	Calc.: $10,000 \times 2.5$	±25,000
Confidence interval as % of visits	Calc.: $(25,000/150,000) \times 100$	±16.7%

Table 13.4 Sample size and population size: small populations

Population size	Minimum sample sizes for confidence interval of ±5% and ±1% on a sample finding of 50%	
	±5%	±1%
Infinite*	384	9,602
10,000,000	384	9,593
5,000,000	384	9,584
1,000,000	384	9,511
500,000	384	9,422
100,000	383	8,761
50,000	381	8,056
25,000	378	6,938
20,000	377	6,488
10,000	370	4,899
5000	357	3,288
2000	322	1,655
1000	278	906
500	217	475
200	132	196
100	80	99
50	44	50

* As in Figures 13.1 and 13.2 and formula in Appendix 17.2

are presented since, as shown in Table 13.1, the 50 per cent finding is the most demanding in terms of sample size: for a given sample size, the confidence intervals for other findings – for example, 30/70% – are always smaller. The table first indicates the sample size for an infinite population and it can be seen that the sample sizes are the same as indicated for a ±5% per cent or ±1% per cent confidence interval in the first column of Table 13.2. The details of the formula relating confidence intervals to population size can be found in Krejcie and Morgan (1970).

Weighting

Situations where weighting of survey or count data may be required have been referred to at various points in this chapter. In Chapter 16 the procedures for implementing weighting using the SPSS computer package are outlined. Here we discuss the principles involved. Take the example of the data shown in Table 13.5. In the sample of 45 interviews the number of interviews is spread fairly equally through the day, whereas more than half the actual visitors are counted around the middle of the day (this information having been obtained by observation/counts). This can be a source of bias in the sample, since the mid-day visitors may differ from the others in their characteristics or opinions and they will be under-represented in the sample. The aim of weighting is to produce a weighted sample with a distribution similar to that of the actual visitors.

One approach is to 'gross up' the sample numbers to reflect the actual numbers – e.g. the 9–11 am group is weighted by $25 \div 10 = 2.5$, the 11–1 pm group is weighted by $240 \div 12 = 20$, and so on, as shown in Table 13.6.

Table 13.5 Interview/usage data from a site/visitor survey

	Interviews		Total visitors (counts)	
Time	Number	%	Number	%
9–11 am	10	22.2	25	5.7
11.01–1 pm	12	26.7	240	55.2
1.01–3 pm	11	24.4	110	25.3
3.01–5 pm	12	26.7	60	2.7
Total	45	100.0	435	100.0

Table 13.6 Weighting

	A	B	C	D
Time	No. of interviews	No. of visitors	Weighting factors	Weighted sample no.
Source:	Survey	Counts	B/A	C × A
9–11 am	10	25	2.5	25
11.01–1 pm	12	240	20.0	240
1.01–3 pm	11	110	10.0	110
3.01–5pm	12	60	5.0	60
Total	45	435		435

The weighting factors can be fed into the computer for the weighting to be done automatically (see Chapter 16). The initial weighting factors are equal to the user number divided by the sample number for that time period. The weighted sample therefore is made to resemble the overall user numbers. It should be noted, however, that the sample size is still 45, not 435! If statistical tests are to be carried out then it would be advisable to multiply the weighting factors by 0.103 (45/435) to bring the weighted sample total back to 45.

In this example the basis of the weighting relates to the pattern of visits over the course of the day, which happened to be information which was available in relation to this particular type of survey. Any other data available on the population could be used – for example, if age structure is available from the census, then age groups rather than time periods might be used.

Sampling for qualitative research

Qualitative research generally makes no claim to quantitative representativeness and, by definition, does not involve statistical calculation demanding prescribed levels of precision (see Chapter 9). Generally, therefore, the quantitative considerations outlined above are not relevant to qualitative research. This is not to say that representativeness is ignored entirely. As Henderson (2006: 172) puts it: 'The researcher using the qualitative approach is not concerned about adequate numbers or random selection, but with trying to present a working picture of the broader social structure drawn from interviews, observations or text.' Thus, if the population being studied includes young and old people, then both young and old people will be included in the sample, but the sample will not necessarily reflect the *proportions* of young and old in the study population.

Miles and Huberman (1994: 28) list 16 'strategies' for qualitative sampling. Some of these are presented in Figure 13.2.

Method	Characteristics
Convenience	Use of conveniently located persons or organisations – e.g. friends, colleagues, students, organisations in the neighbourhood, visitors to local cultural venue or event.
Criterion	Individuals selected on the basis of a key criterion – e.g. age group, membership of an organisation, purchasers of a certain type of recorded music.
Homogeneous	Deliberately selecting a relatively homogeneous sub-set of the population – e.g. university-educated male musicians aged 20–30.
Opportunistic	Similar to 'convenience' but involves taking advantage of opportunities as they arise – e.g. studying a major event taking place locally, or a venue where the researcher works.
Maximum variation	Deliberately studying contrasting cases: opposite of 'homogeneous'.
Purposeful	Similar to 'criterion' but may involve other considerations, such as 'maximum variation' or typicality.
Snowball	Interviewees used as a source of suggestions for additional contacts.
Stratified purposeful	Selection of a range of cases based on set criteria, e.g. representatives of a range of age groups or nationalities.

Figure 13.2 Selected qualitative sampling methods

In the research report, the qualitative sampling methods used should be adequately described. In all cases, just how individuals are selected and contacted should be described. For example, if the 'criterion' sampling method was used, what was the actual criterion used and how were the people who met the criterion contacted? If a 'snowball' method was used, how was it started? If 'convenience' sampling was used, what was the convenience factor – friendship, family, colleagues, students, neighbours?

There are no generally hard and fast rules for determining the appropriate sample size in qualitative research. One criterion used in quantitative research also applies, namely the available budget and time. Some of the sampling methods listed in Figure 13.2 point towards a minimum sample size, for example the range of groups to be covered in the 'criterion' and 'stratified-purposeful' methods. In grounded theory research, the sample size may be determined by the process of 'saturation', that is, the point at which further subjects stop producing new themes or theoretical categories (Charmaz, 2006: 113).

Summary

This chapter covers the topic of sampling, which is the process of selecting a proportion of the population of subjects for study. It also examines the implications of sampling for data analysis. Two key issues are considered: *representativeness* of samples, and *sample size*. The researcher seeks representativeness by following the principles of *random sampling*, which means that, as near as possible, every member of the population has an equal chance of being selected. Different types of survey involve different practical procedures for seeking to achieve random sampling. If a sample has been randomly selected, the question still arises as to the extent to which the statistical findings from the sample truly reflect the population.

Statistical procedures have been developed to assess the level of probability that a sample finding lies within a certain margin of the true population value. This margin is known as a *confidence interval* and its size is related to the size of the sample, regardless of the size of the population – the larger the sample, the smaller the confidence interval or margin of statistical error. The necessary sample size for a study therefore depends on the precision required in the results, the detail of the analysis to be undertaken and the available budget. Finally, the chapter considers the practice of *weighting* to correct a sample for known bias, and methods for qualitative sampling.

TEST QUESTIONS

1. Define random sampling.
2. What is the opposite of a random/representative sample?
3. What is multi-stage sampling and why is it used?
4. What is a confidence interval?
5. What determines the size of the sample to be used in a study?
6. What is weighting?
7. Name three possible approaches to sampling for qualitative research.

EXERCISES

1. Examine two published arts/events research reports or journal articles with empirical content and identify the procedures used to ensure a random sample and how the sample sizes used are justified.

2. Using the reports in exercise 1, produce confidence intervals for a range of percentage statistics occurring in the reports.

3. In the example comparing classical and rock music preferences under 'Detail of proposed analysis', above, what would the confidence intervals be if the sample size was 4,000?

4. Examine the results from a national cultural participation survey or a published survey of visitors to a major event and produce confidence intervals for a number of the key findings.

Resources

Sampling and the statistical implications of sampling are addressed in numerous statistics textbooks, for example: Kidder (1981) Chapter 4; Spatz and Johnston (1989), Chapter 6.

Sampling for telephone interviews: Lepowski *et al.* (2008); problem of mobile phones: Link and Lai (2011).

References

Charmaz, K. (2006) *Constructing Grounded Theory*. London: Sage.

Henderson, K. A. (2006) *Dimensions of Choice: A Qualitative Approach to Recreation, Parks, and Leisure Research*, Second Edition. State College, PA: Venture.

Kidder, L. (1981) *Selltiz, Wrightsman and Cook's Research Methods in Social Relations*. New York: Holt, Rinehart and Winston.

Krejcie, R. V. and Morgan, D. W. (1970) Determining sample size for research activities. *Educational and Psychological Measurement*, 30(4), 607–610.

Lepkowski, J. M., Tucker, C., Brick, J. M., de Leeuw, E. and Japec, L. (eds) (2008) *Advances in Telephone Survey Methodology*. New York: John Wiley.

Link, M. W. and Lai, J. W. (2011) Cell-phone-only households and problems of differential nonresponse using address-based sampling design. *Public Opinion Quarterly*, 75(4), 613–635.

Miles, M. B. and Huberman, A. M. (1994) *Qualitative Data Analysis*, Second Edition. Thousand Oaks, CA: Sage.

Spatz, C. and Johnston, J. O. (1989) *Basic Statistics: Tales of Distribution*, Fourth Edition. Pacific Grove, CA: Brooks/Cole Publishing.

Appendix 13.1
Suggested appendix on sample size and confidence intervals

This is suggested wording for an appendix or note to be included in research reports based on sample data. Suppose the survey has a sample size of 500.

Statistical note

All sample surveys are subject to a margin of statistical error. The margins of error, or 'confidence intervals' for this survey, with a sample of 500, are as follows:

Finding from the survey	95% confidence interval
50%	± 4.4%
40% or 60%	± 4.3%
30% or 70%	± 4.0%
20% or 80%	± 3.5%
10% or 90%	± 2.6%
5% or 95%	± 1.9%
1% or 99%	± 0.9%

This means, for example, that if 20 per cent of the sample are found to have a particular characteristic, there is an estimated 95 per cent chance that the true population percentage lies in the range 20 ± 3.5, i.e. between 16.5 per cent and 23.5 per cent.

These margins of error have been taken into account in the analyses in this report.

PART 3

Data analysis

This part of the book considers analysis of data in various forms and from various sources and so each of the four chapters has particular links with corresponding chapters in Part 2. Other Part 2 chapters, namely Observation (Chapter 8), Experimental research (Chapter 11), The case study method (Chapter 12) and Sampling: quantitative and qualitative (Chapter 13), are linked to all four of the Part 3 chapters in various ways.

- Chapter 14, Analysing secondary data, provides examples of the use of some of the types of data source discussed in Chapter 7.

- Chapter 15, Analysing qualitative data, considers both manual and computer-aided analysis of the type of data discussed in Chapter 9.

- Chapter 16, Analysing quantitative data, continues where Chapter 10 left off, examining the use of both spreadsheet programs and a statistical computer package for the analysis of questionnaire-based survey data.

- Chapter 17, Statistical analysis, relates particularly to the questionnaire-based data discussed in Chapters 10 and 16, and also to Chapter 11, Experimental methods.

Chapter 14

Analysing secondary data

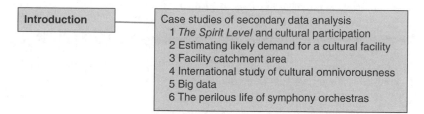

Introduction

This chapter builds on Chapter 7, in which the secondary data phenomenon and its various forms and sources are described. There are no specific analytical techniques or computer packages associated with such data, given its diversity. Most of the quantitative data is susceptible to relatively simple spreadsheet analysis. Where re-analysis of survey data is involved, the procedures outlined in Chapters 16 and 17 will apply. Similarly, for qualitative data, the procedures in Chapter 15 will apply. In this chapter, therefore, the aim is not to address the detail of analytical procedures but to provide summaries of examples of practical and imaginative uses of secondary data for arts/events research purposes. The case studies and data types are summarised in Figure 14.1, which includes reference to a relevant case study in an earlier chapter.

Type of data (see Chapter 7)	Case study
Administrative/management	14.3 Facility catchment area
	14.5 Big data
	14.6 Symphony orchestras
National participation surveys	12.1 Theatre-going
	14.1 Cultural participation
	14.2 Estimating demand
	14.4 Cultural omnivorousness
Economic/industry	14.1 Income inequality
Population census	14.2 Estimating demand
Documentary	14.6 Symphony orchestras
Opportunism	14.1 Cultural participation

Figure 14.1 Summary of secondary data analysis case studies and data types

CASE STUDY 14.1

The Spirit Level and cultural participation

The Spirit Level

In *The Spirit Level: Why More Equal Societies Almost Always Do Better*, Wilkinson and Pickett (2009, 2010) use cross-national secondary data from the United Nations and other sources to make the case that the more equal the distribution of income in a country, the more favourable are the outcomes on a range of indicators of human well-being, including life expectancy, infant mortality, physical and mental health, educational performance and the level of crime.

The book concentrates mainly on the 21 countries with the highest per capita national incomes, with Portugal, Greece and Israel at the lower end and Norway and the USA at the upper end. This selection is made because, it is argued, up to an income of about $15,000 per head, happiness and well-being tend to increase with income; above that level happiness and well-being are related not to income levels but, it is claimed, to the degree of income inequality within the society. For each country, inequality is measured by the ratio of the average income of the top 20 per cent of households to that of the bottom 20 per cent, income being net of income tax and benefits and adjusted for size of household. This measure identifies the USA, Portugal, the UK, New Zealand and Australia as the most unequal countries and Japan and the Scandinavian countries, Norway, Finland, Sweden and Denmark, as the most equal.

Table 14.1 Income inequality and cultural participation, Europe, 2007

	Income inequality (Gini coefficient)	Cultural participation*
Austria (AUT)	0.26	329
Belgium (BEL)	0.26	320
Bulgaria (BUL)	0.35	172
Cyprus (CYP)	0.30	209
Czech Rep. (CZE)	0.25	356
Denmark (DNK)	0.25	452
Estonia (EST)	0.33	371
Finland (FIN)	0.26	410
France (FRA)	0.27	306
Germany (GER)	0.30	338
Greece (GRE)	0.34	214
Hungary (HUN)	0.26	272
Ireland (IRL)	0.31	359
Italy (ITA)	0.32	284
Latvia (LAT)	0.35	353
Lithuania (LIT)	0.34	277
Luxembourg (LUX)	0.27	367
Malta (MALT)	0.26	278
Netherlands (NEL)	0.28	435
Poland (POL)	0.32	250
Portugal (POR)	0.37	211
Romania (ROM)	0.38	197
Slovakia (SLOVK)	0.25	347
Slovenia (SLOVN)	0.23	350
Spain (SPA)	0.31	282
Sweden (SWE)	0.23	458
United Kingdom (UK)	0.33	357

* Cultural = Sum of percentage participation rates for: visiting cinema, ballet/dance/opera, theatre, concert, public library, historic monuments, etc., museums/galleries, spectating at a live sport event, book reading.
Source: Participation: European Commission (2007); Gini coeff.: Eurstat: http://epp.eurostat.ec.europa.eu (varies from 0 (complete equality) to 1 (extreme inequality)).

Case study 14.1 (*continued*)

While the methodology used and the conclusions drawn by Wilkinson and Pickett have not been without their critics (see Veal, 2014 for summary), they have attracted considerable attention and raise some interesting questions regarding social welfare in economically advanced societies.

Cultural participation

Wilkinson and Pickett's book does not, however, include cultural participation indicators. It is possible to remedy this deficiency with data on cultural participation, which is the purpose of this case study.

Table 14.1 shows data on cultural participation for the 27 European Union countries (as at 2007) from a Eurobarometer survey, measured by the sum of the percentage participation rates for each country for ten cultural activities, so it has a maximum value of 1,000. Szlendak and Karwacki (2012) conducted a similar study using the same data source, but analysed just three of the cultural activities separately, and for just 22 of the countries. The measure of income inequality is not the one used by Wilkinson and Pickett but the more common *Gini coefficient*, which has an extreme value of zero for complete equality, where, theoretically, every household has the same income, and a value of 1.0 for the maximum inequality, where, again theoretically, one household has all the income.

In Figure 14.2 these data are plotted on a graph in similar format to that used by Wilkinson and Pickett. This was done using the 'scatterplot' facility in a spreadsheet (also, in the case of Microsoft Excel, a 'macro' to add country labels to the data points). It can be seen that there is a downward-sloping relationship: that is, the greater the level of inequality, the less the level of cultural participation. The figure also includes a measure of the strength of the relationship, an R^2 of 0.37, which is statistically significant, that is, unlikely to be due to chance (see Chapter 17).

This suggests that, in addition to the traditional social welfare measure used by Wilkinson and Pickett, cultural participation may be affected by the degree of income inequality in a community. This could be

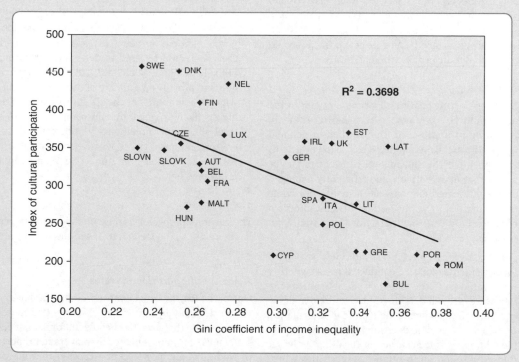

Figure 14.2 Relationship between income inequality and cultural participation, Europe, 2007

Data source: see Table 14.1

Case study 14.1 (*continued*)

explored further, in a number of ways, including examination of individual activities, other variables as influences on variations in participation levels between countries (e.g. average income, levels of education), and theoretical explanations for the variations observed. These possibilities are not pursued here (but see Veal, 2014).

This case study is an example of the use of national participation survey data (in this case international) and economic data (income inequality). It can be seen as opportunistic, in that the analysis arose as a result of the publication *The Spirit Level* and the availability of the Eurobarometer data.

CASE STUDY 14.2

Estimating likely demand for a cultural facility

The problem

A developer or local council is considering whether to build a cinema on a particular site in a town centre, as part of a multi-purpose leisure complex. Cinema is used in this example, but the methodology could be applied equally to other types of facility. The town has a population of 100,000 and already has two 400-seat cinemas. The developer wishes to know what demand exists in the area for such a facility. A range of approaches could be considered to investigate this question.

Possibilities

- *Examine existing facilities*: Existing cinemas in the area could be examined to see whether they are over-used or under-used, that is whether demand is already being adequately met. However, this may not give the full answer, since it might be found that imaginatively and efficiently managed and well-located cinemas are heavily used while others are not. It might also be difficult to obtain commercially sensitive data from potential competitors.

- *Conduct resident survey*: An interview survey of local residents could be conducted to ask whether they would go to the cinema if suitable new facilities were provided. The results could not, however, be relied on as the main piece of information on which to base the decision because, while people's honesty and accuracy in recalling activities might be relied on in relation to activities which they have actually undertaken, asking them to predict their behaviour in hypothetical future situations is risky.

- *Examine similar communities*: Communities of similar size and type could be examined to see what levels of cinema provision they have and how well they are used. This could be somewhat 'hit and miss' because it is not easy to find comparable communities and some of the data required, being commercially 'sensitive', may not be readily available.

- *Use of secondary data*: Secondary data – an appropriate national survey (NS) and the Population Census – could be used to determine an estimate of likely demand for cinema visits in the area. The aim is to provide an estimate of the level of demand which a community of the size of that in the study area is likely to generate and compare it with the level of demand already likely to be catered for by existing cinemas, to see whether or not there is a surplus of demand over supply. Such an approach is outlined here.

The approach

The general approach is represented diagrammatically in Figure 14.3. The steps A to H are discussed in turn below.

A Age-specific participation rates

One of the features of cinema attendance is that it varies considerably by age. Cinema is attended more by young people than by older people. If, for example, the study town contains a higher than average proportion of young people, it would be expected that it would produce a higher than average demand for cinema, and vice versa. The NS gives information on the percentage of people of different ages who go to the cinema,

Case study 14.2 (*continued*)

as shown in Table 14.2. It can be seen that teenagers are almost six times as likely to attend the cinema as the over 60s. The particular NS deals only with people aged 16 and over. Obviously children under that age do go to the cinema, but it may be that there is sufficient demand for an additional cinema even without taking account of the under 16s, so the under 16s can be ignored for the moment, returning to them only if necessary.

B Population by age groups

Suppose the census gives the population of the town as 100,000 and the population aged 16 and over as 80,000. In Table 14.3 the age structure of the national population aged 16 and over is compared with that of the study town. Clearly the town has a much younger age profile than the national average, with only just over half the proportion of over-55s and correspondingly larger proportions in the young age groups. So it is obviously advisable to give consideration to the question of age structure.

C Estimate total demand from local population

Table 14.4 indicates how demand for cinema attendance would be estimated: attendances are estimated for each age group and summed, giving a total of 6,543 attendances per week.

D Estimate of typical facility capacity

For this exercise it is assumed that a typical 400-seat cinema auditorium requires 1,500 ticket sales a week to be viable.

E Estimate capacity of existing facilities

Two cinemas already exist in the town. If they have a seating capacity of 400 each, then they would together be accommodating some 3,000 visits a week for viability.

F Compare

The total estimated demand is 6,500 visits per week, and the existing cinemas have a capacity of 3,000 per week.

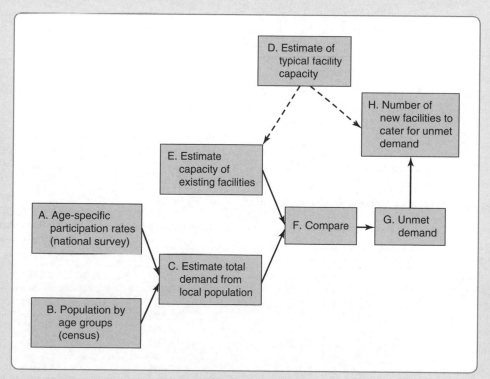

Figure 14.3 Estimating likely demand for a leisure facility

Case study 14.2 (*continued*)

Table 14.2 Cinema attendance by age

Age group	% of age group who go to the cinema in an average week (from national survey)
14–19 years	14.9
20–24	11.5
25–29	7.4
30–39	5.2
40–49	4.8
50–59	3.5
60+	2.5
Total/average	6.6

Source: Hypothetical data.

G. Unmet demand

Unmet demand can therefore be estimated as about 3,500 visits per week.

H Number of new facilities to cater for unmet demand

It would take two typical 400-seat cinemas to cater for the unmet demand – that is, it is estimated that the town could support an additional two cinemas.

Comment

The above approach does not predict demand precisely, it merely indicates a 'ball park' demand figure. A well-managed and programmed cinema might draw far more demand than is estimated. The national survey attendance rates refer to average attendances across the country, so clearly there are places where higher attendance rates occur and places where lower rates occur. What the exercise indicates is that, on the basis of data to hand, 6,500 cinema attendances a week seem likely. This appears to be a simple and crude calculation, but quite often investors – in the public and private sectors – fail to carry out even this sort of simple calculation to check on 'ball park' demand figures; investments are made on the basis of personal hunch, and then surprise is expressed when demand fails to materialise.

Table 14.3 Study town and national age structure compared

Age groups	National population: census data %	Study town population: census data %
14–19	12.5	19.5
20–24	11.9	19.0
25–29	10.6	14.2
30–39	20.1	21.1
40–49	14.2	9.0
50–59	11.8	7.7
60+	18.9	9.5
Total	100.0	100.0

Source: Hypothetical data.

Table 14.4 Estimating demand for cinema attendance

Data source:	% of age group participating per week (X) National survey	Town population (Y) Census	Estimated demand (visits per week) XY/100
14–19 years	14.9	15,600	2,324
20–24	11.5	15,200	1,748
25–29	7.4	11,360	841
30–39	5.2	16,880	878
40–49	4.8	7,200	346
50–59	3.5	6,160	216
60+	2.5	7,600	190
Total/average	8.2	80,000	6,543

Case study 14.2 (*continued*)

Forecasting note: to provide a simple forecast of future demand for, say, the year 2020 it would be necessary merely to insert population forecasts for the year 2020 into the second column of Table 14.4 and rework the calculations.

Economic note: while the exercise here has been outlined in terms of 'number of users or customers', use of household expenditure data, such as that discussed in Chapter 7, could convert the unit of analysis into expenditure.

CASE STUDY 14.3

Facility catchment area

Cultural facilities and events often generate information on visitors' addresses which can be used to study the *catchment area* or *market area* – an important aspect of planning and management. Many cultural facilities have membership or subscriber lists. Cultural tourism businesses that provide residential facilities typically have details of patrons' home addresses. Figure 14.4 shows how such data can be plotted on a map to produce a visual representation of the catchment or market area of the facility. Such information can be used either to concentrate marketing to increase sales in the exist-

ing area, or to focus marketing outside the identified area in order to extend the catchment or market area.

When very large numbers are involved it may be necessary to sample membership or customer lists – for example, selecting every fifth or tenth member or patron on the list.

While this case study is used to illustrate the use of secondary data, catchment areas can also be based on survey data, which will be necessary if existing information on client addresses is not available (see Chapter 10, particularly discussion of user/site surveys).

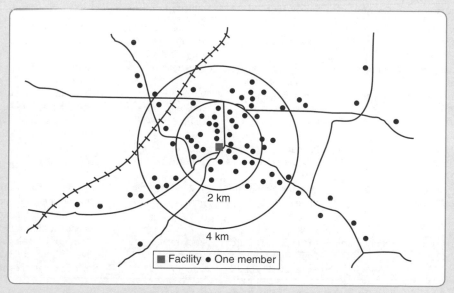

Figure 14.4 Catchment/market area

CASE STUDY 14.4

International study of cultural omnivorousness

There are three competing theoretical perspectives on the relationship between cultural consumption/participation and social class or status.

- The traditional *homology* perspective, associated with Bourdieu (1984) and Gans (1999), is that the hierarchy of social classes, typically based on occupational status, is associated with a corresponding hierarchy of cultural participation.

- The *individualisation* perspective, associated with Giddens (1991) and Beck (1992), is that in Western society the breaking down of traditional ties of solidarity, such as class and community, and the widespread availability of cultural products, results in less predictable and more random or fragmented patterns of cultural consumption.

- The *omnivore–univore* perspective, originated by Peterson and Simkus (1992) in a secondary analysis of US data, observes that those in higher-status occupations, rather than being confined to 'elite' tastes tend to have wide-ranging tastes across the cultural spectrum, while those in lower-status occu-

pations have a comparatively narrow range of tastes – for example, in the case of music, often being confined to a single 'low-status' genre.

The three competing perspectives have spawned a mass of supportive and critical international empirical research. It is not possible to explore all this material here, but we draw attention to one particular collaborative project, led by Tak Win Chan and John Goldthorpe of Oxford University. The project, funded by the British Economic and Social Research Council and the Arts and Humanities Research Council, involved researchers in six countries exploring these perspectives through secondary analysis of existing national survey data-sets. The results were published in a special issue of the journal *Poetics* and details are shown in Figure 14.5. It can be seen that the results are mixed, with only limited support for the pure form of the omnivore–univore perspective. Some of the statistical techniques used in the studies – such as multiple regression and multiple classification analysis – are quite complex and are discussed further in Chapter 17.

Authors	Country	Survey source	Activity focus	Findings (method)*
Alderson *et al.* (2007)	USA	General Social Survey, 2002	Attending performing arts, museums/galleries, reading novels	Confirms omnivore–univore perspective (LCA)
Budoki (2007)	Hungary	Way of Life and Time Use Survey, 2000	Book reading	Confirms homology perspective (MR)
Chan and Goldthorpe (2007)	England	Arts in England Survey, 2001	Visual arts consumption + cultural festival	Questions all three perspectives. In visual arts, for low-status subjects inactive replaces univore (LCA)
Coulangeon and Lemel (2007)	France	Permanent Survey on Living Conditions, 2003†	Taste in music genres	Confirms social elite as omnivorous (MCA)
Katz-Gerro *et al.* (2007)	Israel	Unnamed national survey, 2006†	Taste in music genres	Disconfirms individualisation perspective, but taste is affected by more factors than economic class (MR)
Kraaykamp, *et al.* (2007)	Nether-lands	Family Survey Dutch Population, 1992, 1998, 2000, 2003	Book reading, TV watching	Confirms homology perspective, but participation related to own and partner's status (MR)

Figure 14.5 Studies of cultural consumption/taste and social status

† In these cases the analysis may not be secondary in the strict sense because the authors appear to have been involved with the original data collection.

* LCA = latent class analysis, MCA = multiple correspondence analysis, MR = multiple regression – see discussion in Chapter 17.

CASE STUDY 14.5

Big data

'Big data' is the analysis of large electronic/digital data-sets, typically arising from electronic records of customer activity (see Chapter 5). Some short case studies/examples from the literature illustrate the emerging potential of the phenomenon.

A Book sales

In its early days, the large online bookseller Amazon published book reviews and recommendations on its site, from a panel of knowledgeable book critics (Mayer-Schönberger and Cukier, 2013: 50–52). It was then realised that the company could use the information it held on buying patterns to make recommendations to customers. Initially, it was based on other shoppers' buying patterns, but this generated too large and diverse a list of recommendations. Later (and what customers see on the Amazon website now), the recommendations were based on associations between a number of the characteristics of the products – for example, unlike a simple browser search, the book recommendations do not confuse 'the arts' with 'martial arts'. Once the new system was installed, sales soared and the book critics were made redundant.

B The long tail

While the term 'long tail' was coined quite recently by Anderson (2004), the idea is long-established in the marketing of cultural products, notably books, music recordings and films, as illustrated in Figure 14.6. Benghozi and Benhamou (2010: 47) refer to data on book sales in France which show bestsellers, with sales of over 5000, accounting for just 16 per cent of titles but 83 per cent of sales, while low sellers (less than 800) account for 43 per cent of titles but only two per cent of sales. For the traditional industrial/business model, involving printing technology requiring minimum print runs to be economic and the physical shipping of books to booksellers, this has been a problem. But digitised books and online sales transform the situation, not only are physical production and distribution costs massively reduced, but the reduced prices and globalised ease of purchase tend to *fatten the tail*. But at the same time, the low production costs allow more low-selling products to come onto the market and production-on-demand allows low selling, niche products to continue to be available long after they would have been discontinued under previous business models, thus *lengthening the tail*.

So much for the theory. In practice, some research suggests, for cultural products such as books and CDs, the online environment has not reduced the dominance of bestsellers in the marketplace and, for some consumers, the long tail may be a negative rather than a

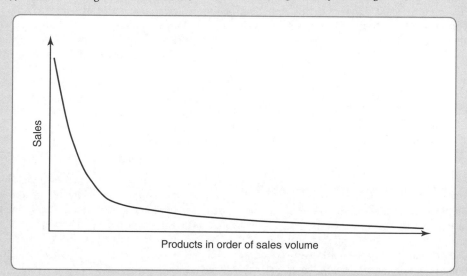

Figure 14.6 The long tail

Case study 14.5 (*continued*)

positive – there can be such a thing as too much choice (Benghozi and Benhamou, 2010; Hjorth-Anderson, 2007). Since choice is often seen as the hallmark of the market system, this type of research, using this type of big data, may be a key contributor to understanding consumer behaviour in the digital age.

C Culturomics

Using the Google Books digitised database, Michel *et al.* (2011) content-analysed data on 5 million books (500 billion words) published between 1800 and 2000 to examine aspects of cultural change as reflected in the printed word – a practice termed *culturomics*. Examples of graphics produced in the paper include the patterns of occurrence of mentions of celebrity names, artists, concepts and philosophies. An online application is available for researchers to do their own searches of words or phrases ('ngrams') – see Resources section.

D Social media

The principles of big data can be extended beyond corporate databases to social media or social network sites. For certain cultural phenomena, information and commentary on media such as Facebook, YouTube and Twitter provide a large and interesting source of data on the development of the phenomenon (e.g. a movie, music group, event). Social media monitoring software, such as Google Analytics and Alterian SM2, is available for business and researchers to utilise this source. An example of its use in research is Flinn and Frew's (2013) study of the social media coverage of the 2010 Glastonbury Festival of Contemporary Performing Arts. However, social media monitoring is just one source of information in the article, which draws on other media (television coverage, festival website) and methods (participant observation) and places considerable emphasis on theoretical interpretation.

CASE STUDY 14.6

The perilous life of symphony orchestras

Flanagan's (2012) book *The Perilous Life of Symphony Orchestras* was published against a background of increasingly frequent financial crises, including bankruptcies, of US orchestras. It is based entirely on secondary data, from three main sources:

- the League of American Orchestras and Opera America, which regularly collects data on the finances and operations of US symphony orchestras and opera companies;

- publicly available data on the tax returns of not-for-profit organisations (for example, via www.guidestar.org);

- data from the National Endowment for the Arts (NEA) on national arts audiences (see Chapter 7).

Another essential background is the phenomenon of the *cost disease* afflicting the arts, as identified by Baumol and Bowen (1966) almost 50 years ago. This is the problem that, while other parts of the economy are able to increase efficiency through the use of technology,

this is not possible in the case of the performing arts – for example, it takes just as long and just as many musicians to play a Mozart concerto now as it took when Mozart composed it. This means that arts organisations everywhere will continue to face cost problems.

The book begins with a simple model of symphony orchestra expenses, as shown in Figure 14.7. It identifies the basic problem, of a gap between the revenues and expenses arising from putting on performances and the need to fill the gap with *non-performance income*, from government, philanthropy or investment income from endowments.

A brief summary of the main findings:

- Symphony orchestras' own ticket sales data and NEA survey data indicate that audiences have been declining for 20 years, despite increasing levels of education in the population and increasing expenditure on marketing.

- Consequently, the relative contribution of ticket sales to total revenue is in decline, even though

Case study 14.6 (*continued*)

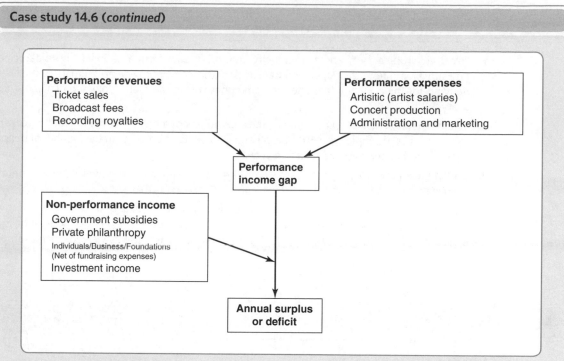

Figure 14.7 Symphony orchestra finances
Sources: Flanagan (2012: 17, modified).

ticket prices have increased faster than consumer prices generally.

- The relative contribution of government support to revenue has also declined.

- Greater reliance has therefore been placed on private support and investment income – but these fluctuate with economic conditions.

- Musicians' salaries have risen faster than wages generally and are higher than in other countries.

- The financial viability of an orchestra is dependent on the size and wealth of its host community.

Flanagan concludes that the structural problems caused by the cost disease are likely to continue and that while no single measure will solve the problem, a number of measures could ameliorate it. However, his suggestion that musician salary levels are part of the problem drew a sharp attack from the chairperson of the musicians' union (Ridge, 2012).

Summary

The chapter presents six case studies demonstrating potential uses of secondary data in policy, management and social research situations, including a cross-national examination of income inequality and cultural participation; a method for estimating demand for a new cultural facility in a local community; assessment of the catchment area of a cultural facility; a summary of international research on the cultural univore–omnivore thesis; examples of 'big data' analysis; and a study of the finances of US symphony orchestras.

EXERCISES

1. Select a cultural activity and a community and, using data from a national leisure participation survey and from the Population Census (see Chapter 7), provide an estimate of the likely demand for the activity in the selected community, using the methodology outlined in Case study 14.2.

2. In relation to exercise 1, what would be the implications of a predicted increase of 15 per cent in the number of people aged 60 and over and a 15 per cent decrease in the number of people aged 25 and under, over the next five years?

3. Undertake an exercise similar to Case study 14.4 for a leisure facility for which you can obtain user/member address data.

4. Select an activity from a national cultural survey and provide a profile of the activity, indicating the overall level of participation and how participation is related to age, gender, occupation and education (this is similar to exercise 12.1 in Chapter 12, where it was viewed as an example of a case study).

Resources

Websites

Culturomics, Harvard University: www.culturomics.org/cultural-observatory-at-harvard
Google Books Ngram Viewer: http://books.google.com/ngrams/

Publications

- Secondary data sources: see Chapter 7 Resources section.
- Big data/the long tail: Anderson (2008), Mayer-Schönberger and Cukier (2013).
- Cultural omnivorousness: extension of research in Case study 14.4: Chan (2010).
- Demand planning methods: Veal (2010).
- Examples:
  - arts amateur participation analysis using US General Social Survey: Brooks (2002)
  - opera: (demand model): Laamanen (2012)
  - orchestras: Flanagan (2012)

References

Alderson, A. S., Junisbai, A. and Heacock, I. (2007) Social status and cultural consumptions in the United States. *Poetics*, 35(2–3), 191–212.

Anderson, C. (2008) *The Long Tail: Why the Future of Business is Selling Less of More*. New York: Hyperion.

Baumol, W. J. and Bowen, W. G. (1966) *Performing Arts: The Economic Dilemma*. Cambridge, MA: MIT Press.

Beck, U. (1992) Beyond status and class? In *Risk Society: Towards a New Modernity*, London: Sage, 91–102 (originally published in German in 1986, Frankfurt: Suhrkamp Verlag).

Benghozi, P.-J. and Benhamou, F. (2010) The long tail: myth or reality? *International Journal of Arts Management*, 12(3), 43–53.

Bourdieu, P. (1984) *Distinction: A Social Critique of the Judgement of Taste*. London: Routledge.

Brooks, A. C. (2002) Artists as amateurs and volunteers. *Nonprofit Management and Leadership*, 13(1), 5–15.

Bukodi, E. (2007) Social stratification and cultural consumption in Hungary: book readership. *Poetics*, 35(2–3), 112–131.

Chan, T. W. (ed.) (2010) *Social Status and Cultural Consumption*. Cambridge: Cambridge University Press.

Chan, T. W. and Goldthorpe, J. H. (2007) Social stratification and cultural consumption: the visual arts in England. *Poetics*, 35(2), 168–190.

Coulangeon, P. and Lemel, Y. (2007) Is 'distinction' really outdated? Questioning the meaning of omnivoration of musical taste in contemporary France. *Poetics*, 35(1), 93–111.

European Commission (2007) *European Cultural Values: Special Eurobarometer 278*. Brussels: European Commission, available at: http://ec.europa.eu/public_opinion/archives/eb_special_en.htm

Flanagan, R. J. (2012) *The Perilous Life of Symphony Orchestras: Artistic Triumphs and Economic Challenges*. New Haven, CN: Yale University Press.

Flinn, J. and Frew, M. (2013) Glastonbury: managing the mystification of festivity. *Leisure Studies*, on-line: DOI: 10.1080/0261 02614367.2012.751121.

Gans, H. J. (1999) *Popular Culture and High Culture: An Analysis and Evaluation of Taste*, Revised Edition. New York: Basic Books.

Giddens, A. (1991) *Modernity and Self-Identity: Self and Society in the Late Modern Age*. Cambridge: Polity.

Hjorth-Anderson, C. (2007) Review of Chris Anderson, *The Long Tail. Journal of Cultural Economics*, 31(3), 235–237.

Katz-Gerro, T., Raz, S. and Yaish, M. (2007) Class, status, and the intergenerational transmission of musical tastes in Israel. *Poetics*, 35(2–3), 152–167.

Kraaykamp, G., van Eijck, K., Ultee, W. and van Rees, K. (2007) Status and media use in the Netherlands: do partners affect media taste? *Poetics*, 35(2–3), 132–151.

Laamanen, J.-P. (2012) Estimating demand for opera using sales system data: the case of Finnish National Opera. *Journal of Cultural Economics*, 37(4), 417–32.

Mayer-Schönberger, V. and Cukier, K. (2013) *Big Data: A Revolution that Will Transform How We Live, Work and Think*. London: John Murray.

Michel, J.-B., Shen, Y. K. and Aiden, A. P. (2011) Quantitative analysis of culture using millions of digitized books. *Science*, 331(1), 176–182.

Peterson, R. A. and Simkus, A. (1992) How musical tastes mark occupational status groups. In M. Lamont and M. Fournier (eds), *Cultivating Differences*. Chicago, IL: University of Chicago Press, pp. 152–186.

Ridge, B. (2012) The perilous life of symphony orchestras: artistic triumphs and economic challenges: a book review. *Senzo Sordino: Official Publication of the International Conference of Orchestra and Opera Musicians*, 50(1), 8–9.

Szlendak, T. and Karwacki, A. (2012) Do the Swedes really aspire to sense and the Portuguese to status? Cultural activity and income gap in the member states of the European Union. *International Sociology*, 27(6), 807–826.

Veal, A. J. (2010) *Leisure, Sport and Tourism: Politics, Policy and Planning*. Wallingford: CABI Publishing.

Veal, A. J. (2014 under review) Leisure, income inequality and the Veblen effect: cross-national analysis of leisure time and sport and cultural activity. See book website for publication details.

Wilkinson, R. and Pickett, K. (2009) *The Spirit Level: Why More Equal Societies Almost Always Do Better*. London: Allen Lane.

Wilkinson, R. and Pickett, K. (2010) *The Spirit Level: Why Equal Societies Is Better for Everyone*. London: Penguin.

Chapter 15

Analysing qualitative data

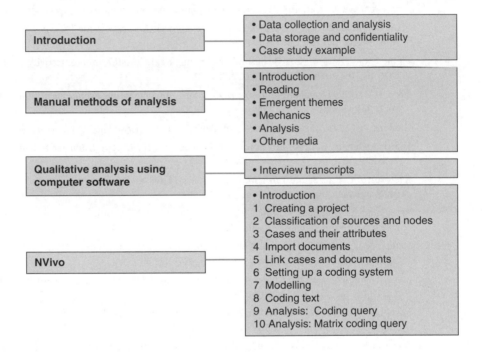

| Introduction | | • Data collection and analysis
• Data storage and confidentiality
• Case study example |

| Manual methods of analysis | | • Introduction
• Reading
• Emergent themes
• Mechanics
• Analysis
• Other media |

| Qualitative analysis using computer software | | • Interview transcripts |

| NVivo | | • Introduction
1 Creating a project
2 Classification of sources and nodes
3 Cases and their attributes
4 Import documents
5 Link cases and documents
6 Setting up a coding system
7 Modelling
8 Coding text
9 Analysis: Coding query
10 Analysis: Matrix coding query |

Introduction

Data collection and analysis

This chapter addresses the task of analysing qualitative data. It is sometimes difficult to separate the collection and analysis processes for qualitative research, at least in a temporal sense (see Chapter 9), but there is nevertheless a clear difference between certain data-collection activities, such as interviewing someone with an audio-recorder, and certain analysis activities, such as poring over typed interview transcripts. While quantitative research can be inductive and qualitative research can be deductive (see Chapter 2), the qualitative approach lends itself to a more inductive process, especially when conducted on a small scale. This difference is illustrated in Figure 15.1, which presents variations on the circular process of research depicted in Figure 2.5.

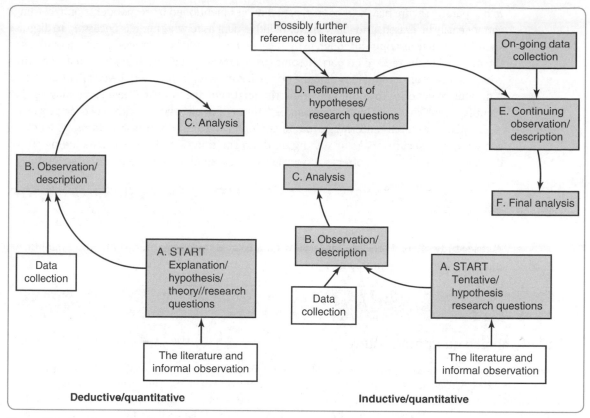

Figure 15.1 Circular model of the research process in qualitative and quantitative contexts

Traditionally, qualitative data were analysed by manual means, and this continues, but in recent years computer software has become available to aid the process. Computers replicate and speed up some of the more mechanical aspects of the manual processes but, of course, the task of interpretation remains with the researcher. The chapter first discusses the question of data storage and confidentiality and then considers manual analysis methods and computer-based methods in turn. Since the most common form of qualitative data is interview or focus group transcripts or notes, the following discussions are based on this form of data. Most of the procedures nevertheless apply, in adapted form, to other forms of data, such as printed materials from organisational archives or mass/social media material.

Data storage and confidentiality

Regardless of whether qualitative data are analysed manually or by computer, consideration should be given to the security and confidentiality of transcripts and tapes, particularly if sensitive material is involved. This raises ethical issues (see Chapter 4).

As a precaution, research material should ideally not be labelled with real names of organisations or people. Fictitious names or codes should be created. If it is felt that it will be necessary to relate recordings and transcripts back to original respondents at some later date, for example for second interviews, the list relating fictitious identities to real identities should be kept in a separate, secure place. Of course, actual names mentioned by respondents on recordings cannot easily be erased, and it is a matter of judgement as to whether it is necessary to disguise such names in transcripts, although in most cases they should be disguised in any quotations of the material in the research report. In some cases, however, it is necessary to create transcripts which can be more anonymous than the original. For example, an interviewee might say, 'I find it difficult to get on with John' – the transcript might change 'John' to 'David', but may need to identify John/David's position – for example, 'I find it difficult to get on with David [Supervisor]'.

Digitised research material stored on computer hard drives and other storage media is subject to the security risks of any digitised information. Some software, including NVivo discussed in this chapter, offers password protection, which may be a useful precaution.

Case study example

A case study of some in-depth interview data is used in the chapter to illustrate qualitative data analysis, both manual and by computer, as shown in Case study 15.1.

CASE STUDY 15.1

Activity choice qualitative study

Figure 15.2 presents a simple conceptual framework for studying cultural activity choice. It is based on a model presented by Brandenburg *et al.* (1982) and further developed in Veal (1995) and suggests that individuals' choice of cultural activity is influenced by background characteristics and experiences, present constraints and personal factors, but also by key events which trigger participation.

While the model is explored qualitatively in this chapter, it could be explored quantitatively, for example by means of a questionnaire, but that would be likely to require prior definition of the three sets of influences and a set of key events. Further, since any one of the three groups could involve a substantial list of items (e.g. background/experience, parental influence, school experience, higher education experience, geography/climate, activities experienced), the analysis task would be daunting. A qualitative approach would enable the various factors and influences to be identified and analysed in a more exploratory manner. Interviews could be conducted using a checklist of the sort presented in Figure 9.4.

Figure 15.3 contains short extracts from three interviews with individuals about their activity

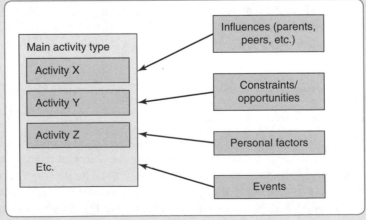

Figure 15.2 Outline conceptual framework for a study of activity choice

Case study 15.1 (*continued*)

choices. The term 'cultural activity' would need to be discussed with interviewees at the beginning of the process. Indeed, discovering what the term means to people could be a significant part of the research. The researcher might wish to restrict the definition used in the rest of the interview or may wish to work with whatever definition each respondent comes up with, including this in the analysis process.

The comments in the first column of the transcripts are explained in the chapter. These transcripts are used to illustrate manual and computer analysis of texts. The aim is to demonstrate the mechanics of analysis in a way that could be readily replicated by the student. The length of the transcript extracts and their number has therefore been limited. Thus the substantive outcomes are incidental and not particularly meaningful taken in isolation. In a complete research exercise, full transcripts, running to many pages, would be involved and, although we are dealing with qualitative research, the number of interviews/transcripts in a study of this type would normally be more than three.

Mark (Age 22, Male, Student, Income £8k)

Q. What would you say is your most time-consuming cultural activity outside of the home at present?

Act.: Pub bands
Constraint: Commitments: football, keeping fit, time, money

Well, I would say it's going to hear pub bands. I'm in a football team, so during the season, because of training twice a week and needing to be fairly serious about keeping fit, I don't do much else: I probably only see a band about once a fortnight. I don't have the time or the money to do much more.

Q. How did you get interested pub bands?

Influence: Mate

A mate of mine was in a band for a while and I used to be roped in almost as a roadie. So I got to know some of the other band members.

Variety, informality

Q. Why do you think you are attracted to pub music?

It's varied, often quite original, and it's informal – you can drop in and out.

Donna (Age 27, Female, FT Employed, Income £19k)

Q. What would you say is your most time-consuming cultural activity outside of the home at present?

Act.: Socialising

Just socialising I would say … you know, going out for a meal or a drink with friends … I go to the gym once or twice a week … and I like to swim a bit in the summer, but they don't take up much time overall.

Q. When did you first start going out socially on a regular basis?

Event: Earning money
Influence: Peers

I was about 16, I guess: the parents were a bit restrictive, but once I started earning a bit of money at weekends I managed to go out at least twice a week – to parties and to the cinema and stuff … my mum and dad didn't have any money to give me, so it wasn't until I started to work part-time that I could go out, sort of regularly. I've always had a fairly close-knit group of friends, girlfriends, about the same age as me, who've always gone out together … even with boyfriends – and one husband – arriving on the scene and disappearing from time to time!

Q. What limits the number of times you go out socialising in a week?

Constraint: Time, Money

Time and money! But mostly it's time these days 'cos we don't always spend a lot.

Q. What are the essential ingredients for a good night out?

Personal: Social – informal
Constraint: Time

It's all about people … people you know and people you might meet! Things like good food – and drink – or good music are important, but the enjoyment comes from doing it with your friends and knowing they have the same sorts of tastes and the same sense of fun. I am serious enough at work, I couldn't imagine myself spending a lot of time with some team sport with serious training and all that: I just don't have the time – or the inclination!

Case study 15.1 (*continued*)

Lee (Age 23, Male, FT Employed, Income £22k)

Event: Girlfriend
Personal: Anti-routine

Q. *What would you say is your most time-consuming cultural activity outside of the home at present?*

It varies. I don't have any set pattern. Up until a couple of weeks ago I was going out with this girl and, apart from going round each other's house, we spent a lot of time going out, one way or another – to the cinema, pub, walking, shopping – it varied. Now that's stopped, it's still a bit of a mixture, but with various friends. I hate routine, so I don't get involved with anything regular.

Q. *So what single thing – from among the mixture of things you do – would you say you spent most time doing in the last week?*

Act.: Cinema

In the last week? Well, I haven't been out that much. It would have to be the movies: I went twice and one of them was one of those late-night double billers – about four hours.

Q. *Are you a movie buff?*

Event: Good review

I wouldn't go that far, but I like movies. I read reviews and that. The movie I saw on Tuesday had a lot of hype and I saw two or three good reviews. For once, the hype was justified: it was really good. Really good: better than the reviews – and that doesn't happen often.

Figure 15.3 Interview transcript extracts

Manual methods of analysis

Introduction

There are various ways of analysing interview transcripts or notes. The essence of any analysis procedure must be to return to the terms of reference, the conceptual framework and the research questions or hypotheses of the research (see Chapter 3). The information gathered should be sorted through and evaluated in relation to the concepts identified in the conceptual framework, the research questions posed or the hypotheses put forward. In qualitative research, those original ideas may be tentative and fluid. Questions and/or hypotheses and definition and operationalisation of concepts may be detailed or general; the more detailed and specific they are, the more likely it is that they will influence the initial stages of the analysis. Conversely, the more general and tentative they are, the more likely it is that the data-analysis process will influence their development and refinement.

Data gathering, hypothesis formulation and the identification of concepts is a two-way, evolving process. Ideas are refined and revised in the light of the information gathered, as described in relation to the *recursive* approach and *grounded theory* approach (see Figure 9.1). In Chapter 3 it is noted that the development of a conceptual framework and of research questions or hypotheses is the most difficult and challenging part of a research project.

In addition to the problem of ordering and summarising the data conceptually, the researcher is faced with the very practical problem of just how to approach the pile of interview notes or transcripts.

Reading

The basic activity in qualitative analysis is reading of notes, transcripts, documents or listening to or viewing audio and video materials. In what follows, it is assumed that the material being analysed is text – while practical adaptations are necessary for audio and video material, the principles are the same. The reading is done firstly in light of initial research questions and/or hypotheses and/or those which have evolved during the data-collection process.

Emergent themes

A typical approach to qualitative analysis is to search for *emergent themes* – the equivalent of *variables* in quantitative research. Indeed, it has been argued, for example by Dupuis (1999), that the practice mimics too closely the positivistic approach to research which many proponents of qualitative methods disparage. There may be a temptation to begin adopting a quasi-quantitative approach to the process, identifying as themes only those which arise from the transcripts of a number of interviewees. Clearly this would be inconsistent with the qualitative approach: a theme that emerges from just one interview is as valid as one that emerges from ten. The criterion for identification should be the extent to which the theme appears to be salient to the interviewee.

The themes may arise from the conceptual framework and research questions, and therefore be consciously searched for in a deductive way, or they may emerge unprompted in a more inductive way. Typically, both processes will be at work.

Themes that emerge from the transcripts are 'flagged' in the left-hand margin of the transcripts in Figure 15.3. The researcher's judgement of the strength with which the views are expressed could be indicated here with one or more plus or minus signs. It is clear that other themes might be identified and alternative terms might be used for the items that are identified, illustrating the personal and subjective nature of qualitative analysis.

The 'developed' conceptual framework presented in Figure 15.4 shows how some of the themes/concepts/factors and relationships emerging from the interviews might begin to be incorporated into the conceptual framework. On the basis of information from short abstracts

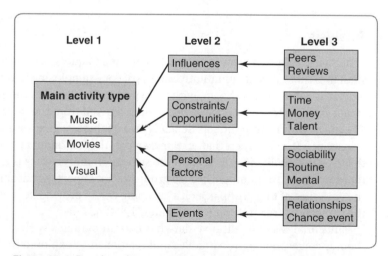

Figure 15.4 Developed conceptual framework for qualitative study of activity choice

from three interviews, the conceptual framework is developed but not fully developed; it represents work in progress. The 'levels' referred to relate to discussion of computer-aided analysis discussed later in the chapter.

Mechanics

The initial steps in qualitative analysis involve fairly methodical procedures to classify and organise the information collected.

Analysis can be done by hand on hard-copy transcripts, which should have a wide margin on one side to accommodate the 'flagging' of themes as discussed above. Colour coding can be used in the flagging process and 'Post-it' notes may also be used to mark key sections.

Standard word-processor packages can be of considerable assistance in the analysis process. The space for flagging can then be secured using the 'columns' or tables facility in the word processor. Word-processing packages also have facilities for:

- adding 'Comments' (e.g. in the 'Track changes' facility in Word);
- blocking text with colour, underlining or bold;
- 'searching' to locate key words and phrases;
- paragraph and/or line numbering;
- coding and cross-referencing using indexing procedures.

These procedures can keep track of topics across a number of interviews, but also of topics that are covered several times in the same interview. A particular focus of the analysis may be related not only to particular substantive topics raised by the interviewer, and therefore related to particular questions, but also to, for example, underlying attitudes expressed by interviewees, which might arise at any time in an interview.

The index becomes the basis for further analysis and writing up the results of the analysis: being able to locate points in the transcripts where themes are expressed enables the researcher to check the wording used by respondents and explore context and related sentiments, and facilitates the location of suitable quotations to illustrate the write-up of the results.

Analysis

In qualitative data analysis it is possible to use techniques and presentation methods that are similar to those used in quantitative analysis. For example, in Figure 15.5 an analysis similar to a cross-tabulation is shown, with 12 hypothetical interviewees 'plotted' on a two-dimensional space based on two variables/themes derived from the interviews referred to above. The placing of the respondents depends on a qualitative assessment based on the interview transcripts. It can be seen that, in the example, the respondents fall into four groups. Given that this is a qualitative survey and the sample of interviewees is unlikely to be statistically representative, the numbers in each group are not important but simply the identification of the existence of four groups. Such a grouping would provide the basis for further analysis of the transcripts (see Huberman and Miles, 1994: 437).

Thus analysis of qualitative data has certain parallels with quantitative analysis, with themes corresponding to variables and relationships explored in ways that parallel cross-tabulation and correlation. But they are parallels only, not equivalents. Whereas quantitative analysis generally seeks to establish whether certain observations and relationships are

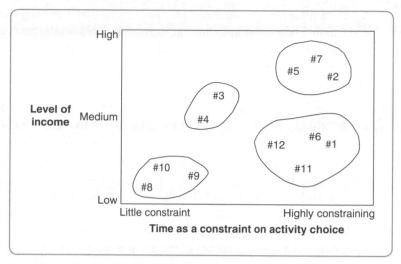

Figure 15.5 'Crosstabulation' of qualitative data

Numbers refer to individual interviewees.

generally true in the wider population on the basis of statistical probability, qualitative analysis seeks to establish the existence of relationships on the basis of what individual people say and do. If only one person or organisation in the study is shown to behave in a certain way as a result of certain influences, this is a valid finding for qualitative research – the question of just how widespread such behaviour is in the wider society becomes a matter for other types of research.

Miles and Huberman (1994) offer a range of data-sorting, presentation and analysis techniques for individual subjects – 'within-case' – and for grouping or comparing a number of subjects – 'cross-case'. In a number of instances they emulate quantitative analysis, as in the example of crosstabulation above. For example, interviewees' various experiences or actions may be grouped into a typology and further grouped by the time period in which they took place. This may be done diagrammatically or in tabular form and may be deductive, relating experience patterns of a theoretically derived conceptual framework, or inductive, with conceptual frameworks, models or networks being developed from the data.

Detailed analysis may be less important when the purpose of in-depth or informal interviews is to provide input into the design of a formal questionnaire. In that case the interviewer will generally make a series of notes arising from the interview that is likely to be of relevance to the questionnaire design process, and can also provide input to the design process from memory, as long as the questionnaire design work is undertaken fairly soon after the interviews.

Other media

Other media call for different approaches. English (1988), for example, discusses the use of the camera in research in an education context. Photographing teacher–child relationships in the classroom, he first takes quite wide-angled views, comparable to asking broad introductory questions in an interview, then examines the photographs and discovers unforeseen phenomena, such as the way teachers have created particular environments to prompt children to engage in different sorts of learning behaviour – comparable to the themes emerging from examination of transcripts. He discusses further challenges concerning the selecting and framing of photographs and the effect of choices on the function of the photograph in conveying information. Again, some of these challenges have parallels in the selection and composing of verbal material.

Qualitative analysis using computer software – introduction

When the researcher is faced with a substantial number of lengthy documents to analyse, the decision may be taken to ease the laborious process of coding and analysing by making use of one of the computer-aided qualitative data analysis software (CAQDAS) packages now available. As with statistical packages, it takes time to learn how to use qualitative analysis packages and to set up a system for an individual project, so a decision has to be made, on the basis of the size and complexity of the documentary material to be analysed, as to whether that investment of time will result in a net time saving, compared with manual analysis. However, consideration should be given to the fact that once an analysis system has been set up, more analysis can be undertaken relatively quickly, possibly resulting in a better quality of output than may have been possible using manual methods. Further, looking to the future, a computerised analysis system can more easily be returned to at future dates for additional interrogation. Finally, even if the amount of data in a given project does not justify setting up a computerised analysis system, a smaller project may be an easier vehicle for learning to use and gain experience with a package, and familiarity and experience with a computer package merits an entry on a person's *curriculum vitae*.

It has been noted above that standard word-processing packages such as Microsoft Word offer facilities that can aid in sorting and locating material in transcripts. The standard word-processing package is, however, limited in its capabilities for this purpose. A number of purpose-designed CAQDAS packages are now on the market. One of the most commonly used, demonstrated here, is NVivo, part of a stable of packages from QSR (Qualitative Solutions and Research Pty Ltd), which includes N6, an updated version of the well-known NUD*IST, and XSight designed for market researchers. Details of these and other packages can be found on the QSR website – see the Resources section.

Interview transcripts

As with the manual analysis discussed above, the extracts of interview transcripts from the activity choice project presented in Case study 15.1 are used to demonstrate the operation of NVivo here. An ideal way for readers to engage with this section is to replicate the processes outlined on a computer. In what follows it is assumed that the reader has access to a computer with NVivo installed.

Readers who wish to replicate the procedures should first either type the text of the transcripts into three files or download them from the book's website. A small font and wide margins are advised for ease of viewing on the NVivo screen. They should be in files named: Mark.doc, Donna.doc and Lee.doc. The suffix .docx (or .doc) indicates Word format, but NVivo will also accept text format (suffix .txt), rich text format (.rtf) or portable document format (.pdf). The files are introduced in the procedure 'Importing internal documents', discussed below.

Introduction

NVivo is one of the most widely used CAQDAS packages. The software enables the researcher to index and coordinate the analysis of text stored as computer files. This includes primary material, such as interview transcripts and field notes, and other material such as newspaper clippings, company reports and video clips. In addition it assists in shaping and understanding data and in developing and testing theoretical assumptions about the data.

It is not possible in a short summary such as this to present all the features of a package – this is done in the online tutorials on the QSR website (see Resources section) and 'Help' built into the package, and in specialist texts, such as that by Patricia Bazeley (2007). Just ten NVivo (Version 10) procedures, considered to be sufficient to get started with the package, are outlined here, as shown in Figure 15.6.

Starting up

The NVivo opening window is divided into two sections, 'Get started' and 'Community', the latter containing news, tips and videos. The 'Get started' section includes a list of 'Recent Projects', where a demonstration environmental change project is already installed, and where your project(s) will in due course be listed. It also includes 'New Project', which is where we begin.

Creating a new Project

Procedures

To demonstrate the system, we start with Create Project. This involves creating a named location for a research project, into which the documents to be analysed, such as interview transcripts, will be added. The NVivo procedures to create a project for the Activity Choice project are shown in Figure 15.7.

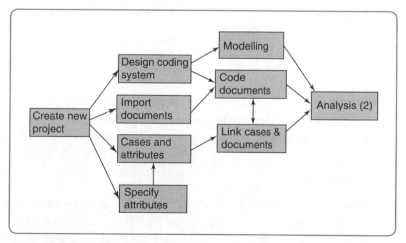

Figure 15.6 NVivo procedures covered

1. Click on *New Project.*
2. In the Title box enter: ActivityChoice.
3. Click on *OK.*
4. A file name *ActivityChoice.nvp* automatically appears at the top of the screen – it will have a default 'My documents' location on your computer but this can be altered by clicking on *Browse* and specifying a location of choice.
5. The screen appears, as shown below.
6. Along the top of the screen is a menu ribbon with a number of 'tabs'. All of the procedures that are noted in Figures 15.8 to 15.17 can be undertaken by clicking on the icons under these tabs.
7. The screen is divided into three main sections:
   - *Navigation View (NV),* on the left, has eight menus (*Sources, Nodes, Classifications, Collections, Queries, Reports, Models* and *Folders*) – clicking on any one of these reveals a sub-menu: a;
   - *List View (LV),* in the main, right-hand part of the screen, in which corresponding information will be presented;
   - menu tabs at the top of the screen.

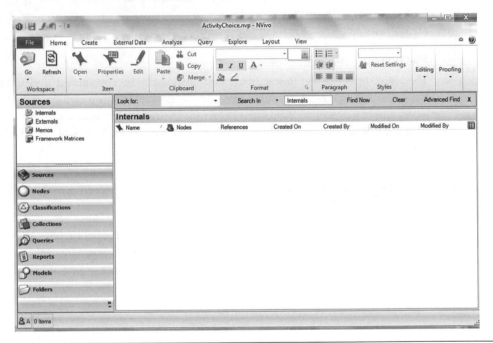

Figure 15.7 Create NVivo project procedure
Source: Reproduced with kind permission from QSR International.

Saving

During an NVivo session, the program will periodically remind the user to save the current version of the project. Backup copies should also be created at the end of a session.

Attributes

Attributes of subjects/cases involved in a study can be recorded as for variables in a quantitative study. At the top of the transcripts (in Figure 15.3) we have four items of information for each respondent – age, gender, employment status and income – and these can be recorded as a set of attributes in the NVivo system, as shown in Figure 15.8.

1. Click on *Classifications* in the main menu (bottom left of the screen): the *Source Classifications* screen appears.
2. Under the *Create* tab click on Classifications: a New Classification dialogue box appears. Enter the name Case, then click on *OK*.
3. Click on *Node Classifications* in the *Navigation View* area, then right click on the new *Case* node classification that now appears in the *List View* area and select *New Attribute*. (This can also be done from the menu ribbon: Create > Attribute.)
4. In the *New Attribute* dialogue box, enter the name *Gender*.
5. Click on the *Values* tab:
   - 'Unassigned' and 'Not applicable' default values are already in place;
   - click on *Add* and type in the value *Male;*
   - click on *Add* again and type in *Female*, then click on *OK;*
   - the attribute *Gender* should now be listed under *Case*.
6. Repeat steps 3–5 for the attribute *Empstat* (employment status), with values *FT Employed* and *Student*.
7. Repeat steps 3 and 4 for the attributes *Age* and *Income*, changing the *Type* from *Text* to *Integer*. Step 5 is not necessary because these are uncoded numerical variables.
8. The four attributes, *Age, Empstat, Gender, Income,* should now be listed under *Case*. The attributes can be sorted alphabetically by clicking the header: *Name*.

Figure 15.8 Classification of nodes – procedure

Cases and their attributes

We can now introduce our three interviewees, as *cases,* and record their individual socio-demographic attributes. Procedures are shown in Figure 15.9.

Importing documents

Information on the three interviews and their attributes has been imported into the Activity Choice project system and the three transcript files must also be imported, as shown in Figure 15.10. It will be seen that other types of material can be incorporated, including sound

1. Click on *Nodes* in the bottom left-hand corner of the screen, then right click *Nodes* in the *Navigation View* and select *New Folder*. (Create > New Folder.)
2. In the *New Folder* dialogue box enter *Cases,* then click on *OK*.
3. Click on *Cases* in the *Navigation View*. Right click in the blank area of the *List View* area and select *New Node*. (*Create* > *Node*.)
4. In the *New Node* dialogue box enter the name *Mark*.
5. Still in the *New Node* dialogue box, click on the *Attribute Values* tab, then select *Case* classification. The four attributes are listed:
   a for *Age* and *Income:* key in Mark's age in years (22) and income in £000s (8);
   b from the drop-down lists of values for *Gender* and *Empstat*, select *Male* and *Student* respectively. Then click on *OK*.
6. Repeat steps 3–5 for Donna and Lee.
7. Save the project to disk using *File > Save* on the menu ribbon.
8. Click *Explore > Node Classification Sheet*, then select *Case:* the three cases and their attributes appear in a spreadsheet-style table as below.
9. The *Case/Attributes* data can be presented in spreadsheet format, so if the information is already held in spreadsheet format, the spreadsheet can be imported into NVivo, replacing the above procedure. This is achieved via: *External Data > Classification Sheets > Browse* where the location of the spreadsheet file is stored.
10. Conversely, the Casebook can be exported to a spreadsheet file via the same *External Data* tab but selecting the furthest right *Classification Sheets* icon.

Figure 15.9 Cases and attributes – procedure
Source: Reproduced with kind permission from QSR International.

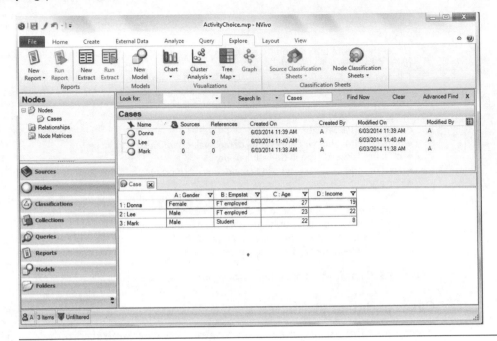

Figure 15.9 *(continued)*

1. In the *Navigation View* area, click on *Sources*.
2. In the menu that appears above, click on *Internals*.
3. On the menu ribbon click *Create > Folder*.
4. In the *New Folder* dialogue box enter the name *Interviews* and click *OK*.
5. *Interviews* now appears as a sub-folder to the *Internals* folder in the *Sources* menu to the left.
6. Click on *Interviews,* then on the menu ribbon click *External Data > Documents*.
7. In the *Import Internals* dialogue box, click on *Browse* to locate Mark.doc and click on *OK*.
8. The *Document Properties* dialogue box appears: click on *OK*.
9. The file name Mark.doc should now be listed in the *Internals* List View area, with its date of creation.
10. Repeat steps 7–9 for Donna.doc and Lee.doc.
11. All three files should now be listed.
12. Save the modified project file.

Figure 15.10 Importing documents – procedure

and video material and external material such as links to websites. This demonstration is confined to dealing with text documents generated internally as part of the research project.

Linking cases and documents

The interview transcript files are linked with the three interviewees/cases – Mark, Donna and Lee – already identified in the system, as shown in Figure 15.11.

Setting up a coding system

As with questionnaires, documents such as interview transcripts must be *coded* in order to be analysed by computer. This involves setting up a *coding system*. A coding system can develop

1. In the Navigation View area, click on *Sources*, then *Internals > Interviews* on the menu, so that the three files appear in List View, under the heading *Interviews*.
2. Click on the file icon on the left of the *Mark* file to highlight it.
3. On the menu ribbon, select *Analyze > Existing Nodes*.
4. The *Select Project Items* dialogue box appears under *Nodes*. Select Cases and the list of three files will appear.
5. Check Mark and click on OK.
6. Repeat steps 2–5 for *Donna* and *Lee*.
7. The three cases/interviewees, with their attributes, are now linked with their respective interview transcripts – if you go to *Nodes > Cases* and click on one of the files, you will see in the Display View area that the link is noted on the top of the transcript.

Figure 15.11 Linking documents and cases – procedure

and evolve as the research progresses, but it has to start somewhere. In the section on manual coding above, the 'flagging' process is similar to the coding process involved here. On the basis of an initial conceptual framework (Figure 15.2) and reading short extracts from three interview transcripts, it was possible to develop a coding system which is displayed in the notes in Figure 15.3 and reflected in the more developed conceptual framework in Figure 15.4. In a fully fledged project the researcher would go on to read and code the full interview transcripts of the three example interviewees and other interviewees as well, and would apply the flagging/coding system to the other texts and further develop the system in an inductive way. Coding systems using NVivo are developed in the same way. In the example below, the codes developed in the manual process are entered into the Activity Choice project to demonstrate the beginnings of a coding system.

The grouping of related concepts, as shown in Figure 15.4, is referred to in NVivo as *Tree Nodes*. Free-floating concepts, which have not been linked to any tree structure, are referred to as *Free Nodes*. The procedures in Figure 15.12 describe the process for entering information presented in Figure 15.4 into the project file. The relevance of the three *levels* mentioned in Figure 15.4 should become apparent in this process.

1. In the Navigation View area, click on *Nodes*.
2. Click on *Nodes* in the sub menu, then *Create > Folder*.
3. In the *New Folder* dialogue box enter *Free Nodes*, then click on *OK*.
4. Repeat steps 2-3 again, this time enter *Tree Nodes*.
5. In the *Nodes* menu click on *Tree Nodes*.
6. Right click in the List View area and select *New Node* (or, *Create > Node*). Type in the name *Main Activity* and click on *OK*. Main Activity is now listed under *Tree Nodes*.
7. Highlight *Main Activity* and click *Create > Node*, then in the *New Node* dialog box type in the name *Activity type* and click on *OK*. *Activity type* should now be listed under *Main Activity*.
8. Highlight *Activity type* and click *Create > Node*, enter *Music* and click on *OK*.
9. Repeat step 8, adding *Movies and Visual* – *Music, Movies and Visual* should now be listed under *Activity type*.
10. Repeat step 7 for: Influences, Constraints, Personal and Events.
11. Repeat steps 7-8 for:
    a. *Influences*: *Peers, Reviews*
    b. *Constraints*: *Time, Money, Talent*
    c. *Personal*: *Sociability, Routine, Mental*.
    d. *Events*: Relationships, Chance event
12. The screen should then appear as follows.

Figure 15.12 Setting up a coding system – procedure
Source: Reproduced with kind permission from QSR International.

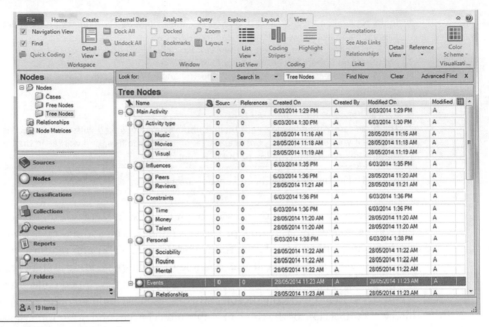

Figure 15.12 *(continued)*

Modelling

The coding system can be depicted diagrammatically as a *model*. The procedures and output are shown in Figure 15.13. Here the model is depicted generically. Later it is shown how the way the model works for an individual case can be depicted.

The following NVivo procedures show how the coding system can be presented diagrammatically as a model.

1. In the Navigation View area select *Nodes* and then *Tree Nodes* from the menu: the *Main Activity* node specified in Figure 15.12 will appear in the List View area.
2. In the Navigation View area, select *Models*, which will now replace *Tree Nodes* in the List View area.
3. Right click in the List View area and from the menu, select *New Model*. (*Explore > New Model*)
4. In the *New Model* dialog box enter a name for the model eg. *Model 1*, and click on *OK*.
5. A workspace for *Model 1* appears below in the Detail View area. A new *Model* tab is also available with a selection of shapes. NB. The workspace can be expanded to full screen by clicking *View > Undock All*.
6. Before working with the model click on *Click to edit* in the top of the work space.
7. Right click in the work space and, from the drop-down menu, select *Add Project Items*. (*Model > Add Project Items*).
8. In the *Select Project Items* dialog box, double-click on the icon next to *Nodes* (not the adjacent tick-box) to bring up extra options. Highlight *Tree Nodes*
9. Main Activity appears in the space to the right: check the tick box and click on OK.
10. The *Add Associated Data dialog box appears:* check *Children*, then click on *OK*.
11. The first part of the graphic, circles containing *Main Activity* and its sub-nodes: Activity type, Influences etc. appears in the workspace.
12. Right click on the Activity type shape and repeat step 10: the three activity types, Music, Movies, Visual, appear as below.
13. Click on Influences and repeat step 10.
14. This can be repeated for all factors, but it will be necessary to click, resize and drag and the shapes around to fit them appropriately into the work space.

Figure 15.13 Modelling – procedure

Source: Reproduced with kind permission from QSR International.

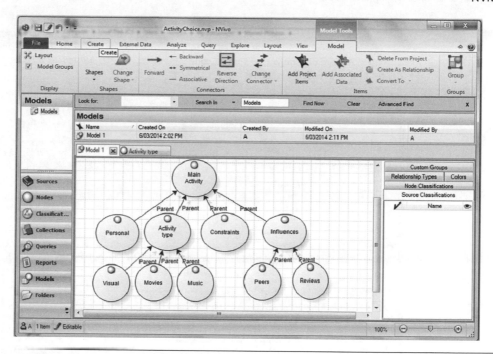

Figure 15.13 *(continued)*

Coding text

Once a coding system has been set up, documents, such as interview transcripts, can be coded. This process is outlined in Figure 15.14.

1. In the Navigation View area, select *Sources,* then *Internals> Interviews* in the sub menu. The three interview transcript files should appear in the List View area.
2. Double click on *Mark* and the transcript should appear below in the Display View area.
3. A section of text is coded by highlighting: to have this highlighting indicated visually on the text after it has been coded select: *View > Highlight > Coding for All Nodes.* Select *Modify Selected Items* to indicate which code category you want highlighted.
4. The coding can also be indicated visually with *Coding stripes* which appear in the space to the right of the text. To activate this select: *View > Coding Stripes > Nodes Most Coding.* (It will be noted that two coding stripes are already in place: one indicates that the Mark transcript as a whole is coded to the *Case* Mark and the other is a 'coding density' stripe which relates to the amount of coding).
5. To code the activity 'going to hear pub bands" as the Main Activity in Mark's transcript:
    a. Highlight the text *going to hear pub bands.*
    b. On the menu ribbon, select *Analyze> Existing Nodes:* the *Select Project Items* dialog box should appear (Alternatively right-click and select *Code Selection > Code Selection At Existing Nodes*).
    c. In this dialog box: select *Tree Nodes – Main Activity* should appear.
    d. Click on the + to the left of *Main Activity* and the factors, *Personal, Influence, Activity type,* etc. will be listed below.
    e. Click on the + to the left of *Activity type* and, *Movies, Music, Visual* will be listed below.
    f. Select *Music* using the tick-box and click on OK.
    g. The text should appear highlighted and a Music stripe should appear in the right hand space.

Figure 15.14 Coding text – procedure

Source: Reproduced with kind permission from QSR International.

(continued)

6. Repeat step 5 for:
   - 'I don't have the time or the money to do much more': code as *Constraints > Time;*
   - 'I don't have the time or the money to do much more': code as *Constraints > Money;*
   - text: 'A mate of mine was in a band' coded: *Personal: code as Influences > Peers*
7. The result should appear as below.

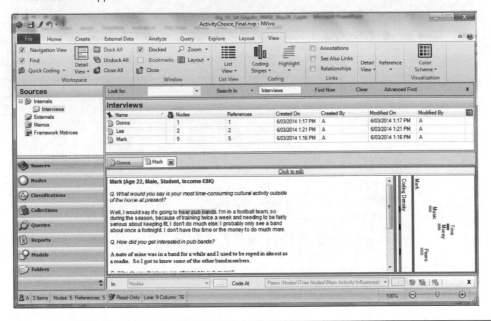

Figure 15.14 *(continued)*

This illustration uses the coding system developed above, which arose from the manual analysis and theoretical framework outlined earlier in the chapter, but the coder is not restricted to this framework: additional codes/nodes can be added as you go along. This reflects the qualitative methodology and is of course very likely to arise with longer interview transcripts. The procedure involves selecting 'New node' in Figure 15.12.

Project summary

The Activity Choice project information is now assembled and coded, as summarised in Figure 15.15. Analysis involves exploring the content of the coded interview transcripts and the cases and their attributes.

Analysis

Software packages invariably include a wide range of procedures which it is impossible to cover in a short summary such as this. Here we cover two basic analysis procedures/issues which will be sufficient to get the researcher started. In reality, these procedures do not encompass data analysis as such, which is concerned with identifying relationships and meanings, discussed in a limited way in the manual analysis section above. The procedures covered here are related to data processing so that the analysis can begin. Two procedures are described below: *coding query* and *matrix coding query.*

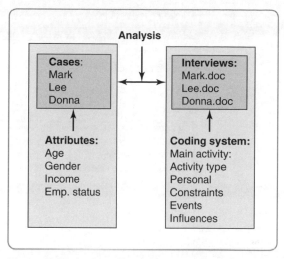

Figure 15.15 Activity Choice project summary

Coding query

One of the simplest forms of analysis is to obtain a listing of all the sections of text coded in a certain way. Thus a listing of all passages in the transcripts coded with Cultural as the Main Activity is obtained as shown in Figure 15.16.

Rather than searching for text coded as a node in the coding system it is possible to search for any item of specified text. This would involve selecting *Text Search* instead of *Coding* at step 2 in Figure 15.16.

Matrix coding query

The *coding query* can be seen as the equivalent of a frequency count in questionnaire survey analysis; the equivalent of a crosstabulation is a *Matrix coding query*. Figure 15.17 shows the procedure for conducting such an analysis in the Activity Choice project to separate cultural participants by gender.

To select all the text that has been coded Cultural as *Main Activity:*

1. In the Navigation View area, select *Queries:* the List View area will now be headed *Queries.*
2. Right click in the List View area and select *New Query > Coding* (or *Query > Coding* from the menu ribbon).
3. A *Coding Query* dialogue box appears offering selection by *Node* or by *Any node where* (which refers to attributes).
4. To select by the *Node* 'Cultural', click on *Select* and click on the + to the left of *Nodes.* Then click on *Tree Nodes > Main Activity > Activity Type > Cultural > OK.*
5. Click on *Run* and a listing will appear in the Detail View area with the names of the cases, Mark and Donna, and a printout of the relevant text, as shown below.
6. The results of this query can be saved for future reference. Click *Query > Store Query Results* and type in a name, e.g. Query Cultural. This material can subsequently be accessed when required via the Navigation View area: *Queries > Results.*

Figure 15.16 Queries – procedure

Source: Reproduced with kind permission from QSR International.

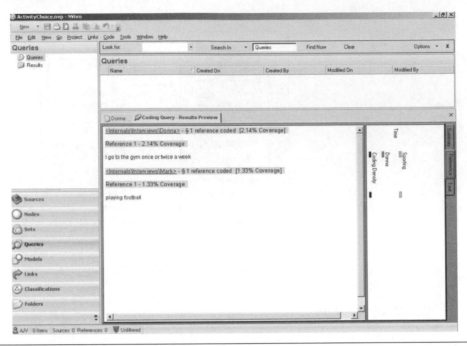

Figure 15.16 *(continued)*

To divide interviewees engaging in cultural activities into males and females:

1. In the Navigation View area, select *Queries:* the List View area will now be headed *Queries.*
2. Right click in the List View area and select *New Query > Matrix Coding* (or *Query > Matrix Coding* from the menu ribbon).
3. In the *Matrix Coding Query* dialogue box, under *Matrix Coding Criteria* and *Rows* and *Define More Rows: Selected Items* will be displayed.
4. Click on the *Select* button on the right. The *Select Project Items* dialogue box will appear.
5. In this dialogue box click on the + to the left of *Nodes,* then highlight *Tree Nodes* to bring up *Main Activity,* then tick the box next to *Cultural* (as in Figure 15.14 steps 5d–f) and click on *OK.*
6. On returning to the *Matrix Coding Query* dialogue box, click on *Add to List* and *Nodes\Tree Nodes\ Main Activity\Activity Type\Cultural* will appear under *Name.*
7. Click the *Columns* tab and under *Define More Columns* select *Attribute Condition > Select.*
8. In the *Coding Search Item* dialogue box click on *Select.*
9. In the *Select Project Items* dialogue box click on *Node Classifications > Case > Gender OK.*
10. The *Coding Search Item* dialogue box automatically indicates the *Gender* Attribute condition as 'equals value' and 'Male'. Click on *OK.*
11. On returning to the *Matrix Coding Query* dialogue box click on *Add to List* and *Case: Gender = Male* will appear under name.
12. Repeat steps 7–11 but in step 10 change the value to 'Female'.
13. Click on *Run* and the results will be displayed in a table as follows (it may be necessary to widen the columns to display the labels in full):

	A : Case: Gender = Male	B : Case: Gender = Female
1 : Cultural	1	1

14. This shows one male and one female coded as taking part in cultural activity as their main activity: double clicking in the cells containing the numbers will bring up the relevant coded text.

Figure 15.17 Matrix coding query – procedure

Summary

The chapter is divided into two sections dealing respectively with manual and computer-aided analysis methods for qualitative data.

Manual methods of data analysis involve 'flagging' issues or themes that emerge in texts such as interview transcripts. Such issues or themes may relate to an existing draft conceptual framework, to research questions and/or hypotheses or, in a 'grounded theory', inductive approach they may be used to build up a conceptual framework from the data. Since texts are invariably available as word-processed files, it is noted that certain features of word-processor packages, such as 'search' and 'list' or 'index', can be used to assist in the 'flagging' process. This provides a link to the custom-made Computer Aided Qualitative Data Analysis Software (CAQDAS) packages.

The second part of the chapter introduces the NVivo package, covering the setting up of a project file and a coding system, coding of data and some elementary analysis procedures. While the package has a large range of capabilities – including the handling of data other than interview transcripts – just a limited range of analysis procedures is presented in this short outline, but it is believed this is adequate for the qualitative researcher to make a start with computer-aided data analysis.

TEST QUESTIONS

1. What are the two major activities involved in manual analysis of qualitative data?
2. What word-processor procedures might be used in 'manual' analysis of qualitative data?
3. What is the difference between a 'Node' and a 'Document' in NVivo?
4. What is the difference between a 'Node' and a 'Source' in NVivo?

EXERCISES

1. Download from the book website the three transcript files for the Activity Choice project used above – or type them out from Figure 15.3 – and replicate the coding and analyses presented above. This can be done manually or by using NVivo.
2. Run the NVivo tutorials included with the package, particularly exploring features of NVivo not presented in this chapter.
3. Select an example of a quantitative and a qualitative research report from a recent edition of one of the arts or events journals and consider whether the qualitative research project could have been approached using quantitative methods and whether the quantitative project could have been approached using qualitative methods.
4. Using the issues of a newspaper for one week, provide a qualitative and quantitative analysis of the coverage of a topic of interest, such as the environment, ethnic minorities, women and cultural activity or overseas locations.

Resources

Websites

- NVivo website: www.qsrinternational.com/ – includes a downloadable bibliography on qualitative data analysis sources.
- CATPAC – text analysis package – www.galileoco.com/N_catpac.asp
- *Qualitative Research* journal: http://qrj.sagepub.com/
- The Qualitative Report (portal): www.nova.edu/ssss/QR/web.html

Publications

- *Analysis of qualitative data generally:* Miles and Huberman (1994).
- *Use of computer software packages* in qualitative data analysis: Miles and Weitzman (1994), Richards and Richards (1994).
- *Use of NVivo software:* Bazeley (2007), Gibbs (2002 – does not include latest version of NVivo); in grounded theory: Hutchison *et al.* (2010).
- Examples:
  - use of NVivo in a meta-analysis of findings of qualitative research: Thomas *et al.* (2004)
  - museum: ethnographic/reflexive study of visitor/researcher behaviour: Noy (2011)
  - museum signage and visitor behaviour, observational: Jeanneret *et al.* (2010)
  - museums: consulting children: Dockett *et al.* (2011)
  - participant observation: events: Mackellar (2013)

References

Bazeley, P. (2007) *Qualitative Data Analysis with NVivo.* Thousand Oaks, CA: Sage.

Brandenburg, J., Greiner, W., Hamilton-Smith, E., Scholker, H., Senior, R. and Webb, J. (1982) A conceptual model of how people adopt recreation activities. *Leisure Studies*, 1(3), 263–276.

Dockett, S., Main, S. and Kelly, L. (2011) Consulting young children: experiences from a museum. *Visitor Studies*, 13(1), 13–33.

Dupuis, S. (1999) Naked truths: towards a reflexive methodology in leisure research. *Leisure Sciences*, 21(1), 43–64.

English, F. W. (1988) The utility of the camera in qualitative inquiry. *Educational Researcher*, 17(May), 8–15.

Gibbs, G. R. (2002) *Qualitative Data Analysis: Explorations with NVivo.* Maidenhead: Open University Press.

Huberman, A. M. and Miles, M. B. (1994) Data management and analysis methods. In N. K. Denzin and Y. S Lincoln (eds), *Handbook of Qualitative Research.* Thousand Oaks, CA: Sage, 428–444.

Hutchison, A. J., Johnston, L. H. and Breckon, J. D. (2010) Using QSR-NVivo to facilitate the development of a grounded theory project: an account of a worked example. *International Journal of Social Research Methodology*, 13(4), 283–302.

Jeanneret, Y., Depoux, A., Luckerhoff, J., Vitabo, V. and Jacobi, D. (2010) Written signage and reading practices of the public in a fine arts museum. *Museum Management and Curatorship*, 25(1), 53–67.

Mackellar, J. (2013) Participant observation at events: theory, practice and potential. *International Journal of Event and Festival Management*, 4(1), 56–65.

Miles, M. B. and Huberman, A. M. (1994) *Qualitative Data Analysis*, Second Edition. Thousand Oaks, CA: Sage.

Miles, M. and Weitzman, E. (1994) *Computer Programs for Qualitative Data Analysis.* Thousand Oaks, CA: Sage.

Noy, C. (2011) The aesthetics of qualitative (re)search: performing ethnography at a heritage museum. *Qualitative Inquiry*, 17(10), 917–929.

Richards, T. J. and Richards, L. (1994) Using computers in qualitative research. In N. K. Denzin and Y. S Lincoln (eds), *Handbook of Qualitative Research*, Thousand Oaks, CA: Sage, 445–462.

Thomas, J., Harden, A. and Oakley, A. (2004) Integrating qualitative research with trials in systematic reviews. *British Medical Journal*, 328(7446), 1010–1012.

Veal, A. J. (1995) Leisure studies: frameworks for analysis. In H. Ruskin and A. Sivan (eds), *Leisure Education: Towards the 21st Century.* Provo, UT: Brigham Young University Press, pp. 124–136.

Chapter 16

Analysing quantitative data

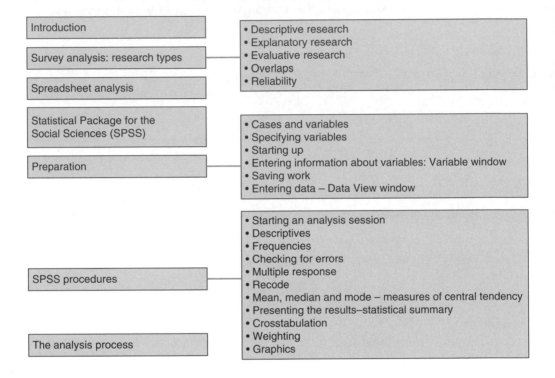

Introduction

In this chapter the analysis of questionnaire survey data is addressed using two types of computer package:

- *spreadsheets*: the most widespread computer application used for general data analysis – Microsoft Excel is used to demonstrate certain analysis procedures;
- *statistical packages*: used to analyse statistical data in a research context – one of the most widely used packages is the IBM®/SPSS® Statistics Software (SPSS)* and this is used

---

* SPSS Inc. was acquired by IBM in October, 2009.

here for demonstration purposes. Other packages include Minitab, BMD (Biomedical Data analysis), SAS (Statistical Analysis System) and Turbostats.

The analysis processes are demonstrated using the simple Campus Entertainment questionnaire in Figure 10.20 in Chapter 10, and the coded data from the questionnaire as shown in Figure 10.21.

Before addressing the mechanics of data analysis, however, the typology of research introduced in Chapter 1 is discussed in relation to the analysis process.

Survey data analysis and types of research

Research can be of three kinds: descriptive, explanatory and evaluative (see Chapter 1). These types of research and their relationship to survey analysis are summarised in Figure 16.1 and discussed in turn below.

Descriptive research

Descriptive research usually involves the presentation of information in a fairly simple form. Of the analytical procedures described in this chapter, the two most appropriate for descriptive research are:

- *frequencies*, which present counts and percentages of responses for single variables; and
- *means*, which present averages for numerical variables.

Explanatory research

Descriptive data do not, of themselves, explain anything. To explain the patterns in data or relationships between phenomena represented by the data it is necessary to consider the question of *causality* – how to determine whether A is caused by B. In Chapter 3 it was noted that to establish causality it is necessary to fulfil four criteria: association, time priority, non-spurious relation and rationale.

- *Associations* between variables can be explored using such procedures as *crosstabulations* between two or more variables (described in this chapter) and *regression* between a dependent variable and one or more independent variables (see Chapter 17).

Research type	Analytical procedures
Descriptive	Frequencies (counts, percentages), Means
Explanatory	Crosstabulation, Comparison of means, Regression
Evaluative	Frequencies – compared with targets or benchmarks
	Crosstabulations – comparing visitor/customer groups
	Means – compared with targets or benchmarks

Figure 16.1 Research types and analytical procedures

- *Time priority* involves establishing that for A to be the cause of B it must take place before B – this is sometimes testable in social science research and is sometimes obvious, but is generally more appropriate for the conditions of the natural science laboratory.

- *Non-spurious* relationships are those that 'make sense' theoretically (that is, the relationship between A and B is not mediated by a third, extraneous variable C) and are not just a 'fluke' of the data. This can be approached using survey analysis techniques. For example, if it is found that cultural expenditure is inversely related to age for the whole sample and this relationship is also found for, say, men and women separately, and for other sub-groups – even random sub-samples – this suggests a non-spurious relationship.

- *Rationale*, or *theory*, is of course not produced by computer analysis but should be integral to the research design. Whether the research may be *deductive* or *inductive* (see Chapter 3), *explanation*, or the establishment of causality, is not complete without some sort of rational, conceptual explanation of the relationships found.

The Campus Entertainment questionnaire offers only limited scope for explanatory research. For example, differences in attitudes between the various student groups – full-time and part-time or different age groups, for example – may indicate that varying expectations from campus entertainment may be a function of student group characteristics.

The particular procedures that are appropriate for explanatory analysis and are covered in this chapter are the production of crosstabulations, which facilitates examination of the relationship between two or more variables based on frequencies, and the examination of the means of two or more variables. These procedures can establish whether or not statistical relationships exist between variables, but whether or not they are spurious and/or supported by theory involves reference to the theoretical or conceptual framework.

Evaluative research

Evaluative research basically involves comparisons between survey findings and some benchmark derived from expectations, past figures, other similar facilities or programmes or target performance standards. The analysis called for, therefore, is relatively simple, generally involving comparisons between findings from the survey and some benchmark value.

The example questionnaire could be used for evaluative purposes – for example, a low level of use of any of the services listed in question 2 could imply that the existing service is not performing well in meeting the demands of students and low levels of use by particular groups could indicate a failure to meet the needs of all groups.

Overlaps

Analysis does not always fall exclusively into one of the above three modes. For example, in presenting a descriptive account of the example Campus Entertainment results, it would be natural to provide a breakdown of the participation patterns and preferences of the four student groups included. While this could be descriptive in form, it would begin at least to hint at explanation, in that any differences in the groups' patterns of behaviour or opinions would seem to call for explanation; the analysis would be saying 'these groups are different' and would be implicitly posing the question 'why?'. In so far as the providers of campus services might have a remit to serve all sections of the student community, the descriptive data could be used in evaluating management.

Validity and reliability

It has been noted that some attempt at testing validity – whether the data are measuring what they are intended to measure – can be achieved in the design of questionnaires (see Chapter 10). Reliability – whether similar results would be obtained if the research were replicated – is a difficult issue in the social sciences, but an approach can be made at the analysis stage. While statistical procedures are well suited to establishing the magnitude and strength of associations, the question of the reliability of such associations is more complex. Unlike the natural sciences, it is not always possible, for practical or resource reasons, to replicate research in the social sciences to establish reliability. While reference to previous research reported in the literature can be relevant and helpful in this respect, in fact, the changing pattern of human behaviour over time and space means that consistency with previous research findings is by no means a guarantee of reliability – indeed, it is the tracking of change that is often the aim of social research.

If the sample is large enough, one approach to reliability is to split the sample into two or more sub-samples on a random basis, or on the basis of a selected variable, and see whether the results for the sub-samples are the same as for the sample as a whole. In the SPSS package this can be achieved using the procedure *split file*: the procedure is not covered here but is relatively straightforward to operate.

Spreadsheet analysis

This section does not provide a guide to elementary spreadsheet procedures, only to procedures specific to analysis of the type of data produced from questionnaire surveys.

The shaded part of Figure 16.2 reproduces, in spreadsheet format, the data for 15 completed questionnaires from Figure 10.21. There is one change: the expenditure variable (*spend*) has been shifted to the end to sit alongside *age*, since both are uncoded numerical variables, which are treated individually below. The unshaded part is produced by the *Frequency* procedure provided in Excel and this is described in Figure 16.3.

Spreadsheet analysis is suitable for a small data-set when simple frequency tables are required. But for larger data-sets, particularly longer questionnaires, and more complex analyses, a statistical software package, as outlined below, is advisable.

	A qno	B status	C movie	D drama	E rock	F jazz	G cheap	H hours	I qual	J meet	K time	L relax	M social	N meaning	O sug1	P sug2	Q sug3	R gend	S	T age	U	V spend
1	qno	status	movie	drama	rock	jazz	cheap	hours	qual	meet	time	relax	social	meaning	sug1	sug2	sug3	gend		age		spend
2	1	2	1	1	0	0	1	4	2	3	5	3	3	1	1			1		18		100
3	2	2	1	1	1	0		4	2	3	5	2	3	1	2	1		1		19		50
4	3	3	1	0	0	0	2	5	1	3	4	2	2	2	3	4		2		19		250
5	4	4	0	0	0	0	2	3	1	4	5	3	2	2	1	2	4	1		22		25
6	5	3	1	0	0	1	2	4	3	2	5	3	3	1				2		24		55
7	6	3	1	1	1	0	2	4	1	3	5	2	3	1	2			2		20		40
8	7	2	1	0	0	0	3	2	1	4	5	2	3	2	3			2		20		150
9	8	2	1	0	1	0	3	4	2	1	5	1	2	2	4	5		1		21		250
10	9	4	0	1	0	0	1	5	2	3	4	2	3	2				1		21		300
11	10	3	1	1	0	0	2	3	1	5	4	1	2	1	1	1		2		21		100
12	11	3	1	1	1	1	2	3	1	4	5	2	2	1	2	3		2		19		75
13	12	2	1	0	0	0	1	4	3	2	5	2	3	1				1		22		50
14	13	1	1	0	1	0	1	5	2	3	4	2	3	2	1	2		2		21		55
15	14	3	1	1	0	0	2	4	1	3	5	3	3	2	4			2		20		75
16	15	1	1	1	0	0	3	2	1	5	4	3	3	1	1	2	5	1		20		150
17																						
18	Code	Freq	Freq	Freq	Freq	Freq	Freq	Freq	Freq	Freq	Freq	Freq	Freq	Freq	Freq	Freq	Freq	Freq	Cat.	Freq	Cat.	Freq
19	0	0	2	7	10	13	0	0	0	0	0	0	0	0	0	0	0	0	19	4	74	6
20	1	2	13	8	5	2	6	0	8	1	0	2	0	8	5	2	0	7	21	8	100	4
21	2	5	0	0	0	0	6	2	5	2	0	8	5	7	3	3	0	8	23	2	200	2
22	3	6	0	0	0	0	3	3	2	7	5	5	10	0	2	1	0	0		1		3
23	4	2	0	0	0	0	0	7	0	3	5	0	0	0	2	1	1	0				
24	5	0	0	0	0	0	0	3	0	2	10	0	0	0	0	1	1	0				
25	Total	15	15	15	15	15	15	15	15	15	15	15	15	15	12	8	2	15		15		15
26	Averages																			20.5		115

Figure 16.2 Questionnaire survey data: spreadsheet analysis

1 Type: **Code** in cell A18.
2 Type **Freq** in cell B18.
3 Type the codes **0, 1, 2, 3, 4, 5** in cells A19 to A24 respectively (0–5 covers all the codes used by variables *status* to *gend*).
4 Select cells B19 to B24 (the cells in which the results of the frequency counts will be placed).
5 Type the following 'array formula' in the 'formula bar' (not shown in Figure 16.1):
   (a) =**FREQUENCY(B2:B16,$A19:$A24)** and then press Ctrl + Shift + Enter together.
   (b) The results will appear as shown in cells B19 to B24 in Figure 16.1.
   (c) Note: – When you have typed=FR Excel will offer you a pop-up FREQUENCY which you can select with a double click.
      – You can *select* the cells B2:B16 rather than typing the cell references manually.
      – The $A format is used in $A19:$A24 because the codes in cells A19:A24 will be utilised for all 17 coded variables so, in spreadsheet parlance, an absolute rather than a relative column location must be specified.
      – General instructions on the use of the FREQUENCY formula are provided by the Excel Help facility.
6 The heading in cell B18 and the formulae in cells B19:B24 can now be copied to produce the frequencies for the other 16 variables: copy cells B19:B24 as one array and paste into cells C19:R24 in one 'copy and paste' operation.
7 Create totals in row 24 using normal spreadsheet procedures.
8 Example results, for *status*, are as follows:

Category	No.
Full-time student with no regular paid work	2
Full-time student with some regular paid work	5
Part-time student with full-time job	6
Part-time student – other	2
Total	15

9 For each variable percentages can be created from the frequencies, and graphics can be created from the frequencies or the percentages using normal spreadsheet procedures.
10 Type category groupings for the non-coded variables, *age* and *spend*, in cells S19:S21 and U19:U21 respectively.

   – cell S19: 19 indicates a group aged 19 and under
   – cell S20: 21 indicates a group aged 20–21
   – cell S21: 23 indicates a group aged 22–23
   – cell S22: 25 indicates a group aged 24–25 (if blank, indicates '24 and over')

11 Select cells T19:T22, then type the following 'array formula' in the 'formula bar' (not shown in Figure 16.1):
   – =FREQUENCY(T2:T16, S19:S22) (note: $S is not required, because the information is only being used for one variable) and then press Ctrl+Shift+Enter together.

   – The results will appear as shown in cells T19 to T22 in Figure 16.1.
12 Results for *age* are therefore:

Age	No.
18–19	4
20–21	8
22–23	2
24–25	1

13 A similar process can be followed for the variable *spend*.
14 Totals, percentages and graphics can be produced as for the other variables. In addition, for the two non-coded variables, averages may be calculated.

Figure 16.3 Questionnaire survey data: spreadsheet analysis steps

IBM SPSS Statistics Software (SPSS)

The main part of the chapter is organised as a step-by-step introductory manual for operating the IBM SPSS Statistics Software (SPSS) software package. It is envisaged that the reader will have access to a computer with SPSS available on it, so that the procedures described here can be tried out in practice.

The question arises: at what point is it worthwhile to invest time and energy in mastering a computer package for survey analysis, rather than relying on a spreadsheet program, with which many people are already familiar? This, of course, depends on the scale and complexity of the task at hand and the likely future career path of the researcher. It is clear that a specialist survey package has far more capabilities than a spreadsheet, as this chapter and the next demonstrate. It should be noted that basic coding and data preparation are identical for both approaches and the basic data file is interchangeable between a spreadsheet and a survey analysis package such as SPSS. As noted in relation to qualitative software (Chapter 15), it is also the case that familiarity and experience with a computer package merit an entry on a person's *curriculum vitae*.

SPSS for Windows is the version of the package that is available for personal computers using the Microsoft Windows system, but it is also available for Mac OS and Linux systems. Version 20 of the package is referred to here. Most universities provide access to the software and further details and information on specialist guides can be found on the SPSS Inc. web-site (see Resources section at the end of the chapter).

A full list of SPSS procedures can be found in the online SPSS manual, which is included in the software package. In this chapter five analysis procedures only are described:

● *Descriptives* – key descriptive statistics for specified variables;

● *Frequencies* – counts and percentages of individual variables;

● *Crosstabs* – the crosstabulation of two or more variables;

● *Means* – obtaining means/averages of appropriate variables;

● *Graphs* – the production of charts and graphs.

The areas covered in this chapter and the statistical procedures covered in Chapter 17 are summarised in Figure 16.4.

The chapter deals with the analysis of data from questionnaire surveys. But SPSS can be used to analyse data from other sources also; the data simply need to be in the variables/ cases spreadsheet format indicated in Figure 16.2. Furthermore, although the package is ideally suited to dealing with numerical data, it can also handle non-numerical data. Any data organised on the basis of *cases* and a common range of *variables* for each case can be analysed using the package (cases and variables are defined below).

The chapter does not deal with procedures for logging into a computer, file handling or the installation of the SPSS software onto the computer; it is assumed that SPSS for Windows is already installed on a computer available to the reader. The information in the chapter provides an introduction to the basics only.

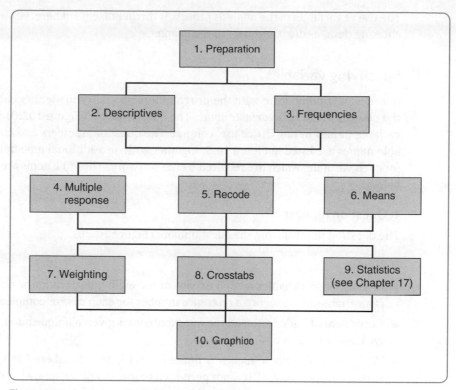

Figure 16.4 Survey analysis – overview

Preparation

Cases and variables

Statistical analysis packages deal with data which are organised in terms of cases and variables.

- A *case* is a single example of the phenomenon being studied and for which data have been collected – for example, an individual member of a community who has been interviewed; a visitor to a theatre or festival; an employee of a company; a visitor to a country; a cultural organisation; or a country. A sample is made up of a number of cases.

- A *variable* is an item of information that is available for all or some of the cases, which can take on different values or categories – for example:

  - the gender of an individual, which can take on the category 'male' or 'female';
  - the salary of an employee, which can be any monetary value;
  - the number of employees of a company; or
  - the population of a country, where the sample is of countries (as in Case study 14.1).

The use of variables in the analysis process is further discussed here, while cases arise when entering data, as discussed later in the chapter.

Specifying variables

In order to communicate with the program it is necessary to identify each item of data in the questionnaire by a *variable name*. The questionnaire (Figure 10.20) is annotated with variable names in the 'Office use' column. The question numbers and corresponding variable names are listed in Figure 16.5, together with an additional nine items of information for each variable, which are required by the software. These 11 items are discussed in turn below.

1 Question number

The question number from the questionnaire (Figure 10.20).

2 Name

- In addition to variables related to each of the eight questions in the questionnaire, there is a variable *qno* to record a reference number for each case or completed questionnaire.
- Every item of information on the questionnaire is given a unique name (no two variables with the same name).
- The length of variable names is limited to 64 letters/numbers (no spaces), beginning with a letter or @, #, $. It is not permitted to use any of the following for variable names because the SPSS program already uses these names for other purposes and would get confused:

ALL AND BY EQ GE GT LE LT NE NOT OR TO WITH

Three possible systems for naming variables are:

- the practice adopted here, which is to use variable names which are full or shortened versions of how the item might be described – for example, *status* for student status, and *sug1* for improvement suggestion 1;
- use a generalised name such as *var*; so a questionnaire with five variables would have variable names: *var1*, *var2*, *var3*, *var4*, *var5*;
- use of question numbers as in the questionnaire – for example, *Q1*, *Q2a*, *Q2b* and so on.

Question 6 should be noted. It is an open-ended question and respondents might wish to give any number of answers. In this case the designer of the questionnaire has assigned three variables to record up to three answers (*sug1*, *sug2*, *sug3*), on the assumption that a maximum of three answers would be given by any one respondent. Not all respondents will necessarily give three answers – this is no problem, because *sug2* and/or *sug3* can be left blank. Some may, however, give more than three answers, in which case it would not be possible to record the fourth and subsequent answers and that information would be lost. If more than a handful of respondents give more than three answers then a fourth variable (*sug4*) could be added. The decision on how many answers to allow for must depend on a preliminary scanning of the questionnaires (possibly in a pilot study). As an open-ended question, the coding system for question 6 applies to all three variables and was devised from the range of free-form answers as discussed in Chapter 10 (Figure 10.19).

Question No.*	Name*	Type	Width**	Decimal places	Label	Values, Value labels	Missing values	Columns	Alignment	Measure/Data type
	qno	Numeric	4	0	Questionnaire number	None	None	4	Right	Scale
1.	status	Numeric	1	0	Student status	1 F/T student: no work 2 F/T student: working 3 P/T student: F/T job 4 P/T student: other	None	4	Right	Nominal
2.	movie	Numeric	1	0	Campus movie in last 4 wks	1 Yes 0 No	None	4	Right	Nominal
	drama	Numeric	1	0	Campus theatre in last 4 wks	as for movie	None	4	Right	Nominal
	rock	Numeric	1	0	Campus rock in last 4 wks	as for movie	None	4	Right	Nominal
	jazz	Numeric	1	0	Campus jazz session in last 4 wks	as for movie	None	4	Right	Nominal
3.	cheap	Numeric	1	0	Free/cheap (rank)	None	None	4	Right	Ordinal
	hours	Numeric	1	0	Times (rank)	None	None	4	Right	Ordinal
	qual	Numeric	1	0	Quality of facilities (rank)	None	None	4	Right	Ordinal
	meet	Numeric	1	0	Socialising (rank)	None	None	4	Right	Ordinal
	time	Numeric	1	0	Time available (rank)	None	None	4	Right	Ordinal
4.	spend	Numeric	4	0	Expenditure on entertainment/month	None	None	4	Right	Scale
5.	relax	Numeric	1	0	Relaxation – importance	3 Very important 2 Important 1 Not at all important	None	4	Right	Scale
	social	Numeric	1	0	Social interaction – importance		None	4	Right	Scale
	meaning	Numeric	1	0	Meaningful – importance		None	4	Right	Scale
6.	sug 1	Numeric	2	0	Improvement suggestion – 1	1 Programme contents 2 Timing 3 Facilities 4 Costs 5 Organisation	None	4	Right	Nominal
	sug 2	Numeric	2	0	Improvement suggestion – 2		None	4	Right	Nominal
	sug 3	Numeric	2	0	Improvement suggestion – 3		None	4	Right	Nominal
7.	gender	Numeric	1	0	Gender	1 Male 2 Female	None	4	Right	Nominal
8.	age	Numeric	2	0	Age	None	None	4	Right	Scale

*From Figure 10.19; **max. no. of characters; § See Figure 10.18 for derivation of coding system.

Figure 16.5 Variable names, labels and values

3 Type

All the variables in the Campus Entertainment survey questionnaire are numeric – that is, they can only be numbers. Other possibilities exist, including *date* and *string*, the latter meaning text comprising any combination of letters and numbers, but these options are not pursued here.

4 Width

Width specifies the maximum number of digits for the value of a variable. In the Campus Entertainment survey questionnaire, all variables are single-digit except two:

- *qno*: width will depend on the size of the sample – here a width of four digits is suggested, indicating a maximum possible sample size of 9999;
- *cost*: width has been put at four, suggesting maximum possible individual fortnightly expenditure on entertainment of £9999 – which should accommodate all respondents!

5 Decimal places

None of the variables in the Campus Entertainment survey questionnaire includes *decimal places*, so the number of decimal places is set to zero for all of them. Many variables could, however, include decimals, e.g. a person's height, or dollars/cents, pounds/pence, such as money spent on a ticket.

6 Label

The variable *label* is fuller and more descriptive than the variable *name*, and there is no restriction on content or length. It can be included in output tables, making them more readily understandable by the reader. This is often necessary with long questionnaires with many variables, and particularly when the short variable *names* are not immediately recognisable.

7 Value labels

Value labels identify the codes used for each variable, e.g. for *gend*, 1 = male and 2 = female. In the case of the Campus Entertainment survey:

- the questionnaire number is just a reference number so it has no value labels;
- variables based on questions 1, 2 and 5 have specific codes or values (1, 2, 3, etc.) with value labels as specified in the questionnaire;
- variables based on question 3 are ranks from 1 to 5 – they have therefore been specified in Figure 16.5 as having no value labels. In fact, the values for these variables could be given value labels as follows: 1 = 'First', 2 = 'Second', 3 = 'Third', 4 = 'Fourth', 5 = 'Fifth';
- the variable *spend* is an uncoded numerical sum of money and *age* is a number of years – they therefore have no value labels;
- the values/labels for the open-ended question, 6, were derived as shown in Chapter 10 (Figure 10.19).

8 Missing values

If a respondent does not answer a question in a questionnaire, the data entry may be left blank, or a 'No answer' or 'Not applicable' code may be provided. The software will automatically treat a blank in the data as a 'missing value', but specific 'No answer' and 'Not applicable' codes can be provided by the researcher and specified as *missing values*. The implications are that missing values are excluded when means and percentages are being calculated. In the Campus Entertainment survey data:

- the phenomenon of missing values becomes apparent in the case of variables *sug1*, *sug2* and *sug3*, since some respondents offer no suggestions at all, many offer only one and very few offer three – so there are usually numerous blanks in the data, particularly for *sug2* and *sug3*;

- in the case of the four variables associated with question 2, it would be possible for non-use of services to be left as a blank, giving rise to missing values, but in this case non-use has been coded as a zero.

The *missing value* phenomenon is not pursued in detail in this chapter but is apparent in a number of the outputs from SPSS provided in this chapter and Chapter 17.

9 Columns

The number of columns or digits per variable is a presentational matter concerning the layout of the spreadsheet-style 'Data view' screen discussed below. A variable can be displayed with any number of columns regardless of the specified width of the underlying variable. In the Campus Entertainment survey example, the specification is four columns for all variables, enabling all the data to be viewed on the 'Data view' screen at once, without scrolling left–right, on most computer screens.

10 Alignment

Alignment is also presentational. As in a spreadsheet, or table, numerical data are easier to read if aligned to the right in a cell, while text is often more suitably aligned to the left.

11 Measure

Data can be divided into *nominal*, *ordinal* and *scale* types.

- *Nominal data* are made up of non-numerical categories, such as the status categories in question 1 and 'Yes/No' in question 2 of the example questionnaire. In this situation, while numerical codes are used in computer analysis, they have no numerical meaning – for example, code 2 is not 'half' of code 4 – the 1/0 codes could equally well be 6 and 7, A and B, or X and Y. It does not make sense, therefore, to calculate, for example, an average or mean of *nominal data* codes.

- *Ordinal data* reflect an ordering or ranking, as in question 3 of the example questionnaire; the 1, 2, 3 in this question represent the order of importance, but rank 3 cannot be interpreted as being '3 times as high as' rank 1. It is, however, possible to take an average or mean rank – for example, to speak of an 'average ranking'.

- *Scale data* are fully numerical – as in questions 4 (*spend*) and 8 (*age*) of the example questionnaire. Numerical information, such as a person's expenditure or age, is scale data. In this case an answer of 4 is twice as high as an answer of 2 and calculation of averages or means would clearly be appropriate.

The data type, or type of measure, of a variable affects the range of statistical analysis that can be performed and the appropriate formats for graphical presentation, and these are discussed later, particularly in Chapter 17. In Figure 16.5 each variable is identified as nominal, ordinal or scale, as follows:

- *qno* is identified as a scale variable, although it will not be used in analysis;
- variables from questions 1, 2, 6 and 7 are nominal;
- variables from question 3 are ordinal;
- the question 4 variable, spend and question 8 variable, age are scale variables;
- question 5 variables are 'Likert-style' variables, and are specified as scale variables.

Variables arising from attitude/Likert variables have been used extensively in psychological and market research and have come to be seen as effectively scale variables when, in reality, they are just ordinal. Means are therefore accepted as an appropriate form of analysis when using such variables. The scores of 1 to 3 in question 5 in the Campus Entertainment survey questionnaire can be treated as numerical indicators of the level of importance respondents attach to the items listed. The means can be interpreted as average 'scores' on importance. It is possible to add scores together in some circumstances.

Starting up

To start an SPSS Statistics session on a computer, activate the program as indicated in Figure 16.6. Switch to the *Variable View* screen to start the process outlined below.

Entering information about variables – Variable View window

The information about the variables arising from a questionnaire, as shown in Figure 16.5 above, must be typed into the *Variable View* window. The result of this exercise for the Campus Entertainment questionnaire is as shown in Figure 16.8. It should be noted that for variables with identical value labels, the value labels can be copied and pasted.

Saving work

As with any computer work, the file should be saved to hard disk or a memory stick from time to time during the course of preparation and when completed, and a backup copy should be made. The suffix for an SPSS datafile is.sav, so the example file could be called CampusEntertainment.sav. Once the file is saved, the title 'CampusEntertainment' appears at the top of the screen.

---

1   Start SPSS Statistics on your computer using the appropriate screen icon or Start and All Programs.
2   The dialogue box headed *SPSS Statistics*, with the question *What would you like to do?*, is presented.
3   Click on *Type in data*, then *OK*.
4   The *Data View* window, which will receive the data, and the *Variable View* window, which will receive information about the variables, should now be available, as in Figure 16.7. You can switch between them using the tab at the bottom of the screen.

Figure 16.6 Starting an SPSS session

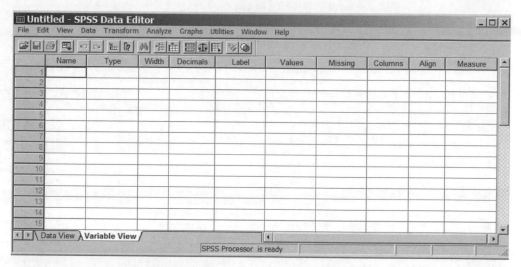

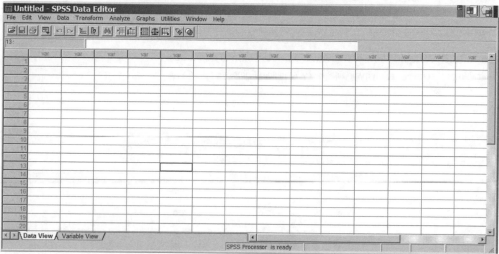

Figure 16.7 Blank Variable View and Data View windows

Source: Reprint courtesy of International Business Machines Corporation.

Entering data – Data View window

Switching to the *Data View* window reveals that the variable names entered via the *Variable View* window have automatically been put in place and the system is ready to receive data. Data from the questionnaires can now be keyed in: one row on the screen per questionnaire, or *case*. Figure 16.9 shows the *Data View* window with data from the 15 cases/questionnaires shown in Figure 10.21. While a sample of 15 would generally be seen as too small for a typical leisure/tourism survey, it is used here for demonstration purposes.

It can be seen that this is similar to the spreadsheet data file shown in Figure 16.2. Indeed, if the data have already been typed into a spreadsheet and saved in a file, this file can be uploaded directly by SPSS. To do this, go to File> Open> Data and, in the 'Open Data' dialogue box, locate the file and change the 'Files of type' to the appropriate type – e.g. Excel.

Once the *Data View* and *Variable View* windows have been completed and the file saved, you are ready to begin analysis.

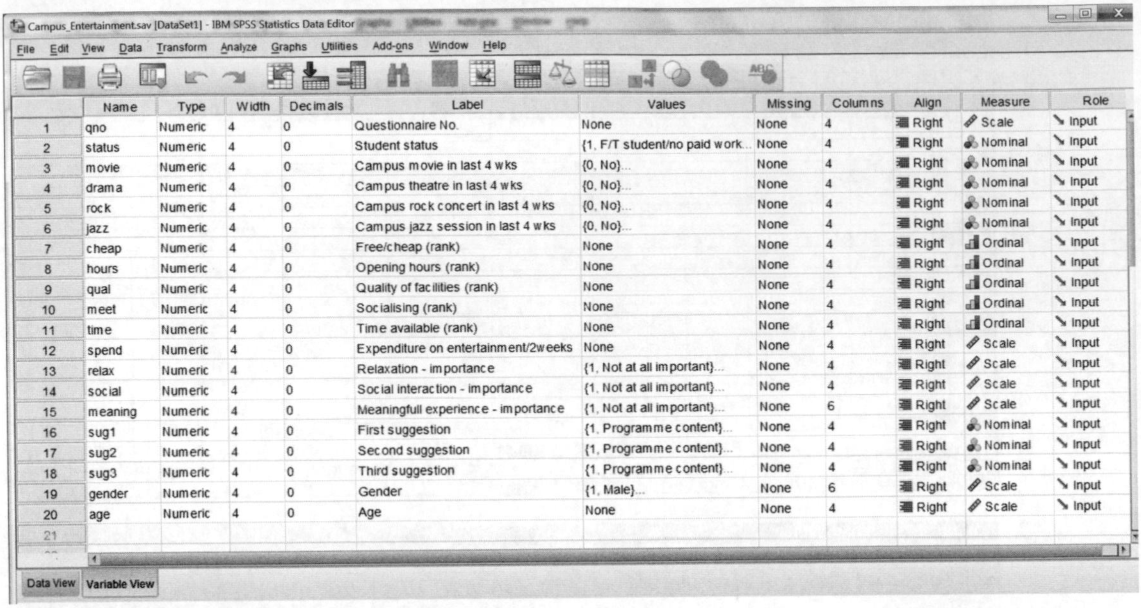

	Name	Type	Width	Decimals	Label	Values	Missing	Columns	Align	Measure	Role
1	qno	Numeric	4	0	Questionnaire No.	None	None	4	Right	Scale	Input
2	status	Numeric	4	0	Student status	{1, F/T student/no paid work...	None	4	Right	Nominal	Input
3	movie	Numeric	4	0	Campus movie in last 4 wks	{0, No}...	None	4	Right	Nominal	Input
4	drama	Numeric	4	0	Campus theatre in last 4 wks	{0, No}...	None	4	Right	Nominal	Input
5	rock	Numeric	4	0	Campus rock concert in last 4 wks	{0, No}...	None	4	Right	Nominal	Input
6	jazz	Numeric	4	0	Campus jazz session in last 4 wks	{0, No}...	None	4	Right	Nominal	Input
7	cheap	Numeric	4	0	Free/cheap (rank)	None	None	4	Right	Ordinal	Input
8	hours	Numeric	4	0	Opening hours (rank)	None	None	4	Right	Ordinal	Input
9	qual	Numeric	4	0	Quality of facilities (rank)	None	None	4	Right	Ordinal	Input
10	meet	Numeric	4	0	Socialising (rank)	None	None	4	Right	Ordinal	Input
11	time	Numeric	4	0	Time available (rank)	None	None	4	Right	Ordinal	Input
12	spend	Numeric	4	0	Expenditure on entertainment/2weeks	None	None	4	Right	Scale	Input
13	relax	Numeric	4	0	Relaxation - importance	{1, Not at all important}...	None	4	Right	Scale	Input
14	social	Numeric	4	0	Social interaction - importance	{1, Not at all important}...	None	4	Right	Scale	Input
15	meaning	Numeric	4	0	Meaningfull experience - importance	{1, Not at all important}...	None	6	Right	Scale	Input
16	sug1	Numeric	4	0	First suggestion	{1, Programme content}...	None	4	Right	Nominal	Input
17	sug2	Numeric	4	0	Second suggestion	{1, Programme content}...	None	4	Right	Nominal	Input
18	sug3	Numeric	4	0	Third suggestion	{1, Programme content}...	None	4	Right	Nominal	Input
19	gender	Numeric	4	0	Gender	{1, Male}...	None	6	Right	Scale	Input
20	age	Numeric	4	0	Age	None	None	4	Right	Scale	Input

Figure 16.8 Variable View window with variable names and labels

Source: Reprint courtesy of International Business Machines Corporation.

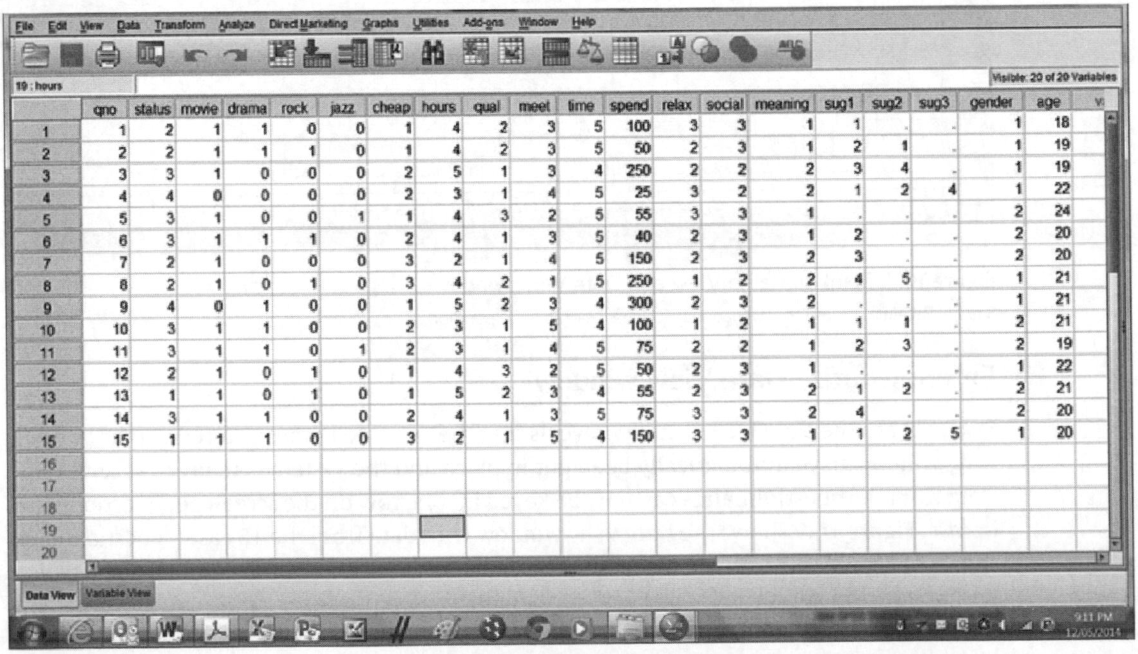

	qno	status	movie	drama	rock	jazz	cheap	hours	qual	meet	time	spend	relax	social	meaning	sug1	sug2	sug3	gender	age
1	1	2	1	1	0	0	1	4	2	3	5	100	3	3	1	1	.	.	1	18
2	2	2	1	1	1	0	1	4	2	3	5	50	2	3	1	2	1	.	1	19
3	3	3	1	0	0	0	2	5	1	3	4	250	2	2	2	3	4	.	1	19
4	4	4	0	0	0	0	2	3	1	4	5	25	3	2	2	1	2	4	1	22
5	5	3	1	0	0	1	1	4	3	2	5	55	3	3	1	.	.	.	2	24
6	6	3	1	1	1	0	2	4	1	3	5	40	2	3	1	2	.	.	2	20
7	7	2	1	0	0	0	3	2	1	4	5	150	2	3	2	3	.	.	2	20
8	8	2	1	0	1	0	3	4	2	1	5	250	1	2	2	4	5	.	1	21
9	9	4	0	1	0	0	1	5	2	3	4	300	2	3	2	.	.	.	1	21
10	10	3	1	1	0	0	2	3	1	5	4	100	1	2	1	1	1	.	2	21
11	11	3	1	1	0	1	2	3	1	4	5	75	2	2	1	2	3	.	2	19
12	12	2	1	0	1	0	1	4	3	2	5	50	2	3	1	.	.	.	1	22
13	13	1	1	0	1	0	1	5	2	3	4	55	2	3	2	1	2	.	2	21
14	14	3	1	1	0	0	2	4	1	3	5	75	3	3	2	4	.	.	2	20
15	15	1	1	1	0	0	3	2	1	5	4	150	3	3	1	1	2	5	1	20

Figure 16.9 Data View window with data from questionnaires/cases

Source: Reprint courtesy of International Business Machines Corporation.

SPSS procedures

Starting an analysis session

The data file with which you are dealing may already be on screen (as in Figure 16.5) if you have just completed typing in data. If not, and in subsequent sessions, you will need to open the file, as shown in Figure 16.10.

1 Start SPSS Statistics on your computer using the appropriate screen icon or *Start* and *All Programs*.
2 The dialogue box headed *SPSS Statistics,* with the question *What would you like to do?,* is presented.
3 If this is the computer on which you set up your SPSS file it may be listed in the *Open an existing data source* window – e.g. CampusEntertainment.sav – and you can select by clicking on it. If your file is not displayed, select *More files…* and locate your file in the appropriate location.
4 The completed *Data View* and *Variable View* windows should now be available.

Figure 16.10 Procedure starting an SPSS analysis session

Descriptives

The *Descriptives* procedure produces a range of statistics for specified variables. It is a useful initial procedure to run as a check for certain minimal information for all variables. The details for running the procedure and an example of the resultant output are shown in Figure 16.11. In the example used, five statistics are produced for each variable (except *qno*).

Procedure

1 Select *Analyze* then *Descriptive Statistics* then *Descriptives*.
2 Select all variables except *qno* and transfer them to the *Variable(s)* box.
3 Select Options and ensure that the following are ticked: *Mean, St. Deviation, Minimum, Maximum,* then click on *Continue*.
4 Click on *OK* to produce the following output.

Output

	N	Minimum	Maximum	Mean	Std. Deviation
Descriptive Statistics					
Student status	15	1	4	2.53	.915
Campus movie, last 4 wks	15	0	1	.87	.352
Campus theatre, last 4 wks	15	0	1	.53	.516
Campus rock concert, last 4 wks	15	0	1	.33	.488
Campus jazz session, last 4 wks	15	0	1	.13	.352
Free/cheap (rank)	15	1	3	1.80	.775
Times (rank)	15	2	5	3.73	.961
Quality of facilities (rank)	15	1	3	1.60	.737
Socialising (rank)	15	1	5	3.20	1.082
Time available (rank)	15	4	5	4.67	.488
Entertainment exp./month	15	25	300	115.00	87.076
Relaxation – importance	15	1	3	2.20	.676
Social interaction – importance	15	2	3	2.67	.488
Meaningful experience – importance	15	1	2	1.47	.516
First suggestion	12	1	4	2.08	1.165
Second suggestion	8	1	5	2.50	1.414
Third suggestion	2	4	5	4.50	.707
Gender	15	1	2	1.47	.516
Age	15	18	24	20.47	1.506

Figure 16.11 Descriptives procedure and output

N – total count

The total count is 15 for all variables except the second and third suggestion since only 12 respondents offered a second suggestion and only 8 offered a third; for the others these variables were blank.

Minimum and Maximum

For coded variables, this is a check that nothing has been miscoded outside the coding range, e.g. 1–3. For the non-coded numerical variables, the maximum and minimum provided may be a useful finding.

Mean

The mean, or average, is the sum of all the values for that variable divided by the number of responses (N) for that variable. It is one measure of the idea of the 'middle' or 'central tendency' of the values for a variable for this sample; other measures of central tendency are discussed under the *Frequencies* procedure below.

The mean is generally a useful statistic for:

- numerical variables – in this case, mean expenditure is £115 and the mean age of the sample members is 20.47 years;

- ordinal variables – for example, the average rank for the *cheap* variable is 1.8.

In general, this is not a useful statistic for nominal/coded variables, but there are exceptions:

- Likert scales – Relaxation, Social interaction, Meaningful experience: as discussed in Chapter 10, the score can be seen as an index of importance, so the mean is an indicator of the average level of importance for the sample: thus in this example, Social interaction (2.67) is the most important and Meaningful experience (1.47) is the least important.

- 1–0 variables (campus movie, drama, rock, jazz): since non-users score zero, the mean is effectively the number of users divided by the total, which is the proportion of users: thus, for example, the proportion of for attendance at campus movies is 0.87 or 87 per cent.

Standard deviation

The standard deviation is a measure of the spread of values around the mean. In this example, among the variables which respondents were asked to rank: for the Time availability, the standard deviation is 0.488, while that for Socialising is 1.082; this makes sense when we see from the maximum/minimum that for the former all responses were either 4 or 5, whereas for the latter they ranged from 1 to 5. The standard deviation is discussed further in Chapter 17.

Frequencies

The Frequencies procedure is the simplest form of descriptive analysis: it merely produces counts and percentages for individual variables – for example, the numbers and percentages of respondents registered in each student status group. The procedure can be run for one variable at a time or for a number of variables.

Frequencies for one variable

The steps to obtain a table for the variable *status* are set out in Figure 16.12, together with the resultant output. The *Output* window presents two tables. The first, *Statistics*, indicates the number of 'valid cases' on which the analysis is based – in this case 15. The second table, headed *Student status,* shows:

- *Frequency* – count of the numbers of students is each status group;
- *Percent* converts frequency numbers into percentages;
- *Valid percent* is explained below under 'missing values';
- *Cumulative percent* adds percentages cumulatively – which may be useful for a variable like *spend* or *age*, but is not particularly useful for the variable *status*.

Frequencies for a number of variables

Frequency tables for all the variables can be obtained by transferring all the variables (except *qno*) into the *Variable(s)* box in Step 2 in Figure 16.12. Running frequency tables for all variables is a common early instruction in survey analysis: it is a good way of obtaining an overview of the results and checking that all is well with the data. The results of this exercise for the example questionnaire are in Appendix 16.1.

It should be noted that the list of variables in the *Frequencies* dialogue box can appear in the form of variable *names* or the longer variable *labels* and can be arranged in the order they appear in the Variable View window or alphabetically. To change these settings, go to *Edit>*

Procedure

1 Select *Analyze* from the menu bar at the top of the screen, then *Descriptive Statistics*, then *Frequencies*. This opens the *Frequencies* dialogue box.
2 In the *Frequencies* dialogue box:
   (a) select the variable *status* by highlighting it. Then click on the right arrow to transfer it to the *Variable(s)* box for analysis;
   (b) make sure that *Display frequency tables* is ticked;
   (c) select *OK* and the results will appear in a new *Output* window as shown below.

Output

Statistics: Student status

N	Valid	15
	Missing	0

Student status

		Frequency	Percent	Valid percent	Cumulative percent
Valid	F/T student/no paid work	2	13.3	13.3	13.3
	F/T student/paid work	5	33.3	33.3	46.7
	P/T student – F/T job	6	40.0	40.0	86.7
	P/T student/other	2	13.3	13.3	100.0
	total	15	100.0	100.0	

Figure 16.12 Frequencies for one variable: procedure and output

Options> General> Variable Lists. Changes to the format of output tables can also be made here. The changes will not be implemented until the file has been saved and closed and then re-started.

Checking for errors

After obtaining the *Descriptives* and/or *Frequencies* printout for all variables check through the results to see if there are any errors. This could be, for example, in the form of an invalid code or an unexpected missing value. The error must be traced in the data file and corrected, perhaps by reference back to the original questionnaire. The data must then be corrected on the data window and the *Frequencies* table for that variable run again. The corrected, 'clean' data file should then be saved and backed up.

Multiple response

Questions 2 and 6 in the example questionnaire are *multiple response* questions. They are single questions with a number of possible responses and must be analysed using a number of variables. Particular 'multiple response' analysis procedures are available in SPSS to handle their particular characteristics. There are two types of multiple response question:

- *multiple response – dichotomous*: question 2 on campus activity is a dichotomous variable, because each answer category is essentially a yes/no (two values) variable; any one respondent could tick one, two, three or all four boxes, so each is a separate variable;

- *multiple response – categories*: question 6 on suggestions for improvements has three variables, sug1, sug2, sug3, each coded with the same five category values, as discussed earlier.

It can be seen from Appendix 16.1 that the normal *Frequencies* procedure produces output for these questions in a rather inconvenient format – four tables for question 2 and three tables for question 6. The multiple response procedure combines multiple responses into a single table for each question. The procedure is operated as shown in Figure 16.13, together

---

Procedure

1 Select *Analyze*, then *Multiple Response* then *Define Variable Sets.*

Multiple response – dichotomous	Multiple response – categories
2 Transfer movie, drama, rock and jazz into the *Variables in Set* box.	2 Put sug1, sug2, sug3 into the *Variables in Set* box.
3 Under the *Variables are coded as…* box, select *Dichotomies*.	3 Under Variables are coded as… select *Categories*.
4 Enter 1 in the *Counted value* box.	4 Enter Range 1 through 5.
5 Give the 'set' a Name – e.g. acts.	5 Add Name, e.g. sugs.
6 Add a Label – e.g. Cultural activities.	6 Add Label, e.g. Suggestions for improvement.
7 Select *Add*.	7 Select *Add*.
8 A new variable, *$acts*, is listed automatically.	8 A new variable $sugs is listed automatically.
9 Select *Close*.	9 Select *Close*.

To produce a table:
10 Select *Analyze*.
11 Select *Multiple Response*.
12 Select *Frequencies* and use the new variable.

Figure 16.13 Multiple response procedures and output

Output

Group: $acts – Cultural activities (Value tabulated = 1)

Dichotomy label	Name	Count	Pct of responses	Pct of cases
Campus movie in last 4 wks	movie	13	46.4	92.9
Campus theatre in last 4 wks	drama	8	28.6	57.1
Campus rock concert in last 4 wks	rock	5	17.9	35.7
Campus jazz session in last 4 wks	jazz	2	7.1	14.3
Total responses		28	100.0	200.0
1 missing cases; 14 valid cases				

Group: $sug – Suggestions for improvement

Category label	Code	Count	Pct of responses	Pct of cases
Programme content	1	7	31.8	58.3
Timing	2	6	27.3	50.0
Facilities	3	3	13.6	25.0
Costs	4	4	18.2	33.3
Organisation	5	2	9.1	16.7
Total responses	22	100.0	183.3	
3 missing cases; 12 valid cases				

Figure 16.13 *(continued)*

with the results – one table for question 2 and one for question 6. It should be noted that percentages are given which relate to the number of respondents and to the number of responses – which of these to use depends on the aims of the research.

Recode

As the name implies, *Recode* is a procedure that can be used to change the codes of variable values. The procedure can be applied to scale, ordinal or nominal variables. This might be done for a number of reasons:

- presentational purposes, when there are a large number of categories and several contain small numbers of responses;
- theoretical purposes, when different parts of the analysis call for different groupings of response categories;
- for comparative reasons, when comparisons with previous research require different groupings;
- for statistical reasons, as discussed in Chapter 17.

Recode with scale and ordinal variables

Scale and ordinal variables are not pre-coded – the actual value given by respondents is recorded in the data file, not a code. In the case of scale variables in particular, this means that the *Frequencies* procedure produces a table with one line for every value in the data-set – as can be seen in Appendix 16.1 for variables *spend* and *age*. With large samples this can produce impractically large tables with possibly hundreds of lines, which would be unreadable and unmanageable, particularly for crosstabulation (discussed below). *Recoded,* grouped versions of such variables can be produced using the method demonstrated in the first part of Figure 16.14.

Part I: scale or ordinal variables

Example: recode the variable *spend* into four groups as follows:

Proposed groupings	New code	Value labels
0–50	1	£0–50
51–100	2	£51–100
101–200	3	£101–200
201+	4	£201 and over

Procedure

1. From the top of the screen, select *Transform*, then *Recode into Different Variables*.
2. Select the variable to be recoded, *spend,* and transfer to the *Numeric variable --> Output variable* box.
3. In the *Output Variable* box, add a *Name* (e.g. *spendr*) and *Label* (e.g. *Spend on entertainment – recoded*).
4. Select *Old and New Values*.
5. In the *Old Value* box select *Range*. In the first box enter 1 and in the second box, enter *50*.
6. In the *Value* box, enter *1*, then click on Add. The Old–New box should now contain '1 thru 50 -- > 1'.
7. Repeat steps 5 and 6 for: 51 through 100 – Value 2; and 101 through 200 – Value 3.
8. Select Range through Highest: enter 201. In the Value box enter 4, then click on Add.
   The Old–New box should now contain: 1 thru 50->1, 51 thru 100 --> 2, 101 thru 200--> 3, 201 thru Highest --> 4.
9. Select Continue.
10. Select Change, then OK. The new variable now appears on the Data View and Variable View screens.
11. Add *Value Labels*, as above, via the *Variable View* window, as for any variable.
12. *Save* the data file with the new variable, if you will want to use it again.
13. Produce a *Frequencies* table for the recoded variable *spendr* in the usual way, to produce the output below.

Output: Spend recoded

	Frequency	Percent	Valid percent	Cumulative percent
£0–50	4	26.7	26.7	26.7
£51–100	6	40.0	40.0	66.7
£101–200	2	13.3	13.3	80.0
£201+	3	20.0	20.0	100.0
Total	15	100.0	100.0	

Part 2: For string (pre-coded) variables

Example: recode the variable *status* into two groups as follows:

Current coding	New code	Value labels
1 F/T student – no work 2 F/T student – working	1	Full-time student
3 P/T student – F/T job 4 P/T student – other	2	Part-time student

Procedure

1–3. Repeat steps 1–3 above, using: variable *status*; recoded variable name *statusr;* and label *Status – recoded*.
4. Select *Old and New Values*.
5. In the *Old Value* box select *Range*. In the first box enter 1 and in the second box, enter *2*.
6. In the *Value* box, enter *1*, then click on *Add*. The *Old–New* box should now contain '1 thru 2-> 1.
7. Repeat steps 5 and 6 for: 3 through *4 – Value 2*. The *Old–New* box also now contains '3 thru 4-> 2.
8. Select *Continue*.
9. Select *Change*, then *OK*. The new variable now appears on the *Data View* and *Variable View* screens.
10. Add *Value Labels*, as above, via the *Variable View* window, as for any variable.
11. *Save* the data file with the new variable, if you will want to use it again.
12. Produce a *Frequencies* table for the recoded variable *statusr* in the usual way, to produce the output below.

Figure 16.14 Recode procedures and output

Output: Status recoded

	Frequency	Percent	Valid percent	Cumulative percent
Full-time student	7	46.7	46.7	46.7
Part-time student	8	53.3	53.3	100.0
Total	15	100.0	100.0	

Figure 16.14 *(continued)*

Ordinal variables, such as those in question 3, can be recoded – for example, ranks first and second could be grouped together, and third and fourth could be grouped together, and so on. Similarly, Likert-type variables, as in question 5, can be recoded – for example, grouping 'very important' and 'important' together.

It might be asked: if a scale variable is to be grouped anyway, why not present groupings in the questionnaire, where respondents can tick a box? This is often done, but the advantage of not having the variable pre-coded is that it is possible to be flexible about what groupings are required and it is also possible to use such procedures as *Means* and *Regression*, which is not generally possible with pre-coded or nominal variables.

Recode with nominal/pre-coded variables

It is also possible to change the groupings of nominal or pre-coded variables using *Recode*. For instance, analysis could be conducted comparing all full-time students and all part-time students – that is, two groups rather than four. This is illustrated in the second part of Figure 16.14.

Mean, median and mode – measures of central tendency

We have already considered the idea of measures of central tendency and the mean in the discussion of *Descriptives* above. As noted there, a mean is the same as an average and is appropriate for scale or ordinal data only, not for nominal variables with codes which represent qualitative categories, except for the exceptions discussed above.

Here we also consider two other measures of central tendency:

- the *median*, which is the value for which there are as many members of the sample above as there are below; and

- the mode, which is the value that contains the largest number of sample members.

Two procedures are available in SPSS for producing means, as shown in Figure 16.15.

- Method 1 uses a feature of the *Frequencies* procedure:
  - Example 1a shows that:
    - mean expenditure on entertainment among the sample is £115;
    - the median value is £75, which is lower than the mean because there are more people in the lower expenditure categories than in the higher categories;
    - the mode is £50, £75, £100, £200 and £250, since all these values have two responses.
  - Example 1b demonstrates the use of the procedure for producing mean scores for Likert-type scales – the median does not have a lot of meaning, but the mode, which is the most popular value for each variable, may be meaningful and useful in some situations.

Method 1. Using *Frequencies* procedure

a. Scale variable

1 Select *Analyze*, then *Descriptive Statistics*, then *Frequencies*.
2 Select *spend* and transfer to the *Variable(s)* box.
3 Select *Statistics* and click on *Mean, Median* and *Mode*.
4 Select *Continue*.
5 Select *OK* to run the *Frequencies* in the normal way.

Output (Frequency table not reproduced)

Statistics: Expenditure on entertainment/month

N	Valid	15
	Missing	0
Mean		115.00
Median		75.00
Mode		50a

a Multiple modes exist. The smallest value is shown.

b. Attitude statements/Likert scales.

Using the procedure as in a. above, produce means for the three variables *relax, social* and *mental* results in output is as follows.

Output (Frequency table not reproduced)

		Relaxation – importance	Social interaction – importance	Meaningful experience – importance
N	Valid	15	15	15
	Missing	0	0	0
Mean		2.20	2.67	1.47
Median		2.0	3.0	1.0
Mode		2	3	1

Method 2. Using *Means* procedure

a. Scale variable

1 Select *Analyze*, then *Compare Means*, then *Means*.
2 Select *status* and put it into the *Independent list** box.
3 Select *spend* and put it into the *Dependent list** box.
4 Select *OK*. Means and standard deviations for each course group are produced, as below, showing different values for different groups.

(* The idea of dependent and independent variables and standard deviations are discussed in Chapter 12.)

Output

Expenditure on entertainment/week

Student status	Mean	N	Std. deviation
F/T student/no paid work	102.50	2	67.175
F/T student/paid work	120.00	5	83.666
P/T student – F/T job	99.17	6	76.643
P/T student/Other	162.50	2	194.454
Total	115.00	15	87.076

Figure 16.15 Means procedures and output

- Method 2 uses the *Means* procedure which produces means for sub-groups as well as for the whole sample. For example, in Figure 16.15, mean expenditures on entertainment are shown for students of different statuses. Note that this moves beyond description into the area of possible explanation, since it reveals that a student's full-time/part-time status and employment status may lead to different levels of expenditure.

Presenting the results: statistical summary

The layout of the frequency tables produced by the software contains more detail than is necessary for most reports. It is recommended that a *Statistical summary* be prepared for inclusion in any report, rather than include a copy of the computer printout. The summary must be prepared with a word processor, either typing it out afresh or editing the saved *SPSS Output* file. For example, the output from the *Frequencies, Recodes, Multiple response* and *Means* analysis covered so far could be summarised as in Figure 16.16.

Sample size	15
Student status	%
F/T student/no paid work	13.3
F/T student/paid work	33.3
P/T student – F/T job	40.0
P/T student/Other	13.3
Total	100.0
Campus cultural activity in the last 4 weeks	%
Movie	86.7
Theatre	53.3
Rock concert	33.3
Jazz session	13.3
Importance of factors in campus services	**Mean rank**
Free/cheap	1.8
Times	3.7
Quality of facilities	1.6
Socialising	3.2
Time available	4.7
Expenditure on entertainment, etc./week	%
£0–50	26.7
£51–100	40.0
£101–200	13.3
Over £200	20.0
Average expenditure/week	£115.00
Suggestions for improvements	**% of cases**
Comments on programme content	58.3
Comments on timing	50.0
Comments on facilities	25.0
Comments on costs	33.3
Comments on organisation	16.7
Gender	%
Male	53.3
Female	46.3
Age	%
18–19	26.7
20–21	53.4
22 and over	20.0

Importance of factors in campus services

	Very important	Important	Not important	Mean score*
	%	%	%	
Relaxation	33.3	53.3	13.3	2.2
Social interaction	66.7	33.3	0.0	2.7
Meaningful experience	0.0	46.7	53.3	1.5

(* 3 = very important, 2 = important, 1= not important)

Figure 16.16 Campus Entertainment Survey 2012: statistical summary

The following should be noted about the summary:

- The results from *multiple response* variables are presented in single tables.
- Recoded versions of *spend* and *age* are included.
- The mean *spend* and *age* and the mean scores for the attitude/Likert-type variables come from the *Means* procedure discussed above.
- It is generally not necessary to include raw frequency counts as well as percentages in reports, since the sample size is indicated: readers of the summary can work out the raw numbers for themselves if required.

Crosstabulation

Introduction

After calculation of frequencies and means, the most commonly used procedure in survey analysis is probably crosstabulation. This relates two or more variables to produce tables of the sort commonly encountered in social research. In analysing the relationships between variables, crosstabulation marks another move from purely descriptive to explanatory analysis. The *SPSS Crosstabs* procedure and output are demonstrated in Part 1 of Figure 16.17.

Rows and columns

Having been specified as the *row* variable in Figure 16.17 Part 1, *status* appears down the side of the table, while the *column* variable, *rock*, appears across the top. Specifying the two variables the other way round would produce a table with *status* across the top and *rock* down the side.

Percentages

In most cases percentages rather than just the raw figures are required in tables. The Part 1 procedure includes percentages only for the row and column totals (which are the same as the percentages in the *Frequencies* tables for the individual variables). The cells in the body of the table contain only counts of the raw numbers, not percentages. To produce percentages in the body of the table it is necessary to specify the 'cell contents'. There are four relevant options for individual cell contents:

- counts;
- row percentages – where percentages add to 100 going across a row;
- column percentages – where percentages add to 100 going down the column;
- total percentages – where all cell percentages add to 100.

The choice of which percentages to use depends on the context and the purpose of the analysis – it generally becomes apparent in the course of discussing the contents of a table; often 'trial and error' is involved in testing out the use of particular percentages in particular situations. The procedures for producing percentages in *Crosstabs* are as shown in Part 2 of Figure 16.17.

Three-way crosstabulations

Often three-way crosstabulations are required. For example, the above table could be further sub-divided by gender. This is demonstrated in Part 3 of Figure 16.17. Further sub-division is possible, although often the sample size places limits on how far this can go.

Part 1: Crosstabs – counts only

Procedure

1   Select *Analyze*, then *Descriptive Statistics*, then *Crosstabs*.
2   Transfer *rock* to the *Columns* box.
3   Transfer *status* to the *Rows* box.
4   Select *OK*. Output is as below.

Output

Student status × Campus rock concert in last 4 wks Crosstabulation

		Campus rock concert in last 4 wks		Total
		No	Yes	
Student status	F/T student/no paid work	1	1	2
	F/T student/paid work	3	2	5
	P/T student – F/T job	2	4	6
	P/T student/Other	1	1	2
Total		7	8	15

Part 2: Crosstabs – with percentages

Procedure

1 Repeat steps 1–3 above.
4 In the *Crosstabs* dialogue box select *Cells*. The *Crosstabs: Cell Display* dialogue box is presented.
5 In the *Counts* box click on the tick in the Observed box to make it disappear (NB: omit this step if you wish to retain counts as well as adding percentages).
6 In the *Percentages*, select *Row*.
7 Select *Continue* then *OK*. Output appears as follows.

Output

Student status × Campus rock concert in last 4 wks Crosstabulation

		Campus rock concert in last 4 wks		Total
		No	Yes	
Student status	F/T student/no paid work	50.0%	50.0%	100.0%
	F/T student/paid work	60.0%	40.0%	100.0%
	P/T student – F/T job	33.3%	66.7%	100.0%
	P/T student/Other	50.0%	50.0%	100.0%
Total		46.7%	53.3%	100.0%

Part 3: Three-way crosstabulation

Procedure

1 Repeat steps 1–3 in Part 1 above.
4 In the *Crosstabs* dialogue box: transfer *gender* into the *Layer* box.
5 Select *OK* to produce output as follows.

Output

Student status × Campus rock concert in last 4 wks × Gender Crosstabulation

Gender			Campus rock concert in last 4 wks		Total
			No	Yes	
Male	Student status	F/T student/no paid work	1	1	2
		P/T student – F/T job	2	3	5
		P/T student/Other	0	1	1
	Total		3	5	8
Female	Student status	F/T student/paid work	3	2	5
		P/T student – F/T job	0	1	1
		P/T student/Other	1	0	1
	Total		4	3	7

Figure 16.17 Crosstabs procedures and output

405

Weighting

The weighting of data to correct for biased samples is discussed in Chapter 13, where the procedure for calculating a weighting factor is discussed. The simplest way of introducing a weighting factor to the SPSS process is to add the weights as an additional variable. For example, the 'weighting' variable might be called *wt* and the weights typed into the data file like any other item of data.

To weight data, select *Data* and use the *Weight Cases* feature, specifying the appropriate variable (e.g. *wt*) as weighting variable. To save having to type in the weights for every respondent, SPSS provides a logical procedure. For example, if all Masters course students are to be given a weight of 1.3, it is possible to indicate this in the *Weight Cases* procedure. It is not intended to explain the detail of this procedure here – the reader is referred to the *Help* facility in the *Weight Cases* dialogue box.

Graphics

Graphical presentation of data is an aid to communication in most situations: for example, most people can see trends and patterns in data more easily in graphic form. Computer packages generally offer the following graphic formats for data presentation:

- scattergram
- bar graph;
- stacked bar graph;
- pie chart;
- line graph.

Computers can produce all four formats from any one set of data. But all formats are not equally appropriate for all data types: the appropriate type of graphic depends on the type of data or level of measurement involved. The data types therefore lend themselves to different graphical treatment. The relationships between these types of data and permitted graphical types are summarised in Figure 16.18.

- The *bar graph* or *histogram* deals with categories for each bar, so any scale variable must first be divided into groups – using the *Recode* procedure. The 'stacked' bar graph includes information on two variables – the graphical equivalent of the crosstabulation.

- The *pie chart* is just that: it divides something into sections like a pie. The segments making up the pie chart must therefore add up to some sort of meaningful total – often the total sample or 100 per cent.

- The *line graph* is the most constrained and is used more generally in more quantified research. Strictly speaking, they should be used only with *scale* variables.
  - A line graph with a single scale variable indicates the distribution of a variable although, for the type of data in the example survey, this is probably best done by means of a bar chart.
  - A line graph can be used to show the relationship between two scale variables – with one variable on each axis. However, a fitted *regression* line, as discussed in Chapter 17, is generally more meaningful than a line traced through all observation points, as would happen with a line graph.

Data characteristics	Data type		
	Nominal	Ordinal	Scale
	Qualitative categories	Ranks	Numerical
Example questions in Figure10.21	1, 2, 6	3, 5	4
Mean/average possible	No	Yes	Yes
Types of graphics			
Bar graph	Yes	Yes	Yes*
Pie chart	Yes	Yes	Yes*
Line graph	No	No	Yes
Scattergram	No	No	Yes

* Grouped

Figure 16.18 Data types and graphics

- A *scattergram* is based on two scale variables, but involves just plots of the observation points, rather than drawing a line through them. This may be overcome by use of a 'best fit' line based on regression (see Chapter 17).

Graphics are easily produced in SPSS using an optional feature of the *Frequencies* command, but this is not very flexible. A better option is the *Graphs* facility. Examples of graphics output from this facility are shown in Figure 16.19. It is not proposed to consider graphics procedures in detail here; details can be found in the SPSS Graphs Help facility.

a. Bar chart
1. Select *Graphs* at the top of the screen, then *Legacy Dialogs*.
2. Select *Bar* and then *Simple* then *Define* to produce the dialog box: *Define Simple Bar: Summaries for Groups of Cases*.
3. Transfer *status* to the *Category Axis* box.
4. Select *N of cases* or *% of cases*. In example here, *% of cases* has been selected.
5. Select *OK* to produce the bar chart.

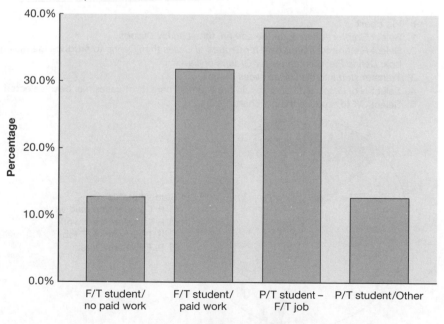

Figure 16.19 Graphics procedures and output

b. Stacked bar chart

1. Select *Graphs* at the top of the screen, then *Legacy Dialogs*.
2. Select *Bar* and then *Stacked* then *Define* to produce the dialog box: *Define Stack Bar: Summaries for Groups of Cases*.
3. Transfer *status* to the *Category axis* box and *gender* to the *Define Stacks by* box.
4. Select *N of cases* or *% of cases*. In the example here, *N of cases* has been selected.
5. Select *OK* to produce the stacked bar chart.

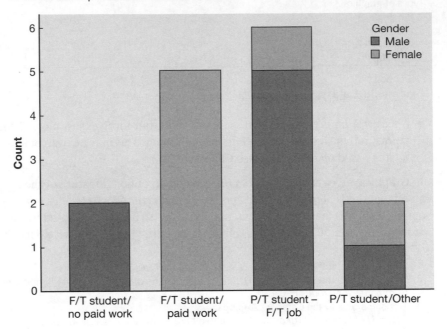

c. Pie chart

1. Select *Graphs* at the top of the screen, then *Legacy Dialogs*.
2. Select *Pie* and then *Summary for Groups of Cases* then *Define* to produce the dialog box: *Define Pie: Summaries for Groups of Cases*.
3. Transfer *status* to the *Define slices by* box.
4. Select *N of cases* or *% of cases*. In the example here, N of cases has been selected.
5. Select *OK* to produce the pie chart.

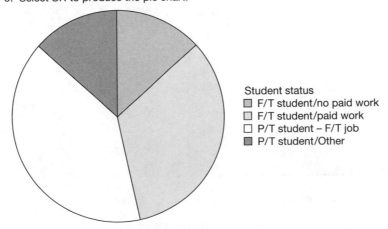

Figure 16.19 *(continued)*

d. Line graph
1. Select *Graphs* at the top of the screen, then *Legacy Dialogs*.
2. Select *Line* and then *Simple* then *Define* to produce the dialog box: *Define Simple Line: Summaries for Groups of Cases*.
3. Transfer *age* to the *Category axis* box.
4. Select *N of cases* or *% of cases*. In the example here, *N of cases* has been selected.
5. Select *OK* to produce the graphic d.

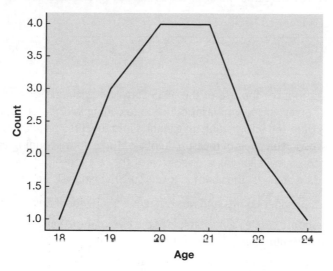

e. Scattergram
1. Select *Graphs* at the top of the screen, then *Legacy Dialogs*.
2. Select *Scatter/Dot* and then *Simple Scatter,* then *Define* to produce the dialog box: *Simple Scatterplot.*
3. Transfer *spend* to the *Y-axis* box and *age* to the *X-axis* box.
4. Select *OK* to produce graphic e.

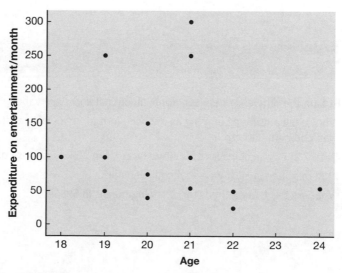

Figure 16.19 *(continued)*

The analysis process

The above is only a brief introduction to the mechanics of survey, and similar, data analysis. While SPSS is capable of much more sophisticated analyses, mastery of the procedures presented here can provide a sound basis for a viable programme of analysis.

Summary

This chapter introduces the use of the SPSS software package for analysis of data from a questionnaire survey. Based on the introduction to coding in Chapter 10, the process of introducing survey data and information on variables into the SPSS package is demonstrated. This includes a discussion of levels of measurement and three corresponding variable types: nominal, ordinal and scale. Following a discussion of the relationship between types of research and types of data analysis, the chapter covers six SPSS analysis procedures:

- *Frequencies* provides counts and percentages for individual and multiple variables.
- *Multiple response* creates single tables for the two or more variables arising from questions with multiple responses.
- *Recode* is used to create groups for scale variables and regroup pre-coded variables.
- *Means* calculates the means or averages of variables and compares means for sub-samples.
- *Crosstabs* creates crosstabulations or frequency tables showing the relationships between two or more variables.
- *Weight* is used to weight data according to some criterion variable, as discussed in Chapter 10.
- *Graphs* produces graphical representations of data in various forms, including bar charts, pie charts, line graphs and scattergrams.

TEST QUESTIONS

1. Explain the difference between nominal, ordinal and scale variables and give examples.
2. What is the advantage of using an uncoded format for a scale variable in a questionnaire, rather than coding it into groups?
3. Outline the characteristics of the two types of multiple response question.
4. Why might an analyst wish to recode variables?
5. What are the two methods for obtaining means in SPSS?

EXERCISES

1. The major exercise for this chapter is to replicate the analyses presented in the chapter. This can be done by typing the data and variable definition data in Figures 16.8 and 16.9 or downloading the data from the book website and carrying out the instructions for the various procedures in the chapter.

2. Repeat each of the procedures in exercise 1 using at least one different variable in each procedure.

3. Conduct a survey of students using the questionnaire in Figure 10.21 and analyse the data using SPSS, following the analysis procedures outlined in this chapter.

Resources

Regarding SPSS:

- Access and guidance: It is envisaged that most readers will have access to a teacher/tutor to assist as problems arise. The SPSS package itself includes a tutorial for beginners and there are numerous books available on the use of SPSS, as indicated below. In higher-education institutions SPSS, as with other computer packages, is generally made available in computer laboratories on licence. Further training is available in SPSS, and other survey packages, through universities, commercial computer training organisations and the SPSS company itself in major centres around the world.

- The SPSS website is at: www.SPSS.com

- There are a number of guides on the use of SPSS, for example: Carver and Nash (2011), Coakes and Ong (2011), George and Mallery (2010), Pallant (2007).

- Regarding questionnaire survey analysis generally:

    o It is difficult to locate published research reports that give full details of questionnaire surveys and their analysis. While many journal articles are based on survey research, they typically do not provide a copy of the questionnaire and give only a brief summary of the analysis process – often only part of the analysis arising from the data. (But see sources for examples of complete questionnaires in the Resources section of Chapter 10.)

    o Few commercially published books are based primarily on questionnaire survey data and even when they are, full details are not always provided.

    o Government-sponsored survey reports, by the government statistical agency or other agencies, often contain these details, although inevitably they are generally either purely descriptive or related in a fairly straightforward manner to policy issues. Such reports are inconsistently available in libraries, but are sometimes available on the internet, as indicated in the Resources section of Chapter 10.

- Regarding surveys in the arts/events:

    o national surveys: see Resources sections of Chapters 7 and 10
    o Example: museums: Schuster (1995)

References

Carver, R. H. and Nash, J. G. (2011) *Doing Data Analysis with SPSS Version 18.0.* Pacific Grove, CA: Duxbury Press.

Coakes, S. J. and Ong, C. (2011) *SPSS Version 18.0 for Windows: Analysis without Anguish.* Brisbane: John Wiley and Sons.

George, D. and Mallery, P. (2010) *SPSS for Windows Step by Step: A Simple Guide and Reference, 18.0 Update.* Boston, MA: Prentice Hall.

Pallant, J. F. (2007) *SPSS Survival Manual: A Step by Step Guide to Data Analysis Using SPSS*, Third Edition. Sydney: Allen and Unwin.

Schuster, J. M. D. (1995) The public interest in the art museum's public. In S. Pearce (ed.), *Art in Museums.* London: Athlone, pp. 109–142.

Appendix 16.1
Frequencies output file

Statistics (only scale and ordinal variables included here to show means)

	Cheap	Hours	Qual	Meet	Time	Spend	Relax	Social	Meaning
N Valid	15	15	15	15	15	15	15	15	15
Missing	0	0	0	0	0	0	0	0	0
Mean	1.8	3.73	1.6	3.2	4.67	115	2.2	1.67	1.47

Student status

		Frequency	Percent	Valid Percent	Cumulative Percent
Valid	F/T student/no paid work	2	13.3	13.3	13.3
	F/T student/paid work	5	33.3	33.3	46.7
	P/T student – F/T job	6	40.0	40.0	86.7
	P/T student/Other	2	13.3	13.3	100.0
	Total	15	100.0	100.0	

Campus movie in last 4 wks

		Frequency	Percent	Valid Percent	Cumulative Percent
Valid	No	2	13.3	13.3	13.3
	Yes	13	86.7	86.7	100.0
	Total	15	100.0	100.0	

Campus theatre in last 4 wks

		Frequency	Percent	Valid Percent	Cumulative Percent
Valid	No	7	46.7	46.7	46.7
	Yes	8	53.3	53.3	100.0
	Total	15	100.0	100.0	

Campus rock concert in last 4 wks

		Frequency	Percent	Valid Percent	Cumulative Percent
Valid	No	10	66.7	66.7	66.7
	Yes	5	33.3	33.3	100.0
	Total	15	100.0	100.0	

Campus jazz session in last 4 wks

		Frequency	Percent	Valid Percent	Cumulative Percent
Valid	No	13	86.7	86.7	86.7
	Yes	2	13.3	13.3	100.0
	Total	15	100.0	100.0	

Free/cheap (rank)

		Frequency	Percent	Valid Percent	Cumulative Percent
Valid	1	6	40.0	40.0	40.0
	2	6	40.0	40.0	80
	3	3	20.0	20.0	100.0
	Total	15	100.0	100.0	

Times (rank)

		Frequency	Percent	Valid Percent	Cumulative Percent
Valid	2	2	13.3	13.3	13.3
	3	3	20.0	20.0	33.3
	4	7	46.7	46.7	80.0
	5	3	20.0	20.0	100.0
	Total	15	100.0	100.0	

Quality of facilities (rank)

		Frequency	Percent	Valid Percent	Cumulative Percent
Valid	1	8	53.3	53.3	53.3
	2	5	33.3	33.3	86.7
	3	2	13.3	13.3	100.0
	Total	15	100.0	100.0	

Socialising (rank)

		Frequency	Percent	Valid Percent	Cumulative Percent
Valid	1	1	6.7	6.7	6.7
	2	2	13.3	13.3	20.0
	3	7	46.7	46.7	66.7
	4	3	20.0	20.0	86.7
	5	2	13.3	13.3	100.0
	Total	15	100.0	100.0	

Time available (rank)

		Frequency	Percent	Valid Percent	Cumulative Percent
Valid	4	5	33.3	33.3	33.3
	5	10	66.7	66.7	100.0
	Total	15	100.0	100.0	

Expenditure on entertainment/month

		Frequency	Percent	Valid Percent	Cumulative Percent
Valid	25	1	6.7	6.7	6.7
	40	1	6.7	6.7	13.3
	50	2	13.3	13.3	26.7
	55	2	13.3	13.3	40.0
	75	2	13.3	13.3	53.3
	100	2	13.3	13.3	66.7
	150	2	13.3	13.3	80.0
	250	2	13.3	13.3	93.3
	300	1	6.7	6.7	100.0
	Total	15	100.0	100.0	

Relaxation – importance

		Frequency	Percent	Valid Percent	Cumulative Percent
Valid	Very important	2	13.3	13.3	13.3
	Important	8	53.3	53.3	66.7
	Not at all important	5	33.3	33.3	100.0
	Total	15	100.0	100.0	

Social interaction – importance

		Frequency	Percent	Valid Percent	Cumulative Percent
Valid	Important	5	33.3	33.3	33.3
	Not at all important	10	66.7	66.7	100.0
	Total	15	100.0	100.0	

Meaningful experience – importance

		Frequency	Percent	Valid Percent	Cumulative Percent
Valid	Very important	8	53.3	53.3	53.3
	Important	7	46.7	46.7	100.0
	Total	15	100.0	100.0	

Improvement suggestion – 1

		Frequency	Percent	Valid Percent	Cumulative Percent
Valid	Programme content	5	33.3	41.7	41.7
	Timing	3	20.0	25.0	66.7
	Facilities	2	13.3	16.7	83.3
	Costs	2	13.3	16.7	100.0
	Total	12	80.0	100.0	
Missing	System	3	20.0		
Total		15	100.0		

Improvement suggestion – 2

		Frequency	Percent	Valid Percent	Cumulative Percent
Valid	Programme content	2	13.3	25.0	25
	Timing	3	20.0	37.5	62.5
	Facilities	1	6.7	12.5	75
	Costs	1	6.7	12.5	87.5
	Organisation	1	6.7	12.5	100.0
	Total	8	53.3	100.0	
Missing	System	7	46.7		
Total		15	100.0		

Improvement suggestion – 3

		Frequency	Percent	Valid Percent	Cumulative Percent
Valid	Costs	1	6.7	50.0	50
	Organisation	1	6.7	50.0	100.0
	Total	2	13.3	100.0	
Missing	System	13	86.7		
Total		15	100.0		

Gender

		Frequency	Percent	Valid Percent	Cumulative Percent
Valid	Male	8	53.3	53.3	53.3
	Female	7	46.7	46.7	100.0
	Total	15	100.0	100.0	

Age

		Frequency	Percent	Valid Percent	Cumulative Percent
Valid	18	1	6.7	6.7	6.7
	19	3	20.0	20.0	26.7
	20	4	26.7	26.7	53.3
	21	4	26.7	26.7	80
	22	2	13.3	13.3	93.3
	24	1	6.7	6.7	100.0
	Total	15	100.0	100.0	

Chapter 17

Statistical analysis

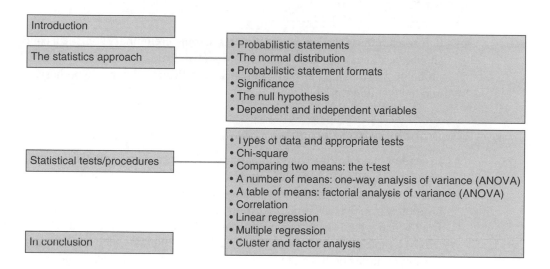

Introduction	
The statistics approach	• Probabilistic statements • The normal distribution • Probabilistic statement formats • Significance • The null hypothesis • Dependent and independent variables
Statistical tests/procedures	• Types of data and appropriate tests • Chi-square • Comparing two means: the t-test • A number of means: one-way analysis of variance (ANOVA) • A table of means: factorial analysis of variance (ANOVA) • Correlation • Linear regression • Multiple regression • Cluster and factor analysis
In conclusion	

Introduction

This chapter provides an introduction to statistics, building on the outline of sampling theory presented in Chapter 13 and the introduction to the SPSS package in Chapter 16. It is only an introduction: it is not intended to be a complete course in statistics. There are many textbooks covering approximately the same ground as covered here, but in more detail and more depth, and reference to some of these texts is given in the Resources section at the end of the chapter. The outline of survey analysis in Chapter 16 deals with quantification and the generation and analysis of statistical information, but this chapter is concerned with more than just quantification. Given that, as discussed in Chapter 13, data based on samples are subject to a margin of error when generalising to the population from which they were drawn, this chapter examines how the accuracy of sample-based statistical data can be assessed and in particular how relationships between variables might be analysed and their statistical significance determined.

After dealing with some general concepts related to the statistical method, the chapter covers a number of statistical tests which are appropriate for different types of data. These tests are the chi-square test, the t-test, analysis of variance, correlation, linear and multiple regression and multivariate analysis, including factor and cluster analysis. In each case the SPSS procedures for carrying out the tests are described. At the end of some of the SPSS procedure sections and at the end of the chapter as a whole some other procedures which are used in some cultural/events research are discussed in general terms but not followed up in detail, including multiple correspondences analysis, structural equation modelling, binary logistic regression analysis and odds ratios.

The statistics approach

Before examining particular statistical tests, some preliminary statistical concepts and ideas should be discussed, namely the idea of probabilistic statements, the normal distribution, probabilistic statement formats, statistical significance, the null hypothesis, and dependent and independent variables.

Probabilistic statements

In general, the science of 'inferential statistics' seeks to make *probabilistic* statements about a population on the basis of information available from a sample drawn from that population. The statements are probabilistic because, as discussed in Chapter 13, it is not possible to be absolutely sure that any randomly drawn sample is precisely representative of the population from which it has been drawn, so we can only estimate the probability that results obtained from a sample are true of the population. The 'statements' which might be made on the basis of sample survey findings can be descriptive, comparative or relational:

- descriptive: for example: 20 per cent of adults prefer classical music;
- comparative: for example: 20 per cent prefer classical music, but 30 per cent prefer rock music;
- relational: for example: 25 per cent of people with high incomes prefer classical music but only 10 per cent of people with low incomes do so – there is a positive relationship between preference for classical music and income.

If they are based on data from samples, such statements cannot be made without qualification. The sample may indicate these findings, but it is not certain that they apply precisely to the population from which the sample is drawn, because there is always an element of doubt about any sample. Inferential statistics modifies the above example statements to be of the form:

- we can be 95 per cent confident that the proportion of adults who prefer classical music is between 16.5 per cent and 23.5 per cent;
- the proportion of adults who prefer rock music is significantly higher than the proportion who prefer classical music (at the 95 per cent level of probability);
- there is a positive relationship between level of income and the preference for classical music (at the 95 per cent level).

The normal distribution

Descriptive statements and 'confidence intervals' are discussed in general terms in Chapter 13 in relation to the issue of sample size. The probability or confidence interval statement is based on the theoretical idea of drawing repeated samples of the same size from the same population. The sample drawn in any one piece of research is only one of a large number of possible samples that might have been drawn. If a large number of samples could be drawn, such an exercise would produce a variety of results, some very unrepresentative of the population but most, assuming random sampling procedures are used, tending to produce results close to the true population values. Statistical theory – which we are unable to explore in detail here – is able to quantify this tendency, so that we can say that, in 95 or 99 out of 100 of such samples, the values found from the sample will fall within a certain range either side of the true population value – hence the idea of 'confidence intervals' as discussed in Chapter 13.

The theory relates to the bell-shaped 'normal distribution' that would result if repeated samples were drawn and the values of a statistic (for example, the proportion who prefer classical music) plotted, as shown in Figure 17.1. The 'normal curve' that would result if a very large number of samples were to be drawn was shown in Figure 13.1 in Chapter 13. The population value of a statistic (such as a percentage or the average of a variable) lies at the centre of the distribution and the value of the statistic found from a sample in a particular research project is just one among the many sample possibilities. The probabilistic statement is made on the basis of this distribution, which has theoretically known properties for different samples and measures, such as percentages and means.

This idea of levels of probability about the accuracy of sample findings based on the theoretical possibility of drawing many samples is common to most of the statistical procedures examined in this chapter.

Probabilistic statement formats

It is customary in social research to use probability levels of 95 per cent or 99 per cent – and occasionally 90 per cent or 99.9 per cent. As probability estimates these can be interpreted exactly as in everyday language – for example, when we say '90 per cent certain', '50:50' or '9 times out of 10' we are making probabilistic statements. So, if a survey finding is *significant* (a concept discussed further below) at the '99 per cent level', we are saying that we believe there is a 99 per cent chance that what we have found is true of the population – there is therefore, conversely, a 1 per cent chance that what we have found is *not* true. If we can only say that something is significant at the lower 95 per cent level, we are less confident – there is a 5 per cent chance that what we have found is not true. Thus, the terminology *highly significant* is sometimes used in relation to findings at the 99 per cent level and *significant* is used for the 95 per cent level.

In some cases, instead of the computer-generated results of statistical tests using these conventional cut-off points, they present the exact probability – for example, it might be found that a result is significant at the 96.5 per cent level or the 82.5 per cent level. It is then left up to the researcher to judge whether such levels are acceptable.

Note also that sometimes the result is expressed as 1 per cent and sometimes as 99 per cent, or as 5 per cent rather than 95 per cent. A further variation is to express the probability as a proportion rather than a percentage – for example, 0.05 rather than 5 per cent, or 0.01 rather than 1 per cent. Similarly, the exact calculations may be expressed as proportions, for example 0.035 rather than 3.5 per cent or 96.5 per cent.

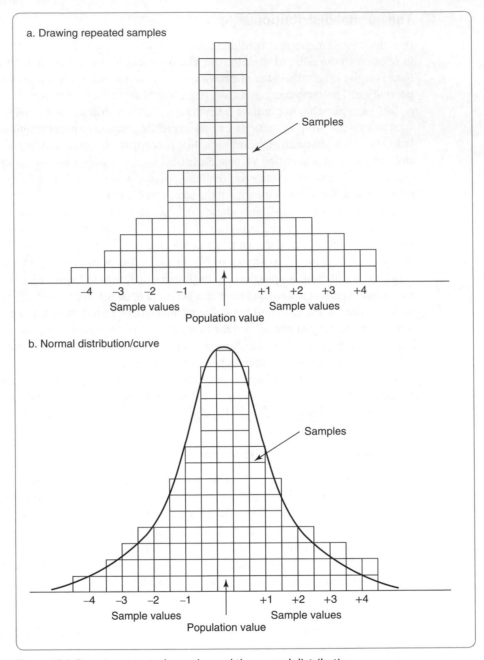

Figure 17.1 Drawing repeated samples and the normal distribution

In the following, therefore, in each row the three forms are equivalent:

5%	95%	0.05
1%	99%	0.01
0.1%	99.9%	0.001
3.5%	96.5%	0.035
7.5%	92.5%	0.075

In computer printouts from computer packages such as SPSS, if the probability is below .0005 it sometimes comes out as .000 because it is printed only to three decimal places. In some research reports and computer printouts results that are significant at the 5 per cent level are indicated by * and those significant at the 1 per cent level are indicated by **.

In the examples and discussions in this chapter, the 5 per cent/95 per cent value is used as the criterion level for tests of significance.

Significance

The second common feature of statistical tests and procedures is that they deal with the idea of *significance*. A significant difference or relationship is one which is unlikely to have happened by chance. So, for example, the bigger the difference between two sample percentages, the more likely it is that the difference is real and not just a statistical chance happening.

For example, if it was found from a sample that 21 per cent of women preferred classical music but only 19 per cent of men did so, we would be inclined, even from a common-sense point of view, to say that the difference is not significant. If another sample were selected, we would not be surprised to find a larger difference between the two figures, for them to be exactly the same or even the opposite way round: it is 'too close to call'. However, whether or not such a small difference is statistically significant depends on the sample size. If the findings were based on a small sample, say around 100 people, 50 men and 50 women, the difference would not be significant – the chances of getting a different result from a different sample of 100 people from the same population would be high – one person more or less in each group would change the percentage difference by two. But if the sample were large – say 1,000 men and 1,000 women – then it might be found to be statistically significant: it would take changes of ten persons to change the percentages by one. So if the result is based on such a large sample we can be much more confident that it is 'real' and would be reproduced if another sample of similar size were drawn.

Statistical theory enables us to quantify and assess 'significance' – that is, to say what sizes of differences are significant for what sizes of sample.

Statistical significance should not, however, be confused with theoretical, social, policy or managerial significance. In a discussion of the idea of experiments to explore the effect of arts education on educational performance generally, Eisner (1998: 11) argues: 'Appraising the educational effects of an experiment is not merely a matter of finding statistically significant differences between groups or correlations that are statistically significant. The differences, if differences are found, must also be educationally significant'. If, for example, the above finding about men's and women's taste in music was based on a sample of, say, 10,000 people, it would be statistically significant, but this does not make the difference significant in any social sense. For all practical purposes, on the basis of such findings, we would say that men's and women's musical tastes are the same or very similar. This is an important point to bear in mind when reading research results based on statistics; large samples can produce many 'statistically significant' findings, but that does not necessarily make them 'significant' in any other way.

The null hypothesis

A common feature of the statistical method is the concept of the *null hypothesis*, referred to by the symbol H_0. It is based on the idea of setting up two mutually incompatible hypotheses, so that only one can be true. If one proposition is true then the other is untrue. The null hypothesis usually proposes that there is *no difference* between two observed values or that there is *no relationship* between variables. There are therefore two possibilities:

H_0 – null hypothesis: there is *no* significant difference or relationship;

H_1 – alternative hypothesis: there *is* a significant difference or relationship.

Usually it is the alternative hypothesis, H_1, that the researcher is interested in, but statistical theory explores the implications of the null hypothesis.

In terms of the types of research approach discussed in Chapter 2, this is very much a deductive approach: the hypothesis is set up in advance of the analysis. However, as noted in Chapter 2, this may be set in the context of an exploratory or even inductive project in which a number of relationships are explored but the testing of each relationship is set up as a deductive process.

The use of the null hypothesis idea can be illustrated by example. Suppose, in a study of music tastes, using a sample of 1,000 adults, part of the study focuses on the relative popularity of classical and rock music. The null hypothesis would be that the participation levels are the same.

H_0 – preference levels for classical and rock music are the same;

H_1 – preference levels for classical and rock music are significantly different.

Suppose it is found that 200 (20 per cent) prefer classical music and 200 (20 per cent) prefer rock. Clearly there is no difference between the two figures; they are consistent with the null hypothesis. The null hypothesis is accepted and the alternative hypothesis is rejected.

But suppose the number preferring classical music was found to be 201 (20.1 per cent) and the number preferring rock was 120 (12.0 per cent). Would we reject the null hypothesis and accept the alternative, that the preference levels for classical and rock music are the same? From what we know of samples, clearly not: this would be too close to call. Such a small difference between the two figures would still be consistent with the null hypothesis. So how big would the difference have to be before we reject the null hypothesis and accept that there is significant difference? A difference of 5, 10, 15? This is where statistical theory comes in, to provide a test of what is and is not a significant difference. And this is basically what the rest of this chapter is all about: providing tests of the relationship between sample findings and the null hypothesis for different situations. The null hypothesis is used in each of the tests examined.

Dependent and independent variables

The terminology *dependent variable* and *independent variable* is discussed in Chapter 1 and is frequently used in statistical analysis. If there is a significant relationship between a dependent and an independent variable, the implication is that changes in the former are caused by changes in the latter: the independent variable influences the dependent variable.

For example, if it is suggested that the level of preference for classical music is influenced by a person's income level, then preference for classical music is the dependent variable and income is the independent variable. Even though a certain level of income does not *cause* people to prefer classical music, it makes more sense to suggest that level of income facilitates or constrains the level of preference for classical music than to suggest the opposite. So it makes some sense to talk of preference for classical music being dependent on income. One variable can be dependent on a number of independent variables, as illustrated in Figure 17.2 – for example, it may be hypothesised that preference for classical music is dependent on income *and* education *and* age.

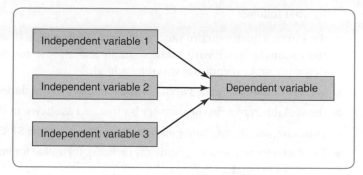

Figure 17.2 Dependent and independent variables

Statistical tests

Types of data and appropriate tests

The idea of levels of measurement, or types of data, was introduced in Chapter 16, when nominal, ordinal and scale data were discussed. The higher the level of measurement, the greater the range of analysis that can be carried out on the data. For example, it is possible to calculate means/averages of ordinal and scale measures, but not of nominal data. Consequently, different statistical tests are associated with different levels of measurement. The rest of the chapter sets out different statistical tests to be used in different situations, as summarised in Figure 17.3. The tests all relate to comparisons between variables and relationships between variables. The appropriate type of test to be used depends on the format of the data, the level of measurement and the number of variables involved.

Task	Format of data	No. of variables	Types of variable	Test
Relationship between 2 variables	Crosstabulation	2	Nominal	Chi-square
Difference between 2 means: paired	Means: whole sample	2	Two scale/ordinal	t-test – paired
independent samples	Means: for 2 sub-groups	2	1. scale/ordinal (means) 2. nominal (2 groups only)	t-test – independent samples
Relationship between: 2 variables	Means for 3+ sub-groups	2	1. scale/ordinal (means) 2. nominal (3+groups)	One-way analysis of variance
3 or more variables	Means: crosstabulated	3+	1. scale/ordinal (means) 2. two or more nominal	Factorial analysis of variance
Relationship between 2 variables	Individual measures	2	Two scale/ordinal	Correlation
Linear relationship between 2 variables	Individual measures	2	Two scale/ordinal	Linear regression
Linear relationship between 3+ variables	Individual measures	3+	3+ scale/ordinal	Multiple regression
Relationships between large numbers of variables	Individual measures	Many	Large numbers of scale/ordinal	Factor analysis Cluster analysis, etc.

Figure 17.3 Types of data and types of statistical test

In what follows:

- data from a questionnaire survey similar to that used in Chapter 16 are used to illustrate the various tests, but with a larger sample and income and additional cultural/event participation and expenditure variables added;
- listings of the questions, variables and data used are included as Appendix 17.1;
- the variable *statusr* in the data-set is produced as shown in Figure 16.13 part 2;
- as in Chapter 16, the examples have been created using SPSS for Windows, Version 20;
- for readers who are mathematically inclined, formulae for various of the test statistics are shown in Appendix 17.2.

Chi-square

Introduction

The chi-square test (symbol: χ^2, pronounced ky, to rhyme with sky) can be used in a number of situations, but its use is demonstrated here in relation to crosstabulations of two nominal variables – the familiar tables produced from such packages as SPSS. When examining crosstabulations it is possible to use 'common sense' and an underlying knowledge of the size of confidence intervals, as discussed in Chapter 13, to make an approximate judgement as to whether there is any sort of relationship between the two variables involved in the table. However, unless the pattern is clear, it can be difficult to judge whether the overall differences are significant. The chi-square test is designed to achieve this.

Null hypothesis

The null hypothesis is that *there is no difference in student full-time/part-time status between male and female respondents*: that is:

H_0 – there is *no* relationship between student status and gender in the population of students;

H_1 – there *is* a relationship between status and gender in the population of students.

Note that the proposition being tested can therefore be expressed in three ways, as shown in Figure 17.4.

Procedures

Figure 17.5 shows the SPSS procedures to obtain a crosstabulation with a chi-square test, and the resultant output. The example chosen relates student full-time/part-time status (*statusr*) to gender (*gender*). The interpretation of this output is discussed below.

Option 1	Option 2	Option 3
Null hypothesis (H_0): there is no relationship between full-time/part-time status and gender in the population of students.	Male and female proportions with full-time/part-time status in the population of students are the same.	Observed and expected values are not significantly different.
Alternative hypothesis (H_1): there is a relationship between full-time/part-time status and gender in the population of students.	Male and female proportions with full-time/part-time status in the population of students are different.	Observed and expected values are significantly different.

Figure 17.4 Alternative expressions of hypotheses

Procedure

1 Select *Analyze*, then *Descriptive Statistics*, then *Crosstabs*.
2 Transfer the variable *statusr* to the *Row(s)* box and *gender* to the *Column(s)* box.
3 Select *Statistics,* then, in the *Crosstabs: Statistics* dialogue box, select *Chi-square* then *Continue*.
4 Select *Cells*, then, in the *Crosstabs: Cells Display* dialogue box:
   – in *Counts*: select *Observed* and *Expected;*
   – in *Percentages*: select *Column* then *Continue*.
5 Select *OK* to produce the output below (*Case Processing Summary* table omitted).

Output
Student status recoded* Gender Crosstabulation

			Gender		
			Male	Female	Total
Student status recoded	Full-time	Count	18	9	27
		Expected Count	13.5	13.5	27.0
		% within Gender	66.7%	33.3%	54.0%
	Part-time	Count	7	16	23
		Expected Count	11.5	11.5	23.0
		% within Gender	30.4%	69.5%	46.0%
Total		Count	25	25	50
		Expected Count	25.0	25.0	50.0
		% within Student status recoded	50.0%	50.0%	100.0%

Chi-Square Tests **(key items highlighted)**

	Value	df	Asymp. Sig. (2-sided)	Exact Sig. (2-sided)	Exact Sig. (1-sided)
Pearson Chi-Square	**6.522** (a)	1	.011		
Continuity Correction (b)	5.153	1	.023		
Likelihood Ratio	6.676	1	.010		
Fisher's Exact Test				.022	.011
Linear-by-Linear Association	6.391	1	.011		
N of Valid Cases	50				

(a) 0 cells (.0%) have expected count less than 5. The minimum expected count is 11.50.
(b) Computed only for a 2 × 2 table.

Figure 17.5 Chi-square test – procedures

Expected frequencies

The cells of the table include counts and row percentages, as discussed in relation to crosstabulations in Chapter 16. But they also include *expected counts*. These are the counts that would be expected if the null hypothesis were true – that is, if there was no difference between males and females in the proportions with full-time/part-time status. In this case we have an equal number of men and women in the sample, so the expected values show a 50:50 split for each status.

The value of chi-square

Chi-square is a statistic based on the sum of the differences between the counts and the expected counts: the greater this sum, the greater the value of chi-square. However, if the differences between the observed and expected counts in the table are simply added, it will be found that the positives cancel out the negatives, giving zero. Chi-square is therefore based on the sum of the *squared* values of the differences. The SPSS package calculates the value of chi-square, so it is not necessary for the reader to know the details of the formula. It is sufficient to understand that chi-square is a statistical measure of the difference between the observed and expected counts in the table.

In the example in Figure 17.5, the value of chi-square is 6.522. We are using the 'Pearson' value, devised by the statistician Karl Pearson – the other values (Continuity Correction, Likelihood Ratio, Fisher's Exact Test and Linear-by-Linear Association) do not concern us here.

Interpretation

How should this value of chi-square be interpreted? We have noted that the greater the difference between the observed and expected values, the greater the value of chi-square. Our null hypothesis is that there is *no* difference between the two sets of values (chi-square would be zero). But clearly, we would accept some *minor* differences between two sets of values and still accept the null hypothesis. But just how big would the differences have to be before we would reject the null hypothesis and conclude that there *is* a difference between male and female full-time/part-time status?

For a given size of table (in this case two cells by two) statisticians have been able to calculate the likelihood of obtaining various values of chi-square when the null hypothesis is true. As with the normal distribution discussed above, this is based on the theoretical possibility of drawing lots of samples of the same size. This is illustrated in Figure 17.6. It shows that, for a particular table size, if the null hypothesis is true, some differences in observed and expected counts can be expected from most samples drawn from a given population, so a range of values of chi-square can be expected. Most values of chi-square would be expected to be fairly small; some larger values would occur, but only rarely – they are unlikely.

Therefore, any value of chi-square in the range to the right of the 5 per cent point in the figure is considered unlikely and inconsistent with the null hypothesis: we *reject* the null hypothesis. If it is in the range to the left of the 5 per cent point we *accept* the null hypothesis.

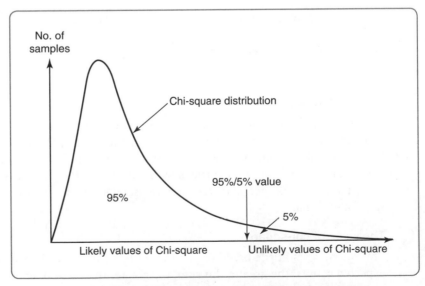

Figure 17.6 Distribution of chi-square assuming null hypothesis is true

In Figure 17.5, the output tells us the value of chi-square for the table: 6.522. It also indicates the likelihood, or probability, of this value: 0.011, or 1.1 per cent. Our value of chi-square is therefore an unlikely one (it has a likelihood of less than 5 per cent), so we reject the null hypothesis and conclude that there *is* a significant difference between the proportion of full-time/part-time status for male and female students.

Degrees of freedom

The values of chi-square depend on the table size, which is indirectly measured by the *degrees of freedom*. Degrees of freedom are calculated by: the number of rows minus one multiplied by the number of columns minus one. So, for the table in Figure 17.5, the degrees of freedom are: $(2 - 1) \times (2 - 1) = 1 \times 1 = 1$. This is shown in the output table under *df*.

Expected counts rule

One rule for the application of chi-square is that there should not be more than one-fifth of the cells of the table with *expected counts* of less than 5, and none with an *expected count* of less than 1. The output indicates whether such cells exist. Note (a) at the bottom of the table indicates that no cells have an expected count of less than 5 and the minimum expected count is 11.5, so there is no problem. If necessary, grouping of some of the values by recoding can be used to reduce the number of cells and thus increase the expected frequencies. In fact, this was done in the example with the recoded variable – if the analysis is run with the original unrecoded *status* variable, the test infringes the expected counts rule and is invalid.

Reporting

How should the results of statistical tests such as chi-square be reported? Four solutions can be considered, as follows:

1. Include the results of the test in the table in the research report, as in Figure 17.7. The commentary might then merely say: 'The relationship between full-time/part-time status and gender was significant at the 5 per cent level'.

2. Include the test results in the text, for example: 'The relationship between full-time/part-time status and gender was significant at the 5 per cent level ($\chi^2 = 6.5$, 1 DF)'.

3. Make the statistics less intrusive by including a note in the report or paper indicating that all tests were conducted at the 5 per cent level and that test values are included in the tables, or are listed in an appendix, or even excluded altogether for non-technical audiences.

4. Use the * and ** approach to indicate significant and highly significant results in tables, as discussed above.

Table 1 Full-time/part-time status by gender

	Male	Female	Total
Status			%
Full-time student	66.7	33.3	54.0
Part-time student	30.4	69.6	46.0
Total	100.0	100.0	100.0
Sample size:	25	25	50

Figure 17.7 Presentation of chi-square test results

$\chi^2 = 6.52$, DF 1, significant at the 5% level

427

Comparing two means: the t-test

Introduction

So far we have dealt only with proportions or percentages, either singly or in crosstabulations, but many research results are in the form of averages – for example, the average age of a group of participants in an activity, the average cultural tourism expenditure of visitors from different countries, or the average score of a group on a Likert scale. In statistical parlance an average is referred to as a *mean*. Means can be calculated only for ordinal and scale variables, not nominal variables.

The simplest form of analysis is to compare two means to see whether they are significantly different. For example, we might want to test whether the average age of classical music fans in a sample is significantly different from that of the rock music fans, or whether the average amount spent on culture by a group of people is greater or less than the amount they spend on going out for meals. In this situation the null hypothesis is expressed as follows:

H_0 – null hypothesis: there is *no* difference between the means;

H_1 – alternative hypothesis: there *is* a difference between the means.

For this situation, rather than chi-square, a statistic referred to as 't' is calculated, but the interpretation is similar. This is based on a formula involving the sample size and the two means to be compared. If there is *no* difference between two means in the population (H_0) then, for a given sample size, t has a known 'distribution' of likely values, as illustrated in Figure 17.8 in comparison with the chi-square distribution. High values are rare, so if the value from a sample is high – in the top 5 per cent of values for that sample size – then we reject H_0 and accept H_1; that is, we conclude that there is a significant difference at the 5 per cent level of probability respectively. Note that because t can take on negative or positive values there are two 'tails' to its distribution – hence the reference to 'two-tailed test' in some of the output discussed below.

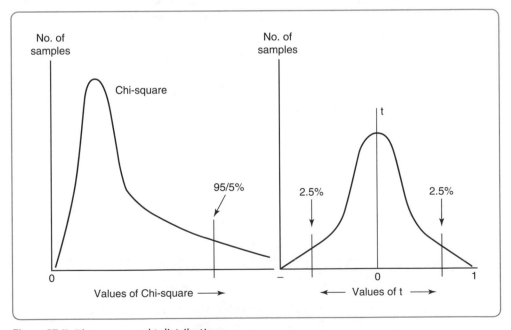

Figure 17.8 Chi-square and t distributions

There are two situations where we might want to compare means:

A To compare the means of two variables that apply to the whole sample – for example, comparing the average amount spent on cultural activity with the average amount spent on dining out (for everybody in the sample). This is known as a *paired samples test*.

B To compare the means of one variable for two sub-groups – for example, comparing the average age of men in the sample with that of women. The sample is divided into two sub-groups, men and women; this is known as a *group* or *independent samples test*.

A. Paired samples test

Figure 17.9 presents two examples of the paired samples test. The SPSS output provides a range of statistics with which we are not concerned here, including a correlation, which is discussed later in the chapter. The items we are interested in are depicted in bold in Figure 17.9.

Example 1 compares the frequency of downloading music with the frequency of buying other items online.

- The people in the sample downloaded music on average 12.2 times in six months and bought other items online on average 9.8 times, a difference of 2.4 – the question is whether this difference is significant.
- The value of t is 1.245 and its (two-tail) significance is 0.219 or 21.9 per cent.
- The result is consistent with the null hypothesis (0.219 is much higher than 0.05).
- So we accept the null hypothesis, that the difference between the the level of buying of other items online and attending live music events is *not* significant.

Example 2 compares the frequency of buying other items online and attending live music events. In this case:

- the difference in the mean frequencies is 3.26;
- the value of t is 2.431;
- its significance level is 0.019, which is below 0.05;
- so we reject the null hypothesis and conclude that there *is* a significant difference between the level of downloading of music and buying of other items online.

B. Independent samples test

Figure 17.10 compares levels of expenditure on entertainment by male and female students.

- For males expenditure is £110 and for males it is £138.60, a difference of £28.60;
- t has a value of −1.25 and a significance level of 0.219;
- since 0.219 is above 0.05, this is consistent with the null hypothesis, so we accept that there is no significant difference between the two expenditure figures.

A number of means: one-way analysis of variance (ANOVA)

Introduction

The t-test was used to examine differences between means two at a time. *Analysis of variance (ANOVA)* is used to examine more than two means at a time. This begins to resemble the crosstabulation process, but with means appearing in the cells of the table instead of counts.

Procedure

1 Select *Analyze*, then *Compare Means*.
2 Select *Paired Samples T-Test*.
3 Highlight the first variable to be compared and transfer to the *Paired variables* box, then transfer the second variable.
4 Select *OK* to obtain t-test output.

Output

Example 1: Downloaded music and Bought other items online

Paired Samples Statistics

		Mean	N	Std. Deviation	Std. Error Mean
Pair 1	Downloaded music	12.20	50	13.095	1.85 2
	Bought other items online	9.80	50	8.804	1.245

Paired Samples Correlations (IGNORE)

		N	Correlation	Sig.
Pair 1	Downloaded music and Bought other items online	50	.274	.054

Paired Samples Test

		Paired Differences					t	df	Sig. (2-tailed)
		Mean	Std. Deivation	Std. Error Mean	95% Confidence Interval of the Difference				
					Lower	Upper			
Pair 1	Downloaded music – Bought other items online	2.400	13.631	1.928	−1.474	6.274	1.245	49	.219

Example 2: Buy items online and Live music events

Paired Samples Statistics

		Mean	N	Std. Deviation	Std. Error Mean
Pair 1	Bought other items online	9.80	50	8.804	1.245
	Live music events	6.54	50	3.157	0.446

Paired Samples Correlations – IGNORE

		N	Correlation	Sig.
Pair 1	But items online and Live music events	50	−.044	.759

Paired Samples Test

		Paired Differences					t	df	Sig. (2-tailed)
		Mean	Std. Deviation	Std. Error Mean	95% Confidence Interval of the Difference				
					Lower	Upper			
Pair 1	Bought other items online – Live music events	3.26	9.484	1.341	0.565	5.955	2.431	49	.019

Figure 17.9 Comparing means: t-test: paired samples – procedures.

Procedure

1 Select *Analyze* and then *Compare Means*.
2 Select *Independent Samples T-Test*.
3 Select the variable for which the mean is required (*spend*) and transfer to *Test variables* box.
4 Select the variable to be used to divide the sample into two groups (*gender*) and transfer to *Grouping variable* box.
5 Select *Define groups* and enter the values used to divide the sample into two groups (in the example: 1 for Male and 2 for Female). Select *Continue* and the two values appear in brackets following the name of the grouping variable: gender(1,2).
6 Select *OK* to obtain t-test.

Output
Group Statistics

	Gender	N	Mean	Std. Deviation	Std. Error Mean
Ent. expenditure, £ p.a.	Male	25	110.00	77.607	15.521
	Female	25	138.60	84.613	16.923

Independent Samples Test

	Levene's Test for Equality of Variances		t-test for Equality of Means							
	F	Sig.	t	df	Sig. (2-tailed)	Mean Difference	Std. Error Difference	95% Confidence Interval of the Difference		
								Lower	Upper	
Equal variances assumed	.431	.514	−1.245	48	.219	−28.600	22.963	−74.770	17.570	
Equal variances not assumed			−1.245	47.646	.219	−28.600	22.963	−74.779	17.579	

Figure 17.10 Comparing means: t-test: independent samples – procedures

An example is shown in Figure 17.11, which compares mean online and live cultural activities for the various student status groups. Here the question we seek to answer with ANOVA is whether, for each activity item, the mean for the different groups of students is different from the overall mean – that is, whether participation is related to student status.

Null hypothesis

*The null hyp*othesis is therefore that all the means are equal to the overall mean. How different must the group means be from the overall mean before we reject this hypothesis?

Variance

Whether or not the means are in effect from one population (with one mean) or from different sub-populations (with different means) depends not only on the differences between the means but also on the 'spread', or *variance*, of the cases upon which they are based. Figure 17.12 shows four examples of three means, with the associated spread of cases around them.

A The means are well spaced and there is little overlap in the cases – there *is* a significant difference between the means.

B The means are closer together and there is considerable overlap, suggesting that they may be from the same population.

Procedure

To obtain a table showing the means to be compared:

1   Select *Analyze* and then *Compare Means*.
2   Select *Means*.
3   Select the variables for which the mean is required (musicdl, musiclv, festiv, buyol) and transfer to the *Dependent list* box.
4   Select variable for grouping (*status*) and transfer to the *Independent list* box.
5   In *Options* ensure that *Mean* and *Number of cases* are in the *Cell statistics* box.
6   Select *OK* to produce the output.

Output

Student status		Download music	Live music events	Cultural festival visits	Buy other items online	Mobile phone exp.
F/T student/no paid work	Mean	9.69	2.62	9.77	6.46	328.46
	N	13	13	13	13	13
F/T student/paid work	Mean	9.64	2.93	8.64	4.00	342.50
	N	14	14	14	14	14
P/T student – F/T job	Mean	19.06	2.25	8.63	8.19	425.63
	N	16	16	16	16	16
P/T student/Other	Mean	6.29	3.29	14.86	8.00	752.86
	N	7	7	7	7	7
Total	Mean	12.20	2.68	9.80	6.54	422.90
	N	50	50	50	50	

Figure 17.11 Comparing a range of means – procedures

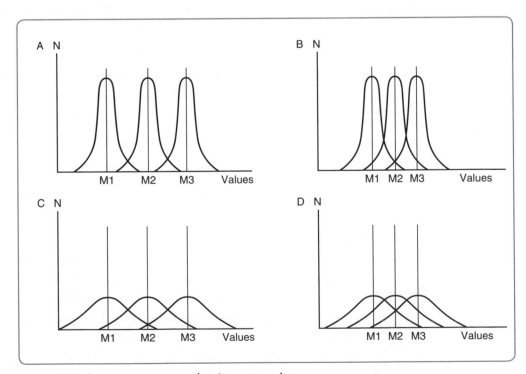

Figure 17.12 Comparing means and variance procedures

C The means are spaced as in A, but the spread around the means is greater and so overlap is considerable, suggesting uncertainty as to whether or not the means are significantly different.

D The worst case of overlap, so we can be fairly certain that the three sets of data are from the same population.

A visual presentation of this type of information, although in a different format, can be obtained using the *Boxplot* feature within the *Graphs* procedure of SPSS.

The 'spread' of sample values is referred to as the *variance* and can be measured by adding up the differences between the scores of individual cases and the mean score.

Analysis of variance

Whether or not the means are significantly different from the overall mean depends on:

1. the spread of the separate sub-group means around the overall mean – the *between groups* variance – the greater the between groups variance, the greater the likelihood of significant difference; and

2. the spread of each of the sub-group cases around the sub-group mean – the *within groups* variance – the greater the within groups variance, the less the likelihood of significant difference.

Analysis of variance is based on the ratio of these two measures, which produces a statistic referred to as F. As with the other statistics examined, values of F for a given number of degrees of freedom (based on sample sizes and number of groups) have a known probability distribution in the null hypothesis situation. High values are unlikely and result in the rejection of the null hypothesis.

Procedures for analysis of variance

The SPSS procedures for analysis of variance and examples of output are shown in Figure 17.13.

In Figure 17.13, it can be seen that:

- for the first three activities significance is above 0.05, so the null hypothesis is accepted and it is concluded that participation in these activities is not related to student status;

- for the last two activities, significance is below 0.05, so the null hypothesis is rejected and we conclude that there is a relationship between these activities and student status.

A table of means: factorial analysis of variance (ANOVA)

Introduction

As with one-way analysis of variance, factorial analysis of variance deals with means. But while the former deals with means of groups determined on the basis of one variable, the latter is designed for sets of means grouped by more than one classifying variable, or 'factor'. An example is shown in Figure 17.14, which presents a table of mean frequency of festival attendance by status and gender, in raw and simplified form, with no statistical test at this stage. It can be seen that:

- there is little difference in frequency of attendance by status, with the lowest mean frequency 2.6 and the highest 3.3;

433

Procedure

1 Select *Analyze* and then *Compare Means*.
2 Select *One-way ANOVA*.
3 Select variables for which means are required (musicdl, musiclv, festiv, buyol, *fees)* and put in the *Dependent list* box.
4 Select variable for grouping (*status*) and put in the *Independent list* box.
5 Select *OK* to produce the output.

Output

ANOVA

		Sum of Squares	df	Mean Square	F	Sig.
Download music	Between Groups	1171.650	3	390.550	2.485	.072
	Within Groups	7230.350	46	157.182		
	Total	8402.000	49			
Live music events	Between Groups	6.446	3	2.149	.411	.746
	Within Groups	240.434	46	5.227		
	Total	246.880	49			
Cultural festival visits	Between Groups	219.871	3	73.290	.942	.428
	Within Groups	3578.129	46	77.785		
	Total	3798.000	49			
Bought other items online	Between Groups	148.752	3	49.584	6.715	.001
	Within Groups	339.668	46	7.384		
	Total	488.420	49			
Mobile phone fees	Between Groups	968661.162	3	322887.054	6.644	.001
	Within Groups	2235593.338	46	48599.855		
	Total	3204254.500	49			

Figure 17.13 One-way analysis of variance – procedures

● there is little difference in frequency of attendance by gender (male 2.2, female 3.1);

● when the two variables are put together, considerable differences emerge, with the lowest mean frequency at 1.4 and the highest at 5.4.

Analysis of variance examines this 'crosstabulation of means' and determines whether the differences revealed are significant. As with the one-way analysis of variance, the procedure examines the differences between group means and the spread of values within groups.

Null hypothesis

The null hypothesis is that there is no interaction between the variables – that the level of festival-going of the students in the various categories is not affected by gender. A table of 'expected counts' consistent with the null hypothesis could be produced as for the chi-square example, but the values would be means rather than numbers of cases.

Procedures for factorial analysis of variance

Figure 17.15 shows the results of a factorial analysis of variance on the above data. The bold F probabilities indicate the relationship between:

● cultural festival visits and status alone is not significant (Sig. = 0.250);

● cultural festival visits and gender is not significant (Sig. = 0.242);

● cultural festival visits and status and gender together is significant at the 5 per cent level (Sig. = 0.019) – so the null hypothesis is rejected: the interaction between gender and status with regard to cultural festival going is significant at the 5 per cent level.

Procedure

1 Select *Analyze* then *Compare Means* then *Means*.
2 Select *festiv* and transfer to the *Dependent list* box.
3 Select *status* and transfer to the *Independent list* box.
4 Click on *Next* to get *Layer 2 of 2*, then *gender* and transfer to the *Independent list* box.
5 Select *OK* to obtain the output.

Output

Cultural festival visits

Student status	Gender	Mean	N	Std. Deviation
F/T student/no paid work	Male	3.11	9	1.833
	Female	1.50	4	2.380
	Total	2.62	13	2.063
F/T student/paid work	Male	1.56	9	1.130
	Female	5.40	5	2.191
	Total	2.93	14	2.433
P/T student – F/T job	Male	1.40	5	2.074
	Female	2.64	11	2.730
	Total	2.25	16	2.543
P/T student/Other	Male	3.50	2	2.121
	Female	3.20	5	1.643
	Total	3.29	7	1.604
Total	Male	2.24	25	1.786
	Female	3.12	25	2.587
	Total	2.68	50	2.245

How the above might be presented in a report

Table 1: Cultural festival visits by status and gender

| Course | Mean number of visits in six months | | |
	Male	Female	Total
F/T student/no paid work	3.1	1.5	2.6
F/T student/paid work	1.6	5.4	2.9
P/T student – F/T job	1.4	2.6	2.3
P/T student/Other	3.5	3.2	3.3
Total	2.2	3.1	2.7

Figure 17.14 A table of means – procedures

Correlation

Correlation can be used to examine the relationships between two or more ordinal or scale variables. If two variables are related in a systematic way they are said to be *correlated*. They can be:

● positively correlated (as one variable increases, so does the other);

● negatively correlated (as one variable increases, the other decreases); or

● uncorrelated (there is no relationship between the variables).

It is often helpful to think of correlation in visual terms. Relationships between income and the four variables are shown in Figure 17.16, illustrating a variety of types of correlation. The graphics were produced using the SPSS graphics *Scatterplot* procedure discussed in Chapter 16. Each dot represents one person (or case or observation). The correlation coefficients, *r*, are explained below.

Relating to data in Figure 17.14.
Procedure

1 Select *Analyze* then *General Linear Model*.
2 Select *Univariate*.
3 Select the *Dependent* variable – the one for which the means are to be calculated (festiv). Select the *Fixed Factors* – the two variables affecting the dependent variable (*status* and *gender*).
4 Click on the *Post Hoc* box and in the dialogue box transfer *status* and *gender* to the *Post Hoc tests for:* box, then select *LSD*, then click *Continue*.
5 Select *OK* to obtain the output.

Output
Tests of Between-Subjects Effects
Dependent Variable: Cultural festival visits (**key items in bold**)

Source	Type III Sum of Squares	df	Mean Square	F	Sig.
Corrected Model	66.523(a)	7	9.503	2.213	.052
Intercept	299.090	1	299.090	69.650	.000
status	18.308	3	6.103	**1.421**	**.250**
gender	6.041	1	6.041	**1.407**	**.242**
status* gender	47.424	3	15.808	**3.681**	**.019**
Error	180.357	42	4.294		
Total	606.000	50			
Corrected Total	246.880	49			

a R Squared = .269 (Adjusted R Squared = .148)

Figure 17.15 Factorial analysis of variance – procedures

Correlation coefficient (r)

Correlation can be measured by means of the *correlation coefficient*, usually represented by the letter r. The coefficient has the following characteristics:

- zero if there is no relationship between two variables;
- +1.0 if there is perfect positive correlation between two variables;
- −1.0 if there is perfect negative correlation between two variables;
- between 0 and +1.0 if there is some positive correlation;
- between 0 and −1.0 if there is some negative correlation;
- the closer the coefficient is to 1.0, the higher the correlation, e.g.:
  - 0.9 is a high positive correlation;
  - 0.2 is a low positive correlation;
  - −0.8 is a high negative correlation.

The correlation coefficient is calculated by measuring how far each data point is from the mean of each of the two variables and multiplying the two differences. In Figure 17.17 it can be seen that the result will be a positive number for data points in the top right-hand and bottom left-hand quadrants (B and C) and negative for data points in the other two quadrants (A and D). The calculations are shown for two of the data points by way of illustration. If most of the data points are in quadrants B and C a positive correlation will result, while if most of the data points are in A and D a negative correlation will result. If the data points are widely scattered in all four quadrants, then the negatives cancel out the positives, resulting in a low value for the correlation. This explains in very broad terms the basis of the positive and negative correlations, and high and low correlations. It is beyond the scope of this book to explain how the 'perfect' correlation is made to equal one, but, for those with the requisite mathematics, this can be deduced from the formula for r, which is given in Appendix 17.2.

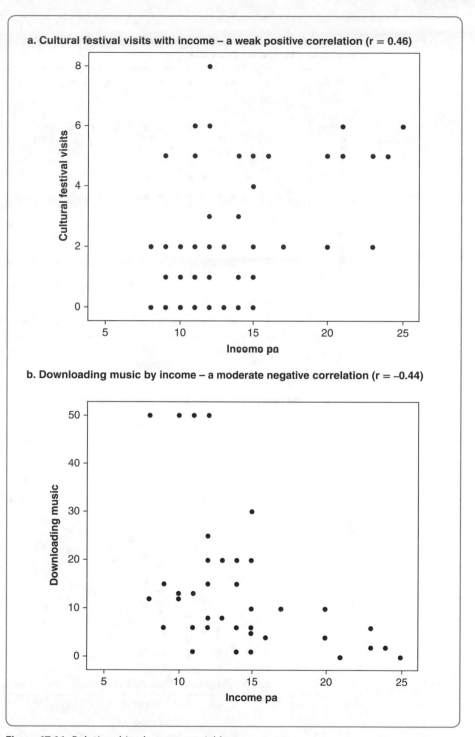

Figure 17.16 Relationships between variables

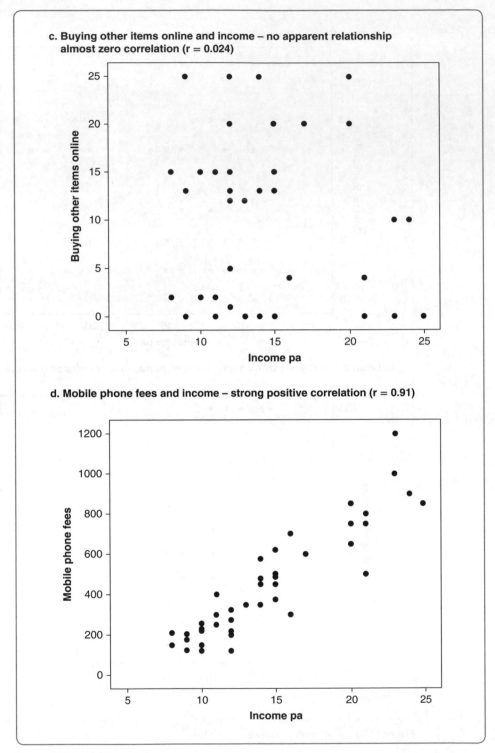

Figure 17.16 *(continued)*

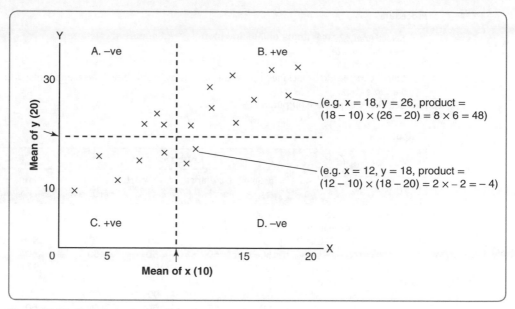

Figure 17.17 Correlation procedures

Significance of r

The *significance* of a correlation coefficient depends on its size, as discussed above, and also the sample size, and is assessed by means of a t-test.

Null hypothesis

The null hypothesis is that the correlation is zero. The t-test therefore indicates only whether the correlation coefficient is significantly different from zero. Quite low coefficients can emerge as 'significant' if the sample is large enough.

Procedures for correlation

The SPSS procedures for producing correlation coefficients between pairs of variables are shown in Figure 17.18. The output is in the form of a symmetrical matrix, so that, for example, the correlation between downloading music and income is the same as between income and downloading music. For each pair of variables, the output includes:

- the correlation coefficient;
- the sample size (the number in brackets); and
- the significance – the probability related to the t-test. The starring system discussed above is used to indicate significance at the 5 per cent and 1 per cent levels. As with other tests, if the probability is below the 0.05 or 0.01 levels we reject the null hypothesis and conclude that the correlation is significantly different from zero, at the 5 per cent or 1 per cent level respectively.

Procedure

1 Select *Analyze*.
2 Select *Correlate*.
3 Select *Bivariate*.
4 Select variables to be included (*inc*, musicdl, musiclv, festiv, buyol, *fees*) and transfer to the *Variables* box.
5 Select *OK* to produce output.

Output

		Correlations					
		Income pa	Download music	Live music visits	Cultural festivals	Buy other items online	Mobile phone fees
Income pa	Pearson Correlation	1.000	−.439**	.076	.460**	.024	.915**
	Sig. (2-tailed)	.	.001	.598	.001	.866	.000
	N	50	50	50	50	50	50
Download music	Pearson Correlation	−.439**	1.000	.454**	−.679**	.274	−.368**
	Sig. (2-tailed)	.001	.	.001	.000	.054	.008
	N	50	50	50	50	50	50
Live music events	Pearson Correlation	.076	.454**	1.000	−.286*	−.044	.119
	Sig. (2-tailed)	.598	.001	.	.044	.759	.410
	N	50	50	50	50	50	50
Cultural festivals	Pearson Correlation	.460**	−.679**	−.286*	1.000	−.292*	.379**
	Sig. (2-tailed)	.001	.000	.044	.	.039	.007
	N	50	50	50	50	50	50
Buy other items online	Pearson Correlation	.024	.274	−.044	−.292*	1.000	.058
	Sig. (2-tailed)	.866	.054	.759	.039	.	.688
	N	50	50	50	50	50	50
Mobile phone fees	Pearson Correlation	.915**	−.368**	.119	.379	.058	1.000
	Sig. (2-tailed)	.000	.008	.410	.007	.688	.
	N	50	50	50	50	50	50

* Correlation is significant at the 0.05 level (2-tailed).
** Correlation is significant at the 0.01 level (2-tailed).

Figure 17.18 Correlation matrix – procedures

Linear regression

Introduction

Linear regression takes us one step further in this type of quantitative analysis – in the direction of 'prediction'. If the correlation between two variables is consistent enough, one variable can be used to predict or estimate the other. In particular, easily measured variables (such as age or income) can be used to predict variables that are more difficult or costly to measure (such as participation in cultural activities). For example, knowledge of the relationship between age and cultural participation can be used in planning cultural facilities for a community: the future age structure of the community can be relatively easily estimated and with this information future demand for cultural activities can be estimated.

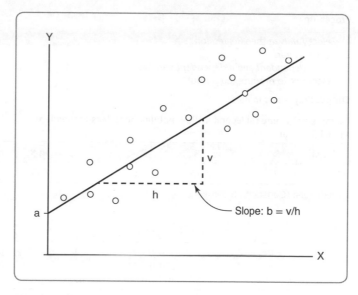

Figure 17.19 Regression line

The procedures described here are just one format in which the relationships between variables of interest can be examined. If the variables can be quantified, then the techniques enable the strength and nature of the relationship to be quantified also.

Regression model

To predict one variable on the basis of another a *model* or equation is needed of the type:

Cultural participation rate = *some number* multiplied by AGE

Suppose participation is measured in terms of the number of visits or days participation for some activity over the course of a year. Regression analysis produces an equation of the form:

Days participation = a + b × AGE

The *coefficients* or *parameters*, a and b, are determined from examination of existing data, using regression analysis. The process of finding out the values of the parameters or coefficients is referred to as *calibration* of the model.

In general terms this is represented by the equation: y = a + bx, where y stands for participation and x stands for age. Note that here *participation* is the dependent variable and AGE is the independent variable.

In visual terms this describes a 'regression line' fitted through the data, with 'intercept' or 'constant' of *a* and 'slope' of *b*, as shown in Figure 17.19. The regression procedure finds the 'line of best fit' by finding the line that minimises the sum of the (squared) differences between it and the data points, and specifies this line by giving values for a and b.

Procedures for regression

Examples of regression output from SPSS are shown in Figure 17.20. The program produces a large amount of output with which we are not concerned here – only the items in bold are discussed. However, the output illustrates the point that regression is an involved process and only the broad outlines are dealt with in this book. The output relates to multiple regression,

441

Procedure

1 Select *Analyze* then *Regression*.
2 Select *Linear*.
3 Select *dependent* and *independent* variables.
4 Select *OK* to produce the output.

Output (key items in bold)

Example 1: Income (independent) by mobile phone fees (dependent)

Model Summary

Model	R	R Square	Adjusted R Square	Std. Error of the Estimate
1	**.915**	**.836**	.833	104.51

a Predictors: (Constant), Income pa

ANOVA

Model		Sum of Squares	df	Mean Square	F	Sig.
1	Regression	2679971.336	1	2679971.336	**245.361**	**.000**
	Residual	524283.164	48	10922.566		
	Total	3204254.500	49			

a Predictors: (Constant), Income pa b Dependent Variable: Mobile phone fees

Coefficients

		Unstandardised Coeffs		Standardised Coeffs	t	Sig.
Model		B	Std. Error	Beta		
1	(Constant)	−323.493	49.890		−6.484	.000
	Income pa	**52.563**	3.356	.915	15.664	.000

a Dependent Variable: Mobile phone fees

Example 2: Income (independent) by festival visits (dependent)

Model Summary

Model	R	R Square	Adjusted R Square	Std. Error of the Estimate
1	**.460**	**.212**	.195	2.01

a Predictors: (Constant), Income pa

ANOVA

Model		Sum of Squares	df	Mean Square	F	Sig.
1	Regression	52.284	1	52.284	**12.896**	**.001**
	Residual	194.596	48	4.054		
	Total	246.880	49			

a Predictors: (Constant), Income pa b Dependent Variable: Cultural festival visits

Coefficients

		Unstandardised Coeffs		Standardised Coeffs	t	Sig.
Model		B	Std. Error	Beta		
1	(Constant)	−.617	.961		−.642	.524
	Income pa	**.232**	.065	.460	3.591	.001

a Dependent Variable: Cultural festival visits

Figure 17.20 Regression analysis – procedures

Procedure

1 Select *Analyze* the *Regression* then *Curve Estimation*.
2 Select *fees* then transfer to *Dependents* box and *inc* and transfer to *Independents* box.
3 Select *OK* to produce output.

Output

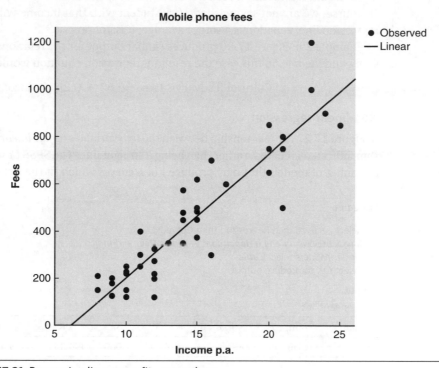

Figure 17.21 Regression line: curve fit – procedure

which involves more than one independent variable, as discussed in the next section, but here we have only one independent variable, income.

The items we are interested in are the value of the regression coefficient, R (similar to the correlation coefficient, r), the value of R^2, which is an indicator of how well the data fit the regression line, its test of significance, and the coefficients listed under B. For Example 1 in Figure 17.20, the relationship between income and mobile phone fees:

- the value of R is 0.915;

- R^2 is 0.836;

- probability (as measured by an F test) is 0.000, which makes it highly significant;

- the constant (a) is −323.493 and the coefficient of slope (b) for income is 52.563.

The regression equation is therefore:

Mobile phone fees (£ per 6 months) = −323.493 + 52.563 × income (in £000s pa)

This regression line can be plotted onto a graph, as shown in Figure 17.21, using the SPSS *Curve estimation* procedure.

With this equation, if we knew a student's income we could estimate their level of mobile phone fees, either by reading it off the graph or calculating it. For example, for a student with an income of £10,000 a year:

$$\text{Mobile phone fees} = -323.49 + 52.56 \times 10 = -323.49 + 525.60 = £202.11$$

So we would estimate that such a student would spend £202 on mobile phone fees in a year. Of course, we are not saying that every student with that income will spend this sum: the regression line/equation is a sort of average; it is not precise.

Example 2 in Figure 17.20 produces similar output for the relationship between festival-going and income. In this case the resultant regression equation would be:

$$\text{Cultural festival visits} = -0.62 + 0.23 \times \text{income}$$

Non-linear regression

In Figure 17.22 the relationship between the two variables is *non-linear* – that is, the relationship indicated is curved, rather than being a straight line. The SPSS *Curve fit* procedure offers a number of models that may produce lines/curves which fit the data better than a simple

Procedure

1 Select *Analyze* then Regression then Curve Fit.
2 Select depend*ent* and *independent* variables (*fees* and *inc*).
3 Under *Models* select *Cubic*.
4 Select *OK* to produce output.

Output

Independent: inc

Dependent	Mth	Rsq	d.f.	F	Sigf	b0	b1	b2	b3
hols	CUB	.843	46	82.43	.000	494.351	−113.10	10.5471	−.2118

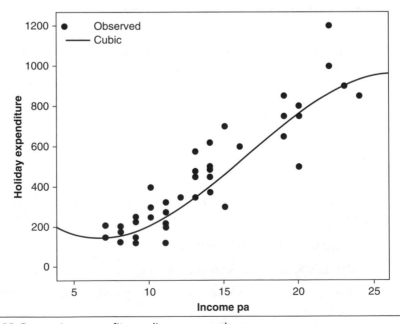

Figure 17.22 Regression: curve fit, non-linear – procedures

straight line. Theory or trial and error may lead to a suitable model. In Figure 17.22 a 'cubic' model is presented, in which the independent variable is raised to the power of three – this results in the curved line indicated and a small increase in the value of R^2 to 0.843.

This emphasises the importance of examining the data *visually,* as done here, and not relying just on correlation coefficients.

Multiple regression

Multiple regression is linear regression involving more than one independent variable. For example, we might hypothesise that cultural participation is dependent not just on income but also on age. Thus our model, or regression equation, would be:

$$\text{Cultural participation} = a + b \times \text{income} + c \times \text{age}$$

In linear regression, as discussed above, the procedure fits a straight line to the data – the line of best fit. In multiple regression the procedure fits a surface to the data – the surface of best fit. It is possible to visualise this in three dimensions (one dependent and two independent variables), with the axes forming a three-dimensional box, the observations suspended in space and the regression surface being a flat plane somewhere within the box (SPSS offers a 3-D graphical option to represent this in the *Scattergram* procedure). When additional variables are included, then four, five or 'n' dimensions are involved and it is not possible to visualise the process, but the mathematical principles used to establish the regression equation are the same.

An example, in which festival-going is related to income and age, is shown in Figure 17.23. It will be noticed that the value of R has risen from 0.46 in the single variable case (Figure 17.20, Example 2) to 0.5799, indicating an improvement in the 'fit' of the data to the model. The model equation is now:

$$\text{Cultural festival visits} = -0.3.49 + 0.056 \times \text{income} + 0.0227 \times \text{age}$$

It is possible, in theory, to continue to add variables to the equation. This should be done with caution, however, since it frequently involves *multi-collinearity,* where the independent variables are themselves inter-correlated. The 'independent' variables should be, as far as possible, just that: independent. Various tests exist to check for this phenomenon. Often, in cultural activity, a large number of variables is involved, many inter-correlated but each contributing something to the phenomenon under investigation. Multivariate analysis procedures, such as cluster and factor analysis, discussed below, are designed partly to overcome these problems.

Structural equation modelling

A technique often used in sport research is *structural equation modelling (SEM)*, or *path analysis,* in which a network of equations is established to model a particular social process. Rather than a single relationship, the models proposed and tested typically include a number of inter-connected relationships, as indicated in Figure 17.24. Each relationship is represented by an equation. Data is gathered on the values of each variable for a sample of subjects and one of the special computer packages which are available to undertake SEM (see Resources section) is used to provide estimates of the strengths of the relationships (a–d).

One form of SEM is *hierarchical modelling,* which recognises that data-sets are often structured hierarchically – for example, in a study of professional artists, members of

Procedure

1. Select *Analyze* then *Regression* then *Linear*.
2. Transfer *festiv* to *dependent* box and *age, income* to *independents* box.
3. At *Method*, select *Enter* for all the selected variables to be included immediately, or *Stepwise* for the program to select and include variables in order of influence.
4. Select *OK* to produce the output.

Output

Variables Entered/Removed[b]

Model	Variables Entered	Variables Removed	Method
1	**Age, Income pa**[a]	.	Enter

a All requested variables entered. b Dependent Variable: Cultural festival visits

Model Summary

Model	R	R Square	Adjusted R Square	Std. Error of the Estimate
1	.580a	.336	.308	1.87

a Predictors: (Constant), Age, Income pa

ANOVA[b]

Model		Sum of Squares	df	Mean Square	F	Sig.
1	Regression	83.023	2	41.512	11.907	.000a
	Residual	163.857	47	3.486		
	Total	246.880	49			

a Predictors: (Constant), Age, Income pa b Dependent Variable: Cultural festival visits

Coefficients[a]

		Unstandardised Coefficients		Standardised coefficients	t	Sig.
Model		B	Std. Error	Beta		
1	(Constant)	−3.493	1.316		−2.654	.011
	Income pa	.056	.084	.111	.662	.511
	Age	.227	.076	.497	2.969	.005

a Dependent Variable: Cultural festival visits

Figure 17.23 Multiple regression – procedures

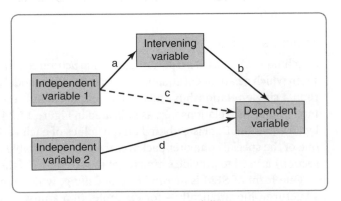

Figure 17.24 Structural equation modelling

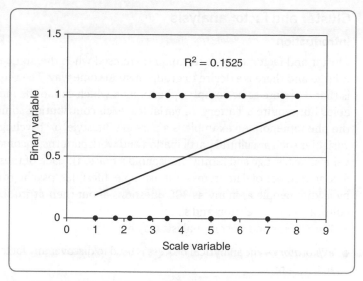

Figure 17.25 Binary and scale variable graphic

a particular performing arts organisation have their own age, educational background, personality, etc., but they share the characteristics of the organisation (scale, prestige, programme, etc.). So in any analysis, it may be advisable to recognise the existence of people with common organisational characteristics. Special computer packages and procedures are available to undertake SEM and hierarchical modelling, as indicated in the Resources section.

Binary logistic regression analysis and odds ratios

Data in binary form – for example, male/female or participant/non-participant – can be quantified by use of one and zero. Mathematically, statistics such as means and correlation coefficients can be calculated, but they violate some of the principles behind statistical tests, such as the assumption that data are normally distributed. The oddity of the data can be seen in Figure 17.25, which portrays one scale variable and one binary variable, with a regression line and correlation coefficient indicated. If the scale variable were to be replaced by a second binary variable, all the cases would be located at four points only: 0,0; 0,1; 1,1; and 1,0.

Binary logistic regression is designed to cope with these situations. The relationship is described by *odds ratios*. An odds ratio describes the relative strength of the association between independent variables and categories of the dependent variables. For example, in examining the relationship between cultural participation (yes/no) and gender (male/female), odds ratios of 1.4 for females and 0.6 for males would indicate that females are 1.4 times more likely to participate in cultural activity than males and males are 0.6 times as likely to participate as females. The advantage of binary logistic regression over, for example, a series of chi-square tests is that all independent variables can be modelled in a single procedure with the odds ratios for each being considered against each other. Sources/examples are provided in the Resources section.

Cluster and factor analysis

Introduction

Cluster and factor analysis techniques are used when the number of independent variables is large and there is a desire to group them in some way. The theoretical counterpart to this is that there are some complex phenomena which cannot be measured by one or two variables but require a 'battery' of variables, each contributing some aspect to the make-up of the phenomenon. An example is a person's 'lifestyle' or 'psychographic' group (made up of variables such as cultural participation and work patterns, income and expenditure patterns, values, tastes, age and family/household situation). Each of these is often researched using a large number of data items – for example, lifestyles/psychographics have been measured by asking people as many as 300 questions about their attitudes to work, politics, morals, cultural activity, religion and so on.

Both factor and cluster analysis may be:

- *exploratory* – the analytical process is used to discover any factors/clusters which may exist in the data; or
- *confirmatory* – the analytical process is used to test the existence of one or more hypothesised clusters or factors.

Factor analysis

Factor analysis is based on the idea that certain variables 'go together', in that people with a high score on one variable also tend to have a high score on certain others, which might then form a group – for example, people who go to the theatre might also visit galleries; people with strong pro-environment views might be found to favour certain types of holiday. Analysis of this type of phenomenon can be approached using a simple, manual technique involving a correlation matrix of the variables (as outlined above), as illustrated in Figure 17.26, which is based on Australian data of arts/events participation. Three groupings of activities are produced by linking activities with the activity with which they have their highest correlation coefficient, indicated in the figure, which measures the extent to which participants in one activity also participate in the other.

This procedure takes account of the highest correlation only. But variables will have a range of lower-order relationships with each other which are difficult to take account of using this

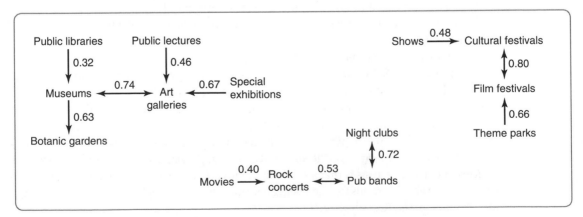

Figure 17.26 Simple manual factor analysis

Source: Re-analysis of data from Bennett *et al*. (1999). Numbers are correlation coefficients.

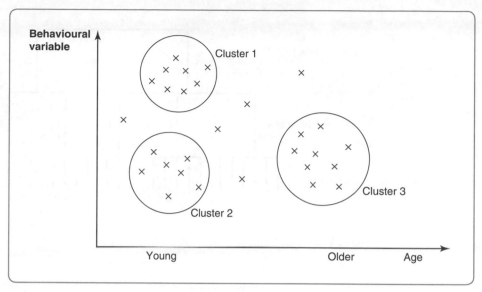

Figure 17.27 Plots of 'clusters'

manual method. A number of lower order correlations may, cumulatively, be more significant than a single highest correlation. Factor analysis is a mathematical procedure that groups the variables taking account of all the correlations. The mathematical details of the method are beyond the scope of this book, but sources and examples are indicated in the Resources section.

Cluster analysis

Cluster analysis is another 'grouping' procedure, but it focuses on the individuals directly rather than the variables. Imagine a situation with two variables, a behavioural variable and age, and data points (individuals) plotted in the usual way, as shown in Figure 17.27. It can be seen that there are three broad 'clusters' of respondents – two young clusters and one older cluster. Each of these clusters might form, for example, particular market segments. With just two variables and a few observations it is relatively simple to identify clusters visually. But with more variables and hundreds of cases this would be more difficult.

Cluster analysis involves giving the computer a set of rules for building clusters. It first calculates the 'distances' between data points, in terms of a range of specified variables. Points that are closest together are put into a first-round 'cluster' and a new 'point' halfway between the two is put in their place. The process is repeated to form a second round of clustering, and a third and fourth and so on, until there are only two 'points' left. The result is usually illustrated by a 'dendrogram', of the sort shown in Figure 17.28.

Multiple correspondence analysis

Factor and cluster analysis can be applied only to scale/numerical data – for example, frequency of participation. While some mathematical operations can be undertaken with binary variables (participant/non-participant = 1/0) and Likert-type variables, when more complex nominal variables are involved, for example social class or ethnicity, this is not possible. Multiple correspondence analysis (MCA) is a procedure that overcomes this difficulty: it is a form of cluster analysis for nominal data. Again, the detail is beyond the scope of this book, but sources and examples are given in the Resources section.

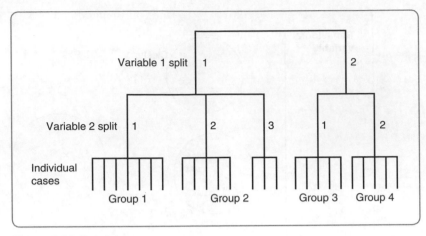

Figure 17.28 Dendrogram

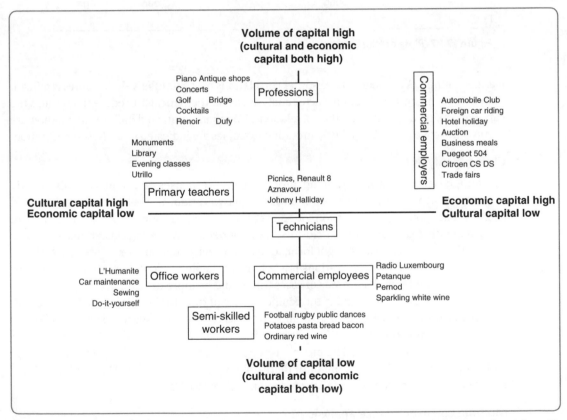

Figure 17.29 Multiple correspondence analysis: from Pierre Bourdieu's diagram of the spaces of social position and lifestyle

Source: Redrawn excerpt from Bourdieu (1984: 128).

MCA has been used extensively in analysis of cultural participation patterns in recent years, partly as a result of the significance of the work of French sociologist Pierre Bourdieu, who used the technique in his seminal work *Distinction* (Bourdieu, 1984). In this study Bourdieu used MCA to plot various occupational/social classes in French society along with their typical patterns of cultural tastes and consumption in a space defined by cultural and economic capital. An extract from a much larger diagram is shown in Figure 17.29.

More recent examples of the use of MCA in cultural research are the British replication of Bourdieu's study by Bennett *et al.* (2009) and studies referred to in Case study 14.6, although a number of the latter use a similar analytical technique, latent class analysis (McCutcheon, 1987).

In conclusion

Much arts/events research, even of a quantitative nature, is conducted without the use of the techniques covered in this chapter. This is a reflection of the descriptive nature of some of the research in the field, as discussed in Chapter 1, the nature of the data involved and the needs of the audience or client for the research. Often the need is for 'broad brush' research findings: accuracy is required but not a high level of precision. Contrast this with medical research, where precision can be a matter of life or death. To some extent the level of use of statistical techniques is related to disciplinary and geographical/cultural/academic traditions.

Some arts/events researchers could therefore find that they rarely make use of the techniques presented in this chapter, but they should be able to interpret research reports that do make use of them, and they should be able to utilise them if called upon, even if specialised advice has to be sought.

As stressed throughout this book, data collection and analysis should be determined by a theoretical, conceptual or evaluative framework. At the analysis stage the researcher should, ideally, not be wondering what to relate to what, and choosing variables and analyses in an *ad hoc* manner. While a certain amount of inductive exploration and even serendipity is inevitable, ideally there should be a basic analysis plan from the beginning. Key variables and the question of relationships between them should have been thought about in advance, for example as a result of an early 'concept mapping' exercise. Thus, while the examples given in this chapter may appear *ad hoc* and 'data driven', in a real research project the procedures used should be theory driven or problem or hypothesis driven.

Summary

This chapter builds on Chapter 13, which introduces the idea of sampling and its effects, and on Chapter 16, which deals with the analysis of questionnaire survey data using the package SPSS. Here, the principles and processes involved in statistical analysis are introduced. The phenomenon of statistics, in this context, does not refer just to quantification but to the processes required to generalise from findings from samples to the wider population. Statistical concepts are initially introduced, including the idea of probabilistic statements, the normal distribution, significance, the null hypothesis, and dependent and independent variables. The chapter then outlines SPSS procedures and presents outputs for a number of statistical tests, as follows:

- chi-square – for examining the relationship between two variables in frequency table;
- the t-test – for comparing the significance of the difference between two means;

- one-way analysis of variance (ANOVA) – for examining the relationship between two variables as expressed by a set of means;
- factorial analysis of variance (ANOVA) – for examining the relationship between one dependent variable and two independent variables based on means;
- correlation – the relationship between two scale variables;
- linear regression – which establishes the 'line of best fit' between two variables;
- multiple regression – which examines the relationship between one dependent variable and two or more independent variables, including discussion of structural equation modelling;
- cluster and factor analysis – which deal with summarising the relationships among large numbers of variables, including discussion of multiple correspondence analysis.

TEST QUESTIONS/EXERCISES

It is suggested that readers replicate the various analyses set out in this chapter, first using the data in Appendix 17.1 and then using their own data-set. This can be based on data which may have been collected for Chapter 16, but will involve adding a range of scale variables to the questionnaire, similar to those listed in Appendix 17.1.

Resources

Websites

SPSS software: www.spss.com.
Structural equation modelling (SEM):

- Semnet discussion group: www2.gsu.edu/~mkteer/semnet.html
- Amos software: www.spss.com/amos/
- Lisrel software: www.ssicentral.com/lisrel/index.html

Publications

There are many excellent statistics textbooks available which cover the range of techniques included in this chapter and, of course, much more. Texts vary in terms of the degree of familiarity with algebra that they assume on the part of the reader, so readers with limited mathematical knowledge should 'shop around' to find a text that deals with the topic in conceptual terms rather than in detailed mathematical terms. However, a certain amount of mathematical aptitude is, of course, essential.

- Binary logistic regression: Pampel (2000).
- Cluster analysis: Bowen and Daniels (2005).
- Factor analysis: examples of use: audience segmentation: Nevin and Cavusgil (1987); personality of performing arts venues: Ouellet *et al.* (2008); museum service quality scale: Raajpoot *et al.* (2010).

- Hierarchical modelling: Todd *et al.* (2005); young people and performing arts: Martin *et al.* (2012).

- Latent class analysis: McCutcheon (1987); examples of use: see Case study 14.6 and Chan (2010); cities and culture: Van der Ark and Richards (2006); highbrow/lowbrow reading: Van Rees *et al.* (1999); museum visitation: Burke *et al.* (2010).

- Multiple correspondence analysis: Le Roux and Rouanet (2010); examples of use: Bourdieu (1984), Bennett *et al.* (2009), Coulangeon (2013), Nantel and Colbert (1992) and see Case study 14.6 and Chan (2010).

- Odds ratios: example of use: Hand (2009).

- Structural equation modelling (SEM): Kline (2005); festivals: Kim *et al.* (2010); museum visitors: Carmen de Rojas and Carmen Camarero (2006), Hanquinet and Savage (2012).

References

Bennett, T., Emmison, M. and Frow, J. (1999) *Accounting for Tastes: Australian Everyday Cultures*. Melbourne: Cambridge University Press.

Bennett, T., Savage, M., Silva, E., Warde, A., Gayo-Cal, M. and Wright, D. (2009) *Culture, Class, Distinction*. London: Routledge

Bourdieu, P. (1984) *Distinction: A Social Critique of the Judgment of Taste*. London: Routledge and Kegan Paul.

Bowen, H. E. and Daniels, M. J. (2005) Does the music matter? Motivations for attending a music festival. *Event Management*, 9(2), 155–164.

Burke, P. F., Burton, C., Huybers, T., Islam, T., Louviere, J. J. and Wise, C. (2010) The scale-adjusted latent class model: application to museum visitation. *Tourism Analysis*, 15(2), 147–165.

Carmen de Rojas, M. del and Carmen Camarero, M. del (2006) Experience and satisfactions of visitors to museums and cultural exhibitions. *International Review on Public and Non-Profit Marketing*, 3(1), 49–65.

Chan, T. W. (ed.) (2010) *Social Status and Cultural Consumption*. Cambridge: Cambridge University Press.

Coulangeon, P. (2013) Changing policies, challenging theories and persisting inequalities: social disparities in cultural participation in France from 1981 to 2008. *Poetics*, 41(2), 177–209.

Eisner, E. W. (1998) Does experience in the arts boost academic achievement? *Art Education*, 51(1), 7–15.

Hand, C. (2009) Modelling patterns of attendance at performing arts events: the case of music in the United Kingdom. *Creative Industries Journal*, 2(3), 259–271.

Hanquinet, L. and Savage, M. (2012) 'Educative leisure' and the art museum. *Museum and Society*, 10(1), 42–59.

Kim, Y. H., Kim, M., Ruetzler, T. and Taylor, J. (2010) An examination of festival attendees' behavior using SEM. *International Journal of Event and Festival Management*, 1(1), 86–95.

Kline, R. B. (2005) *Principles and Practice of Structural Equation Modelling*, Second Edition. New York: Guilford Press.

Le Roux, B. and Rouanet, H. (2010) *Multiple Correspondence Analysis*. Thousand Oaks, CA: Sage.

Martin, A. J., Anderson, M. and Adams, R.-J. (2012) What determines young people's engagement with performing arts events? *Leisure Sciences*, 34(4), 314–331.

McCutcheon, A. L. (1987) *Latent Class Analysis*. Newbury Park, CA: Sage.

Nantel, J. A. and Colbert, F. (1992) Positioning cultural arts products in the market. *Journal of Cultural Economics*, 16(2), 63–71.

Nevin, J. R. and Cavusgil, S. T. (1987) Audience segments for the performing arts. In J. H. Donnelly and W. R. George (eds), *Marketing of Services*. Chicago, IL: American Marketing Association, pp. 126–128.

Ouellet, J.-F., Savard, M.-A. and Colbert, F. (2008) The personality of performing arts venues: development of a measurement scale. *International Journal of Arts Management*, 10(3), 49–59.

Pampel, F. C. (2000) *Logistic Regression: A Primer*. Thousand Oaks, CA: Sage.

Raajpoot, N., Koh, K. and Jackson, A. (2010) Developing a scale to measure service quality: an exploratory study. *International Journal of Arts Management*, 12(3), 54–69.

Todd, S. Y., Crook, T. R. and Barilla, A. G. (2005) Hierarchical linear modelling of multilevel data. *Journal of Sport Management*, 19(4), 387–403.

Van der Ark, L. A. and Richards, G. (2006) Attractiveness of cultural activities in European cities: a latent class approach. *Tourism Management*, 27(6), 1408–1413.

Van Rees, K., Vermunt, J. and Verboord, M. (1999) Cultural classifications under discussion: latent class analysis of highbrow and lowbrow reading. *Poetics*, 26(4), 349–365.

Appendix 17.1
Details of example data file used – variable details and data

Additional questions (added to the questionnaire in Figure 10.20)

7 What is your approximate gross income per year: £_____ | ___ inc
                                                                     |
8 Approximately how many times have you engaged in the following |
   activities in the last 6 months? |
                                                                     |
   Downloaded music from the internet   ____ times | ___ musicdl
   Been to a live music event   ____ times | ___ musiclv
   Been to any sort of cultural festival ____ times | ___ festiv
   Bought items online   ____ times | ___ buyol

9 Approximately how much did you spend in total on |
   mobile phone fees in the last 6 months?   £_____ | ___ fees

Name	Type	Width	Decimals	Lab	Values	Missing	Columns	Align	Measure
qno	Numeric	5	0	Questionnaire number	None	None	8	Right	Scale
status	Numeric	5	0	Student status	1 F/T study no work, 2 F/T some work, 3 P/T study, F/T job 4 P/T other	None	8	Right	Nominal
movie	Numeric	5	0	Campus movie in last 4 wks	0 No 1 Yes	None	8	Right	Nominal
drama	Numeric	5	0	Campus theatre in last 4 wks	0 No 1 Yes	None	8	Right	Nominal
rock	Numeric	5	0	Campus rock concert in last 4 wks	0 No 1 Yes	None	8	Right	Nominal
jazz	Numeric	5	0	Campus jazz session in last 4 wks	0 No 1 Yes	None	8	Right	Nominal
cheap	Numeric	5	0	Free/cheap (rank)	None	None	8	Right	Ordinal
hours	Numeric	5	0	Times (rank)	None	None	8	Right	Ordinal
qual	Numeric	5	0	Quality of facilities (rank)	None	None	8	Right	Ordinal
meet	Numeric	5	0	Socialising (rank)	None	None	8	Right	Ordinal
time	Numeric	5	0	Time available (rank)	None	None	8	Right	Ordinal
spend	Numeric	5	0	Expenditure on entertainment/month	None	None	8	Right	Scale
relax	Numeric	5	0	Relaxation – importance	1 Not Important 2 Important 3 Very Important	None	8	Right	Scale
social	Numeric	5	0	Social interaction – importance	As above	None	8	Right	Scale
meaning	Numeric	5	0	Meaningful experience	As above	None	8	Right	Scale
sug1	Numeric	5	0	First suggestion	1 Programme content 2 Timing 3 Facilities, 4 Costs 5 Organisation	None	8	Right	Nominal
sug2	Numeric	5	0	Second suggestion		None	8	Right	Nominal
sug3	Numeric	5	0	Third suggestion		None	8	Right	Nominal
age	Numeric	5	0	Age	None	None	8	Right	Scale
gender	Numeric	5	0	Gender	1 male 2 Female	None	8	Right	Nominal
inc	Numeric	5	0	Income pa, $000s	None	None	8	Right	Scale
musicdl	Numeric	5	0	Download music from Internet: 6 months	None	None	8	Right	Scale
musiclv	Numeric	5	0	Live music events: 6 months	None	None	8	Right	Scale
festiv	Numeric	5	0	Cultural festival visits: 6 months	None	None	8	Right	Scale
buyol	Numeric	5	0	Buy other items online: 6 months	None	None	8	Right	Scale
mobfees	Numeric	5	0	Mobile phone fees: 6 months	None	None	8	Right	Scale
statusr	Numeric	5	0	Student status – recoded	1 Full-time 2 Part-time	None	7	Right	Nominal

Data

Qno	status	movie	drama	rock	jazz	cheap	hours	qual	meet	time	spend	relax	social	meaning	sug1	sug2	sug3	age	gender	inc	musicdl	musiclv	festive	buyol	mobfees
1	2	1	1	0	0	1	4	2	3	5	100	3	3	1	1			18	1	12	25	8	1	5	220
2	2	1	1	1	0	1	4	2	3	5	50	2	3	1	2	1		23	1	15	30	10	0	15	485
3	3	1	0	0	0	2	5	1	3	4	250	2	2	2	3	4		28	2	15	5	2	4	20	450
4	4	0	0	0	0	2	3	1	4	5	25	3	2	2	1	2	4	35	2	21	0	12	5	4	750
5	3	1	0	0	1	1	4	3	2	5	55	3	3	1				29	2	20	4	4	5	25	650
6	3	1	0	0	0	2	4	1	3	5	40	2	3	2	2			29	1	14	20	8	0	0	480
7	2	1	0	1	0	3	2	1	4	5	150	2	3	2	3	5		23	2	11	6	3	6	0	250
8	2	1	1	0	0	3	4	2	1	5	250	1	2	2	4			22	1	12	8	1	0	12	120
9	4	0	0	0	0	1	5	2	3	4	300	2	3	2		3		22	2	15	10	6	0	20	450
10	3	1	1	0	0	2	3	1	5	4	100	1	2	1	2			19	2	12	50	10	0	15	220
11	3	0	0	0	1	3	3	3	4	5	75	2	2	2		2		20	1	11	13	9	1	2	300
12	2	1	0	0	0	1	4	2	2	5	50	2	3	2	1	5	5	19	1	14	6	5	3	13	575
13	1	1	0	1	0	1	5	1	3	4	55	2	3	2	4			21	2	11	1	7	5	0	300
14	3	1	1	0	0	2	4	1	3	5	75	3	3	2	1	2		35	2	25	0	9	6	0	850
15	1	1	0	0	0	3	2	2	5	4	150	3	3	2	4	3		22	2	9	15	6	1	25	200
16	2	1	0	0	0	3	4	1	2	5	200	1	2	2			4	28	2	12	6	2	8	1	220
17	1	0	1	0	0	1	5	2	3	4	175	2	3	2	1			20	1	12	20	11	0	20	275
18	1	1	0	1	0	2	3	1	5	4	100	1	2	2	1	5		21	2	8	12	8	2	2	150
19	4	1	0	0	1	2	3	3	4	5	105	2	3	2	2			32	1	23	4	10	5	10	1200
20	1	1	1	0	0	1	4	1	2	5	50	2	2	2	3			23	1	16	6	0	5	4	300
21	1	1	0	1	0	3	2	2	4	5	150	2	3	2	4	1		18	1	11	8	3	2	0	250
22	2	0	0	0	0	3	4	2	1	5	250	1	2	2				25	2	12	10	6	2	12	325
23	4	1	1	0	0	1	5	1	3	4	300	2	3	2	1	3		22	2	17	50	12	2	20	600
24	3	1	1	0	0	2	3	1	5	4	100	1	2	1	2			29	1	11	13	9	0	15	400
25	3	1	1	0	1	2	3	3	4	5	75	2	2	2				23	1	10	6	9	1	2	230
26	2	1	0	1	0	1	4	3	2	5	50	2	3	1				19	2	9	6	5	5	13	125

457

Qno	status	movie	drama	rock	jazz	cheap	hours	qual	meet	time	spend	relax	social	meaning	sug1	sug2	sug3	age	gender	inc	musicdl	musiclv	festive	buyol	mobfees
27	1	1	0	1	0	1	5	2	3	4	55	2	3	2	1	2	·	21	1	14	1	7	5	0	350
28	3	1	1	1	0	2	4	1	3	5	75	3	3	2	1	·	·	35	2	21	0	9	6	0	500
29	1	1	1	0	0	3	2	1	5	4	150	3	3	1	4	2	5	22	1	12	15	6	1	25	200
30	3	1	0	0	1	1	4	3	2	5	55	3	3	1	1	·	·	29	1	20	4	4	5	25	850
31	3	1	1	0	0	2	4	1	3	5	40	2	3	1	·	·	·	20	1	13	20	8	0	0	350
32	2	1	0	0	0	3	2	1	4	5	150	2	3	2	2	·	·	23	1	23	6	3	2	0	1000
33	2	1	0	1	0	3	4	2	1	5	250	1	2	2	3	5	·	25	2	12	8	4	6	12	275
34	4	0	1	0	0	1	5	2	3	4	300	2	3	2	4	·	·	22	1	20	10	6	2	20	750
35	3	1	1	0	1	2	3	1	5	4	100	1	2	1	·	1	·	19	2	10	50	10	0	15	150
36	3	1	1	1	0	2	3	1	4	5	75	2	2	1	1	3	·	20	2	10	13	9	1	2	250
37	2	1	0	1	0	1	4	3	2	5	50	2	3	1	2	·	·	19	1	15	6	5	1	13	450
38	1	1	0	0	0	1	5	2	3	4	55	2	3	2	·	2	·	21	1	15	1	7	5	0	500
39	3	1	1	0	0	2	4	1	3	5	75	3	3	1	4	·	·	35	2	21	0	9	6	0	800
40	1	1	1	1	0	3	2	1	5	4	150	3	3	2	1	2	5	22	2	14	15	6	1	25	450
41	1	0	0	0	1	1	5	2	3	4	175	2	2	1	·	·	·	20	1	15	20	11	0	20	375
42	4	1	0	1	0	2	3	1	5	4	100	1	3	2	1	3	4	21	1	10	12	8	2	2	220
43	1	1	1	0	0	2	3	1	4	5	105	2	2	1	2	·	·	32	2	24	2	10	5	10	900
44	2	1	0	0	0	1	4	3	2	5	50	2	3	1	3	·	·	28	2	16	4	4	5	4	700
45	2	0	0	0	0	3	2	2	4	5	150	3	2	2	4	5	·	23	1	9	6	3	2	0	180
46	4	1	1	0	0	3	4	1	1	5	250	1	3	2	·	·	·	25	2	13	8	1	2	12	350
47	3	1	1	0	0	1	5	2	3	4	300	2	3	2	1	1	·	22	2	15	10	6	2	20	620
48	3	1	1	0	0	2	3	1	5	5	100	1	2	1	1	1	·	19	2	8	50	10	0	15	210
49	3	1	1	0	1	2	3	1	4	4	75	2	2	1	2	3	·	20	2	10	13	9	1	2	120
50	2	1	0	1	0	1	4	3	2	5	50	2	3	1	·	·	·	19	1	12	6	5	3	13	220

Appendix 17.2
Statistical formulae

95 per cent confidence interval for normal distribution for percentage p

$$\text{C.I.} = 1.96\sqrt{\frac{p(100 - p)}{n - 1}}$$

where n = sample size

Chi-square

$$\chi^2 = \sqrt{\Sigma((O - E)/E)^2}$$

t for difference between means

$$t = \sqrt{\frac{(\overline{x}_1 - \overline{x}_2)}{(s_1^2/n_1 + s_2^2/n_1)}}$$

Standard deviation

$$SD = \sqrt{\frac{\Sigma(x - \overline{x})^2}{n}}$$

Correlation coefficient

$$r = \sqrt{\frac{\Sigma(x - \overline{x})(y - \hat{y}))^2}{(s_1^2/n_1 + s_2^2/n_2)}}$$

Value of t for correlation coefficient

$$t = r\sqrt{(N - 2)/(1 - r)^2}$$

PART 4

Communicating results

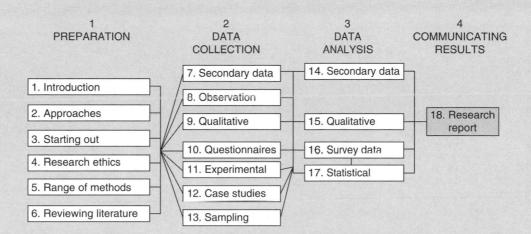

1
PREPARATION

2
DATA
COLLECTION

3
DATA
ANALYSIS

4
COMMUNICATING
RESULTS

1. Introduction

2. Approaches

3. Starting out

4. Research ethics

5. Range of methods

6. Reviewing literature

7. Secondary data

8. Observation

9. Qualitative

10. Questionnaires

11. Experimental

12. Case studies

13. Sampling

14. Secondary data

15. Qualitative

16. Survey data

17. Statistical

18. Research
report

Chapter 18

Research reports and presentations

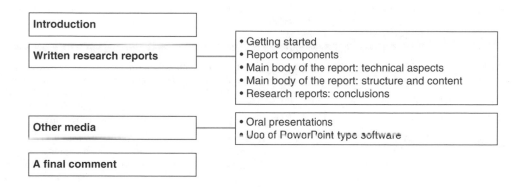

Introduction

| Written research reports | • Getting started
• Report components
• Main body of the report: technical aspects
• Main body of the report: structure and content
• Research reports: conclusions |

| Other media | • Oral presentations
• Use of PowerPoint type software |

| A final comment |

Introduction

This chapter outlines key aspects of the reporting of research results. It concentrates primarily on the preparation and presentation of written research reports, including discussion of content, structure and layout, and considers the varying requirements and conventions of different reporting formats, including academic articles, consultancy reports, books and theses. It concludes with a brief consideration of non-written formats, particularly the oral presentation.

Written research reports

Written reports of research are a key element of the world of policy making, planning and management. Applied studies of the sort discussed in Chapter 1, namely feasibility studies, marketing plans, cultural needs studies, cultural development plans, event strategies, market research studies and performance appraisals, all tend to be presented in the form of written reports. The results of academic studies are produced in the form of articles, reports, books or theses/dissertations. In this chapter we deal with three formats: policy/planning/management project reports, academic articles and theses. The first of these may arise in a policy/planning/management organisational context or may arise from a funded academic project when the researcher reports to the funding body; this style of report is referred to as

Characteristic	Policy/planning/ management project report	Academic article	Thesis
Authors	In-house staff, external consultants or funded academics	Academics	Honours, masters or doctoral students
Content	Report of commissioned or grant-funded project	Report of academic research	Report of academic research
Brief	Provided by commissioning organisation or outlined in grant application	Generally self-generated (although may arise from commissioned work)	Generally self-generated (although may arise in part from grant-funded project)
Quality assurance	In-house: internal. Consultants/academics: reputation of consultants/ researchers	Anonymous refereeing process (see Chapter 1)	Supervision + examination by external examiners
Readership	Professional policy makers/ planners/managers and possibly elected or appointed board/ council/committee members	Primarily academics	Primarily academic
Published status	May or may not be publicly available	Publicly available (often online) in published academic journals	Publicly available in libraries and, recently, online; findings generally published in summary form in one or more academic articles
Length	Varies	In the social/management sciences, including arts/events studies, generally 5,000–7,000 words	In the social/management sciences, including arts/events studies: Honours: c. 20,000 words Masters: c. 40,000 words PhD: c. 70,000 words +
Emphasis	Emphasis on findings rather than links with the literature/theory and methodology (although the latter must be described)	Methodology, theory, literature as important as the findings	Methodology, theory, literature as important as the findings

Figure 18.1 Types of research report

a *project report* in the discussion below. Project reports prepared for a policy or practitioner readership are referred to as *management/policy reports*. In the academic context, in North America the word dissertation is generally used rather than thesis. The main distinguishing characteristics of the three styles of report are summarised in Figure 18.1.

The medium is the message and in this case the medium is the written report. The ability to prepare a report and to recognise good-quality and poor-quality reports should be seen as a key element in the skills of the researcher and manager. While form is no substitute for good content, a report that is poorly presented can undermine or even negate good content. While most of the researcher's attention should of course be focused on achieving high-quality, substantive content, the general presentational and structural aspects raised in this chapter also merit serious attention.

Getting started

In discussing research proposals in Chapter 3 it was noted that researchers invariably leave too little time for report writing. Even when adequate time has been allocated in the timetable, this is often whittled away and the writing of the report is delayed, leaving too little time. There is a tendency to put off report writing because it is difficult and it is often felt that, with just a little more data analysis or a little more reading of the literature, the process of writing the report will become easier. This is rarely the case – it is invariably difficult!

A regrettably common practice is for writers of research reports to spend a great deal of their depleted time, with the deadline looming, writing and preparing material which could have been attended to much earlier in the process. There are often large parts of any report that can be written before data analysis is complete, or even started. Such parts include the introduction, statement of objectives, outline of theoretical or evaluative framework, literature review and description of the methodology. In addition, time-consuming activities such as arranging for maps, illustrations and cover designs to be produced need not be left until the last minute. One way to start the process is to open files for each section/chapter of the report, including 'preliminaries' (acknowledgements, preface, etc.) and 'end matter' (appendices, bibliography, etc.) and begin placing relevant material (notes, drafts, illustrations) in them from the beginning.

Report components

Reports generally include standard components, although some are unique to certain report styles, as shown in Figure 18.2. The components listed are discussed in turn below

Cover

For a project report the cover should include minimal information, such as title, author(s) and publisher or sponsor. The lavishness and design content will vary with the context and the resources available.

If the report is available for sale it should include an International Standard Book Number (ISBN) on the back cover. The ISBN is a 13-digit product identifier for books and other published materials used by publishers, booksellers and libraries. The ISBN system is overseen by the London-based International ISBN Agency and registered with the International Organization for Standardization (ISO) in Geneva. ISBNs are allocated by National ISBN Agencies, which are often national libraries which, under national legislation, generally receive free deposit copies of all publications produced in their country. The ISBN makes it easy to order publications through booksellers and ensures that the publication is catalogued in library systems around the world.

Title page

The title page is the first page inside the cover of a project report. It may include much the same information as the cover or considerably more detail, as indicated in Figure 18.2. In some cases, as in commercially published books, some of the detail is provided on the reverse of the title page.

List of contents

A list of contents is required in project reports and theses and may include just chapter titles, but usually also full details of sub-sections. An example of a contents list is shown in Figure 18.3. Word-processor packages include procedures for compiling tables of contents and lists, such as tables and diagrams.

Component	Content	Management/Planning/Research report	Academic article	Thesis
Cover	• Title of report • Author(s) • Institution/publisher • ISBN (if published), back cover	All items listed left	Not applicable	Prescribed by university regulations
Title page	• Title of report • Author(s) • Institution/publisher, including address, phone, fax numbers, email, website* • Sponsoring body (e.g. 'Report to the Arts Council') • Date of publication* • If the report is for sale: ISBN*. (* sometimes on reverse of title page)	All items listed left	Submitted article includes cover page containing: • Title of article • Author(s) • Institutional affiliation • Contact details (Page omitted by editors when article is sent for anonymous refereeing).	Prescribed by university regulations
Contents page(s)	See Figure 18.3 for example	As in Figure 18.3	Not applicable.	As in Figure 18.2 but less detailed section numbering
Summary	Summary of *whole* report, including background, aims, methods, main findings, conclusions and (where applicable) recommendations	Executive Summary: Length: 20 pp report: ½–1 page 21–50 pp report: 3–4 pp 50–100 pp report: 5–6 pp	Abstract: Length: typically about 300 words.	Synopsis: Length: typically 3–5 pages
Preface/Foreword	Optional. Contains background information, sometimes an explanation of authors' involvement with the project. Or may be by a significant individual not directly involved in the project. Not applicable in academic article, where such information may be included in an endnote.			
Acknowledgements	• Funding organisations • Liaison officers of funding organisations • Members of steering committees • Organisations/individuals providing access to information, etc. • Staff employed (e.g. including interviewers, coders, computer programmers, secretaries, word processors) • Individuals (including academic supervisors) who have given advice, commented on report drafts, etc. • (Collectively) Individuals who responded to questionnaires, etc.			
Main body of report	Discussed separately			
Appendices	Text/statistical material included for the record but which, because of its size, would interrupt the flow if included in the main body of the report			

Figure 18.2 Report style and components

C O N T E N T S

Page

Executive summary...(i)
Preface ....(iii)
Acknowledgements ....(iv)

1. INTRODUCTION 1
   1.1 Background to the study 1
   1.2 The nature of the problem...3
   1.3 Aims of the study 4
   1.4 Outline of the report 4

2. LITERATURE REVIEW..5
   2.1 Research on youth and the arts generally 5
   2.2 Research on student arts engagement 8
   2.3 Conclusions: the state of knowledge on students and the arts.....................10
   2.4 Questions still to be answered 12

3. METHODOLOGY 13
   3.1 Data requirements..13
   3.2 Selection of methods 15
   3.3 Secondary data: sources and proposed analysis 16
   3.4 In-depth interviews 18
   3.5 Questionnaire survey..19
   3.6 Pilot survey..21

4. STUDENT ARTS ENGAGEMENT IN THE 21ˢᵗ CENTURY...22
   4.1 Data sources..22
   4.2 Students at school 22
   4.4 Students at college/university..25
   4.5 Conclusions 27

5. STUDENT WORK AND ARTS/LEISURE PATTERNS
   5.1 Sample characteristics..29
   5.2 Attitudes towards academic work..30
   5.3 Attitudes towards paid work..32
   5.4 Attitudes towards the arts and leisure 34
   5.4 Work, leisure and the arts: a synthesis 37

6. SUMMARY AND CONCLUSIONS 40
   6.1 Summary..40
   6.2 Conclusions...42

REFERENCES 44
APPENDICES
     1. Copy of questionnaire..49
     2. In-depth interview checklist..51
     3. Census data on student population 53
     4. Survey statistical summary...56

LIST OF TABLES
     1.1 Title...xx
     1.2 Title...xx
     Etc.
LIST OF DIAGRAMS/ILLUSTRATIONS
     1.1 Title ....yy
     1.2 Title ....yy
     Etc.

Figure 18.3 Example report list of contents

Summary – executive summary/abstract/synopsis

A summary is required for all three styles of report except for very short project reports. The summary is called *executive summary*, *abstract* or *synopsis*, depending on the context. The typical length also varies, depending on the context.

An executive summary is sometimes thought of as the summary for the 'busy executive' who does not have time to read the whole report, but really refers to the idea that it should contain information necessary to take executive action on the basis of the report.

A summary should contain a summary of the *whole* report, article or thesis, as indicated in Figure 18.2; it is not the introduction. The summary should, of course, be written last.

Preface/foreword

Prefaces or forewords are used for a variety of purposes. Usually they explain the origins of the study and outline any qualifications or limitations. Acknowledgements of assistance may be included if there is no separate 'acknowledgements' section. Sometimes a significant individual is asked to write a foreword, such as the director of an institution, a government minister or an eminent academic.

Acknowledgements

It is clearly a matter of courtesy to acknowledge any assistance received during the course of a research project. People and institutions which might be acknowledged are listed in Figure 18.2.

Main body of the report – technical aspects

Clearly the main body of the report is its most important component. The substantive content is discussed in the next section; here we consider a number of technical aspects of organisation and presentation, as listed in Figure 18.4.

Section numbering

In project reports it is usual to number not only the major sections/chapters but also subsections within chapters, as shown in the example in Figure 18.3. Once a numbering system is established it should be carried through consistently throughout the report. Word-processor packages provide 'style' templates to facilitate this process.

In project reports, section numbers may extend to several levels, for example within section 4.2 there could be sub-sections: 4.2.1, 4.2.2, etc. Further levels can become cumbersome and

- Section numbering
- Paragraph numbering
- 'Dot point' lists
- Page numbering
- Headers/footers
- Heading hierarchy
- Typing layout/spacing
- Tables and statistical tests
- Presentation of tables and graphics
- Referencing
- Which person?

Figure 18.4 Main body of report: technical aspects

are generally not required throughout the report, so if there is an occasional need for further sub-sections it is often advisable to use a simple a. b. c. or (i), (ii), (iii), etc.

Journal articles rarely include section numbering; when it is included it is typically for one level only.

In theses, chapters are numbered, and possibly one level of sections within chapters, but sub-section numbering is not generally used.

Paragraph numbering

In some reports, notably government reports, paragraphs are individually numbered, although this is rare. This can be useful for reference purposes when a report is being discussed in committees, etc. Paragraphs can be numbered in a single series for the whole report or chapter by chapter: in chapter 1: paragraphs 1.1, 1.2, 1.3, etc.; in chapter 2: paragraphs 2.1, 2.2, 2.3, etc. and so on.

'Dot point' lists

Dot point lists are common in project reports, and quite common in the other reporting formats. This device can assist the reader to understand the structure of the material and assists in visual scanning of a document. Project reports are often discussed in committee or written comments are offered in various consultation exercises, and this process is eased by dot point lists, although numbered lists may be even more helpful: it is easier to refer to and to locate 'Item **5**' than 'the fifth dot point'.

Where possible, grammatical rules should be followed in dot point lists. For example, the introduction and complete dot point list in Figure 18.5 are, in effect, all one sentence. There are therefore no capital letters at the beginning of each item, semi-colons at the end of each list item, 'and' after the penultimate item and a full-stop at the end of the list. This principle is difficult to follow when the individual dot points are lengthy, perhaps themselves involving more than one sentence: in this case each dot point in a sequence should be treated as one or more complete sentences with capital letters and full-stops. Some publishers' 'house-styles', however, now omit the semi-colons, in effect treating the dot points grammatically as a series of headings.

Page numbering

One problem in putting together long reports, especially when different authors are responsible for different sections, is to organise page numbering so that it follows on from chapter to chapter. This can be eased by numbering each chapter separately, for example: Chapter 1: pages 1.1, 1.2, 1.3, etc.; Chapter 2: pages 2.1, 2.2, 2.3, etc. and so on. Such a numbering system can also aid readers to find their way around a report. Word processors can be made to produce page numbers in this form.

It is general practice for the title page, contents page(s), acknowledgements and executive summary pages to be numbered as a group using roman numerals (as in this book) and

---

In preparing a research report, the author should take account of:

- the likely readership;
- the requirements of the funding agency, as indicated in the study brief;
- printing or other distribution format;
- likely costs; and
- delivery of a clear message.

Figure 18.5 Dot point list example

for the main body of the report to start at page 1 with normal numbers. Word processors can facilitate this.

Headers/footers

Word-processing packages provide a facility to include a running header or footer across the top or bottom of each page. This can be used to indicate sections or chapters, as in this book, or, in the case of a consultancy report, can be used to indicate title and authorship of the report, perhaps even displaying the consultancy logo on each page.

Heading hierarchy

In the main body of the report a hierarchy of heading styles should be used, with the major chapter/section headings being in the most prominent style and with decreasing emphasis for sub-section headings. For example:

1. Chapter Titles
1.1 Section Headings
1.1.1 Sub-section Headings

Such a convention helps readers to know where they are in a document. When a team is involved in writing a report it is clearly sensible to agree these heading styles in advance. Word-processor systems provide a range of report 'styles' which standardise heading formats and section numbering systems, linked to the assembly of tables of contents.

Typing layout/spacing

Essays and books tend to use the convention of starting new paragraphs by indenting the first line. Report style is to separate paragraphs by a blank line and not to indent the first line. Report style also tends to have more headings. For a document in report style it is usual to leave wide margins, which raises the question as to whether it is necessary to print documents in 1.5 or double-space format or whether single spacing is adequate (and more environmentally friendly!). Different journals have different format specifications for submission of articles, usually indicated in the journal itself and/or on the journal website. Universities provide their own guidelines for the layout of theses.

Tables, graphics and statistical tests

Balance: When presenting the results of quantitative research, an appropriate balance must be struck between the use of tables, graphics and text. In most cases, large or complex tables are consigned to appendices, with simplified and/or graphical versions included in the body of the report. It may be appropriate to place all tables in appendices and provide only 'reader-friendly' graphics in the body of the report. The decision on which approach to use depends partly on the complexity of the data to be presented, but mainly on the type of audience.

Tables, graphics and text each have a distinctive role to play in the presentation of the study findings:

- tables provide information;
- graphics illustrate that information so that patterns can be seen in a visual way;
- the text should be telling a story or developing an argument and 'orchestrating' tables and graphics to support that task.

Table X. Participation in cultural activities, persons aged 16+ England, 2003		
	% Participating in 12 months prior to interview	
Activity	Males	Females
Reading for pleasure	67	78
Bought a novel/book	43	56
Dance (not for fitness)	5	7
Play musical instrument for own pleasure	11	8
Play musical instrument for an audience	4	2

Source: compiled from Fenn *et al.* (2004: 47)

Commentary A

The table indicates that, of the five activities listed, women are more active in three – reading for pleasure (78% compared with 67% for men), buying novels/books (56% compared with 43%) and dancing (not for fitness) (7% compared with 5%) – while men are more active in two – playing a musical instrument for their own pleasure (11% compared with 8% for women) and for an audience (4% compared with 2%).

Commentary B

Women are substantially more active in the two most popular activities listed, reading for pleasure and buying books/novels. While men are more active in playing musical instruments, for their own pleasure and for others, this is a minority activity, involving less than 10% of the population.

Figure 18.6 Table and commentaries

There seems to be little point in the text of a report simply repeating what is in a table or graphic. At the least the text should highlight the main features of the data; ideally it should develop an argument or draw conclusions based on the data. In the example in Figure 18.6, Commentary A does little more than repeat what is in the table: it says nothing to the reader about the difference between men's and women's participation patterns, which is presumably the purpose of the exercise. Commentary B, however, is more informative, pointing out particular features of the data in the table.

Statistical tests: In the more quantitative disciplines there is a convention that, in academic reports such as journal articles and theses, the detailed results of statistical tests, such as those discussed in Chapter 17, should be mentioned in the text, even if the information is also available in a table. Thus, for example, a sentence in the text might read: 'Mean monthly frequency of participation by men (2.1) is significantly higher than for women (1.7, t = 5.6, p < 0001)'. Clearly the information in brackets 'clutters' the text and makes it less 'reader-friendly' if there are a number of such insertions; it seems unnecessary to include it in the text if it can be seen in the table; and the t-test information may be meaningless to readers without statistical knowledge. In less quantitative fields it is not necessary to include the information in brackets, particularly the t-test result, in the text if it is available in a table. In management/policy reports, results of statistical tests are often not included at all, even though they may have been carried out, although such terms as 'significantly different' or 'not significantly different' may be used.

Presentation of tables and graphics

Graphics and tables should, as far as possible, be complete in themselves; that is, the title should be informative and the columns, rows or axes should be fully labelled so that the reader can understand them without necessarily referring to the text. The table in Figure 18.6

follows these principles. Thus tables or graphics presenting data from cultural participation surveys or other data sources should include information on:

- the geographical area/community/country to which the data refer;
- the year(s) to which the data refer or the year collected;
- gender and age range of the sample or population to which the data relate;
- sample size, where relevant;
- units of measurement.

Reproductions of secondary data should indicate the source of data, but tables or graphics presenting results from the primary data collection of the study, such as a survey, do not need to indicate this on every table and diagram. Nevertheless, some consultants tend to do this for intellectual property reasons so that if a user copies just one table or diagram then its source is still indicated.

Referencing

References to the literature and other sources in academic reports should follow the referencing conventions set out in Chapter 6. This may, however, be inappropriate for the non-academic readerships of management/policy reports. While sources should be acknowledged in such reports, it is generally appropriate to do so in an unobtrusive manner – for example, by use of endnotes or footnotes rather than the author/date reference style. In some management/policy reports the 'review of the literature' is relegated to an appendix with just the conclusions being presented in the body of the report.

Which person?

In academic reports, it is conventional to report the conduct and findings of research in an 'impersonal style' – for example, to say: 'A survey was conducted' rather than 'I/we conducted a survey' and 'It was found that…' rather than 'I/we found that…'. Some believe that this attempt to appear 'scientific' is inappropriate in the social sciences, particularly in qualitative research where the researcher personally engages with the research subjects. First-person accounts are therefore sometimes, but not commonly, used in some arts/event research reports. The first-person plural is also quite commonly used by consultants in management/policy reports, especially when the consultants wish to convey the impression that they are bringing particular personal and team skills and experience to bear on a project.

The impersonal style can appear odd or pretentious when authors refer to their own work. Thus, for Smith to say, 'Smith (2002) has argued that cultural consumption is class-based' seems odd, and even for Smith to say, 'The author has argued that cultural consumption is class-based (Smith, 2002)' seems pretentious. The solution in such a situation is either for Smith to use the first person – 'I have argued that cultural consumption is class-based (Smith, 2002)' – or to 'de-centre' the author – 'It has been argued that cultural consumption is class-based (Smith, 2002)'.

Main body of the report – structure and content

Structure

It could be said that the three most important aspects of a research report are 1. structure, 2. structure and 3. structure! The *structure* of a report is of fundamental importance and needs to be thoroughly considered and discussed, particularly when a team is involved. While all reports have certain structural features in common, the important aspects of any one report concern the underlying argument and how that relates to the objectives of the study and any data collection and analysis involved. This is linked fundamentally to the *research objectives*, the *theoretical or evaluative framework* and the *overall research strategy*, as discussed in Chapter 3.

Before writing starts it is of course necessary to decide and agree on the report structure and format, but it can also be useful to decide and agree target word lengths for each chapter or section. While an agreed structure is a necessary starting point, it is also necessary to be flexible. As drafting gets under way it may be found that what was originally conceived as one chapter needs to be divided into two or three chapters, or what was thought of as a separate chapter can be incorporated into another chapter or into an appendix. Throughout, consideration needs to be given to the overall length of the report, in terms of words or pages.

When a questionnaire survey is involved, there is a tendency for some authors to structure the presentation according to the sequence of questions in the questionnaire and, correspondingly, the sequence of tables as they are produced by the computer. This is not an appropriate way to proceed. Questionnaires are structured for ease of interview, for the convenience of interviewer and/or respondent: they do not provide a suitable sequence and structure for a report. The report should be structured around the substance of the research problem.

The table of contents, as shown in Figure 18.3, indicates the formal broad structure of the report to the reader. The example relates to project reports and theses, which tend to be lengthy and to be divided into chapters and have tables of contents. Journal articles are shorter and do not have tables of contents, but structure is still important. There is a conventional overall structure for journal articles involving about seven sections, as shown in Figure 18.7. This structure is not hard and fast; in particular, not all articles are empirical, so 'methods' and 'results' sections relating to data collection are not universal.

In the case of a project report, the contents page indicates the general organisation of the report and should make the reader aware of the structure. But this is rarely enough: it must be *explained* – often more than once. Being clear in your mind about structure is one thing; conveying it to the reader can be quite another. Thus it is good practice, particularly in the case of a lengthy report/thesis, to provide an outline of the structure of the whole report in the introductory chapter and outlines of each chapter in the introduction to each chapter. Summaries are useful at the end of each chapter and these can be revisited and summarised at the end of the report when drawing together conclusions. It is advisable to provide numerous references backwards and forwards, as reminders to the reader as to where you are in the overall 'story' of the report.

When a list of 'factors', 'issues' or 'topics' is about to be discussed, one by one, it is useful to list these factors or issues and then summarise at the end of the section to indicate what the review of factors or issues has achieved.

- Background/introduction/justification for the research/nature of the problem/issue
- Review of the literature
- Specific outline of problem/issue/hypotheses
- Methods
- Results
- Conclusions
- References

Figure 18.7 Conventional academic article structure

Articles are shorter, of course, so organising the structure is less of a logistical challenge. There is no table of contents as such, although the abstract – typically just a paragraph – is usually printed at the beginning of an article and should give some impression of structure. But the logic and structure should also be explained within the article proper.

Between methods and results

All empirical research reports, regardless of format, should include a clear summary of the methods used to gather data. In journal articles the description is often quite short, because of the limitation of word length. In management/policy reports the description may be short in the body of the report because of the type of readership, but there is scope to provide more detail in appendices. In a thesis an extensive and explicit description of methods used is essential.

In all formats, but particularly in a thesis, the *choice* of methods should also be discussed. Why was a particular method selected? What alternatives were considered and why were they rejected? Such a discussion should be related to the nature of the research questions/hypotheses. It is not sufficient merely to list the characteristics and merits of the methods chosen, but to indicate why those particular characteristics were appropriate in this particular project. Factors to consider in selecting a research method are discussed at the end of Chapter 5 and these should be referred to in justifying the choice of method.

Part of the reporting of results of empirical research involves provision of some very basic information on the success of the chosen data-collection method in achieving a suitable sample of subjects for study. Since this is technical in nature and not concerned directly with the substantive findings, it can be reported in the 'methods' section, although it is often reported as the first part of the 'results' section. This component of the report should provide information on:

- the size of the sample achieved;
- response rates and an indication as to whether they are deemed to be acceptable and are likely to have caused bias;
- characteristics of the sample, particularly where they indicate the representativeness of the sample – thus a sample from a household or community survey might be compared with the known age/gender structure of the local population from the Population Census data for the area, while the age structure of a site survey sample might be compared with junior/adult ticket sales ratios or information from other similar surveys;
- any measures taken to correct sample bias by means of weighting, and a description of that process (see Chapter 10).

While these comments relate particularly to quantitative research involving surveys, the same principles, concerning information on the nature of the sample of subjects under study, apply in all forms of empirical research, qualitative as well as quantitative and non-survey-based as well as survey-based.

Audiences and style

The style, format and length of a report are largely influenced by the type of audience at which it is aimed. The amount of technical jargon used and the detail with which data are presented will be affected by this question of audience. Audiences may be of three kinds:

- *Popular audience:* Consisting of members of the general public who might read a report of research in a newspaper or magazine – full research reports are therefore not generally written for a popular readership.

- *Decision makers:* Groups, such as elected members of councils, government ministers, members of boards of trusts, companies or clubs, or senior executives, who may not have a detailed knowledge of a particular field, or may have a particular type of knowledge, which might be technical, managerial, policy-related or political.

- *Experts:* Professionals or academics who are familiar with the broad subject matter of the research.

Report functions: narrative and record

A research report can be thought of in two ways: first the report as *narrative* and, second, the report as *record*. Balancing these demands as the report is being put together can be a major challenge.

Narrative

The report as *narrative* refers to the idea that a report has to tell a story to the reader. The writer of the report therefore needs to think of the flow of the argument – the 'story' – in the same way that the writer of a novel has to consider the flow of the plot. The report as narrative may call for presentation of only simplified factual information or key features of the data, possibly in graphical form, to demonstrate and illustrate the argument. The narrative of a research report usually develops as indicated in Figure 18.8. The items listed may emerge

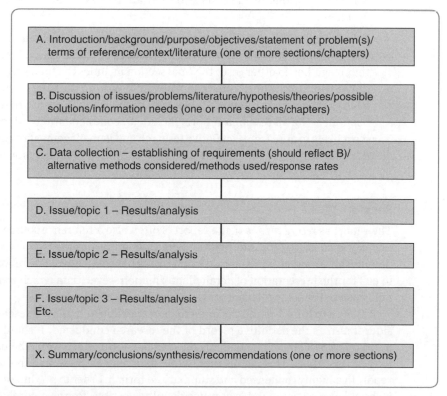

Figure 18.8 Report as narrative – structure

in a variety of chapter/section configurations. For example, sections A and B could be one chapter/section or three or four, depending on the complexity of the project.

A Introduction. The introductory section(s) should reflect the considerations which emerged in the initial steps in the planning stages of a project (components 1, 2 and 6 in Figure 3.1). The term 'context' is used to include the environment in which the research is situated, including any initial literature review which may be involved.

B Discussion of issues, etc. It is important that the relation between data requirements and the research questions and theoretical or evaluative framework be explained, as discussed in Chapter 3. It should be clear from the discussion why the data are being collected: how this relates to the planning/policy/management/theoretical issues raised and how it was anticipated that the information collected would solve or shed light on the problems/issues raised or aid decision-making.

C Data collection/methodology. This should be described in detail; it should be clear why particular techniques were chosen, how samples or subjects were selected, and what data-collection instruments were used. Where sample surveys are involved, full information should be given on response rates and sample sizes obtained and some indication given of the consequences in terms of potential bias, as discussed above, and confidence intervals, as discussed in Chapter 13. These technical aspects of the results of any survey work can be included in the methodology section of the report or in the first of the results sections, and in some cases in appendices.

D, E, F, etc. Results/analysis sections. These should ideally be structured by the earlier conceptual or theoretical discussion (B) around issues and elements of the research problem.

X Summary/conclusions. Sometimes conclusions are fully set out in the results/analysis section(s) and all that is required in the final conclusions section is to reiterate and draw them together. In other cases the final section includes the final stage of analysis and the drawing of conclusions from that analysis. In writing the final section it is vital to refer back to the terms of reference/objectives of the study to ensure that all objectives have been met. Not all research reports include 'recommendations'. Recommendations are most likely to arise from evaluative research and in management research where the brief has explicitly asked for them. It should, of course, be clear to whom such recommendations are addressed.

Record

The report as *record* means that a report is often also a reference source where future readers may wish to look for information. Being a good record may involve including extensive detailed information, which would interfere with the narrative. The report as record is likely to call for the presentation of detailed information – even data which were collected but did not prove particularly relevant for the overall study conclusions.

It is wise to think beyond the immediate readership and use of a research report and consider it also as the definitive record of the research conducted. It should therefore contain a summary of all the relevant data collected in a form which would be useful for any future user of the report. This means that, while data may be presented in the main body of the report in a highly condensed and summarised form in order to produce a readable narrative, it should also be presented in as much detail as possible 'for the record'. To avoid interfering with the narrative, data included for record purposes can be placed in appendices or, when large amounts of data are involved, in a separate statistical volume.

In the case of questionnaire survey data it can be a good idea to provide a statistical appendix that includes tables from all the questions in the order they appear in the questionnaire (see Figure 16.16). Any reader interested in a specific aspect of the data is then able to locate and use it. The main body of the report can be structured around issues, unconstrained by the structure of the questionnaire.

The possibility arises that some of the recording functions discussed above can be devolved to a website. In some disciplines, as noted in Chapters 1 and 4, publications require original data to be publicly available online, so such online repositories could also include items such as detailed statistical results and copies of research instruments.

Research reports: conclusion

Ultimately the writing of a good research report is an art and a skill that develops with practice. Reports can be improved enormously as a result of comments from others – often because the writer has been 'too close' to the report for too long to be able to see glaring faults or omissions. The researcher/writer can also usually spot opportunities for improvement if he or she takes a short break and returns to the draft report with 'fresh eyes'.

Finally, checking and double checking the report for typing, spelling and typographical errors is well worth the laborious effort!

Other media

While the written report is still the most common medium for the communication of research results, this is likely to change in future. In particular, the researcher is often required to present final or interim results of research in person and some sort of audio-visual aids are usually advisable, including handouts, posters, computers and audio-visual devices. The most common medium is the oral presentation aided by computer-based visuals using such packages as Microsoft PowerPoint.

Oral presentations

An important point to bear in mind is the obvious fact that the audio-visual presentation is not the same as a written report. The presentation must be designed as a medium/message in its own right. The information to be presented must fit into the time allotted and be suitable for the medium and the audience. Therefore a conscious selection of material must be made. This will normally be explained at the beginning of the presentation, but constant references to what is not being covered in the presentation because of lack of time are an indication of an unprofessional approach. For example, if there are six 'key findings' from a study, rather than rushing to cover all six it is in most cases better to say to an audience: 'There are six findings from the study and in this presentation I am going to concentrate on the three most important/relevant to this audience'.

It goes without saying that the presenter should practise presenting the material to ensure that it fits into the time allotted. Such practice sessions can be seen as the equivalent of various drafts of the written report. Typically it is necessary to be selective in making such a presentation. Judgement must be used in deciding what to include and what to leave out. As with the writing of abstracts and synopses, this can be a considerable challenge. Practice runs help in this process. Programs such as PowerPoint include a 'rehearse timings' procedure which helps in deciding how long to spend on particular parts of the presentation and what to leave out on grounds of time.

Reading from a prepared script is rarely as successful as talking directly to an audience, using the computer slides and/or notes as a guide. However, if a prepared script is being used, then practising the presentation, to ensure the presenter is familiar with the script, is even more advisable so that frequent eye contact can still be made with the audience.

Arranging, and reviewing, audio-visual recordings of practice runs of a presentation can pay dividends.

Use of PowerPoint-type software

Most of the readers of this book are students, who sit through hundreds of PowerPoint-type presentations during the course of their studies. Students are therefore experienced judges of what is and is not a good presentation. These notes distil just a few of the do's and don'ts.

- Do not stand in front of the screen!
- Do not overcrowd slides. The standard slide templates available in programs such as PowerPoint provide a default font size and a default number of dot points on a slide. This is for a good reason. Viewing an image when preparing it on a personal computer screen from less than a metre is different from viewing the same image projected on a screen in a lecture hall or meeting room. Thus, while a table or graphic with 30 lines of data may be readable in a printed report and on a personal computer screen, it may not be readable to someone 20 metres from a projection screen. In such a situation the most important, say, ten lines of the table or items in the graphic must be selected, or the table or graphic must be divided into two or more sequential slides. As an example, the PowerPoint slides available for this book include eight slides for Figure 18.3: one containing the main chapter/section headings only (the headings in capital letters) and one each for the detail of each chapter/section and the references, appendices, etc. One of the worst things to hear from a presenter is: 'You probably won't be able to read this from the back of the room but…' A practice run-through with a full-size screen viewed from the back of a room is advisable.
- Use graphics. The PowerPoint-type presentation is a visual medium. Ideally, therefore, graphical images should be mixed with verbal material. Photographs, and even video material, from the research process and/or relating to the research subject can make a presentation 'come alive'. However, excessive use of such material can be a distraction and may limit time available for presentation of key material. A balance must be struck.
- Be careful about colour. Maximum contrast aids viewing. Yellow lettering on an orange background may look effective in close-up on a computer screen but could be unreadable when projected. Lighting conditions in rooms vary and projector colour definition can also vary: it is better to play it safe. Similarly, some photographs that look good on a small screen may not be very impressive when projected.
- Use the dynamic features of the program. PowerPoint-type programs include 'animation'. While items flying into view from all directions may be a distraction, the sequential appearance of, for example, items in a dot-point list at least concentrates the viewer/listener

on the item the presenter is talking about. This works even more effectively with graphics. Again, using an example from the PowerPoint slides made available with this book: in the case of Figure 3.1, which summarises the ten components of the research process, the ten boxes appear sequentially, so that the presenter can talk to each component in turn as it appears.

Summary

This chapter considers the preparation of what is generally the final outcome of a research project, namely a written report. It considers the varying demands of three types of report: the policy/planning/management/research project report, the academic journal article and the thesis, each with different audiences, different constraints and different conventions. The chapter reviews the various ancillary components of a report, including the cover, cover page, title page, list of contents, synopsis/abstract/executive summary, preface/foreword and acknowledgements. It then considers the main body of the report in terms of technical aspects, largely to do with format, and structure and content. Structure is emphasised as the key feature of a research report, particularly in their longer formats. Finally, some do's and don'ts are offered in regard to computer-aided oral presentations.

A final comment

Research is a creative process which, in the words of Norbert Elias, with which we began this text, aims to 'make known something previously unknown to human beings ... to advance human knowledge, to make it more certain or better fitting ... the aim is ... discovery'. It is hoped that this book will provide some assistance in that process of discovery and that the reader will enjoy some of the satisfactions and rewards that can come from worthwhile research.

TEST QUESTIONS/EXERCISES

No specific exercises are offered here. By now the reader should be capable of venturing into the world of research by carrying out a research project from beginning to end.

Resources

The best reading relevant to this chapter is the critical reading of research reports. As regards non-print media, most readers of this book have ample opportunity in the course of their academic and/or professional lives to see good and bad examples of audio-visual presentations from which they can discern good and bad practice!

- General: Miles and Huberman (1994, Chapter 12, 298–306).
- Qualitative research: Wolcott (2008).

References

Fenn, C., Bridgwood, A. and Dust, K. (2004) *Arts in England 2003: Attendance, Participation and Attitudes, Research Report 37*. London: Arts Council England.

Miles, M. B. and Huberman, A. M. (1994) *Qualitative Data Analysis*, Second Edition. Thousand Oaks, CA: Sage.

Wolcott, H. F. (2008) *Writing up Qualitative Research*, Third Edition. Thousand Oaks, CA: Sage.

Index

a priori theory 221
abuse of results in policy/practice 104
academic journal articles 18–19
   list of main refereed journals 18–19
   peer review 18, 19
   refeering 18, 19
   reviewing 18, 19
academic research 55
   disciplinary field 59–60
   funding 15, 17, 79
   motivation for 14–15
   research proposals 79
access to information held by public bodies
     103–4
access to research information, ethical issues
     103–4
'accountability' 10
acknowledgements 103, 466, 468
ACORN classification 124, 125
action research 115–17, 304
activity choice qualitative study 360–2
administrative/management data 179–80
advertising coupons 119
aerial photography 210–11
age, and questionnaire design 268
age range, participation surveys 185
Alderson, A.S. 352
Amazon 353
ambulatory assessment 120
American Marketing Association, *Marketing Scales
     Handbook* 126
analysis of results, ethical issues 102–3
Anderson, C. 118
Andreotti, L. 207
anonymous questionnaire-based surveys, ethics guidelines
     98
anonymous subjects 99
anthropology, and arts and events research 31
appendices 466
applied research 32, 38
art/health projects 299
artistic – economic dichotomy 317–18
arts, meaning of 4
Arts Council England, Target Group Index 182
Arts in England 181
arts festivals 10
arts leaders' entrepreneurship 318–19
arts/events publications 147–8
attitude/opinion questions 266, 273–5
   attitude statements 274, 275, 278

formats 273–5
   Likert scales 273–5
   ranking 274, 275
   repertory grid 275
   semantic differential 274, 275
Australia
   Bureau of Statistics 181, 182, 185
   General Social Survey 244
   Household Expenditure Survey 186
   More than Bums on Seats survey 181, 182
   NHMRC code 89
   NHMRC National Ethics Application Form 91
   Nugent Report 22
   participation surveys 182
   population census 189
   theatre attendance 316–17
   time-use surveys 185, 186
Australia Council 168, 182
authenticity 45
author/date referencing system 154, 156–7
   advantages and disadvantages 157, 159
   basic features 156
   compared with footnote or endnote referencing system
     159
   specifics and quotations 156–7
   style variation 156
author's opinions or beliefs 152
authorship 103
automatic counters 210
Auvinen, T. 317–18
average *see* mean

Bachman, J.G. 283
balanced scorecard analysis 130
bar graph produced in SPSS 406,
     407–8
Baum, M. 8
BBC
   Great British Class Survey 121
   time-use surveys 185
beaches 204
Beck, U. 352
behaviour
   effects of experimental research 294, 295
   monitoring changing patterns 7
Bekkers, R. 302
Belfiore, E. 90
Bennett, A. 315–16
Bennett, R. 252
Bereson, R. 58

bibliographies 144–5, 147
    compiling and maintaining 149, 154
    examples 162
    inclusive 150
'big data' 116, 117–18
    secondary data analysis 353–4
binary logistic regression analysis 447
biographical research 121, 221, 229
    memory work 229
    nature 229
    oral history 229
    personal domain histories 229
biological research 98
Bitgood, S. 300
Black, N. 305
Bolstein, R. 301–2
book sales 118, 353
Bourdieu, P. 122, 284, 352, 450–1
brainstorming 56
Brandenburg, J. 360
bricolage 37, 230
briefs 10, 80–2
Bryman, A. 36, 229
budget 71
Budoki, E. 352
'bums on seats' 128, 171

Caltabiano, M.L. 283
captive group surveys 114, 243, 257–8, 259
    by interview 258
    conduct 257–8
    nature 257
    respondent completion 257, 258
car registration numbers 208
case study method of research 110, 115, 309–23
    activity profile – theatre attendance 316–17
    analysis 315–16
    arts leaders' entrepreneurship 318–19
    case selection 314
    data gathering 314–15
    definitions 310–11
    demographic and geographic levels 311
    descriptive research 312
    design and conduct 313–15
    evaluative research 312, 313
    explanatory research 312, 313
    merits 313
    museums, failure of 319–20
    music production and consumption 318
    opera house management 317–18
    in practice 316–20
    reliability 313
    scale 311
    temporal consistency 315
    theory and policy 312
    unit of analysis 314, 315
    validity 311–13
case study research 121
catchment area 255

causality 7, 34–5, 381–2
    associations 381
    non-spurious relationships 382
    rationale 382
    time priority 382
CCTV 210, 211
Chan, T.W. 352
Charmaz, K. 40, 223
Chase, D. 283
chi-square, formula 459
chi-square test 423, 424–7, 451
    degrees of freedom 427
    expected counts rule 427
    interpretation 426–7
    null hypothesis 424
    reporting 427
    uses 424
    value 425–6
Chiaravalloti, F. 90
children 258
    behaviour 200
    ethical issues 94, 95
    observational research 212
    participation surveys 185
    proxy interviews 185
Chiozzi, G. 207
cinema, estimating likely demand 349, 350
circular model of research process 39–40
Clavio, G. 228
climate research 103, 104
cluster analysis 448, 449
    dendrogram 449, 450
coding 278–81
    open-ended questions 278, 279
    pre-coded questions 278
    recording coded information 278–81
Comedia 298
commercial organisations, motivation for research 14, 15
commissioning research 16
complaints, visitor surveys 256
Computer Assisted Telephone Interviewing (CATI) 247, 327
computer-aided qualitative data analysis software
    (CAQDAS) 366
    see also NVivo
concept map 62–3
conceptual framework
    case study 75–6, 77
    decision-making models 67
    defining concepts 64
    description 60
    devising 60–5
    examples
        customer service quality study 66
        market research study 66
    identifying/listing concepts 63–4
    operationalisation of concepts 64–5
    for qualitative study 363–4
    as a quantifiable model 65
    relationship between concepts 62–3

conducting questionnaire surveys 284–7
  fieldwork arrangements – planning 284–6
  permissions 284
  pilot survey 286–7
  recruitment of interviewers and supervisors 286
conducting research 72–3
conference presentations/papers 20
confidence intervals 419
  and normal curve 331, 332
  population estimates 335
  reporting on 334, 341
  and sample size 331–3
  and visit numbers 35
confidentiality 99–102, 276, 359–60
conjoint analysis 13, 116, 118, 302, 303
consensus study 122, 150
consent, informed see informed consent
consent form, example 97
conservative stance 58
constructivist approaches 36
consultants 79
  motivation/purpose for research 14, 17
content analysis 116, 118–19, 151
contents, table of 465, 466, 467, 473
contributors to research project, acknowledgement 103,
    466, 468
control group 293
conversion studies 116, 119
cordon surveys 116, 120
correlation 123, 435–40
  coefficient (r) 436, 439, 459
  null hypothesis 439
  positive and negative 436
  procedures 439–40
  uses 435
Cosper, R. 303
cost disease 354
cost-benefit analysis 13, 130
Coulangeon, P. 352
Council of Europe, participation surveys 180, 181
counting heads 117, 128–9, 171–2, 173, 199, 200–1
  use of clicker device 201
  use of infra-red devices 201, 210
  where no entrance fee 200–1
counting sheets 208–9
coupon surveys 116, 119
cover 465, 466
critical approaches 32, 33–4, 36
Crompton, J.L. 102
cross-disciplinary, meaning of term 30
cross-tabulation 364, 365, 404–5
crowd behaviour 95
Csikszentmihalyi, M. 120
cultural, use of term 4
cultural consumption/taste and social status,
    secondary data analysis 352
cultural indicators 175
cultural maps/mapping 20, 175–9
  populating 176, 177

  toolkits 176, 193
cultural needs studies 21
cultural observatories, motivation/purpose for research
    14, 17
cultural participation, secondary data analysis 346, 347–8
cultural statistics 172–5
  UNESCO Framework 173–5
cultural tourism 4, 21, 246
culture, meaning of 4
culturomics 354
Cushman, G. 181
customer service quality study, conceptual framework 66
cyclists 210

data, ethics 92
data analysis
  observational research 209
  secondary see separate entry
  techniques to be used 70–1
  see also qualitative data analysis
data availability/access, and methods of research 131
data collection method, disclosure in report 474
data collection process, risk of harm 98–9
data gathering 16
  case study method of research 314–15
data, personally identifiable, protection of ID 100–2
data processors, appointment and training 286
data storage and handling 73–4
  anonymous subjects 99
  and confidentiality 359–60
  identified subjects 99–100
  partial anonymity 99
  password-protected access 99
  risk of harm 99–102
databases, specialist 146
Dean, 223–4
Debenedetti, S. 212
deception, ethical issues 97
decision-making, alternative products 302
decision-making models, conceptual framwork 67
deduction 32, 39–42
  case studies 41
Delphi technique 116, 119
demand for cultural facility, estimating 348–51
demand forecasting 130
dendrogram 449, 450
Denzin, N.K. 36
dependent variables 293, 422–3
Dept of Culture, Media and Sport
  Cultural Mapping Document 176, 187, 188
  social inclusion report 298
  Taking Part Survey 182, 185
descriptive research 6–7, 32, 34
  survey data analysis 381
  why required 7
deviant behaviour, observational research 203
diary methods see time-use surveys
digital data, password-protected access 99
digital sources 190

digital tracking 120
Dillman, D.A. 250
disciplinary field, identifying 59–60
disciplinary traditions 30–1
discourse analysis 116, 119
discovery 5, 6
discrete choice experiments (DCEs) 297, 302–4
    case studies 303–4
    cultural events 303
    repeat visits to museums 303–4
documentary sources 190
    examples 190
dot point lists 469
Duffy, M.E. 128
Dupuis, S. 225, 363–4

e-surveys 243, 248, 252–4
    advantages 253
    disadvantages 253–4
    junk mail 254
    nature and conduct 252–3
    types of 253
    user/site/visitor survey combo 253, 257
Eagleman, A.N. 228
ecological momentary assessment (EMA) 120
economic impact analysis 13, 22
economic status, and questionnaire design 269–70
economics 31
Eisner, E.W. 102, 421
electoral registers 326
electronic databases, disadvantages 144–5
electronic storage 73–4
electronically aided research
    digital tracking 120
    Electronically Activated Recorder 120
    experience sampling method (ESM) 116, 120
Elias, N. 5, 6
emancipatory research 34
emergent themes – search for 363–4
empirical research 32, 38–9
employment in cultural industry 187, 188
en route surveys 116, 120
encyclopedias, specialist, examples 147–8
endnote referencing system *see* footnote or endnote refer-
    encing system
engagement in arts, typology of individual 168–9
English, F.W. 365–6
entrance fees, where none charged 200–1
environment 31
environmental appraisal 11–12
environmental impact 22
environmental and social impact analysis 13
epistemology 32, 33
et al 161
ethical issues
    access to research information 103–4
    authorship 103
    big data 118
    captive groups 94–5

children 94, 95
deception 97
examples 89–90
freedom of choice 94–6
honesty/rigour in analysis and interpretation 102–3
honesty/rigour in reporting 103
informed consent 96–8
and methods of research 132
observation 94, 95
official surveys 94, 95
participant observation 96
performance evaluation 89–90
plagiarism 103
policy-related research 93
researcher competence 94
risk of harm 96, 98–102
sample size 102–3
sensitive topics 97
social benefit 93–4
and stages in research process – summary 92
use and abuse of results in policy/practice 104
ethics 88–107
    anonymous vs identifiable data 92
    Application for Ethics Approval Form 91
    clearance 71
    codes 91
    general principles 92
    guidelines for anonymous questionnaire-based surveys
        98
    institutional oversight of research ethics 90–1
    NHMRC code 89
ethics committees, universities 90–1
ethnic group, and questionnaire design 272
ethnographic research 36, 230
ethnography 221
European Commission, participation surveys 182
evaluation 13, 299
evaluative research 8, 32, 34
    survey data analysis 382
    uses 8
Evans, G. 176
events studies
    scope of 4
    use of aerial photography 211
evidence-based policy 8, 18, 130
exaggeration 240–1
exhibit labels, case study 300
exhibit layout
    case study 300
    changing 297, 299–300
exhibition development 305
    research in stages of 13
expenditure per visit 170, 171
experience sampling method (ESM) 116, 120
experimental research 32, 42, 110, 114, 292–308
    action research 304
    case study – exhibit layout and labels 300
    case study – experimenting with research methods 297,
        301–2

changing layout/design of exhibits 297, 299–300
classic (true) design 293–4
components 293
control group 293
dependent variable 293
discrete choice experiments (DCEs) 297, 302–4
effects on behaviour 294, 295
field experiments vs laboratory experiments 295
independent variable 293
observation/measurement 297
physical models 305
policy/management experimental projects 297–9
principles of 293–4
qualitative methods 304–5
quasi-experimental designs 295–7, 298
sampling – random assignment 330
threats to validity 294–5
treatment or experimental group 293
validity 294–5
explanatory research 7–8, 32, 34
survey data analysis 381–2
uses 7–8
exploratory research *see* descriptive research
exploratory review 150
exports for cultural industry 187, 188
expression of interest 80

face-to-face interviewing 242
facility catchment area, secondary data analysis 351
facility use, research design process – case study 75–8
factor analysis 40, 448–9
factorial analysis of variance 423, 433–5
null hypothesis 434
procedures 434–5, 436
Falk, J.H. 300
false names, use of 100
falsification of results 102
'fast leisure' 75, 76
feasibility studies 21
feedback 13
Feist, A. 190
feminism 34
Fenn, C. 75
fieldwork planning 70, 284–6
data processors – appointment and training 286
identity badges/letters 286
instructions for interviewers 285
insurance 285
permissions 284
printing 285
quotations 286
recruitment 286
training 286
film 228
filters 277
Fiske, J. 204
Flanagan, R.J. 354–5
Flinn, J. 354
focus groups 221, 226–7

Foord, J. 176
football fans 204
footnote or endnote referencing system 157–9
advantages and disadvantages 159
basic features 157–8
compared with author/date referencing system 159
multiple references 158
specifics and quotations 158–9
forecasting studies 22
foreward 466, 468
free open-air events 16
freedom of choice
captive groups 94–5
children 94, 95
ethical issues 94–6
observational research 94, 95
official surveys 94, 95
participant observation 96
freedom of information 100
Frew, M. 354
funding 15, 17–18

galleries 200–2, 204
Gans, H.J. 352
Garcia, B. 15
gender, and questionnaire design 268
General Lifestyle Survey 244
geography, and arts and events research 31
George, A.L. 315–16
Gerring, J. 310, 312
Giddens, A. 33, 352
Gini coefficient 347
Glaser, B. 221
Global Positioning Systems (GPS) 120, 210
Glotova, O. 219
goals 10, 13
Goffman, I. 204
Goldthorpe, J.H. 352
Google 146
Google Books 118, 354
Google Scholar 147
Goulding, C. 204
government
motivation for research 14, 15
policy-related research – ethical issues 93
policy/planning/management reports 20
research funding 17, 18
government-sponsored research 55
Grant, D. 204
graphical presentation of data using SPSS 406–9
bar graph (histogram) 406, 407–8
line graph 406, 409
pie chart 406, 408
scattergram 406, 409
graphics in report 470–2
Greenwood, D.J. 117
Grichting, W.L. 283
grounded theory 221

group interviews 221
Guba, E. 36, 43, 45

Hagedorn, R. 34
Hantrais, L. 181
harm, risk of 96, 98–102
    data collection process 98–9
    data storage and handling 99–102
    publication of results 102
Harmonised European Time Use Survey 185
Harvard Business School 309
Harvard system *see* author/date referencing system
Hastie, P. 219
Hawthorne effect 294, 295
headers/footers 470
heading hierarchy 470
health 299
Hedges, B. 229
Hemingway, J.L. 8
Henderson, K.A. 45, 337
heritage, meaning of 4
heritage buildings, reuse 305
hermeneutics 118, 151
hidden agenda 81
hierarchical modelling 445–7
Hirschi, K.D. 300
histogram produced in SPSS 406
historical research 116, 121
history 31
Hodder, I. 228
holistic view 43
host communities, impact on 299
household expenditure – cultural items 186–7
household surveys 114, 243–5
    advantages 243
    conduct 244
    interviewer completed 259, 261
    introductory remarks 276
    national 245
    nature 243
    omnibus surveys 243, 244
    range of information 266, 272
    sampling 326–7
    time-use 243, 245
household type, and questionnaire design 271
housing information, and questionnaire design 273
Huberman, A.M. 60, 61, 219–20, 337–8, 365
hypothesis 43
    description 39
    versus research questions format 65–6
hypothetical – deductive model 33

Iacocca, L. 229
ibid 161
identity badges/letters 286
ideological/political motivations 57
impact studies 22
importance – performance analysis 13, 130
in-depth interviews 71, 221, 222–6

checklist 223, 224
informal/unstructured approach 225
interventions by interviewer 225
interview process 223–6
nature 222
recording 226
standardised approach 224–5
uses 222–3
inclusive/evaluative/systematic reviews 150
income, and questionnaire design 270
income inequality
    Gini coefficient 347
    secondary data analysis 346–8
independent variables 293, 422–3
indexes, specialist 146
induction 32, 39–42
industry, research funding 18, 55
industry/sector studies 22
informal areas/facilities
    observational research 200–2
    spatial/functional patterns 201–2
information
    how well public informed 123
    list of requirements 68–9
    'on/off the record' 100
information needs, case study 78
information for participants, checklist 97
information, recording, observational research
        208–9
information, sources of 145–8
    arts/events publications 147–8
    bibliographies 147
    Google Scholar 147
    internet 146–7
    library catalogues 145–6
    obtaining copies of material 148–9
    reference lists 148
    specialist indexes and databases 146
    unpublished research 148
information-gathering methods
    examples 70
    techniques to be used 70
informed consent 96–8, 231
    consent form – example 97
    information for participants – checklist 97
infra-red beams 201, 210
institutional oversight of research ethics 90–1
instrumental review 151
insurance 285
intensity 170, 171
inter-disciplinary, meaning of term 30
inter-library loan service 148–9
intercept surveys 116, 120
internet 228
    references 155
    searching on 146–7
    see also e-surveys
interpretation of results, ethical issues 102–3
interpretive approaches 32, 33, 36

interviewers
    interventions by 225
    quality checks on 273
    recruitment 286
    training 328
    written instructions for 285
interviews, protection of ID 101
introductory remarks, questionnaire design
    276
Irwin, R.L. 302
ISBN 465
ISI Web of Knowledge 146

Jackson, R. 228
James, J.M. 301–2
jargon 219
Jeanneret, Y. 212
journal articles 473
junk mail 254

Kamphorst, T.J. 181
Karttunen, S. 91
Karwacki, A. 347
Katz-Gerro, T. 352
Kelly, G. 126
key performance indicators (KPIs) 130
    cultural indicators 175
key service dimensions (KSDs) 76
Kinsley, B.L. 303
Kline, R.B. 41
Kraaykamp, G. 352

Labovitz, S. 34
latent class analysis 116, 122
Latin abbreviations 160–1
Lavers, G.R. 231–2
Lee, A.S. 34
leisure facility, estimating likely demand 348–51
Lemel, Y. 352
Lenskyj, H.J. 58
Levin, M. 117
libraries 148–9
    inter-library loan service 148–9
library catalogues 145–6
life-cycle stage, and questionnaire design 272
lifestyle research see psychographic/lifestyle research
lifestyle studies 21
Liker 279, 280
Likert scales 273–5, 278, 396
Lincoln, Y. 36, 43, 45, 91
line graph produced in SPSS 406, 409
linear regression 423, 440–5
    line of best fit 441
    non-linear 444–5
    procedures 441–4
literature, role in research 58, 59, 143–4
literature reviews 58–60, 110, 111, 143–64, 168
    content analysis 151
    critical and creative reading 151–2

exploratory 150
hermeneutics 151
inclusive bibliography 150
inclusive/evaluative/systematic reviews 150,
    152
instrumental 151
meta-analysis 150, 153–4
meta-evaluation 153, 154
meta-interpretation 153, 154
meta-review 153
published and unpublished research 59
questions to ask 151
reporting styles 151–2
summarising 152–3
and types of literature 152
types of 149–51
see also bibliographies; information, sources of; refer-
    encing
local/non-local participation 171, 172
logic model 130
longitudinal research/studies 116, 121
    protection of ID 101
'long tail' 118, 353

McPhail, T. 228
Madden, G. 0, 175
magazine articles 152
Maher, J.K. 95
mail surveys 114, 243, 248–52
    accompanying letter 250
    identifying non-respondents 100
    introductory remarks 276
    length of questionnaire 249
    nature 248–9
    non-response – analysis of 252
    postage-paid reply envelope 250
    protection of ID 100, 101
    questionnaire design/presentation/complexity
        249–50
    range of information 266
    reminders/follow-ups 250–1
    response pattern 251
    response rate – factors affecting 249–51
    response rate – required 251–2
    rewards/incentives 250, 301–2
    sampling 329
    and user/site/visitor survey combo 252, 257
management
    motivation/purpose for research 14, 16
    use of term 9
    see also policy-making, planning and management
        processes
management reports see policy/planning/management
    reports
Mann, M.E. 104
map/mapping 62–3, 116, 175–9
marital status, and questionnaire design 270
market area 351
market profiles 20–1

market research 21
  conceptual framework 66
  information needs 69
  and telephone surveys 247
market segmentation 21, 130
  questionnaire design 275
marketing plans 21
Marsh, P. 204
mass media coverage 228
Matarasso, F. 8, 298
mean
  definition 396
  one-way analysis of variance (ANOVA) 423, 429, 431–3
  t-test 423, 428–9
measurement, experimental research 297
measuring engagement in cultural activity/events 168–71
  counting heads 171–2, 173
  cultural mapping 175–9
  cultural statistics 172–5
  expenditure per visit 170, 171
  individual engagement – typology 168–9
  intensity 170, 171
  local/non-local participation 171, 172
  number of participants 169, 170
  participation rate 169, 170
  professional involvement 170, 171
  spatial dimensions 171, 173
  time spent 170, 171
  volume of activity 170, 171
media, as source for research project 53, 55–6
media reader/viewer/listener surveys 116, 121–2
median, definition 401
medical patients 95
medical research 98
memory work 229
Mercer, C. 176
meta-analysis 116, 122, 150, 153–4
meta-evaluation 153
meta-interpretation 153, 154
meta-review 153, 154
methodology 32, 33
methods of research
  case study method 110, 115
  choosing method – considerations 129–32
  and data availability/access 131
  and ethics 132
  existing sources 110, 111
  experimental method 110, 114
  'just thinking' 110–11
  literature/systematic reviews 110, 111
  multiple methods see multiple research methods
  observation 110, 111–12
  policy/management-related research-based techniques 129, 130
  and previous research 131
  qualitative 110, 112–13
  questionnaire-based surveys 110, 113–14
  reasons for studying 8–9
  and research question and hypothesis 130–1

  and resources 131
  scholarship 110
  and time and timing 131
  and uses/users of findings 132
  and validity, reliability and trustworthiness 131–2
  see also subsidiary/cross-cutting research techniques
Michel, J.-B. 354
Miles, M.B. 60, 61, 219–20, 337–8, 365
mission statement 10
mobile phones 247, 248, 327
mobility 273
mode, definition 401
monitoring and evaluation process 13
monographs 20
Montford, A.W. 104
multi-collinearity 445
multi-disciplinary, meaning of term 30
multiple classification analysis 116, 122
multiple correspondence analysis 449–51
  uses 450–1
multiple regression 423, 445–7
  binary logistic regression analysis 447
  description 445
  procedures 445, 446
  structural equation modelling 445–7
multiple research methods 117, 127–9
  counting heads 117, 128–9
  triangulation 117, 128, 129
Munsters, W. 204
museums 4, 10, 16, 204
  attendance figures 89, 200–2
  ethical issues 89, 90
  facility use case study 75–8
  failure 319–20
  movement patterns 201–2
  observation studies 201–2, 212
  repeat visits 303–4
  restitution of cultural heritage 90
music production and consumption 318
Myers–Briggs personality scale 126
mystery shopping 203–4

National Arts Council 10
National Arts Index 175
national surveys 245
  telephone surveys 248
naturalistic research 32, 42–3
neo-liberal strance 58
neo-Marxism 58
netnography 116, 122
network analysis 116, 122–3
New Labour Government, social inclusion 297–9
newspaper articles, referencing 155
newspapers 152
NHMRC
  ethics code 89
  National Ethics Application Form 91
non-empirical research, definition 32
non-financial measures of output/supply 187, 188

non-profit organisations, motivation for research 14, 15
non-ticketed sites 329–30
non-visitors 256–7
normal curve, and confidence intervals 331, 332
normal distribution 419, 420
null hypothesis 421–2
Nurse Rainbolt, G. 301
NVivo 360, 367–76
    analysis 374–6
    attributes of subjects 368–9
    backup copies 368
    classification of nodes 369
    coding query 375
    coding text 373–4
    creating new project 367–8
    description 367
    Free Nodes 371
    importing documents 369–70
    linking cases and documents 370, 371
    matrix coding query 375–6
    modelling 372–3
    project summary 374, 375
    setting up coding system 370–2
    starting up 367
    Tree Nodes 371

objectives 13, 68
objectivism 34
objectivity 34, 43
observational research 44, 110, 111–12, 198–216
    aerial photography 210–11
    automatic counters 210
    case studies 212
    children's behaviour 200, 212
    complementary research 204
    conducting observation 209
    counting sheets 208–9
    data analysis 209
    deviant behaviour 203
    everyday life 204
    experimental research 297
    Global Positioning Systems (GPS) 210
    informal areas/facilities 200–2
    main elements 205–9
    mystery shopping 203–4
    observation decision 207–8
    observation point – choice of 205–6
    participant observation 199, 208
    qualitative complementarity 204
    quantitative complementarity 204
    recording information 208–9
    site – choice of 205
    site – use of term 205
    situations 200
    social behaviour 204
    still photography and video 211
    technology – use of 209–11
    time-lapse photography 211
    types of 199

visitor profiles 202–3
zone – use of term 205
zones – division of site into 208
observed data 32, 44
occupation, and questionnaire design 269–70
odds ratio 447
Office for National Statistics
    Arts in England 182
    population census 188–9
    socio-economic groupings 269
office use column 277
official surveys, ethical issues 94, 95
Olympic Games 299
O'Malley, P.M. 283
omnibus surveys 243, 244
omnivore – univore perspective 352
online surveys, protection of ID 101
on-site surveys see visitor/user/on-site surveys
one-way analysis of variance (ANOVA) 423, 429, 431–3
    null hypothesis 431
    procedure 433, 434
    use 429
    variance 431
online survey 114
ontology 32, 33
op cit 161
open-ended questions 114, 239, 263–4, 267
    advantages 263
    coding 278, 279
    disadvantages 264–5
opera house management 317–18
opinion polls 93
opinion questions see attitude/opinion questions
Oppenheim, A.N. 241
opportunism, as source for research project 56
opportunistic research 190
options
    developing 12
    evaluation 12–13
oral presentations of report 477–8
    use of PowerPoint-type software 478–9

page numbering 469–70
panel studies 116, 123
paragraph numbering 469
parking charges 201
Parr, M.G.W. 8
partial anonymity 99
participant observation 199, 208, 221, 227
participants, number of 169, 170
participation rate 169, 170
participation surveys 180–5
    age range 185
    composite international publications 180–1
    national surveys 181–3
    participation reference period 184
    sample size 184
    social/demographic characteristics 185
    validity and reliability 183

participatory research 37
Pearce, P.L. 201–2
pedestrian movements 95, 210
peer review 18, 19
perceptual mapping 116, 123–4
performance evaluation 130
    ethical considerations 89–90
performance indicators 8
Perlis, V. 229
personal constructs 275
personal domain histories 229
personal interest, as source for research project 53–4
personal records, rights of access 73
Peterson, K.I. 219
Peterson, R.A. 318, 352
photography 365–6
    aerial 210–11
    time-lapse 211
    use on observational research 210–11
physical models 305
Piber, M. 90
Pickett, K., *The Spirit Level*. 346–8
pie chart produced in SPSS 406, 408
Pieper, J. 152
pilot projects 297
pilot survey 286–7
    de-briefing 287
plagiarism 103
plan, implementation 13
planning reports *see* policy/planning/management
        reports
planning a research project 51–74
    budget 71
    communication of findings 73
    conducting research 72–3
    data analysis – techniques to be used 70–1
    data storage 73–4
    deciding research questions 65–8
    decision strategy 69–71
    devising conceptual framework 60–5
    ethics clearance 71
    fieldwork 70
    identififcation of project elements/stages 69–70
    information-gathering techniques to be used 70
    list of information requirements 68–9
    literature review 58–60
    selection of topic 53–8
    summary 52
    timetable 71
plans
    use of term 9
    see also policy-making, planning and management
        processes
Poetics 352
policies
    use of term 9
    see also policy-making, planning and management
        processes
policy or management issue problem 53, 55

policy options 12
    evaluation 12–13
policy-making, planning and management processes 9–13
    examples 10
    rational – comprehensive model *see* rational –
        comprehensive planning/management process
    tasks and associated research – example 12
policy/management experimental projects 297–9
policy/management-related research
    purpose 58
    techniques 129, 130
policy/planning/management reports
    cultural maps 20
    cultural needs studies 21
    cultural tourism strategies 21
    examples of published reports 20, 24–5
    feasibility studies 21
    forecasting studies 22
    government 20
    impact studies 22
    industry/sector studies 22
    on internet 20
    lifestyle studies 21
    market profiles 20–1
    market research 21
    market segmentation 21
    marketing plans 21
    position statements 20
    psychographic studies 21
    types of 20–2
political/policy science 31
politicians 90
politics
    opinion polls 247
    push polling 93–4
popular culture 4
population, definition 325
population census 68, 94, 188–90, 238, 328
    data available 189
    secondary data analysis 348–51
    uses 190
population estimates, confidence intervals 335
position statements 20
positivism 32, 33, 36
post-positivism 32, 33, 36
post-test observation 300
postal surveys *see* mail surveys
Power-Point type software 478–9
'PQ Method' 125
pragmatism 32, 37
pre-coded/closed questions 263–4, 267, 278
    advantages 264
pre-test observation 300
prediction 7–8, 440
preface 466, 468
presentations of report 477–8
    use of PowerPoint-type software 478–9
primary data 32, 43–4
printing 285

privacy 73, 99, 100, 248
  big data 118
private trusts/foundations, research funding 18
probabilistics statements 418
  formats 419, 420
professional involvement 170, 171
professional journal articles 19
project planning *see* planning a research project
projective techniques 116, 124, 211
pseudonyms 100, 101
psychographic/lifestyle research 21, 116, 124, 125
  ACORN classification 124, 125
  VALS typology 124, 125
psychological research 98
psychology 31
public policy 121
public-sector clients, ethical considerations 90
purpose of research 57, 68
  policy/management-related research 58
push polling 93–4

Q methodology 116, 124–5
qualitative data, in-depth interviews 71
qualitative data analysis 221, 358–79
  case studies – activity choice 360–2
  crosstabulation of data 364, 365
  developed conceptual framework 363–4
  emergent themes – search for 363–4
  manual methods 362–6
  mechanics 364
  reading 363
  using computer software 366–76
  word-processing packages 364
  see also NVivo
qualitative methods, experimental research 304–5
qualitative research 73, 110, 112–13, 217–36
  biographical research 221, 229
  case study – *English Life and Leisure* 231–2
  compared with quantitative research 36, 61, 112
  conceptual framework 61
  description 32, 35–6
  ethnography 221, 230
  focus groups 221, 226–7
  grounds for using 218
  group interviews 221
  in-depth interviews 221, 222–6
  limitations 219–20
  merits 218–19
  nature of 218
  participant observation 221, 227
  process 220–1
  researcher as research instrument 221
  sampling 230, 337–8
  sequential and recursive approaches 220
  summary of data collection methods 113
  summary of methods 221
  textual analysis 221, 228–9
  trustworthiness 231
  uses 219

validity 230
  when appropriate 112
quantitative data analysis *see* survey data analysis
quantitative modelling 65, 116, 125
quantitative research
  compared with qualitative research 36, 112
  deductive approach 40, 41
  description 32, 35–6
  ethical issues 102
  exclusion of outliers 102
  hypothetical – deductive approach 35
  inductive approach 35, 40–1
  sequential and recursive approaches 220
  statistical approach 35
quasi-experimental designs 295–7, 298
  experiments compared with research 296
  types of 295–6
questionnaire design 258–77
  activities/event/place questions 265–8
  attitude/opinion questions 266, 273–5
  case studies – short questionnaires 259–62
  filters 277
  household survey – interviewer completed 259, 261
  and information to be gathered 265
  intensity of involvement 268
  introductory remarks 276
  layout 277
  length 277
  market segments 275
  media use questions 268
  office use column 277
  open-ended questions 263–4, 267
  pre-coded/closed questions 263–4, 267
  question order 276–7
  reference period 267
  respondent characteristics *see separate entry*
  site survey – interviewer-completed 259, 262
  summary of process 258–9
  tick boxes and codes 277
  visitor/street survey: respondent-completed
    259, 260
  wording of questions 262–3
questionnaire-based data
  validity *see* validity of questionnaire-based data
  see also survey data
questionnaire-based surveys 110, 113–14, 237–91
  accuracy of recall 241
  captive group 243, 257–8
  coding *see separate entry*
  conducting *see* conducting questionnaire surveys
  definitions 238
  e-surveys 243, 248, 252–4
  exaggeration 240–1
  face-to-face interviewing 242
  household 243–5
  interviewer-completed 113, 241–2, 244, 276
  limitations 240–2
  mail surveys 243, 248–52
  merits 239–40

questionnaire-based surveys (*continued*)
  omnibus 243, 244
  open-ended questions 114, 239
  qualities 239–40
  respondent-completed 113, 242, 244, 276, 328
  sampling 238, 241
  self-reported data 240–1
  sensitive topics 241
  street surveys 243, 245–6
  telephone surveys 242, 243, 246–8
  terminology 238
  time-use 243, 245
  types of 114, 243
  under-reporting 240–1
  uses 238–9, 240
  visitor profiles 202–3
  visitor/user/on-site surveys 243, 254–7
  when used 114
questions
  deciding on 65–8, 76, 77
  open-ended 263–5, 267, 278, 279
  pre-coded/closed 263–4, 267, 278
  primary and secondary questions 68
  versus hypothesis format 65–6
  when research topic specified 67
  when research topic vague 67–8
  see also questionnaire design
quota sampling 246, 328–9
quotations, obtaining 286

random sampling 325–6
rational – comprehensive planning/management process
    10–13
  environmental appraisal 11–12
  implementation of plan or strategy 13
  monitor/evaluate/feedback 13
  options – developing 12
  options – evaluation 12–13
  planning approach, deciding 11
  set values/missions/goals 10
  stakeholder consultation 12
  strategy/goals/objectives – deciding 13
  terms of reference/brief 10
re-analysis of research data 111
recall 267
  accuracy 241
reference lists 148
reference period, questionnaire design 267
referencing 154–61, 472
  excessive 160
  formats – examples 155
  internet references 155
  Latin abbreviations 160–1
  newspaper articles 155
  purpose 154
  recording 154–5
  second-hand references 160
  standard/generic formats 154
  systems *see separate entry*

referencing systems 156–60
  author/date (Harvard) system 154, 156–7
  comparison of 159
  footnote or endnote system 157–9
reflexivity 32, 38
reliability 32, 45
Rentschler, R. 318–19
repertory grid 116, 126, 275
reporting styles 151–2
research
  and arts practice 32, 37
  defining 5
  descriptive 6–7
  evaluative 8
  explanatory 7–8
  reasons for studying 8–9
  types of 6–8
  see also scientific research; social science research
research agendas 53, 56, 84
research formats 18–22
  academic journal articles 18–19
  books 20
  conference presentations/papers 20
  policy/planning/management reports 20–2
  professional journal articles 19
research literature, as source for research project 53, 54–5
research methods *see* methods of research
research outputs *see* research formats
research process
  case study 75–8
  in real world 74–5
research proposals 79–82
  responsive 79, 80–2
  self-generated 79–80
research reports
  oral presentations 477–8
  statistical notes – sample size and confidence intervals
    334–5, 341
  types of 464
  use of PowerPoint-type software 478–9
  see also written research reports
researcher competence, ethical issues 94
residential location, and questionnaire design 272–3
resource auditing/mapping 130
resources, and methods of research 131
respondent characteristics 266, 268–73
  age 268
  economic status 269–70
  ethnic group 272
  gender 268
  group type and size 271
  household type 271
  housing information 273
  income 270
  life-cycle stage 272
  marital status 270
  occupation 269–70
  residential location 272–3
  socio-economic group/class 269–70

transport 273
trip origin 272–3
responsive research proposals 79, 80–2
checklist 82
content 81–2
results, publication of
ethical issues 102, 103
negative or non-findings 102
risk of harm 102
revenue for cultural industry 187, 188
reviewing the literature *see* literature reviews
Rojek, C. 75, 76, 228, 229
Rowntree, B.S. 231–2

Sallent, O. 123
sample, definition 325
sample size 330–6
and budget 334
ethical issues 102–3
and level of precision – confidence intervals 331–3
participation surveys 184
reporting issues 334–5, 341
small populations 335–6
and type of analysis 333–4
sampling 324–41
biased 325
clustered 326, 327
complex events studies 329–30
disclosure in report 474
household surveys 326–7
mail surveys 329
multi-stage 326
qualitative research 337–8
questionnaire-based surveys 238, 241
quota 328–9
random 325–6, 330
representativeness 325–30
self 329
street surveys 246, 328
telephone surveys 247, 327
visitor/user/on-site surveys 327–8
weighting 328, 336–7
Saren, M. 204
scales 116, 126
examples 127
scattergram produced in SPSS 406, 409
scenarios 302
scholarship 110
Schuster, J.M. 8, 173, 175, 181
scientific research, description 5–6
Screven, C.G. 13, 300, 305
Scullion, A. 15
second-hand references 160
secondary data 7, 32, 43–4, 110, 111, 178–97
administrative/management data 179–80
advantages and disadvantages of using 178, 179
documentary sources 190
employment in cultural industry 187, 188
exports for cultural industry 187, 188

household expenditure – cultural items 186–7
national cultural/events participation surveys 180–5
national time-use surveys 185–6
non-financial measures of output/supply 187, 188
opportunistic research 190
population census 188–90
revenue for cultural industry 187, 188
types of – list 178–9
secondary data analysis 121
big data 116, 117–18
secondary data analysis – case studies
'big data' 353–4
cultural consumption/taste and social status 352
cultural participation 346, 347–8
economic data 346–8
estimating demand for cultural facility 348–51
facility catchment area 351
income inequality 346–8
national participation surveys 346–51, 352
opportunism 346–8
population census 348–51
symphony orchestras' finances 354–5
section numbering 468–9
self-generated research proposals 79–80
self-reported data 32, 44, 240–1
sensitive topics 241
service quality 75, 76
SERVQUAL 75, 76, 130
significance 421
'significant', use of term 419
Silberberg, T. 89
Simkus, A. 352
site or user survey 114
social behaviour, observational research 204
social benefit, as ethical issue 93–4
social concern 53, 55
social impact 22
social inclusion 297–9
social media 354
social network analysis 123
social psychology, and arts and events research 31
social science research, description 5–6
socio-demographic characteristics 20, 185
socio-demographic profile, visitor surveys 255–6
socio-economic group/class, and questionnaire design 269–70
socio-psychological research 98–9
sociology 31
sociometry 123
specialist indexes and databases 146
'spin' 90
sport, social inclusion 298–9
Sport England, Active People Survey 182, 183
sport research, structural equation modelling 445–7
spreadsheet analysis 383–5
stakeholder consultation 12

standard deviation
   definition 396
   formula 459
standard error 331
standpoint reearch 34
statistical analysis 417–58
   chi-square test 423, 424–7, 451, 459
   cluster analysis 448, 449, 451
   correlation 423, 435–40, 451
   dependent variables 422–3
   factor analysis 448–9, 451
   factorial analysis of variance 423, 433–5, 451
   independent variables 422–3
   linear regression 423, 440–5, 451
   multiple correspondence analysis 449–51
   multiple regression 423, 445–7, 451
   normal distribution 419, 420
   null hypothesis 421–2
   one-way analysis of variance (ANOVA) 423, 429, 431–3, 451
   probabilistics statements 418, 419, 420
   significance 421
   t-test 423, 428–9, 451
   types of data and appropriate tests 423–4
Statistical Package for the Social Sciences (SPSS) 386–410
   cases – definition and examples 387
   crosstabs 386
   crosstabulation 404–5
   descriptives 386
   descriptives procedure 395–6
   entering data – Data View window 393–4
   errors – checking for 398
   frequencies 386
   frequencies procedure 397–8
   graphics 406–9
   graphs 386
   mean 386, 396, 401–2
   measures of central tendency 396, 401–2
   median 401
   mode 401
   multiple response questions 398–9
   overview 387
   presentation of results: statistical summary 403–4
   recode procedure 399–401
   resources 411
   saving work 392
   standard deviation 396
   starting up 392
   uses 386
   variables – definition and examples 387
   variables – entering information (Variable View window) 392, 393
   variables – specifying 388–92
   weighting 506
statistical tests in report 471
Stebbins, R.A. 169
Stephenson, W. 124
Stokowski, P.A. 123
Stone, A.A. 284

strategy, implementation 13
strategy decisions 13
   case study 78
Strauss, A.L. 221
street surveys 114, 243, 245–6, 272
   conduct 246
   duration of interview 246
   limitations 246
   nature 245
   quota sampling 246
   sampling 246, 328
structural equation modelling 41, 445–7
   hierarchical modelling 445–7
students 79
   motivation for research 14, 15
   participation in research project 95, 258
subject, meaning of term 22–3
subjectivism 34
subjectivity 43
subsidiary/cross-cutting research techniques 115–27
   action research 115–17
   big data 116, 117–18
   conjoint analysis 116, 118
   content analysis 116, 118–19
   conversion studies 116, 119
   cordon surveys 116, 120
   coupon surveys 116, 119
   Delphi technique 116, 119
   discourse analysis 116, 119
   en route surveys 116, 120
   experience sampling method (ESM) 116, 120
   historical research 116, 121
   intercept surveys 116, 120
   latent class analysis 116, 122
   list of 116–17
   longitudinal studies 116, 121
   mapping techniques 116
   media reader/viewer/listener surveys 116, 121–2
   meta-analysis 116, 122
   multiple classification analysis 116, 122
   netnography 116, 122
   network analysis 116, 122–3
   panel studies 116, 123
   perceptual mapping 116, 123–4
   projective techniques 116, 124
   psychographic/lifestyle research 116, 124, 125
   Q methodology 116, 124–5
   quantitative modelling 116, 125
   repertory grid 116, 126
   scales 116, 126
   time-use surveys 117, 126–7
   visitor conversation research 117, 127
   web-based research 117, 127
summary of report 466, 468
survey, meaning of term 238
survey data
   as appendices in report 477
   validity and reliability 383

survey data analysis 380–416
  descriptive research 381
  evaluative research 382
  explanatory research 381–2
  spreadsheet analysis 383–5
  SPSS *see* Statistical Package for the Social Sciences (SPSS)
  and types of research 381–3
symphony orchestras' finances 354–5
systematic reviewing 122
systematic view 43
Szlendak, T. 347

t-test 423, 428–9
  independent samples (group) test 429, 431
  paired samples test 429, 430
  two-tailed 428, 429
tables 470–2
telephone surveys 114, 242, 243, 246–8
  advantages 246, 247
  CATI 247
  conduct 247–8
  costs 248
  duration of interview 247
  limitations 247
  mobile phones 247, 248
  national 245, 248
  nature 246–7
  privacy 248
  protection of ID 101
  range of information 266
  representativeness 247, 248
  response levels 247, 248
  sampling 247, 327
television 204
tenders 55, 80–2
terms of reference 10
text, use of term 228
textbooks 20, 152
textual analysis 221, 228–9
  film 228
  internet 228
  mass media coverage 228
  material culture 228–9
theatres 16, 316–17
theoretical research 32, 38
thesis 15, 79
tick boxes 277
ticket sales 329
time and timing, and methods of research 131
time-lapse photography 211
time-use surveys 117, 120, 126–7, 185–6, 243, 245
  diary of activities 185–6
timetable for project 71, 72
title page 465, 466
topic of research, sources 53–8
  brainstorming 56

examples from different sources – summary 53
  ideological/political motivations 57
  knowledge for its own sake 57
  opportunism 56
  personal interest 53–4
  policy or management issue problem 53, 55
  popular/media 53, 55–6
  published research agendas 53, 56, 84
  and purpose of research 57
  research literature 53, 54–5
  social concern 53, 55
tourism questions 267
traffic management 95, 271
transformative research 34
transport, and questionnaire design 273
triangulation 117, 128, 129
trip origin, and questionnaire design 272–3
'trip', defining 267
trustworthiness 32, 45

UK
  Expenditure and Food Survey 186
  Mass Observation (1930's and 1940s) 204
  participation surveys 182
  time use 185, 186
UN
  Human Development Index 175
  Intergovernmental Panel on Climate Change 122, 150
under-reporting 240–1
UNESCO
  Framework for Cultural Statistics 173–5
  Multinational Comparative Time-Budget Research project 185
unfunded research 17
universities
  Application for Ethics Approval Form 91
  ethics committees 90–1
  research funding 17
unobtrusive techniques 44, 111–12
  meaning of term 199
unpublished research 59, 148
Urban Institute, Arts and Cultural Indicators Project 176–8
USA
  National Council on Public Polls 93
  National Endowment for the Arts 56, 182
  participation surveys 181, 182
use of results in policy/practice 104
user surveys *see* visitor/user/on-site surveys
uses/users of findings, and methods of research 132

validity 32, 44–5
  case study method of research 311–13
  experimental research 294–5
  external 44, 230
  internal 44, 230
  qualitative research 230
  survey data 383

validity of questionnaire-based data 282–4
    checking 282
    comparison of time periods 283
    dummy questions 283
    problems – taking account of 284
    semi-disguised duplication of questions 283
    threats to 282
    use of alternative data source 283–4
VALS typology 124, 125
variable, meaning of term 23
variance
    factorial analysis 423, 433–5
    one-way analysis (ANOVA) 423, 429, 431–3
Veal, A.J. 360
vehicle counts 201, 210
vehicle occupancy 271
video, use on observational research 210–11
virtual research 122
visitor circulation 301
visitor conversation research 117, 127, 201
visitor expenditure 302
visitor group type and size 271
visitor numbers 117, 128–9, 171–2, 199, 200–1, 239
    confidence intervals 35
visitor opinions 256
visitor profiles 202–3
visitor studies 19
visitor/street survey: respondent-completed 259, 260
visitor/user/on-site surveys 243, 254–7
    by interview 254–5, 327–8
    catchment area 255
    conduct 254–5
    and e-survey combo 253, 257
    introductory remarks 276
    ISUM 327
    and mail combo 252, 257
    nature 254
    non-visitors 256–7
    questionnaire design 271
    range of information 266, 272–3
    respondent completion 254, 328
    sampling 327–8
    socio-demographic profile 255–6
    uses 255
    USIM 327, 328
    visitor opinions 256
visits, repeat 303–4
Visual Sociology 211

Voderer, P. 228
volume of activity 170, 171, 300

web-based research 117, 127
weighting
    sampling 336–7
    using SPSS 506
Whyte, W.F. 225
Wikipedia 147
Wilkinson, R., *The Spirit Level.* 346–8
word-processing packages 364, 366
written research reports 73, 463–77
    acknowledgements 466, 468
    appendices 466
    audiences and style 474–5
    chapter summaries 473
    components 465–8
    conclusions 477
    contents, table of 465, 466, 467, 473
    cover 465, 466
    data collection method 474
    dot point lists 469
    headers/footers 470
    heading hierarchy 470
    impersonal style 472
    journal articles 473
    main body – structure and content 472–7
    main body – technical aspects 468–72
    narrative – structure 475–6
    page numbering 469–70
    paragraph numbering 469
    preface /foreward 466, 468
    as record 476–7
    referencing 472
    sampling 474
    section numbering 468–9
    starting 464–5
    statistical tests 471
    summary 466, 468
    survey data as appendices 477
    tables and graphics 470–2
    title page 465, 466
    typing layout/spacing 470

Yin, R.K. 310, 315

Zillmann, D. 228